Prophets, Prophecy, and
Ancient Israelite Historiography

To the Canadian Society of Biblical Studies

For its ongoing commitment to support and promote
biblical scholarship within the Canadian context.

Prophets, Prophecy, and Ancient Israelite Historiography

edited by

MARK J. BODA and LISSA M. WRAY BEAL

Winona Lake, Indiana
EISENBRAUNS
2013

Copyright © 2013 Eisenbrauns
All rights reserved.
Printed in the United States of America.

www.eisenbrauns.com

Library of Congress Cataloging-in-Publication Data

Prophets, prophecy, and ancient Israelite historiography / edited by Mark J. Boda and Lissa M. Wray Beal.
  p. cm.
  "This volume found its impetus in the Ancient Historiography Seminar / Groupe de Travail sur l'Historiographie Ancienne at the 2009 Annual meeting of the Canadian Society of Biblical Studies / Societe canadienne des Etudes bibliques, where several of the essays were originally presented."
  Includes bibliographical references and index.
  ISBN 978-1-57506-257-0 (hardback : alk. paper)
  1. Prophecy—Judaism—History—To 1500—Congresses.
2. Judaism—Historiography—Congresses. 3. Jews—History—To 70 A.D.—Historiography—Congresses. 4. Bible. O.T. Prophets—Criticism, interpretation, etc.—Congresses. 5. Bible. O.T.—Historiography—Congresses. I. Boda, Mark J. II. Wray Beal, Lissa M.
  BS1198.P76 2013
  221.9′50072—dc23
                                                                2012045745

The paper used in this publication meets the minimum requirements of the American National Standard for Information Sciences—Permanence of Paper for Printed Library Materials. ANSI Z39.48-1984.™♾

Contents

Introduction vii

Part 1
Prophets and Prophecy in Israelite Historiographic Books

"Face to Face": Moses as Prophet in Exodus 11:1–12:28 3
   Bernon Lee

The Shaping of a Prophet:
   Joshua in the Deuteronomistic History 23
   Gordon Oeste

Recycling Heaven's Words: Receiving and Retrieving Divine
   Revelation in the Historiography of Judges 43
   Mark J. Boda

Samuel Agonistes: A Conflicted Prophet's Resistance to God
   and Contribution to the Failure of Israel's First King . . . 69
   J. Richard Middleton

Prophecy as Prediction in Biblical Historiography 93
   John Van Seters

Jeroboam and the Prophets in 1 Kings 11–14:
   Prophetic Word for Two Kingdoms 105
   Lissa M. Wray Beal

Presumptuous Prophets Participating in a
   Deuteronomic Debate 125
   K. L. Noll

Prophecy Influencing History:
   Dialogism in the Chronicler's Ahaz Narrative 143
   Paul S. Evans

Chronicles and Its Reshaping of Memories of
   Monarchic Period Prophets: Some Observations 167
   Ehud Ben Zvi

Deus ex Machina and Plot Construction in Ezra 1–6 189
   Lisbeth S. Fried

Is the Governor Also among the Prophets? Parsing the
    Purposes of Jeremiah in the Memory of Nehemiah 209
  DAVID SHEPHERD

The Use and Non-Use of Prophetic Literature in
    Hellenistic Jewish Historiography 229
  ANDREW W. PITTS

Part 2
Historiography in Israelite Prophetic Books

The Poetics of History and the Prophecy of Deutero-Isaiah . . . 253
  DANIELLE DUPERREAULT

Personal Missives and National History:
    The Relationship between Jeremiah 29 and 36. 275
  MARK LEUCHTER

Ezekiel's Perspective of Israel's History:
    Selective Revisionism? 295
  BRIAN PETERSON

The Ordering of the Twelve as Israel's Historiography 315
  GRACE KO

The "Exilic" Prophecy of Daniel 7: Does It Reflect
    Late Pre-Maccabean or Early Hellenistic Historiography? . 333
  RALPH J. KORNER

(Re)Visionary History: Historiography and Religious Identity
    in the Animal Apocalypse 355
  COLIN M. TOFFELMIRE

Index of Authors 375
Index of Scripture 382

Introduction

"So, a prophet, a priest, and a king walk into a bar."

One might expect that a line such as this begins a familiar genre in which each of the characters voices a boast, the second out-doing the first, and the third delivering a classic punchline. But a closer look at this opening line reveals that, although the joke begins in a familiar place, it leads in significantly different directions. The characters are not the usual suspects: current business, world, or religious leaders. And it is this difference that affords fresh and insightful reflection.

Now, while we do not liken the present volume to this genre, *Prophets and Prophecy and Ancient Israelite Historiography* frames its study in such a way that fresh and insightful reflection results. The volume grows out of an awareness of a deep divide that exists between the traditions of historiography and prophecy in the scholarly study of the Hebrew Bible. This separation between the prophetic and historiographic traditions of the Hebrew Bible certainly does not originate with von Rad, but he voiced it in his Old Testament theology. For him, the historical traditions evident in the great Hebrew historiographic works of the Hexateuch, the Deuteronomistic History, and the Chronicler's history were undermined by the prophets who looked to new divine activity.[1] The division of his Old Testament theology into two volumes, the first dealing with the theology of Israel's historical traditions and the second with the theology of Israel's prophetic traditions, highlighted his juxtaposition of the two streams.

This volume is an attempt to show the close relationship between these two traditions within the literature of the Hebrew Bible, first by showing the role that prophets play within the great Hebrew historiographic works and second by the role that historiography plays within the great Hebrew prophetic works. A glance at the table of contents shows that this collection of essays ranges broadly and, as suggested, takes one into surprising areas. Beginning with the Hebrew Bible's narrative recitation of Israel's past, the collection also engages the Hebrew Bible's prophetic traditions and even moves beyond to apocalyptic literature. The exploration reveals

---

1. See G. von Rad, *Old Testament Theology* (trans. D. M. G. Stalker; 2 vols.; New York: Harper & Row, 1962–65) 1:v, vii, 127–28.

that, together, the historiographic and prophetic records speak to Israel's past, appropriating it, shaping it, and drawing out its implications for new generations and new situations: to wit, presenting a historiographical record in the midst of prophetic ministry. The extension of the study avoids a kind of "pan-prophetism" and even a "pan-historiography" by holding to its dual exploration of prophets and historiography. Where these two are found, this book seeks to provide an invitation to new thought and further exploration.

Perhaps such a far-reaching grasp for historiography is not ill considered in a context such as ancient Israel's. Its primary events, its tradents, its redactors, all worked in a milieu charged with the reality and the expectation of Yhwh's word in Israel's history. Once the prophetic ministry was considered heard, the community was attentive to any repetition. Early or late, in assenting or dissenting cadence, Israel's history and writing were marked by the phenomenon. It could do no more but consider its present life as well as its past history in terms of prophetic ministries and words such as these. Who Israel was, was marked by these words, communicated to an anticipatory people. It is, therefore, no wonder that its own record of its life should be indelibly marked by the event.

This collection is a collaboration of scholars who identify with Canada, either because is is their contry of origin or they serve its academy. The volume found its impetus in the Ancient Historiography Seminar / Groupe de Travail sur l'Historiographie Ancienne at the 2009 Annual Meeting of the Canadian Society of Biblical Studies / Société canadienne des Études bibliques, where several of the essays were originally presented. True to the nature of the Canadian Society of Biblical Studies, the volume includes offerings by both junior and senior scholars and displays a collegial openness to varying methodologies and viewpoints.

The first section of the volume is titled "Prophets and Prophecy in Israelite Historiographic Books," and offerings focus on specific books or prophetic characters. Bernon Lee takes up the dialogic interplay in the speeches of Moses and God in Exod 11:1–12:28 concerning Passover rites. Lee demonstrates the Bakhtinian polyphony by which each interlocutor forwards the language, imagery, and concepts of the other in new directions and, in the interchange between the exemplary prophet and God, Second Temple scribes find inspiration for fresh acts of interpretation.

Gordon Oeste's chapter considers Joshua as a prophet-like figure. Beginning in the deuteronomic definitions of prophecy and working through the book of Joshua, Oeste's synchronic reading notes the various ways in which the succession narrative and Joshua's words and actions present him as the true spiritual, military, covenantal, and intercessory successor who both parallels and completes Moses' career. Finally, Oeste notes that the prophet-like role of Joshua fills a lacuna in the DH, enabling each era from Moses to the monarchy to be represented with prophetic leadership.

Mark J. Boda reveals two very different presentations of the mediation of the divine word in the canonical book of Judges. In the cyclical core (2:6–16:31), the declaration of the divine word invariably occurs through mediation of some divine figure. In the epilogic ending (chaps. 17–21), no such figures appear, and the authenticity and clarity of God's word is thus generally suspect. Each form of mediation being presented in the introduction (1:1–2:5) draws together the two sections of the book of Judges, revealing the importance to the book's redactors of the proper mediation of the divine word.

J. Richard Middleton tackles the interpretive problem of Saul's rejection and provides a nuanced portrayal of the prophet Samuel *vis à vis* God, the monarchy, and Saul. Through several interrelated theses, Middleton suggests it is the prophet's human fragility that provides possibilities to unravel the text's complexities. Samuel's resistance ultimately precludes him as adequately representing God's intent; furthermore, Samuel *Agonistes* effects change in both God and in the subsequent exercise of the prophetic office.

Understanding the prophetic oracles in the corpus as ideologically driven, fictional imitations, John Van Seters examines three narratives (Saul's rejection [1 Sam 15:1–16:3] and subsequent interaction with the ghost of Samuel [1 Sam 28: 3–25], the David and Bathsheba narrative [2 Sam 11:1–12:25], and the man of God from Bethel [1 Kings 13]). He understands each to proffer a dissenting voice that belies the theological weight implicit in a Deuteronomistic theology of history sometimes discerned in a prophecy-fulfillment schema posited for the DH.

Lissa Wray Beal views the four prophetic pericopes in 1 Kings 11–14 not as discrete pericopes whose fulfilments are individually considered in the subsequent narrative; rather, as a coherent set bounded by narrative cues, they speak prophetically on cultic and monarchic issues for both the ongoing Northern Kingdom and the Southern Kingdom initially addressed in the Solomonic Narrative. Only the fall of the Northern Kingdom reactivates direct prophetic address to the Southern Kingdom in the remaining chapters of its history.

Kurt L. Noll reads the DH as a creative fiction that stands as an exploration of theological problems and possibilities for an elite group of educated readers who dissented from the teachings about prophecy in earlier religious texts such as Deuteronomy. The thesis examines simple and complex prediction and fulfillment formulas, with particular attention paid to the Micaiah narrative (1 Kings 22) as undermining the teaching regarding prophecy in the deuteronomic work.

Employing Bakhtinian dialogism, Paul S. Evans explores a fruitful methodology by which to explain specific divergences between the Chronicler's account of Ahaz (2 Chronicles 28) and that found in its putative Vorlage in 2 Kings 16. Evans extends the dialogism in a third direction and includes Isaiah 7 as one of the Chronicler's sources. He calls for his demonstrated methodology as one means by which literary studies and historical-critical studies can profitably interact, translating the findings of each paradigm into usable data.

Ehud ben Zvi's essay explores five central issues regarding social memory within the Chronicler's Persian-period social setting. Addressing, among other topics, the success of the monarchic prophets, the temporal relevance of their message, and the wide range of potential intermediaries, he shows that the Chronicler worked from the ideological trends of his own era in an effort to rebalance the social memory of monarchic prophets and prophecy.

Two offerings explore prophets and prophecy within the historiographical books of Ezra–Nehemiah. Lisbeth S. Fried discusses the temple-building narrative in Ezra 1–6 as comporting with the common events and ideology of ancient Near Eastern historiographical temple-building accounts. However, Fried's work reveals that the account has been rhetorically revised toward Aristotelian rules of tragic drama, including the creation of the protagonist, the plot structure, and the *deus ex machina* of the prophetic voices of Haggai and Zechariah (Ezra 5:1). In these ways, the author heightened the drama of the historiographical account. David Shepherd's work uncovers the ways in which Nehemiah's Memoir presents his ministry as fulfillment of the prophetic programme contained in the Jeremianic tradition. Shepherd carefully builds an argument that resonances such as Nehemiah's physical rebuilding of Jerusalem, his encounters with false prophets, and the shape and content of his prayers all are uniquely associated with Jeremiah's own commission, encounters with false prophets, and traditions of prayer.

Finally, this section is rounded out by Andrew W. Pitts's exploration of the use of prophetic literature within Hellenistic Jewish historiography. He posits that it is the background of Hellenistic citation practices that best explains those of the Jewish historians. Moving on a chronological continuum from *Jubilees* to 1 Esdras to 1–2 Maccabees to Josephus, Pitts traces the developing techniques of Jewish citation of biblical prophetic materials, particularly the instances when this sort of citation occurred.

In the volume's second section, "Historiography in Israelite Prophetic Books," Danielle Duperreault's work enters the Achaemenid world of Deutero-Isaiah, where, through the prophetic "Word," Isaiah reformulates historical consciousness. The 'Word' becomes the generative thread that enables a continuous, chronological, and typological link from the distant past to the postexilic present. Through this "Word," Duperreault explores Deutero-Isaiah's identity formation and vision of change for his own community.

Mark Leuchter examines the personal missives in Jeremiah 29 as exemplary of the redactional process described in Jeremiah 36. The redacted missives carry rhetorical and lexical hallmarks of the Jeremianic corpus, and the layers reveal that the redacted prophetic message applies not only to the captives of 597 but to all the post-597 communities who endured the exile. The missive's historiographical form reveals a redactional impetus that weaves the disparate traditions—as the communities who treasured them—into a unified whole, thus addressing a nation.

Brian Peterson turns to Ezekiel, the last of the Major Prophets, and reviews his radical and negative revisions of Israel's history in chaps. 16, 20, and 23. Tracing the revisions to alternate versions available to the prophet, Peterson plumbs the impetus behind Ezekiel's historiographic revisioning, placing it in the exilic experience of God's people, out of which Ezekiel is commissioned to generate hope in God's continuing sovereignty and grace.

Grace Ko's offering on the canonical Book of the Twelve considers the overall historiographical presentation of the collection and Habakkuk's placement within it. Working with a U-shaped comedic framework, Ko explores the framework's editorial markers of chronology and thematics and considers how these markers set Habakkuk at the framework's nadir. Its unique position within the framework is understood to cohere with its genre category of lament and enables the righteous to pose questions of theodicy.

In the book of Daniel, Ralph J. Korner considers the implications of identifying the "little horn" of Daniel 7 with Ptolemy I Soter. Korner argues that Daniel 7 functions as a symbolic history of Judean events in a Hellenistic era and that chap. 7 can be linked literarily to Aramaic Daniel 2–7. Thus, Korner posits an implicit appropriation of Aramaic Daniel's assumptions of divine determinacy into Hebrew Daniel, creating hope of divine deliverance for a new Jewish generation living under oppression.

The inclusion of Colin M. Toffelmire's exploration of the *Animal Apocalypse* considers the work as ancient historiography set within Enoch's prophetic vision. Within the prophetic vision, the pseudonymous author links the sufferings of the Seleucid-era audience to Israel's ancient past and describes the present conflict in Priestly categories. Toffelmire argues that in this way the author frames present identity in terms of a distant past that issues a call to religious and military resistance.

Working as co-editors with 16 other contributors and the work represented in this volume, we have been struck often by the scope and expertise of our Canadian colleagues. Learning from them in conference and reading their many publications has enriched our own scholarly exploration; it is a joy working with them. To the Canadian Society of Biblical Studies, and the Historiography section that has for several years shared papers and published on various aspects of ancient historiography, it is particularly encouraging to work within this uniquely Canadian context. Perhaps one never leaves the open spaces and cosmopolitan cities of Canada—they have shaped us as people and, perhaps, as scholars. We dedicate this volume to the Canadian Society of Biblical Studies in appreciation for its ongoing commitment to support and promote biblical scholarship within the Canadian context.

Thanks is extended to our respective academic institutions—McMaster Divinity College in Hamilton, Ontario, and Providence Theological Seminary in Otterburne, Manitoba, for research encouragement and funding, which helps to make projects such as this possible. Finally, hearty thanks is due to Shannon Baines, who has faithfully toiled over the stylistic details of these essays, dotting *i*s and crossing *t*s and generally bringing the work of scholars into publishable form—a daunting task well done!

So, we anticipate the next meeting of the Canadian Society of Biblical Studies. Let the "prophets, priests, and kings walk into bars"—the surprising results are the stuff of good scholarship!

Part I

Prophets and Prophecy in Israelite Historiographic Books

"Face to Face":
Moses as Prophet in Exodus 11:1–12:28

BERNON LEE

Recent research on the literature of the Second Temple period has shown Moses to be a spirit of innovation in the interpretation of ancient traditions. By association with the prophet *par excellence*, the affinity of the scribal establishment for religious renewal through interpretation finds legitimacy.[1] In Moses, the prophetic imagination finds inspiration for engaging divine communiques, prophetic and legal, as enshrined in texts of prestige from days of yore.[2] Most recently, J. Watts and M. Zvi Brettler have traced this impulse back to the Pentateuch, finding in its texture

---

1. See E. Mroczek, "Moses, David and Scribal Revelation: Preservation and Renewal in Second Temple Jewish Textual Traditions," in *The Significance of Sinai: Traditions about Sinai and Divine Revelation in Judaism and Christianity* (ed. G. J. Brooke, H. Najman, and L. T. Stuckenbruck; Themes in Biblical Narrative 12; Leiden: Brill, 2008) 112. Mroczek's argument proceeds with reference to *Jub.* 1:5–7, 1:26–2:1. For a similar perspective see H. Najman, "Interpretation as Primordial Writing: Jubilees and Its Authority Conferring Strategies," *JSJ* 30 (1999) 406–8; idem, *Seconding Sinai: The Development of Mosaic Discourse in Second Temple Judaism* (Supplements to the Journal for the Study of Judaism 77; Leiden: Brill, 2003) 12–25.

2. For Moses as a paradigm for the eschatological prophet in the Dead Sea Scrolls, see G. J. Brooke, "Moving Mountains: From Sinai to Jerusalem," in *The Significance of Sinai: Traditions about Sinai and Divine Revelation in Judaism and Christianity* (ed. G. J. Brooke, H. Najman and L. T. Stuckenbruck; Leiden: Brill, 2008) 81–84; Marcus Tso, "The Giving of the Torah at Sinai and the Ethics of the Qumran Community," in *The Significance of Sinai: Traditions about Sinai and Divine Revelation in Judaism and Christianity* (ed. G. J. Brooke, H. Najman, and L. T. Stuckenbruck; Themes in Biblical Narrative 12; Leiden: Brill, 2008) 123. Brooke's comments stem from an analysis of portions from 4Q174, 4Q175, and 4Q177. Elsewhere, Brooke explores the prophetic imagination in rewritten prophetic texts at Qumran ("Prophecy and Prophets in the Dead Sea Scrolls: Looking Backwards and Forwards," in *Prophets, Prophecy, and Prophetic Texts in Second Temple Judaism* [ed. M. H. Floyd and R. D. Haak; LHBOTS 427; New York: T. & T. Clark, 2006] 151–65; see especially pp. 154–56). According to Brooke, the profuse deployment of biblical prophetic texts coupled with the absence of any argument for legitimacy, as seen in *Pseudo-Ezekiel* [a–d] (4Q385, 4Q385b, 4Q386, 4Q388) and the *Jeremiah Apocrypha* A–C[a–f] (4Q383, 4Q384, 4Q385a, 4Q387, 4Q387a, 4Q388a, 4Q389, 4Q389a, 4Q390), betrays the assumption of a prophetic function by the authors of these texts. These writers, in spelling out for their contexts

subtle discretions of Moses in legal promulgation. A tension, sometimes stark, opens up between the voices of the prophet and God.[3]

In this essay, I explore prophetic engagement with divine proclamation in the Pentateuch by pursuing a comparison of the speeches of Moses and God in Exod 11:1–12:28. While the work of others, Watts and Brettler, for example, pursues the interaction between these figures, I shall seek these connections within a single smaller stretch of the text. The analysis will proceed in four parts (Exod 11:1–10, 12:1–13, 12:14–20, 12:21–28), each a segment of speech on a distinct topic. I shall argue that each interlocutor picks up the language, imagery, and concepts of the other, extending the nuances of previous speeches in novel directions.[4] Departures such as these from previous rhetorical directions often take the form of conceptions absent in, or marginal to, preceding utterances, promoting these novel arguments as concerns central to the discourse at hand. Within this rich network of exchange, the prophet may become, at times, an affront to divine communication, while remaining the face of God to the people. The voice of God exhibits similar tendencies in relation to the prophet's speech. The result is a portrayal of the prophet in Moses consistent with a dialogical approach to prophetic practice, one cherished and enshrined in the ideals of ancient Israelite scribal practice up through the period of the Second Temple.[5]

---

meanings incipient in and inherent to earlier prophetic visions, were no less engaged in prophecy.

3. J. W. Watts, "The Legal Characterization of Moses in the Rhetoric of the Pentateuch," *JBL* 117 (1998) 418–22; M. Zvi Brettler, "'Fire, Cloud and Deep Darkness' (Deuteronomy 5:22): Deuteronomy's Recasting of Revelation," in *The Significance of Sinai: Traditions about Sinai and Divine Revelation in Judaism and Christianity* (ed. G. J. Brooke, H. Najman, and L. T. Stuckenbruck; Themes in Biblical Narrative 12; Leiden: Brill, 2008) 22–27. Watts and Brettler stand at the end of a long line of scholars investigating the legal innovations in the book of Deuteronomy. Watts, in particular, pursues a distinction between the roles of Moses as prophet and scribe; acts of interpretation and innovation belong, properly, in the latter role. This boundary, in my analysis, is porous.

4. While my analysis will take note of the speaker for each segment of speech, I shall consider direct quotations of divine speech within the speeches of the prophet to belong to the perspective of the prophet. This approach is useful, especially, when distinctions in the prophet's communication of divine instruction occur in comparison with a preceding speech by God on the same subject: the distance between the two voices becomes evident.

5. As the choice of terms here may betray, M. Bakhtin's conception of "polyphony" in the novel inspires my thoughts on this matter. All utterances, by this conception, are multivoiced, a conglomeration reflecting the religious, socioeconomic, ideological, and other variations representative of other voices in dialogical tension within a work. For a demonstration of Bakhtin's approach in reading Dostoevsky's novels,

Exodus 11:1–10:
One Last Smiting for Egypt

A series of three speeches announces the intention of Israel's god to smite Egypt's firstborn children. The divine speeches initiating the despoilment of Egypt (Exod 11:1–3) and anticipating Pharaoh's stubbornness (Exod 11:9–10) enclose the prophet's communication of divine intent (Exod 11:4–8).

Many scholars consider the direction for Egypt's despoilment (Exod 11:1–3) to come from a separate source (usually E), an intrusion on the exchange between Moses and Pharaoh (Exod 11:4–8 picking up from the end of chap. 10).[6] The effect of this editorial insertion disrupting the dialog between Moses and Pharaoh is a measure of irony: Pharaoh's steadfast refusal to grant the divine request is juxtaposed with a forecast of the monarch's reversal of his own position (Exod 11:1–3). The impact of Pharaoh's hardened demeanor wanes beside (the anticipated vision of) the snapshot of his desperate plea for Israel's departure, with gifts to boot.[7] The achievement of this colossal victory over Pharaoh, however, must wait: the Egyptian remains resolute at the conclusion of the chapter.

The interpolation of Exod 11:1–3 has a second literary effect. The direction for Moses to speak to Israel in Exod 11:2a leads, quite naturally, to the expectation that the words beginning with Exod 11:4b address Israel. The first-person pronoun (אני) in v. 4b has God as its antecedent: on the heels of

---

see M. Bakhtin, *Problems of Dostoevsky's Poetics* (trans. C. Emerson; Theory and History of Literature 8; Minneapolis: University of Minnesota Press, 1984). For a comprehensive and systematic introduction to the often-complex thinking of Bakhtin, see M. Holquist, *Dialogism: Bakhtin and His World* (New Accents; London: Routledge, 1990); S. Vice, *Introducing Bakhtin* (New York: Manchester University Press, 1997). For a concise overview and application in biblical studies, see B. Green, *Mikhail Bakhtin and Biblical Scholarship: An Introduction* (SemeiaSt 38; Atlanta: Society of Biblical Literature, 2000).

6. Among others, A. H. McNeile, *The Book of Exodus* (Westminster Commentaries; London: Methuen, 1908) 60; B. D. Eerdmans, *Das Buch Exodus* (Giessen: Alfred Töpelmann, 1910) 29; S. R. Driver, *The Book of Exodus* (Cambridge Bible for Schools and Colleges; Cambridge: Cambridge University Press, 1953) 84; B. S. Childs, *The Book of Exodus: A Critical Theological Commentary* (OTL; Louisville: Westminster, 1974) 160–62. The portion of Exod 11:4–8 is thought to derive from J. For a concise overview of literary problems in Exod 11:1–10, see M. Noth, *Exodus* (trans. J. S. Bowden; OTL; Philadelphia: Westminster, 1962) 92–93; J. I. Durham, *Exodus* (WBC 3; Waco: Word, 1987) 146–47.

7. Childs, *The Book of Exodus*, 161–62. For an argument along similar lines, see W. Janzen, *Exodus* (Believers Church Bible Commentary; Waterloo: Herald, 2000) 134; T. Fretheim, *Exodus* (IBC; Louisville: Westminster John Knox, 1991) 131.

the direction to speak for God to Israel (Exod 11:1–3), Moses introduces his words as those of God (Exod 11:4a). The deployment of the plural in the second-person form תדעון ('[that] you [pl.] might know') of v. 7b is supportive of the impression that Israel is the object of the address. The use of a plural form seems incongruous with the perception of Pharaoh as the sole addressee. However, if the members of Pharaoh's court (mentioned later in v. 8) are included with Pharaoh as the party addressed, then the plural designation would be appropriate in Exod 11:7b.[8] Certainly, the absence of a designated addressee in the introduction to the prophet's speech (Exod 11:4a) should not exclude Pharaoh and his subjects from the list of possible recipients of the prophet's communication. Nevertheless, the preponderance of the direction to address Israel in the preceding speech by God (Exod 11:1–3) fortifies the impression, if only tentative, of Israel as addressee from Exod 11:4b on. In the perception of readers making their way through Exod 11:1–10, this is a viable, even preferable, option. Exod 11:8–9, however, overturns this presumption: these verses refer to Pharaoh in the second person, designating his subjects with the phrase 'all your servants' (כל־עבדיך). Clearly, Pharaoh is the one addressed at this point.[9] In light of the seamless transition between vv. 7 and 8 (that is, no introduction to a fresh unit of speech by the narrator), readers are compelled to reevaluate, retroactively, the object of Moses' address in vv. 4b–7.

Alongside the now-emergent clarity of the addressee in Exod 11:8 is the cessation of any direct citation of divine speech by the prophet. The first-person pronominal elements ("to me" twice) find Moses as their referent, even as Moses is the subject of אצא ('I shall go forth'; v. 8). Clearly, the prophet is speaking for himself. Divested of oracular function, the naked voice of the prophet emerges. This unmarked transition is disconcerting. As such, the speech of Moses in Exod 11:4b–8 exemplifies the prophetic

---

8. More recently, this has been suggested by C. Houtman, *Exodus* (trans. S. Woudstra; 3 vols.; Kampen: Kok, 1996) 2:134; and W. H. C. Propp, *Exodus 1–18: A New Translation with Introduction and Commentary* (AB 2; New Haven: Yale University Press, 1999) 344. Propp goes as far as to include the Israelites and readers as addressees.

9. F. V. Winnett (*The Mosaic Tradition* [Near and Middle East Series 1; Toronto: University of Toronto Press, 1949] 11–12) would include Exod 10:28–29 between Exod 11:8a and 11:8b in an earlier version of the text. See also J. Van Seters, *The Life of Moses: The Yahwist as Historian in Exodus–Numbers* (Louisville: Westminster John Knox, 1994) 108; P. Heinisch, *Das Buch Exodus* (Bonn: Hanstein, 1934) 95–96. For Winnett, the clauses of Exod 10:28–29 were removed to their present location by P in order to mark a conclusion to the story of the plagues at the end of chap. 10. Subsequently, Exod 11:9–10 was composed to set the inauguration of the Passover within the context of a final (tenth) plague.

voice as a mixture of the divine voice with the prophet's own; that is, the speech as a whole is an index to the hybrid nature of prophetic discourse. Here, the boundary between prophet and deity is not easily discerned.

While the voices merge in the course of the prophet's speech, the juxtaposition of that same speech with the unmediated words of God in vv. 1–3 points to distinction between the two. Moses, in conveying divine intention to the people, emphasizes the exception of Israel from the destructive designs of God (v. 7). The divine speech on the same subject omits this emphasis, confining itself to securing Israel's material welfare at Egypt's expense (v. 2). God's intention in initiating this action is related to the enhancement of the prophet's stature (v. 3).

Succinctly stated, my argument in the analysis of Exod 11:1–10 is as follows. The tapestry of speeches in Exod 11:1–10 generates ambiguities regarding the identities of addressor and addressee. Progression through the passage fosters the genesis of assumptions, which suffer reevaluation. Who, exactly, is speaking to whom? The various indexes of disparate sources become, in the present composite text, points of redirection for readerly speculation as to the recipient of the speech. One effect of this literary artistry, if it be that, is the perceived convergence of the voices of the prophet and the deity. The rhetorical trajectories of the two speakers, however, maintain a degree of disparity. The prophet and God speak on similar subjects with different emphases, and the tension, if subtle, can be felt between the units of speech. If the accomplishment of Exod 11:1–10 is to raise awareness of both the conflation and the distinction of the voices, it remains to be seen how these opposing tendencies will play out in subsequent speeches.

Exodus 12:1–13: Instructions for Israel's First Passover

The instructions for the selection of an animal for the Passover meal, its preparation, and its consumption appear as unmediated divine speech (Exod 12:1–13); God speaks for himself. This speech, in tandem with a latter portion of the previous chapter (Exod 11:4–10), forms a chiasm:

A		Egypt will be smitten (Exod 11:4–6)
	B	Israel will be set apart from the destruction (Exod 11:7–8)
	X	Egypt will remain resolute (Exod 11:9–10)
	B′	the Passover meal; the setting apart of Israel (Exod 12:1–11)
A′		Egypt will be smitten, but not Israel (Exod 12:12–13)

The chiastic pattern suggests that Exod 12:1–13 responds to elements in the closing verses of Exod 11:1–10. Pharaoh's staunch resistance is the turning point (X) in the chiasmus. This central point, Pharaoh's stubbornness, is enclosed by divine resolution to shatter Egypt's resolve (A, A′). Caught between the contest of divine wills—Pharaoh and Israel's god—is Israel's safety and destiny, the concern of Exod 11:7–8 and 12:1–11 (B, B′). Exod 12:1–11 develops a method for establishing Israel's distinction. The response of Exod 12:1–13 to Exod 11:4–10, therefore, is to explain the way in which the security of Israel is to be achieved. This is the achievement of chiasmus in Exod 11:4–12:13.

Beyond the framework of this chiastic structure, other elements serve to advance the rhetoric of God's speech in Exod 12:1–13. This speech is part of a larger segment of text (Exod 12:1–20) considered by many to derive from the Priestly pen.[10] By comparison, pre-Priestly material on Passover preparations (Exod 12:21–23) focuses narrowly on the blood rite at the thresholds of Israelite homes. The Priestly version in Exod 12:1–13 is replete with references to the act of eating (אכל). In this short space, אכל appears seven times: vv. 4b, 7b, 8a, 8b, 9a, 11a, 11b. The verb is placed within instructions prescribing the time (v. 8a), location (v. 7b), and manner for the consumption of the sacrificial portion (vv. 11a, 11b), its method of preparation (v. 9a), accompanying foods (v. 8b), and the number of participants at each meal (v. 4b). Also prominent in the passage are the multiple instances of בית ('house').[11] The clauses that contain the term display concerns similar to those with reference to eating: the number of participants in the slaughter and consumption of each animal (vv. 3b [both instances], 4a, and 4b); the location for its consumption (v. 7b). The case of v. 13b stands out through its unique focus on the blood of the beast as a marker of Israelite households, a matter also of concern in v. 7b. By and large, the clauses using either term (or both terms) all together

---

10. Among others, Noth, *Exodus*, 94; Childs, *The Book of Exodus*, 184; Propp, *Exodus 1–18*, 379–80. Both Childs and Propp offer a concise outline of the distinctive characteristics of P's version of the Passover ritual in comparison to the pre-Priestly version in Exod 12:21–23; see also McNeile, *The Book of Exodus*, 63.

11. The clauses of Exod 12:1–13 attest to a semantic range in the use of the term 'house' (בית). While בית in vv. 3b (two times), 4a, and 4b refers to members of a household, 'the houses' (הבתים) in vv. 7b and 13a almost certainly designate the physical structures of the domiciles. Shimon Bar-On ("Zur literarkritischen Analyse von Ex 12,21–27," *ZAW* 107 [1995] 23–25) has noted the repeated use of the term, and finds in the similar prominence of "house" in Exod 12:22–27a indication that Exod 12:22–27a followed Exod 12:7 at an earlier stage in the development of the text.

designate the procedural, temporal, and local boundaries governing the preparation and consumption of the meal.[12]

The clauses invoking the images of consumption and domiciles are part of a larger network of statements within Exod 12:1–13 tracing the spatio-temporal boundaries of the Passover meal. The members of the household should partake of the sacred portion within the physical structure of the domicile (Exod 12:7b) and during the night of the 14th day of the first month (Exod 12:8a; cf. Exod 12:6). Even as dawn marks the terminus of the temporal boundary (Exod 12:10), the entrance to every Israelite household, the doorposts (המזוזות) and the lintel (המשקוף), marks the locus of the meal (Exod 12:7). In keeping with protocols for sacred meals elsewhere (see Exod 34:25; 29:34; Lev 7:15, 17; 8:32; 22:29–30; Deut 16:4), the prescriptions proscribe consumption beyond a designated place and time.[13] The Passover meal, by this conception, is a special meal, taking place in a special place and time. Not unlike the utterances with reference to households and ingestion, the conceptions of sacred space and time will find new direction as God's speech further unfolds.

A restatement of the impending nocturnal act of destruction (Exod 12:12–13) stands at the close of the instructions for the Passover. Echoes of the prophet's initial announcement in Exod 11:4–8 may be found in the divine speech at hand. The terrifying divine visitation is located, once again, 'in the land of Egypt' (בארץ מצרים) and designated as an event of the night (בלילה הזה, 'on this night'). As in the communication of Moses (Exod 11:5), the object of destruction will be 'the firstborn in the land of Egypt' (בכור בארץ מצרים), 'human' (אדם) and 'beast' (בהמה).[14] The Mosaic turns of phrase, so it seems, resonate with God! Absent in Exod 12:1–13, however, is any extensive prospection regarding the humiliating

---

12. As the divine speech moves on to introduce a commemorative festival (Festival of Unleavened Bread) in Exod 12:14–20, the reprisal of these terms (אכל and בית) promote a narrower, particular interest, a subset within the broader spectrum of significance.

13. The function of proscriptions such as these as indicators of the sacred and elevated status of these ritualized acts of consumption is favored by the majority: e.g., J. B. Segal, *The Hebrew Passover from the Earliest Times to* A.D. *70* (London Oriental Series 12; London: Oxford University Press, 1963) 207; Propp, *Exodus 1–18*, 396–97; Houtman, *Exodus*, 2:181. Additionally, R. de Vaux (*Les Sacrifices de l'Ancien Testament* [Paris: Gabalda, 1961] 12) links the restriction of consumption to the night and the disposal of leftovers to breaking camp at dawn within nomadic practice, the original context for the rite.

14. The designation of the object of destruction in Exod 12:12 may be read as an abbreviation of the longer statement in Exod 11:5, maintaining the categories (animal and human) of the preceding expression (Exod 11:5).

capitulation of Pharaoh and his courtiers (Exod 11:8). Nor are there elaborate images of Egypt's suffering (Exod 11:6) and Israel's security (Exod 11:7). Instead, we find the inclusion of the Egyptian pantheon as an object of defeat (Exod 12:12b). Also extraneous to the forecast of Moses in Exod 11:4–8 is the indication of the blood on the threshold as a sign (Exod 12:13a) and, of course, the extensive ritual that spawns that sign. But perhaps the most prominent rhetorical shift in the divine forecast of the destruction of Egypt's offspring may be found in the series of first-person verbal forms emphasizing God as the agent of destruction: "For *I will pass through* ((ועברתי the land of Egypt that night, and *I will strike down* (והכיתי) every firstborn . . . *I will execute* (אעשה) judgments . . . when *I see* (וראיתי) the blood, *I will pass* (ופסחתי) over you" (Exod 12:12–13).[15] In contrast, the single direct representation of God as the agent of destruction in a participial phrase (אני יוצא 'I, going forth') in Exod 11:4 appears anemic.[16]

In sum, the speech of God up to this point seconds the prophet's previous assurance of a distinction between Egypt and Israel (Exod 12:13; see Exod 11:7). In light of Exod 12:13, the prescriptions for the preparation of the Passover meal may be perceived as an elaboration on the method

---

15. The emphasis on divine agency has been noted by several scholars: U. Cassuto, *A Commentary on the Book of Exodus* (trans. I. Abrahams; Publications of the Perry Foundation for Biblical Research in the Hebrew University of Jerusalem; Jerusalem: Magnes, 1967) 140; Childs, *The Book of Exodus*, 192; Van Seters, *The Life of Moses*, 116. The translations of the Hebrew into English consisting of segments beyond a single clause, here and throughout this essay, are from the NRSV. The emphasis is mine. Contrary to the NRSV, I consider the sense 'to protect' for פסח to suit the context of the passage (see Gen 9:16; Isa 31:5).

16. The preference for the abstract infinitival expression למשחית ('to destroy') in Exod 12:13b instead of the personified agent of destruction, המשחית ('the destroyer'; see also 2 Sam 24:16; 1 Chr 21:12) in Exod 12:23b may indicate P's aversion to the idea of ministering angels. See R. E. Friedman, *Who Wrote the Bible?* (Englewood Cliffs, NJ: Prentice Hall, 1987); Propp, *Exod 1–18*, 401–2). Priestly reservation in matters of this sort, as it turns out, contributes to the rhetorical direction of the passage in emphasizing God as the agent of destruction. No other 'destroyer' (המשחית) exists in the speech of Exod 12:1–13 to steal the show from Israel's national deity. However, H. G. May ("The Relation of the Passover to the Festival of Unleavened Cakes," *JBL* 55 [1936] 70) contends, with reference to Exod 13:14, 15 and Deut 6:20, that Israel's god is often indistinguishable from the extraterrestrial agents of his will. Reference to such beings, in his view, does not diminish divine participation. May's contention presents no problem to my argument here. The function of emphasis inherent to the selection of certain lexical or grammatical forms over others does not presume the absence of the object of amplification in a text under comparison. In fact, the opposite is the case. The proliferation of first-person verbs and the choice of the infinitive construct למשחית embolden a notion (divine initiative) already present in surrounding texts. Emphasis, in this capacity, draws attention to something present already in a work.

of this distinction, though not exclusively. The correspondence of Exod 12:1–11 (B′) to Exod 11:7–8 (B) in the chiastic setup of Exod 11:1–12:13 would support this interpretation. But even as the deity echoes Moses in word(s) and thought, he fortifies the perception of his own position as the prime mover in this initiative. As the one forging Israel's (and Egypt's) fate, God authors and prescribes a course of action that will create in space and time a structure that will separate Israel from its captors.

Exodus 12:14–20: *Instructions for the Festival of Unleavened Bread*

The divine speech proceeds in Exod 12:14–20 with instructions for the Festival of Unleavened Bread. With the exclusion of Exod 12:14, chiasmus governs this segment of speech:[17]

A   Seven days (שבעת ימים) you shall eat unleavened bread; on the first day you shall remove leaven from your houses, for whoever eats leavened bread (כי כל־אכל חמץ) from the first day until the seventh day shall be cut off (ונכרתה הנפש ההוא) from Israel (Exod 12:15).

    B   *On the first day* you shall hold a solemn assembly, *and on the seventh day* a solemn assembly; no work shall be done on those days; only what everyone must eat, that alone may be prepared by you (Exod 12:16).

       X   You shall observe the festival of unleavened bread, for on this very day I brought your companies out of the land of Egypt: you shall observe this day throughout your generations as a perpetual ordinance (Exod 12:17).

    B′   *In the first month from the evening of the fourteenth day until the evening of the twenty-first day*, you shall eat unleavened bread (Exod 12:18).

A′   For seven days (שבעת ימים) no leaven shall be found in your houses; for whoever eats what is leavened (כי כל־אכל מחמצה) shall be cut off (ונכרתה הנפש ההוא) from the congregation of Israel, whether an alien or the native of the land. You shall eat nothing leavened; in all your settlements you shall eat unleavened bread (Exod 12:19–20).

The assignment of the festival as a commemorative gesture to the impending deliverance of Israel (Exod 12:17) stands at the center of the chiasmus

---

17. Emphasis in the text below is mine. As elsewhere in this essay, the translation into English is from the NRSV.

(X). This single statement forges the connection with the preceding prescriptions for the Passover meal.

Farthest removed from the center of the structure are similar injunctions against the consumption of leaven under penalty of excommunication (Exod 12:15 [A]; Exod 12:19–20 [A']).[18] The cluster of similar phrases across both units (see Hebrew text in parentheses) reinforces the thematic correspondence between the units at this level (A, A').[19]

Two seemingly disparate subjects—two solemn gatherings at the extremities of the duration for the festival (Exod 12:16) and the avoidance of leaven (Exod 12:18)—take up residence one level removed from the center (B, B'). These units share a preference for designations of a temporal duration that denote the beginning and the end of the period of time (see emphasized text in B and B' above). In contrast, the units of the outermost ring (A, A') deploy a single phrase ('seven days', שבעת ימים) to designate a duration without explicit indication of the boundaries (beginning and end) of that period. The fruit of the comparison between B and B', orchestrated by the literary pattern of the passage, is the recognition of an analogous relationship between abstinence from leaven (B') and cessation from labor (B). Associations with Gen 2:2–3 and Exod 20:8–11 through similar concerns with periods of seven days and cessation (שבת) from labor (מלאכה) reinforce the perception that abstinence from leaven is an exceptional activity within a specific time. The network of correspondences grows.

The reference to structures of inclusion (and exclusion) in the passage as a whole (Exod 12:14–20) is, of course, reminiscent of previous spatio-temporal constructions in Exod 12:1–13. By this point, the respect for boundaries of time and space is familiar. Perhaps in this aspect the festival commemorates the Passover event, and remembering the Passover event (the inception of the exodus) is, after all, the central purpose behind the festival, the point of the chiastic structure. What more can one say about connections with the preceding instructions for the Passover meal?

---

18. The progression of thought in both statements is identical: a call to abstain from leaven leading into a stipulated consequence for failure to abstain.

19. I. Knohl (*The Sanctuary of Silence: The Priestly Torah and the Holiness School* [Minneapolis: Fortress, 1995] 21) finds in Exod 12:18–20 a chiastic structure that places the grave consequence of excommunication in focus: command to eat unleavened bread (v. 18); prohibition of leaven (v. 19a); consequence of excommunication (v. 19b); prohibition of leaven (v. 20a); command to eat unleavened bread (v. 20b). Combining the focuses of both chiastic constructions in the passage leads to an understanding of Passover observance/remembrance as inclusion in the congregation of Israel, a state diametrically opposed to that of excommunication.

Beyond thematic similarities (to which I shall return) are similarities in vocabulary.[20] The repeated references to 'house' (בית) and eating (אכל) in Exod 12:1–13 appear again here in this segment of divine speech. In fact, U. Cassuto has noted that the sevenfold repetition of אכל in Exod 12:1–13 is matched in Exod 12:14–20.[21] Without exception, the object of consumption in the seven instances of the verb in Exod 12:1–13 is a portion of the designated sacrificial beast (vv. 4b, 7b, 8a, 8b, 9a, 11a, 11b). This stands in contrast to the passage at hand. Here, in Exod 12:14–20 the object of consumption, with the exception of the case in v. 17a, is the unleavened cakes (מצות; vv. 15a, 18a, 20b) or the proscribed article with leaven (חמץ/מחמצת; vv. 15b, 19b, 20a). Not surprisingly, instructions for the Festival of Unleavened Bread (Exod 12:14–20) contain numerous references to a baked item as the object of consumption. Exod 12:14–20, in its constitution, substitutes leavened cakes for the beast of the Passover meal as the direct object of consumption. But the recurrence of a series of clauses deploying the verb אכל begs comparison with Exod 12:1–13, and comparison yields another similarity: temporal restrictions.

'House' (בית) shows up two times in the passage at hand (Exod 12:15a, 19a). Both instances of the noun are in statements calling for the removal of leaven (שאר) from the home within prescribed periods ("on the first day"; "for seven days") a concern of the outermost bracket (A, A′) in the chiastic order of Exod 12:14–20. As was the case in the instructions for the Passover meal, the prescriptions for the Festival of Unleavened Bread involves the collocation of בית and אכל in a spatiotemporal scheme of exclusion. The point is this: the Festival of Unleavened Bread is like the Passover meal, which is a type of Sabbath (by association with Gen 2:2–3 and Exod 20:8–11). The genesis of broad and abstract categories transcends the particularities of the individual rituals. The conjunction of the two appears seamless.[22]

---

20. The postulation that the festival was a celebration of the harvest and only subsequently related to the Passover has been rehearsed elsewhere: J. Morgenstern, "The origins of Massoth and the Massoth Festival," *AJT* 21 (1917) 275–93; J. Pedersen, *Israel: Its Life and Culture* (2 vols.; London: Oxford University Press, 1940) 2:399–401; R. de Vaux, *Ancient Israel: Its Life and Institutions* (trans. J. McHugh; London: Darton, Longman, & Todd, 1961) 490–92. The details of that theory are not the concern of this study but only the connections, albeit artificial and secondary, forged in the conjunction of Exod 12:1–13 and 14–20, and the inconcinnities that remain for readers encountering the text.

21. Cassuto, *A Commentary on the Book of Exodus*, 140.

22. Even the chronological irregularities in the speech of Exod 12:1–20 participates in bridging the two rites. One might ask: does 'this day' (היום הזה) in Exod 12:14a refer

To summarize the divine contributions in Exod 12:1–20 as a whole, the voice of God is emphatic, even exclusive, in speaking about divine initiative in Israel's deliverance. In pursuing this initiative, God spells out a method for the distinction of Israel from Egypt, a matter also of concern for the prophet (Exod 11:4–8). This method involves both the Passover rite and the Festival of Unleavened Bread. Broad similarities bring a measure of coherence to both rites. Essential to this resemblance is a spatio-temporal scheme that locates specified items beyond select boundaries. Table 1 represents the correspondences among the various prescriptions in the speech. Similarities in language pave the way for similar ideas, drawing lines of correspondence across separate rituals. The speech of God is beginning to look like a house of mirrors, multiplying rituals even as the speech reflects the interests of Moses. Now, what will the prophet say to all this?

Exodus 12:21–28:
Instructions for the Passover, Once Again

The voice of Moses returns to communicate the instructions for the Passover rite to the people. The discourse follows a general outline witnessed in the earlier speech of the deity: selection and slaughter of an animal (Exod 12:21b; see 12:3b–6); blood application (Exod 12:22; see 12:7); slaughter of Egyptian firstborn, but Israel escapes destruction (Exod 12:23; see 12:12–13).[23] Along with the familiar sequence of prescribed actions are words and phrases known from previous instructions for the

---

to the day of the Passover meal, the destruction, the departure (see Exod 12:17), or the inception of the Festival of Unleavened Bread (Exod 12:18)? The list of activities straddles two days (14 and 15 Nisan). By formal resemblance, היום הזה echoes other temporal phrases in surrounding texts. Looking backward from Exod 12:14a, היום הזה picks up החדש הזה ('this month' in Exod 12:1a [the start of the year that commemorates the exodus]) and בלילה הזה ('on this night' in Exod 12:8a, 12a [the night of the Passover meal and of the destruction, respectively]). Looking ahead from Exod 12:14a, היום הזה designates the day of Israel's departure (15 Nisan) in Exod 12:17a, b, which the festival (its inception slated for 14 Nisan according to Exod 12:18) commemorates. The cluster of similar temporal expressions draws together the various activities of both days, underscoring the temporal confusion. Confusion, however, may be in order in a speech that seeks to confuse two rituals. Several commentators follow this trend when they suggest that 'this day' in Exod 12:14a refers to both days loosely: Childs, *Exodus*, 197; Durham, *Exodus*, 157–58; Knohl, *The Sanctuary of Silence*, 19–20. A similar fastidious attention to temporal delimitations, even if inaccurate, straddles both acts of ritual. The fusion of the start of both rites is also the accomplishment of Ezek 45:21, as Knohl points out, but in contrast to Lev 23:5–8 and Num 28:16–18.

23. G. W. Coats, *Exodus 1–18* (FOTL 2a; Grand Rapids: Eerdmans, 1999) 83.

Table 1. Corresponding Prescriptions in Exodus 12:1–20

Activity	Spatial Boundaries	Temporal Boundaries	Excluded Activities or Things
consumption of Passover sacrifice	in the house	during the night	eating leftovers at dawn
consumption of unleavened cakes	in the house	for seven days	eating leaven (nonconforming member of community to be excommunicated)
Sabbath observance	none	on the first and seventh days in a seven-day period	labor

event. The choice animal is taken (לקח; v. 21b; see vv. 3b, 5b) and slaughtered (שחט, v. 21b; see v. 6b). God passes through the land (עבר; v. 23a; see v. 12a); he sees (ראה; v. 23a; see v. 13a) and passes over/protects (פסח, v. 23b; see v. 13a) from destruction/the destroyer (המשחית, v. 23b; see למשחית in v. 13b). Again, there is talk of doorposts, the lintel (המזוזות, המשקוף, v. 22a; see v. 7a), houses (בית, vv. 22b, 23b, 27a, 27b; see vv. 3b, 4a, 4b, 7b, 13b, 15a, 19a) and restrictions until dawn (עד־בקר, v. 22b; see v. 10). The images are well known, and the action is predictable.

Beyond the familiar turns of phrase and sequence of action are the unique pursuits of the prophet's communication of divine instruction. Shorn of interest in the preparation and consumption of the sacrificial beast (see Exod 12:8–11; 'eating' [אכל] does not show up in this speech), Moses expands on instructions for the application of the blood of the sacrificial beast (Exod 12:22).[24] As with the Festival of Unleavened Bread, the ritual of the Passover here becomes an object for future religious attention, and directions for informing posterity of the meaning of the rite ensue (Exod 12:24–28).

---

24. The unique properties of Exod 12:21–28 and the assignment of the bulk of it by many to a pre-Priestly stratum have been flagged in an earlier part of this essay (see p. 9 n. 14). While the narrow focus on the blood rite is unique to Exod 12:21–23, the literary, lexical, and thematic links with the Priestly prescriptions of Exod 12:1–13 (some of which have just been mentioned above) have led some to seek the origins of Exod 12:21–28 in the same Priestly source. See May, "The Relation of the Passover," 71–73; B. N. Wambacq, "Les Origines de la Pesah Israélite," *Bib* 57 (1976) 316–18; Coats, *Exodus 1–18*, 82-83; Van Seters, *The Life of Moses*, 115–16; Bar-On, "Zur literarkritischen Analyse," 22.

The speech of Moses here makes a contribution to the structures of space and time established in previous communication. In the final clause of Exod 12:22, every Israelite is cautioned against leaving the house prior to dawn. Perhaps, this would bring the transgressing individual into the realm of the destroyer, and that individual (or the offspring) would forfeit the protection extended through participation in the ritual. The temporal boundary of dawn (עד־בקר 'until dawn') is reminiscent of the requirement to confine consumption of the meal to the night in Exod 12:10: according to this commandment, all leftovers are to be disposed of by burning at dawn. The common phrase across both statements suggests a connection between the prescriptions in the grand scheme of things: the Israelite stepping outdoors in the night (Exod 12:22) matches the post-dawn Israelite diner (Exod 12:10). Both activities, in different ways, stand outside stipulated boundaries. Through Exod 12:10, the transgressing Israelite of Exod 12:22 joins the list of designated items excluded by the (still-)growing spatiotemporal scheme of the broader literary context.

A second initiative in this speech of the prophet is the direction of focus toward the threshold of Israelite homes. This focus is a concomitant feature of the emphasis on the blood rite. The return to the subject of blood application in Exod 12:22 is marked by the reprisal of שתי המזוזת ('the two doorposts') and המשקוף ('the lintel') in reversed sequence (see Exod 12:7a).[25] Moses tarries at this point in the procedure, lingering on details in the method of application (the immersion of the applicator in blood, touching it to parts of the threshold) and the requisite instruments for the task (a bundle of marjoram, a receptacle for the blood), all extraneous to the preceding instructions in Exod 12:1–13. The reader's imagination is arrested and fixed on the entrance to the house.[26] The choice of the ambivalent term סף 'bowl' or 'threshold' becomes one more index to the

---

25. So noted in ibid., 22 n. 25.

26. Several scholars have noted here the significance of the threshold as the transit place between the benign spaces of the house and the external environment populated by malevolent forces: B. M. Levinson, *Deuteronomy and the Hermeneutics of Legal Innovation* (New York: Oxford University Press, 1997) 58–59; Houtman, *Exodus*, 175–76; Propp, *Exodus 1–18*, 434–39. In Exod 12:22, the administration of blood to ward off the onslaught of the destroyer from outside the house seems superfluous in the light of Exod 11:4–7 (see also Exod 4:24–26); there, God recognizes Israelite homes without need for a sign. Propp finds a ritual similar to the Passover in the Muslim rite of *fidya*. The latter is an undertaking in times of danger (transition, disease, and so on) for the community. Blood from a slain beast is applied to various objects, including doorways, for the purpose of protecting those inside. Houtman observes similarities between the blood rite of the Passover and the Jewish practice of attaching scrolls of scriptural passages to doorposts (see Deut 6:5; 11:20), and also the Christian practice of installing crucifixes in the same location.

point of transition between the outside and the inside of the home.²⁷ As though readers would miss the first indication of the source of the blood (בדם אשר־בסף 'in the blood that is in/on the basin/threshold'), the prescriptions return them to this fact (מן־הדם אשר בסף 'from the blood that is in/on the basin/threshold') in the very next sentence. Even so, there is more direction for attention to the threshold.

The choice of the phrase מפתח ביתו ('from the door of his house') in the warning against wandering outdoors on the night of the Passover is surprising. The earlier reference to evacuation (of leaven) from the area within the house in Exod 12:15a designates this space by מבתיכם ('from your houses'). A similar prepositional phrase here in Exod 12:22, מביתו ('from his house'), would not alter the sense of the clause. The expanded phrase מפתח ביתו ('from the door of his house') with the inclusion of פתח in Exod 12:22b stands out. On its own, this slight departure from the form of the earlier expression is insignificant. But, again, there is more to suggest a concerted effort to elevate the prominence of the threshold in the prophet's speech.

The prophet's reprisal of the smiting of the firstborn in Exod 12:23, while following the same sequence of action in Exod 12:12–13, inserts a similar focus on the entrance to the house. This particular interest of Exod 12:23 is evident in comparison with the corresponding material in the earlier unmediated words of God (Exod 12:13).²⁸

וראה את־הדם על־המשקוף ועל שתי המזוזת ופסח יהוה על־הפתח	When he sees the blood *on the lintel and the two doorposts*, the Lord will pass over *that door*. (Exod 12:23)
וראיתי את־הדם ופסחתי עלכם	When I see the blood, I will pass *over you*. (Exod 12:13)

---

27. Both meanings are possible. The concept of a receptacle is appropriate to 2 Sam 17:28, 2 Kgs 12:14, and Jer 52:19. 'Doorway' would suit the contexts of Judg 19:27, Isa 6:4, and Amos 9:1. The Aramaic versions prefer the idea of a receptacle, while LXX and *Vulg.* designate a doorway. Similarly, scholars are divided on this matter. In favor of 'threshold,' with the implication that the slaughter takes place by the entrance, are A. M. Honeyman, "Hebrew סַף 'Basin, Goblet,'" *JTS* 37 (1936) 59; Houtman, *Exodus*, 193; and Levinson, *Deuteronomy and the Hermeneutics of Legal Innovation*, 59. Others consider 'receptacle' a better fit: McNeile, *The Book of Exodus*, 72; Segal, *The Hebrew Passover*, 158 n. 1; Propp, *Exodus 1–18*, 408. The former option suits the degree of attention to the threshold in Exod 12:21–24. The alternative ('receptacle'), however, would not subtract from my argument here. The image of a doorway would remain a possibility, a playful offering through the choice of the ambiguous term for readers that would perceive a connection with the broader literary context.

28. Emphasis in the following material cited is mine.

The prophet's rendition of the deity's statement appends a prepositional phrase ("on the lintel and the two doorposts") and, in the very next clause, substitutes one prepositional phrase ("over that door") for another ("over you"). As is the case elsewhere in the passage, the prophet's choice of words brings to the foreground the entrances of Israelite homes.

What might be the prophet's purpose in taking the words of God on this novel trajectory? The answer may lie in a comparison of the clauses immediately following those just cited above.

ולא יתן המשחית לבא אל־ בתיכם לנגף	. . . and will not allow *the destroyer to enter your houses* to strike you down. (Exod 12:23)
ולא־יהיה בכם נגף למשחית בהכתי בארץ מצרים	. . . and no plague shall destroy you when I strike the land of Egypt. (Exod 12:13)

While attention to differences between these verses has focused on the personification of destruction (המשחית) in Exod 12:23, the additional imagery of (the destroyer's) movement across the threshold (see emphasized text) in Exod 12:23, largely, has not been explored.[29] The barring of the destroyer (המשחית) by a product of the slaughter of an animal (the blood) gains significance by the recognition of a pun on שחט (to slay) in המשחית (from the root שחת).[30] By this phonetic resonance, the slaughtered (שחט; see vv. 6b and 21b) beast within the house is likened to the victim of the destroyer (המשחית) outside the home. The two acts of destruction appear as parallel movements in two mutually exclusive realms. Therefore, it becomes conceivable through this imagery that the slaying of the beast obviates the necessity for the slaughter of an Israelite firstborn within the home; destruction (from the root שחת) is checked at the door by recognition that slaughter (שחט) already has taken place within the house.[31] Just as the destructive intentions of the destroyer are confined to the outside

---

29. This surplus in Exod 12:23 is matched by the (prohibited) opposite movement of an Israelite through the doorway toward the outside of the house in the preceding verse (Exod 12:22b).

30. R. Friedman (*Commentary on the Torah: With a New Translation and the Hebrew Text* [San Francisco: HarperSanFrancisco, 2001] 207) notes the pun and its ironic import: "the Israelites are to slaughter (root שחט) the lamb so as to keep out the destroyer (root שחת)."

31. The idea of the slaughter of the lamb as a substitute for the death of the Israelite firstborn is implied in the allowance for the redemption of a child with the offer of an animal in Exod 13:14–15. Of course, the suggestion of a vicarious function for the slaughter, here in Exod 12:22–24, is the product of one interpretation of the imagery, and further removed from the implication of a substitution in Exod 13:14–15. Other postulations for the accomplishment of the Passover sacrifice and blood manipulation in Exod 12:22–24, beyond an apotropaic function, include the related functions of

(Exod 12:23), so are the protective powers of the sacrifice to the inside (Exod 12:22b). Symmetry and mutual exclusion, therefore, are the contributions of the prophet's modifications to the spatiotemporal constructs of the Passover meal.

In summary, the prophet's speech within Exod 12:21–28 states that Israelites outside their houses on the night of the Passover are out of bounds. The recurrence of "until morning" suggests this transgression is in the same category as that of eating leftovers from the Passover sacrifice and, by analogy, that of other proscribed activities within designated times (consuming leaven, working). In his emphasis on the blood rite, Moses creates an analogy between the destruction indoors and outdoors by a focus on the boundary between the two spaces. The same analogy is reinforced by the phonetic resemblance between two verbal roots for destruction (שחט/שחת) and the clear delineation of the realm for each act of slaughter. This correspondence between the two realms generates the possible interpretation that the slaughter of the Passover animal may stand in lieu of the death of a child in the house.

The Space between Prophet and Deity:
Some Remarks in Conclusion

This essay began with observations that literature up through the period of the Second Temple invokes Moses as an exemplary prophet. Inherent to this reference is the understanding that prophetic activity is a (sometimes-contentious) conversation with voices past, divine or otherwise. Following the lead of Watts and Brettler in their work on the Pentateuch, I find this affinity for mutual adaptation and modification in the fabric of speeches in Exod 11:1–12:28. There, a pastiche of speeches initiates a blending of the voices of God and prophet (Exod 11:1–10). In the initial exchange, the prophet shifts emphasis to Israel's exclusion from divine wrath (Exod 11:4–8), following God's initial announcement of the Passover event (Exod 11:1–3). This is accomplished by swift transitions between speeches without clear introduction and by grammatical incongruities. These collaborate in the genesis of ambiguity of identity in addressor and addressee. Between readerly conjecture and reevaluation, the realization dawns that an intercalation of divine and prophetic voices permeates the unit of speech.

---

purification (Segal, *The Hebrew Passover*, 157–62, 185–86; Lev 14:2–9, Num 19:2–10, and Ezek 45:18–20) and reconciliation (Heinisch, *Das Buch Exodus*, 101–2).

The next burst of divine communication (Exod 12:1–13), as though to confirm this instinct in reading, carries with it the prophet's assurance to the people and his choice of terms; but alongside agreement with the prophetic proclamation is the direction of attention to God's own initiative behind Israel's deliverance. This stands over and against the prophet's slight representation of that fact.

The structures of exclusion germane to the prescribed procedure for the Passover meal carry over into that of the Festival of Unleavened Bread (Exod 12:14–20). The specifications of space, time and the entities they exclude in each unique rite line up together. A spatiotemporal paradigm emerges. The prophet's distinct concerns, when his voice returns, are to include the unwary Israelite who wanders outdoors in the list of excluded entities, and to reenvision the slaughter of the Passover lamb as a counterpart to the slaughter of the Egyptian offspring beyond the boundaries of Israelite homes.

Therefore, the series of speeches in Exod 11:1–12:28 is a concatenation of units deploying similar language, imagery, and concepts; each subsequent unit squeezes fresh significance from this common stock. Things of less import (for example, divine agency in Israel's deliverance), or nonexistent in earlier speeches (for example, the slain lamb in the house as counterpart to the slain offspring outside the house), find themselves central subjects in subsequent discourse. Through a network of analogies, the significance of concepts grows: new boundaries of time and space are added and the list of excluded entities/activities grows. One rite is fashioned in the image of another; one set of requirements for conformity resembles a previous set. The semblance of coherence emerges. The prophet speaks through the words of God, and God through the prophet's; words and the traces of previous meanings in those words are twisted in the mouth of each other and present new meanings. In this manner, both prophetic and divine speech is perverse, a deviation from previous direction. But it is this perversion that animates the imagination, as the reader revisits older nuances in earlier utterances, seeking out the points of aberration. Did Moses, in his announcement of divine intent in Exod 11:4–8, anticipate the need for a sign to distinguish Israelite homes from others (Exod 12:13)? Does God's vision for the preparation and consumption of the Passover lamb (Exod 12:12–13) envision these actions as a likeness to the slaughter that will take place beyond the houses of the Israelites, as the prophet would suggest (Exod 12:22–23)? Are there other ways of comprehension beyond those proposed? The contingency of each act of interpretation becomes stimulus for further speculation. Within the interstices of the dialectic between God and Moses, scribes find inspiration for fresh acts of interpretation and a basis for a recasting of prophetic vision and religious sensibility. In Moses, once again, prophets and scribes find themselves face-to-face with God.

The Shaping of a Prophet: Joshua in the Deuteronomistic History

Gordon Oeste

The book of Joshua is unique in the Deuteronomistic History (DH) in that it alone makes no direct mention of prophets or prophetic activity.[1] Yet prophets play a key role throughout the rest of the DH.[2] Moreover, Deut 18:15, 18, indicates that Yahweh would raise up a prophet like Moses, while Deut 31:7–8 describes Joshua as Moses' successor. Later interpreters saw prophetic elements in the portrayal of Joshua. Interpreters such as Sirach (46:1), Josephus, the Qumran Community (4Q175, 4Q379, 4Q522), the Samaritan tradition, and various early church fathers[3] viewed Joshua through prophetic lenses. Joshua's canonical position among the Former Prophets is also suggestive.[4] This essay will utilize a synchronic, theological reading of the DH to argue that, though the DH never explicitly calls Joshua a prophet, the portrayal of the figure of Joshua in the DH is presented in a way that suggests that Joshua fulfills a "prophet-like" role in the book of Joshua and the DH.

---

1. The only exception is Josh 14:6, referring to Moses as the "man of God," a prophetic title; see T. C. Butler, *Joshua* (WBC 7; Waco: Word, 1983) 173. J. Blenkinsopp (*A History of Prophecy in Israel* [rev. ed.; Louisville: Westminster John Knox, 1983, 1996] 51) attributes the absence of prophetic presence in Joshua to Dtr's concept of charismatic succession.

2. See M. A. O'Brien, "The 'Deuteronomistic History' as a Story of Israel's Leaders," *ABR* 37 (1989) 14–34.

3. *Josephus*: See L. H. Feldman, "Josephus's Portrait of Joshua," *HTR* 82 (1989) 351–76. *Samaritan tradition*: See E. Noort, ("Der Reissende Wolf—Josua in Überlieferung und Geschichte," in *Congress Volume Leiden 2004* [ed. André Lemaire; VTSup 109; Leiden: Brill, 2006] 166), though the main emphasis in the Samaritan tradition is on Joshua as ideal ruler. *Church fathers*: Eupolemos in Eusebius, *Praep. ev.* 9.30.1; *Barn.* 12.8; *Sib. Or.* 2.241–45 and possibly 5.256–59; noted in E. Noort, "Joshua: The History of Reception and Hermeneutics," in *Past, Present, Future: The Deuteronomistic History and the Prophets* (ed. J. C. de Moor and H. F. van Rooy; OTS 44; Leiden: Brill, 2000) 212–14.

4. See S. B. Chapman, *The Law and the Prophets: A Study in Old Testament Canon Formation* (FAT 27; Tübingen: Mohr Siebeck, 2000) 166–87.

Prophecy in the Book of Deuteronomy

The theology of the book of Joshua draws heavily on the book of Deuteronomy.[5] Deuteronomy, however, nowhere provides a comprehensive definition of prophecy, a full description of the prophetic role, or what qualified as prophecy in ancient Israel. Instead, it presents some broad parameters within which Israelite prophecy was to function. In a paraenetic speech (Deut 12:32–13:5[13:1–6]), Deuteronomy delimits prophecy negatively, describing what false prophets do. False prophets utilize signs and/or wonders to validate their prophecies, not unlike true prophets of Yahweh (e.g., Deut 34:11, 1 Kgs 13:3, Ezek 24:20–24). However, false prophets utilize these phenomena to validate a call to pursue other gods (נלכה אחרי אלהים אחרים 13:2[3]). This is tantamount to advocating rebellion (דבר סרה 13:5[6]) against Yahweh. True prophets advocate the pursuit of Yahweh (אחרי יהוה אלהיכם תלכו 13:4[5]), expressed through a series of six verbs (walk, fear, keep, obey, serve, hold fast), which bear strong similarity to those used in ancient vassal treaties and together exemplify complete obedience to Yahweh.[6] Thus, the laws in Deuteronomy 13 defining illegitimate prophetic activity fall within the larger context of covenant keeping and covenant breaking.[7]

Deut 18:9–22 serves as the capstone for a much broader series of regulations (Deut 16:18–18:22) dealing with the responsibilities of various leadership positions in ancient Israel. The inclusion of prophets among these leadership positions intimates the central role the prophets played in the deuteronomic vision of Israel's ideal society,[8] and by extension, the DH. Deut 18:9–22 contains three related sections. The first (Deut 18:9–13), warns Israel away from following a list of abominable Canaanite practices (תועבות). With the possible exception of the one who makes his

---

5. G. J. Wenham, "The Deuteronomic Theology of the Book of Joshua," *JBL* 90 (1971) 140–48.

6. About ancient vassal treaties, see R. D. Nelson, *Deuteronomy* (OTL; Louisville: Westminster John Knox, 2002) 170–71. Regarding obedience, Deuteronomy 13 describes three groups of people who may entice a fellow Israelite to follow other gods: (1) prophets or dreamers; (2) close family members; and (3) rebellious city leaders. Ancient vassal treaties specifically warn of religious leaders, close family members, and influential urban rebels as potential advocates of defection from political treaties. See M. Weinfeld, *Deuteronomy and the Deuteronomic School* (Oxford: Oxford University Press, 1972; repr., Winona Lake, IN: Eisenbrauns, 1992) 91–100.

7. G. McConville (*Deuteronomy* [AOT; Downers Grove, IL: InterVarsity, 2002] 235) notes that the covenantal background of Deuteronomy 13 accounts for various features of the chapter: the danger of conspiracy to defect from the covenant, the need for denunciation, and the call to "love" Yahweh/the suzerain.

8. R. Wilson, *Prophecy and Society in Ancient Israel* (Philadelphia: Fortress, 1980) 160.

children "pass through the fire," each of these practices concerns consultation with specialists seeking information from or manipulation of the divine realm.[9]

In contrast to these illegitimate means of ascertaining the divine will, Deut 18:15–19 specifies the legitimate means by which Israel could receive communication from the divine realm—prophecy originating from Yahweh. Here, Deut 18:18 emphasizes that true prophets will follow the prototype of Moses and exhibit three key characteristics: (1) Yahweh will raise up (קוּם) the prophet, (2) he must be a fellow Israelite (אָח), and (3) Yahweh will put his words into the prophet's mouth so that he can communicate all of Yahweh's words to the people. This stress on Yahweh's raising up the prophet and placing his words in the prophet's mouth underlines the prophet's authority while also acknowledging his/her subordination to Yahweh. Deuteronomy 18 further emphasizes the prophet's authority through the fourfold repetition of the verb שׁמע 'listen' (18:14, 15, 16, 19). While the Canaanite nations *listen* to those who practice illegitimate methods of divine mediation (18:14), Israel must instead *listen* to the prophet like Moses who mediates the words of Yahweh (18:15, 19), or Yahweh himself will deal with him. Thus, Deut 18:15–19 characterizes prophetic activity as the intermediation of Yahweh's words or instructions,[10] though this mediation is constrained by Yahweh's word and Moses' shadow.

Most commentators recognize that the use of the singular "prophet" in 18:15, 18 does not denote one specific future prophet (see "son" in 2 Sam 7:14), but instead points to a series of prophets arising at Yahweh's initiative throughout Israel's history, though likely not denoting a specific prophetic 'office' passed down from prophet to prophet.[11] H. Barstad,

---

9. Ibid., 161; see Nelson, *Deuteronomy*, 232. The fact that the other six practices listed in Deut 18:10–11 relate to some form of consultation with the divine realm suggests that the one who causes his children to "pass through the fire" also falls within this category (see 2 Kgs 17:17; 21:6).

10. D. Petersen ("Defining Prophecy and Prophetic Literature," in *Prophecy in Its Ancient Near Eastern Context: Mesopotamian, Biblical, and Arabian Perspectives* [ed. Marti Nissinen; SBLSymS 13; Atlanta: Society of Biblical Literature, 2000] 33–44) recognizes the broad scope of prophetic activity in ancient Israel and the ANE and concludes that viewing prophets as intermediaries between the divine and human realms best conveys the essence of prophetic activity.

11. On the notion of prophets arising throughout Israel's history, see S. R. Driver, *A Critical and Exegetical Commentary on Deuteronomy* (ICC; Edinburgh: T. & T. Clark, 1895) 227; A. D. H. Mayes, *Deuteronomy* (NCB; London: Oliphants / Greenwood, SC: Attic, 1979) 282; P. Miller, *Deuteronomy* (IBC; Louisville: Westminster John Knox, 1990) 155; Nelson, *Deuteronomy*, 234–35. R. P. Carroll ("The Elijah-Elisha Sagas: Some Remarks on Prophetic Succession in Ancient Israel," *VT* 19 [1969] 414)

however, has argued that the implied referent of Deuteronomy 18—the prophet like Moses—is Joshua.[12] While Barstad's proposal has merit and Deuteronomy does portray Joshua as Moses' successor, Deuteronomy does not explicitly designate Joshua as Moses' *prophetic* successor.[13] Furthermore, the rather broadly painted picture of prophecy in Deuteronomy opens up additional possibilities for referents beyond Joshua.[14]

The final section of Deut 18:9–22 (18:20–22) builds on Deut 13:1–6 with its description of illegitimate prophecy. Deut 13:1–6 characterized a false prophet as someone who advocated obedience to other gods. Deut 18:20–22 now characterizes false prophecy more closely and in line with the preceding description of a prophet like Moses. Here, a false prophet not only advocates the worship of other deities, but unlike a true prophet, also presumes to speak on Yahweh's behalf (18:20) when Yahweh has not spoken. When prophecies such as these fail to come true, they expose the prophet as false and make him/her liable to the death penalty (18:21–22). In this way, Deuteronomy 18 builds on Deuteronomy 13, further specifying the criteria for identifying true prophets of Yahweh, while also creating an expectation for a prophetic successor to Moses.

The final reference to prophets and prophecy in Deuteronomy stands in relation to the death of Moses (Deut 34:10–12). Significantly, the defining characterization of Moses, despite his other roles within the book, is that of prophet.[15] The link with the false prophets of Deut 13:1[2], who also produce signs and wonders (האתות והמופתים, 34:11), further emphasizes this characterization. Moreover, the language of Deut 34:10 echoes Deut 18:15, 18, so that in this characterization of Moses, Deuteronomy draws

---

presents evidence for the existence of prophetic succession based on a Mosaic model in the Elijah-Elisha stories, though it remains unclear how widely this was practiced. There is not enough evidence to support a conclusion of the existence of a formal prophetic office passed on through direct succession.

12. H. M. Barstad, "The Understanding of the Prophets in Deuteronomy," *SJOT* 8 (1994) 236–51.

13. For further response, see K. Jeppesen ("Is Deuteronomy Hostile Towards Prophets?" *SJOT* 8 [1994] 252–56) and especially S. Tengström ("Moses and the Prophets in the Deuteronomistic History," *SJOT* 8 [1994] 257–66).

14. E.g., Jeremiah. See the examples given in Nelson (*Deuteronomy*, 234 n. 9); M. Köckert, "Zum literargeschichtlichen ort des Prophetengesetzes Dtn 18 zwischen dem Jeremiabuch und Dtn 13," in *Liebe und Gebot: Studium zum Deuteronomium* (ed. R. G. Kratz and H. Spieckermann; FRLANT 190; Göttingen: Vandenhoeck & Ruprecht, 2000) 80–100; and W. H. Schmidt, "Das Prophetengesetz Dtn 18,9–22 im Kontext Erzählender Literatur," in *Deuteronomy and Deuteronomic Literature* (ed. M. Vervenne and J. Lust; BETL 133; Leuven: Peeters, 1977) 55–69.

15. McConville, *Deuteronomy*, 477.

together the various prophetic regulations within the book, embodying them in the person of Moses, the true prophet of Yahweh.

ולא קם נביא עוד בישראל כמשה	נביא אקים להם מקרב אחיהם כמוך
No prophet has again arisen in Israel like Moses. (Deut 34:10)	I will raise up for them a prophet from among their brothers like you. (Deut 18:18)

S. Chapman points out that the actions attributed to Moses in Deut 34:10–12 are characteristic of God's actions throughout the book of Deuteronomy. The final verses of the book may then reflect the phenomenon of dual agency (human and divine) that so often typifies prophetic speech and actions.[16] He also points out that phrases from Deut 34:10–12, such as "signs and wonders" and "a mighty hand," are also associated with other biblical prophets.[17] In this way, "a typology is established in these verses that functions with regard to the *prophets* rather than any other individual or group, extending Moses' authority to them at the same time that it also serves to set him apart."[18]

In summary, Deuteronomy defines prophecy broadly and largely negatively, connecting false prophecy with the worship of other gods. When prophecy is defined positively, it is always in connection with Moses. Moses is portrayed as the consummate prophetic spokesman and paradigmatic intermediary of Yahweh who exhibits his unique prophetic status through the signs and wonders performed during the exodus events. Moreover, Deuteronomy anticipates unnamed prophetic successors to Moses, though not his equal.

Joshua as Moses' Successor in Deuteronomy

The book of Deuteronomy culminates with the death of Moses (Deut 34:10–12). However, Deuteronomy designates Joshua as Moses' successor. N. Lohfink, followed by C. Schäfer-Lichtenberger, points out that the theological portrait of Joshua's succession progresses step-by-step in Deuteronomy, culminating with Joshua's installation in Josh 1:7–9.[19] Schäfer-

---

16. E.g., the alteration of first and third person speech—Exod 6:9–10; Deut 1:6–8, 42; 3:2; 5:5–6; 9:13; Judg 6:8; 1 Sam 10:18; 1 Kgs 20:13; and so on.

17. Chapman, *The Law and the Prophets*, 125–26 and nn. 72, 73 (e.g., Ezek 20:34, Isa 8:18, Jer 32:21).

18. Ibid., 124.

19. N. Lohfink, "The Deuteronomistic Picture of the Transfer of Authority from Moses to Joshua: A Contribution to an Old Testament Theology of Office," in *Theology of the Pentateuch: Themes of the Priestly Narrative and Deuteronomy* (trans. L. Malone;

Lichtenberger observes that Deuteronomy begins by describing Joshua's subordinate status as "one standing before" (העמד לפניך) Moses (1:38).[20] However, in Deut 31:7–8, Moses publically encourages Joshua and acknowledges him as his successor, charging him with the task of facilitating Israel's possession of the promised land and assuring him of Yahweh's presence. Then, privately, Yahweh reassures Joshua of his presence and charges him with the taking of the land (31:14–15, 23). This private charge is only repeated before all Israel in Josh 1:7–9. Having officially designated Joshua, Deut 32:44 then gives Moses and Joshua similar status but only acknowledges Joshua's full assumption of leadership at Moses' death (34:9).

Deut 34:9–10 juxtaposes Moses and Joshua, inviting comparisons between them. While emphasizing Moses' incomparability among the prophets, Deut 34:10 also assumes prophetic successors to Moses. Additionally, the overlap in language with Deut 18:15–19 recalls Yahweh's promise to raise up a prophet like Moses. This account is juxtaposed with the description of Joshua's assumption of Israel's leadership (Deut 34:9) as Moses' duly appointed successor. This then raises questions for the audience. If Deut 18:15–19 creates the expectation that Yahweh will raise up prophetic successors to Moses, and Joshua is specifically designated as Moses' successor, then does Joshua's succession also include prophetic elements? If the portrayal of Moses in Deuteronomy ultimately defines his career in prophetic terms, might we expect a similar portrayal of Joshua, his successor who is named in the previous verse? These questions prepare readers for the portrait of Joshua that we encounter in the book of Joshua.

Joshua as Moses' Successor in the Book of Joshua

G. Wenham has pointed to the book of Joshua's strong theological and linguistic dependence on the book of Deuteronomy,[21] centred particularly

---

Edinburgh: T. & T. Clark, 1994) 234–47; C. Schäfer-Lichtenberger, "Joschua und Elischa: Ideal-Typen von Führerschaft in Israel," in *Wünschet Jerusalem Frieden: Collected Communications of the XIIth Congress of the International Organization for the Study of the Old Testament, Jerusalem, 1986* (ed. M. Augustin and K.-D. Schunck; BEATAJ 13; Frankfurt am Main: Peter Lang, 1988) 274–75; idem, "'Josua' und 'Elisha'—eine biblische Argumentation zur Begründung der Autorität und Legitimität des Nachfolgers," *ZAW* 101 (1989) 206–10. See Deut 1:37–38; 3:21–22, 28; 31:2–6, 7–8, 14–15, 23; Josh 1:2–9.

20. Schäfer-Lichtenberger, "Joschua und Elischa: Ideal-Typen von Führerschaft in Israel," 275–77. This parallels the subordinate status of Abraham (Gen 18:22) and Israel (Deut 29:14) before Yahweh.

21. For a discussion of redactional layers in Joshua, see R. Nelson, *Joshua* (OTL; Louisville: Westminster John Knox, 1997) 5–9; and V. Fritz, *Das Buch Joshua* (HAT 7; Tübingen: Mohr Siebeck, 1994) 3–9.

on the role of Joshua.²² Indeed, Joshua 1 does look back to the transfer of office from Moses to Joshua reported in Deut 31:7–8 and 34:9 and highlights the central role of the Mosaic Torah for Joshua's leadership.²³ But it also looks forward, introducing two key roles (also intimated in Deut 31:7–8) for Joshua that will concern the rest of the book: Joshua as military leader and Joshua as land divider (confirmed in 13:1, 7), thereby portraying Joshua as the full-fledged successor to Moses.²⁴

N. Lohfink noted the key role in Joshua's succession played by Josh 1:6–9, which repeats the language of Deut 31:6–7, 23, suggesting that it contained an "installation formula" for inducting leaders into office.²⁵ J. R. Porter, followed by R. Nelson,²⁶ developed Lohfink's observations, connecting Josh 1:6–9 to the transmission of office in royal contexts. However, S. Chapman has pointed out that the language of Josh 1:6–9 most closely resembles the language of a war oracle, though the overall portrait of Joshua does include some royal parallels.²⁷ In any case, Josh 1:6–9 links Joshua to Deuteronomy, emphasizing Joshua as Moses' successor.²⁸

---

22. Wenham notes five motifs that link the two books in Joshua 1: holy war, land and its distribution, the unity of Israel, Joshua as Moses' successor, and the covenant and the Law of Moses (Wenham, "The Deuteronomic Theology of the Book of Joshua," 140–48). See also J. F. D. Creach, *Joshua* (Interpretation; Louisville: Westminster John Knox, 2003) 6–9; L. D. Hawk, *Joshua* (BO; Collegeville, MN: Liturgical Press, 2000) xxiv–xxviii, 1, 3–4; Butler, *Joshua*, xx–xxi. "It is clearly a fundamental concern of the editor to demonstrate that Joshua was the divinely appointed and authenticated successor to Moses" (Wenham, "The Deuteronomic Theology of the Book of Joshua," 145).

23. C. Schäfer-Lichtenberger, *Josua und Salomo: Eine Studie zu Autorität und Legitimität des Nachfolgers im Alten Testament* (VTSup 58; Leiden: Brill, 1995) 191.

24. Lohfink, "The Deuteronomistic Picture of the Transfer of Authority," 236–7.

25. Ibid., 241. The formula included the following elements: (1) "formula of encouragement" (חזק ואמץ), (2) "statement of task" (introduced by כי אתה), and (3) "formula of support" (key element: עמך יהוה).

26. J. R. Porter, "The Succession of Joshua," in *Proclamation and Presence: Old Testament Essays in Honour of Gwynne Henton Davies* (ed. J. I. Durham and J. R. Porter; Macon, GA: Mercer University Press, 1983) 102–32, esp. pp. 108–11; R. Nelson, "Josiah in the Book of Joshua," *JBL* 100 (1981) 531–40, esp. pp. 531–32.

27. S. B. Chapman, "Joshua Son of Nun: Presentation of a Prophet," in *Thus Says the Lord: Essays on the Former and Latter Prophets in Honor of Robert R. Wilson* (ed. J. J. Ahn and S. L. Cook; LHBOTS 502; New York: T. & T. Clark, 2009) 13–26, esp. pp. 18–20, 24–25; following L. Rowlett, *Joshua and the Rhetoric of Violence: A New Historicist Analysis* (JSOTSup 226; Sheffield: Sheffield Academic Press, 1996) 116–19, 121–55; and M. Weinfeld (*Deuteronomy and the Deuteronomic School*, 45–51). D. J. McCarthy ("An Installation Genre?" *JBL* 90 [1971] 31–41, esp. p. 35) pointed out that when one considers other, partial uses of the formulas, the evidence does not point toward its use in a particular genre. Lohfink also acknowledged parallels with war oracles ("The Deuteronomistic Picture of the Transfer of Authority," 241–42).

28. Nelson notes the following connections between the two figures: Joshua is Moses' attendant (Josh 1:1), Joshua assumes Yahweh's promises to Moses (1:3–4; see

Additionally, the larger sequence of events in Josh 1:2–18 may further develop the portrayal of Joshua as Moses' successor. In Josh 1:2, Yahweh speaks to Joshua, instructing him to prepare the people to cross over the Jordan. Joshua then verbally conveys the gist of Yahweh's words to Israel's leaders (1:11). In this way, Joshua's role as Yahweh's intermediary mirrors that of his predecessor.[29] This sequence also broadly conforms to the sequence specified in Deut 18:15, 18 for a prophet like Moses, which can be outlined as in table 1.

The emphasis on Joshua as Moses' successor in the book of Joshua extends to the various ways in which the career of Joshua parallels that of Moses. These parallels can be briefly outlined as follows:[30] the sending of spies (Joshua 2 // Numbers 13–14); the crossing of the Jordan and the Red Sea (Josh 3:13 // Exod 15:8; Josh 3:17 // Exod 14:21–22, 29); the erection of 12 stones as a memorial, prompting children to ask "what are these stones?" and the Passover memorial, prompting children to ask "what is this observance to you?" (Josh 4:22–24 // Exod 12:26); the circumcision of the uncircumcised (Josh 5:2–7 // Exod 4:24–26); the celebration of the Passover (Josh 5:10 // Exod 12; 13:5); intercession after sin (Josh 7:7–9 // Deut 9:25–29); the hardening of the enemy's heart (Josh 11:20 // Exod 9:12); the holding aloft of a javelin/hands to secure victory (Josh 8:18–23 // Exod 17:10–13); and Joshua's farewell speeches approximate Moses' repeated final exhortations (Joshua 23, 24 // Deuteronomy 31, 33). Additionally, we could note how the book parallels Moses' military victories (Josh 12:1–6) with Joshua's military victories (Josh 12:7–24) and Moses' allotments (Deut 3:12–20; Josh 13:8) with Joshua's allotments (Joshua 14–19), while in Josh 22:7, Moses assigns half of Manasseh's land and Joshua assigns the other half, completing Moses' work. Moreover, Joshua fulfills the instructions of Moses:[31] keeping the covenant ceremony at Mt. Ebal and Mt. Gerizim (Deut 27:2–8 // Josh 8:30–35), apportioning cities of refuge (Deut 19:1–3 // Josh 20:1–20), and keeping the Mosaic ban (Deut 7:1–5, 20:1–10 // Josh 6:17).

This portrait clearly depicts Joshua as Moses' successor, taking up his spiritual, military, covenantal, and intercessory roles. Thus, both the Dtr[n] and Dtr redactors portray Joshua as Moses' successor. Joshua's career not

---

Deut 11:24), Yahweh's presence as it was with Moses (1:5, 17; see Deut 2:7), and the people's obedience to both leaders (1:17; *Joshua*, 30–31).

29. See Yahweh's instructions to Moses, which he then relays to Israel: Exod 6:2–9; 7:19–20; Deut 1:42–43; 4:13–14; 5:4–5, 27, 31; 6:1; 31:19–22.

30. See Wenham, "The Deuteronomic Theology of the Book of Joshua," 146.

31. P. J. Kissling, *Reliable Characters in the Primary History: Profiles of Moses, Joshua, Elijah and Elisha* (JSOTSup 224; Sheffield: Sheffield Academic Press, 1996) 89.

Table 1. Joshua as Moses' Successor in Joshua and Deuteronomy

"I will raise up (אקים Hiphil) a prophet from their midst like you." (Deut 18:18)	"Moses my servant is dead. Now arise." (קום Qal imperative, Josh 1:2)
"I will set my words in his mouth." (Deut 18:18)	"Yahweh said to Joshua . . . cross over this Jordan." (Josh 1:1, 2)ᵃ
"He will tell them all that I command (צוה) him." (Deut 18:18)	"Then Joshua commanded (צוה) the officers of the people . . . in three days, you will cross over this Jordan." (Josh 1:10–11)
"Yahweh your God will raise up a prophet from your midst like me. You must listen (תשמעון) to him." (Deut 18:15)	"We will do everything you have commanded us and we will go wherever you send us. Just as we listened to Moses, so we will listen (נשמע) to you." (Josh 1:17)

a. Yahweh's instructions to cross over the Jordan in 1:1–2 are then taken up and relayed to Israel in 1:10–11, so that Yahweh's words form the essence of Joshua's words to the people. In light of Josh 1:6–9, Yahweh's setting his words in Joshua's mouth may also take the form of obedience to the commands of Moses as specified in the Mosaic Torah (e.g., Joshua's application of Moses words in Deut 3:18–20 to the Transjordan tribes—Josh 1:12–15).

only parallels that of his predecessor but completes it. Joshua, like Moses, is an amalgam of roles, though the reiteration of obedience to Moses and the Mosaic Torah subordinate Joshua to Moses', and Yahweh's, ultimate authority (see Josh 11:15).[32] Thus, if Dtr rendered the theological portrait of Joshua to parallel that of Moses so that Joshua takes up the roles ascribed to Moses in Deuteronomy, could it also be possible that Dtr was concerned to portray Joshua as also implicitly taking on a "prophet like Moses" role, much like the one anticipated in Deut 18:15–18 and hinted at in Joshua 1?

Joshua as Prophet in the Book of Joshua

We must begin by acknowledging that the book of Joshua never explicitly describes Joshua as a prophet. However, the portrayal of Joshua's words and actions at times add a prophet-like sheen to his character. This prophet-like picture does not stem from any one passage, though it does become most prophet-like in Joshua 24. Moreover, the portrayals, in and

---

32. Schäfer-Lichtenberger, *Josua und Salomo*, 209–20.

of themselves, are not explicitly prophetic, and it is more in the sum of these portrayals that an image of Joshua as prophet emerges.

Joshua's Prophet-like Speech

The portrayal of Joshua in the book of Joshua shares several speech patterns common to prophetic speech. J. Creach, followed by Chapman,[33] notes how Joshua's call to Israel to 'draw near and hear the words of Yahweh your God' (גשו הנה ושמעו את־דברי יהוה אלהיכם; 3:9) mirrors the opening words of later prophetic oracles (see Isa 1:10; Jer 2:4; Hos 4:1; Amos 3:1, 4:1). C. Westermann points out that the *conveyance formula* ('I have given . . . into your hand', נתתי בידך, and its variants), which he classifies as a subtype of the salvation oracle, appears throughout Joshua.[34] Initially, Yahweh assures Joshua with these words (6:2, 8:1, 10:8), but in the succeeding narratives, Joshua turns around and conveys these same words to Israel (6:16, 8:18, 10:19), an act later connected with the prophets during the monarchic period in the DH (1 Kgs 20:13, 28; 22:6, 12, 15; 2 Kgs 3:18). The book of Joshua also twice employs the messenger formula (כה אמר יהוה 'thus says Yahweh'), once in Yahweh's directives (7:13) and once as part of Joshua's speech (24:2). Although this formula derives from the speech of messengers,[35] it becomes characteristic of prophetic speech in the DH (e.g. 1 Sam 2:27; 10:18; 15:2; 2 Sam 7:5; 12:7; 1 Kgs 11:31; 12:24; 13:2, 21; 20:13; 22:11; 2 Kgs 2:21; 7:1; 19:6; 20:1; 22:15).

Joshua's intercession on Israel's behalf after Aachan's sin (Josh 7:6–8) echoes the intercession of Moses and Samuel.[36] In response to Aachan's sin and Joshua's prayer (Josh 7:1–9), Yahweh instructs Joshua to call Israel to account using the form of a prophetic judgment speech (7:13–15).[37] The introduction (v. 13a) is followed by the messenger formula (v. 13b, "Thus says the Lord, the God of Israel") and the accusation "a banned object is in your midst, O Israel" (v. 13c), along with its development, "You cannot stand before your enemy until you remove the banned object from your midst" (v. 13d). Josh 7:14 then describes Yahweh's intervention in the situation while 7:15 relates the results of his intervention.

---

33. Creach, *Joshua*, 54; Chapman, "Joshua Son of Nun," 22–23.

34. C. Westermann, *Prophetic Oracles of Salvation in the Old Testament* (trans. K. Crim; Louisville: Westminster John Knox, 1991) 24–25. See Josh 2:24; 6:2; 8:1, 7; 18; 10:8, 19, 30, 32; 11:8; 21:44; 24:8, 11.

35. E.g., 1 Kgs 2:30, 2 Kgs 18:19.

36. See Exod. 32:11–13, 1 Sam 12:19–25.

37. Idem, *Basic Forms of Prophetic Speech* (trans. H. White; Louisville: Westminster John Knox, 1991) 169–81; see Nelson, *Joshua*, 105. Butler also sees a lawsuit form in 7:10–12 (*Joshua*, 80).

Joshua's Prophet-like Predictions

Prophetic oracles in ancient Israel could at times include elements relating Yahweh's will regarding the immediate future, whether concerning judgment or salvation. These oracles were usually directed toward the immediate future but could include a length of time between the announcement and its fulfillment.[38] At times, prophets might refer to signs in the future in order to coincide with or authenticate their words (Deut 13:1; 1 Sam 2:34; 1 Kgs 13:3, 5). The Dtr portrait of Joshua includes a number of instances where Joshua's words anticipate the future words or actions of Yahweh.

The plot structure of Joshua 3–4 is notoriously difficult and marked with numerous digressions and parentheses.[39] In Josh 3:8, Yahweh tells Joshua to instruct the priests to stand in the water when they reach the river's edge. We have already noted the prophetic tenor of Josh 3:9. Joshua then expands on Yahweh's words, predicting that, when the priests' feet touch the water, the flow of the Jordan will be cut off (3:13). This then happens in 3:15–16 (see 4:18), authenticating Yahweh's and Joshua's words (4:14, 24). Moreover, Joshua's declaration that Yahweh would do wonders (נפלאות) in their midst (3:5) precedes the entire scene and points toward Yahweh's coming salvific actions on Israel's behalf.[40]

Josh 6:26 records Joshua's curse on the city of Jericho. While curses are not uttered exclusively by prophets (e.g., Judg 9:57, 17:2; 2 Sam 16:9), Westermann notes the close connection between curses and prophetic woe oracles.[41] Moreover, Dtr reads the fulfillment of Joshua's words as a prophetic expression of Yahweh's will (1 Kgs 16:34).[42] Similarly, Joshua's prediction, despite Israel's protestations, that Israel would be unable to

---

38. Westermann, *Basic Forms of Prophetic Speech*, 170–71.
39. Nelson concludes that multiple hands must be at work here (*Joshua*, 53–71). For a different perspective, see Hawk (*Joshua*, 53–62).
40. See R. Albertz, "פלא, *pl*'" (ed. E. Jenni and C. Westermann; 2 vols; THAT; Munich: Chr. Kaiser, 1976) 2:413–20, esp. 416–18.
41. Westermann, *Basic Forms of Prophetic Speech*, 194–98; E. Gerstenberger, "The Woe-Oracles of the Prophets," *JBL* 81 (1962) 258–59.
42. See Hawk, *Joshua*, 104. Also the expression אשר דבר ביד יהושע בן־נון 'which [Yahweh] spoke through Joshua son of Nun' (1 Kgs 16:34), not only interprets the words of Joshua as those of Yahweh, but "אשר דבר ביד x" and its variants are used elsewhere only with those known as prophets: Moses (Exod 9:35; Lev 10:11; Num 17:5 [16:40]; 27:23; Josh 20:2; 1 Kgs 8:53, 56; see 2 Chr 35:6); Ahijah (1 Kgs 12:15, 14:18, 15:29; 2 Chr 10:15); Jehu the prophet (1 Kgs 16:12); Elijah (1 Kgs 17:16; 2 Kgs 9:36, 10:10); Jonah (2 Kgs 14:25); the prophets (2 Kgs 17:23, 24:2; see Ezek 38:17; Zech 7:7, 12); Isaiah (Isa 20:2); Jeremiah (Jer 37:2, 50:1); see Hag 1:1, 3; 2:1; Mal 1:1.

serve Yahweh (24:19–20) finds fulfillment in Judg 2:1–5, 2:10–11, 3:6–8, and 10:13–14, shortly after Joshua's death.

Joshua's Prophet-like Sign-Acts

The prophets of ancient Israel used a variety of nonverbal, symbolic actions to embody or dramatize a particular element of their message.[43] K. Friebel, in his study of Jeremiah and Ezekiel's sign-acts, describes sign-acts as "nonverbal behaviours (i.e. bodily movements, gestures and paralanguage) whose primary purpose was communicative and interactive."[44] These sign-acts were part of the prophet's arsenal of persuasive means and were performed in an attempt to convince the audience of a message given by Yahweh. They arose in response to the exigencies of the moment and functioned essentially as nonverbal persuasion or rhetoric, intended to change the viewing audience's belief and/or behaviors.[45] Sign-acts included not only physical behaviors but could also incorporate the use of "artifacts" or props.[46] Friebel also suggests that prophetic sign-acts are a subset of the larger category 'signs' (אותות) and 'wonders' (מופתים), for signs need not be performative or nonverbal.[47]

The portrayal of Joshua includes the performance of a number of sign-acts. When Israel was about to cross over the Jordan, Joshua attempted to persuade Israel of Yahweh's immediate and future presence (Josh 3:10) as they entered the land. In response to Yahweh instructions (3:8), Joshua pointed to the advance of the ark of the covenant into the Jordan and the subsequent interruption of the flow of the Jordan as the visible sign of Yahweh's invisible presence and assurance of his future work (3:10–13).[48]

The portrayal of Israel's defeat of a coalition of five Amorite kings in Joshua 10 serves as a literary precursor to the description of Israel's southern campaign. Significantly, Joshua uses a symbolic act to embolden his troops. When the five kings are brought before Joshua, he instructs his army commanders to put their feet on the necks of the kings, a common

---

43. E.g., 1 Sam 16:13; 1 Kgs 11:29–33, 13:1–5, 20:35–43; and the corpus of sign-acts performed by Jeremiah and Ezekiel.

44. K. Friebel, *Jeremiah's and Ezekiel's Sign-Acts: Rhetorical Nonverbal Communication* (JSOTSup 283; Sheffield: Sheffield Academic Press, 1999) 14.

45. Ibid., 30, 40, 53–57, 59. See the list on pp. 24–25 for examples of sign-acts in Jeremiah and Ezekiel.

46. Ibid., 40.

47. Ibid., 27–31, esp. p. 30 n. 58. Examples of nonperformative signs in Joshua are Josh 4:4–7, 22:26–28, 24:26–27.

48. Creach points to the ongoing significance of the Jordan crossing for the prophets, where Elisha's striking of the Jordan with Elijah's mantle and crossing over symbolized his assumption of Elijah's prophetic role (*Joshua*, 43–44).

royal act indicating unconditional surrender. Here, however, the act has been democratized,[49] persuading Israel of Yahweh's guarantee of their victory (10:22–25). Joshua's elevation of a sword (8:18) during the battle of Ai may also have served a similar persuasive function.[50]

Not all sign-acts, however, are necessarily prophetic in nature. The distinction between prophetic and nonprophetic sign-acts for Friebel presumably lies in the context of their performance (religious vs. nonreligious settings) and in performance by prophets.[51] The "Yahweh-war" context of Joshua 1–11 blurs the distinction between "religious" and "nonreligious" settings,[52] however, and because the prophet-like aspects of Joshua's leadership depend on other elements of the portrayal of Joshua, these sign-acts become "prophetic" only in light of other factors.

Joshua as Prophet in Joshua 24

The depiction of Joshua as prophet culminates in Joshua 24.[53] The redactional history of Joshua 24 is debated,[54] though commentators agree that the chapter is not a covenant renewal ceremony but a report—and hence adaptation—of a covenant renewal ceremony.[55] However, Josh 24:1–28 also exhibits a number of general similarities with prophetic speech: the use of the messenger formula ("Thus says the Lord"), the switch from the indicative statements of 24:2–13 to the imperatives in 24:14, an alternation between first-person speech (24:2–13) and third-person speech (24:14–28), and a general adversarial stance[56] are typical of prophetic speech.

---

49. Nelson, *Joshua*, 146.
50. Creach suggests that the sword exemplifies how Yahweh will bring victory to Israel (*Joshua*, 78).
51. Note that Friebel does not formally set out to define the distinction between prophetic and nonprophetic sign-acts (*Jeremiah's and Ezekiel's Sign-Acts*, 61–69). Examples of biblical nonprophetic sign-acts are 1 Sam 11:1–7; 20:20–22, 35–39.
52. See R. Hess, *Joshua* (TOTC; Downers Grove, IL: InterVarsity, 1996) 46–51.
53. See Chapman, "Joshua Son of Nun," 21–22.
54. See the discussion in W. T. Koopmans, *Joshua 24 as Poetic Narrative* (JSOTSup 93; Sheffield: JSOT Press, 1990) 1–163. Koopmans points out that Joshua 24 does not use standard Dtr phraseology or content and was probably composed at some point prior to the final composition of the DH, and probably prior to Joshua 23 (pp. 411–12).
55. R. L. Hubbard, *Joshua* (NIVAC; Grand Rapids: Zondervan, 2009) 548; Butler, *Joshua*, 266; Nelson, *Joshua*, 267; contra K. Baltzer, *The Covenant Formulary in Old Testament, Jewish, and Early Christian Writings* (trans. D. E. Green; Oxford: Blackwell, 1971) 19–26.
56. *Indicative-to-imperative switch*: See Westermann, *Basic Forms of Prophetic Speech*, 106–9. *First-person/third-person alternation*: ibid., 171. *Adversarial stance*: Hawk, *Joshua*, 264.

In addition to the similarity of Joshua's farewell speech to that of Moses in Deuteronomy 31, several others features of Joshua 24 find correspondence in the speeches of prophetic figures in the DH (table 2). Additionally, Joshua's prediction of Israel's inability to serve Yahweh (Josh 24:19–20) may serve as an adaptation of prophetic judgment speech: accusation—"You are not able to serve Yahweh, for he is a holy and jealous god" (v. 19a); intervention of God—"He will not forgive your rebellion and your sins" (v. 19b); development of the accusation—"For you will forsake Yahweh and serve other gods" (v. 20a); results of the intervention—"And he will turn and bring disaster on you and make an end of you after he has been good to you" (v. 20b).[57] As a preemptive judgment speech, Joshua's words then highlight the very serious nature of the commitment Israel is undertaking here. Thus, taken together, the structure and phraseology of these verses correspond to prophetic speeches in the DH, particularly those of Moses in Deuteronomy and Samuel in 1 Samuel 12, suggesting Joshua 24 may have been shaped to reflect a prophetic tenor.[58]

The coda to Joshua's career (24:28–32) compares him with Moses in three respects: (1) Joshua's lifespan (110 years versus Moses' 120—Deut 34:7); (2) Joshua's burial in the land (versus Moses' burial outside the land—Deut 34:6); and (3) attribution of the title "servant of Yahweh" (Deut 34:5; see Josh 1:1). These similar elements invite comparison between the careers of Moses and Joshua. Joshua 24 portrays Joshua as achieving a similar, though slightly subordinate, status to that of his predecessor, Moses, and his career culminates with a speech that includes multiple prophet-like elements. Moses' career in Deuteronomy was summed up in prophetic terms and anticipates the ministry of other prophets who are like Moses, though not his equal (Deut 34:10; see 18:15–18). In light of the juxtaposition of the careers of Joshua and Moses in Joshua 24 and the anticipation in Deuteronomy of a prophet like Moses, we might ask if the portrayal of Joshua in the book of Joshua could indeed qualify him as a fulfillment of that anticipation.

When Joshua 24 is taken together with the other prophet-like elements of Joshua's portrayal in the book of Joshua, it seems as though Joshua

---

57. Westermann, *Basic Forms of Prophetic Speech*, 169–81. The form usually develops from an accumulation of sin, which may be implied in 24:14–15, though here the judgment speech functions preemptively rather than retrospectively (see Judg 2:12–13; 10:6–16).

58. For additional examples of the prophet-like quality of Joshua 24, see Chapman ("Joshua Son of Nun," 21–22; idem, *The Law and the Prophets*, 184–85) and Creach (*Joshua*, 120).

Table 2. Joshua 24 and Prophetic Speeches of DH

Joshua 24	Prophetic Speech
Joshua's national, historical recap and speech (24:2–24)	national, historically oriented speeches: Deut 1–3; Judg 6:7–10; 1 Sam 7:2–17; 10:17–27, 11:14–12:25[a]
imperatives following speech in 24:14–15: עבד, ירא[b]	imperatives of Moses (Deut 6:13; 10:20) and Samuel (1 Sam 12:24): עבד, ירא
choose "this day" (24:15)[c]	choose "this day" (Deut 30:18–19; see 1 Kgs 18:21)
Israel—"far be it from us" (24:16)[d]	Samuel—"far be it from me" (1 Sam 12:23)
'great signs' (אותות) in exodus event (24:10)	'signs and wonders' (אותות ומפתים) in exodus event (Deut 4:34, 6:22, 7:19, 26:8, 29:3)
use of the key verbs (עבד: 24:2, 14 [4×], 15, 16, 17, 18, 19, 20, 21, 22, 24, 29, 31; הסיר: 24:14, 23; העלה: 24:17)[e]	use of the key verbs (עבד: 64× in Deuteronomy; 1 Sam 12:10; הסיר: 1 Sam 7:3, 4; העלה: Judg 6:8; 1 Sam 10:18; 12:6)

    a. See Koopmans *Joshua 24 as Poetic Narrative*, 370–92. The narrator's speech in 2 Kgs 17:7–23 may serve a similar function in some respects, though unlike the other speeches, it is not set in a direct confrontation with the people of Israel.
    b. Hubbard, *Joshua*, 554–55.
    c. Ibid., 555.
    d. Ibid.
    e. C. Brekelmans, "Joshua XXIV: Its Place and Function," in *Congress Volume: Leuven, 1989* (ed. J. A. Emerton; VTSup 43; Leiden: Brill, 1991) 7.

does fit the criteria of Deut 18:15–22 for a prophetic successor to Moses: (1) Josh 1:1–9 establishes Joshua's credentials as raised up by Yahweh (Deut 18:15, 18).[59] (2) Joshua's place "among his brothers" (Deut 18:15, 18) is secured not only by his leadership position, but also by his burial in his own נחלה 'inheritance', the symbol of covenant-community membership[60] (Josh 19:49–50 and 24:30, emphasized through the parallel with the burial of the patriarch Joseph in his נחלה, 24:32). (3) Joshua's faithful

    59. Yahweh's commission begins with the command to arise (קום—Josh 1:2). Deut 18:15, 18 indicates that Yahweh will raise up (קום) a prophet in Israel. The usage in Josh 1:2 spurs Joshua to cross the Jordan, but the rhetorical associations of this verb at Joshua's inauguration by Yahweh (not Moses; see Deut 31:7–8) are surely not coincidental.
    60. See C. J. H. Wright, *Old Testament Ethics for the People of God* (Downers Grove, IL: InterVarsity, 2004) 76–99.

conveyance of the commands of Yahweh and Moses (Josh 11:12, 15, 23; 15:13; 17:4; 22:9, 24:2–13; see 14:2, 5; 21:2, 8) also fits the criteria of a prophet like Moses (see Deut 18:18). (4) Joshua's insistence on complete fidelity to Yahweh (Josh 22:5, 23:7–8, 24:2–28) also parallels the requirements of a true prophet (Deut 13:1–5, 18:20). (5) His accurate predictions (Josh 3:5, 13–16; 6:26; 1 Kgs 16:34; 24:19–20; and Judg 2:1–5, 10–11; 3:6–8; 10:13–14) also comport with Mosaic requirements (Deut 18:21–22). Thus, Joshua fulfills all of the traits required of a prophet who is like Moses, implying that, among the varied roles attributed to Joshua, we should add the role of "prophet like Moses."[61]

Joshua, Prophets, and Leaders in the Deuteronomistic History

The portrait of Joshua in the book of Joshua incorporates a variety of roles (e.g., military leader, land divider) and depicts him as Moses' successor, which includes prophet-like characteristics. These prophet-like characteristics appear throughout the book, and like the portrait of his predecessor in Deuteronomy, culminate in a final prophet-like portrayal. The fact that Joshua is not called a prophet but is portrayed in a prophet-like manner and as fulfilling the Dtn criteria for a prophet after the prototype of Moses may then affect our understanding of the theology of leadership in the DH and the historiographical impulses that propelled Dtr.

C. Brekelmans has noted how Joshua 24 looks both backward to Deuteronomy and forward to 1 Samuel 7–12 through similarities of both form and content.[62] He observed many similarities between the historical surveys of Joshua 24 and 1 Samuel 12[63] and noticed that after 1 Samuel 12, this particular form of prophetic admonition disappears from the DH. Moreover, the paraenetic speeches of Joshua 24 and 1 Samuel 12 resemble each other, 1 Samuel 12 bringing Joshua 24 up to date and so forming a kind of inclusio.[64] Significantly, if our observations hold, both are prophetic speeches that close an era of leadership in the DH. M. Noth, when observing the theological structure of the DH, highlighted a concern for periodization and described its composition in relation to these eras.[65] M. O'Brien further refined Noth's schema, suggesting three eras

---

61. See the conclusion of Creach, "In this final chapter [Josh 24] it appears that he has taken his place as the prophet 'like Moses' spoken of in Deuteronomy 18:15" (*Joshua*, 120).
62. Brekelmans, "Joshua XXIV," 4–9.
63. See also Koopmans, *Joshua 24 as Poetic Narrative*, 379–92.
64. Breckelmans, "Joshua XXIV," 8–9.
65. M. Noth, *The Deuteronomistic History* (trans. J. Doull et al.; JSOTSup 15; Sheffield: JSOT Press, 1981) 9; see chaps. 5–9. These periods included: the Mosaic era, the

(Moses–Joshua, Judges–Samuel, and the post-Samuel era), though the repetition of the formula "after the death of *X*" (Josh 1:1, Judg 1:1) and the use of speeches to conclude the eras of Moses, Joshua, and the judges (which includes Samuel as the last judge—1 Sam 7:15–17) suggests a separate era under Joshua. O'Brien pointed out that prophets served as key leaders in each era but that in the final era leadership roles were divided between prophets and kings.[66] However, P. Dutcher-Walls notes how the era spanning Moses to Samuel (until the bifurcation of leadership roles) was typified by leaders embodying not only prophetic but a variety of other leadership roles.[67]

If we take these observations together, we can describe the portrayal of leadership in the DH as in table 3.[68] If the DH is periodized in this manner, each era, with the exception of the era of Joshua, contains leaders whose roles included a prophetic element.[69] We have noted that the portrait of leaders in the DH up to the time of Samuel included an amalgam of roles including that of prophet. Thus, if, as we have argued, the portrayal of Joshua included a prophetic element, then each era of the DH would include a prophetic type of leader.

---

occupation of the land under Joshua, the judges era, the era of Saul, David, and Solomon, and the period of the kings.

66. O'Brien, "The 'Deuteronomistic History' as a Story of Israel's Leaders," 18, 24–26.

67. P. Dutcher-Walls ("Dtr Leadership Transitions," unpublished manuscript, 1) points out that Moses and Samuel both embody multiple, parallel roles. Significantly, these leaders come at the beginning and at the end of the eras before the bifurcation of leadership roles into prophet and king after the time of Samuel. Moses was lawgiver (throughout Deuteronomy); warrior/leader (see his battle direction in Deuteronomy 2–3); narrator of salvation history (Deuteronomy 2–3); judge (administered justice, Deut 1:9–19, 17:8–13; see 17:14–20); prophet relating the words of Yahweh (Deut 18:15–22; 34:10); appointer of new leaders (Deut 31:7–8); and priest organizing the mediation between the people and Yahweh (Deut 5; 18:1–8). Similarly, Samuel acted as lawgiver (1 Sam 10:25); interpreter of the law (1 Sam 12:14–15, 20–25); warrior/leader (1 Sam 7:7–11); judge (1 Sam 7:6, 15–16; 12:3–4); prophet (1 Sam 3:20; 8:6–7, 21–22; 13:13; 15:1, 10); priest (apprentice to Eli in 1 Samuel 1–2); and narrator of salvation history (1 Sam 12:6–13). Leaders during the time of Joshua and the judges embody some, but not all, of these roles; see the conclusions of L. Grabbe ("Prophets, Priests, Diviners and Sages in Ancient Israel," in *Of Prophets' Visions and the Wisdom of Sages: Essays in Honour of R. Norman Whybray on His Seventieth Birthday* [ed. H. A. McKay and D. J. A. Clines; JSOTSup 162; Sheffield: Sheffield Academic Press, 1993] 53–54) about multiple roles for "pre-classical prophets."

68. I am indebted to P. Dutcher-Walls (unpublished manuscript, p. 1) for this general outline, with slight adaptation.

69. Deborah (Judg 4:4–5) and the unnamed prophet (Judg 6:8–10) may serve as representatives of this style of leadership in the book of Judges.

Table 3. Leadership in the Deuteronomistic History

Reference	Deuteronomy 1–34	Joshua 1–24	Judges 1– 1 Samuel 12	1 Samuel 13– 2 Kings 25
Era	era of Moses	era of Joshua	era of the Judges	era of kings and prophets
Leader	Moses	Joshua	judges (Samuel, Deborah)	kings prophets

The fact that Joshua is never directly described as a prophet but is portrayed, in addition to other roles, in a prophet-like manner after the prototype of Moses may also be suggestive of some of the historiographical impulses behind the shaping of the DH. If one accepts the portrayal of Joshua as including prophet-like elements that qualify him as a type of prophetic successor to Moses during the era of Israel's emergence in the land, it suggests an attempt by Dtr to show a general succession of prophetic figures in the vein of Moses throughout Israel's early history. The evidence supports not the existence of a prophetic office but rather an attempt to highlight prophetic and prophet-like individuals in Israel's early history who helped shape Israel's Yahwistic ethos and helped Israel to maintain a fidelity to Yahweh.

The particular emphasis in the book of Joshua is Israel's fidelity and obedience to Yahweh (e.g., Josh 4:10, 11:15, 24:31) during this period of military success (e.g., Josh 11:22), under a leader who spoke with prophet-like authority and predicted Israel's inability to serve Yahweh faithfully (Josh 24:19–20). This sort of emphasis highlights Israel's later disobedience to prophetic critiques of Israel's fidelity to Yahweh during the period of the monarchy (e.g., 2 Sam 12:1–14; 1 Kgs 13:1–3, 18:21; 2 Kgs 9:6–10; etc.). The portrayal of Joshua as prophet-like allows Dtr to present prophetic figures in each of Israel's major historical periods who exemplified the ideal of fidelity to Yahweh and his word and who warned Israel of the dangers of infidelity. This then gives additional legitimacy to Dtr's prophetic critiques of Israel's fidelity to Yahweh during the period of the monarchy, which resulted in the loss of its land and opened the door to Dtr's calls for a return to Yahweh.[70]

---

70. A. Campbell and M. O'Brien (*Unfolding the Deuteronomistic History: Origins, Upgrades, Present Text* [Minneapolis: Fortress, 2000] 19–20) suggest that an exilic edition of the DH emphasized Israel's responsibility for failing to listen to the prophets and their failure to obey the law of Yahweh. See also the positive example of Josiah's obedience to the Torah in 2 Kings 22–23 contrasted with the negative assessment by

Conclusion

The book of Deuteronomy clearly presents Joshua as Moses' successor. The book also sets up expectations for a prophetic successor after the Mosaic archetype (Deut 18:15, 18). The book of Joshua underscores Joshua's succession of Moses through Yahweh's commission (1:2–9), the use of narrative comparisons (e.g., Josh 4:14, 22:7) and plot parallels, and Joshua's obedience to Moses' commands (e.g., Josh 17:4). The portrayal of Joshua also suggests that this succession included the assumption of prophet-like characteristics through its depiction of Joshua's prophet-like actions and words, culminating in Joshua 24. The inclusion of a prophet-like role among the various leadership "hats" worn by Joshua then also brings the book of Joshua into closer line with the theological portrait of leadership in the DH. Leaders in each premonarchic era of the DH, like Moses, Samuel, and Joshua, are portrayed as an amalgam of various leadership roles in ancient Israel. It is during the period of the monarchy that leadership roles diversify into prophetic and kingly-political leadership roles.

Dtr of Israel's obedience to the warnings of the prophets with regard to the Torah in 2 Kgs 17:13.

On Dtr's call to return to Yaweh, see H. W. Wolff, "The Kerygma of the Deuteronomistic Historical Work," in *Reconsidering Israel and Judah: Recent Studies on the Deuteronomistic History* (ed. G. N. Knoppers and G. McConville; Sources for Biblical and Theological Study 8; Winona Lake, IN: Eisenbrauns, 2000) 62–78.

Recycling Heaven's Words: Receiving and Retrieving Divine Revelation in the Historiography of Judges

Mark J. Boda

There is little question that the word of Yhwh is a major theme within what critical scholars have called the Deuteronomistic History and Jewish tradition knows as the Former Prophets. Attention is consistently paid in these books to the way in which the people have or have not obeyed the word of God delivered through Moses in the Torah. Prophets constantly appear to speak words from Yhwh, calling the people back to the covenant.

It is not then surprising to find at various intervals in the book of Judges evidence of words from the deity breaking into the narratives. This aspect of Judges, however, has not been studied globally, especially to discern regular patterns that appear in the two major sections of Judges, that is, the cyclical core of Judg 2:6–16:31 and the concluding narratives in Judges 17–21.

This essay investigates the role of intermediaries of the divine word within the historiographic structure of the book of Judges. It will reveal that a word from the deity is a major feature in the book's historical presentation. However, this examination will highlight the significant difference between the two major sections of Judges (2:6–16:31 and chaps. 17–21) in their presentation of this mediation of the divine word and then argue that the introduction to the book as a whole (Judg 1:1–2:5) is designed with both of these approaches in mind. The essay will treat each of the two major sections of Judges in order before concluding with a comparison and contrast between the sections and a consideration of the introductory chapter.

Author's note: With thanks to Sara Locke, Daniel Block, and Trent Butler for helpful comments on an earlier draft of this essay.

Receiving Heavenly Messages
in the Cyclical Core of Judges (2:6–16:31)

It is well known that the inner core of the book of Judges is dominated by a historiographic structure often identified as a cycle.[1] Some have suggested that this cycle comprises five stages that include sin, punishment, crying out, salvation, and quiet, while others suggest a four-part cycle by excluding quiet or a six-part cycle by including the element of the raising up of the deliverer.[2] At the outset, I would like to suggest a six-part cycle that includes sin, discipline, distress, salvation, peace, and death.

Sin. In every cycle, the beginning of the sin stage is signaled by the phrase "then the children of Israel (again) did evil in the sight of Y<small>HWH</small>" (2:11a; 3:7, 12; 4:1; 6:1; 10:6; 13:1).[3] Other vocabulary that is repeated in a more limited way includes *forget, serve, forsake, follow, bow down,* and *play the harlot* (mostly in chaps. 2, 3, and 10).

Discipline. The discipline stage nearly always employs either the collocation "give into the hands of" (נתן ביד; 2:14, 6:1, 13:1) or "sold into the hands of" (מכר ביד; 2:14, 3:8, 4:2, 10:7),[4] and always lists the period of years the Israelites endured the discipline (3:8, 14; 4:3; 6:1; 10:8; 13:1; see 9:22). On a few occasions, a depiction of the anger of Y<small>HWH</small> signals the beginning of the stage (2:12, 14, 20; 3:8; 10:7).

Distress. The distress stage nearly always depicts the cry of Israel to God (זעק, צעק; 2:18; 3:9, 15; 4:3; 6:6, 7; 10:10) and sometimes the condition of Israel (2:15, 6:6, 10:9).

Salvation. The salvation stage is the most diverse. Most common is a reference to the raising up of a judge/deliverer (קום Hiphil; 2:16, 18; 3:9, 15; 10:1), an element that is left out in the Gideon and Samson narratives,

---

1. See R. H. O'Connell, *The Rhetoric of the Book of Judges* (VTSup 63; Leiden: Brill, 1996) 26 n. 18.

2. *Five-part cycle*: E.g., Y. Amit, *The Book of Judges: The Art of Editing* (Biblical Interpretation Series 38; Leiden: Brill, 1999) 36–37. F. E. Greenspahn ("The Theology of the Framework of Judges," *VT* 36 [1986] 388) speaks of five basic clauses in the framework: did evil, sold them, cried out, they were humbled before, and there was peace.

Four-part cycle: E.g., G. W. Trompf, "Notions of Historical Recurrence in Classic Hebrew Historiography," in *Studies in the Historical Books of the Old Testament* (ed. J. A. Emerton; VTSup 30; Leiden: Brill, 1979) 219–20.

Six-part cycle: A. D. Mayes, *The Story of Israel between Settlement and Exile: A Redactional Study of the Deuteronomistic History* (London: SCM, 1983) 61–62; see D. M. Gunn, "Joshua and Judges," in *The Literary Guide to the Bible* (ed. R. Alter and F. Kermode; Cambridge, MA: Belknap, 1987) 104–5.

3. ויספו בני ישראל לעשות הרע בעיני יהוה or ויעשו בני־ישראל את־הרע בעיני יהוה.

4. Judg 3:12 speaks of Y<small>HWH</small> strengthening the foreign king.

most likely because a more detailed account of the divine episode that raised up the judge/deliverer is provided. In four cases, the word *subdued* signals the defeat of the enemy (כנע, 3:30, 4:23, 8:28, 11:33), and in five cases, reference is made to God's strengthening the hand of Israel against their enemy (4:24), delivering Israel from the hand of their enemy (2:18), or giving their enemy into their hand (3:10, 11:32, 12:3). There are also several references to the presence (יהוה עם; 2:18, 6:12) or Spirit of YHWH enabling the judge/deliverer (רוח־יהוה; 3:10; 6:34; 11:29; 13:25; 14:6, 19; 15:14; 16:25; compare 9:23).

Rest. The rest stage employs one of two formulas (but never both): the rest of the land formula (שקט; 3:11, 30; 4:31; 8:28) or the length of the judge/deliverer's reign formula (2:18; 10:2, 3; 12:7; 15:20; 16:31).

Death. The death stage comprises one or both of the following formulas: the death formula, which notes that the judge died (מות; 2:19; 3:11; 4:1; 8:32–33; 10:2, 5; 12:7; see 16:30) and/or the burial formula (קבר; 8:32; 10:2, 5; 12:7; 16:31).

This pattern, however, should not be treated as merely a cycle that returns to the same point from which it began. It is better described as a downward spiral because the cycles disintegrate as the book progresses.[5]

The following analysis highlights an additional element that appears in nearly all of the cyclical accounts just prior to the salvation of the people from their condition of distress: the declaration of the word of YHWH.

Gideon (Judges 6:1–8:32)

The Gideon cycle (6:1–8:32) begins in typical fashion with the declaration that Israel had done evil in the sight of YHWH (sin, 6:1a), which results in YHWH giving them into the hands of the foreign power Midian (discipline, 6:1b) and ultimately in Israel's distressed condition (6:6a) which prompts their cry (6:6b). God's response to this cry, however, is not to raise up a deliverer/judge as found in what is often seen as the paradigmatic account of Othniel in 3:7–11 (see 3:9b).[6] Instead, YHWH sends איש נביא

---

5. See D. I. Block, *Judges, Ruth* (NAC 6; Nashville: Broadman & Holman, 1999) 391, which notes how Israel's response is missing in the Samson account. T. C. Butler (*Judges* [Nashville: Thomas Nelson, 2009] lviii–lix), emphasizes the diversity in the schema in order "to argue that this is a purposeful element of the writer's style so that style and content both show the growing disaster that was Israel and their relationship to God" (personal communication). See ibid., 482–84, table I.2 in the appendix. Butler focuses more on vocabulary than elements, which are my focus in this article.

6. For the role of the Othniel account, see Amit, *Art*, 161; B. G. Webb, *The Book of the Judges: An Integrated Reading* (JSOTSup 46; Sheffield: JSOT Press, 1987) 127; M. Z. Brettler, "The Book of Judges: Literature as Politics," *JBL* 108 (1989)

('a man, a prophet') who delivers a message according to the form of the classic prophetic judgment speech.[7] This speech begins by rehearsing YHWH's gracious act of delivering the people from Egypt and giving them possession of the promised land only to end with a reminder of his warning about and condemnation of their false worship. The message does not mention impending judgment or call for human response but rather provides for the community the reason for their present predicament.[8]

The abrupt ending to the message of the one called איש נביא ('a man, a prophet') is followed immediately by the appearance of another figure with a closely related title: מלאך יהוה ('messenger of YHWH').[9] Verse 11 appears to be the continuation of the narrative backbone which began with the introductory clause ויהי כי ('now it came about when') followed by the two waw-consecutive prefix conjugations in v. 8 (וישלח . . . ויאמר, "then he sent . . . then he said").[10] This ambiguity links together these two traditionally separate pericopes (6:6–10 and 6:11–25) and, as a result, the figures.

405–6; J. C. Exum, "The Center Cannot Hold: Thematic and Textual Instabilities in Judges," *CBQ* 52 (1990) 411; R. B. Chisholm, "The Role of Women in the Rhetorical Strategy of the Book of Judges," in *Integrity of Heart, Skillfulness of Hands: Biblical and Leadership Studies in Honor of Donald K. Campbell* (ed. C. H. Dyer and R. B. Zuck; Grand Rapids: Baker, 1994) 37. Too-close attention to this account has led to lack of attention to the role of the word of the deity in the most of the other accounts.

7. Block, *Judges*, 255–56; Butler, *Judges*, 199.

8. Judg 6:7–10 does not appear in 4QJudg[a], which has suggested to some an earlier phase in the development of the book (A. G. Auld, "Gideon: Hacking at the Heart of the Old Testament," *VT* 39 [1989] 257–67; J. C. Trebolle Barrera, "Textual Variants in *4qJudg*[a] and the Textual and Editorial History of the Book of Judges [1]," *RevQ* 14 [1989] 229–45; E. Tov, *Textual Criticism of the Hebrew Bible* [2nd ed.; Minneapolis: Fortress / Assen: Van Gorcum, 2001] 135–36, 344–45; E. C. Ulrich, *The Dead Sea Scrolls and the Origins of the Bible* [Studies in the Dead Sea Scrolls and Related Literature; Grand Rapids: Eerdmans / Leiden: Brill, 1999] 105–6), but more likely it is simply a scribal error (see especially O'Connell, *Rhetoric*, 147 n. 178; see N. Fernández Marcos, "The Hebrew and Greek Texts of Judges," in *The Earliest Text of the Hebrew Bible: The Relationship between the Masoretic Text and the Hebrew Base of the Septuagint Reconsidered* [ed. A. Schenker; SBLSCS 52; Atlanta: Society of Biblical Literature, 2003] 1–16; N. Fernández Marcos, "The Genuine Text of Judges," in *Sôfer Mahir: Essays in Honour of Adrian Schenker* [ed. Y. Goldman, A. van der Kooij, and R. D. Weis; VTSup 110; Leiden: Brill, 2006] 33–45 [with thanks to S. Locke]). On the role of this prophet and his message within the Gideon narrative, see L. R. Martin, "The Intrusive Prophet: The Narrative Function of the Nameless Prophet in Judges 6," *Journal for Semitics* 16 (2007) 113–40.

9. See Isa 44:26; Hag 2:13; Mal 1:1; 3:1; 2 Chr 36:15, 16; possibly Isa 42:19; Qoh 5:5; Job 33:23. In other contexts, however, this term is used for a heavenly being (Gen 48:16; Exod 23:20, 33:2; Hos 12:5).

10. See R. L. Heller, *Narrative Structure and Discourse Constellations: An Analysis of Clause Function in Biblical Hebrew Prose* (HSS 55; Winona Lake, IN: Eisenbrauns, 2004).

Table 1. Gideon's Response to the Messenger

Judges 6:8–9	Judges 6:13
וישלח יהוה איש נביא אל־בני ישראל ויאמר להם כה־אמר <u>יהוה</u> אלהי ישראל אנכי <u>העליתי אתכם ממצרים</u> ואציא אתכם מבית עבדים ואצל אתכם מיד מצרים ומיד כל־לחציכם ואגרש אותם מפניכם <u>ואתנה</u> לכם את־ארצם	ויאמר אליו גדעון בי אדני ויש יהוה עמנו ולמה מצאתנו כל־זאת ואיה כל־נפלאתיו אשר ספרו־לנו אבותינו לאמר הלא <u>ממצרים העלנו יהוה</u> ועתה נטשנו יהוה <u>ויתננו</u> בכף־מדין
Then Yhwh sent a man, a prophet, to the children of Israel and he said to them, "Thus has said Yhwh, God of Israel, 'I myself brought you up from Egypt and I brought you out from the house of servitude, and I rescued you from the power of Egypt and from the power of all your oppressors and I drove them out before you and I gave you their land.'"	Then Gideon said to him, "If I may sir, if Yhwh is with us, why has all this happened to us? Where are all his miracles which our ancestors recounted to us, saying, 'Did not Yhwh bring us up out of Egypt?' But now Yhwh has abandoned us and has handed us over into the power of Midian."

The messenger of Yhwh figure in 6:11–25 now delivers a more positive message ("Yhwh is with you, O valiant warrior," v. 12) to the one chosen to deliver Israel in the present circumstances. It is interesting that Gideon's initial response to the messenger figure challenges the message that had been delivered through the איש נביא figure in 6:6–10 (see table 1). Gideon's response appears to link the earlier message of איש נביא with this מלאך יהוה, showing a recognition of their common master, if not identity.[11] But no sooner does the narrator present Gideon's response than this character is depicted as Yhwh himself (v. 14), a designation that appears to be in view throughout vv. 14–19, as the figure shifts from speaking about Yhwh in the third person ("Yhwh is with you," v. 12) to first person ("Have I not sent you?" v. 14; "Surely I will be with you," v. 16). With v. 20, however, the identity of the character shifts back to מלאך יהוה, who performs a miracle. This prompts Gideon to fear for his life, because he has seen what he calls מלאך יהוה face to face, even though he is addressing אדני יהוה ('Lord Yhwh', v. 22) who is identified as the one who reassures Gideon in v. 23 that he will not die. After this point, Gideon continues to hear the voice of

---

11. On this ambiguity see Butler, *Judges*, 200.

God throughout the account of salvation (6:25–27, 7:2–11), but there is no more reference to a prophet or messenger of Yhwh.[12]

The account of Gideon provides more details in the Judges cycle between the typical elements of depiction of the distress of the people and the raising up of the chosen judge/deliverer for Israel. In between these two typical elements the narrator depicts a figure (or figures) associated with the deity who deliver(s) a negative word to the people, confronting them for their lack of fidelity to Yhwh's commands, while giving a positive word to the deliverer, who will soon deliver the people from their distress.

Jephthah (Judges 10:6–12:7)

The sin formula signals the beginning of the Jephthah cycle in 10:6. The depiction of the sin of the people is one of the most extensive in the book, providing details on the character of the people's evil which included 'serving' (עבד) a long list of Canaanite gods while 'forsaking' (עזב) Yhwh and not 'serving' (עבד) him.[13] As expected, this prompts a disciplinary response from Yhwh, whose 'anger' (אף יהוה) burns before he 'sells' (מכר) them into the power of foreign overlords (Philistines, Ammonites), for 18 years. In this distressed condition, the people finally cry out to Yhwh for help and, for the only time in the book, confess their sin (however, see 1 Sam 12:8–11). Yhwh's response to this cry, however, is unexpected. One might suppose that this admission of sin would prompt an act of divine salvation, but instead Yhwh announces judgment on the people.[14] Like the speech delivered through the prophet to Gideon in 6:8–10, the speech in 10:11–14 begins by rehearsing Yhwh's past deliverance of the distressed people beginning with the rescue from Egypt and expanding to Canaanite foes. Yhwh then declares his exasperation with the people's forsaking him and serving other gods, refusing to deliver them and encouraging them

---

12. It must be noted that Yhwh uses a dream in 7:13–15, an avenue of revelation often associated with the prophetic in the OT, to relate his word to Gideon (see 7:9–11).

13. K. Latvus (*Anger and Ideology: The Anger of God in Joshua and Judges in Relation to Deuteronomy and the Priestly Writings* [JSOTSup 279; Sheffield: Sheffield Academic Press, 1998] 43–44) notes the striking similarities between 10:6–16 (in terms of vocabulary and structure) and the paradigmatic 2:11–19 and 3:7–11; see O'Connell, *Rhetoric*, 178; M. Sjöberg, *Wrestling with Textual Violence: The Jephthah Narrative in Antiquity and Modernity* (The Bible in the Modern World 4; Sheffield: Sheffield Phoenix, 2006) 30.

14. See further my *Severe Mercy: Sin and Its Remedy in the Old Testament* (Siphrut: Literature and Theology of the Hebrew Scriptures 1; Winona Lake, IN: Eisenbrauns, 2009).

instead to cry out to their Canaanite gods for deliverance. The people persist, however, confessing again their culpability, inviting divine discipline, and then repenting by putting away their gods and serving YHWH. While there is some debate over the meaning of the final line in 10:16,[15] what follows this encounter between YHWH and Israel is a depiction of Israel's salvation from their enemy through Jephthah.

The account of Jephthah, therefore, has a divine message at the same juncture as the account of Gideon, that is, after the cry of a distressed Israel and before the redemptive act of YHWH in raising up a deliverer for the people. In this case, however, the messenger is YHWH himself.[16]

Samson (Judges 13:1–16:31)

Although the account of Samson contains the least formulaic language of the previous cycles, Judg 13:1 carefully follows the formulas, announcing that the Israelites once again did evil in the sight of YHWH, an act that prompts YHWH's discipline as he gives them into the hands of the Philistines for 40 years. In the cyclical template, what should follow is the distressed cry of the Israelites, but the Samson account is the only of the main six cycles that lacks this element. Instead, what follows in Judges 13 is a narrative account strikingly similar to what stands between the depictions of distress and of salvation in the Gideon account. A figure identified by the narrator as מלאך־יהוה appears to a barren woman, declaring that she would give birth to a child who would deliver Israel from the power of the Philistines (13:2–5). While the woman describes this figure as possessing a form כמראה מלאך האלהים ('like the appearance of the messenger of God', 13:6), and the narrator continues to identify the figure this way in 13:9, 13, 15–18, 20–21,[17] it is interesting that, as in the Gideon account, a title often associated with prophets, איש האלהים ('man of God', Deut 33:1;

---

15. Contrast Webb, *Judges*, 45–48; O'Connell, *Rhetoric*, 186–87; Block, *Judges*, 348; D. Janzen, "Why the Deuteronomist Told about the Sacrifice of Jephthah's Daughter," *JSOT* 29 (2005) 347; with R. D. Haak, "A Study and New Interpretation of *qsr nps*," *JBL* 101 (1982) 161–67; T. E. Fretheim, *The Suffering of God: An Old Testament Perspective* (OBT 14; Philadelphia: Fortress, 1984) 129; J. C. McCann, *Judges* (IBC; Louisville: Westminster John Knox, 2002) 78–79, over whether this suggests YHWH's gracious response or judgmental rejection.

16. It must be noted, however, that like Samson the judge-deliverer Jephthah himself does not receive a message from God directly as did Barak and Gideon, evidence of the progressive downward spiral of 2:6–16:31; see Webb, *Judges*, 65.

17. The way the messenger figure seeks to elude self-revelation is reminiscent of the encounter between Jacob and the "man" who is also called "God" in Gen 32:30. So also the elusive self-revelation of YHWH in the book of Exodus (see Exod 3:13–15, 4:13–15, 6:3, 33:12–34:7). See Amit, *Art*, 292, 302.

Josh 14:6; 1 Sam 2:27, 9:6–7; 1 Kgs 12:22, 13:1–2), is used by the woman and her husband to describe this figure (13:6, 8; see 13:10, 11).[18] Further similarities to the Gideon account are seen in the fact that this couple offer a meat and grain offering on a rock (13:19; compare 6:20) and that the figure performs some kind of miracle in relation to the offerings (13:20; compare 6:21), which confirms the figure's heavenly status (13:21; compare 6:22). In both cases, there is a close identification of the figure with Yhwh himself as the main characters in each fear for their lives for having seen God (13:22–23; compare 6:22–23), only to have these fears immediately calmed (13:23; compare 6:23). The Samson story bears striking similarities to the Gideon account,[19] with a figure called "the messenger of Yhwh," and with ambiguous links to both Yhwh and prophets, arising at the narrative juncture just prior to the raising up of a deliverer for Israel. In contrast to the Gideon account, however, this messenger figure in chap. 13 does not announce judgment against Israel as does the איש נביא ('a man, a prophet') in 6:8–10.

These three accounts (Gideon, Jephthah, Samson), thus, all depict a prophetic-messenger-deity figure arising in the narrative gap between the discipline and salvation of the people. In two cases, the people's cry comes prior to the appearance of this figure, while in one case this element is absent entirely from the account. While the accounts of Jephthah and Samson are extremely different in their presentation of this prophetic-messenger-deity figure, that of Gideon contains striking similarities to both of these later accounts.

Barak (Judges 4:1–5:31)

The account of Barak in Judges 4–5 begins with the typical formulas, noting Israel's sin (4:1), Yhwh's discipline (4:2), and Israel's distressed condition and cry (4:3). Relying on the first two cycles (Othniel and Ehud), one might expect a deliverer to be raised up in response to the people's cry, and at first sight this seems to be the case as the reader is introduced to Deborah, who is described as שפטה את־ישראל בעת ההיא ('judging Israel at that time,' 4:4). The description of this "judging" in 4:5 (למשפט 'for judgment'), however, is unlike what has been encountered to this point

---

18. Notice how according to the narrator the husband Manoah did not recognize this figure as "the messenger of Yhwh," suggesting that there is a distinction between "man of God" and "messenger of Yhwh."

19. For a full discussion of the similarities between the two accounts, see Webb, *Judges*, 164; Amit, *Art*, 289–90; V. H. Matthews, *Judges and Ruth* (New Cambridge Bible Commentary; Cambridge: Cambridge University Press, 2004) 142.

in the book of Judges and also in the accounts which follow.[20] No other judge in this book actually does "judging" activity. A further complication arises as the account depicts Deborah sending for and summoning another individual, Barak, to lead the Israelites into battle in order to deliver Israel from the foreign oppressor (4:6–9).[21] While her warning to the timid Barak that YHWH will sell Sisera into the hands of a woman initially creates an expectation that she will ultimately function like other "judges" in the book, these expectations are dashed as that woman turns out to be Jael, not Deborah herself.

It appears that Deborah functions here in a manner consonant with the title the narrator has given her: אשה נביאה ('a woman, a prophet') who would dispense justice through prophetic inquiry under a palm tree in the southern Ephraimite hill country.[22] A prophetic figure would be dispensing justice (למשפט) because this figure could seek the will of the deity and so offer the correct decision in difficult cases.[23] Furthermore, the phrase used at the end of 4:5 is one that may be linked to the reception of a divine oracle.[24] Her role is not leadership in battle but rather to be messenger

---

20. E. Assis, "Man, Woman and God in Judg 4," *SJOT* 20 (2006) 110–24.

21. See A. Brenner, "A Triangle and a Rhombus in Narrative Structure: A Proposed Integrative Reading of Judges 4 and 5," *VT* 40 (1990) 129–38, for how the relationship between Deborah and Barak (as one initiates and the other completes) is a typical motif in this narrative in Judges.

22. One cannot help but see the striking similarity between the title given by the narrator to the prophetic figure in the account of Gideon in Judg 6:8 (איש נביא) and the title given to Deborah in 4:4 (אשה נביאה); see Block, *Judges*, 254; T. J. Schneider, *Judges* (Berit Olam; Collegeville, MN: Liturgical Press, 2000) 102; W. Bluedorn, *Yahweh Versus Baalism: A Theological Reading of the Gideon-Abimelech Narrative* (JSOTSup 329; Sheffield: Sheffield Academic Press, 2001) 62; Butler, *Judges*, 197. Another striking prophetic connection between Deborah and the Gideon account is that the "messenger of YHWH" in 6:11 also sits under a tree ("the oak of Ophrah"). See Bluedorn, *Yahweh*, 70–71. At the least one must admit that Deborah's status as "judge" is ambiguous as per Amit, *Art*, 204–6. Although, see Block, *Judges*, 191–200. Notice also the combination of judge and prophet in the later transitional character of Samuel (1 Samuel 3, 7).

23. See further K. Spronk ("Deborah, a Prophetess: The Meaning and Background of Judges 4:4–5," in *Elusive Prophet: The Prophet as a Historical Person, Literary Character and Anonymous Artist* [ed. J. C. D. Moor; OtSt 45; Leiden: Brill, 2001] 236–38), who notes the use of מִשְׁפָּט also in Judg 13:12 as related to an oracle from a messenger of YHWH (see also *KTU* 1.124), although it is not necessary to see here ancestral cult practice. See also S. Niditch, *Judges: A Commentary* (OTL; Louisville: Westminster John Knox, 2008) 2–3.

24. See D. I. Block, "Deborah among the Judges: The Perspective of the Hebrew Historian," in *Faith, Tradition, and History* (Winona Lake, IN: Eisenbrauns, 1994) 229–53; idem, "Why Deborah's Different," *BRev* 17 (2001) 34–40, 49–52; Spronk, "Deborah," 236.

of Yhwh's will to those who would lead the army, first by commissioning the leader[25] and then by providing divine directions for the timing and method of battle. In response to an inquiry of the people looking for justice from God for the abuses of Jabin and Sisera, she sets the enactment of justice in motion by summoning Barak and then instructing him as to when to enter battle against Sisera according to Yhwh's military strategy.[26]

Similar to the accounts of Gideon and Samson, the account of Barak includes the depiction of a prophetic-messenger figure who speaks on behalf of and has access to the will of Yhwh. This depiction follows the description of the distressed condition and cry of the people and immediately prior to the appearance of a deliverer to save Israel from their distress.

Abimelech (Judges 8:33–10:2)

The relationship between the Abimelech episode in Judges 9 and the cyclical accounts of the judges throughout Judg 2:6–16:31 is uncertain and highly debated. Clearly, the account does not contain the same lexical formulas that appear throughout the six major accounts, and yet, if one considers the material immediately preceding and following Judges 9, a case can be made for the presence of most of the basic rhetorical rhythms of the major cycles: sin (8:33–35), discipline (9:1–22), salvation (9:23–10:1), rest (10:2a), and the judge's death (10:2b). This would make this episode in Judg 8:33–10:2 technically the account of Tola, with Abimelech functioning in the cycle in the role of the foreign oppressor, odd for one who is an Israelite brother, but most likely a statement about the appropriateness of a kingship model fashioned after the nations.

Like the account of Samson, there is no depiction of the distress and cry of the people. However, after the depiction of the equivalent of the "discipline" phase of the cyclical pattern, that is, the account of Abimelech's treachery and murder of Gideon's sons at Ophrah in 9:1–6 and prior to the beginning of the salvation in 9:23–10:1, there appears a speech delivered by the sole survivor of Abimelech's purge, Jotham, the youngest son of Gideon, in 9:7–22. This speech is addressed to the lords of Shechem from the lofty safety of Mount Gerizim, where covenant blessings were first delivered to Israel after their entrance into the land (Deut 11:29, 30; chaps. 27–28; see Josh 8:33–35).

Jotham's speech begins with the call to his hearers to listen to him so that God may listen to them. His position on Mount Gerizim along with

---

25. See Block, *Judges*, 191–94, for 4:4–10 as call narrative.
26. See the far more extensive treatment of Deborah as prophet rather than judge in idem, "Deborah among the Judges," 229–53.

the implicit assumption that he speaks for the deity, in that heeding his voice will be essential to the deity's heeding theirs, suggests that he is functioning here as an intermediary of divine revelation.[27] The use of a parable (fable) would fit with prophetic speech (see 2 Sam 12:1–15), and the fable concludes with a clear announcement of judgment against Abimelech and the lords of Shechem, one that presages the demise of both parties in the narrative that follows.

Thus, although in some ways contrasting the major cyclical accounts of the judges, on a deeper level there are points of connection, and once again, like the major accounts of Barak, Gideon, Jephthah, and Samson, a divine intermediary figure appears at the juncture in the narrative between discipline and salvation.

Ehud (Judges 3:12–30)

The initial accounts of Othniel and Ehud do not appear to contain this element of the word of YHWH, which is so key to the other accounts in Judges. In the account of Othniel, the element of sin (3:7) prompts the discipline of YHWH (3:8), to which the Israelites respond by crying (3:9a). This, in turn, prompts YHWH to raise up a deliverer (3:9b) whose victory results in rest (3:11a) until the death of the judge (3:11b). The account of Ehud follows suit, employing the elements of sin (3:12a), discipline (3:12b–14), distress (3:15a), salvation (3:15b–30a), and rest (3:30b), with the death of the judge held off until the beginning of the account of Barak (4:1). However, in light of the evidence presented above, it is interesting that in this account just prior to Ehud's act of salvation proper, once again there appears a divine intermediary figure. After presenting the tribute to Eglon, Ehud appears to return home with his servants, but we are told that when he reaches the idols which were at Gilgal, he returned alone to address Eglon. Ehud describes what he has for Eglon as a דבר־סתר ('secret message', 3:19), later qualified as דבר־אלהים ('a message from God/gods', 3:20). The mention of the idols at Gilgal is essential to this ruse, suggesting that Ehud has received something from a deity while at Gilgal.[28] The secret divine message, however, is from YHWH and is in the form of a cubit of sharpened metal hidden beneath his robe.

---

27. See now Butler, *Judges*, 239, who notes the parallel between Jotham and the prophet of Judg 6:7–10.

28. See Judg 2:1–5, which suggests that Gilgal was a cult center where messages from the deity originated. Possibly, the idols refer to the use of the cult center by Eglon (J. Gray, *Joshua, Judges, Ruth* [NCB; Grand Rapids: Eerdmans, 1986] 263–64; R. G. Boling, *Judges* [AB 6a; Garden City, NY.: Doubleday, 1975] 86; L. K. Handy, "Uneasy

While not identical to the other accounts, once again, a divine intermediary is essential to the transition between the cry and salvation of the people.

Summary (Judges 2:6–16:31)

It appears then that in nearly all of the major accounts of the judges, a speech from a divine intermediary appears at the juncture in the account just prior to the salvation of the people. This speech functions in a variety of ways, sometimes as a message of judgment to the people as a whole explaining the discipline they are experiencing (the first Gideon, Jephthah) and at other times as a message of salvation associated with the circumstances essential to the rescue of the nation (the second Gideon, Samson, Barak). Sometimes these are mixed, as a message of judgment is delivered to more limited groups whose demise will lead to salvation for the nation (Abimelech, Ehud). The identity of the divine intermediary is diverse, ranging from Yhwh himself (Jephthah), to ambiguous prophetic-messenger-divine figures (Gideon, Samson), to a prince (Abimelech), to a judge (Ehud).

The absence of this speech from a divine intermediary element within what is often considered the paradigmatic account of Othniel may have prompted most past scholars to exclude it from the basic elements of the cyclical pattern. So also this divine intermediary element is not found as a regular component within the cycles described in the introductory sections in 2:6–3:6. However, there are places where the word of God does play a role, first, subtly in the statement of 2:15 that the discipline they experienced was כאשר דבר יהוה וכאשר נשבע יהוה להם ('as Yhwh had spoken and as Yhwh had sworn to them') and, second, explicitly in 2:20–22 in the direct divine speech in which Yhwh determines to leave nations in the land to test Israel.

In any case, the lack of this divine intermediary element in possibly only one (Othniel) major account suggests that it was important to the writer(s) and it may be the missing seventh stage of the cycle (now reaching perfection!). It is interesting that the "distress" element is missing from at least one (Samson) if not two (if one includes Abimelech) accounts, and yet this has not been considered reason enough to remove this element from the basic cycle. I would suggest that the appearance of a divine intermediary

---

Laughter: Ehud and Eglon as Ethnic Humor," *SJOT* 6 [1992] 237), thus Eglon would assume this message was from his own god(s) (Matthews, *Judges*, 61; Butler, *Judges*, 71). On secrecy, royalty, and deity, see A. Lenzi, *Secrecy and the Gods: Secret Knowledge in Ancient Mesopotamia and Biblical Israel* (SAAS; Helsinki: Neo-Assyrian Text Corpus Project, 2008).

is a key element within the basic historiographic structure of the major accounts of the judges in Judg 2:6–16:31.

Retrieving Heavenly Messages in the Concluding Narratives of Judges (Chapters 17–21)

Refrains (Judges 17:6, 18:1, 19:1, 21:25)

With Judges 17, the cyclical pattern that has dominated the narratives throughout 2:6–16:31 is left behind.[29] What binds these final five chapters together is a refrain incorporated at four intervals in the narrative complex, two in each of the two main narratives, with the first near the beginning of the first story concerning Micah and the Danites, the second at a key juncture in this story (as the narrative shifts from a focus on Micah to the tribe of Dan), and the third and fourth at the beginning and end of the second story concerning the Levite's concubine and the Benjaminites.[30]

(17:6)	בימים ההם אין מלך בישראל איש הישר בעיניו יעשה
(18:1)	בימים ההם אין מלך בישראל
(19:1)	ויהי בימים ההם ומלך אין בישראל
(21:25)	בימים ההם אין מלך בישראל איש הישר בעיניו יעשה

In those days there was no king in Israel. (Each did what was right in their own eyes.)

This refrain highlights the driving purpose of this section of Judges, that is, to show that the conditions depicted are somehow connected to the absence of a king in Israel.[31] The narrator's theological summary of the condition of Israel in the cyclical pattern was

---

29. This does not preclude connectivity between the cyclical core of Judg 2:6–16:31 and the concluding chapters, 17–21; see R. G. Bowman, "Narrative Criticism of Judges: Human Purpose in Conflict with Divine Presence," in *Judges and Method* (ed. G. A. Yee; Minneapolis: Fortress, 1995) 17–44; G. T. K. Wong, *Compositional Strategy of the Book of Judges: An Inductive, Rhetorical Study* (VTSup 111; Leiden: Brill, 2006) 69–141. For connections between Judges 16 and 17, see M. A. Sweeney, "Davidic Polemics in the Book of Judges," *VT* 47 (1997) 517–29. There are, however, even greater connections between Judges 17–18 and 19–21; see P. E. Satterthwaite, "'No King in Israel': Narrative Criticism and Judges 17–21," *TynBul* 44 (1993) 75–88; O'Connell, *Rhetoric*, 264–65; Sweeney, "Davidic Polemics"; Block, *Judges*, 474–75, 515.

30. O'Connell (*Rhetoric*, 265) notes how the overall pattern of the refrain's placement creates a symmetrical pattern (full refrain, short refrain, short refrain, full refrain). Notice also the use of ויהי to signal the juncture between the two main narratives; see Heller, *Narrative Structure*.

31. That the lack of kingship is uppermost in the narrator's/redactor's mind is seen in the fact that this part of the refrain is what is repeated each time. While most see here a reference to human kingship, and most likely Davidic kingship, others favor

(3:7, 6:1) ויעשו בני־ישראל (את־)הרע בעיני יהוה
(3:12, 4:1, 10:6, 13:1) ויספו בני ישראל לעשות הרע בעיני יהוה

Now the children of Israel (again) did the evil in the eyes of YHWH.

However, in the concluding narrative complex it is

איש הישר בעיניו יעשה[32]

Each did what was right in their own eyes.

This latter refrain is an inner-biblical allusion to Deuteronomy 12, a passage focused on the mandated centralization of worship in Israel at a single shrine after Israel's conquest of the land.[33] According to this passage in Deuteronomy, the worship patterns of Israel in the wilderness are likened to Canaanite practices that took place at המקמות ('places') located על־ההרים הרמים ועל־הגבעות ותחת כל־עץ רענן ('on the high mountains and on the hills and under every leafy tree', 12:2). When they entered the promised land, they were to destroy all of these worship sites and instead seek YHWH at the central place YHWH would choose for his name to dwell among the tribes (12:5).[34] Moses' instruction in 12:8 is thus:

---

the idea that YHWH's kingship is in focus. For a summary of the various views, see G. T. K. Wong, "Is There a Direct Pro-Judah Polemic in Judges?" *SJOT* 19 (2005) 84–110; idem, *Compositional Strategy*, 191–223.

32. See resonances of this phrase in Exod 15:26; Deut 6:18; 12:25, 28; 13:19; 21:9; 1 Kgs 15:5, 11; 22:43; 2 Kgs 10:30; 12:3; 14:3; 15:3, 34; 16:2; 18:3; 22:2; 2 Chr 14:1; 20:32; 24:2; 25:2; 26:4; 27:2; 28:1; 29:2; 34:2; לעשות הישר בעיני יהוה. ועשית הישר והטוב בעיני יהוה; תעשה הטוב והישר בעיני יהוה אלהיך;אלהיך.

33. O'Connell, *Rhetoric*, 235; A. D. H. Mayes, "Deuteronomistic Royal Ideology in Judges 17–1," *Biblical Interpretation* 9 (2001) 255. This connection to Deuteronomy 12 is true not only of the refrain but also of Judges 17–18 as a whole; for evidence of this, see O'Connell, *Rhetoric*, 239–40; Matthews, *Judges*, 172. For connections to various laws in Deuteronomy, see E. A. Mueller, *The Micah Story: A Morality Tale in the Book of Judges* (Studies in Biblical Literature 34; New York: Peter Lang, 2001) 126; N. Na'aman, "The Danite Campaign Northward (Judges XVII–XVIII) and the Migration of the Phocaeans to Massalia (Strabo IV 1, 4)," *VT* 55 (2005) 52. This evidence challenges earlier attempts to distance the bracket around the book of Judges (1:1–2:5; chaps. 17–21) from the deuteronomic tradition (as per M. Noth, *Überlieferungsgeschichtliche Studien* [Halle: Max Niemeyer, 1943] 52–53, 59–60).

34. There is some debate over the translation of Deut 12:5, that is, whether they are to "seek" YHWH at the chosen place (e.g., NASB) or "seek" YHWH for the chosen place (e.g., NIV, NRSV). Most have taken the term דרש here in the sense of making pilgrimage (see Gen 25:22, Deut 18:11, 1 Sam 9:9, Amos 5:5, 2 Chr 1:5), thus favoring the former understanding (see A. D. H. Mayes, *Deuteronomy* [NCB; London: Oliphants / Greenwood, SC: Attic, 1979] 223; J. H. Tigay, *Deuteronomy* [JPS Torah Commentary; Philadelphia: Jewish Publication Society, 1996] 120, 365 n. 17; D. L. Christensen, *Deuteronomy 1:1–21:9, Revised* [Nashville: Thomas Nelson, 2001] 243),

לא תעשון ככל אשר אנחנו עשים פה היום איש כל־הישר בעיניו

You shall not do according to all which we are doing here today, each (according to) all which is right in their own eyes.

In light of this, the narrator/redactor of Judges 17–21 summarizes the conditions of this time as related to the lack of a central worship shrine within Israel. This is then linked to the lack of royal patronage, suggesting that Davidic establishment of Jerusalem as the location of the central shrine is in view in this refrain. With this larger narratival purpose in view, one should look at the details of the narratives to see how they contribute to the establishment of the key problem that will be solved by the emergence of kingship.

Micah and the Danites (Judges 17–18)

It is obvious that a lack of centralized worship is in view in the first narrative in chaps. 17–18 concerning Micah and the Danites. There, one finds the establishment of an unorthodox local shrine within a family unit, a Levite roaming about the land looking for employment, a tribe stealing the shrine's paraphernalia and Levite and establishing their own shrine in the north that will not only rival the Jerusalem temple but ultimately lead to the exile of the Northern Kingdom. This story fits well with this overarching theme of cultic centralization.

Micah expresses his purpose in having this priest in the final verse of chap. 17: "Now I know that Yhwh will deal well with me, because I have [there is to me] the Levite as a priest." The priest will grant Micah access to the heavenly realms in order that he might experience material blessing (see Gen 12:16; Exod 1:20). The Danites as well understand the role of this priest and his shrine. When they happen upon this fully functioning shrine in 18:3–6, they take the opportunity to make an inquiry of God (or the gods) to determine if their mission to find a new site for their tribe would be successful.

---

although others favor the latter (J. G. Millar, *Now Choose Life: Theology and Ethics in Deuteronomy* [New Studies in Biblical Theology; Grand Rapids: Eerdmans, 1999] 110; R. D. Nelson, *Deuteronomy: A Commentary* [OTL; Louisville: Westminster John Knox, 2002] 142). This seeking, however, may best be understood as "seeking spiritual direction from" as in "inquire from," per other uses in which אל follows דרש, which is used for both orthodox and unorthodox inquiry: Deut 18:11 ("one who seeks [דרש אל] the dead"); Isa 8:19 ("Seek [דרש אל] the mediums and the spiritists who whisper and mutter, should not a people seek [דרש אל] its God?"); Isa 19:3 ("they will seek [דרש אל] idols, and ghosts, and mediums and spiritists"). The verb דרש is also used with accusative for inquiring of Yhwh: Gen 25:22, Exod 18:15, and possibly Ps 77:3.

Such inquiries (שאל) of God in relation to a military expedition are common in the Hebrew Bible (Judg 1:1; 20:18, 23, 27; 1 Sam 10:22; 14:37; 22:10, 13, 15; 23:2, 4; 28:6; 30:8; 2 Sam 2:1; 5:19, 23). However, in this case, there are reasons to question the validity of the Levite's answer.[35] First, in the narrative presentation, the Levite's response is given very quickly after the request is made by the Danites, raising questions over its authenticity.[36] Second, the priest makes "no claim to divine inspiration."[37] Third, no details on how the will of God was ascertained by the Levite are provided. Fourth, while the first part of the Levite's response is clearly positive (לכו לשלום 'Go in peace'),[38] the second part, which provides the basis for this action, is ambiguous: נכח יהוה דרככם אשר תלכו־בה ('in front of YHWH is your way in which you are going'). The collocation נכח יהוה could refer to something agreeable or disagreeable to God (see Ezek 14:3–4, 7; Jer 17:16; Lam 2:19; Amos 9:4).[39] Finally, because within the larger context of Judges it is clear that the Danites' failure to conquer their tribal territory is considered the lowest point in the conquest account in Judges 1 and prompts the divine judgment of Judg 2:1–5, there is little reason to expect YHWH to bless the Danites' migration north. These ambiguities raise serious questions over the validity of the Levite's message as a word from YHWH.

The Levite, Concubine, Gibeah, and Israel's Civil War (Judges 19–21)

While the connection between the first narrative in chaps. 17–18 and the larger narratival purpose of chaps. 17–21 is clear, this cannot be said, at least initially, of the second narrative in chaps. 19–21. This narrative, which focuses on the horrendous treatment of the Levite's Bethlehemite

---

35. See especially D. I. Block ("What Has Delphi to Do with Samaria? Ambiguity and Delusion in Israelite Prophecy," in *Writing and Ancient Near Eastern Society: Papers in Honour of Alan R. Millard* [ed. P. Bienkowski, C. Mee, and E. Slater; LHBOTS 426; London: T. & T. Clark, 2005] 199–200), who compares the inquiry here to that of Ahab's inquiry of the Baal prophets in 1 Kgs 22:5–6; see Schneider, *Judges*, 237; Mueller, *Micah*, 68; Butler, *Judges*, 393–94; contra J. S. Bray, *Sacred Dan: Religious Tradition and Cultic Practice in Judges 17–18* (LHBOTS 449; New York: T. & T. Clark, 2006) 36.

36. See Schneider, *Judges*, 237; Mueller, *Micah*, 68.

37. Block, "Delphi," 200.

38. It appears that the reconnaissance team takes this as an indication of God's approval; see 18:10, "for God has given it into your hand."

39. R. Polzin, *Moses and the Deuteronomist* (A Literary Study of the Deuteronomic History 1; New York: Seabury, 1980) 198; Exum, "Center," 427; G. A. Yee, "Ideological Criticism: Judges 17–21 and the Dismembered Body," in *Judges and Method* (Minneapolis: Fortress, 1995) 159; and especially Block, "Delphi," 200.

concubine during an overnight sojourn in Gibeah, seems to showcase the traditional understanding that the phrase "everyone did what was right in their own eyes" indicates moral anarchy or ethical relativism.[40] While the ethical breakdown displayed in the death of the concubine as well as the ultimate destruction of Jabesh-gilead and the capture of the virgins at Shiloh reveal the moral implications of the absence of a centralized cult, the focus on the centralized cult is subtly maintained.[41]

Judges 19

First, the narrator begins by depicting once again a Levite who is roaming about the land, sojourning first in a remote section of the tribal territory of Ephraim but ultimately traveling to Bethlehem in Judah to retrieve his concubine. While it may be legitimate for a Levite to be doing this, the striking similarity to the clearly unorthodox practice of the Levite in chaps. 17–18 casts a shadow over this second figure. Furthermore, in his conversation with the elderly man in Gibeah, the Levite seems to equate the "house of Yhwh" with his home in the "remote part of the hill country of Ephraim" (19:18; see 19:27).[42] It appears that, like the Levite in chaps. 17–18, this Levite is functioning at an independent shrine.

Second, much is made of the Levite's refusal to turn aside to spend the night in Jerusalem. In 19:10–12, Jerusalem is clearly identified as Jebus and considered a dangerous place for the Levite and his party to sojourn because it was controlled by foreigners, ironic in light of their ultimate treatment in Benjaminite Gibeah. This emphasis on Jerusalem in the hands of foreigners is a reminder of a period before its establishment as the central shrine in Israel.

Judges 20

As the story moves from the local to the national level in chap. 20, there is growing confusion over the location where inquiry was made of God and also over the legitimacy of the answer.[43] While the books of Joshua and Samuel consistently place the אהל מועד ('tent of meeting') at Shiloh,[44] the location where Israel was to seek Yhwh, worshiping and inquiring of

---

40. See O'Connell, *Rhetoric*, 235, 242, for this shift from religious to ethical anarchy.

41. See Mueller (*Micah*, 126), who wisely notes signs of ethical anarchy in chaps. 17–18, thus revealing that both are in view throughout chaps. 17–21.

42. So also in 19:9, his father-in-law is portrayed as understanding that the Levite was going home (לאהלך).

43. See S. S. Brooks, "Was There a Concubine at Gibeah," *BAIAS* 15 (1996) 31.

44. Josh 18:1; 19:51; 21:2; 22:9; 1 Sam 1:3; 2:22; 3:21; 4:4, 12; see משכן in Josh 22:29; היכל יהוה in 1 Sam 3:3; בית־יהוה in 1 Sam 3:15.

him, the account of the civil war between Benjamin and the rest of Israel in Judges 20 is unclear on the precise locations where the various inquiries took place. This ambiguity can be found from the start of chap. 20 as the Israelites 'assemble as one to Yhwh at Mizpah' (ותקהל העדה כאיש אחד אל־יהוה המצפה . . ., vv. 1, 3; see 21:5).[45] The narrator provides a detailed description of the deliberations among the Israelites and the request for the Israelites to 'give your advice and counsel here' (הבו לכם דבר ועצה הלם, v. 7). The advice that is given is clear: they will unite against the city of Gibeah (vv. 9–11). Strikingly missing, however, is any mention of inquiry of Yhwh throughout these deliberations among a group that had assembled "to Yhwh." Furthermore, the claim that Yhwh was "at Mizpah" introduces questions over whether this was the legitimate cult center identified with Shiloh in Joshua and Samuel.

Eventually, inquiry is described, but not until the account of the battle proper in vv. 18–48. This account is presented in three phases (vv. 18–21, 22–25, 26–48), each of which comprises three elements: Israel's inquiry of Yhwh (vv. 18, 23, 26–28),[46] the arraying of troop formations (vv. 19–20, 22, 29–30), and the battle (vv. 21, 24–25, 31–48).[47] In the second phase, the first and second elements are reversed.

In the first phase (v. 18), the Israelites go to בית־אל (Bethel) to inquire of God (the gods).[48] It is possible, however, that this is not the name of the town Bethel but is merely a reference to the shrine; but with the absence of the town name, Shiloh, this is ambiguous at best.[49] There, they ask a

---

45. The words "to Yhwh" signal "turning to God for direction" (Butler, *Judges*, 440); contra T. L. Brensinger (*Judges* [Believers Church Bible Commentary; Scottdale, PA: Herald, 1999] 202), who distinguishes between Mizpah as "place of assembly" and Bethel as place "where oracles are sought."

46. On the form and style of the "war oracle," see Block, "Delphi," 193–202.

47. On the role of the repetitive material in vv. 36b–48, as a narrative technique rather than evidence of multiple sources (C. F. Burney, *The Book of Judges with Introduction and Notes* [2nd ed.; London: Rivingtons, 1920] 447; Gray, *Judges*, 379–81; J. A. Soggin, *Judges: A Commentary* [OTL; Philadelphia: Westminster, 1981] 293–94; C. Niessen and G. Hentschel, "Der Bruderkrieg Zwischen Israel und Benjamin [Ri 20]," *Bib* 89 [2008] 17–38), see E. J. Revell, "The Battle with Benjamin (Judges XX 29–48) and Hebrew Narrative Techniques," *VT* 35 (1985) 430; P. E. Satterthwaite, "Narrative Artistry in the Composition of Judges XX 29ff," *VT* 42 (1992) 80–89; and Matthews, *Judges*, 196.

48. The collocation שאל ב indicates consulting the spiritual realm, whether through legitimate (Judg 1:1; 18:5; 1 Sam 10:22; 14:37; 22:10, 13, 15; 23:2, 4; 28:6; 30:8; 2 Sam 2:1; 5:19, 23; 1 Chr 14:10) or illegitimate (1 Chr 10:13 through a medium; Ezek 21:26 through teraphim; Hos 4:12 through wooden idols) means.

49. In light of the note at the end of chap. 18 that the first story traces the origins of the far northern cult center of the northern Israelite kingdom at Dan, the reader is

question strikingly similar to what was asked at the outset of the book of Judges (see 1:1):

(20:18) מי יעלה־לנו בתחלה למלחמה עם־בני בנימן
(1:1) מי יעלה־לנו אל־הכנעני בתחלה להלחם בו
Who will go up for us at first to engage in battle with the Benjaminites? (20:18)
Who will go up for us against the Canaanites at first to engage in battle against them? (1:1)

Although the basic answer is the same, it is expressed differently:

(20:18) יהודה בתחלה
(1:2) יהודה יעלה הנה נתתי את־הארץ בידו
Judah, at first (20:18)
Judah will go up. Indeed, I have given the land into his hand. (1:2)

In contrast to Yhwh's answer in 1:2, the answer in chap. 20 is short and gives no indication as to the potential success of the mission. Interestingly, the battle that followed was unsuccessful, casting doubt over the efficacy of the inquiry.[50]

Although defeated in Gibeah, the Israelites are not ready yet to abandon their mission. The second phase begins not with an inquiry as expected, but rather with a depiction of the Israelites encouraging one another and arraying for battle 'in the place where they had arrayed themselves on the first day' (במקום אשר־ערכו שם ביום הראשון), that is, at Gibeah (v. 22). Almost as an afterthought in v. 23 are they described as once again going up before Yhwh to make inquiry. The precise location of this inquiry is not given. Although it is possible that it refers to a return to Bethel from Gibeah, the fact that according to v. 22 they were already arrayed for battle suggests that their inquiry took place outside Gibeah as they were awaiting the battle. There is clearly greater intensity in this inquiry, because now the Israelites "weep before Yhwh until evening"; there is possibly some question as to the legitimacy of this action, because the Benjaminites are referred to as 'my brother' (אחי, v. 23).[51] Although the answer from Yhwh once again gives clear direction (עלו אליו 'go up against him'), there is still no guarantee of success in battle. Once again, the Israelite army is soundly defeated by the Benjaminites.

---

not surprised to see mention in chaps. 19–21 of Bethel, the location of the far southern cult center of the northern Israelite kingdom.

50. Check on Exum, "Center," 429; D. M. Hudson, "Living in a Land of Epithets: Anonymity in Judges 19–21," *JSOT* 62 (1994) 49.

51. See Satterthwaite, "Narrative Artistry."

This raises the intensity of the third and final phase of the battle. Now the entire army returns to Bethel, where they weep, fast, and present offerings to Yhwh (v. 26). The content of their inquiry is also more refined, as they not only ask whether they should go into battle but add at the end a negative option as well: אִם־אֶחְדָּל ('or shall I cease?'). The narrator now makes explicit reference to the presence of the ark and the legitimate priestly line (Phinehas son of Eleazar, son of Aaron).[52] Yhwh's answer now is not only clear, but there is a promise of success (v. 28).[53]

This series of battles raises questions about the efficacy and legitimacy of inquiring of Yhwh throughout this war. One option is to link the problem to the use of inappropriate locations. The tribal deliberation in 20:1–17 identifies Mizpah with the location of God's presence, while the battle account in 20:18–48 links the location to Bethel on two occasions and leaves the location ambiguous in a third with strong indications that it was at Mizpah.[54] It may be that the location of the inquiries of vv. 18–48 is Shiloh, but this is left ambiguous.

Another option is to blame the failures on inappropriate protocols for inquiry. The tribal deliberations in 20:1–17 completely ignore Yhwh as a source for inquiry even though the people have assembled "to Yhwh" (20:1). It is clear that by the time inquiry is made the plan of action is assumed. This is made clear in the first inquiry, which assumes the legitimacy of the mission[55] while ignoring the appropriate mourning and sacrificial rites (v. 18). The second inquiry asks about the legitimacy of the mission and incorporates mourning rites (v. 23), but appears to be done after the legitimacy of the mission is a foregone conclusion (v. 22). Furthermore, the inquiry does not include a negative option or sacrificial rites. It is in the third inquiry that nearly all the key elements align: the entire army

---

52. Contrast on this 18:5–6 and esp. 18:30–31; see Butler (*Judges*, 446), who argues that the narrator admits that Bethel had legitimate status at one time, "but only when it could claim the proper religious accoutrements, namely, the proper sacrifices, the proper symbols of divine presence, and the proper priesthood."

53. On the progression of these inquiries, see Satterthwaite, "Narrative Artistry," 82; see further Block, "Delphi," 196, for the contrast between 20:23 and 20:28, especially in terms of the "committal formula." Block compares Josh 20:28 here to 2 Sam 5:19.

54. Boling, *Judges*, 285, argued that the Bethel of 20:18 is merely a shrine located at Mizpah, while the Bethel of 20:26–28 is the central shrine found at Bethel and attended by the Aaronide Phinehas. However, this distinction seems arbitrary, for there is no difference in the Hebrew text between these two words that would justify it. There appears to be some ambiguity over the location of the inquiry, but this seems to be true of all three of the locations.

55. See Webb, *Judges*, 193.

is involved, both mourning and sacrificial rites are practiced, the proper means of inquiry are explicitly noted (at ark, mediated by Phinehas), and an explicit request with both positive and negative options is used. This narrative progression suggests a community uninterested at the outset in the need for inquiry and then untrained in appropriate protocol for inquiry.[56] Furthermore, the ambiguity regarding the location of inquiry, especially the reference to Mizpah and Bethel and the lack of reference to any location in the second inquiry, suggests confusion over centralization of worship. These two issues, location and protocol, are of great concern in deuteronomic literature, that is, the place and means of worship must be sanctioned by Yhwh. The people will not be allowed to do as they see fit (see Deut 12:8).

Judges 21

The devastating victory over the Benjaminites, however, only heightens the dilemma of Israel as they must now deal with the near loss of Benjamin as a tribe within their nation. As they deal with this crisis, they are portrayed as confused about or displaying disregard for proper protocols and locations for inquiry.

Judg 21:1, 5b reveals that, while they were before Yhwh at Mizpah, the Israelites took two oaths, one not to give their daughters to Benjaminites in marriage and another to put to death any who had not assembled with them at Mizpah. The narrative tension of chap. 21 revolves around these two oaths, which are strikingly absent from the narrative of chap. 20.[57] In the intervening verses between these two descriptions of oaths at Mizpah lies a description of two inquiries of God at Bethel (21:2–5a) which echoes the description of the final and successful inquiry that brought Israelite victory over Benjamin in 20:26. The first inquiry in 21:2–3 focuses on the crisis created by the first oath taken at Mizpah (21:1), and the second inquiry in 21:4–5a focuses on the crisis created by the second oath taken at Mizpah (21:5b).

The narrative in 21:6–14 appears to provide details of the inquiries introduced in 21:1–5. The section divides into two parts, beginning with the issue of the imminent loss of the tribe of Benjamin due to the Israelite's oath (21:6b–7) which is resolved (21:13–15) by giving attention to the second issue of the identity of those absent from the Mizpah assembly

---

56. Ibid.
57. For the folly of an oath such as this in the heat of battle, see the story of Jephthah in 11:30–31 and Wong, *Compositional Strategy*, 132–35; Sjöberg, *Wrestling*, 62.

(21:8–12). What is striking throughout 21:6–14 is the complete absence of the voice of Yhwh and the focus instead on the deliberations and actions of the assembly,[58] a return to their practice already observed in 20:1–17.

The Israelites' solution to provide Jabesh-Gileadite women as wives for the remnant of Benjamin, however, is inadequate according to 21:14.[59] This time, it is clear that Yhwh is irrelevant to their deliberations. Not only do they now blame Yhwh directly for the crisis in the loss of the tribe (contrast 21:3, 6), but there is no reference to an inquiry of Yhwh or of any accompanying rites. Instead, the elders' question in 21:16–18 is answered by the solution offered by the assembly in 21:19–23. That solution interestingly revolves around capturing young women participating in a cultic dance at the central sanctuary at Shiloh and solves the dilemma by ignoring their oath taken before Yhwh through devious means.[60] It is interesting that this is the first reference to Shiloh within the book, and it is clear that the Israelites have little respect for it as a sacred site, using a sacred event at the site to break their oath and steal away unsuspecting young women in the process.[61]

Judges 21 continues the trend already observed in Judges 20. The location of worship of Yhwh is identified as Mizpah, Bethel, and Shiloh. Protocols for inquiry of Yhwh seem to be followed, and yet the solutions are all provided by discussion among the congregation. No wonder the chapter ends with the reminder that, as the Israelites each return to their own tribes, families, and inheritances, everyone was doing what was right in their own eyes (21:24–25).

Summary (Judges 17–21)

While one cannot ignore the ethical crisis depicted throughout Judges 17–21, it is clear that this ethical crisis is related to a crisis in centralization

---

58. O'Connell, *Rhetoric*, 255; Webb, *Judges*, 195; see Block, *Judges*, 571, who writes: "God does not answer, and the people are thrown back on their resources."

59. That 21:15–23 is a continuation of the earlier dilemma and deliberations is clear by the lexical links between 21:6 and 21:15.

60. Leveraging, as Matthews (*Judges*, 199–200) suggests, Torah rape-capture laws (Deut 22:28–29; see Exod 22:16–17); see Exum, "Center," 430–31; A. Bach, "Rereading the Body Politic: Women and Violence in Judges 21," *Biblical Interpretation* 6 (1998) 1–19; E. Eynikel, "Judges 19–21, an 'Appendix': Rape, Murder, War and Abduction," *Communio viatorum* 47 (2005) 113; Niditch, *Judges*, 211.

61. The fact that the young women are called "daughters of Shiloh" rather than "daughters of Israel" may even indicate their status as permanent servants of the sanctuary akin to Canaanite cult prostitution (see Block, *Judges*, 581), further denigrating the role of Shiloh.

of cult. This reflects the narrator's viewpoint as communicated through the summary statement in 17:6 and 21:25, "everyone did what was right in their own eyes," a phrase echoing the concern of Deut 12:8. The narratives consistently raise questions about the appropriate location[62] and protocols for inquiry. Israel is tempted to use the cult for its own means and to follow its own deliberative methods. The only successful inquiry occurs in Judg 20:26 and there involves the Aaronide priesthood and ark, even though their location remains ambiguous.

For the narrator, this depiction of inquiry and centralization of cult raises the need for centralized royal rule (17:6, 18:1, 19:1, 21:25). At the same time, however, it does cast some questions over the accuracy of priestly means for discerning the will of Yhwh. This is especially notable in comparison with the methods for ascertaining the will of Yhwh in the cyclical core of the book (2:6–16:31).

Conclusion

This study of the book of Judges has revealed that the two main sections of Judges, Judg 2:6–16:31 and Judg 17:1–21:25, each display radically different conduits for the revelation of heavenly words. In Judg 2:6–16:31 people are confronted by heavenly words delivered through Yhwh, a prophet/man of God, or a messenger figure whose heavenly origin is suggested. There is at times an ambiguous relationship between these three categories.[63] This word is delivered always just prior to the beginning of the salvation of the people from their predicament and often after the people's cry of distress to Yhwh. The word that is delivered is always clear and normative.

Judg 17:1–21:25 never depicts a prophetic or messenger figure delivering the word of Yhwh. Instead, the word of God is delivered only after an inquiry by the people. At times, priestly figures and cult sites are connected to the reception of these heavenly words. In many cases, what begins as an inquiry of the will of Yhwh ends up as a point of departure for the community's own deliberations. The authenticity and clarity of the word that is delivered is often questionable.

Many have noted how the cyclical core of the book of Judges constitutes a descending spiral that hits its lowest point in the "leadership" of Samson in chaps. 13–16. Furthermore, chaps. 17–21 are often treated

---

62. See Brooks for the ambiguity surrounding the location of the inquiries ("Concubine," 31).

63. For evidence of this ambiguity elsewhere in the Hebrew Bible see my "Messengers of Hope in Haggai–Malachi," *JSOT* 32 (2007) 113–31.

as the conditions that arise (at least in terms of the literary presentation) in the wake of the failure of the leadership of the judges. The loss of a word directly from Yhwh and the uncertainty of the word gained through inquiry in chaps. 17–21 suggests that, for the person(s) responsible for Judges, priestly inquiry was dangerous, especially if practiced at cult sites other than that sanctioned by the official priesthood. If heavenly words were needed outside the cult center, this would have to come through prophet-messengers.[64]

It is interesting that the first introduction to the book of Judges in 1:1–2:5 is bracketed by the two types of heavenly mediation found in the two main sections of Judges that follow. This introduction begins with a mediation akin to that found in Judges 17–21, as the Israelites make inquiry of Yhwh to ascertain who should be the first to engage the Canaanites in battle.[65] While the answer is clear (יהודה יעלה 'Judah will go up') and promising (הנה נתתי את־הארץ בידו 'indeed I have given the land into his hand'), it is interesting that Judah turns to Simeon to assist him in this task (1:3), a response not even intimated in the divine answer.[66] While the inquiry in 1:1–2 appears to be normative, the people's response foreshadows some of the problems related to inquiries throughout chaps. 17–21.

At the conclusion to the first introduction to Judges in 2:1–5, the narrator depicts a confrontation that resulted from the people's disobedience

---

64. Block observes that "the silence of the priesthood in the book of Judges is deafening. But just because the people were in spiritual decline, it does not follow that Yhwh abandoned his people totally. He still had his representative" ("Deborah among the Judges," 252). According to Block, that representative was the prophet (in his case, Deborah). It may be that there is an anti-priestly rhetoric in Judges, although the introduction of the Aaronides in 20:27–28 before the only successful inquiry that appears to contrast the northern Mushite priesthood in 18:30, suggests that there is a role for the priesthood at the centralized sanctuary.

65. The vocabulary used in 1:1–2 (שאל ב) is clearly linked to that used in 20:18 (see O'Connell, *Rhetoric*, 242, 261; Amit, *Art*, 353–55). Schneider (*Judges*, 4) argues that this does not specify whether the Israelites made inquiry through priestly means (Urim and Thummim; see Num 27:21) or prophetic means. However, in Judges when this term is used, a prophetic figure is never explicitly in view whereas a priestly figure is often in view (Judg 1:1; 18:5; 20:18, 23, 27). See also elsewhere in the Hebrew Bible: שאל ביהוה (1 Sam 10:22; 22:10; 23:2, 4; 28:6; 30:8; 2 Sam 2:1; 5:19, 23), שאל באלהים (1 Sam 14:37; 22:13, 15; 1 Chr 14:10); cf. שאל in Num 27:21 (for Eleazar's Urim); and for illegitimate consultation of a medium (1 Chr 10:13); Teraphim (Ezek 21:26[21]); and an idol (Hos 4:12); also Josh 9:14. Possibly Isa 7:11 and 30:1–2 could be a case where a prophet is in view, but even this is not clear.

66. See L. R. Klein (*The Triumph of Irony in the Book of Judges* [Bible and Literature Series 14; Decatur, GA: Almond, 1988] 23) and Matthews (*Judges*, 38) who consider this evidence of compromise.

to the command to remove the Canaanites from the land, disobedience that is traced progressively throughout chap. 1. This confrontation involves a figure named "the messenger of Yhwh" (מלאך־יהוה) who travels from Gilgal to Bochim to deliver a message in the first-person voice of Yhwh.[67] While the speech is strikingly similar to the messages delivered by the prophet in Judg 6:8–10 and Yhwh in 10:11–14,[68] the title of the figure is the same as that used of those who appeared to Gideon in 6:11–24 and Samson's parents in 13:3–23, and the use of first-person speech connects the figure to Yhwh.[69] Once again, there is ambiguity in the depiction of this figure. This divine word of judgment explains the sinful idolatrous pattern that will dominate the cyclical core of Judg 2:6–16:31 while foreshadowing the various means by which heavenly words will be mediated to the people throughout the cycles.[70]

By including the two main processes by which the people of Israel receive and/or request heavenly words, the first introduction in 1:1–2:5 draws together the two main sections of Judges. This is further evidence that, for the person(s) responsible for the book of Judges, properly receiving and retrieving heaven's words were important issues.

---

67. The mention of Gilgal adds yet another possible cultic center into the mix; see Amos 4:4; 5:5; Hos 4:15; 9:15; 12:11; Block, *Judges*, 111. Possibly Bokim refers to Bethel (Webb, *Judges*, 105; Y. Amit, "Hidden Polemic in the Conquest of Dan: Judges 17–18," *VT* 40 [1990] 19; Amit, *Art*, 353; O'Connell, *Rhetoric*, 242; Wong, *Compositional Strategy*, 40–42).

68. Webb, *Judges*, 102.

69. On this ambiguity, see ibid., 145, 239 n. 81; Bluedorn, *Yahweh*, 66–67.

70. For connectivity between 2:1–5 and the cyclical accounts, see O'Connell, *Rhetoric*, 71–72. There are also connections to chaps. 17–21, esp. with the common language of 21:1–5 (Amit, *Art*, 353; O'Connell, *Rhetoric*, 242; Wong, *Compositional Strategy*, 40–42).

Samuel Agonistes:
A Conflicted Prophet's Resistance to God and Contribution to the Failure of Israel's First King

J. Richard Middleton

As one of the three central characters in 1 and 2 Samuel, and the one after whom the book is named, the prophet Samuel occupies a prominent place in the narrative, second only to Israel's first two kings. Although Samuel is not the only prophet mentioned in the book, the others are, by comparison, bit players. An unnamed "man of God" predicts the demise of the priestly house of Eli (1 Samuel 2), while the prophet Gad guides David in his flight from Saul (1 Sam 22:3) and later brings God's word of judgment against David for the census (2 Samuel 24). Somewhat more prominent is Nathan, who communicates God's promise of a dynasty for David (2 Samuel 7) and later brings God's message of judgment (and forgiveness) for David's adultery and murder (2 Samuel 12).

Yet Samuel's role is considerably more significant than any of these. From the report of his birth (1 Sam 1:20) to his early years (1 Sam 2:18–26 and chap. 3), we are put on notice that Samuel's life will be significant for the story that follows. Samuel is first called a prophet in 1 Sam 3:20 and his prophetic actions are prominent in significant blocks of narrative (1 Samuel 7–13, 15–16), focusing on the origin of the monarchy and the rise and fall of Saul, Israel's first king, with two brief reprises (in 1 Samuel 19, when he protects David from Saul, and in 1 Samuel 28, when Saul summons him for a postmortem consultation). His death is reported in 1 Sam 25:1 and 28:1.

Author's note: I am grateful to Roberts Wesleyan College for supporting the development of this essay with a 2006 Professional Activity Grant. Portions of this essay were presented at the meeting of the Canadian Society of Biblical Studies at York University in Toronto, in May 2006, and at two annual meetings of the Society of Biblical Literature: in Washington, DC, November 2006, and in Atlanta, November 2010.

The Interpretive Problem of Saul's Rejection

The issue for this essay is Samuel's role in the demise of Saul. The problem (which has long troubled interpreters of the book) is God's evident favoritism shown toward David, given God's earlier summary rejection of Saul. God's quite-different treatment of the first two kings of Israel seems patently unfair. While Saul is rejected from being king and refused forgiveness even when he confesses his sin (1 Samuel 15), David receives an unconditional covenant from God (2 Samuel 7) and his sin is immediately forgiven when he confesses (2 Samuel 12). Further, while the ostensible reason given for Saul's rejection in 1 Samuel 15 is his failure to eradicate the Amalekites in holy war (because he spares the Amalekite king and takes spoil), David twice attacks the Amalekites without eradicating them (while taking spoil) and is never condemned for this (1 Samuel 27 and 30).

There are two standard approaches to interpreting the differing treatment that Saul and David receive in the narrative of Samuel. One common explanation appeals to David's superior fit for kingship, given Saul's ineptitude or outright sin. This explanation assumes that God (and the narrative of Samuel) judges Saul unfit for kingship by his actions, while celebrating David's rise to the throne with a positive evaluation of his character and accomplishments. The second approach appeals to God's sovereign election of David as the decisive factor in the rejection of Saul. This reading assumes that God discards Saul in order to orchestrate providentially David's rise to power.

Both approaches, the moralistic and the providential, are problematic. The idea that Saul merits rejection by his own actions is difficult to support from a close reading of the narrative. Not only does the text fail to provide any clear, compelling basis for his rejection (as we shall see), but the later portrayal of David is far from unambiguously positive. Indeed, one version of the providential approach acknowledges these difficulties and therefore understands the text of Samuel as basically a deuteronomic *apologia* for David, which requires the narrative to get Saul out of the way as soon as possible (even on trumped-up charges, if necessary). If the first approach is simply naive in its reading of the text, the trouble with the second approach is that it makes God morally abhorrent, or at least hopelessly inconsistent and arbitrary. Indeed, one Old Testament scholar calls the God revealed in 1 and 2 Samuel "a capricious story-world character" who undermines "all piety, all theodicy, all doctrine."[1]

---

1. K. N. Noll, "Review of T. W. Cartledge, *1 and 2 Samuel* (Smyth & Helwys Bible Commentary; Macon, GA: Smyth & Helwys, 2001) and A. F. Campbell, *1 Sam-*

Beyond these problems, both approaches (the moralistic and the providential) are seriously deficient in failing to factor in the complex characterization of the prophet Samuel throughout chaps. 8–15.[2] It is my thesis that attention to the nuanced portrayal of Samuel as a conflicted character vis-à-vis God, the monarchy, and Saul personally might make better sense of the complexities of the text, and might even (dare I say it) make sense theologically. This essay thus questions one fundamental assumption in many traditional readings of the rejection of Saul, namely, that Samuel adequately represents God's intent. It will be my task to show not just that Samuel misrepresents God but where this misrepresentation is rooted.[3]

Samuel's Character Zone (Prior to Saul's Rejection in Chapter 15)

Let us begin with what we know of Samuel prior to 1 Samuel 15, especially in relation to Saul and to the kingship, generally.

The Similarity of the Names Samuel and Saul (1 Samuel 1)

First of all, there is the strange similarity of the names Samuel (שְׁמוּאֵל) and Saul (שָׁאוּל)—separated by only one consonant in Hebrew. Samuel's mother, Hannah, gives the derivation of his name (in 1:20) as the verb שאל ('to ask'), explaining that she had asked him of YHWH. But it is actually Saul's name that is more clearly and obviously derived from this verbal root. Indeed, Saul (שָׁאוּל) is the Qal passive participle of שאל (and means

---

uel (FOTL 7; Grand Rapids: Eerdmans, 2003)," in *Interpretation* 58 (2004) 404.

2. A growing number of scholarly works that address Saul's downfall are suspicious of the character of Samuel, attributing to him a significant role in Saul's rejection. Three of the most recent (with important resonances to my own approach) are T. Czövek, *Three Seasons of Charismatic Leadership: A Literary-Critical and Theological Interpretation of the Narrative of Saul, David and Solomon* (Regnum Studies in Mission; Milton Keynes: Paternoster, 2006), esp. pp. 41–100; K. Bodner, *1 Samuel: A Narrative Commentary* (Hebrew Bible Monographs 19; Sheffield: Sheffield Phoenix, 2008); and M. J. Steussy, *Samuel and His God* (Studies on Personalities of the Old Testament; Columbia: University of South Carolina Press, 2010). Special thanks to Bodner for many stimulating conversations about Samuel, Saul, and David over the years, and to Steussy for allowing me prepublication access to her manuscript.

3. Although my critical reading of the prophet Samuel is similar at many points to that of many interpreters (including Czövek, Bodner, and Steussy), I distinguish more sharply than most between the point of view of YHWH and that of Samuel. My suspicious reading of Samuel is not limited to the narrative prior to chap. 15 but spills over even into chap. 15. I thus read YHWH and Samuel as consistently at odds right until the end. A fuller exposition of my interpretation of the role of Samuel in the rejection of Saul will be provided in my forthcoming commentary: *1 and 2 Samuel* (Abingdon Old Testament Commentaries; Nashville: Abingdon, forthcoming).

either 'asked' or 'lent', depending on the context). Thus, it is supremely ironic that Hannah (in 1:28) says that as long as Samuel lives he is lent (שָׁאוּל) to YHWH (that is, he is *Saul* to YHWH). The very similarity of their names, then, may put us on notice of a certain rivalry of identification between Samuel and Saul. And, indeed, it turns out they are rivals for the leadership of Israel, as the later narrative shows.

Samuel's Initial Resistance to the Monarchy (1 Samuel 8)

Their rivalry, however, predates Saul's appearance on the scene; it lodges initially not in a person, but in the very idea of the monarchy. When the people ask (שׁאל) for a king in chap. 8, Samuel objects in no uncertain terms. Even after God concedes to the people's request, Samuel is unconvinced. We may surmise that Samuel's objection is both theological and personal. Theologically, he interprets the request for a king (as does one important strand of biblical faith) as a rejection of YHWH's rule over Israel. But that he objects even after YHWH decides to allow the monarchy suggests that Samuel has other motivations. He seems to realize that his unique and privileged position of leadership in Israel will now be threatened.

The depth of Samuel's resistance to the monarchy is evident if we attend to the structure of chap. 8. Twice in this chapter, we find a cycle of speeches in which the elders of the people make their request for a king to Samuel, which he reports to God, who then gives him instructions, followed by Samuel's return to the elders to relay what God has said. The two cases of slippage between God's instructions and Samuel's response are telling.

In the first cycle (8:4–18), God's response to the people's request is prefaced by his comment to Samuel not to take it personally (it is God, not Samuel, whom the people are rejecting). Then God instructs Samuel to listen to (that is, heed or obey) the people's voice, while also warning them about the dangers of the monarchy (8:7–9). Listening to the people's voice "in all that they say to you" (8:7) implies giving them a king.[4] While Samuel warns them in a rather lengthy speech about the dangers of the monarchy (8:10–18), he does *not* appoint a king for them.

This leads to the elders' second request for a king, and the cycle starts over (8:19–22). God again tells Samuel to listen to or heed/obey the people's voice (8:21), and this time God adds the explicit instruction "and appoint them a king" (8:22a), just in case he did not get it the first time.

---

4. Thus, the NAB appropriately translates the phrase (in 8:7, 9, and 21) as 'grant their request', while the NJPSV renders it 'heed their demand'.

But Samuel's only response is an almost brusque dismissal of the people (8:22b). He is simply not ready to appoint a king. Indeed, Samuel's disobedience to the voice of God is so glaring that the New Living Translation is embarrassed by it and therefore inserts that Samuel "agreed" before he sent the people home. But he pointedly does not.

Samuel's Delay in Installing Saul as King (1 Samuel 9–11)

Samuel only anoints a king for Israel at the end of chap. 9 after God's explicit instructions to anoint Saul. Even then, Samuel drags out the installation of Saul as king into three stages, each of which contains elements that suggest Samuel's prejudicial attitude toward kingship. First, there is a secret anointing, with no witnesses (9:26–10:1), followed by the public casting of lots at Mizpah (10:17–27), to discover who the new king will be (as if Saul had not already been anointed). Beyond the fact of the delay, the casting of lots is how Achan was found to be the one guilty of breaking holy war regulations in Josh 7:16–18. So the use of this technique for choosing Israel's king looks like a public relations stunt to prejudice the people against Saul at the outset. It even suggests that Samuel has *already* judged Saul guilty of the disobedience of chap. 15.

Finally, we have the formal confirmation or renewal of the kingship at Gilgal at the end of the following chapter (11:14–15). That Samuel waits until after Saul's victory in defending Jabesh-Gilead against the Ammonites suggests that he could not simply trust Yhwh's choice of Saul, but had to gain confirmation for himself that the bumbling farmer-king was up to the task of legitimate rule.

While this three-stage installation of Saul may be taken as an indication of multiple sources, each of which conceived Saul's coming to kingship differently, I am interested in the narrator's framing of Saul's installation as king (whatever the underlying sources) as a long, drawn-out process, which certainly suggests Samuel's reticence in having Saul come to the throne.

Samuel's Convoluted and Contradictory Instructions to Saul
(1 Samuel 10)

A key component of Samuel's resistance to passing on the leadership of Israel to Saul is a series of seemingly arbitrary, covert instructions he gives Saul at the secret anointing, which seem intended to keep Saul under his thumb. The instructions (the first three of which are called "signs") may be summarized as follows.

First, Saul will find two men at Rachel's tomb in the region of Benjamin who will convey certain information to him from his father (10:2). Then he will meet three men going to Bethel who are carrying specific items (three kids, three loaves, and a jug of wine); these men will greet him and give him two of the loaves (10:3–4). Then he will come to another location where there is a Philistine prefect and he will there encounter a band of prophets coming from the high place, accompanied by people playing four different types of musical instruments (which are listed). These prophets will be prophesying in an ecstatic state and Saul will be grasped by the spirit of YHWH (and become another man) and will prophesy with them (10:5–7).

If these signs were conveyed to Saul in an unadorned manner, we could well believe that God had given them (through Samuel) as a way to confirm that Saul's momentous transformation from humble farmer to king of Israel had really occurred by divine consent. But the manner of their delivery, full of obfuscation, with a plethora of irrelevant details, suggests a different function. These three sets of signs are actually quite difficult to remember (I've found that my students cannot accurately reproduce all their details even after they have just read them or heard them read aloud). Even granted the superior memory of those in an ancient oral culture, I wonder what the effect of these convoluted instructions would have been on the newly anointed Saul (who may already be wondering why the anointing was done in secret—is he or is he not king?).

But Samuel's final instruction is much simpler. After the third sign is fulfilled, Saul is to do whatever his hand finds to do, for God is with him (10:7). By itself, this instruction suggests that Saul is being confirmed and encouraged in his newfound authority as ruler of Israel. Yet the kicker is what Samuel then adds. Saul is to go to Gilgal and wait there for seven days until Samuel arrives to tell him what to do (10:8). These mixed messages (*do what your hand finds to do* for God is with you; but wait for me seven days and *I will tell you what to do*) suggests that Samuel is manipulating the situation to keep Saul off balance. Having had actually to anoint Saul (against his better judgment), Samuel now wants to keep the new king dependent on himself as the privileged mediator of YHWH's will. Worse, he seems determined to jerk Saul around and so psychologically sabotage his leadership potential.

While Samuel may be setting Saul up for failure, this may not be a purposeful goal on Samuel's part but rather the unreflective expression of his resentment of God's decision to give the people a king and his resentment of Saul, who is, after all, the first concrete embodiment of the monarchy.

Samuel's Speech at Gilgal—Good Theology, Bad Motives? (1 Samuel 12)

Also important is Samuel's speech to the people in chap. 12, which is placed in the context of the confirmation of Saul's kingship at Gilgal. The speech reads like good deuteronomic theology, articulating a conditional covenant between God, on the one side, and the king and the people, on the other, warning them to follow Yhwh or be destroyed (12:14–15, 24–25). Yet this traditional theology is shot through with Samuel's self-serving motives.

What is especially disturbing about Samuel's speech in chapter 12 is that it is given under the pretext of celebrating the confirmation of Saul's kingship on the heels of his victory at Jabesh-Gilead. Yet the speech actually serves to undermine the fledgling monarchy. Having just installed the new king, Samuel makes a last ditch attempt to assert his own position as indispensable and to affirm the evil of the monarchy.

Samuel stresses at the outset that his own leadership has been impeccable (12:3), a claim he gets the people to affirm (12:4–5), thereby implying they did not need a king at all. He even adds his own name to the list of judges beginning with Gideon (12:11), which seems so self-serving that the Syriac Peshitta replaces *Samuel* with *Samson*. Later in the speech, Samuel portrays himself as the people's indispensable intercessor with Yhwh (promising, through an oath, never to cease praying for them) and also as their necessary teacher of the Torah (12:23). In all this, he emphasizes the "evil" of their request for a king (12:17), which he gets them to acknowledge for themselves (12:19), interspersed with a public demonstration of his authoritative standing with God by requesting (and receiving) a visible miracle (12:17–18). The tactic works. The people feared Yhwh, the text says, "and they feared Samuel as well" (12:18). I wonder about the psychological impact of a speech of this sort on Saul, right after the public confirmation of his kingship.

Samuel's Condemnation of Saul for Not Waiting (1 Samuel 13)

This brings us to chap. 13, which begins with the Philistines gathering a massive number of troops to attack Saul and the Israelite army at Michmash. The result is that nearly three-quarters of Saul's troops have deserted due to fear. Having retreated to Gilgal and waited for Samuel for seven days (which seems to allude to Samuel's instruction in 10:8), Saul decides to offer sacrifices to Yhwh (a burnt offering and a communion offering), possibly to win God's favor in the upcoming battle or to encourage the remaining troops by a show of piety. Although we are not explicitly told Saul's motivation, he is clearly doing what his own hand finds to do, in fulfillment of Samuel's prior word to him in 10:8.

But Samuel appears at the very moment Saul completes the first offering and reprimands him for being "foolish" in not keeping the commandment that Yhwh gave him (13:13), though what commandment this might be is unclear from the narrative. Could Samuel be referring back to his own instructions in 10:8 for Saul to wait for him at Gilgal for seven days?[5] There are three problems with this interpretation, none of which rule it out. Indeed, if this interpretation is accurate despite the interpretive difficulties, this just confirms the superbly manipulative role of Samuel.

First of all, chap. 13 opens in the MT by mentioning that *at least* two years have passed since Saul has become king. Verse 1 (missing from the main LXX manuscripts) says that Saul was [word missing] years old when he began to reign and that he reigned for [word missing] *and two years*. Since the Hebrew implies there is a multiple of 10 missing before *and two*, this incident might be placed 12 (or even 22 or 32) years after Samuel's instructions. Are we to believe that this injunction from chap. 10 is still relevant? Why was it not considered fulfilled when Saul went to Gilgal to be installed as king in chap. 11?

But the second problem with this interpretation is that in chap. 13 Saul *does* in fact wait seven days for Samuel, though evidently not till the *very end* of the seventh day, by Samuel's reckoning. Note, however, that from the narrator's point of view not only did Saul wait "the time appointed by Samuel," but "Samuel did *not* come" (13:8). So, if the command in question was the one given in chap. 10 to wait seven days, then not only is Samuel at fault, but he is a master manipulator, who has kept Saul tied up in knots years later, still waiting.

The third problem with this interpretation is that the idea of waiting seven days was certainly no commandment of Yhwh, but *Samuel's* own rather arbitrary instruction to Saul (even the narrator attributes this instruction to Samuel, not God, in 13:8). The emphatic way, therefore, that Samuel frames Saul's purported disobedience is all the more striking: "You have not kept the commandment of Yhwh your God, which he commanded you" (13:13). Does stating it twice make it more authoritative?

Perhaps, then, Saul's sin was that he engaged in priestly functions (offering a sacrifice), in a period when royal and priestly duties were to be kept separate. King Uzziah of Judah, after all, was struck with leprosy when he dared to enter the temple to burn incense at the altar (2 Chr 26:16–21). But not only is the Uzziah incident from a much later era, but we would have to reckon with David's own explicitly priestly actions in 2 Samuel 6, including his liturgical dance in the presence of the ark, fol-

---

5. B. T. Arnold accepts that on the surface Saul's offense is not waiting for Samuel, but he claims that Saul's underlying problem is disobedience to Samuel (and thus to Yhwh). See Arnold, *1 and 2 Samuel* (NIV Application Commentary; Grand Rapids: Zondervan, 2003) 200–201.

lowed by his multiple offering of sacrifices and his blessing of the people. But David receives no reprimand for any of this. Could it be, then, as some commentators suggest, that the issue is that Saul is too superstitious or supercilious about cultic matters? But this is grasping at straws.[6]

The crucial point is that in 1 Samuel 13, Samuel accuses Saul of disobeying not him *but* YHWH, which is, on the face of it, incomprehensible. Now, I have no desire to defend Saul as a paradigm of virtue in the narrative. Although he is sometimes decisive and vigorous in action (such as when he rescues Jabesh-Gilead from Nahash and the Ammonites in chap. 11), he is often portrayed as inept, ignorant or lacking in discernment. Take, for example, the opening scene of chap. 9 about the lost donkeys, or when Saul hides among the baggage at Mizpah in chap. 10, or when his rash oath in chap. 14 precipitates the troops to break food laws and almost costs Jonathan his life.[7] Then later, in chap. 15, he seems to be less than honest in his conversations with Samuel.[8] However, I can find no rational explanation for Saul's supposed disobedience in chap. 13, beyond Samuel's resentment (which has been building for at least two years, if we follow the time-frame of 13:1). As Walter Brueggemann notes: "Samuel cites no commandment that has been broken, nor can we construe one. The commandment that seems to have been broken is, 'Thou shalt not violate Samuel's authority.'"[9]

Indeed, Samuel goes on to say that because of this (unspecified) act of disobedience, Saul's kingdom will not stand. Instead, YHWH has *already* sought for himself a man after his own heart, says Samuel, and has appointed him as ruler over Israel (13:14). While commentators often as-

---

6. V. Philips Long cogently argues that Saul's infraction at Gilgal in chap. 13 is not cultic. See Long, *The Reign and Rejection of King Saul: A Case for Literary and Theological Coherence* (SBLDS 118; Atlanta: Scholars Press, 1989), chap. 2. However, Long's construal of the infraction as disobedience or insubordination to YHWH through the divinely authorized prophet is valid only if we understand this as *Samuel's* twisted point of view and neither that of the narrator nor of God.

7. Saul's rash oath may, however, be attributed to the fallout of Samuel's condemnation in chap. 13; it could be overcompensation for a sense of guilt in not living up to Samuel's standards. Czövek likewise suggests that "the purpose of 1 Samuel 14 is to portray a king handicapped due to the incident in chap. 13" (*Three Seasons of Charismatic Leadership*, 38).

8. Saul (like Samuel) is a complex, multidimensional character, whose "character zone" is dynamic and changes over time. He moves from bumbling farmer to confident king/military deliver and then to an increasingly constricted/conflicted person, gradually deconstructing under Samuel's manipulation.

9. W. Brueggemann, *First and Second Samuel* (IBC; Louisville: Westmister John Knox, 1990) 100.

sume that this is prophetic foreshadowing of David (three chapters early), I read Samuel's words of condemnation, including the claim to know God's mind on the matter of a replacement for Saul, quite differently. Given what we have seen of his conflicted character and motives so far, I take this as a bit of extemporaneous bluster on Samuel's part.

The relevant question, in my opinion, is not what Saul did wrong (here the text simply does not help us), but what effect Samuel's forceful condemnation has on Saul's psyche. Indeed, it is possible that God chose Saul (9:15–17) precisely because he wanted a humble farmer as Israel's first king, someone who had no aspirations to power and could therefore be expected to rule without the sort of oppression Samuel warned the people of in chap. 8. But this sort of farmer king would require significant mentoring to achieve the leadership qualities and administrative competence (not to mention knowledge of Yhwh) required for the job, something he does *not* get from Samuel. Thus, I have to wonder whether Samuel's use of his prophetic office to manipulate Saul does not push Saul (who is initially a rather inept figure, without much self-confidence) farther over the edge, into the sort of emotional instability that begins to surface after David comes on the scene.

The Role of Samuel in God's Rejection of Saul (1 Samuel 15)

We now come to 1 Samuel 15, perhaps the most complex chapter in the book. Instead of carefully working though the chapter, highlighting the many ambiguities and tensions, space constraints require me to proceed differently. Here I simply advance a series of intertwined interpretive claims or theses that together constitute my hypothesis concerning the rejection of Saul and God's later (seeming) favoritism toward David. The final thesis will explore Samuel's fundamental failure in his prophetic function *vis-à-vis* Saul, by comparing him with Moses, the paradigmatic prophet.

Thesis 1. Samuel has maintained inappropriate control over Saul, instead of mentoring the fledgling king into becoming a leader in his own right.

Samuel's misuse of the authority of his prophetic office to maintain control over both Saul and the people, which has been sabotaging Saul's fledgling kingship, is evident also in chap. 15, which opens with Samuel emphasizing his own role in anointing Saul king. "It was *me*," he says (the personal pronoun is emphatic), "whom Yhwh sent to anoint you king over Israel" (15:1). This assertion of prophetic priority and authority is striking, because Samuel had previously *resisted* anointing Saul as king.

Now he is emphatically taking the credit. So Samuel's very first statement to Saul ought to raise questions about his motivations. Is he reminding Saul who is really in control here, so that Saul will not even *think* of questioning his instructions (in Yhwh's name) to execute holy war against the Amalekites (15:2–3)?

After the battle, when Samuel questions Saul about the sound of sheep and cattle that he hears (15:14), Saul explains that the people spared some of the best animals to sacrifice to Yhwh "your God" (15:15). This is the first of three references that Saul makes in this chapter to Yhwh as *Samuel's God* (also 15:21 and 30). This telling phraseology certainly indicts Saul for his sense of distance from the God of Israel (I have no interest in defending Saul here). But it also suggests that Samuel has been so successful in positioning himself as Yhwh's unique spokesman (in all his dealings with Saul) that Saul has been unable to develop any independent relationship with God. This language thus serves also as an *indictment of Samuel*, who has failed to mentor his replacement adequately.[10] This may also explain why later in the chapter Saul tells Samuel, "I have sinned, for I have transgressed against Yhwh's mouth *and against your words*" (15:24). This close linkage of God and Samuel throughout the chapter suggests that their authority is well-nigh interchangeable in Saul's consciousness.[11]

Thus, far from appropriate mentoring of his successor, Samuel's heavy-handed exercise of prophetic authority over Saul (since their first meeting, in chap. 9) constitutes an illegitimate attempt to maintain control over the fledgling monarchy, which has effectively sabotaged Saul's ability to rule. Indeed, the negative mentoring Saul receives from Samuel leads T. Czövek to conclude that charismatic leaders (such as Saul or David) cannot afford to have mentors at all if they are to be successful.[12]

Thesis 2. Samuel, not God, initiates the rejection of Saul.

Samuel's misuse of prophetic authority (which has been intensifying since chap. 9) culminates in chap. 15 with his instructions to Saul to eradicate the Amalekites. Samuel claims (15:2–3) that he has a word from Yhwh that directs Saul to punish the Amalekites for their ancient sin against

---

10. Note that this same terminology ("your God") was used by the people when addressing Samuel in 12:19.

11. To see just how indispensable Samuel becomes for Saul, we need only think of Saul's desperate attempt to get advice from the dead prophet, even from the grave (1 Samuel 28).

12. Czövek, *Three Seasons of Charismatic Leadership*, 99. On the importance of surrogate father/son relationships (equivalent to mentoring) in 1 Samuel, see D. Jobling, *1 Samuel* (Berit Olam; Collegeville, MN: Liturgical Press, 1998) 105–25.

Israel during the wilderness period (Exod 17:8–16; Deut 25:17–19). Saul and the people are instructed to destroy them totally (חרם). Contrary to what commentators sometimes claim, the חֶרֶם does not always involve the total and immediate destruction of all life (see Num 31:7–12, 17–18; Deut 2:34–35, 20:13–14, 21:10–14; Josh 8:28, 11:7, 9, 14). Yet in this case Saul is instructed quite specifically to "spare" none (1 Sam 15:3).

The central question for us is whether this reactivation of holy war against Israel's ancient enemy is really from God or derives from Samuel's initiative.[13] There is no record in the narrative of God actually giving this particular word to Samuel, so we are left to discern, from his prior actions, if Samuel is a trustworthy character.[14] Given his treatment of Saul leading up to the present chapter, I read Samuel's instructions to destroy Amalek as one more attempt to keep Saul under his thumb, subject to the prophetic will.[15]

One consideration in favor of this reading is that this is a strange assignment to give to Israel's first king, especially as the monarchy is beginning to take root; it looks designed to throw the king off track from the task of governance. If we follow the narrative time of the story, this assignment comes fully three centuries after the original Amalekite incident (assuming a 13th-century date for the exodus). Why reactivate this ancient feud centuries later? No one in Israel is portrayed as even attempting to fulfill this old statute from the wilderness period. If this was an important task for the new king, why is David not given any similar command? Indeed, he attacks the Amalekites (without attempting to eradicate them) on at least two occasions (1 Samuel 27 and 30), while taking spoil (with no rebuke from anyone, neither God nor prophet).

---

13. Many commentators simply accept, without dispute, that this is Y<small>HWH</small>'s command issued through Samuel; for example, P. K. McCarter Jr., *I Samuel: A New Translation with Introduction, Notes and Commentary* (AB 8; Garden City, NY: Doubleday, 1980) 269; R. W. Klein, *1 Samuel* (WBC 10; Waco, TX: Word, 1983) 146. B. C. Birch goes further, however, in his claim that any commentator who suggests that Samuel's instructions were illegitimate is reading contemporary concerns into the text; see B. C. Birch, "The First and Second Books of Samuel," in *The New Interpreter's Bible* (ed. Leander E. Keck et al.; 12 vols.; Nashville: Abingdon, 1998) 2:947–1383, esp. p. 1085.

14. L. Eslinger's suggestion that we should not automatically identify the narrator's point of view with that of the characters in chaps. 8–12 is applicable also to chap. 15; see Eslinger, "Viewpoints and Point of View in 1 Samuel 8–12," *JSOT* 26 (1983) 61–76.

15. M. Steussy, who is typically suspicious of Samuel's motives, accepts the divine origin of this command, because it is introduced with a standard prophetic formula (Steussy, *Samuel and His God*, 68). Note, however, that Hananiah also introduces his prophetic oracles with a similar formula (Jer 28:2, 10), but they are not from Y<small>HWH</small>.

Nevertheless, Saul dutifully musters the troops and attacks the Amalekites, although he does not completely follow Samuel's instructions. He and "the people" spare both Agag the Amalekite king and the best of the animals (15:4–9)—something he was explicitly told *not* to do.[16]

Thesis 3. Samuel thinks God was wrong to allow the monarchy in the first place.

We have already seen that, beyond a specific antimonarchial strain in ancient Israel (that Samuel may indeed share), we cannot discount his personal resentment toward Saul for his sense that his leadership position is threatened. But is it possible that, beyond both these motivations, Samuel's opposition to Saul's kingship is tied to a particular theological understanding of what is appropriate for God? Could it be that Samuel believes that God should not be influenced by human beings, specifically in the case of allowing the monarchy in the first place? Does he think that this sort of mutability is beneath the divine character?

The starting point for this possibility is the intratextual tension *within* chap. 15 concerning the use of the verb 'repent' (נחם in the Niphal stem). In 15:11, Yhwh tells Samuel (privately) that he has "repented" of making Saul king because Saul has turned away from him and has not fulfilled or established his words. That Yhwh has, indeed, "repented" of making Saul king is confirmed by the narrator at the end of the chapter (15:35). However, between these two statements, when Saul confesses his sin and pleads for forgiveness, Samuel tells him (15:29) that God is not a human being that he should "repent" (twice). Indeed, Samuel equates God's repentance with *deception*, thus indicating how reprehensible he finds the idea. The evident contradiction between these two statements about God's "repentance" in the chapter is unlikely to be unintentional in such an astute narrative.[17]

There are, however, at least three typical attempts to avoid interpreting this *prima facie* contradiction as a genuine disagreement between God and Samuel. One way is to take the force of the verb נחם in 15:11 and 35 (as the NLT and the NIV do, following a long tradition) to signify that

---

16. Although Samuel will castigate Saul for sparing the animals, he utters no word of objection to sparing the Amalekite king (the precedent might be the people bringing the king of Ai to Joshua for execution in Josh 8:29).

17. R. Polzin thinks the narrator clearly indicates that Samuel's denial of God's repentance is "off the mark"; see Polzin, *Samuel and the Deuteronomist: A Literary Study of the Deuteronomistic History*, part 2: *1 Samuel* (Bloomington, IN: Indiana University Press, 1989) 142.

God is *sorry* or *grieved* over Saul's kingship, without implying that God has actually changed his mind about Saul.[18] Part of the motivation for this translation (which is linguistically possible) might be a theological attempt to deny that God changes. The trouble is that this solution would require differing translations of נחם in 15:1 and 29, which is unlikely, without further argument.

Furthermore, even if we admit differing translations in 15:11 and 29, so that 15:11 does not imply that God has actually rejected Saul, this would not solve much. It would still put Samuel at odds with God, because God (on this reading) has not explicitly rejected Saul, but Samuel claims unambiguously (twice) that God *has* rejected Saul, using a different (more unambiguous) verb (15:23 and 26). And by the end of the chapter, when the narrator affirms that "Y{\sc hwh} had repented of making Saul king over Israel" (15:35), the meaning is clear—that Saul's kingship is rejected.[19] God has indeed changed his mind. Thus, I am inclined to think that God's original statement of "repentance" in 15:11 actually implies the rejection of Saul's kingship.[20]

A second tack taken by interpreters to avoid a contradiction between Samuel and God is to limit the meaning of Samuel's denial of God's repentance to a claim that God will not change his mind *about rejecting Saul*. That is, having once changed his mind and rejected Saul, God will not go back on that decision.[21] Yet God's rejection of Saul would have been precisely a 'change of mind' on God's part. So we are left with the paradox that God will not change his mind *about changing his mind*! But, *why* not? Why one change and not another?

A final approach that tries to avoid a contradiction between Samuel and God is to take God's lack of repentance in 15:29 as pointing ahead

---

18. Klein also softens the contradiction by translating נחם in 15:11 and 35 as 'am sorry' or 'felt sorry' and in 15:29 as 'change his mind'/'changes his mind' (*1 Samuel*, 144–45).

19. McCarter finds the contradiction between Samuel's words and God's words to be so "blatant" that he suggests v. 29 may be a late addition to the text of chap. 15, possibly derived by Num 23:19, meant to contradict the idea that God does in fact repent (*I Samuel*, 268). Long also feels the force of this "intervening, prima facie contradictory statement" (*The Reign and Rejection of King Saul*, 141).

20. The basis for God's repentance is that Saul has not established/fulfilled God's words, though what particular words these may be is maddeningly unspecified (especially because God's words about repentance in 15:11 are the only words the narrator has God speak in the entire chapter). A surface reading, however, would suggest these words constitute the instruction given by Samuel to eradicate the Amalekites. In the end, the narrative judges Saul to be disobedient to what *he took* to be Y{\sc hwh}'s word.

21. This is McCarter's position (*I Samuel*, 268).

to the election of David (1 Samuel 16), perhaps even to God's unconditional promise to his line (2 Samuel 7).[22] This seems initially plausible because 15:29 directly follows Samuel's statement that God has (already) torn the kingdom from Saul and will give it to someone else who is better than he (15:28)—a covert reference perhaps to David? This approach makes a connection between 1 Sam 15:29 and God's lack of repentance in Balaam's oracle to Balaak in Num 23:19, where repentance is also identified as a human quality and linked to deception.[23] There we are told that God will not repent (נחם) of his commitment to bless Israel (Num 23:20; 24:1). In both cases, then, God refuses to repent of his promise *to bless his chosen* (people or king, as the case may be). Confirmation for this reading is often sought in Pss 110:4 and 132:11, both of which refer to Yhwh's oath to David of which he will not "repent" (whereas the former text uses נחם, the latter uses שוב). So perhaps what God will not change his mind about in 1 Samuel 15 is the election of David.

This interpretation assumes that the deuteronomic author/editor already knows that God is committed to David's line and has Samuel assert that *this* decision is irrevocable. The trouble is that this still does not explain what the basis of Saul's rejection is *from Samuel's point of view*. It is an appeal to the world *behind* the text; but this historical reconstruction does not address with any integrity the text's own narrative world. The question remains: *Why* has God rejected Saul in the first place and become irrevocably committed to David?

At a narrative level, it is highly implausible that Samuel has David in mind when he utters his pronouncements of 1 Sam 15:28 and 29, since David does not appear on the scene until the following chapter, and even then Samuel has a difficult time recognizing him as God's choice. Not only does the Samuel of the narrative have no prior knowledge of David, but the very circumstances that generate Samuel's denial of God's repentance suggest this is an unplanned comment on his part, uttered on the spur of the moment out of indignation and resentment.

---

22. This is the approach of R. W. L. Moberly, "'God Is Not a Human That He Should Repent' (Numbers 23:19 and 1 Samuel 15:29)," in *God in the Fray: A Tribute to Walter Brueggemann* (ed. T. Linafelt and T. K. Beal; Minneapolis: Fortress, 1998) 112–23; and T. E. Fretheim, "Divine Foreknowledge, Divine Constancy, and the Rejection of Saul's Kingship," *CBQ* 47 (1985) 595–602.

23. Although a different word is used for *deception*, Balaam's oracle in Num 23:19 is the closest statement in the Hebrew Bible to 1 Sam 15:29. Balaam's later oracles even proclaim Israel's victory over Agag and Amalek (Num 24:7, 20), thus suggesting some sort of connection to the narrative of 1 Samuel 15.

When Samuel tells Saul that God has rejected him, Saul confesses his sin and pleads unsuccessfully for Samuel's forgiveness (15:23–26). When Samuel turns to leave, Saul grasps Samuel's robe, which tears (15:27). Seizing the moment, Samuel turns this into a symbolic prophetic act, telling Saul that Yhwh has torn the kingdom of Israel from him "today" and will give it to his fellow man who is better than he (15:28).[24] Given that Samuel bases his oracle on an unplanned occurrence (his robe tearing), this is clearly extemporizing on Samuel's part. He is making this up as he goes along.

The extemporizing feel continues as Samuel adds, "and moreover" (וְגַם). We can imagine the prophet wagging his finger at Saul, sputtering with righteous indignation, as he utters what amounts to a run-on sentence in Hebrew: "And what's more . . . the Unchanging One of Israel does not deceive . . . and he does not repent . . . for he is not a human being . . . that he should repent" (15:29). So, there!

It is further intriguing that Samuel's statement of God's lack of repentance in 15:29 is linked to an unusual designation for God (נֵצַח), used as a title or name of God nowhere else in the Bible, and usually translated here as *the Glory* or *the Eternal One* of Israel.[25] It is possible that this title encapsulates Samuel's distinctive theological perspective. Given that the semantic range of נֵצַח (in its nominal, adjectival, and adverbial uses) typically includes *forever, perpetual, unceasing, enduring*,[26] this suggests that Samuel is emphasizing God's temporal transcendence of the human condition. And when linked to the statement that God does not repent, it

---

24. Is there an intended tension between Samuel's statement that God has torn the kingdom from Saul *today* and the fact that it was *the previous night* that God said he "repented" of making Saul king?

25. Whereas the NRSV, NIV, NAB, NLT, NASB, NJPSV render the phrase as 'the Glory of Israel', the New Century Version and Holman Christian Standard Bible have 'the Eternal One of Israel' (compare McCarter, *I Samuel*, 260, who has 'Israel's Everlasting One'). Other variants are 'the Strength of Israel' (KJV) and 'the Faithful One of Israel' (Klein, *1 Samuel*, 145). Although not functioning precisely as a divine title in 1 Chr 29:11, נֵצַח is one of a series of five epithets used there to ascribe glory to God and is often translated in that context as 'victory', presumably because the LXX renders it as *nikē*. The LXX can make no sense, however, of נֵצַח יִשְׂרָאֵל in 1 Sam 15:29 and so has an entirely different phrase at this point ('and Israel shall be divided in two').

26. Verbal uses are a bit different. In the Niphal (which is rare), it also means 'enduring'; but it is more typically used in the Piel (as a participle or infinitive construct), meaning 'to direct' or 'supervise' (esp. in regard to the temple). If applied to God, this might suggest that, along with transcending temporality, God is at the same time sovereign (an ancient precursor to the later doctrine of divine impassibility?).

may well designate God's immutability or unchanging nature.[27] The issue for Samuel thus seems to be a contrast between *God's* character, which is transcendent and unchanging, and *human* mutability.[28]

It seems, therefore, that one of the factors at play in Samuel's opposition to Saul's kingship is a distinctive understanding of what is appropriate for the divine nature. Samuel believes that the God of Israel should not be influenced by human beings.[29] If this reading is correct, it implies that Samuel thinks he knows better than God what God should do. This generates Samuel's resentment toward God for not living up to *his* (Samuel's) expectations, initially in being influenced by the people's request for a king (in chap. 8), but then here (in chap. 15) for changing his mind about Saul's kingship.

Thesis 4. Samuel is himself internally conflicted over the rejection of Saul.

Samuel is in conflict with Saul and he is in conflict with God over allowing the monarchy (and over whether God should/could repent). But beyond this, Samuel seems to be *internally conflicted* over the rejection of Saul. Various dimensions of Samuel's conflicted psyche are manifest in chap. 15.

First of all, we have Samuel's unexplained anger in 15:11. Immediately following God's statement that he has repented of making Saul king, Samuel is angry and cries out to Yhwh all night (15:11). However, we do not know for sure *who* Samuel was angry at, whether God or Saul. Nor do we know *why* he was angry; but we may surmise that he was angry both *at Saul* for his failure as king (specifically for his failure to submit to the divinely authorized prophet) and *at God* for rejecting Saul.[30] Samuel's

---

27. Thus, Bodner's rendering of נֵצַח יִשְׂרָאֵל as 'the Unchanging One of Israel' is an excellent suggestion (*1 Samuel*, 161).

28. Moberly claims that it is unlikely than anyone in the Bible (except perhaps Qoheleth) would deny the possibility of divine repentance as a theological principle, because it is the normative view in Israel's Scripture. He nevertheless admits that this does not rule out the possibility of "particular people at particular times or places disagreeing with the consensus construal" and that this disagreement may "have been preserved within Israel's Scripture despite its departure from the norm" (Moberly, "God Is Not a Human Being That He Should Repent," 115). I believe that here we have precisely this sort of case with the prophet Samuel.

29. Does Samuel read his own inflexibility into the character of God? Most people in leadership positions, if they are religious, tend to see a certain continuity between their own self-image and their understanding of the divine (this may be quite explicit or it may be implicit and unconscious).

30. Some commentators also suggest that Samuel's anger is due to his perceived loss of face with the people, now that the king he had installed (even against his will)

anger at God would stem from his realization that God has once again condescended to act at a human level. In other words, Samuel is upset with Yhwh that he changed his mind in response to Saul's failure, since this compromised Samuel's ideal sense of divine autonomy.

Evidence for Samuel's anger at God may be found in the slippage in Samuel's report to Saul in 15:16–19 of what God had told him the previous night. Samuel actually interrupts Saul so he can report Yhwh's words (15:16). Yet when Samuel speaks (15:17), he pointedly does *not* report what Yhwh actually said (15:10–11). He specifically *omits* telling Saul that God has "repented" of making him king. Instead he castigates Saul for thinking too little of himself, an outburst that makes little sense in the context, but which would have the effect of putting Saul on the defensive.[31] Then, after Saul attempts (unsuccessfully) to defend himself (15:20–21), Samuel utters an oracle in elevated poetic speech, meant to indict Saul for disobedience, even idolatry (15:22–23).[32] It is in this oracle that Samuel first states that God has rejected Saul (in response to Saul's supposed rejection of God).[33]

But the paradox is that Samuel does not seem to grasp the full implications of his own statements. While Samuel avoids stating that God has repented of making Saul king (and will twice *deny* that God repents, in

---

is rejected. Of course, none of these options necessarily rules out the others, given the complex nature of the human psyche.

31. It particularly makes no sense of the fact that someone had just reported to Samuel that Saul was erecting a monument to himself (15:12), which might indicate just the opposite (hubris). Commentators sometimes suggest that Samuel is referring to Saul's self-deprecation at his anointing (9:21); but these words are part of the stereotypically expected response of the call narrative *Gattung* (compare Moses and Jeremiah; Exodus 3 and Jeremiah 1). Indeed, similar self-deprecating words are uttered by David (2 Sam 7:18) and Solomon (1 Kgs 3:7–8) at the cusp of their power. Unlike them, however, Saul actually sounds surprised and sincere in wondering why God chose him.

32. Notice that Samuel harps on idolatry in various speeches he makes to Saul and the people. While his plea in chap. 7 for the people to put away their false gods (7:3) is actually fulfilled (7:4), this is the last time the narrative mentions idolatry as an issue for the people; and Yhwh only mentions idolatry as past disobedience (8:8). Yet, in Samuel's speech of chap. 12, he cites the idolatry of the Judges period (12:10) and exhorts the people to put away their current idols (12:21). And in chap. 15 he identifies disobedience with "teraphim" (a synechdode for idolatry). This might suggest that Samuel is living in the past, and that his typical concerns diverge from that of the narrator. Thanks to my student Mike Micklow for pointing out this intriguing pattern.

33. Notice that the people's rejection of God in 1 Sam 8:7 (also mentioned in 10:9) does not automatically generate God's rejection of them. The question for this essay is why *Saul's* (supposed) rejection of God generates God's rejection of Saul (according to Samuel in 15:23).

15:29), he nevertheless states unequivocally that God has rejected Saul (15:23, repeated in 15:26). But what can it mean that God has rejected Saul, yet he does not repent or change his mind? Does Samuel not understand that either statement (rejection or repentance) implies that God's decisions are influenced by human action (it is, after all, Saul's disobedience that has triggered this change in God)? Or is *rejection* a more abstract term that does not demean God in Samuel's eyes, whereas *repentance* reduces Yhwh to a human level? Could Samuel's theological disagreement with God (if we may ironically call it that) be at cross-purposes with his prophetic judgment against Saul, in a manner of which he is not even aware?

Finally, Samuel's conflicted psyche results not just in his contradictory statements about God's rejection of Saul and his anger in 15:11 (whether at God or Saul or both), but also in his grief or mourning (15:34) over Saul's rejection (despite the fact that he has, in effect, engineered this rejection). I say "in effect" because whatever indictments this essay brings against Samuel for contributing to the demise of Saul, I do not read him as a cold-blooded, calculating sociopath. Rather, Samuel is no different from many people in the real world, who operate out of unexamined and often conflicting beliefs and commitments, with destructive effects on the lives of those around them.

Thesis 5. God has chosen to be constrained by the choice of Samuel as the authoritative representative of God's will.

I have argued that God did not initiate a decision to find someone to replace Saul (chap. 13); the reference to someone after God's heart was an extemporaneous utterance by the prophet, made in anger. Nor did God give a command through Samuel for Saul to destroy the Amalekites (chap. 15); that was Samuel's own invention. However, God clearly ends up backing Samuel on both counts. So the question is: *Why?* Why would God support Samuel's self-serving moves to have Saul rejected, or, to be more precise, Samuel's self-serving moves to keep Saul under his control, which *resulted* in Saul's failure and rejection.

The key text for understanding this matter is 1 Sam 3:19–20, which states (right after the call of Samuel) that Yhwh did not allow any of his words to "fall to the ground," with the result that Samuel was known as a 'faithful' or 'trustworthy' (נֶאֱמָן) prophet throughout all Israel. The very ambiguity of "his words" in 3:19 (Samuel's words? God's words?) reinforces the point. As a prophet, Samuel's words *are* God's words. God is henceforth committed to supporting the prophetic word uttered by

Samuel. Thus, God can legitimately say in 1 Sam 15:11 that Saul has not established *my* words (even though God did not initiate the command about the Amalekite war).

What this means is that God's rejection of Saul ultimately results from God's decision to be constrained by his commitments to human beings, in this case, to Samuel as his authoritative prophet. God committed himself to supporting Samuel's words and he will abide by that commitment.

This view of how God operates helps us understand a major interpretive conundrum between 1 Samuel 2 and 3. Commentators are generally stumped by the fact that whereas chap. 2 expects Samuel to become a priest, he becomes a prophet instead in chap. 3. Samuel's mother dedicates him to God as a priestly replacement for Eli's corrupt sons, then he is apprenticed to Eli at the Shiloh temple, and is portrayed as engaging in priestly duties (clad in a priestly ephod). Yet by the end of chap. 3 Samuel has filled not a priestly, but a *prophetic* office. This shift is precisely an instance of God adapting—here (with foresight)—to the upcoming monarchy. Well aware that kings tend to abuse their power, God changes his plans to have a renewed priesthood (in 2:35 God had promised that he would raise up a 'faithful' or 'trustworthy' [נֶאֱמָן] priest). Instead, God anticipates the people's request for a king and prepares in advance to have an authoritative prophet to balance the power of the king, because that is the more pressing historical need. The trouble is that the prophet misuses his authority and significantly overbalances the king.

But note that the principle at work in God's commitment to support Samuel as an authoritative prophet is the very principle that Samuel cannot accept, namely that God is influenced and affected by human beings. Paradoxically, the fact that God has chosen to support Samuel's word (even when that word does not reflect God's intent) itself contradicts Samuel's idea that God should not be influenced by humans.

Thesis 6: God's commitment to adapt to human needs leads to a change in modus operandi vis-à-vis the next king (and all future kings).

That God has chosen to be constrained by his commitments to the human creature does not only lead God to adapt to Israel's request for a king, by allowing the monarchy and by providing a prophetic voice to balance and oversee this new institution. God's commitment to adapt to human needs leads God to change his *modus operandi* in relation to the next king (and all future kings in the Davidic line). I propose that Yhwh came to the realization through the experience with Samuel that one resentful, crotchety old man (who has the status of an authoritative prophet, whose word God is committed to supporting) can undermine God's own long-term purposes for the covenant people. So God decides to put his relationship with the next king on a different (unconditional) footing.[34] In 2 Samuel 7, Yhwh tells David that while he will discipline any king in his line who is disobedient, he will not take his favor/love (חֶסֶד) from that king, "as I took it from Saul" (2 Sam 7:15). Paradoxically, then, Samuel's inflexibility (his resistance to God changing) has precipitated a further change in God.[35]

Thesis 7. Samuel has not fulfilled the central intercessory role of the prophet vis-à-vis Saul.

The depth of Samuel's culpability in the rejection of Saul comes into even clearer focus when his prophetic role is compared to that of Moses, the paradigmatic prophet (according to Deut 18:15, 17), especially to Moses' intercession on behalf of the people's sin in the episode of the golden calf.[36] In Exodus 32–34, we find Moses interceding on behalf of the people after their sin of idolatry. The parallels between this event and the case of Saul's rejection in 1 Samuel 15 are striking (for both their initial similarities and their ultimate divergence).

In Exodus 20, Yhwh gives the ten commandments through Moses, the second of which (Exod 20:4–6) is an explicit prohibition against idolatry (with a motive clause concerning punishment). Nevertheless, while Moses is away on the mountain, Aaron the priest leads the people in disobedience to this very commandment (they construct and worship a golden calf, Exod 32:1–6), which generates God's word to Moses that the covenant is over and that he has rejected the people (Exod 32:9–10). When confronted by Moses, Aaron refuses to take responsibility for constructing the idol and passes the blame to the people (32:21–24).

In the case of 1 Samuel 15, we have Samuel's *claim* that God has commanded Saul to execute the חֵרֶם against the Amalekites (although no explicit consequences are mentioned for disobedience). In the absence

---

34. This is why the many statements that God was with David (and helped him succeed) should not be taken as affirming God's approval of David's action. The key point is that God's support of David is *unconditional*.

35. Note the parallels to the flood narrative, where the human heart's resistance to change after the flood (compare Gen 6:5 with 8:21) precipitates God's commitment never again to bring a flood as judgment on the whole earth. The inability of humans to change leads God to act differently.

36. Abraham is specifically called a prophet in Gen 20:7 in connection with his prayer on behalf of Abimilech (see also his extended intercession on behalf of Sodom and Gomorrah in Genesis 18). And Jeremiah's prophetic prayers on behalf of Israel are well known. On the intercessory role of Moses, see Michael Widmer, *Moses, God, and the Dynamics of Intercessory Prayer: A Study of Exodus 32–34 and Numbers 13–14* (FAT 2; Tübingen: Mohr Siebeck, 2004).

of Samuel, Saul, the king, leads the people in disobedience (they do not fully execute the חֵרֶם), which generates God's word to Samuel that he has changed his mind about Saul's kingship. When accused by Samuel, Saul tries to avoid responsibility by emphasizing the people's role in sparing the animals (1 Sam 15:15).

But herein lies the fundamental difference between the two accounts. Whereas Moses pleads with God in an extended series of intercessory prayers for God to forgive the people's sin and to change his mind about rejecting them, in 1 Samuel 15 there is absolutely no intercession by Samuel on behalf of Saul.

Moses even explicitly includes the people in the special favor he has with God and uses this as part of his appeal on their behalf (32:31–32; 33:12–13; 34:9), with the result that God "repents" of the evil he was going to perform (32:14) and eventually agrees to accompany Israel on the journey to the promised land (33:16–17). In the end, YHWH offers forgiveness for sin and reestablishes the covenant with Israel on an *unconditional* footing (34:6–7a), a significant change from the conditionality of divine חֶסֶד in the motive clause for the second commandment.[37]

By contrast, Samuel declares that God will *not* change his mind, and he categorically refuses Saul's plea for forgiveness (even though the request for forgiveness would not automatically imply a request for Saul's kingship to be restored). While Moses has to plead with God to change his mind, in Samuel's case it is *the prophet's* mind that is made up.

Further, because of Moses' faithful intercession on behalf of the people, Aaron remains in his role as priest and founder of the priestly line, even after so blatant a sin as idolatry (explicit disloyalty to YHWH). But the lack of (indeed *refusal* of) intercession on Samuel's part results in the rejection of Saul's kingship, and his dynasty comes to nothing. Or perhaps that is too strong a statement, because Samuel's lack of intercession is only the final nail in the coffin. While Samuel's intercession on behalf of Saul may

---

37. Whereas the motive clause for the second commandment (Exod 20:5–6) includes first a statement of punishment for sin followed by an affirmation that God's חֶסֶד will be shown to "a thousand generations" of those who love and obey God, the restatement of this motive clause after Moses' intercessory prayer (Exod 34:6–7) is characterized by three significant changes. First, the order of punishment and love is reversed; love receives the priority. Second, the vocabulary of love by which YHWH is characterized is expanded exponentially to include compassion, grace, and patience (slow to anger), even "abounding" in חֶסֶד and faithfulness. But third, the enactment of חֶסֶד ("to the thousandth generation") has lost any conditionality and is paired with the forgiveness of iniquity/transgression/sin (two of these are terms that Samuel uses in his poetic indictment of Saul in 1 Sam 15:23).

well have averted his rejection, this rejection is actually the result (the final consequence) of Samuel's consistent mistreatment of Saul.

Samuel's refusal to intercede for Saul in chap. 15 (as the final linchpin in a series of manipulative actions) clearly sets him apart from Moses in his paradigmatic prophetic intercession on behalf of Israel's sin. But this refusal is also in direct contradiction to the oath Samuel himself swore in his farewell speech to Saul and the people that he would not "sin against Yhwh" by ceasing to pray for them (1 Sam 12:23). The irony is that Samuel's emphatic oath hoodwinked not just Saul and the people, but many commentators as well, who seem not to have noticed that Samuel reneges on this oath vis-à-vis Saul. The result is that it is typical to find summary statements such as the following: "The tragedy of Saul is in large part the tragedy of his inability to accept God's choice of David and live accordingly."[38] But this is tantamount to blaming the victim. Without defending Saul's actions, just a few changes to the above quotation would make it a much truer statement: The tragedy of *Samuel* is in large part the tragedy of his inability to accept God's choice of *Saul* and live accordingly!

The narrative of Samuel thus does not simply expose the underside of the first two kings of Israel, both of whom are found wanting in significant ways (something widely acknowledged in contemporary scholarship). It exposes also the fragility of the prophetic office in the person of Samuel, who is the foremost representative of this office at the crucial point of transition to the monarchy. Given the negative portrayal of Samuel in the narrative, it is no wonder that after chap. 15 he recedes into the background, with no significant role *vis-à-vis* the new king. His seeming replacement, Nathan, certainly has no relationship with David analogous to Samuel's relationship with Saul. Not only does Nathan have to frame his critique of David's adultery and murder initially in a parable, presumably so that he might even get a hearing (2 Samuel 12), but when Nathan affirms the new king's project to build a house for Yhwh (2 Sam 7:3), he gets Yhwh's word *wrong* and must deliver a revised message (7:4–17). Paradoxically, then, the very prophet who resisted change generated significant transformations in both God and the prophetic office in the book that bears his name.

---

38. Moberly, "God Is Not a Human Being That He Should Repent," 121.

Prophecy as Prediction in Biblical Historiography

John Van Seters

Prophecy plays many different roles within the drama of biblical historiography, but this essay will focus on only one, the role of prophet as the *predictor* of future events within the Dtr corpus and its later literary supplements. Prediction in biblical historiography may be compared with the role of prediction in ancient Near Eastern historical texts, primarily in the form of omens and divination, and in the oracles of the *baru*.[1] In Greek histories, prediction likewise plays a dominant role in the compositional structure of Herodotus's *Histories*, in his use of oracles, mantics, and wise counselors to anticipate future events.[2] Likewise, Xenophon, in his *Anabasis*, makes repeated reference to consulting omens in an effort to predict the outcome of military engagements.[3]

Prophecy, as seen in this comparative context, is first and foremost a revelation from a deity given in an oral form through a devotee of a particular deity, and only secondarily is it transcribed into a written form by a scribe for delivery to a king or person of high rank.[4] The message of

---

1. For contemporary Neo-Assyrian examples of prophecy, see M. Nissinen, *References to Prophecy in Neo-Assyrian Sources* (SAAS 7; Helsinki: Neo-Assyrian Text Corpus Project, 1998). See also on omens and divination F. H. Cryer, *Divination in Ancient Israel and Its Near Eastern Environment: A Socio-historical Investigation* (JSOTSup 142; Sheffield: JSOT Press, 1994); K. L. Sparks, *Ancient Texts for the Study of the Hebrew Bible* (Peabody, MA: Hendrickson, 2005) 216–39.

2. R. Lattimore, "The Wise Adviser in Herodotus," *Classical Philology* 34 (1939) 24–35; J. Van Seters, *In Search of History: Historiography in the Ancient World and the Origins of Biblical History* (New Haven, CT: Yale University Press, 1983) 37, 46–49. Note that in the case of both Herodotus and DtrH the fabricated (?) predictions are used as a structural device for literary purposes.

3. R. Waterfield, *Xenophon's Retreat: Greece, Persia, and the End of the Golden Age* (Cambridge, MA: Harvard University Press, 2006) 42–44.

4. See M. Nissinen, "Spoken, Written, Quoted, and Invented: Orality and Writtenness in Ancient Near Eastern Prophecy," in *Writings and Speech in Israelite and Ancient Near Eastern Prophecy* (ed. E. Ben Zvi and M. H. Floyd; Atlanta: Society of Biblical Literature, 2000) 235–71.

the prophecy is generally limited to the immediate historical context and is rarely considered to have any further relevance. During the course of transmission from oral to written, there is undoubtedly some modification of the original works and scribal stylization. In some instances, the oracle or a summary of its message and meaning is embedded in some other literary form. In the late Neo-Assyrian period, there was a tendency to make collections of some prophetic oracles, primarily having to do with the legitimacy of the royal succession of Esarhaddon and Ashurbanipal.[5] They also find a prominent role within royal inscriptions as oracles of assurance received by the king before important military campaigns and as such, they were predictions of victory. Within this context, it is likely that the original oracle was modified by the scribe to conform it to the predominant style of the royal inscription. These prophecies had little to do with long-term predictions of the ultimate destiny of the dynasty or the nation, such as one encounters in the biblical narrative. This comparative social context deserves very careful consideration in any extended treatment of the subject of prophecy as prediction, but my focus in this essay will be limited to prophecy as prediction in biblical historiography. What this comparative material strongly suggests, however, is that the prophetic oracles within this corpus are primarily fictional imitations used for ideological purposes.

While the biblical narratives do recognize the use of omens manipulated by ephod-wearing priests for the purpose of predicting the outcome of an impending battle,[6] Dtr seems to denigrate the use of divination and gives the primary function of predicting future events to the prophet. This has to do not only with warnings about the consequences of disobedience to the divine will but also with warnings concerning the more long-term destiny of royal dynasties and the fate of the states of Israel and Judah. This is reflected in the so-called "theology of the Dtr history," as spelled out by G. von Rad.[7] For von Rad, the theology of Dtr is tied so closely to the pattern of prophecy in the book of Kings that his focus is almost entirely with this corpus. A notable exception is the account of the divine promise to David through Nathan the prophet in 2 Samuel 7, which is indispensable to the ideological pattern in the rest of the history. This is the pattern in which David is the example of the righteous king for all the

---

5. See S. Parpola, *Assyrian Prophecies* (SAAS 9; Helsinki: Neo-Assyrian Text Corpus Project, 1997).

6. See the detailed treatment in Cryer, *Divination*, 229–305.

7. G. von Rad, "The Deuteronomic Theology of History in *I* and *II Kings*," in *The Problem of the Hexateuch and Other Essays* (trans. E. W. Trueman Dicken; Edinburgh: Oliver & Boyd, 1966) 205–21.

subsequent rulers of Israel and Judah, in contrast to Jeroboam, the first ruler of the Northern Kingdom of Israel, who constitutes the negative model for all the evil kings of Israel and the series of divine judgments against them.

Even though von Rad must begin his discussion with David, most of the book of Samuel constitutes a problem for him because (1) the David presented in the largest part of the David story does not fit the description of the righteous king that is so frequently repeated by Dtr, and (2) the pattern of prophecy and fulfillment tied to obedience to the law is lacking in the rest of the David story. For obvious reasons, von Rad chooses to ignore the story of David and Bathsheba, in which the pattern of prophetic condemnation and a future judgment is certainly present, and I will return to this episode below. The reason von Rad has a problem with the book of Samuel, however, is that he has followed Noth in viewing the account of David's rise and the Succession Narrative as sources used by Dtr, which Dtr then so blatantly contradicts. There is a better solution to this problem.

If I set aside the David story for the moment and look at the earlier part of the book of Samuel, I find that both the youthful Samuel and an unknown "man of God" play a role in passing judgment on the priestly house of Eli, the last judge of Israel, both in terms of his immediate family and the future of its priesthood (1 Sam 2:27–36; 3:1–18). However, it is Samuel as prophet who sets the pattern for the rise and fall of kings and dynasties in the anointing of Saul as the first king and then later passing judgment on Saul's dynasty for disobedience to Yahweh's prophet, and his prediction of Saul's replacement by another (David) who is the divine choice (1 Sam 13:8–15). It is of fundamental importance to Dtr's construction of the identity of the "people of Israel" that David, as a Judean, succeeds Saul, the first Israelite king. Therefore, both Saul's election and subsequent rejection by the prophet Samuel and David's election as Saul's replacement are vital to Dtr's basic theological pattern of history. As I have argued elsewhere,[8] the underlying structure of this early history of the monarchy is Dtr's invention of a united kingdom of David and a common people of Israel, and prophecy plays a major role in this construction. The same prophetic pattern is found in Nathan's promise to David of a perpetual dynasty over Judah in 2 Samuel 7, followed by Ahijah's rejection of the rule of Solomon's successors over the northern tribes of Israel and

---

8. See my book, *The Biblical Saga of King David* (Winona Lake, IN: Eisenbrauns, 2009) 207–69, esp. pp. 268–69.

the election of Jeroboam as a replacement (1 Kgs 11:29–40), followed by the rejection of Jeroboam's house (1 Kgs 14:1–18), and the election of Ba'asha, followed by his subsequent rejection (1 Kgs 15:27–30, 16:1–4), and so on. This is the theological pattern of prophecy that von Rad explores in the book of Kings.

There are, however, three episodes, embedded within the history of the monarchy, making use of this same pattern of prophecy and fulfillment, which seem to contradict violently Dtr's theological pattern. These consist of the following:

1. The rejection of Saul by the deity through Samuel in 1 Sam 15:1–16:13 and the follow-up to this in the story of the medium of Endor in 1 Sam 28:3–25.
2. The David and Bathsheba story in 2 Sam 11:1–12:25.
3. The story of Jeroboam and the man of God from Judah in 1 Kings 13.

In every one of these cases, the pattern of prophecy and fulfillment is taken up and developed in an extended narrative as an elaborate parody or revision of Dtr's theology or ideology of history. Let us look at each in turn.

Turning first to the divine rejection of Saul, space does not permit me to deal with the whole of this story and its parallel in 1 Sam 13:8–15,[9] so I will focus on Saul's dealings with the medium of Endor in 1 Sam 28:3–25. At the very outset of the episode, one is confronted with the remarkable statement that Saul is a reformer who acted in conformity with deuteronomic law, after the manner of Josiah, by getting rid of the mediums in the land. But this very act of piety has rendered Saul vulnerable in a time of crisis, because Yahweh will not answer his inquiries by the use of any of the legitimate means, so he must resort to the use of illegitimate means, namely, employing a medium who has escaped his purge. This is a complete reversal of the Dtr scheme in which the prophet confronts the king when he violates the deuteronomic law and then passes judgment on him. When a king, such as David, does what is pleasing to Yahweh and then petitions the deity (2 Samuel 7), he receives an immediate favorable response from Yahweh through his prophet. But in this case, Saul's act of piety is met with complete silence, and even when the prophet's ghost is forced to respond as a result of the use of a medium, Samuel says nothing about the medium, nor does he acknowledge his religious reforms. He only repeats a prior verdict of judgment from the previous episode in 1 Samuel 15. In contrast to this, in the DtrH even Ahab's acts of contrition after his sentence of judgment win him some reprieve from his harsh sentence (1 Kgs 21:27–29; cf. 1 Sam 15:24–31). Again, in those parallel

---

9. See my detailed discussion in ibid., 121–35.

cases in DtrH where the deity passes sentence on the king and his dynastic succession, the usual Dtr pattern is that the prophet is ordered by the deity to confront the king and pass judgment on him whether the king has summoned him or not. But here, Saul is the one who is eager to appear before Samuel and shows him great reverence. This is a complete parody of Dtr's prediction pattern.

After Saul receives the sentence of impending disaster for himself, his sons, and the whole army of Israel, he is completely devastated. Saul, of course, receives no sympathy from Samuel. Instead, it is the medium who shows him compassion and prepares a lavish feast of fatted calf and freshly baked bread for him and his servants and forces him to eat. In this touching scene of kindness by the outlawed medium who has risked her own life to help him, the author elicits from the reader a feeling of sympathy for the condemned king. This again is hardly what one expects from Dtr.

The second example, the David and Bathsheba story, is likewise a complete caricature of the Dtr pattern of prophecy and fulfillment.[10] In it, Nathan the prophet is sent by Yahweh to pass judgment on David for his adultery with Bathsheba and murder of Uriah. Because the pattern is so obvious here, it is surprising that von Rad makes no comment about it. In terms of content, of course, it flies in the face of the whole royal ideology of Dtr because it certainly contradicts his idealization of David. But it is the deliberately ironic use of the Dtr pattern that concerns us here.

The statement that introduces the scene of prophetic judgment on David's actions is the simple statement "What David did was evil in the eyes of Yahweh" (2 Sam 11:27). Now this statement is completely out of character for this author of the David Saga[11] because he seldom makes any reference to the deity or divine intervention in human affairs. By contrast, a statement of this sort is ubiquitous throughout the Dtr corpus; it introduces periods of apostasy by the Israelites in the time of the judges followed by divine judgment in the form of a foreign oppressor; and in the book of Kings it regularly introduces all the evil kings of Judah and Israel and the threat of judgment on the king, his dynasty, and the nation as a whole. So characteristic of Dtr is this phraseology of "doing what is evil in the eyes of Yahweh," that it has led some scholars to regard such language in the David and Bathsheba story (2 Sam 11:27b, 12:9) as later Dtr additions to an earlier narrative. However, this is unacceptable for two reasons:

---

10. For a larger discussion of the David and Bathsheba story, see ibid., 287–301, with literature cited there.

11. This is my name for the source reflected in the Court History, which I use in my *Biblical Saga*. For the choice of the term *David Saga*, see pp. 39–49.

(1) statements of this sort are integral to the narrative so that they cannot be removed as editorial glosses, and (2) the statement of divine displeasure toward David completely contradicts the frequent statements by Dtr that David did only what was upright in the eyes of Yahweh and was the model for all subsequent kings to follow. What we have in this story instead is the deliberate imitation, by a later writer, of Dtr's phraseology and the prophetic pattern that was used to denounce evil kings, which the story writer applies ironically to David.

A good example of this Dtr prophetic pattern of judgment may be seen in the case of Abijah, the prophet, and Jeroboam, in 1 Kings 14. Abijah is commissioned by Yahweh to address a message to Jeroboam (through his wife). He begins with a résumé of Yahweh's past favors to Jeroboam and then draws a sharp comparison with David as the one who did only what was "right in my eyes." He outlines Jeroboam's crimes and the punishment that will follow, which is twofold: his dynasty will be violently wiped out and the sick child, his son, will not recover but die. In addition, the nation of Israel will also come to an end and be exiled beyond the Euphrates. This same pattern is employed in the David story, with Nathan commissioned by Yahweh to speak to David. Nathan likewise gives David an outline of Yahweh's past favors to David, followed by an accusation of his crimes and a threefold judgment: (1) the sword will never depart from David's House (that is, his dynasty and his realm), (2) there will be a rebellion against him from within his own house in which his wives will be violated in plain sight of all, and (3) Bathsheba's child will die.

Not only is there the same pattern here, as in other places in Dtr, but there is an interesting comparison of details that underlines the irony in the David story. Within the historical résumés, it is emphasized that both David and Jeroboam replaced the previous dynasties (the House of Saul and the House of David, respectively) by direct divine intervention, but both later kings proved to be unworthy of this benefaction by their behavior. The irony comes when the evil of Jeroboam is compared by Dtr with the rectitude and morality of David, a claim that the David Saga completely undermines. There is also the detail about the sick child that dies, which is common to both. This detail suggests that there is a very close relationship between the two accounts, the one mimicking the other. It cannot be argued that this similarity is merely a matter of the use of the same genre. There are too many close similarities with other details drawn from Dtr, especially with the story of Ahab and Naboth's vineyard, that make this argument quite unlikely.[12]

---

12. For these parallels see ibid., 291–96.

Yet there are two major departures from the Dtr prophetic pattern that call for some comment. The first is the interruption of the pattern at the outset by a long parable that is used to lead David into convicting himself for his actions. There is no parallel for this feature or style of presentation in Dtr. By contrast, this is quite similar to the kind of story that the wise woman of Tekoah spins, with very similar results. It suggests that the author of the David Saga regarded wisdom as a form of prophecy and wise counselors as akin to those who spoke the word of God.[13] The second departure has to do with the prediction of the Absalom rebellion, in which the 10 concubines of David would be deliberately violated on the advice of Ahithophel, and this advice is identified as equivalent to consulting "the word of God." What is remarkable is that it is a prophet who predicts the violation of the women as a divine punishment and another person who speaks the "word of God" that makes it all happen. This surely sets the whole Dtr scheme of divine intervention in history, as spelled out by von Rad, on its head!

Finally, one must take seriously the suggestion by the David Saga that, contrary to the whole scheme of Dtr, David was as much responsible for the demise of the Southern Kingdom of Judah as Jeroboam was for the Northern Kingdom of Israel. For the David Saga, the House of David, which means the whole dynasty and the state of Judah, was under constant divine judgment—the sword—until the very end, just as much as Israel was under the curse of Jeroboam until its demise. The rest of the David Saga and the succession of Solomon attempts to make this message very clear. Surely, one of the marks of great literature and a consummate literary artist is seen in the use of irony and parody; and the pleasure in serious entertainment of this sort is to see beyond the use of traditional forms and language in order to grasp the reality that the author is trying to communicate. The story of David and Bathsheba is a case in point.

The third example of a revisionist treatment of the prediction pattern is the story of the man of God from Judah who comes to Bethel to pass judgment on Jeroboam's altar (1 Kings 13). Von Rad includes this within his list of examples from DtrH, and others have followed him in this. Indeed, Frank Cross has made the story of the man of God in 1 Kings 13 and its sequel in 2 Kgs 23:15–20 a key element in their interpretation of the DtrH,[14] but this seems quite unlikely. It is only in the following story

---

13. In Herodotus, there is also a similarity of his use of Delphic orals and the advice of wise counselors.

14. F. M. Cross, *Canaanite Myth and Hebrew Epic* (Cambridge: Harvard University Press, 1973) 274–89, esp. pp. 279–80; also W. K. Lemke, "The Way of Obedience:

in 1 Kings 14, which originally followed 1 Kgs 12:32, that Dtr takes up the pattern of condemning Jeroboam for the sins of establishing the cult places in Dan and Bethel. The story in 1 Kings 13 interrupts this pattern and does not include Jeroboam or his sins of apostasy in setting up the calves—these are not even mentioned—but only the future of the altar that Jeroboam has built. And it is this altar that is destroyed and desecrated in 2 Kgs 23:15–20, not any foreign cult. Indeed, within these two units of the story, there is a complete scarcity of Dtr language and ideology. So something quite different is going on in this "prophetic" story.[15]

I will not repeat what I have said about this story in another place,[16] except to say that any perceptive reader will recognize that it is not the kind of literary masterpiece that one recognizes in the *David Saga*, as reflected in the story of David and Bathsheba. Rather, it is a pastiche of elements borrowed from many other narratives and put together in such a careless and confusing fashion that it is difficult to make out at any point in the story just what is actually going on. I do not wish to deal with these details here, but I will focus instead on the prediction of the man of God concerning the altar and its fulfillment and just what the author intends to say by his use of this pattern. This is not an early prophetic tale incorporated into the history by a late Dtr editor as some have suggested. The many indications of late language and anachronisms make this quite unlikely. Instead, it is a very late tale that has been added to DtrH, making use of the Dtr pattern of prophecy/fulfillment in a radically transformed style and for a very different purpose. Let us now look at this prophecy.

When the man of God comes to give his prophecy, he directs his speech to the altar, in the presence of Jeroboam, and predicts that one day in the future, Josiah will desecrate the altar by sacrificing the priests of the high places on it, then burning human bones on the altar, and finally destroying the altar with the ashes spilling out. He then offers a sign that this will

---

1 Kings 13 and the Structure of the Deuteronomistic History," in *Magnalia Dei: The Mighty Acts of God. In Memoriam G. E. Wright* (ed. F. M. Cross et al.; Garden City, NY: Doubleday, 1976) 301–26; G. N. Knoppers, *Two Nations Under God: The Deuteronomistic History of Solomon and the Dual Monarchies* (2 vols.; HSM 52–53; Atlanta: Scholars Press, 1993–94).

15. See also S. L. McKenzie, *The Trouble with Kings: The Composition of the Book of Kings in the Deuteronomistic History* (VTSup 42; Leiden: Brill, 1991) 51–56.

16. J. Van Seters, "On Reading the Story of the Man of God from Judah in 1 Kings 13," in *The Labour of Reading: Desire, Alienation, and Biblical Interpretation. Festschrift Robert C. Culley* (ed. F. C. Black, R. Boer, and E. Runions; SemeiaSt; Altanta: Scholars Press, 1999) 225–34; idem, "The Deuteronomistic History: Can It Avoid Death by Redaction?" in *The Future of the Deuteronomistic History* (ed. T Römer; BETL 147; Leuven: Peeters, 2000) 213–22.

happen by predicting that the present altar will be destroyed immediately with the ashes spilled out, and this happens without any human agency. Of course, this raises an obvious question: if the altar was in fact destroyed in this miraculous fashion in Jeroboam's time, why did Josiah have to do so again so many centuries later? Nothing is said about its being rebuilt or replaced. But let's not quibble.

We will pass over the intriguing, but thoroughly confusing, not to say badly muddled, account of the encounter between the two prophets, the man of God from Judah and the old prophet from Bethel, except to note that there is no suggestion that Bethel contains any foreign cult. Everyone in Bethel is a worshiper of Yahweh and the deity speaks through the old prophet just as he does through the prophet from Judah. But the old prophet has a further word concerning the prediction that the man of God has just made about the altar. When he brings the body of the man of God back to Bethel for burial, the old prophet instructs his sons to have his bones also buried in the same grave as the man of God, because of his prediction, but it is not clear until one reads the sequel why these instructions were given.

The fulfillment about the destruction of the altar made by Jeroboam at Bethel is given in 2 Kgs 23:15, although once again the text is badly muddled by the inclusion of a remark about "the high place" of Bethel associated with the altar; both are pulled down together (and broken in pieces; see the LXX). The high place is then burned along with an Asherah, although the Asherah is not mentioned as part of Jeroboam's apostasy. What is lacking is any mention of the molten calf of Bethel, as one would certainly expect from Dtr. Some of the language from the surrounding Dtr description of Josiah's reform has been mixed into this account, but the primary focus is on the altar, nonetheless. The desecration of the altar continues in v. 16 with the burning of bones from nearby tombs on the altar, but this, of course, is entirely inconsistent with the notion that the altar has already been destroyed.

When Josiah has finished destroying the altar and desecrating the place with the bones of the dead, he observes a tomb with a marker and is told that it belongs to the grave of the man of God who predicted the destruction of the altar and its desecration, and so he does not permit it to be disturbed. This explains why the old prophet was so concerned to have his bones buried in the same grave as the man of God in the story of 1 Kings 13, because in this way, the prophet's bones were also preserved.

Josiah then proceeds to destroying all the temples of the high places throughout Samaria, slaughtering its priests on the altars of these places, and burning human bones on them, just as he had done with Bethel (vv. 19–20). Now the preceding text in vv. 15–16 did not actually say that Josiah slaughtered the priests of Bethel on the destroyed altar, but this was part of the prediction in 1 Kings 13. But why was such drastic action taken against these priests of the high places in Samaria when this was clearly not the case for the priests of the high places in Judah? The author seems to suggest two reasons: (1) from the very beginning they were not Levitical priests, and (2) after the overthrow of Samaria, when the entire population was replaced by foreigners, all of the high places were taken over by foreign priests worshiping foreign gods, as spelled out in 2 Kgs 17:29–34.[17] Thus, they were worthy of complete eradication by Josiah.

The prediction and outcome that is reflected in the story of the man of God in 1 Kings 13 and its sequel in 2 Kgs 23:15–20 reflects an entirely different purpose from that in DtrH. It takes for granted the centralization of worship demanded by Deuteronomy and reflected in the Josiah reform as it concerns Judah "from Geba to Beersheba" (v. 8), but it completely rejects any participation by the northern region of Samaria and Bethel, in particular, in such a common religious community.

Conclusion

Ever since von Rad's influential study on Dtr's theology of history, as reflected in the prophecy-fulfillment pattern in Kings, scholars have taken this Dtr pattern to reflect the basic OT understanding of history as directed by and under the control of the word of Yahweh. Von Rad concludes his study by stating that

> Israel's history depends upon a few quite simple theological and prophetical propositions concerning the nature of the divine word. It is this [predictive] word of Yahweh, and it alone, which gives to the phenomena of history a purpose and meaning, so binding together into a single whole in the eyes of God its manifold and diverse elements.

The matter, however, is not quite so simple or straightforward. What I have seen is that the pattern is by no means uniform and that it is often used in elaborately constructed parodies to run quite counter to the understanding of Israel's history given to it by Dtr. In addition, the pattern of prediction is used primarily as a structural device in the literary construc-

---

17. There is strong reason to believe that this text is post-Dtr and that it is also part of the same source reflected in 1 Kings 13. See my "Deuteronomistic History," 220–21.

tion of the stories, and, in most cases, it cannot bear the theological weight that is so often given to it. In the stories of Saul, David, Solomon, and Jeroboam, Dtr's views of the origins of the states of Israel and Judah and the link made through predictive prophecy to the rest of Israel's history were strongly contested by later authors, and failure to hear these dissenting voices is a serious mistake in historical criticism.

Jeroboam and the Prophets in 1 Kings 11–14: Prophetic Word for Two Kingdoms

Lissa M. Wray Beal

In 1–2 Kings, Jeroboam is the great villain of the Northern Kingdom. He is promised a sure house as was given David, if only Jeroboam would walk in accordance with the law. Despite this, Jeroboam ascends the throne and immediately disregards the law particularly as it touches on the key aspect of Deuteronomistic worship practices. Due to his flagrant disobedience of the law in respect to worship, Yhwh rejects him. As the history of the Northern Kingdom progresses, his downfall becomes the paradigmatic downfall by which northern rulers are judged and found similarly wanting. In this way, Jeroboam's effect on the history is unmistakable.

Jeroboam's rise and fall is related in 1 Kings 11–14. The prominence of prophets in this corpus is striking, for, since Nathan, prophets have not figured in the narrative. An exploration of the role of prophets in Jeroboam's narrative reveals that Jeroboam stands as more than a historiographical paradigm for the Northern Kingdom. An indelible connection also exists between this narrative and that of the whole monarchic history, both prior to and following Jeroboam's tale.

The treatment in recent literature of the prophetic encounters in 1 Kings 11–14 forms a starting point for this study. Often, each prophetic encounter in 1 Kings 11–14 is treated on its own. Thus, Ahijah's initial encounter with Jeroboam is studied on its own to understand how that encounter relates to Solomon's narrative. Similarly, the man of God's encounter at the Bethel altar is studied on its own to draw connections to Josiah. Further, when scholars do treat the chapters as a narrative whole and the whole's effect on the larger narrative is considered, the direction of consideration moves linearly forward. The relationship of 1 Kings 11–14 to the fall of the Northern Kingdom or to Josiah's reign is thoroughly discussed, but little attention to the preceding Solomonic narrative is evident. Changing both these focuses yields fruitful new understandings of Jeroboam's place in the whole history.

Having considered several examples of the treatment of 1 Kings 11–14, this work will explore (using the MT as a "final form" text) the four prophetic episodes within 1 Kings 11–14: the two confrontations between Ahijah and Jeroboam in 1 Kgs 11:29–39 and 14:1–18 (here, the confrontation involves Jeroboam's wife) and the dual prophetic interactions of 1 Kgs 13:1–10 and 20–25a in which nameless prophets interact with Jeroboam and one another. The four prophetic episodes will be considered as a bounded set, with investigation of the varied means by which this set is held together and how it speaks to the key issues of the Jeroboam narrative. The delineation of the bounded set then leads to a consideration of how that set's themes and motifs are traced throughout 1–2 Kings. Briefly, attention will be given to the set's continuing influence in the historiography of the Northern Kingdom, as well as its narrative conclusion in 2 Kings 23. Greater attention will be given to how the set interacts with Solomon's narrative as well as the set's relation to the Southern Kingdom in the history. 1 Kings 11–14 does narrate the means of judgment on Solomon via the division of the kingdom but unfolds much more than that. Parable-like, it stands as a prophetic demonstration of judgment on Solomon's cultic sins. And thus, looking back to judge Solomon, it also once again looks forward to stand as a prophetic word to the Southern Kingdom for the remainder of 1–2 Kings. By shifting the investigative focus to the broader context of 1 Kings 11–14 rather than focusing solely on its individual prophetic interactions enables new light to be shed on the historiographical intent in the Deuteronomist's (hereafter, Dtr) use of Jeroboam as a paradigm—not only for measuring northern kings, but also for judging Solomon and speaking prophetically to the Southern Kingdom.

Jeroboam's Narrative:
Reading Atomistically and Futuristically

Most often, the connection of the Jeroboam narrative to the larger history is traced through the prophecy-fulfillment schema apparent in 1 Kings 13 and 2 Kings 23. 1 Kings 13 figures prominently in discussions regarding Jeroboam's rule, and that chapter's reference to Josiah's destruction of the Bethel altar makes an obvious connection to the larger (and southern) history. Many commentaries explore the nature and purpose of the prophecy-fulfillment relationship between 1 Kings 13 and 2 Kings 23.[1]

---

1. Several commentators, as part of the discussion of 1 Kings 13, explore its relationship to Josiah's reforms in 2 Kgs 23:15–20, for example, S. de Vries , *1 Kings* (Word 12; Nashville: Thomas Nelson, 2003); J. Gray, *I and II Kings* (OTL; Philadelphia: Westminster, 1970); G. H. Jones, *1 and 2 Kings* (vol. 1; NCBC; Grand Rapids: Eerd-

At times, exploration of the prophecy-fulfillment relationship takes account of its connection to other characters within the history and considers questions of compositional history or literary coherency. For instance, Marvin Sweeney, proposing both a Hezekian and a Josianic edition of the Deuteronomistic History (hereafter, DH), argues that the Jeroboam narrative in its present form includes a prior Hezekian version. That version emphasizes the role of Jeroboam in the collapse of the Northern Kingdom (2 Kings 17), using Jeroboam's unfaithfulness as a foil against which Judah's faithfulness under Hezekiah is contrasted.[2] This edition includes 1 Kings 11 and 14. The Josianic edition adds 1 Kings 13 to "anticipate the narrative concerning Josiah's reforms in 2 Kings 22–23" as well as to question the validity of the promise made to Jeroboam in 1 Kings 11 and reversed in 1 Kings 14.[3] In this reading then, Jeroboam and the prophets serve the interests of later editions to present Jeroboam as a foil to both Hezekiah and Josiah.

Robert Cohn, examining narrative technique in 1 Kings 11–14, explores the composite narrative that now works as a coherent whole "shaped to explain and justify the rise and fall of the man responsible for the division of the kingdom."[4] The narrative stands as a pivot both to fulfill God's word against Solomon and to "point ahead to the end of Jeroboam's short-lived dynasty, of his kingdom, and of his cult."[5] In this reading, the prophecy of the man of God in 1 Kings 13 cites Josiah and anticipates the ultimate destruction of the Jeroboam cult.

Beyond the prophecy-fulfillment schema, 1 Kings 13 also figures prominently in analogical connections drawn between Jeroboam's narrative and the larger history. The interactions between the man of God and the Bethel prophet in 1 Kings 13 are cited as in some way prefiguring the subsequent interactions of Judah and Israel. Many of these studies focus the investigation on 1 Kings 13 as an independent unit without considering its function within the context of 1 Kings 11–14.

In volume two of *Church Dogmatics*, Karl Barth uses the prophetic narrative in 1 Kings 13 to develop his discussion of election. Within that discussion, he posits the prophetic figures as analogical to the Northern

---

mans, 1984); J. Montgomery, *The Book of Kings* (ICC; London: T. & T. Clark, 1986); M. A. Sweeney, *I and II Kings* (OTL; Louisville: Westminster John Knox, 2007); J. T. Walsh, *1 Kings* (Berit Olam; Collegeville, MN: Liturgical Press, 1996).

2. M. A. Sweeney, *King Josiah of Judah: The Lost Messiah of Judah* (New York: Oxford University Press, 2001) 92.

3. Ibid., 90.

4. R. Cohn, "Literary Technique in the Jeroboam Narrative," *ZAW* 97 (1985) 35.

5. Ibid., 35.

and Southern Kingdoms. Working dialectically, Barth proposes that the man of God and the Bethel prophet present two pictures. In the first picture, the man of God from Judah bearing a message against the northern cult positively represents Josiah. Negatively, in his failure to remain faithful to his task he represents Judah's own failure by which it becomes as apostate as Israel. The second picture focuses on the prophet of Bethel and is predominantly negative. In it, the Bethel prophet represents false profession or false prophecy that characterizes Israel's own profession of Yhwh. Positively, the Bethel prophet illustrates that judgment is not immediate against Israel and thus allows time for reform. Further, in that the Bethel prophet takes up the mantle of true prophecy, he attests to Yhwh's own faithfulness to apostate Israel.

Barth's reading is theologically compelling, although some of his exegetical underpinnings are challenged.[6] Particularly, his insight that the prophets stand as representative of others has reappeared several times in subsequent work and is one of the ways that this essay discerns the historiographical intent of Jeroboam's narrative within the larger 1–2 Kings corpus.

Werner Lemke asks after the purpose of 1 Kings 13 within the DH's "structural and ideological framework."[7] While allowing for a compositional history to 1 Kings 13, he argues that it, together with its framework (12:26–33 and 13:33–34), is from Dtr's hand. Tracing key expressions and motifs in the narrative throughout the history, he notes that the narrative connects to other key texts such as 1 Samuel 12 and 2 Kings 17 and

---

6. Barth's reading is his usual exciting unfolding of theological truth. However, his exegesis of the passage is flawed on two primary counts. First, it requires a dichotomy between the man of God as a true prophet of Yhwh and the Bethel prophet as a representative of a professional guild of prophets of the false cult centered in Bethel. The dichotomy between the man of God and the Bethel prophet is foundational to Barth's reading; however, the terms cannot be so distinguished. Rather, they are used interchangeably throughout the history: even individuals such as Moses (Deut 33:1, 34:10), Elijah (1 Kgs 17:18, 18:22), and Elisha (2 Kgs 3:11, 5:8) receive both appellations. Second, Barth's exegesis seems too readily to set aside the initial delineation of the Northern Kingdom as the divine will, and Yhwh's ongoing commitment to that Northern Kingdom as expressive of that will. Despite recognition of Barth's exegetical flaws in several works, there is acknowledgement of the vitality of Barth's insights to his subject of election, and the intriguing way that he seeks to discern this insight in 1 Kings 13. A helpful critique of Barth's exegesis by a scholar who favorably accepts his interpretation is found in D. Bosworth, "Revisiting Karl Barth's Exegesis of 1 Kings 13" *BI* 10 (2002) 366–67.

7. W. Lemke, "The Way of Obedience: 1 Kings 13 and the Structure of the Deuteronomistic History," in *Magnalia Dei: The Mighty Acts of God* (ed. F. M. Cross; Garden City, NY: Doubleday, 1976) 301–26.

23, making the story "in its present context . . . another pivotal passage in the DH, which is illustrative of the Historian's theology and over-all proclamation."[8] Lemke cites several of the themes of the DH he finds in 1 Kings 13: the prophecy-fulfillment schema, the realization of the divine word mediated through the prophets, the condemnation of deviant religious practices, and the primary importance of obedience to the divine will.[9]

Additionally, Lemke understands the man of God from Judah to stand analogically for the nation of Judah:

> Proleptically, the fate of the man of God from Judah points beyond itself to that of the nation. Like the former, Israel too had received a command from Yahweh, as revealed in the Mosaic Torah and reiterated repeatedly by his servants the prophets. Like him, she had rebelled against the mouth of the Lord by turning from her divinely ordained way, thus sealing her ultimate downfall and destruction and confirming the warning which the Deuteronomist had uttered, on the occasion of the institution of the monarchy, through the mouth of the prophet Samuel: "But if you still do wickedly, you shall be swept away, both you and your king" (I Sam 12:25).[10]

Jerome Walsh similarly considers 1 Kings 13 one of the texts that "integrate and unify the whole history."[11] Walsh begins by considering the different interpretive contexts within which 1 Kings 13 may be read. He demonstrates that each different context affects one's interpretation of the narrative. For instance, the emphases of the narrative differ whether one reads the narrative as a self-contained whole, or a component of Jeroboam's narrative. When read in light of the history of the kingdoms, Walsh points out several threads found in 1 Kings 13 that can be traced throughout the history. So, he notes that the evaluation of Jeroboam found in 1 Kgs 13:34 appears regularly throughout the remainder of the (northern) history. Additionally, 1 Kings 13 supports Dtr's concern with prophecy and fulfillment: the man of God predicts Josiah's destruction, and this destruction is fulfilled in 2 Kgs 23:15–16. Similarly, the Bethel prophet predicts the destruction of all the sanctuaries in the cities of Samaria, and 2 Kgs 23:19 cites the fulfillment. Although Walsh does not develop this observation, he, too, briefly addresses the analogical function of the characters in this chapter:

---

8. Ibid., 317.
9. Ibid.
10. Ibid., 317–18.
11. J. T. Walsh, "The Contexts of 1 Kings XIII," *VT* 34 (1989) 366.

The story of prophetic conflict is itself prophetic. The individuals mirror their kingdoms, and their tragedy portends the tragic destiny awaiting Israel and Judah. Israel has become unfaithful. Judah can still speak the word that Israel needs to hear; but if Judah, too, following Israel's lead, compromises its worship (as history shows it will), then both are doomed to overcome their separation only in death. Judah will be buried in an alien land, and Israel will be saved only so far as it is joined to Judah.[12]

Two tendencies become apparent in the scholarship that seeks to understand Jeroboam's narrative in light of the larger history. First, much of the work tends to atomize Jeroboam's story, reading its disparate parts as separately connected to various parts of the history. For instance, 1 Kings 11 is read in relation to the prior narrative as delineating judgment on Solomon by raising up Jeroboam, with 1 Kings 12 demonstrating the outworking of the prophetic word in the division of the kingdom. 1 Kings 13, with its prophecy-fulfillment connection to Josiah, is read in light of 2 Kings 23, while 1 Kings 14, with its judgment on Jeroboam, is read in relation to subsequent evaluations and judgments on northern kings. Rarely is the question asked how 1 Kings 11–14 as a whole relates to the history. Second, beyond the connection of 1 Kings 11 to Solomon's judgment, the narrative tends to be read in relation to the subsequent history; it is not asked how 1 Kings 11–14 as a whole relates to the preceding history of Solomon. What new understandings might be revealed should 1 Kings 11–14 be read as a unit, a "bounded set," and read with an eye not only to the subsequent history, but in relation to the lengthy narrative that precedes it? How might a bounded set such as this answer or correspond to Solomon's story?

The Bounded Set of Prophetic Interactions in 1 Kings 11–14

Four prophetic interactions exist within Jeroboam's narrative (1 Kgs 11:29–39, 13:1–10, 13:20–25a, and 14:1–18).[13] These four interactions can be considered a bounded set that, as a unit, define Jeroboam's reign.

---

12. Walsh, "Contexts," 367–68.
13. The prophetic word of Shemaiah to Rehoboam (1 Kgs 12:22–24) is excluded here because it does not take place in the northern king's circle but is directed to the southern king. Its presence in the bounded set will be addressed later under consideration of the absence of the prophetic word to southern kings within 1–2 Kings. Further, the delineation of the third prophetic interaction (13:20–25a) works with a delineation provided by J. K. Mead, "Kings and Prophets, Donkeys and Lions: Dramatic Shape and Deuteronomistic Rhetoric in 1 Kings XIII," *VT* 49 (1999) 191–205. That delineation is slightly modified here and will be discussed further later in this essay.

Two primary evidences demonstrate the cohesiveness of the four interactions; the first is the presence of signs within each element of the bounded set, and the second is the presence of linguistic and thematic elements that connect the bounded set in a chiastic structure.

First, regarding the presence of signs within the bounded set, the history of the Northern Kingdom contains several prophetic oracles and interactions concerning the rise and fall of subsequent dynasties (Baasha's dynasty in 16:1–4, 7; Ahab's dynasty in 1 Kgs 19:15–18, 21:17–29, and 2 Kgs 9:1–10). Within Jeroboam's narrative, 1 Kgs 11:29–39 and 14:1–18 contain prophetic oracles. Given by Ahijah to Jeroboam, these oracles are concerned (as are the oracles regarding Baasha and Ahab) with dynastic succession. Yet, for all the oracles concerning dynastic succession in the Northern Kingdom, it is striking that only those between Jeroboam and Ahijah contain a sign.[14] The observation is even more acute when one considers that prophetic oracles in the Northern Kingdom often do contain prophetic signs—one considers their prevalence in the Elijah and Elisha narratives, for instance. But when prophetic oracles are given about dynastic succession, signs are strangely absent—except in the case at hand. Thus, the first and last oracles in Jeroboam's narrative give an oracular word concerning dynastic succession and accompany that word with a prophetic sign. Further, these two oracles (the first and last in Jeroboam's narrative) envelope 1 Kgs 13:1–10 and 20–25a and each of these prophetic interactions also contain a sign.[15]

Each of the prophetic signs in 1 Kings 11–14 works to demonstrate the infallibility of YHWH's word regarding rulership, and appropriate cultic practice as prescribed by the law. In 1 Kgs 11:30–31, a prophetic sign

---

14. When accompanying the prophetic word, signs of this sort may be considered efficacious because, together with the divine word, they declare the divine will that will come to pass; alternately, they may be considered nonverbal rhetoric that seeks to persuade the intended audience of the depicted future or call them to act toward that future's fulfillment. See a discussion of the efficacy of sign-acts in D. Block, review of K. Friebel, *Jeremiah's and Ezekiel's Sign-Acts*, *JETS* 44 (2001) 729–31; K. Friebel, "A Hermeneutical Paradigm for Interpreting Prophetic Sign-Actions," *Didaskalia* 12 (2001) 25–45; B. Long, *1 Kings with an Introduction to Historical Literature* (FOTL; Grand Rapids: Eerdmans, 1984) 129; M. Matheney, "Interpretation of Hebrew Prophetic Symbolic Act," *Encounter* 293 (1968) 256–67; W. Stacey, *Prophetic Drama in the Old Testament* (London: Epworth, 1990) 79–82, 262–82.

15. This discussion focuses on the first evidence for the bounded set of oracles within Jeroboam's narrative. That evidence is that each of the prophetic interactions contains a sign. At this point, the discussion puts the four oracles in a relationship of outer envelope and inner core. This relationship will be further explored in the discussion of the second evidence for considering the oracles as a bounded set—that of linguistic and thematic elements that hold the four oracles together in a chiastic structure.

accompanies Ahijah's oracle concerning the transfer of 10 tribes to Jeroboam. Ahijah tears Jeroboam's new mantle into pieces that represent the 12 tribes; 10 of those tribes mark the extent of Jeroboam's rule. By a word play, the sign also signifies loss of sovereignty for Solomon: the consonants of both "mantle" (שלמה) and "Solomon" (שלמה) are identical. The tearing of the mantle unleashes the destruction of Solomon's kingdom and the oracle and sign are fulfilled in the next chapter.

In 1 Kgs 13:3, the man of God, while pronouncing the desecration of the Bethel altar by Josiah, proclaims a sign (מופת): the altar will be split apart and its ashes scattered. The sign is immediately fulfilled as assurance that the prophet's words will come to pass, thus confirming the inevitable destruction of the northern cult. Concomitant with this sign stands another sign intended to emphasize the efficacy of the divine will against Jeroboam and his cult. When Jeroboam attempts to forestall the man of God's words by stretching out his hand against him, the hand is rendered useless. Only through the intercession by the man of God is Jeroboam's hand restored to him, thus confirming the power of Yhwh's representative and his word.

In 1 Kgs 13:20–25a the Bethel prophet proclaims against the man of God that, for his disobedience of the word of Yhwh, he will die but not be buried in his father's tomb. The sign is, of course, summarily executed. The man of God is killed by the lion and his body, rather than being returned for burial in Judah, is interred in the Bethel prophet's own grave. The prophet is judged for his disobedience to Yhwh's word. Jeroboam too is also judged for disobedience, and his dynasty will fail.

A similar sign is proffered in 1 Kgs 14:1–8. When Jeroboam's wife arrives at Ahijah's door seeking assurance of Abijah's restoration to health, Ahijah delivers a judgment oracle against Jeroboam's dynasty. As a sign of the word's certainty, Abijah will die at the return of Jeroboam's wife. Again, the sign is summarily executed and the downfall of Jeroboam's short-lived dynasty is thus assured.

An exploration of the four prophetic interactions reveals that not only the bookend oracles but also the interior oracles contain a sign. Furthermore, each of these signs focalizes around the issue of the rise and fall of Jeroboam. The oracles stand thus as a bounded set—a set that becomes more apparent when the chiastic nature of their arrangement is considered.

The second evidence that suggests the four interactions should be considered a bounded set is the unifying chiastic structure that stretches across the four episodes:

A Ahijah's oracle (11:29–39)
 B Oracle and sign against the Bethel altar (13:1–10)
 B′ Oracle and sign against the man of God as he returns from Bethel (13:20–25a)
A′ Ahijah's oracle (14:1–18)

Each of the outer and inner elements of the chiasm relates to the others by thematic and linguistic connections. Additionally, the elements §B′ and §A′ show connections that relate the oracles and signs to the larger history. To begin, I will outline the connections of §A to §A′ and §B to §B′. Then, we will explore the connection of §B′ to §A′.

The interactions in §A and §A′ both involve Ahijah and specify his connection to Shiloh (11:29; 14:2, 4). Each is conducted in private and gives a prophetic word about Jeroboam's kingship: its rise (1 Kings 11) and its fall (1 Kings 14).

Wordplays echo from passage to passage, suggesting their connectedness. Ahijah takes (לקח) and tears (קרע) the cloak as a sign that YHWH is tearing (קרע) the kingdom from Solomon (11:30-31), and Ahijah's later judgment confirms that YHWH has torn (קרע) the kingdom from the house of David (14:8). The transfer of kingdom to Jeroboam is signaled by the 10 pieces of the mantle given to Jeroboam. The taking of the cloak and its division into 10 pieces is further connected to 1 Kings 14 when Jeroboam's wife takes (לקח) 10 loaves (mirroring the 10 pieces of the cloak) to Ahijah and is told that the kingdom given Jeroboam will be taken from him.

In both instances, the prophetic word concerns the establishment of Jeroboam's rule over Israel (11:37, 14:7). In both instances, its establishment and continuance is dependent on Jeroboam acting as YHWH's servant David, adhering to YHWH's commandments, walking in YHWH's ways, and doing the right in YHWH's eyes (11:38, 14:8). Thus, both encounters concern Jeroboam's dynasty and the means by which it may continue. Initially, Jeroboam's house is appointed with the possibility of a sure house such as given David (11:38), but its final destiny is utter destruction (14:10–11, 14). By extension, in that Jeroboam led Israel into idol worship (14:9, 15–16), all Israel will face the destruction of exile (14:15–16).

As in §A and §A′, the correspondences between §B and §B′ are also thematic and linguistic.[16] Both episodes begin by placing the characters

---

16. The division of 1 Kings 13 is adapted from Mead, "Kings and Prophets," 191–205. Mead reads 1 Kings 13 as two parallel panels spanning 13:1–19, 20–32, pairing vv. 1–10 with vv. 20–25a as I have here. However, rather than aligning vv. 11–19 with

in a specific location, indicated by a *qal* participle ('standing on the altar', 'sitting at the table'; vv. 1, 20). Both the man of God and the Bethel prophet 'cry out' (קרא) and deliver a prophetic oracle of judgment; in each instance, the oracle is preceded by the typical "thus says Yhwh" (vv. 2, 21), a phrase appearing only at these junctures in the chapter. The sign is given (vv. 3, 22) and summarily executed and the narrative portions each end with a threefold repetition of 'by the way' (בדרך; vv. 9–10, 24–25a).

As a whole, the chiasm spans Jeroboam's narrative and provides its major themes. In §A, Jeroboam is promised that he will reign as king over Israel. If conducted in obedience to Yhwh's word, that reign would become a sure house. In §B, Jeroboam, despite the promises of Yhwh, chooses to act in disobedience to Yhwh's word. He seeks to ensure the kingdom not on the basis of Yhwh's word but on the basis of instituting a new cult designed to unify the Northern Kingdom and set it apart from the Southern Kingdom (1 Kgs 12:26–33).[17] The prophetic word against the altar in

---

vv. 25b–32, as does Mead, I read vv. 11–19 and vv. 25b–32 as an envelope around the central panel vv. 20–25a. The envelope structure to this central panel can be diagrammed thus:

A "certain prophet, an old man, dwelling in Bethel" (v. 11)	"they reported it in the city in which the old prophet lived" (v. 25b).
The prophet hears of the man of God (v. 11).	The prophet hears of the man of God (v. 26).
[see v. 14 below; identification awaits initial encounter]	"It is the man of God who rebelled" (v. 26).
"Saddle the donkey for me." They saddled the donkey for him (v. 13).	"Saddle the donkey for me." They saddled it (v. 27).
The prophet "went . . . and found" the man of God (v. 14).	The prophet "went . . . and found" (v. 28).
"Are you the man of God who came from Judah?" (v. 14).	[see v. 26 above; identification made in initial encounter in v. 14 and so precedes the actions of the prophet in this part of the envelope]
Prophet brings man of God home alive (v. 15–18).	Prophet brings man of God home dead (v. 29).
Prophet's word: deceit (v. 18b)	Prophet's words to counter deceit: lament (v. 30) and confirmation of truth of Yhwh's word (v. 31–32).

The crucial observation in both readings, however, is that the core prophetic interactions of the man of God and Jeroboam (vv. 1–10) and the man of God and the Bethel prophet (vv. 20–25a) mirror one another.

17. 1 Kgs 12:26–33 repeatedly emphasizes Jeroboam's personal responsibility for the Bethel altar and cult: he made the altar, the calves, and the festival and appointed the priests. Having done all this against the law, vv. 32–33 thrice emphasizes that Jeroboam "went up to the altar," which he had made in Bethel in order to worship. It is in this

13:1–10 foretells the downfall of the very cult by which Jeroboam sought to establish his kingdom.

§B′ concerns obedience to Yhwh's word and provides crucial connections to the larger narrative. These connections will be explored momentarily. §A′ takes up the issue of the false cult and Jeroboam's dynasty. It is Ahijah's judgment oracle in which the concerns of §A (the promised rule and dynasty) and §B (the false cult) are conjoined.[18] Jeroboam's failure to walk in obedience to Yhwh's word while seeking to establish his kingdom has resulted in cultic failure, provoking Yhwh to anger and causing Israel to sin. It is Jeroboam's cultic failure that results in his loss of rule (1 Kgs 14:7–11, 15–16). Ironically, while God assured Jeroboam's rule, Jeroboam attempted to obtain its assurance by means forbidden him. By these forbidden means, the rule he sought to maintain is lost.

Returning to §B′, it too works within this same movement of royal and cultic establishment and then royal and cultic loss. It does so in a way that connects the narrative both to its immediate context of Jeroboam's reign and to the larger context of Northern and Southern Kingdoms, and, thus, a longer discussion is undertaken to demonstrate the powerful narrative connectors present in §B′.

§B′ contains the judgment oracle of the Bethel prophet against the man of God. In this oracle, the man of God is judged for only one reason—he has disobeyed Yhwh's word (v. 21). The prophet reminds the man of God, "Thus says Yhwh, 'You have disobeyed Yhwh's declaration, and have not kept the commandment which Yhwh your God commanded you.'" His disobedience to Yhwh's word is exactly what Jeroboam has acted out in 1 Kgs 12:25–13:10, and for which Jeroboam is subsequently judged (14:8). Certainly, the disobedience of the man of God has demonstrated itself in a way different from Jeroboam's disobedience: the man of God disobeys Yhwh regarding eating, drinking, and returning to his home, while Jeroboam disobeys Yhwh regarding how he is to conduct his reign. Both, however, act in disobedience to Yhwh's word. In this, the man of God from Judah stands as an analogous figure to Jeroboam. Both have disobeyed; both are judged.[19]

But the man of God stands as a figure of Jeroboam in a second way. The Bethel prophet pronounces a judgment on him: "your corpse shall not

---

context of covenant unfaithfulness that the oracle in 13:1–10 must be heard. Judgment against the altar is judgment against Jeroboam, who made the altar, and thus judgment against his dynasty, which is dependent on his covenant faithfulness.

18. See the previous note which explores the conjunction of cult and dynasty.
19. As detailed in Cohn, "Literary Technique," 34.

come to the grave of your fathers" (13:22). In the same way, Jeroboam is judged. Not only will his house face disaster; not only will every male of his house be cut off, but burial within the honorable confines of the father's graves will be denied to them (14:11, 13).[20]

Thus, the man of God figuring Jeroboam both in his disobedience and in his disposition shows that this prophetic interaction appears at this juncture in Jeroboam's narrative to depict Jeroboam's own fate. The prophetic word of 13:20–25a acts as a bridge, both reiterating the necessity of obedience (as has already been communicated to Jeroboam in 11:38–39), and foreshadowing the judgment for disobedience (as Jeroboam will soon learn in 14:1–18). And, as the man of God's death confirms the prophetic word against his disobedience, so Jeroboam can expect full accomplishment of the prophetic word against him and his house. In this way will YHWH's will be affirmed.

The fate of the man of God prophesied to him by the Bethel prophet also places him as a non-Jeroboam figure, connecting him to Abijah and (later) to Josiah. When the man of God dies, the sign is fulfilled in that he is not buried in his father's tomb. But the sign is mitigated in that he is buried in the Bethel prophet's own tomb. The Bethel prophet makes this provision for the man of God, recognizing the validity of his word against the Bethel altar. The Bethel prophet thus affirms the truth of the man of God's word and his integrity as a servant of YHWH.

The Bethel prophet returns the man of God to his town to mourn (ספד) for him and bury (קבר) him (13:29). The body is subsequently laid in the tomb and once again it is noted that he is mourned (ספד). Finally, after burying (קבר) him, the Bethel prophet instructs his disciples that, on his own death, they are to bury him (קבר) in the grave (קבר) where he is buried (קבר; 13:29–31).

Much is said here regarding mourning and burial. It is notable, then, that in just the next chapter the combination of mourning and burial reappears. In the midst of the judgment oracle against Jeroboam for his continued disobedience against YHWH's word, a respite is given to only one member of Jeroboam's family. His son Abijah will be the only one buried (קבר) and mourned (ספד) by Israel (14:13) because only in him does YHWH find something good. Later, his death precipitates exactly what Ahijah has prophesied: he is buried (קבר) and mourned (ספד; 14:18). Abi-

---

20. The concept of improper burial in the grave of one's fathers, particularly if wild animals tore the body, was a horror in the ancient near eastern culture. See *ANET* 538; M. Cogan, and H. Tadmor, *II Kings* (AB 11; New York: Doubleday, 1988) 107.

jah's death, like that of the man of God, attests to the validity of the prophetic word. The man of God is buried and mourned because his word of judgment against the Bethel altar is true; Abijah is buried and mourned to testify similarly to the truthfulness of Ahijah's word of judgment against Jeroboam.

Abijah's death, however, also speaks of mitigation such as received by the man of God. Just as the man of God's burial in the prophet's tomb mitigates the judgment of nonburial, so Abijah's burial mitigates the judgment of nonburial promised Jeroboam. In each case, recognition of prophetic ministry and recognition of good forestalls the full effect of judgment.

By the end of the bounded set of the four prophetic interactions in 1 Kings 11–14, Jeroboam has been promised a dynasty and received judgment against that same dynasty. The judgment occurs because he fails to obey YHWH's word. Prophetic word and sign judges both Jeroboam's cult (13:1–10) and dynasty (14:1–18). Because fulfillment of the signs involving the altar, the hand, and Abijah have all come to pass, this piece of historiography urges one to consider that the word against the cult and the dynasty will similarly fully come to pass.

Moreover, the word given the man of God by the Bethel prophet has analogously figured the man of God as Jeroboam and, as the fate of the man of God, so will Jeroboam's fate be. And, as the man of God has acted in obedience and thus been honored with burial and mourning, so will those (even of the house of Jeroboam) who are obedient or good receive similar honor. What counts in this case, according to Dtr's economy, is obedience over family or location in Northern or Southern Kingdoms.

The Reflection of the Bounded Set in the Larger History: Northern Kings and Josiah

The prophetic interactions in 1 Kings 11–14 can be considered as a unit. Structurally, linguistically, and thematically, they demonstrate the intertwining of key themes: ongoing rulership and cultic expression. Certainly, these themes are central to the continuing history of the Northern Kingdom. With little exception, each successive northern king is measured according to the paradigm of Jeroboam (1 Kgs 15:26, 30, 34; 16:13, 19, 26, 31; 2 Kgs 10:28–29; 13:2, 11; 14:24; 15:9, 18, 24, 28; 17:2). Additionally, the judgment oracles that are spoken against the northern dynasties of Baasha (16:1–7) and Ahab (21:17–24; see also 2 Kgs 9:7–10) are familially related to the original oracle spoken against Jeroboam's house (1 Kgs 14:7–11). For instance, in each oracle, judgment is rendered against the whole house of the scion, and that judgment is rendered in generalized terminology ("evil" or "calamity" will come against the houses of Jeroboam and Ahab; Yhwh will "sweep" or "consume" the houses of Baasha, Jeroboam, and Ahab), and each oracle reflects the judgment that "every male, both bond and free, will be cut off."[21] In this way, the fate of the Northern Kingdom is sealed by Jeroboam, whose influence and sin is replicated in successive rulers until the exile.

As 1 Kings 13 directs, and as explored in many studies, there is an obvious connection between Jeroboam's narrative and Josiah's narrative in 2 Kings 22–23. There, the king cited in the man of God's prophecy accomplishes the desecration and destruction of Jeroboam's northern cult. An interesting line of inquiry in this regard is the exploration of the signs that mark the bounded set of prophetic interaction as they appear in Josiah's narrative. That is, in §A of the bounded set, the sign is a torn mantle (ויקרעה) as a sign of the loss of kingdom (1 Kgs 11:30); when Josiah hears the words of the book which speak judgment against the kingdom because those words have not been heeded, he too tears his garment (ויקרע את־בגדיו; 2 Kgs 22:11). In §B of the bounded set, the sign of the broken altar signifies the actions that Josiah will take against the altar. Those actions are elaborated in 2 Kgs 23:15–20. Finally, the sign of nonburial in §§B′ and A′ is converted into both burial and mourning in recognition of the prophetic word of the man of God, and of Abijah's goodness. It is interesting, then, that the question of burial figures prominently in Josiah's narrative (2 Kgs 22:20, 23:30). Yhwh promises to gather him to his fathers to be buried in peace in recognition of the fact that he listened to Yhwh's word (*contra* the man of God) and repented (*contra* Jeroboam).[22] The glowing report of Josiah given by Dtr is lament and praise of Josiah after his death and for his great goodness (2 Kgs 23:25). Further exploration of the reappearance of the signs of the bounded set in Josiah's narrative may provide another means of demonstrating that he is presented as the king who wholly reverses Jeroboam's sins, accomplishing what no king before him was able to do. Historiographically, he serves as a bookend to Jeroboam, both reunifying the kingdom and putting an end to the northern cult.

---

21. For a fuller discussion of the familial relationship of the judgment oracles against northern dynasties, see my *Deuteronomist's Prophet: Narrative Control of Approval and Disapproval in the Story of Jehu (2 Kings 9 and 10)* (LHBOTS 478; New York: T. & T. Clark: 2007) 64–66.

22. Further discussion of this connection appears later in this paper under the discussion of the connection of Jeroboam's narrative to Solomon's narrative.

The Reflection of the Bounded Set in the Larger History: Solomon and the Southern Kingdom

What is not often considered in study of the prophetic interactions of Jeroboam's tale is how they relate to the *preceding* narrative. Illuminating connections suggest that Jeroboam-and-the-prophets historiographically function not only to outline the failures of the first northern king, or to set a paradigm for successive kings, or even to set the stage for 2 Kings 17 and its peroration on the fall of the Northern Kingdom. Further, Jeroboam's narrative historiographically functions not only to anticipate and glorify Josiah's actions. Rather, the narrative, standing as it does after Solomon, also speaks a word of judgment against Solomon and demonstrates the fate the Southern Kingdom can anticipate, should Solomon's failures remain unaddressed.

Solomon is not very different from Jeroboam in certain respects. In §A, the first prophetic encounter between Jeroboam and Ahijah, Ahijah calls Jeroboam to the same obedience to which Solomon was called. In 1 Kgs 2:2–4, 3:14, 6:12, and 9:4–6, Solomon is charged with obedience to the law, and his failure in 11:4–6, 10–11 is similarly connected to disobedience to the law. Like Jeroboam, he too is to do all that YHWH commands, to walk in his ways, to do what is right in his eyes, keeping YHWH's statutes and commands as David his father did.[23]

In §B, Jeroboam's cultic sins are encapsulated in his activity at the Bethel altar, and it is his cultic sin that is judged. Within Solomon's narrative, his cultic sins are uppermost and can be traced from his initial, to his final, acts. He begins in 1 Kgs 3:1–3 by marrying a foreign queen who leads his heart astray (11:1). The commencement of his reign is also marked by the fact that he first attends to his palace building project and *then* attends to the Temple project (3:1).[24] As a result, worship on the high places continues. He ends in 1 Kings 11 by multiplying foreign wives who lead him astray, by building temples to foreign gods, and by following these gods.[25] As for Jeroboam, Solomon's cultic sins become the epitome

---

23. Similar observations are found in D. W. van Winkle, "1 Kings XII 25–XIII 34: Jeroboam's Cultic Innovations and the Man of God from Judah" *VT* 46 (1996) 110–11.

24. The order of the projects in 1 Kgs 3:1 reverses the order in which they are related in 1 Kings 6–7. Ensconced in the negative connotations of the balance of 1 Kgs 3:1–3, this reversal also is a negative assessment by Dtr. Thus, the reign of Solomon begins with both overt and subtle references to his questionable priorities and obedience.

25. Solomon cannot be read as beginning well and only ending poorly. The narrative is replete with his failures, either implied or stated, demonstrating that, as great

of disobedience to the law (as defined in 1 Kgs 9:4–6 and expanded on in 11:1–11). Like Jeroboam, Solomon's cultic sins are judged by Yhwh (9:6–9, 11:11–13) with loss of dynasty and rule.

Given that Solomon and Jeroboam are similarly charged, similarly fail, and are similarly judged, the signs given Jeroboam by which Yhwh's judgment is affirmed also speak to the judgment given Solomon. The torn cloak assures the loss of Solomon's rule—indeed, it has already occurred. The broken altar, the man of God buried, and the death of Abijah all affirm the judgment against Jeroboam. But, parable-like, they also affirm the judgment against Solomon, including not only the current loss of rulership to his servant Jeroboam, but the future loss of the nation to exile (9:6–9). The prophetic interactions with Jeroboam affirm Yhwh's judgment to Jeroboam, and by extension they affirm Yhwh's judgment to Solomon (despite Yhwh's promise to David), and so should warn the Southern Kingdom. These prophets are prophets to the Northern Kingdom and, historiographically, to the Southern Kingdom as well.

The signs of the deaths of the man of God and Abijah are mitigated in §§B′ and A′. The man of God is buried honorably and mourned due to the recognition that he initially was obedient to Yhwh's word. Abijah's burial acknowledges his goodness (and perhaps obedience?). If such mitigation is present in Solomon's narrative, it is only proleptic: Yhwh's ongoing commitment to the Davidic covenant suggests such mitigation of judgment, but that mitigation remains future (1 Kgs 11:12–13; see also 11:36, 15:14; 2 Kgs 8:19).

The mitigation may also be considered proleptically in another fashion. Already in Solomon's narrative, Josiah is in view, for it is Josiah who reverses the cultic ills of Solomon.[26] Josiah's death and burial, as in the case of the man of God and Abijah, is accompanied by lament. Can Josiah's

---

as Solomon is, he is not perfect. His failures in the cultic realm are the central means by which Solomon is judged, but the narrative suggests similar disapproval in areas of his wisdom, administration, and politics. Several works take up this sort of reading; see C. Camp, *Wise, Strange and Holy: The Strange Woman and the Making of the Bible* (JSOTSup 320; Sheffield: Sheffield Academic Press, 2000); L. Eslinger, *Into the Hands of the Living God* (Sheffield: Almond, 1989); J. Hays, "Has the Narrator Come to Praise Solomon or to Bury Him? Narrative Subtlety in 1 Kings 1–11," *JSOT* 28 (2003) 149–74; I. W. Provan, *1 and 2 Kings* (NIBC; Peabody, MA: Hendrickson, 1995); Walsh, *1 Kings*.

26. Analogous patterning is particularly apparent in 1–2 Kings. Josiah, as reformer, is analogous to all reformers before him and yet conducts the reforms fully as his predecessors did not. His reforming work "eradicated the cultic sins of Ahab, Ahaz, Manasseh, Solomon, Jeroboam, and even the people of Israel. Josiah, then, is the one who corrects all the cultic sins from Solomon on, thus returning worship to the Deu-

death, then, be considered a mitigation to mirror the mitigation found in 1 Kings 11–14? If so, will Josiah's mitigation be enough to reverse the judgment and save the dynasty (especially given Yhwh's promises to David)?

Unfortunately, neither the mitigation of the burial of the man of God nor of the burial of Abijah accomplishes a reversal of judgment. Similarly, neither is Josiah's death such a complete mitigation. 2 Kgs 23:26–27 quickly precludes this possibility; Manasseh's sins are as Jeroboam's and Ahab's, and even Solomon's. Josiah's obedience, while it reforms the cultic sins of each of these individuals, cannot alter the judgment given to Solomon and confirmed to Manasseh. But in recognition of his goodness and obedience, like Abijah before him, he is buried and mourned.

Finally, to show that the prophet's words to Jeroboam are clearly also words to Solomon and the Southern Kingdom, one can consider the prophetic ministry throughout Kings. It is interesting to note that no prophets speak prophetic oracles prior to the interactions with Jeroboam. Certainly, Nathan does appear in the first two chapters of Kings, but he provides no prophetic words or oracles. No other prophets appear in the rest of Solomon's story (1 Kings 3–11). Yhwh does speak, but does so directly to Solomon in night visions (1 Kgs 3:5–15, 9:1–9), or without any prophetic mediation specified (1 Kgs 6:11–13, 11:11–13).[27]

Within Jeroboam's narrative, one prophetic word is given to a southern king when Shemaiah directs his oracle to Rehoboam (12:22–24). This oracle, however serves only to affirm that the events are Yhwh's judgment against Solomon. In this, Shemaiah only emphasizes what the bounded set proclaims: loss of kingdom follows cultic sin—in this instance, Solomon's cultic sins.

After Jeroboam's narrative and until the fall of the Northern Kingdom, the history adheres to a similar pattern as found in Solomon's narrative: no prophetic interaction or oracles are delivered directly to Judah. During that period, prophets interact with northern kings. On three of those occasions, prophets address northern kings with southern kings present or considered. In two of these references, Jehoshaphat is in attendance with a northern king, and it is the northern king who summons the prophet

---

teronomistic ideal realized at the completion of the Temple" (Wray Beal, *The Deuteronomist's Prophet*, 170; see Sweeney, *King Josiah*, 44).

27. That Yhwh speaks directly to Solomon may be another instance of ironically highlighting Solomon's failure: Yhwh foregoes a prophetic mediator and speaks to the great king directly. Solomon's failure is that the great king does not respond well even to Yhwh's own words!

and whom the prophet responds to and addresses (1 Kgs 22:1–38; 2 Kgs 3:11–19). The third reference is in 2 Kgs 17:13–14 and specifies that Yhwh warned Israel *and Judah* through his prophets. But one looks in vain for these prophets' speaking warning to Judah.

Yet there *is* such warning. It is found in the prophetic interactions in Jeroboam's narrative. They proclaim the certainty that all judgment against his dynasty and cult will come to pass. He is judged because he has not heard and obeyed Yhwh's word. In this light, these interactions answer Solomon's narrative, for Solomon, too, has neither heard nor obeyed Yhwh's word. His judgment will be as certain as Jeroboam's. This warning answers Solomon's narrative and also stands throughout the whole of 1–2 Kings as an indelible historiographical warning to the Southern Kingdom of that coming judgment.

From Jeroboam to 2 Kings 17, the Southern Kingdom is not directly addressed by prophets but receives prophetic warning through the words given Jeroboam. Once the Northern Kingdom falls, however, prophets again begin to address southern kings. Three kings are addressed (Hezekiah, Manasseh, and Josiah), and consideration of these prophetic words adds to the reflection on the historiographical presentation of the prophetic word in Kings.

Hezekiah is lauded as a great Deuteronomistic king (18:3–6) who enacts cultic reform such as not accomplished by any king before him. Following on the heels of the peroration on the fall of the Northern Kingdom which is a warning to the Southern Kingdom and in which cultic malfeasance is blamed for the fall, Hezekiah's reforms must raise the question whether those reforms are sufficient to avoid a similar fate for Judah. The first prophetic words Hezekiah receives reveal that Yhwh favors Hezekiah's reign and will sustain it in the face of foreign threat (2 Kgs 19:6–7, 20–34). Part of the reason Yhwh saves Jerusalem from Assyria is the old promise to David (19:34). A second series of prophetic words come to Hezekiah regarding his impending death (20:1, 4–6) and again promise deliverance from Assyria due to Yhwh's old promise to David (v. 6). Has Hezekiah's cultic reform been sufficient to set aside judgment? Is this reform, in which Hezekiah does what is right as David did (18:3), what fires the persistent prophetic pronouncement that Yhwh has remembered his covenant with David and will act on that covenant?

The third prophetic interaction with Hezekiah (20:16–18) returns to the prophetic theme of exile for Judah. Strangely, however, it does not predicate exile on cultic disobedience. Following so many prophetic words that do predicate exile on cultic disobedience, this word is striking. Is this new reason for exile intended to signal that, while exile will still occur, it will no longer occur for the familiar cultic reasons? Thus, has Hezekiah heeded the warnings cited in 1 Kings 17 and enacted cultic reform so that the weight of the prophetic warning throughout Kings has been set aside? Is exile now to be credited to a new impetus—that of Hezekiah's personal failure to trust Yhwh?

Of course, this is not the case, as the ensuing chapters reveal. But for a brief moment, the historiographical presentation of the prophetic word has raised the question whether the long-iterated words of judgment for cultic sin might indeed be set aside. The final two prophetic words negate any such possibility. Hope raised during Hezekiah's reign is subsequently undone by Manasseh's, whose cultic sins are worse than even Ahab's (21:3, 13). The prophetic word to Manasseh returns to the prophetic byline: Judah will fall due to cultic sin (21:10–15). It is Manasseh's sin that historiographically is cited as the irrevocable turning point to exile (23:26–27). Not even the third king to receive a prophetic word after the Northern Kingdom falls—righteous Josiah, whose cultic reforms are greater even than Hezekiah's (2 Kings 22–23)—can set aside the prophetic judgment proclaimed over Manasseh's rule. Huldah's prophetic word reiterates the familiar refrain, and Judah will be judged as was Israel for its cultic sins (22:15–17). Josiah receives only a personal mitigation in the face of Judah's impending destruction.

Conclusion

Much attention has been given to specific verses or events within Jeroboam's narrative. For instance, the reference to Josiah has drawn obvious attention to 2 Kings 23, while Ahijah's first oracle to Jeroboam has drawn attention to Jeroboam's rise as part of Yhwh's will. Similarly, Ahijah's oracle of judgment against Jeroboam has received attention for its continued appearance in the historiographical presentation of the Northern Kingdom. By focusing attention on the bounded set of the prophetic interactions within Jeroboam's narrative and drawing from that set an overarching prophetic message of the relationship of cultic sins to ongoing rule, one frames differently the question of Jeroboam's relationship to the larger history.

Similarly, by examining the bounded set in its relation to the preceding narrative of Solomon questions how that relationship can be considered. It appears that the prophetic interactions in Jeroboam's narrative speak not only to Jeroboam's own history, the history of the Northern Kingdom, or to the glorification of Josiah. They also speak to Solomon's narrative as parabolic answer to the questions—will the judgments spoken against Solomon truly be enacted? He has lost part of the kingdom to Jeroboam, but will the further judgments take place? If he (like Jeroboam) similarly sins, will he not be similarly judged, and will not that judgment take place as surely as Jeroboam's? The prophets of Jeroboam's narrative provide a resounding "Yes!" to these questions.

And, in this "Yes!" lies a historiographical warning that urges the Southern Kingdom as long as the Northern Kingdom lasts. Within the present form of the text, the prophets to Jeroboam are those that the south should heed. And, as the oracles of those prophets come to pass in the Northern Kingdom, Judah surely should hear their echo. But they do not and therefore, once the Northern Kingdom falls then (and only then) does YHWH begin to speak through his prophets to southern kings.

Solomon did not heed YHWH's direct words; will any king of the south heed YHWH's prophets? If so, he would show himself greater than Solomon. Only Hezekiah and Josiah heed and obey YHWH's prophets and, thus, are kings greater than Solomon. Yet, even their cultic obedience is unable to forestall the prophetic judgment spoken first to Solomon and then to Jeroboam and made inevitable in Manasseh.

Presumptuous Prophets Participating in a Deuteronomic Debate

K. L. Noll

Academe usually treats the Former Prophets as historiographical literature composed by ancient scribes eager to interpret the past in light of their own religious world view. Although this is a reasonable presupposition, it can be refuted from the evidence. This essay suggests that the scribes were not trying to preserve information about, or construct interpretations of, past prophetic figures, nor were they necessarily always expressing their own religious viewpoint. Neither the god that the scribes have constructed nor the prophets they have portrayed were intended to be taken as historically accurate or religiously useful.[1]

Like the Gemara, the Nevi'im mixed old sources and creative inventions, often revising sources beyond recognition or reliable recovery.[2] Also like the Gemara, the Nevi'im do not advance a religious message, but rather preserve the debates of many intellectuals, often with no adjudication of their differences. This analogy with the Gemara is useful but should not be pressed too far. The Nevi'im do not name the voices in their pages, as does the Gemara (albeit not always accurately). Instead, they are collected under a single named prophet in each book of the Latter Prophets, or conformed to the artificial chronological framework and

---

Author's note: This essay is an adaptation of "Neither Prophets nor History Writing in the Nebiim," which I presented to the Ancient Historiography Seminar at the meeting of the Canadian Society of Biblical Studies in Ottawa, May 25, 2009.

1. See also my "Deuteronomistic History or Deuteronomic Debate? (A Thought Experiment)," *JSOT* 31 (2007) 311–45; idem, "Is the Book of Kings Deuteronomistic? And Is It a History?" *SJOT* 21 (2007) 49–72.

2. I do not express a position on the composition of the Bavli; for entry into recent discussion with ample bibliography, see J. L. Rubenstein, *The Culture of the Babylonian Talmud* (Baltimore: Johns Hopkins University Press, 2003); L. Moscovitz, *Talmudic Reasoning: From Casuistics to Conceptualization* (Texts and Studies in Ancient Judaism 89; Tübingen: Mohr Siebeck, 2002); J. L. Rubenstein, ed., *Creation and Composition: The Contribution of the Bavli Redactors (Stammaim) to the Aggada* (Tübingen: Mohr Siebeck, 2005); R. Kalmin, *The Sage in Jewish Society of Late Antiquity* (New York: Routledge, 1999).

fictional narrative voice with which the Former Prophets have been structured. Also, the Nevi'im do not show deference to any religious authority because they were constructed when the proto-Masoretic Torah had not yet been publicly disseminated.[3] Predictably, many passages in the Nevi'im exerted normative authority over the various Judaisms that evolved in later times. Surprisingly, the Nevi'im also included passages that dissent from, or openly mock, early religious texts that later became biblical, such as Deuteronomy; and they go out of their way to present a god who is a caricature of the normal patron god known to the ancient Near East.

Noninductive Diviners and Biblical Prophets

Academe's usual treatment of the Former Prophets as historiographic literature derives from a misconception about narrative verisimilitude, which is especially evident with respect to the role of prophets. There is a gaping chasm between the social phenomenon of prophecy, as it occurred everywhere in the ancient Near East over a span of several thousand years, and the pale reflection of that phenomenon in the creative fiction of the Former Prophets. Ancient Near Eastern prophecy was performed by persons with a recognized status as noninductive diviners, whose roles were defined by the temple communities to which they were in most cases attached, and whose messages were treated in accordance with routine bureaucratic processes.[4] On occasion, a biblical narrative presents a situation familiar from the comparative data, such as the prophet who can see the divine council in 1 Kings 22, or the warriors who consult a diviner in 2 Kings 3. But these creative tales differ from the real-world situations of Mari or Neo-Assyria. A prophet in the Former Prophets is similar to actual ancient noninductive diviners as a television cop is similar to actual police investigators.

This misconception about verisimilitude plays a role in the widespread acceptance of Martin Noth's hypothesis, which depends to a significant degree on the allegedly historiographical motif of prophetic prediction-and-fulfillment.[5] However, the unrealistic god and the equally contrived

---

3. K. L. Noll, "The Evolution of Genre in the Hebrew Anthology," in *Early Christian Literature and Intertextuality*, part 1: *Thematic Studies* (ed. C. A. Evans and H. D. Zacharias; London: T. & T. Clark, 2009) 10–23.

4. M. Nissinen, "What Is Prophecy? An Ancient Near Eastern Perspective," in *Inspired Speech: Prophecy in the Ancient Near East: Essays in Honor of Herbert B. Huffmon* (ed. J. Kaltner and L. Stulman; London: T. & T. Clark, 2004) 17–37 esp. pp. 21–24; see also S. B. Parker, "Official Attitudes toward Prophecy at Mari and in Israel," *VT* 43 (1993) 50–68, esp. pp. 52–67.

5. M. Noth, *The Deuteronomistic History* (trans. J. Doull et al.; JSOTSup 15; Sheffield: JSOT Press, 1981) 68–74; Gerhard von Rad, "The Deuteronomic Theology

nature of the prophetic situations in many of these biblical narratives undermine the thesis. Rather than supporting Noth and his disciples, the prediction-and-fulfillment motif exposes the fictional intention of the Former Prophets. A survey of the Former Prophets demonstrates this thesis.

Simple Prediction-and-Fulfillment Formulas in the Former Prophets

Many prediction-and-fulfillment formulas are not sufficiently complex to play a part in any theological history. One can distinguish simple prediction formulas from complex types by the straightforward nature of the narrative results they achieve. The simple formulas are conventional components of an almost universal storytelling motif. They are distributed throughout the books of Joshua (for instance, Josh 3:5, 6:2–5, 8:1, 10:8, 11:6), Judges (for instance, Judg 6:14, 16; 9:20; 13:3), Samuel (for instance, 1 Sam 9:15–16; 2 Sam 12:14, 24:12–13), and Kings (for instance, 1 Kgs 17:4, 14; 20:13–14, 22, 28; 2 Kgs 4:16; 5:10; 7:1–2).

Each simple prediction is indispensable to its immediate context because it drives the plot, but only occasionally (such as Judg 9:20) does it become the point of its own story, much less the point of a larger, allegedly theological, history spanning four canonical books. For example, it is a narrative necessity that a man of god must establish his credibility by giving instructions or announcing promises that achieve results (for example, 1 Kgs 17:13–16, 2 Kgs 4:16–17), which prepares the reader for a plot complication (1 Kgs 17:17–24, 2 Kgs 4:18–37). That a narrator stresses the prediction's fulfillment in a summary statement does not constitute a theological message, unless one wishes to reduce the notion of "theology" to a meaningless level of common supernatural belief.[6] This would defeat, rather than defend, the thesis that the narrative intends to interpret the past from a specifically defined theological perspective. If one insists on calling these simple formulas historiography, the past they construct is nothing more than myth, a "past" that was reinvented as wondrous. Even

---

of History in I and II Kings," in *The Problem of the Hexateuch and Other Essays* (trans. E. W. Trueman Dicken; London: SCM, 1966) 205–21; W. Dietrich, *Prophetie und Geschichte: Eine redactions-geschichtliche Untersuchung zum deuteronomistischen Geschichtswerk* (FRLANT 108; Göttingen: Vandenhoeck & Ruprecht, 1972); E. Würthwein, *Studien zum deuteronomistischen Geschichtswerk* (BZAW 227; Berlin: de Gruyter, 1994) 80–92.

6. A peculiarity of religiously motivated biblical scholarship is a routine failure with respect to this rather obvious issue. For discussion of an alternative approach, see K. L. Noll, "Was There Doctrinal Dissemination in Early Yahweh Religion?" *BibInt* 16 (2008) 395–427.

that thesis is less than compelling because the prediction formulas are so mundane that the narrator often does not pause to underline their fulfillment (such as Josh 6:5, 20; Judg 13:3, 24; 1 Sam 9:15–17; 2 Kgs 20:5–6).

Complex Prediction-and-Fulfillment Formulas in the Former Prophets

In contrast to the simple formulas, the Former Prophets display about 20 or so (depending on how one counts) complex prediction-narrative clusters. Although there is no absolute distinction to be made between the simple and the complex, a prediction narrative can be viewed as complex if it has consequences that go beyond the immediate narrative context, or if its fulfillment complicates the story narrated by the scroll in which it is found. As such, the complex type often incorporates within it one or more of the simple formulas previously discussed.

The complex formulas can be grouped into three categories of variant narrative techniques and functions:

1. Predictions that are fulfilled exactly as predicted
2. Predictions that are fulfilled in an unexpected or confusing manner that possibly undermines the integrity of the prophet or the god (or both)
3. Predictions that are unfulfilled, or fulfilled in a manner that clearly undermines the integrity of the prophet or the god (or both)

Category 1

The first category might support an interpretation of the Former Prophets as theological history writing, though this can be disputed. Four texts are included in this category: Joshua's curse (Josh 6:26; fulfilled in 1 Kgs 16:34); Elijah's mass murder (2 Kgs 1:2–16; fulfilled in 1:17); Jehu ben Hanani's prophecy (1 Kgs 16:1–4; fulfilled in 16:12); and Manasseh's condemnation (2 Kgs 21:10–15; fulfilled in 24:2).

If a Deuteronomistic prophet is defined as one like Moses, who is able to foretell the future flawlessly while simultaneously affirming the central themes of Deuteronomy, including the need for Torah-obedience, uncompromising monolatry, a military ban for the peoples of "other gods," and a single temple for Yahweh's name, then each of these predictions *might be* interpreted as part of a hypothetical Deuteronomistic History, though difficulties remain.[7] The first (which is a curse, not a prophecy) is the least

---

7. For example, Deuteronomy does not use a cliché to describe the fulfillment of a prophetic promise, with the exception of Deut 9:5b, which appears to be a gloss, but even if it is original, it is is not able to bear the weight of being the model for the

compelling because manuscript variation at Josh 6:26 (the Greek includes a significant plus) and 1 Kgs 16:34 (lacking in Lucianic manuscripts) suggests that these were late glosses. The second, 2 Kgs 1:2–17, was not intended as history writing. While the story's literary merit is worthy of a genius such as Herodotus, it lacks the rhetorical markers of historiographic intention, especially the intrusion of first-person into the third-person narration, which would, for Herodotus, establish a faux critical distance. Most researchers view 2 Kgs 21:10–15 as part of a (nearly) final revision, not part of the original composition.[8] Likewise, 1 Kgs 16:1–4 seems to be a gloss dependent on the very late Masoretic version of 1 Kings 11–14, and thus also not part of the scroll's original narrative.[9] In sum, three of these are glosses, while the other is a fine Deuteronomistic parable, but hardly a history writing.

Category 2

The second group of complex prediction formulas is less consistent with the notion that the Former Prophets constitute theological history writing. I identify six (or eight, depending on how one counts) tales of this kind: Deborah's prophecy (Judg 4:6–9; fulfilled in Judg 4:15–23); oracles against the Elides (1 Sam 2:27–36; see also 3:11–14; fulfilled in 1 Kgs 2:27); Samuel's prediction of the king's customs (1 Sam 8:11–18; fulfilled in 1 Kings 3–10); Samuel's instructions to Saul (1 Sam 10:2–8; fulfilled in 1 Sam 10:9–11 and chaps. 11–16); Nathan's dynastic promise (2 Sam 7:11b–16; fulfilled in 1 Kgs 5–9, 15:4, etc.), with Nathan's condemnation of David's sin (2 Sam 12:7–12; fulfilled in 2 Sam 12:15–23 and chaps. 13–19); and Ahijah's prophecy to Jeroboam (1 Kgs 11:29–39; fulfilled in 1 Kgs 12[13]–14), with Ahijah's condemnation of Jeroboam (1 Kgs 14:1–18; fulfilled in 1 Kgs 15:29 and 2 Kgs 17:21–23).

The common element in this category is the creative use of prediction to *misdirect* the reader's attention, which later delights or baffles the

---

complex use of predictions-and-fulfillments in the Former Prophets (see M. Weinfeld, *Deuteronomy and the Deuteronomic School* [Oxford: Oxford University Press, 1972] 350–54). Given this lack, plus the open hostility Deuteronomy directs against prophets, it is a puzzle why anyone ever associated the prediction-and-fulfillment formulas in the Former Prophets with a hypothetical Deuteronomistic History.

8. F. M. Cross, *Canaanite Myth and Hebrew Epic: Essays in the History of the Religion of Israel* (Cambridge: Harvard University Press, 1973) 274–89; R. D. Nelson, *The Double Redaction of the Deuteronomistic History* (JSOTSup 18; Sheffield: Sheffield Academic Press, 1981) 27–28, 65–69.

9. S. L. McKenzie, *The Trouble with Kings: The Composition of the Book of Kings in the Deuteronomistic History* (VTSup 42; Leiden: Brill, 1991) 64–66.

reader. On a first reading of Judges 4, the "woman" mentioned in v. 9 refers to Deborah, but the introduction of Jael is a delightful O. Henry twist. Similarly, the reader expects Samuel to fulfill the judgment on Eli's house and is bewildered by the later revelation that a minor character plays that role (1 Sam 2:25–26; 8:1–3; 2 Sam 8:17; 1 Kgs 1:7–8; 2:27, 35). The instructions in 1 Sam 10:2–8 seem clear at first reading, so the reader is puzzled by the increasingly ambiguous fulfillment that unfolds, which results in the equally troubling judgment of Saul, in 1 Samuel 11–16. Yahweh's grotesque misinterpretation of the people's request for a king "like the nations" (1 Sam 8:1–10; see Deut 17:14) is followed by an accurate description of King Solomon in 8:11–18, which undermines the god's integrity and underscores the ambiguity that the narrator tries to convey in 1 Kings 1–10.

A creative twist on the motif of prediction-as-misdirection occurs in 2 Samuel 7, where Nathan announces that David's seed shall endure forever as a house (7:13a might be a gloss, since it breaks the waw-consecutive pattern in vv. 12b–13b). The prediction becomes more complex with the tale in 2 Samuel 12, so that a sword shall not depart from David's divinely favored house. By 2 Samuel 13–16, the reader has realized that it is Absalom who can fulfill all predictions simultaneously. Therefore, Absalom's divinely willed demise comes as a shock to the reader, for it indicates that Yahweh has failed (2 Sam 17:14). Meanwhile, Solomon, who is introduced ambiguously in 2 Sam 12:24–25, seems to fulfill the prophecy (1 Kings 5–9), yet the narrator's subtle undermining of Solomon's character serves notice that Yahweh is not a good judge of character and that the Davidic house might not endure "forever" (2 Sam 7:16; compare 1 Sam 2:30).

The complexity in most of these stories derives from revisions and supplementary expansions that can no longer be traced with precision. I doubt that the scribes who rewrote their received texts failed to realize that they were reducing Yahweh to a caricature and undermining the role of prophecy, nor do I deem it plausible to suggest that these scribes believed they were describing the past by deliberately altering their source-texts. They knew they were fictionalizing their sources, and they did not introduce rhetorical structures to convince the reader that their stories were accounts of a genuine past. They were not writing history and they were not writing theology (and they were certainly not writing theological history).

The tale of Rehoboam and Jeroboam illustrates the process of increasing complexity through scribal revision of a preexisting version. John Van Seters demonstrates that some version of 1 Kgs 12:32 was originally followed by 13:34–14:20, and the intervening material is part of a Hellenistic-era revision.[10] But that does not resolve all difficulties. Juha Pakkala views the story of the two golden calves in 12:26–33 as an addition to the story.[11] Similarly, 1 Kings 11 contains a variety of accumulations designed to make Solomon's sins weightier.[12] These are just the most obvious indications of revision, and it seems unlikely that any of us can unscramble this omelet with complete success.

The Old Greek (3 Kgdms 12:24a–z) is not necessarily the earliest version of this tale, but it is the earliest recoverable version.[13] Evil Rehoboam has become king, but Jeroboam had previously proven himself a capable man and "exalted himself to the kingship" (3 Kgdms 12:24b). A reader inclined to view Jeroboam as a legitimate fulfillment of Nathan's oracles (2 Sam 7:14b, 12:10) will be stopped by the blunt divine rejection (12:24g–n). (One might recall that Absalom should have fulfilled Nathan's oracles, but the reader's anticipation of this was defeated at 2 Sam 17:14. In this tale, Yahweh is an incompetent god.) Shemaiah predicts that Jeroboam will, nevertheless, rule ten tribes, and Rehoboam's foolishness fulfills the prophecy (12:24o–z).

The Masoretic chapters of 1 Kings 11–12 and 14 transform the original tale with no regard for the integrity (or possible historical accuracy) of the original. Shemaiah's role is reduced, and Ahijah's is expanded but not improved (11:29–39). The problem is not limited to Ahijah's inability to count to 12 (11:32, 35–36; contrast 3 Kgdms 12:24o; see also 3 Kgdms 12:24x and 1 Kgs 12:21 MT), for Yahweh makes a dynastic promise that the god of the Old Greek's Vorlage would never have offered, a promise that opens the future to a house of Jeroboam like the house of David (11:37–38a). This is shocking in light of Yahweh's prior promises to David. The promise seems to be snatched back by a later gloss in 11:38b–39

---

10. J. Van Seters, "The Deuteronomistic History: Can It Avoid Death by Redaction?" in *The Future of the Deuteronomistic History* (ed. T. Römer; Leuven: Leuven University Press, 2000) 213–22.

11. J. Pakkala, "Jeroboam without Bulls," *ZAW* 120 (2008) 501–25.

12. For the textual data (but a different conclusion), see P. S. F. Van Keulen, *Two Versions of the Solomon Narrative: An Inquiry into the Relationship between MT 1 Kgs. 2–11 and LXX 3 Reg. 2–11* (VTSup 104; Leiden: Brill, 2005) 202–37.

13. A. Schenker, "Jeroboam and the Division of the Kingdom in the Ancient Septuagint: LXX 3 Kingdoms 12.24A-Z, MT 1 Kings 11–12; 14 and the Deuteronomistic History," in *Israel Constructs Its History: Deuteronomistic Historiography in Recent Research* (ed. A. de Pury, T. Römer, J.-D. Macchi; Sheffield: Sheffield Academic Press, 2000) 214–57. For an alternative viewpoint, see M. A. Sweeney, "A Reassessment of the Masoretic and Septuagint Versions of the Jeroboam Narratives in 1 Kings / 3 Kingdoms 11–14," *JSJ* 38 (2007) 165–95.

(lacking in the Greek). With or without the gloss, the promise to Jeroboam complicates the portrait of the story's god by rendering the future contingent on Jeroboam's conduct and calling into question the deity's fidelity to David. The fact that the narrative portrays Jeroboam as an apostate does not alleviate the tension it has created, for he could have lived up to Yahweh's proposed deal. Although this late stage of the tale can be characterized as an awkward attempt to reduce Jeroboam to a Deuteronomistic villain (see also 1 Kgs 15:29, 16:1–4; 2 Kgs 17:21–23), it need not be viewed that way (especially, but not exclusively, because it creates a contingent future in contradiction to Deut 18:22).

At least half of these stories require the reader to distrust the god of the story. In places such as 1 Samuel 8 and 2 Sam 17:14, the author appears to be stressing the point, and it is missed only by those exegetes who presume, a priori, that the divine character is always intended to be in the right. The impious characterization of the deity implies that the tales are intended to be received as creative "thought experiments," much like the book of Job, in which an unreliable god enters into a frivolous bet with a divine underling, then later fails to admit what he has done when he confronts Job.

Unlike the book of Deuteronomy, which seriously exhorts the reader to believe in and obey its unattractive god, the narratives of the Former Prophets rarely present theological interpretations of a "genuine" god. Frequently, this version of Yahweh is a narrative necessity. The tales do not intend to present Yahweh as he would have been worshiped by the scribes who wrote these stories. These Yahwehs are fictions designed to probe the problems created by theism and, at times, to probe the implications of Deuteronomy's idiosyncratic theism.

Category 3

The last group of complex prediction formulas undermines the thesis that the Former Prophets constitute a Deuteronomistic History. Roughly 10 tales fit this category: David's divination at Keilah (1 Sam 23:1–13), the incompetent man of god at Bethel (1 Kings 13, 2 Kgs 23:15–20), tales of King Ahab and the prophets (1 Kgs 17:1–22:40; see also 2 Kgs 9:22–37), Elisha's prophecy concerning Moab (2 Kgs 3:4–27), Elisha's prophecy concerning Hazael (2 Kgs 8:7–15), Elisha's prediction of victory for Joash (2 Kgs 13:14–19, 25b), Jonah ben Amittai's prophecy (2 Kgs 14:25), Isaiah's prophecy concerning Sennacherib (2 Kings 19), Isaiah's predictions concerning Hezekiah and Babylon (2 Kgs 20:1–19), and the prophecy of Huldah (2 Kgs 22:14–20).

Undoubtedly, the tales of category 3 were designed as a "Deuteronomic Debate." A brief discussion of Deuteronomy is necessary, but I will not trace its literary evolution, which was complex. My thesis suggests only that these stories were formulated, in most cases ad hoc, in response to Deuteronomy's teachings about prophets.[14]

Deuteronomy constructs an artificial world in which the fictitious Moses anticipates the coming exile hundreds of years in the future (Deut 4:25–31, 28:64–68, 29:27, 30:1–10).[15] This is precisely the kind of prophetic activity that never occurred in ancient noninductive divination, for this sort of long-distant prediction was as useless as it was impossible.[16] The "genuine" gods of the ancient world did not know the future, for they were invented by flesh-and-blood priests and were therefore limited by the cognitive capacity (not to mention the real-world interests) of those priests.[17] But Moses and his god were different, or so says Deuteronomy, for they knew the future without contingency.

As a text, Deuteronomy could not hope to compete with flesh-and-blood prophets, so it took steps to exclude any possibility that it would ever have to compete with them. This scroll was designed to possess full authority over the community it tries to create.[18] Human power is spread over several offices with the scroll at the center of all decision making (16:18–18:22). Flesh-and-blood prophets are a potential threat to the scroll's authority because their words are beyond any text's ability to anticipate or control.

---

14. In this sense, the evolution of the Former Prophets is analogous to the concept of a rolling corpus (that is to say, a scroll that was randomly supplemented) in Jeremiah, where bits of text gave rise to ad hoc responses. For the concept as it is applied to Jeremiah, see volume 1 of W. M. McKane, *A Critical and Exegetical Commentary on Jeremiah* (2 vols.; ICC; Edinburgh: T. & T. Clark, 1986–96); R. P. Carroll, *Jeremiah: A Commentary* (OTL; Philadelphia: Westminster, 1986); and P. R. Davies, "Potter, Prophet and People: Jeremiah 18 as Parable," *HAR* 11 (1987) 23–33.

15. For the following discussion of Deuteronomy's rhetorical agenda, see K. L. Noll, *Canaan and Israel in Antiquity: An Introduction* (Biblical Seminar Series; London: Sheffield and Continuum, 2001) 277–78.

16. L.-S. Tiemeyer, "Prophecy as a Way of Cancelling Prophecy: The Strategic Uses of Foreknowledge," *ZAW* 117 (2005) 329–50.

17. For example, a "genuine" god, such as Dagan of Terqa, is uncertain about the outcome of battle operations and requires the king to send him updates (letters to the god) in M. Nissinen, *Prophets and Prophecy in the Ancient Near East* (with contributions by C. L. Seow and R. K. Ritner; ed. P. Machinist; SBLWAW 12; Atlanta: Society of Biblical Literature, 2003) 62–64 (#38); see also 2 Kgs 19:1, 14.

18. B. Levinson, "The Reconceptualization of Kingship in Deuteronomy and the Deuteronomistic History's Transformation of Torah," *VT* 51 (2001) 511–34 (esp. pp. 511, 520–23).

Deuteronomy could have attacked prophets in the manner of Ezekiel 13, Jer 23:9–40, or Zech 13:2–6, but it accomplishes a similar goal in a more subtle, and more successful, way. The scroll claims to affirm the dignity of the prophetic office by positioning Moses as the greatest of all prophets (34:10–12; see also 4:10–14; 5:5, 23–33) and by promising to send a prophet "like Moses" in the future (18:15–20). This domesticates prophecy to Deuteronomy's agenda, but the prophet-like-Moses will never arrive. Deuteronomy sets forth a stringent criterion for measuring prophetic validity, a criterion that no human could ever hope to meet and no Iron Age god ever did meet: to be a genuine prophet-like-Moses, one has to predict a noncontingent future (Deut 18:22).[19]

The rhetorical accomplishment of Deuteronomy is profoundly antiprophetic. Because its message is not esoteric, prophetic specialists are never needed to fathom its depths (Deut 30:11–14). (Contrast, for example, the treatment of Jeremiah 25 in Daniel 9.) Everyone can observe Deuteronomy's commands. Indeed, as readers of Deuteronomy, every generation is the generation who stood before Moses and who witnessed the giving of the commandments (5:1–5, 6:20–25, etc.). Real time is dissolved by this rhetoric, and Deuteronomy becomes the voice of Moses, the voice of Yahweh, for all times (Deut 4:2 and 13:1; note the twin roles of Yahweh and Moses, Deut 4:13–14, 5:22).

The scroll of Deuteronomy is the prophet-like-Moses for every generation. To ensure that no human will usurp this status, prophets must predict the future flawlessly (Deut 18:22) or risk condemnation as apostates if their "signs" are too successful (compare the prohibition against adding anything new in 13:1 with the grim attack on miraculous proof by would-be innovators in 13:2–6). Never has there arisen—and every seventh year this affirmation ought to be repeated (Deut 31:10–13)—a human prophet like Moses. This is Deuteronomy's deconstruction of the prophetic office.

---

19. Many researchers are unable to accept the plain sense of Deut 18:22. Representative is R. D. Nelson, who believes that 18:15–22 establishes a line of authoritative prophets, and the wait-and-see criterion "obviously points to an evaluation of long-term performance and general reputation rather than to any specific oracle about which judgment must be made immediately" (Nelson, *Deuteronomy: A Commentary* [OTL; Louisville: Westminster John Knox, 2002] 234–36, quoting p. 236). However, in the real world, it can be assumed that a prophet will predict future events accurately only 50 percent of the time, at best, and even that ratio is possible only if the prophet severely restricts the kind of prediction that is made. If the prophet attempts to increase the odds by formulating the prediction ambiguously, or by relying on probabilities, shrewd observers will realize that this prophet does not possess unusual insight and his or her reputation will collapse. Thus, Nelson's interpretation wrestles only with the text's surface and fails to inquire after the real agenda behind its very existence. This passage logically excludes strategies for rationalization of failure.

The narratives of category 3 mock Deuteronomy, and the polemic is missed only by those who prefer to strain out theological gnats while swallowing satirical camels. In seven cases, these tales underscore their dissent from Deuteronomy with an explicit "punch line" that evokes and ridicules Deut 18:22 and the god it implicitly defines.

1. David's divination at Keilah (1 Sam 23:1–13) demonstrates that a god can know future possibilities but cannot predict the future without contingency, because the future remains entirely contingent on human free action.
2. The tale of 2 Kgs 14:23–27 designates Jonah as "servant of Yahweh," and his prediction even conforms to the mechanical noncontingency of Deut 18:22. Despite these prophet-like-Moses credentials, Jonah serves a god who waives Deuteronomy's requirement for unswerving obedience by supporting an evil king.
3. Elisha's prediction to Hazael becomes, apparently, the motivation for the action that fulfills the prophecy (2 Kgs 8:7–15). In this case, the intention of Deut 18:22 is violated by a story that demonstrates the ambiguity of alleged "fulfillments."
4. The tale of 2 Kgs 13:14–19 describes a king who follows his prophet's instruction perfectly, only to discover that the prophet, though genuinely from Yahweh, has quite deliberately withheld from him information crucial to his own success.
5. In 2 Kgs 20:1–19, Hezekiah's free action reverses a noncontingent prediction of death. Isaiah's newly formulated promise of 15 years is not to be trusted because the god has just displayed his fickleness. Hezekiah shrewdly demands an immediate "sign," just as Mari's prophets were subject to authenticating divination (not miracles, of course, because these occur only in the realm of fiction). In the next scene, Isaiah's usefulness as a Deuteronomistic prophet is again undermined when he predicts, with suitable noncontingency, Babylon's despoiling of Jerusalem. He is brushed off by his king, who offers condescending piety while harboring the entirely realistic cynicism that the prediction is irrelevant to his own life.
6. During the expedition against Moab, Elisha's impressive prediction contains one key flaw: the free action of a Moabite king can, at the last moment, thwart the prediction of victory (2 Kgs 3:4–27).
7. Huldah predicts that King Josiah will die in peace (2 Kgs 22:14–20), but the tale provides an ironic fulfillment worthy of Herodotus: the king dies by the sword of a foreign king without declaration of war (2 Kgs 22:15–20, 23:29).

No two of these tales are alike, yet each undermines Deuteronomy's advice for discerning true prophecy by highlighting an aspect of reality that Deuteronomy failed to anticipate. The attentive reader concludes that prophecy is not a useful phenomenon even when it is genuine. How useful, in that case, was the great Moses, really? These tales are not Deuteronomistic; they are anti-Deuteronomic. They are not historical narratives but ad hoc fictional supplementations probing the intellectual challenges presented by Deuteronomy and its unattractive god, as are the remaining examples in 1 Kings 13, 17–22, and 2 Kings 19.[20]

One can only marvel at the sheer audacity of 1 Kings 13. A genuine prophet of Yahweh is able to predict that a king, whom he names, will appear hundreds of years in the future to attack the altar of Bethel (13:2). But this perfectly Deuteronomistic prophet is not able to discern the truth or falsehood of another prophet's pronouncement and pays for his incompetence with his life (13:11–24). Meanwhile, the second prophet is described as a liar but affirmed by the structure of the narrative as a genuine prophet of Yahweh (13:18b, 21–24). Could the story be constructed any more exquisitely to undermine the advice of Deut 18:22?

The narrative of King Ahab (1 Kgs 16:29–22:40) demonstrates that Yahweh is unreliable, his prophets are not to be trusted, and the advice of Deut 18:22 can destroy a king. A *mise-en-scène* appears in 1 Kgs 20:35–36. This prophet does not preach Torah "like Moses," nor does he predict the future so that his credentials can be confirmed in light of Deut 18:22. Rather, he commands someone to strike him in the face. When this word from Yahweh is quite reasonably *not* obeyed, the punishment is death. This type of prophecy is so alien from Deuteronomy's world view that no human can hope to escape the wrath of a capricious deity. So, too, will be the fate of King Ahab.

Ahab is introduced as a wicked king (16:30–33), but his wickedness is liturgical, not moral: he worships Sidon's god, Baʻal. With respect to morality, Ahab displays a selfish opportunism mixed with a capacity for Stoic commitment to royal duty. He is quick to seize stolen property that falls into his lap (21:16) but is willing to sacrifice his own property to protect the property of his subjects (20:1–12). King Ahab is no saint and has no intention of ever becoming a saint, but he is no fool, and the narrator displays a grudging respect for his character.

Elijah's performance on Mount Carmel puts an end to Ahab's flirtation with Sidon's god (18:20–40).[21] After this, Ahab interacts exclusively with

---

20. I have discussed 2 Kings 19 previously and will not do so here; see my "Evolution of Genre in the Book of Kings: The Story of Sennacherib and Hezekiah as Example," in *The Function of Ancient Historiography in Biblical and Cognate Studies* (ed. P. G. Kirkpatrick and T. Goltz; London: T. & T. Clark International, 2008) 30–56.

21. The characterization of Elijah is complicated. See McKenzie, *Trouble with Kings*, 61–100; and P. J. Kissling, *Reliable Characters in the Primary History: Profiles of Moses, Joshua, Elijah and Elisha* (JSOTSup 224; Sheffield: Sheffield Academic Press, 1996) 96–148.

prophets of Yahweh, though he apparently uses idols (21:26; perhaps idols of Yahweh or Asherah).[22] Jezebel is reduced to empty threats (19:1–3, 18). Ahab never becomes a saint, but confronted by Elijah, Ahab repents (21:27). Confronted by a nameless prophet with no prior record of prophetic accomplishment, Ahab becomes "resentful and sullen" (20:39–43; contrast the original messages in 20:13–14, 22, 28). The reader notes this key element in Ahab's characterization: a judgmental prophet with a proven record elicits repentance (however self-serving the repentance might be), but a judgmental prophet who seems genuine but lacks a proven record produces anxiety from the king. In neither instance does Ahab respond as he is about to respond to Micaiah ben Imlah.[23]

When the king of Israel suggests a splendid little war, Jehoshaphat of Judah recommends noninductive divination (22:5). Four hundred prophets announce victory, but Jehoshaphat seems suspicious (22:6–7). Does he suspect these 400 are false prophets? If so, his suspicion is mistaken. They are not false prophets. They have heard a genuine message from Yahweh (22:22). It happens to be a false message, but it is not a false prophecy.[24] In any case, it is normal procedure in the ancient Near East to test the prophecy, and for that purpose, the king of Israel is willing to summon another prophet (22:8).

Ahab claims to hate Micaiah ben Imlah because Micaiah never prophesies good but only evil (22:8). Some commentators interpret this to mean that the king views prophecy as a charade in which the prophet is expected to say what the king wants to hear.[25] One exegete calls the

---

22. The "idols" of 1 Kgs 21:26 are not Sidon's Baʿal (1 Kgs 16:31–32; 18:19–40; 19:18), but undefined Canaanite gods (see also 2 Kgs 17:12; 21:11, 21; 23:24). In this story world, prior to the time of King Josiah, many regard Yahweh as the henotheistic patron of a pantheon (see also Deut 10:17).

23. The discussion of Micaiah is modified from my "The Deconstruction of Deuteronomism in the Former Prophets: Micaiah ben Imlah as Example," in *Far from Minimal: Celebrating the Work and Influence of Philip R. Davies* (ed. D. Burns and J. W. Rogerson; LHBOTS 484; London: T. & T. Clark, 2012) 325–34. (An editor introduced a typographical error in the essay's first sentence. Please read 18:22, not 18:12.)

24. Oddly, many theologians dismiss the 400 as false prophets. For example, R. W. L. Moberly incorrectly interprets 22:22–23 to mean that the 400 lack moral integrity and even reads Yahweh's desire to deceive (22:20) as though it were a desire to warn the king that he has been deceived (*Prophecy and Discernment* [Cambridge Studies in Christian Doctrine 14; Cambridge: Cambridge University Press, 2006] 109–25, esp. pp. 119–20).

25. For example, B. O. Long asserts that the king is so blinded by personal hatred that he acts against his own interests (*1 Kings with an Introduction to Historical Literature* [FOTL 9; Grand Rapids: Eerdmans, 1984] 235–36). R. D. Nelson's interpretation is closer to what I will offer here, but Nelson also seems to regard Micaiah's status as

prophet Zedekiah (22:11) a "stooge for the crown" and asserts that the 400 prophets "voice conventional jingoistic support for royal policy," but this is eisegesis.[26] It was customary to propose a war and then perform divination, and an ancient reader is unlikely to have perceived the opening scene as anything but routine. Moreover, the king hates Micaiah because this prophet predicts evil, but he does not hate Micaiah because evil has befallen the king. Indeed, Ahab is alive and well, which indicates that any predicted evil has been, at best, slow to arrive. Perhaps there is no need to stand in dread of Micaiah, for he has been, at least from the perspective of Deut 18:22, a false prophet. The plain sense of 22:8 is that King Ahab is willing to seek Jehoshaphat's suggested second opinion, but he is unhappy with the only remaining means for this precaution because Micaiah has been an unreliable prophet.

There are several additional details that demonstrate Micaiah's unreliable status. First, the king's judgmental integrity is confirmed when, later, he must indignantly remind Micaiah of his duty to speak only the truth (22:16). This implies that the king perceived each of Micaiah's previous evil messages to be false prophecies. From the king's perspective, Micaiah's sudden agreement with the 400 implies that he is uncharacteristically speaking a good word for the king *and* characteristically performing the role of a false prophet, for the shrewd king of Israel realizes that good news from this particular prophet is bad news for the king, which in turn contradicts the good news he has received from the reliable 400. Thus, 22:18 is the king's exclamation of relief, knowing that Micaiah has not, after all, stepped out of his typically false character. Micaiah does not dispute the king's description of their past encounters (22:16, 18), so the reader can be certain on this point: Micaiah has been speaking evil, and the king has been perceiving it to be false. Why? The obvious answer is that this king is impressed by prophets with a record of accurate prediction. Micaiah lacks that record.

A second narrative detail undercuts the reader's confidence in Micaiah. A royal servant warns Micaiah that 400 verdicts are on record, but Micaiah responds with indignation (22:13–14). At first, the reader is inclined to be impressed with Micaiah. Yet, at the close of the story, at least half of Micaiah's prediction is left unfulfilled: the prophet Zedekiah has not, so far as the reader knows, fled to an inner room (22:25). The battle did not result

---

a genuine prophet to be beyond question and therefore views the king's conduct with suspicion or surprise (*First and Second Kings* [Int; Atlanta: John Knox, 1987] 145–53).

26. W. Brueggemann, *1 and 2 Kings* (Smyth & Helwys Bible Commentary; Macon, GA: Smyth & Helwys, 2000) 267–76, esp. pp. 268–69.

in some kind of disaster overcoming the city in which Zedekiah resides, nor does the command from the king of Aram imply that the battle ever will escalate to that level (22:31). This demands a reassessment of Micaiah's indignant response to the king's servant (compare Jer 28:15–17). Does Micaiah really speak only what Yahweh tells him, or does Micaiah protest too much? Micaiah's vision of 22:17, if genuine, contradicts Micaiah's prediction of 22:25. If the reader believes that Micaiah speaks the truth in the former (and 22:36 supports this supposition), there is no alternative but to conclude that he functions as a false prophet (as defined by Deut 18:22) in the latter.

It is clear that the ancient author expected the ancient reader to ask whether Micaiah has been a false prophet. Genuine prophets have a record. Micaiah apparently has none. Do not stand in dread of him, says Deut 18:22, and the king of Israel does not stand in dread of Micaiah. He would have ignored Micaiah but for Jehoshaphat's desire for a second opinion, and there is nothing in the text to suggest that this is the kind of king who would ignore genuine prophecy. Moreover, at least part of Micaiah's prediction seems to be false. Should the reader assume the entire prophecy was false? This is possible because the arrow that strikes the king of Israel was shot randomly (22:34), but the possibility raises a dilemma. For if Micaiah's vision of the divine throne was a lie, then perhaps the 400 prophets are liars as well (in spite of their apparent previous record of accuracy). If so, King Ahab never stood a chance, for Yahweh does not reveal anything to him by means of any prophets at all, but merely lets the king go off to battle and certain death. There is nothing in the text to suggest that these 400 think of themselves as anything but genuine. Zedekiah is indignant in 22:24, and nothing in the text causes a reader to doubt Zedekiah's integrity. These 400 prophets are not merely telling the king what he wants to hear. If they are genuine, then Yahweh is a liar. If Micaiah is genuine, then Yahweh is a liar. Only if Micaiah's prophecy is fully false can the 400 be viewed also as false. Which solution is the one desired by the story itself?

After the king's challenge, Micaiah tells a new story (22:17, 19–23), one so absurd that it surely condemns him to the status of false prophet—or does it? "Yahweh," says Micaiah, "has given a lying spirit into the mouth of all these your prophets" (22:23). Yahweh wants the king to die. Moreover, Yahweh permitted the false prophet, Micaiah, to see a vision of this divine conspiracy. Put yourself in the king's sandals for a moment. If Micaiah's claim about the vision is true, then he should *not* have told the king about it. Therefore, if the king chooses to believe Micaiah, he is compelled to believe that Yahweh himself has tried *and failed* to deceive the king, because this formerly false prophet has confessed the genuine divine ruse. In other words, if the king believes Micaiah, then he also believes that Yahweh is incompetent. You are in the king's sandals. Is it reasonable to think your divine patron is incompetent? We have seen already that King Ahab is presented by the text as shrewd. He is also a man who will respect genuine prophecy. In this case, he has 400 reasons to believe that Micaiah's evil message differs not at all from Micaiah's prior evil messages.

King Ahab makes the only proper decision (22:26–27, 29). Micaiah has no credibility. He has been, in the past, a false prophet, and on this occasion he announces a vision that, if true, he should not have announced at all. Therefore, the vision seems to be false and the king is right to dismiss it as such. Thus, in this story, the king of Israel is not defeated by his own hubris. He is defeated by an ingeniously deceptive god who chooses a false prophet to speak a true message that is articulated in such a way that the king is compelled to reject it as false.

The plot of this complex story works *because* the reader is aware of the idea that a genuine prophet foretells the future without contingency and a false prophet does not. That idea is expressed in Deut 18:22 and exposed in this story as false. Yet, the scribe who penned Micaiah's tale has gone to an extreme rarely observed. Not only does he craft a tale in which the genuine prophets speak a divine lie while the false prophet speaks the truth, but he has also structured this surprising story so that Deuteronomy's criterion of noncontingent prophecy is, ironically, upheld. The deity has manipulated the human characters so that nothing remains contingent on human choices. The very god who promised to alter his judgment against Ahab's life (21:28–29) later changed his mind but made use of prophets whose status Ahab was unable to measure (20:41–43; 22:15–28a). King Ahab was the victim of a deliberately deceptive deity (21:19; 22:37–38).[27] There can be no doubt that the story of Ahab emerged through a process of revisions and supplementations to a more basic original narrative;

---

27. Würthwein (*Studien zum Deuteronomistischen Geschichtswerk*, 181) makes a reasonable argument that the battlefield scene exposes the king of Israel as a coward who endangers his vassal, Jehoshaphat, to save himself. However, this king presumes the 400 are genuine and Micaiah is not. In the ancient Near East, it was appropriate to take precautions in the light of a bad omen. Because Jehoshaphat is represented in the story as a vassal, his life is not as valuable, and it was not uncommon for a king to establish a substitute (or "scapegoat") to face these circumstances. In this fictional tale, the king of Israel is characterized not as despicable but as appropriately cautious in light of a bad omen, albeit an improbable one.

therefore, it seems likely that the scribe who made these extensive revisions expected the reader to view this god as a repulsive, fictional thought experiment.

Conclusion

The Bavli tells a story about R. Eliezer, who disagreed with an assembly of rabbis over a point of Halakhah (*Bava Metzi'a* 59b). Through miraculous signs, Eliezer tried to convince the others to see things his way. He caused a carob tree to be uprooted, but the rabbis said that Halakhah is not determined by a carob tree. Likewise, Eliezer made water flow backward and the walls of the synagogue unstable, but the rabbis would not change their mind. Finally, R. Eliezer called on the god of Israel, who spoke from the sky, announcing that Eliezer is right. But the rabbis retorted that Torah is not in heaven (Deut 30:12). Thus, they effectively reduced their own deity to one conversation partner among many and, so the story continues, this god in his heavens laughed and said, "My children have defeated me." In this tale, Halakhah is determined by community consensus and not divine revelation.

Bava Metzi'a 59b echoes the hostility toward prophecy expressed by both Deuteronomy and the Former Prophets. Like the latter, the Gemara's aggadic literature often constructs fictional narratives as thought experiments, probing various difficulties with theism, such as the problem of divine revelation. The two anthologies of literature differ only in the degree to which the storyteller is willing to undermine conventional piety. In this sense, Deuteronomy exerted greater influence on the rabbis than did the anti-deuteronomic tales of the Former Prophets. Especially in cases in which the religious satire was too penetrating, rabbinic piety responded by misreading the plain sense of the Former Prophets. For example, the rabbis could not stomach the radical implication of the Micaiah story. Therefore, they tamed this story by treating Zedekiah and the 400 as false prophets and Micaiah as a trustworthy representative of their god (*b. Sanh.* 89a–b). This aggressive misreading of the text's plain sense remains common even in modern scholarship, but modern scholarship would do well to remember that piety was not universal in the ancient world.

My thesis has been that the Nevi'im were not intended to serve as historiographic literature or authoritative religious literature. They do not attempt to preserve information about real prophets. They frequently revise sources or invent freely in such a way that the reliability of preserved sources is undermined. And they do not teach, proclaim, or defend a particular version of the Yahweh religion. These writings suggest theological problems and possibilities for an elite group of educated readers, but the texts were not intended for dissemination among common Yahweh worshipers and, in fact, were not circulated until quite late, so that most pre-Hellenistic Jews never knew the Nevi'im existed. When public dissemination of these scrolls began (no earlier than the Ptolemaic period and possibly much later), literate Jews brought their own presuppositions to the texts, insisting that they be viewed as sacred, thus limiting what the texts were permitted to "mean."[28]

The notion that the Former Prophets add up either to an interpretation of the past or to a coherent theological message derives from a mistake. It derives from the Bible's 2,000-year status as a revealed "Word of God," an artificial status that has nothing to do with the text but has nevertheless motivated religious readers to find history or theology, or both, where none exists.

---

28. Noll, "The Evolution of Genre in the Hebrew Anthology."

Prophecy Influencing History: Dialogism in the Chronicler's Ahaz Narrative

Paul S. Evans

The Ahaz account in the book of Chronicles (2 Chronicles 28) is an intriguing pericope that serves as a striking example of the freedom with which the Chronicler (hereafter, Chr)[1] reworked his putative Vorlage, 2 Kings 16.[2] Recognition of Chr's reliance on the Deuteronomistic History (hereafter, DH) has aided the interpretation of Chronicles enormously and allowed interpreters to understand better Chr's unique message by focusing on how the book of Chronicles differs from his Vorlage. Deviations of this sort often are understood as the result of Chr's intentional editorial activity and directly related to his ideology. However, in some cases appeal to Chr's ideological reworking of his Vorlage is not able to explain Chr's *Sondergut* fully.[3] In Chr's Ahaz narrative, we find such a case.

When Chr's Ahaz account is compared with the account in 2 Kings 16, considerable differences are apparent. In fact, at first blush the two accounts seem more dissimilar than similar. However, a comparison of the structure/outline of the narrative reveals that Chr was influenced heavily by his Vorlage even here.[4] Both contain a very similar regnal resume, and describe war between Judah, Ephraim, and Aram; Edomite conquests of

---

1. By "the Chronicler," I mean the author(s) of the book of Chronicles.
2. Of course, Auld and Ho argue for a common source behind both Chronicles and the DH rather than a theory of dependence of the former on the latter. See A. G. Auld, *Kings without Privilege: David and Moses in the Story of the Bible's Kings* (Edinburgh: T. & T. Clark, 1994); idem, "What Was the Main Source of the Books of Chronicles?" in *The Chronicler as Author* (ed. M. P. Graham and S. L. McKenzie; JSOTSup 263; Sheffield: JSOT Press, 1999) 91–99; C. Y. S. Ho, "Conjectures and Refutations: Is 1 Samuel XXXI 1–13 Really the Source of 1 Chronicles X 1–12?" *VT* 45 (1995) 82–106.
3. As G. N. Knoppers (*I Chronicles* [AB 12; New York: Doubleday, 2004], 131) writes, "Some of this additional material may be attributed to the author's interpretation or theological reworking of his biblical sources, but much of it cannot be."
4. Both Japhet and Dillard point out that the structure is basically parallel, even if the details differ tremendously. See S. Japhet, *I and II Chronicles: A Commentary*

Judahite lands; Ahaz's appeal to (and monetary gift to) Assyria for aid; Ahaz's cultic offenses; and an explicitly negative evaluation of Ahaz's reign. But despite the structural parallels, each of these sections are augmented, supplemented, or transformed in considerable ways in Chronicles.

It is the contention of this study that Chr did not make these changes out of whole cloth and that these divergences are due to the tensions he perceived within his sources. Two perspectives that illuminate probable reasons for many of the divergences between Chr's Ahaz narrative and that of his Vorlage are evident. First, it appears that his changes often begin with textual clues in 2 Kings 16, which lend themselves to his purposes. Second, many of the more perplexing changes become explicable if we understand Chr to be in dialogue not only with 2 Kings 16 at this point but also the book of Isaiah. Others have acknowledged the possibility that Chr had access to Isaiah when rewriting his history of Israel; however, it is the position of this essay that this suggestion has not been examined sufficiently.[5]

There is good indication that Chr had access to the book of Isaiah, probably in its canonical form. In 2 Chr 32:32, Chr cites the 'vision of Isaiah, son of Amoz' (בחזון ישעיהו בן־אמוץ) as a source for his information on Hezekiah, which Chr says is located in "the book of the Kings of Judah and Israel" (2 Chr 32:32). It is well known that Isaiah 36–39 is nearly identical to 2 Kings 18–20 and it appears that Chr was aware of a relationship between the book of Isaiah and Kings.[6] The Chronicler refers

---

(OTL; London: SCM / Louisville: Westminster John Knox, 1993) 896; R. B. Dillard, *2 Chronicles* (WBC 15; Waco, TX: Word, 1987) 220.

    5. W. Johnstone (*1 and 2 Chronicles* [2 vols.; JSOTSup 253–54; Sheffield: Sheffield Academic Press, 1997] 2:180) actually argues that Chr presupposes not only Dtr's history but the account in the book of Isaiah as well. H. G. M. Williamson (*1 and 2 Chronicles* [New Century Bible Commentary; Grand Rapids: Eerdmans / London: Marshall, Morgan, & Scott, 1982] 348) also mentions in passing the possibility that the Chr was influenced by the book of Isaiah. He writes, "This latter point in particular is in line with, and may have been derived by the Chronicler directly from, the interpretation of the same event in Isa. 7." Japhet denies the likelihood of this. See Japhet, *I and II Chronicles*, 899. Regarding the divergences from his Vorlage in Chr's Ahaz narrative, Dillard suggested that "the writer appears to have been elaborating and interpreting the events reported in the parallel history in accord with some other sources at his disposal; one can only speculate regarding the nature of these additional materials" (*2 Chronicles*, 220). This is similar to the position of the present essay, except that Isaiah (rather than empty speculation) is considered to be another source/voice through which Chr is interpreting his Vorlage.

    6. W. M. Schniedewind, *The Word of God in Transition: From Prophet to Exegete in the Second Temple Period* (JSOTSup 197; Sheffield: Sheffield Academic Press, 1995) 216.

to this source as "the vision (חזון) of Isaiah," which is the natural title of the canonical book of Isaiah because the editorial incipit reads, 'The vision of Isaiah son of Amoz' (בחזון ישעיהו בן־אמוץ). Because editorial superscriptions of this sort are late accompaniments to prophetic books, if not some of the very last additions, Chr's awareness of this title indicates his knowledge of the canonical book already in its edited form. The Chronicler also references Isaiah in 2 Chr 26:22 as being the author of the history of Uzziah, a king under whose reign the book of Isaiah claims the prophet ministered (Isa 1:1). Of course, many doubt whether Isaiah actually served during Uzziah's time, probably especially due to Isaiah 6 being understood as the prophet's call narrative, which occurred when Uzziah died (Isa 6:1).[7] In fact, were it not for the superscription of the book, no one would think that Isaiah served during Uzziah's regency, which strengthens the supposition that Chr had access to the book of Isaiah.

In fact, 2 Chr 32:32 connects "the scroll of the kings of Judah and Israel" to the book of Isaiah, and "the scroll of the kings of Judah and Israel" is explicitly referred to in the Ahaz account (2 Chr 28:26). The Chronicler only refers to this source in this exact way three times in the book of Chronicles,[8] making the connection here quite significant.

These references to the book of Isaiah invite the interpreter to view Chr in dialogue with Isaiah.[9] Therefore, this study will examine the relationship between 2 Kings 16, Isaiah 7, and 2 Chronicles 28, drawing on Bakhtin's ideas of dialogism. C. Mitchell has made a good case for Chronicles being a type of "early exemplar of the novel" and, therefore, for understanding Chronicles as intrinsically dialogic as it responds to the utterances of other works/voices.[10] Following her lead, this study will examine Chronicles as a response to the voice ideas of both the DH and Isaiah. Supposing that Chr was familiar with both the DH and the book of Isaiah, it seems likely he would have seen the potential for these texts/ ideas to quarrel. Bakhtin suggests that ideas are physically "embodied" by an author, and that the author "hears" the dialogical interaction through

---

7. E.g., H. Wildberger, *Isaiah 1–12* (trans. T. H. Trapp; CC; Minneapolis: Fortress, 1991) 3; R. E. Clements, *Isaiah 1–39* (New Century Bible Commentary; Grand Rapids: Eerdmans, 1980) 8.

8. 2 Chr 25:26, 28:26, and 32:32.

9. I do not mean to suggest that Isaiah was the author of the entire book, or even the portions under discussion in this essay, but will refer to Isaiah periodically as either the implied author of these narratives and/or originator of the oracles.

10. C. Mitchell, "The Dialogism of Chronicles," in *The Chronicler as Author* (ed. M. P. Graham and S. L. McKenzie; JSOTSup 263; Sheffield: JSOT Press, 1999) 311–26.

these idea-images.[11] That Chr heard the voice ideas of both Dtr and Isaiah regarding Ahaz's reign does not mean that he merely repeated the material in both (that is, repeated the dialogues known to him), but that he played upon their potential for conflict and dialogue by creatively reworking them into his Ahaz narrative. Rather than viewing Chr as attempting to harmonize the data, we could envision him as placing these ideas at intersections of dialogical conversation, where he saw fit. Thus, he is not privileging one over the other (that is, prioritizing Isaiah over the Deuteronomist [hereafter, Dtr][12] or vice versa), nor is he attempting to replace either text,[13] but instead he answers their dialogue, making room for us to hear the variety of voices in his narrative.

Of course, several other explanations have been offered to explicate the differences between Chr's Ahaz account and that of his Vorlage. However, sometimes explanations determining the purpose of Chr's Ahaz account substitute for real explanations of the specific changes he appears to make from his Vorlage. For instance, H. G. M. Williamson has compared 2 Chronicles 13, when Jeroboam was king in Israel at the time of the schism, with Chr's Ahaz narrative and has argued compellingly that, in the latter, Chr purposed to reverse the situation between the Northern and Southern Kingdoms as presented in the former, and leave both nations in a similar situation of military defeat and exile.[14] Like Jeroboam, Ahaz makes molten images for worship (2 Chr 13:8, 28:2) and worships false gods (2 Chr 13:8–9; 28:10–16, 23).[15] Furthermore, Ahaz even closes

---

11. M. Bakhtin, *Problem of Dostoevsky's Poetics*, 90. Bakhtin wrote of Dostoevsky that he heard "both the loud, recognized, reigning voices of the epoch, that is, the reigning dominant ideas (official and unofficial), as well as voices still weak, ideas not yet fully emerged, latent ideas heard as yet by no one but himself, and ideas that were just beginning to ripen, embryos of future worldviews" (ibid.).

12. By "Dtr," I mean the author(s) of the books of Joshua–Kings.

13. T. Willi, *Die Chronik als Auslegung: Untersuchungen zur literarischen Gestaltung der historischen Überlieferung Israels* (FRLANT 106; Göttingen: Vandenhoeck & Ruprecht, 1972) 56–66, 88; P. R. Ackroyd, "The Chronicler as Exegete," *JSOT* 2 (1977) 21; B. S. Childs, *Introduction to the Old Testament as Scripture* (Philadelphia: Fortress, 1979) 646–47; R. K. Duke, "A Rhetorical Approach to Appreciating the Books of Chronicles," in *The Chronicler as Author* (ed. M. P. Graham and S. L. McKenzie; JSOTSup 263; Sheffield: Sheffield Academic Press, 1999) 109. Contra M. A. Fishbane (*Biblical Interpretation in Ancient Israel* [Oxford: Clarendon, 1988] 381–82), who suggests that Chronicles is attempting to replace the DH.

14. H. G. M. Williamson, *Israel in the Books of Chronicles* (Cambridge; New York: Cambridge University Press, 1977) 114–18; idem, *1 and 2 Chronicles*, 343–50.

15. Japhet notes that the sins of Jeroboam (which Williamson equates with the sin of Ahaz and his molten images to Baalim) is to be distinguished from Canaanite worship in both Dtr's and Chr's views (*I and II Chronicles*, 898).

the temple (2 Chr 28:24), making Abijah's words to Jeroboam claiming orthodoxy for the South (2 Chr 13:11) null and void. Also, at the time of the schism, the South was obedient to a prophet, whereas, in 2 Chronicles 28, the North is obedient to the prophet Oded. In other words, Chr casts Ahaz in the same form as Jeroboam and makes way for the possibility of the unification of Israel by presenting both nations as in similar situations (defeated and partially exiled).

Williamson's argument depends in part on the assumption that Chr supposed that his audience would understand the Northern Kingdom to be exiled at the end of the Ahaz narrative. As is well known, Chr does not narrate the fall of the North as does Dtr (2 Kings 17, 18:9–12). While Judah is clearly narrated as having suffered a partial exile, with captives exiled to Damascus (2 Chr 28:5), Samaria (2 Chr 28:8), and Edom (2 Chr 28:17), there is no explicit mention of an exile of the North. Acknowledging this reality, Williamson believes the exile of the North is implied two chapters later in the invitation that Hezekiah makes to the "remnants who escaped from the hands of the kings of Assyria" (2 Chr 30:6). Williamson argues that, because Hezekiah's invitation occurs in the beginning of his reign, Chr understood the destruction of Samaria and the Assyrian exile of Israel to have occurred during the reign of Ahaz.[16] Of course, in the DH, the fall of Samaria occurs during the reign of Hezekiah and not of Ahaz (2 Kgs 18:9–12). In fact, since the exile of Samaria occurs early on in Hezekiah's regency,[17] it does not follow that Chr is dating this event to the time of Ahaz just because the "remnants" of the exile are mentioned relatively early in Hezekiah's reign.[18] Because most believe that Chr assumes that his readership had knowledge of the DH, this explanation seems tenuous. Nevertheless, many commentators have largely agreed with Williamson's analysis.[19]

---

16. Idem, *Israel in the Books of Chronicles*, 117.

17. As the siege begins the 4th year of Hezekiah's reign and Samaria is taken in his 6th year (2 Kgs 18:9–10).

18. In the DH, this is relatively early in his reign as no other events are narrated until Hezekiah's 14th year (2 Kgs 18:13). If those who would emend 14th to 24th year are correct, the 4th year of his reign appears quite early indeed. See M. Cogan and H. Tadmor, *II Kings: A New Translation with Introduction and Commentary* (AB 11; Garden City, NY: Doubleday, 1988) 228; E. R. Thiele, *Mysterious Numbers of the Hebrew Kings: A Reconstruction of the Chronology of the Kingdoms of Israel and Judah* (Chicago: University of Chicago Press, 1951) 118–40.

19. E.g., S. L. McKenzie, *1–2 Chronicles* (Abingdon Old Testament Commentary; Nashville: Abingdon, 2004) 334; Dillard, *2 Chronicles*, 219; S. J. de Vries, *1 and 2 Chronicles* (FOTL 11; Grand Rapids: Eerdmans, 1989) 366.

While Williamson's observations regarding parallels between 2 Chronicles 13 and 2 Chronicles 28 are helpful in understanding the purpose of the overall presentation of Ahaz and North-South relations in 2 Chronicles 28, in other respects their explanatory power is lacking. Williamson fails to explain all the differences in Chr's account of the war between Judah and Israel and Aram (such as their working independently against Judah rather than as a coalition), leaving him to posit an alternative account of that war to which Chr had access.[20] Thus, in some instances, such as the success of Israel and Aram against Judah in Chronicles, Williamson defends Chr's historicity by speculating that if the Syro-Ephraimite alliance was able to besiege Jerusalem, then they must have had widespread military success in other areas of Judah to allow them to carry out their siege plans.[21] In other words, these divergences are partially explained because they reflect historical reality. However, due to the clear purpose in Chr's account, Williamson also concedes that we can clearly see Chr's own hand in 2 Chronicles 28 and that many of the divergences from 2 Kings 16 may be attributed to Chr's own creative contributions to the narrative.[22]

Seeking to explicate the differences between Chr's Ahaz account and his Vorlage, other scholars have attended to the differences in Chr's account of the war. Regarding Chr's presentation of the military campaigns of Israel and Aram against Judah as separate and independent campaigns (contrary to their acting as a coalition in 2 Kings 16), R. Dillard has suggested that this change was due to the Chr's desire to present the Northern Kingdom in a positive light, which meant he had to omit their alliance with Aram due to the biblical polemic against foreign alliances.[23] However, both the prophet Oded and the people themselves explicitly state that the North is living in sin and rebellion against Yahweh (2 Chr 28:10, 13). Only at the point where they listen to the prophet and confess their sin are they portrayed positively. Therefore, their being in an alliance with Aram previously would not be a problem for Chr's presentation, but would fit with their current circumstance of "sin and guilt" (להסיף על־חטאתינו ועל־אשמתינו; 2 Chr 28:13). One must seek after another reason for Chr's presenting Israel and Aram as independent threats.

Sara Japhet views the story of the North's military success against Judah and their subsequent return of Judahite prisoners as *not* serving Chr's ob-

---

20. Williamson, *1 and 2 Chronicles*, 344, 346.
21. Ibid., 345.
22. Ibid., 344, 346.
23. Dillard, *2 Chronicles*, 221. E.g., 2 Chr 16:2–9, 19:1–2, 22:3–6, 25:6–10. Other instances of biblical condemnation of foreign alliances can be seen in 2 Kgs 17:4; Hos 12:2; Isa 30:1–7; 31:1, 3; Jer 37:6–8; 46:25; Ezek 29:6–7.

jectives in his portrayal of Ahaz because the military oppression of Ahaz's Judah (necessary in light of his wickedness) is contradicted in it.²⁴ Therefore, she views the pericope as derived from one of Chr's other sources and entertains the possibility that Chr is relating different events from those referred to in 2 Kings 16, because there must have been many such military conflicts between these nations at that time that were not mentioned in Kings.²⁵ Be this as it may, historically, neither Japhet nor Williamson explains why Chr *chose* to present Israel and Aram as independent military threats rather than as a coalition.²⁶

While Williamson is probably correct in seeing a connection between 2 Chronicles 13 and 2 Chronicles 28, and scholars' recognition that Chr is purposefully heightening the wickedness of Ahaz in his narrative *vis-à-vis* Dtr's presentation is undoubted, these insights do not further explicate many of the specific changes Chr makes in order to achieve his goals. While acknowledging the tremendous value of the contributions of these scholars, as mentioned above, this study seeks further explanation for Chr's divergences from his 2 Kings 16 source by recognizing his dialogue with both Dtr and the book of Isaiah.

In order to explore the dialogue that Chr responds to and perpetuates, this study will briefly examine the Ahaz narratives in both Dtr and Isaiah and then scrutinize Chronicles in order to understand Chr's presentation of Ahaz. The benefit in viewing Chronicles as in dialogue with both Kings and Isaiah will hopefully be evident in terms of insightful exegesis and may even suggest something in terms of actual sources employed.

Ahaz and the Deuteronomist

In the DH, the presentation of Ahaz begins with his regnal resume, which emphasizes his cultic offenses, fronting their description with a reference to his "passing his son through fire" (2 Kgs 16:3) and sacrificing offerings on the high places (2 Kgs 16:4).²⁷ Following the delineation of his cultic offenses, the siege of Jerusalem by Pekah and Rezin is tersely narrated and concludes with a statement that their attack was unsuccessful (2 Kgs 16:5).²⁸ In this narrative, Aram and Israel clearly act in concert as

---

24. Japhet, *I and II Chronicles*, 900.
25. Ibid., 899.
26. Keeping in mind that all historiographic accounts are selective. After all, if these events were historical, Dtr chose *not* to recount them for his own purposes.
27. Something that previous Judahite kings did not do (only the people were said to have done this; Cogan and Tadmor, *II Kings*, 186).
28. The exact meaning of these statements is unclear because one (ויצרו על־אחז) normally indicates a siege, but the other (ולא יכלו להלחם) seems to indicate that they

a coalition in their military campaign against Judah (2 Kgs 16:5). Also, in the context of this military crisis, Edom is said to have made gains at Judah's expense.[29]

In response to this military crisis, Ahaz then appeals to Tiglath-pileser of Assyria for aid and sends a gift/bribe (שחד) to encourage Assyrian action on his behalf (2 Kgs 16:8). However, there is no explicit negative comment regarding his appropriation of temple treasures.[30] If one examines other instances of Judean monarchs in the DH who act similarly, the lack of negative comment is consistent.[31] Asa draws on the temple riches to bribe the Arameans in 1 Kgs 15:16–22 but is assessed positively in direct statements by the narrator.[32] In 2 Kgs 18:15–16, Hezekiah dips into the temple treasuries in order to secure salvation from the Assyrian threat, yet is not criticized for this and is held up as a model king.[33]

---

were unable to mount an attack. See ibid.

29. Most scholars read אדם for ארם in this verse, arguing that the misreading (and introduction of Rezin's name) comes from 2 Kgs 16:6 into v. 5. See ibid.; V. Fritz, *1 and 2 Kings* (trans. A. Hagedorn; CC; Minneapolis: Fortress, 2003) 342; J. Gray, *1 and 2 Kings: A Commentary* (OTL; Philadelphia: Westminster, 1970) 632.

30. H. Tadmor and M. Cogan ("Ahaz and Tiglath–Pileser in the Book of Kings: Historiographic Considerations," *Bib* 60 [1979] 491–508) have argued that the term 'bribe' שחד "bears negative connotations" and is used in the Ahaz narrative to criticize the king (p. 499). However, the same term is used of Asa, despite the fact he is characterized positively by Dtr.

31. E. T. Mullen ("Crime and Punishment: The Sins of the King and the Despoliation of the Treasuries," *CBQ* 54 [1992] 231–48) has examined instances in which kings seek to survive a military threat through the offering of temple and palace treasuries. He concludes that the account of the despoliation of the treasuries functioned to show the king was being punished for failing to remove the high places—though he notes Hezekiah as an exception (p. 247). However, his view is difficult to accept because various kings who despoiled the treasuries are evaluated differently by the narrator, with some said to have done right in Yahweh's eyes (e.g., Asa). Also the exception of Hezekiah seems enough not to "prove the rule" but break it. N. Na'aman ("The Deuteronomist and Voluntary Servitude to Foreign Powers," *JSOT* 65 [1995] 37–53) has examined these narratives and emphasizes the different circumstances of these kings with some being robbed of treasures (Rehoboam, Amaziah, Jehoiachin), some voluntarily handing over treasure (Asa and Ahaz), and others attempting to avert a threat to Jerusalem (Jehoash and Hezekiah). Na'aman criticizes Mullen's study, concluding that it is doubtful that "these notices consistently serve as a part of the 'punishment' for numerous rulers who failed to remove the high places" (44 n. 18).

32. Still, M. Cogan (*1 Kings: A New Translation with Introduction and Commentary* [AB 10; Garden City, NY: Doubleday, 2001] 402) suggests that it "was likely viewed negatively by Dtr, though this is not specifically stated." In the later book of Chronicles, Asa is characterized negatively (2 Chr 16:1–12), but, interestingly, no explicit connection is made with this negativity and the appropriation of temple treasures.

33. Who "trusted in Yahweh the God of Israel and after him or before him there was no one like him among all the kings of Judah" (2 Kgs 18:5). Interestingly, while

While, unlike Hezekiah and Asa, Ahaz *is* characterized negatively by the narrator (2 Kgs 16:2–4), this criticism is not explicitly linked to his appropriation of temple monetary resources. In fact, the comparison of the accounts of these three kings in the DH would seem to suggest that appropriating the temple treasuries was not necessarily a deplorable action. In fact, Ahaz's actions could be understood as heroic, because by them he is defending Jerusalem and his people.[34]

Ahaz had not done what was right in God's eyes (2 Kgs 16:2), yet, despite the Deuteronomistic tendency for good things to happen to good kings and bad things to bad kings, the result of Ahaz's plea to Assyria appears to break this law of retribution. The text notes that "the king of Assyria listened to him" (2 Kgs 16:9)[35] and quickly took care of Ahaz's enemies. One could hardly hope for a better result. From one perspective, Ahaz's political move proved flawless.

The text then describes Ahaz going to Damascus (to meet with the Assyrian king) and his duplication of the Aramean altar in the Jerusalem temple (2 Kgs 16:10–11). The temple innovation is usually seen as a negative mark on his reign. However, given Dtr's lack of explicit comments[36] denouncing his temple reform, it is possible to read even this portion of the text as reflecting positively on Ahaz.[37]

---

appropriating temple treasuries is never explicitly judged negatively, when Hezekiah shows the Babylonians the non-temple treasuries of Judah, Isaiah levels an extremely negative oracle in response, implying that this action was very wrong. C. T. Begg ("2 Kings 20:12–19 as an Element of the Deuteronomistic History," *CBQ* 48 [1986] 27–38) has drawn attention to the fact that Judean kings who despoil the temple are never explicitly evaluated for their actions, nor "is anything directly said about their evoking retribution from Yahweh . . . [but] Hezekiah's action [of showing the treasures to the Babylonians] does call for a divine response" (p. 33).

34. W. Brueggemann (*1 and 2 Kings* [Smyth & Helwys Bible Commentary; Macon, GA: Smyth & Helwys, 2000] 494) sees Hezekiah's similar actions as positive because "Hezekiah, good king that he is, wants the occupying troops of the empire removed." Na'aman ("Voluntary Servitude," 44) has observed that in the DH "the payment of treasure under threat of siege may have been described in a non–critical tone." Similarly, B. O. Long (*2 Kings* [FOTL 10; Grand Rapids: Eerdmans, 1991] 129) suggests that such payment of treasures was merely "a strategy to relieve military pressure on Jerusalem and to preserve Judah's independence" and not capitulation.

35. A common meaning of the idiom שמע אל is 'to obey' (with אל Gen 28:7, Exod 6:9, Josh 1:17, and 1 Kgs 12:15), which could be implied, making the result of his plea even more shocking in light of his wickedness.

36. Earlier criticisms of the king included Ahaz's passing his son through the fire and sacrificing on the high places, but nothing about his temple innovations.

37. Some commentators view the innovations as (in reality) neutral, or motivated not by syncretistic motives but by attempting to update the 'fashion' of the Jerusalem

In conclusion, we could understand the "voice idea" of Dtr's Ahaz pericope in the following way. Ahaz's cultic offenses (2 Kgs 16:3–4) result (in a good Deuteronomistic fashion) in his being attacked by Aram and Israel (2 Kgs 16:5–6).[38] Bravely, he takes the extreme measure of sacrificing the riches of the temple (which the king had rights and access to) to appeal to the dangerous Assyrian king, Tiglath-pileser (2 Kgs 16:7–8). As a result of his heroism in that regard, the Assyrian king grants his request and delivers Ahaz from his enemies (2 Kgs 16:9). After his salvation experience, he celebrates by renovating the temple and installing a new and improved altar.[39] The orthodox nature of the reform is implied.[40] First, the priest Uriah (a known supporter of Isaiah the prophet; see Isa 8:2) concurs with the temple reform and carries it out, and second, Ahaz's son, Hezekiah, does *not* purge the temple of this new altar, though he even destroys an ancient Mosaic cultic appurtenance (2 Kgs 18:4).[41] Ahaz's officiating at the sacrifice[42] is in line with the precedent of David (2 Sam 6:17–18) and Solomon (1 Kgs 8:63); accordingly, in light of this precedent, these actions should not be viewed as negative. While most commentators[43] view the story of Ahaz's temple renovations as presenting the king in a negative light, it is possible to view them otherwise.

---

temple. Cogan and Tadmor note that "Syrian art and architectural styles" were widespread at the time. See Cogan and Tadmor, *II Kings*, 193.

38. Note the clear Hebrew expression (אז), which begins 2 Kgs 16:5 and explicitly connects the military crisis to his offering of sacrifices on the high places.

39. The problem of the original altar's small size is even mentioned in the text. 1 Kings 8:64 notes that it was too "small" (קטן) for the offerings. Ahaz's altar solved this problem with its larger (הגדול) proportions (2 Kgs 16:15). See J. G. Taylor, *Yahweh and the Sun: Biblical and Archaeological Evidence for Sun Worship in Ancient Israel* (JSOTSup 111; Sheffield: JSOT Press, 1993) 129.

40. As Gray points out, Yahwistic practice is implied, and the sacrifice described on the altar is "a *locus classicus* for sacrifice in the Temple" (*1 and 2 Kings*, 636).

41. Taylor draws attention to the fact that Hezekiah did not tear down Ahaz's altar and suggests it is because Hezekiah was sympathetic to Ahaz's solar Yahwism implied by the altar and Ahaz's sun dial (Taylor, *Yahweh and the Sun*, 164–72).

42. As Cogan and Tadmor point out, "these were inaugural, not everyday, sacrifices" (*II Kings*, 189).

43. Cogan and Tadmor argue that Dtr "recorded this narration in full to bolster his indictment of King Ahaz, whose apostasy he set out in the introduction to the king's reign, vv. 1–4. Ahaz's innovations, by no means idolatrous or syncretistic, are criticized, it would seem, because they upset the order of the Temple as established by Solomon" (*II Kings*, 193). Even in this observation, it is interesting to note that it is by no means clear that the innovations are wrong because they "upset" Solomon's order, as nothing to this effect is mentioned in the text.

Ahaz and the Prophet Isaiah

The Ahaz narrative in the book of Isaiah begins with a summary statement that Israel and Aram had allied themselves against Ahaz of Judah (Isa 7:1). In combination with 2 Kings 16, most biblical historians argue from this text that Aram and Israel formed a "Syro-Ephraimite" alliance against Assyria, which opposed Judah because Ahaz would not join in their cause.[44] This military crisis sets the context for the following story, which narrates a confrontation between the prophet Isaiah and the Davidic king, Ahaz. Isaiah brings unsolicited oracles of encouragement (Isa 7:4–9) to Ahaz, presumably before his appeal to Assyria.[45] Isaiah predicts that the Syro-Ephraimite coalition will actually come to nothing (Isa 7:7) and that Ahaz has nothing to fear (Isa 7:4). Isaiah belittles the kings (Rezin and Pekah) of these enemy nations, suggesting that they, and their capital cities, do not have the legitimacy of Ahaz and Jerusalem.[46] Isaiah cautions that Ahaz must believe (אמן) if he is to be established (אמן), perhaps alluding to the Davidic promise in 2 Sam 7:16 of the Davidic line's perpetuity (that it be "established [אמן] forever").[47]

The narrative continues with Isaiah offering a sign to Ahaz to encourage his trust in the oracle.[48] Ahaz is pictured as refusing to listen to the prophet and refusing the generous offer of a "sign à *la carte*." Therefore, Ahaz is famously given the sign of Immanuel. Whether the sign is a promise of salvation or of judgment has been fiercely debated.[49] Without entering deeply into the debate here, we hold that, because the sign is given in response to Ahaz's unbelief, it seems logical that it would be a threatening sign of judgment.[50] Though the sign includes the assurance that the two kings now plaguing Ahaz will be destroyed (Isa 7:16), the following verse (Isa 7:17) makes clear that days of trouble are ahead for the Davidic monarchy at the hands of the king of Assyria. Whether it was originally a

---

44. J. Begrich, "Der syrisch–efraimitische Krieg und seine weltpolitischen Zusammenhänge," *ZDMG* 83 (1929) 213–37.
45. Clements, *Isaiah 1–39*, 79.
46. Wildberger, *Isaiah 1–12*, 300.
47. Ibid., 302.
48. Though some have suggested that there should be a break between Isa 7:9 and Isa 7:10 indicating a different time and locale for this pericope (e.g., Kaiser), with Wildberger (ibid., 287) we hold that "the sign is clearly connected with the message delivered to Ahaz in vv. 4–9: Signs never have meaning in and of themselves, but only as they are connected with a message from Yahweh."
49. See Wildberger (*Isaiah 1–12*, 279–80) for bibliography regarding the debate.
50. Ibid., 313.

salvation sign, with vv. 17–25 being a late addition, or not, is irrelevant here. The final form of the text clearly portrays difficult times for Ahaz's Judah at the hand of Assyria.

What is also interesting about the judgment oracles following the sign of Immanuel is the insect imagery used in Isa 7:18. A close look at this text is necessary.

> On that day Yahweh will whistle for the fly that is at the ends of the streams of Egypt, and for the bee that is in the land of Assyria.

It is curious that Egypt and Assyria are mentioned together, because historically they never allied together against Judah and, in Ahaz's day, Egypt was not a threat at all. Also, the (scarab) beetle is the normal insect image for Egypt—not the "fly."[51] Seeing this difficulty, some have emended the text to make sense of it, suggesting that Egypt and/or the fly imagery was added secondarily.[52] However, as the text stands, both are mentioned and seem to anticipate trouble for Ahaz from both north (Assyria) and south (the ends of the streams of Egypt). Finally, the oracles conclude with a picture of a time of devastation for Judah, where the countryside is impoverished ("silver" to "thorns," Isa 7:23), invaded by enemies ("bows and arrows," Isa 7:24), unfertile (Isa 7:25), and uncontrolled (Isa 7:25).

Ahaz and the Chronicler

Keeping in mind the distinctives of the Ahaz narrative in both the DH and in the book of Isaiah, this study will now examine Chr's Ahaz account and search for the reasons behind its distinctiveness. As previously noted, Chr's reworking is quite comprehensive. Even in Chr's regnal resume of the king, there are significant changes. First, unlike Dtr, which simply states that Ahaz "walked in the ways of the kings of Israel" (2 Kgs 16:3) it is said that he also made molten images for the Baalim. Second, Chr changes Dtr's note (2 Kgs 16:3) that Ahaz made his son pass through the fire to an assertion that Ahaz "burned" his "sons" (plural) with fire.

---

51. M. Lubetski, "The Land Named for an Insect," in *Thinking towards New Horizons: Collected Communications to the XIXth Congress of the International Organization for the Study of the Old Testament, Ljubljana 2007* (ed. M. Augustin and H. M. Niemann; BEATAJ 55; Frankfurt am Main: Peter Lang, 2007) 103–12; M. Lubetski, "Beetlemania of Bygone Times," *JSOT* 91 (2000) 3–26.

52. Wildberger suggests that the original text did not mention Egypt or the fly imagery, asserting that the reference to Egypt was not in the original text but only added later in the time of Seleucid and Ptolemaic times (*Isaiah 1–12*, 322). Clements suggests that the fly and bee imagery were original, but both referred to Assyria (*Isaiah 1–39*, 90).

While scholars debate what was meant by Dtr's note, Chr removes the ambiguity and interprets the act as being nothing less than child sacrifice and states that Ahaz subjected more than one son to the pagan act. Third, Chr remarks that Ahaz made sacrifices in the valley of the son of Hinnom (2 Chr 28:3). Regarding Ahaz's idol worship, it appears that Chr interpreted Dtr's criticism of Ahaz sacrificing on the high places (2 Kgs 16:4) as worship of idols/foreign gods.[53] While perhaps historically incorrect, it is obvious that Chr used the text as a springboard for his expanded description of Ahaz's wickedness in the regnal resume.[54]

The Condemnation of Appropriating Temple Treasuries

Contrary to 2 Kings 16, the appropriation of temple funds in Ahaz's appeal to Assyria is explicitly condemned in Chr's version, perhaps out of concern for cultic purity and the sanctity of the temple (which Chr emphasizes more than Dtr).[55] It is quite possible that Chr's change in despoliation notices evinces an attempt to impose limitations on royal privileges regarding the temple.[56] This concern may be in dialogue with the voice idea of the day that the ruler had authority over the temple and its

---

53. In line with the later Deuteronomistic view of high places. See I. W. Provan, *Hezekiah and the Books of Kings: A Contribution to the Debate about the Composition of the Deuteronomistic History* (BZAW 172; Berlin: de Gruyter, 1988).

54. The increased emphasis on his sin regarding high places can be seen in 2 Chr 28:25, where it is referenced again and explicitly said to involve the worship of other gods. Perhaps this may have been influenced by Isaiah 7, which refers to all the "hills" being covered with "briers and thorns" (Isa 7:25). If the "briers and thorns" were interpreted by Chr as a reference to being cursed in some way, then this may have led him to see the "high places" as fulfilling this prophecy. Ahaz's idolatrous worship on the "high places" was effectively cursing the "hills" of the country.

55. This has been highlighted by many studies. See G. N. Knoppers, "'The City Yhwh Has Chosen': The Chronicler's Promotion of Jerusalem in Light of Recent Archaeology," in *Jerusalem in Bible and Archaeology: The First Temple Period* (ed. A. G. Vaughn and A. E. Killebrew; SBLSymS 18; Atlanta: Society of Biblical Literature, 2003) 307–26; N. Dennerlein, *Die Bedeutung Jerusalems in den Chronikbüchern* (BEATAJ 46; Frankfurt am Main: Peter Lang, 1999); P. C. Beentjes, "Jerusalem in the Book of Chronicles," in *The Centrality of Jerusalem: Historical Perspectives* (ed. M. Poorthuis and C. Safrai; Kampen: Kok Pharos, 1996) 15–28; M. Selmen, "Jerusalem in Chronicles," in *Zion, City of Our God* (ed. R. S. Hess and G. J. Wenham; Grand Rapids: Eerdmans, 1999) 43–56; and I. Kalimi, *An Ancient Israelite Historian: Studies in the Chronicler, His Time, Place and Writing* (SSN 46; Assen: Van Gorcum, 2005) 125–39.

56. In another article, I have suggested this possibility, arguing that Chr's explicit statements condemning this sort of temple despoliation, his negative characterization of the offending monarch (contrary to the king's characterization in the DH), and his omissions of temple despoliation notices all reveal the negative disposition of the book of Chronicles in this regard and his desire to limit royal control over temple treasuries

treasuries, as evidenced in the Persian practice of the "king's chest" which was a tax-collection device where part of the temple income was diverted from the sanctuary and handed on to the ruler.[57] In order to counter this idea, Chr quarrels with it by limiting even a Davidic king's privileges in regard to the temple treasuries. This concern can be seen in the deletion of Hezekiah's analogous actions in 2 Chronicles 32 in order to present that monarch in a positive light.

Ahaz's Temple Innovations as Worship of Aramean Gods

As we have seen, Chr presents Ahaz as worshiping Aramean gods after he appeals to Assyria. This is contrary to 2 Kings 16, which presents even Ahaz's reproduction of the Aramean altar in Jerusalem as meant for use in orthodox worship of Yahweh.[58] Why then did Chr view Ahaz as worshiping Aramean gods? Even at this point, Chr may have been following the lead of his Vorlage. First, the fact that Ahaz saw the Aramean altar may have suggested to Chr that Ahaz was participating in Aramean worship while there. After all, on what other occasion would Ahaz have viewed the altar, if he was not present at a cultic worship service? Second, 2 Kgs 16:10 suggests that Ahaz spent significant time in Damascus. Ahaz was there long enough to view the Aramean altar and send plans back to Jerusalem for the priest to have an identical altar constructed there. What is more, Dtr asserts that the construction of the altar was completed *before* Ahaz returned to Jerusalem (2 Kgs 16:11). The Chronicler probably understood this to mean that Ahaz was absent from Judah for an extended period of time. No other king of Israel or Judah is presented in the DH as abdicating his capital for any length of time, making this a unique episode.

In an ancient Near Eastern mindset, to dwell in a new land meant there was no opportunity to worship the god of the old land. Even in 2 Sam 26:19, when David is on the run from Saul, this understanding is reflected in David's speech when he complains "they have driven me out today, so that I cannot have a share in Yahweh's possession, saying, 'Go serve other

---

(P. S. Evans, "The Function of the Chronicler's Temple Despoliation Notices in Light of Imperial Realities in Yehud," *JBL* 129 [2010] 31–47).

57. J. Schaper, "The Jerusalem Temple as an Instrument of the Achaemenid Fiscal Administration," *VT* 45 (1995) 528–39. See A. Lemaire ("New Aramaic Ostraca from Idumea and Their Historical Interpretation," in *Judah and the Judeans in the Persian Period* [ed. O. Lipschits and M. Oeming; Winona Lake, IN: Eisenbrauns, 2006] 413–56), who discusses some Aramaic ostraca that he argues are important for understanding Achaemenid administration and the collection of taxes.

58. As Gray points out, Yahwistic practice is implied and the sacrifice described on the altar is "a *locus classicus* for sacrifice in the Temple" (*1 and 2 Kings*, 636).

gods.'" To dwell in another land is to worship the god of that land. Chr may have understood Ahaz's absence from Judah and his sojourn in Damascus as indicating that he worshiped the gods of Aram.

Ahaz's sojourn in a foreign land and his concern with foreign religious practice find an interesting parallel in the story of Nabonidus, the last king of Babylon.[59] As is well known, Nabonidus left Babylon for an extended period of time to reside in Teima (Arabia). He is well known for neglecting the worship of the main Babylonian god, Marduk, in favor of the moon god, Sîn.[60] These actions led to his character defamation and an infamous reputation (utilized by Cyrus in his propaganda campaign against the Babylonian monarchy) that alienated him from the powerful Marduk priesthood. When Nabonidus returned to Babylon from Teima, he overtly asserted his religious beliefs and undertook religious reforms promoting Sîn, which included the building of a temple for the moon god.[61] What is more, one account[62] notes that Nabonidus actually cancelled the New Year's festival at that time.[63] As the festival was dedicated to Marduk and included the purification of the *akītu* temple,[64] the cancelling of the festival was an extreme measure. The Cyrus Cylinder further claims that Nabonidus "put an end to the regular offerings" and even "did away with the worship of Marduk."[65] Thus, Nabonidus' building of temples to other deities and his excessive measures against the Marduk cult could have been seen by Chr as analogous to Ahaz's building of altars to foreign gods in Jerusalem and his closing of the "house of Yahweh" (2 Chr 28:24). While it is unlikely that Dtr knew of Nabonidus's story, because he probably wrote before Nabonidus's reign,[66] the parallel is striking. The Chronicler, on the other hand, would doubtless have known about Nabonidus,[67] and

---

59. For Nabonidus, see P.–A. Beaulieu, *The Reign of Nabonidus, King of Babylon, 556–539 B.C.* (Yale Near Eastern Researches 10; New Haven, CT: Yale University Press, 1989).

60. See P.–A. Beaulieu, trans.,"The Sippar Cylinder of Nabonidus" (*COS* 2.123A: 310–13).

61. Beaulieu, *The Reign of Nabonidus*, 204. He also repaired temples for the warrior goddess Anunitu and the sun god Šamaš in Sippar.

62. The inscription of Adad–guppi, referred to as the "Verse Account" by Beaulieu. For the text, see ibid., 206–7.

63. Ibid., 206.

64. J. Klein, "Akitu," *ABD* 1:138–40.

65. M. Cogan, trans., "Cyrus Cylinder" (*COS* 2.124: 314–16).

66. Assuming a preexilic (Cross and others) or exilic (Noth and others) Dtr.

67. Note his knowledge of the Cyrus decree (2 Chr 36:23). The Cyrus cylinder explicitly references Nabonidus as the king who "did not revere" Marduk but "put

this may have influenced him to understand Ahaz as being analogous to the infamous Babylonian king in this way.

The Philistine Campaign against Judah

Another interesting divergence between 2 Chronicles 28 and 2 Kings 16 is Chr's attributing the Philistines with a successful campaign against Judah during Ahaz's reign (2 Chr 28:18). This Philistine campaign has no parallel in 2 Kings 16. Some have surmised that the alliance against Assyria at this time was broader than just Aram and Israel and that Philistia was part of the coalition and may have attacked Judah for not joining in their cause.[68] If this is so, it is interesting that Dtr chose to omit reference to it.

While it may be that Chr relied on an unknown source for this information,[69] and that it is historically accurate, his *choosing* to include it in the Ahaz pericope may be due to his dialogue with the book of Isaiah. Isaiah predicted that along with Assyrian trouble will come a threat from the "end of the springs of Egypt" (Isa 7:18). While Egypt was not a threat to Ahaz during this time, the phrase is sufficiently ambiguous to signify Philistia to Chr. It is worth noting that the threat comes from the vicinity of Egypt and is not Egypt itself.[70] In 2 Chr 9:26 "the land of the Philistines" is paralleled with the "border (גבול) of Egypt," and geographically, they are basically adjacent.[71]

---

an end to the regular offerings . . . [and] did away with the worship of Marduk." See M. Cogan, trans., "Cyrus Cylinder," (*COS* 2.124: 314–16).

68. D. J. Wiseman, "A Fragmentary Inscription of Tiglath–Pileser III from Nimrud," *Iraq* 18 (1956) 17–29, here, p. 25; and Cogan and Tadmor, *II Kings*, 191.

69. Williamson suggests that "Since these matters are not demanded by the Chronicler's message nor suggested by any other passage (beyond a possible hint in 2 Kgs 16:6), it may be confidently concluded that he had access to a separate and valuable alternative source" (*1 and 2 Chronicles*, 345). While this possibility cannot be disproved, if Chr includes this story due to the influence of Isaiah, perhaps some of the need for a separate source to explain this evaporates. Of course, others also posit these sources. See Dillard, *2 Chronicles*, 220; and Japhet, *I and II Chronicles*, 900.

70. The word 'end' (קצה) may indicate the edge, extremity, or border of Egypt, not Egypt itself. See "קצה," *HALOT* 3:1120–21.

71. I. Kalimi (*The Reshaping of Ancient Israelite History in Chronicles* [Winona Lake, IN: Eisenbrauns, 2005] 110) has examined this phrase from 2 Chr 9:26 (ועד־ארץ פלשתים ועד גבול מצרים) in detail and concluded that Chr was indicating "two parallel geographic defining characteristics of the southwest border of the kingdom of Solomon." The boundaries of the promised land are often delineated as the land of Egypt in the south, even though Canaan does not really border on Egypt. Even in the portrayal of Solomon's kingdom (1 Kgs 5:1), the boundaries only approach this limit. The southern border of the promised land is often described as being the 'Wadi of Egypt' (נחלה מצרים; see Num 34:5, Josh 15:47, 1 Kgs 8:65, Isa 27:12). Similarly, Gen 15:18

Whether the Isaian oracle originally intended Philistia to be understood or not, there is a distinct possibility that Chr could have interpreted it that way.[72] In fact, the chronological progression of military campaigns in Chr's narrative follows that of their mention in the prophecy of Isa 7:18: first, "the fly at the ends of the springs of Egypt," that is, Philistia (2 Chr 28:18), then, second, "the bee which is in the land of Assyria," that is, Tiglath-Pileser (2 Chr 28:20). This probability is strengthened by the fact that this threat is called the "fly (זבוב) from the ends of the streams of Egypt" and one of the most famous gods of Philistia is Baal-zebub, "Master of the flies," known as the god of Ekron (2 Kgs 1:2, 3, 6, 16). In fact, in the entire HB/OT, the word זבוב is used almost exclusively in reference to the god of Ekron. It is found only twice elsewhere: in Isa 7:18 and Qoh 10:1. Therefore, it is likely that Chr made the connection between "fly" and Philistia due to this Ekron deity. Interestingly, the villages the Philistines are said to have taken at this time (2 Chr 28:18) are within the vicinity of Ekron (from Ekron Beth-shemesh is fewer than 7 miles, Soco fewer than 9 miles, and Gimzo fewer than 12 miles). Baal-zebub rules the "flies" in Ekron, who invade Ahaz's Judah, as prophesied by Isaiah.

The Syro-Ephraimite Threat

The Chronicler's distinctives are significant in the description of the war between Judah and its northern neighbors, Israel and Aram. As already noted, 2 Kings 16 and Isaiah both present Israel and Aram as forming a coalition and their military campaign against Judah as unsuccessful (2 Kgs 16:5). However, Chr presents them as working independently as separate enemies of Ahaz who successfully defeat him (2 Chr 28:5). This defeat of Ahaz is even elaborated on by the addition of a nonsynoptic story (2 Chr 28:8–15) of Israel's successful campaign against Judah (and the prisoners they took), and the prophetic response it generates. Understanding Chr as being in dialogue with Isaiah may explicate some of Chr's divergences here.

---

describes the promised land as reaching to the נהר 'river' of Egypt, which could refer to the eastern part of the Nile (Y. Aharoni, *The Land of the Bible: A Historical Geography* [2nd ed.; Philadelphia: Westminster, 1979] 59).

72. It is even possible that Chr augmented Edom's role against Judah during this time due to this ambiguous phrase. Perhaps Chr saw the prophecy as indicating trouble from the south—including Philistia *and* Edom. Note that Edom and Egypt are lumped together in Jer 9:26 as "those with shaven temples who live in the desert." An interesting translation issue with Jer 9:26 is seen where פצוצי פאה ('shaven temples') was translated by Rashi and Kimḥi as 'fringe of the desert' (קצה = קצצה) using קצה to indicate Edom. (Also in Joel 3:19, Egypt and Edom are listed together and condemned together.)

Separating the Syro-Ephraimite Coalition

In Isa 7:7–9, the prophet predicts that the Syro-Ephraimite coalition will come to nothing (which agrees with the statement of 2 Kgs 16:5 that Aram and Israel could not prevail against Ahaz). However, due to Ahaz's wickedness, Chr saw it necessary to present Ahaz as defeated by his enemies and suffering immediate retribution. Therefore, in order to acknowledge the voice idea in Isaiah's prophecy (that the coalition will not succeed), Chr could only present separate and independent attacks from these nations as successful. This allowed Isaiah's prediction (Isa 7:7) to be sustained as the *coalition* "did not happen" (ולא תהיה).[73]

The Chronicler's dialogue with Isaiah can also be heard in the way that Chr refers to the kings of Israel and Aram. Rezin's name is never mentioned, and Pekah ben Remaliah is never referred to as the king of Israel/Ephraim in 2 Chronicles 28. In fact, in the pericope about the return of prisoners from the North, the king of Israel is conspicuously absent from the narrative. When debating about what to do after the prophetic message, the king is not consulted, but only the chiefs of the Ephraimites (2 Chr 28:12). These anomalies may also be explained if Chr was acknowledging Isaiah's belittlement of both of these kings in Isaiah 7, where Pekah and Rezin are pejoratively referred to as "smouldering stumps of firebrand" (Isa 7:4) and the prophet links the failure of the coalition to the fact that "the head of Samaria is the son of Remaliah" (Isa 7:9).[74] Due to these *ad hominem* arguments in Isaiah 7, Chr hesitates to acknowledge the regency of these monarchs and omits them from his story. Thus, the positive actions of Samaria in 2 Chronicles 28 are done without consultation (or mention) of the king, and Pekah is denied the title of king, even in his introduction in the narrative (2 Chr 28:6).

The Exile of the North

Regarding Williamson's contention that Chr understood both the North and the South as being in partial exile at the end of 2 Chronicles 28, realization of Chr's dialogue with Isaiah 7 supports this conclusion. If Chr was in dialogue with Isaiah, Chr's understanding of the exile of the

---

73. The interpretation of Isaiah and Kings by Chr is in line with Childs's comments that the Chr "sought to explore the outer limits that the texts allowed in order to reconcile differences" (Childs, *Introduction to the Old Testament as Scripture*, 648).

74. Of course, Rezin is referred in analogously negative ways in Isaiah 7, which may explain why his name is not mentioned by Chr, who instead calls him "the king of Aram." Due to Isaiah's negative presentation of these kings, Israel's king is denied kingship and Rezin is denied his name.

North as being imminent (or having occurred) in the time of Ahaz may have been influenced by Isa 7:8, which, in the context of the prophet's oracles to Ahaz, mentions that "Ephraim will be shattered from being a people." This prediction, of course, states that, within 65 years, Ephraim would be exiled while in reality it occurred much sooner than this, leading some scholars to suggest this is a genuine, but inaccurate prophecy.[75] However, 65 years is 5 years shorter than the lifespan given to humans (Ps 90:10), so Chr may have interpreted it as meaning within one person's lifespan—that is, Ahaz's lifespan. This may have led him to infer the exile of the North in Ahaz's day.

Ahaz's Appeal to Assyria

Interestingly, the efficacy of Ahaz's appeal to Assyria in the context of the Syro-Ephraimite coalition is reversed in Chronicles *vis-à-vis* 2 Kings 16.[76] Instead of resulting in Ahaz's deliverance from Aram and Israel as in 2 Kings 16, the appeal in 2 Chronicles 28 results in Assyrian oppression. Perhaps the greatest benefit exegetically in recognizing Chr's dialogue with Kings *and* Isaiah is its ability to explain this difference. The Chronicler doubtless sensed the tension between Isaiah's predictions in this regard and Dtr's presentation of historical events. Isaiah emphasized the need for Ahaz to have faith in Yahweh or he would not stand at all (Isa 7:9). The prophet also clearly predicts that Assyria will trouble Ahaz severely (Isa 7:17), but Dtr presented the appeal as essentially successful (2 Kgs 16:9), ending the Syro-Ephraimite threat as Assyria came to his aid. Sensing the antagonism between these voice ideas, Chr makes these texts quarrel by making Isaiah's ideas dialogue with Dtr's ideas in 2 Chronicles 28.[77] The Chronicler answers the positions of both texts through his presentation of Ahaz's lack of faith (that is, his appeal to Assyria) as resulting in Assyrian oppression, in accordance with Isaiah's oracles.

---

75. See Wildberger, *Isaiah 1–12*, 301.

76. The occasion of Ahaz's appeal to Assyria appears to be the same in Chronicles as the temporal marker 'at that time' בעת ההיא (v. 16) appears to refer back to Syro–Ephraimite defeats in 2 Chr 28:5–7 (Aram) and 2 Chr 28:8 (Israel). So Japhet, *I and II Chronicles*, 905; contra Dillard, *2 Chronicles*, 223; Williamson, *1 and 2 Chronicles*, 345, and the NRSV rendering, which views Philistia and Edom as the cause for the appeal through translating ועוד in v. 17 as "for."

77. Another possible influence of Isaiah 7 on Chr's Ahaz narrative is his statement that "Yahweh humbled Judah on account of Ahaz" (2 Chr 28:19). This may be influenced by the imagery of the land being impoverished in Isaiah 7, where the land is "humbled" because hills are now infertile, thorns grow in place of good crops, and cattle wander wild (Isa 7:23–25).

The Insertion of the Prophetic Story

As is well known, Isaiah 7 describes Ahaz as rejecting the prophetic word of Isaiah.[78] However, 2 Kings 16 does not recount the episode or present Ahaz as spurning prophetic revelation. Therefore, Chr inserted a story about the apostate North being obedient to the prophet, in order to make a contrast with Ahaz's prophetic rejection in Isaiah 7. Furthermore, acknowledging Dtr's voice idea that Ahaz *did* escape some military threat, Chr includes the story of Israel's returning prisoners to Judah, which, in line with Isaiah's voice idea, only occurs due to an act of faith (Northern obedience to the prophet Oded). Thus, Isaiah's caution that faith is needed in order to survive is affirmed as true, though in this case it is the North who shows this faith.[79]

It is quite clear that Chr would equate obedience to a prophet with "standing in faith" (אמן). In fact, Chr's dialogue with Isaiah can also be seen in 2 Chronicles 20, when Jehoshaphat's speech to his people parallels Isaiah's exhortation to Ahaz during the Syro-Ephraimite crisis in Isa 7:9. The situation in 2 Chronicles 20 and Isaiah 7 is similar, as in both narratives: a coalition of foreign nations is threatening the Judahite king (Isa 7:1, 2 Chr 20:1), the king is afraid (Isa 7:2, 2 Chr 20:3), and a prophet encourages the king (Isa 7:3–9, 2 Chr 20:14–17). In a very similar situation, unlike Ahaz, Jehoshaphat chooses to trust in Yahweh. The double-voiced nature of Jehoshaphat's speech is clearly perceived by the twofold use of the verb אמן in 2 Chr 20:20. In the entire Old Testament, only here and in Isa 7:9 is the verb employed twice in one sentence, and both employ the word in exactly the same sense. Isaiah cautions Ahaz that "if you do not stand firm in faith (תאמינו), you will not stand firm (תאמנו)" (Isa 7:9). Analogously, in Chronicles, after the prophetic message, Jehoshaphat urges the people to "Stand firm in faith (האמינו) in Yahweh your God, and you will stand firm (תאמנו). Have faith (האמינו) in His prophets, and prosper!" The wording clearly resounds with the voice of Isaiah, only in this instance, Jehoshaphat is the king heeding this advice. The parallel nature of these two texts reveals an interpretive stance by Chr that understands having faith (תאמינו) as meaning "obeying God's prophet."

---

78. It is possible that the presentation of Ahaz as spurning the prophetic word in Isaiah 7 may have contributed to Chr's rationale for presenting Ahaz as the worst king of Judah and the nadir of the Jerusalem cult.

79. The notion that the faith of one can aid another is not foreign to biblical texts as the suffering servant suffers vicariously for others (Isaiah 53), the presence of 10 good men would save Sodom and Gomorrah (Genesis 18), and in the DH, God allows Abijam's son to succeed him, not for his own sake, but for "David's sake" (1 Kgs 15:4).

In 2 Chronicles 28, although Ahaz fails to listen to the prophet and have faith, the Northerners do just that.

The Chronicler's Sources and His Method

As Mitchell has asserted, "the reader of Chronicles does not have to know Samuel–Kings [and I would add, Isaiah] in order to get the message of Chronicles. But the reader of Chronicles who also knows Samuel–Kings [and Isaiah] can appreciate the dialogue between the [three]."[80] Thus far, this essay has suggested that viewing Chronicles as dialogic is fruitful for explicating many of Chr's specific divergences from 2 Kings 16. However, the implications of this study could be taken a step further and be brought to bear on our understanding of both Chr's method and the sources he employed in constructing his Ahaz narrative.

Thus far in scholarship, the appropriation of Bakhtinian insights for biblical studies has been relegated to what we might call ahistorical studies.[81] That is, their weight has never been regarded as contributing to the historical question regarding the composition or authorship of biblical narratives.[82] However, though Bahktinian studies have ignored historically minded studies, the converse is equally true.[83] This state of affairs

---

80. Mitchell, "Dialogism of Chronicles," 326.

81. E.g., ibid., 311–26; F. O. Garcia-Treto, "The Fall of the House: A Carnivalesque Reading of 2 Kings 9 and 10," in *Reading Between Texts: Intertextuality and the Hebrew Bible* (ed. D. N. Fewell; Louisville: Westminster John Knox, 1992) 153–71; B. Green, *How Are the Mighty Fallen? A Dialogical Study of King Saul in 1 Samuel* (JSOTSup 365; London: Sheffield Academic Press, 2003); K. Bodner, *David Observed: A King in the Eyes of His Court* (Hebrew Bible Monographs 5; Sheffield: Sheffield Phoenix, 2005).

82. R. Polzin (*Moses and the Deuteronomist: A Literary Study of the Deuteronomistic History: Part One: Deuteronomy, Joshua, Judges* [New York: Seabury, 1980]; idem, *Samuel and the Deuteronomist: A Literary Study of the Deuteronomistic History*, part 2: *1 Samuel* [San Francisco: Harper & Row, 1989]; idem, *David and the Deuteronomist: A Literary Study of the Deuteronomistic History*, part 3: *2 Samuel* [Bloomington: Indiana University Press, 1993]) has frequently criticized previous historical-critical work on the DH on the basis of his literary reading, which incorporates Bakhtinian insights. However, while he points out weaknesses in previous reconstructions of the history of the text, Polzin never offers an alternative reconstruction or theory regarding the origins of the text. While decrying the source-critical approach, Polzin offers no arguments for an alternative but only "presumes" the text makes sense, "however worked-over the text is scribally and hermeneutically, and however deficient it is text-critically" (*Samuel and the Deuteronomist*, 17).

83. R. Polzin ("1 Samuel: Biblical Studies and the Humanities," *RelSRev* 15 [1989] 297–306) speculates that biblical scholarship often ignores rhetorical studies "under the assumption that if you don't *do* literary history you oughtn't to knock it" (p. 304).

is not uncommon in regard to many new literary studies and their older historical-critical counterparts. However, as J. Barton has stated, "It is in the interests of all students of the Old Testament that historical and literary critics should somehow be brought to inhabit the same world [and] that most of the texts they interpret need *both* historical *and* literary skill if they are to be adequately interpreted."[84] Though Barton did not mean Bahktinian analysis particularly when he referred to "literary" methods, his statement is still appropriate in this regard. Rather than each of these criticisms ignoring scholarship based on different assumptions, biblical scholarship is in need of some way to translate the results of both paradigms into usable data. Therefore, in conclusion, I would propose that the evidence gleaned in this study's Bahktinian analysis of 2 Chronicles 28 strongly suggests that Chr employed Isaiah 7 as a source for his narrative and that this realization should be considered when assessing both Chr's method and his narrative as a historical document.[85]

Several proposals have been put forward for explaining Chr's method and the nature of his work. The Chronicler has been viewed as an exegete (an interpreter of texts), as a historian (relying on texts and sources, many of which are unknown to us today), or as a theologian (who contributed creatively to the narrative in order to make the story fit his theological ends).[86] While each of these proposals has merit, each also has limits,

---

84. J. Barton, "Historical Criticism and Literary Interpretation: Is There Any Common Ground?" in *Crossing the Boundaries: Essays in Biblical Interpretation in Honour of Michael D. Goulder* (ed. S. E. Porter, P. Joyce, and D. E. Orton; BibInt 8; Leiden: Brill, 1994) 3–15, here, p. 15.

85. However, this is not to say that the use of a prophetic book as a source immediately undermines its historical value as modern historians of ancient Israel glean historical information from prophetic books. Clearly, the prophetic books are rooted in history and many oracles refer to historical events. After all, Dtr's Ahaz account says nothing about Ahaz being pressured to join the Syro-Ephraimite coalition or their plan to dethrone Ahaz and put the son of Tabeel on the throne, only Isaiah 7 records this. However, many scholars deem this to be good historical information. Some even read this information into the Kings narrative. E.g., P. R. Davies, *The Origins of Biblical Israel* (LHBOTS 485; New York: T. & T. Clark, 2007) 142.

86. *Exegete*: Willi, *Die Chronik als Auslegung*. *Historian*: I. Kalimi, "Was the Chronicler a Historian?" in *The Chronicler as Historian* (ed. M. P. Graham, S. L. McKenzie, and K. G. Hoglund; JSOTSup 238; Sheffield: Sheffield Academic Press, 1997). *Theologian*: P. R. Ackroyd, *The Chronicler in His Age* (JSOTSup 101; Sheffield: JSOT Press, 1991); R. J. Coggins, *The First and Second Books of the Chronicles* (Cambridge: Cambridge University Press, 1976) 3–5; W. Johnstone, *1 and 2 Chronicles*, 1:9–10, 23; K. G. Hoglund, "The Chronicler as Historian: A Comparativist Perspective," in *The Chronicler as Historian* (ed. M. P. Graham et al.; JSOTSup 238; Sheffield: Sheffield Academic Press, 1997) 19–29.

and the insights of each proposal are not mutually exclusive.[87] This study, which strongly suggests that Chr employed Isaiah 7 as a source for his Ahaz narrative, may contribute to an appraisal of these scholarly proposals of Chr as exegete, historian, or theologian. As exegete, Chr interpreted his sources, which must be conceived as more than Samuel–Kings and must include the book of Isaiah. As historian, Chr took seriously the prophetic witness in Isaiah, assuming the historical value of its narrative and, more significantly, the trustworthiness of Isaiah's predictions concerning the outcome of Ahaz's policies. As theologian, he undertook to present the message of Isaiah that only through faith would salvation come—even the faith of those from the apostate North.

Thus, Chr's high view of the prophetic word of Isaiah (for both historical and theological ends) shows him to be both a hearer and doer of the word as his historiographical method put into practice Jehoshaphat's dictum, "Stand firm in [Yahweh's] prophets, and prosper!" (2 Chr 20:20).

---

87. As McKenzie points out, in ancient historiography a distinction between history and theology did not exist (*1–2 Chronicles*, 34).

Chronicles and Its Reshaping of Memories of Monarchic Period Prophets: Some Observations

Ehud Ben Zvi

Several important studies on prophets in Chronicles have appeared in recent years.[1] Of course, these studies built on a significant corpus of research that deals directly or indirectly with these matters since the early 1970s.[2] Many issues have figured prominently in this now-substantial

---

1. E.g., Y. Amit, "The Role of Prophecy and Prophets in the Chronicler's World," in *Prophets, Prophecy, and Prophetic Texts in Second Temple Judaism* (ed. M. H. Floyd and R. D. Haak; OTS 427; London: T. & T. Clark, 2006) 80–101. In fact, this is an updated version of the work by the same title published in *Beth Miqra* 93 (1983) 113–33 [Hebrew], which was overlooked in research, for the most part; P. C. Beentjes, *Tradition and Transformation in the Book of Chronicles* (SSN 52; Leiden: Brill, 2008), esp. pp. 90–98 and 129–39 (pp. 129–39 consist of a revised version of Beentjes, "Prophets in the Book of Chronicles" in *The Elusive Prophet: The Prophet as a Historical Person, Literary Character, and Anonymous Artist* [ed. J. C. de Moor; OTS 45; Leiden: Brill, 2001] 45–53); E. S. Gerstenberger, "Prophetie in den Chronikbüchern: Jahwes Wort in zweierlei Gestalt?," in *Schriftprophetie: Festschrift für Jörg Jeremias zum 65. Geburtstag* (ed. F. Hartenstein, J. Krispenz, and A. Schart; Neukirchen-Vluyn: Neukirchener Verlag, 2004) 351–67; L. C. Jonker "The Chronicler and the Prophets: Who Were His Authoritative Sources?" in *What Was Authoritative for Chronicles?* (ed. E. Ben Zvi and D. V. Edelman; Winona Lake, IN: Eisenbrauns, 2011) 145–64; A. Warhurst, "What Was Prophetic for the Chronicler?," in *What Was Authoritative for Chronicles?* (ed. E. Ben Zvi and D. V. Edelman; Winona Lake, IN: Eisenbrauns, 2011) 165–82.

2. E.g., T. Willi, *Die Chronik als Auslegung: Untersuchungen zur literarischen Gestaltung der historischen Überlieferung Israels* (FRLANT 106; Göttingen: Vandenhoeck & Ruprecht, 1972); J. D. Newsome, "Toward a New Understanding of the Chronicler and His Purposes," *JBL* 94 (1975) 201–17; S. Japhet, *The Ideology of the Book of Chronicles and Its Place in Biblical Thought* (BEATAJ 9; 2nd ed.; Frankfurt am Main: Peter Lang, 1997; first published in Hebrew: Jerusalem: Bialik, 1977); D. L. Petersen, *Late Israelite Prophecy: Studies in Deutero-prophetic Literature and in Chronicles* (SBLMS 23; Missoula, MT: Scholars Press, 1977) 55–96; I. L. Seeligmann, "Die Auffassung von der Prophetie in der Deuteronomistischen und Chronistischen Geschichtsschreibung," *VT* 29 (1978) 254–84; J. P. Weinberg, "Die 'ausser kanonischen Prophezeiungen,'" *Acta Antiqua* 26 (1978) 387–404; R. Micheel, *Die Seher- und Prophetenüberlieferungen in der Chronik* (BBET 18; Frankfurt am Main: Peter Lang, 1983); S. J. de Vries, "The Forms of Prophetic Address in Chronicles," *HAR* 10 (1986) 15–36; C. T. Begg, "The

corpus. Among them, one may mention: (1) the role and status of historical prophets at the time of the author(s) of Chronicles, including the question of whether ("classical") prophecy had ceased at that time, or even what a statement such as this may mean; (2) Chronicles' representations of prophets as "preachers" and/or "historians"; (3) the sources that the author(s) of Chronicles may have used or purposefully ignored when writing about prophets and prophecy; (4) the question of who is a prophet in Chronicles, and the related issues of "ad hoc" or "temporary" prophets, Levitical singers as prophets, and whether divinely inspired messengers were conceptually understood as "prophets"; (5) prophecy and cult; and (6) the status of prophetic utterances vis à vis Mosaic Torah and the general question of what was authoritative for Chronicles. Every (or almost every) contemporary work on Chronicles and prophets/prophecy has implicitly or explicitly dealt with or assumed a position on these issues.

This essay is no exception, but its main goal is not to revisit these debates but to explore the issue of Chronicles and prophecy/prophets from a perspective informed by a strong focus on social memory. What did Chronicles, or better, what did the reading and rereading of Chronicles

---

Classical Prophets in the Chronistic History," *BZ* 32 (1988) 100–107; idem, "The Chronicler's Non-mention of Elisha," *BN* 45 (1988) 100–107; R. A. Mason, *Preaching the Tradition: Homily and Hermeneutics after the Exile* (Cambridge: Cambridge University Press, 1990); J. Kegler, "Prophetengestalten im Deuteronomistischen Geschichtswerk und in den Chronikbüchern: Ein Beitrag zur Kompositions- und Redaktionsgeschichte der Chronikbücher," *ZAW* 105 (1993) 481–97; H. F. van Rooy, "Prophet and Society in the Persian Period according to Chronicles," in *Second Temple Studies*, vol. 2: *Temple Community in the Persian Period* (ed. T. C. Eskenazi and K. H. Richards; JSOTSup 175; Sheffield: Sheffield Academic Press, 1994) 163–79; J. B. Burns, "Is Neco Also among the Prophets?" *Proceedings, Eastern Great Lakes and Midwest Biblical Society* 14 (1994) 113–22; W. M. Schniedewind, *The Word of God in Transition: From Prophet to Exegete in the Second Temple Period* (JSOTSup 197; Sheffield: Sheffield Academic Press, 1995); idem, "Prophets and Prophecy in the Books of Chronicles," in *The Chronicler as Historian* (ed. M. P. Graham, K. G. Hoglund, and S. L. McKenzie; JSOTSup 238; Sheffield: Sheffield Academic Press, 1997) 204–24; P. Höffken, "Der Prophet Jesaja beim Chronisten," *BN* 81 (1996) 82–90; R. W. Klein, "Prophets and Prophecy in the Books of Chronicles," *TBT* 36 (1998) 227–32; G. N. Knoppers, "Review of W. M. Schniedewind, *The Word of God in Transition: From Prophet to Exegete in the Second Temple Period*," *JJS* 49 (1998) 133–35; A. Hanspach *Inspirierte Interpreten: Das Prophetenverständnis der Chronikbücher und sein Ort in der Religion und Literatur zur Zeit des Zweiten Tempels* (Arbeiten zu Text und Sprache im Alte Testament 64; St. Otillien: EOS, 2000). An earlier and foundational work was, of course, G. von Rad ("The Levitical Sermon in I and II Chronicles," in *The Problem of the Hexateuch and Other Essays* [G. von Rad; Edinburgh: Oliver & Boyd, 1966] 267–80); idem, "Die levitische Predigt in den Büchern der Chronik," in *Festschrift für Otto Procksch* (ed. A. Alt; Leipzig: Deichertsche Verlag und Hinrichssche Buchhandlung, 1934) 113–24.

within the Jerusalem-centered community of the late Persian (or perhaps, early Hellenistic) period, within which the book emerged, contribute to social memory in that community, or at least among its literati, in terms of *their* memories about the prophets of the monarchic period?[3]

I would like to stress that the focus here is not on particular memories about individual prophets but on the image of what a "monarchic-period prophet" looked like[4] and its importance in terms of social memory for the community within which Chronicles emerged.

Chronicles, like any other historiographical or prophetic book within the repertoire of ancient Israel/Yehud, was meant to evoke memory, to bring *particular* figures of the past to the present of the community and to allow members of the latter to shape and vicariously visit specific sites of memory (that is, people, places, events), which were construed through communally (more or less) shared acts of imagination as they read and reread the book. But bringing prophetic personages to the present of the community had to go hand in hand with and, in fact, necessitated at the level of general discourse the existence of a concept (or prototype) of what a "monarchic period prophetic persona" looked like, or, in other words and from a slightly different perspective, of a social memory of what monarchic prophets as a group were about.[5]

---

3. The question whether the book emerged in the late Persian period or early Hellenistic does not have a significant bearing on the observations advanced here. For the sake of convenience, I will continue referring to the era in which the book emerged and in which one is to find its primary readership as "late Persian period," but with an understanding that the early Hellenistic era is also a possibility. In fact, it is worth considering whether strong distinctions between the two are not based on a misguided use of external historical events (as opposed to social developments internal to the relevant society) as a base for historical periodization. After all, how drastic was the change in Judah, its society, and, as appropriate in this essay, its ideological discourse, when Alexander became the "last Achaemenid emperor"? (The characterization of Alexander as the "last Achaemenid" was advanced by P. Briant in 1979 ("Des Achéménides aux rois hellénistiques: Continuités et ruptures," *Rois, tributs et paysans: études sur les formations tributaires du Moyen-Orient ancient* [Annales littéraires de l'Université de Besançon 269 / Centre de recherches d'histoire ancienne 43; Paris: Les Belles lettres, 1982] 291–330) and was accepted by many since then, for example, M. A. Dandamaev, *A Political History of the Achaemenid Empire* (trans. W. J. Vogelsang; Leiden: Brill, 1989) 331.

4. That is, in more precise terms, the focus is on the socially shared prototype of what a "monarchic period prophet" looked like, or, if one wishes, on the (mental or cognitive) concept associated with "monarchic prophet" within the relevant community.

5. There is no doubt that memories of particular prophets (for example, Isaiah) contributed to the creation of that prototype, but one has to take into account that these memories are by necessity very individualized, and many features, events, and the like associated with a particular figure are unique to that personage. On some of these

Given the importance of prophecy and prophets in the intellectual discourse of the Yehudite literati, this social memory could not but play an important role and much was at stake in its shaping. The very existence of the corpus of prophetic books, the centrality of figures such as Isaiah, Jeremiah, and Moses, who is also characterized as a prophet, attests to that matter and so does the prominent role of prophets in both Samuel–Kings and Chronicles.

At this point, it is important to stress that social memory cannot be identified with any book, since it is not a book. Moreover, it cannot be identified with what evolved in the minds of an 'appropriately-socialized' individual as s/he read any single book, even if s/he did so within a socially accepted ideology and mode of reading. Instead, social, comprehensive memory may be understood as a large, integrative system or array of multiple social memories and sites of memories constantly informing each other. This array included memories evoked and relived through multiple readings of multiple books. In each of these readings, the literati could not but bring to bear the social and socially agreed knowledge that they possessed, and in a text-centered community, this implied many authoritative texts, concepts, and images in addition to those explicitly mentioned in the book they were reading. This being so, to understand the ways in which Chronicles contributed to the reshaping of the conceptual range of what a monarchic-period prophet was about, one must deal with the general discourse of the period and with the *Sitz im Diskurs* of Chronicles' images and positions. This is hardly surprising because readings of texts are always advanced within a general social discourse, and it is within that discourse that they are imbued with significance. To be sure, it is the text *as read* by the community that counts toward any reconstruction of the contribution of the book to the community's social memory.

In sum, images of monarchic prophets and prophecies were evoked through reading and rereading the book. These images served as memorials, that is, as sites of memory that existed in the minds of the readers, but which were socially shared. The Chronicler[6] asked his implied and primary (re)readers—hereafter, for the sake of simplicity, target readers or

---

matters, from the perspective of the book of Kings, see my "'The Prophets': Generic Prophets and Their Role in the Construction of the Image of the 'Prophets of Old' within the Postmonarchic Readership of the Book of Kings," *ZAW* 116 (2004) 555–67.

6. By "Chronicler," I mean the implied author of the book as construed by its primary or intended readership; in other words, the communicator or communicative voice they "heard" when they read the book. (Given the gender constructions of the period, this Chronicler was most likely imagined as male.)

target readership—to visit and revisit these sites of memory. The questions at the center of this essay are: What did these visits "do" to and for the community? What difference did these visits, and indirectly the book of Chronicles, make in society in terms of social memory?

The target readers of Chronicles developed and encountered the mentioned sites of memory, that is, textually evoked memorials that in turn embodied, reminded them, and above all drew their attention to particular sets of attributes that the community associated with their implicit concept of "monarchic prophet." As they did so, they had no choice but at times to reinforce and at times to draw attention away from the attributes that were embodied and communicated by other images evoked by different books.

Thus, the approach I am advancing here must take into account the *Sitz im Diskurs* of the readings of the text of Chronicles within its target readership in the late Persian period[7] but also must address the question of mindshare in the historical community, or to be more precise, in the approximation of the historical community that its texts suggests to us.[8] In practical ways, this means that an approach that raises the question of what effect Chronicles had on social memory in the late Persian period should bring up time and again the question of whether and how Chronicles reshaped or rebalanced the relative mindshare of features or common topoi associated with the images of the monarchic prophets.[9]

---

7. The definition of "Chronicler" advanced above is consistent with this approach.

8. There is no access to the actual community of flesh-and-blood Israelites, but historians can reconstruct "textual communities," which in turn are likely to reflect, even if in very imperfect ways, the actual communities of readers or at the very least their own image of themselves. See L. C. Jonker, "What Constitutes Society? Yehud's Self-Understanding in the Late Persian Era as Reflected in the Books of Chronicles," *JBL* 127 (2008) 703–24; and my own discussions about the partial resemblance between intended and actual readerships in Yehud and the possibility of approximating in some ways ancient readings, for example, "Is the Twelve Hypothesis Likely from an Ancient Readers' Perspective?" in *Two Sides of a Coin: Juxtaposing Views on Interpreting the Book of the Twelve/the Twelve Prophetic Books* (ed. E. Ben Zvi and J. D. Nogalski; Analecta Gorgiana 201; Piscataway, NJ: Gorgias, 2009) 47–96, esp. pp. 54–63.

9. It is worth noting that, unlike some present-day marketing struggles over consumers' mindshare, in which one company may set as its goal to obliterate the mindshare of its competitor, the tendency in Yehud was toward balancing mindshare. Chronicles was not aimed at convincing people that they should not read Kings or Samuel but sought to offer complementary memories that informed and were informed by those evoked by Kings or Samuel. Tendencies toward mainly monochromous memories and ideologies are more likely to develop within sectarian groups defining themselves and their boundaries and struggling against each other than within socially cohesive societies. In the latter, social cohesion is supported by both a centralization of resources and a significant range of allowed variety, which in turn is not seen as "dangerous" due to

A full, comprehensive study of all these features and topoi is beyond the scope of any paper or even of a single monograph. To make the study manageable in the present setting, five issues have been selected. These are central enough, however, to carry, at the least, the potential to make a significant contribution to a better understanding of both social memory within Yehudite Israel and its intellectual discourse and thus to contribute to the intellectual history of the period.

Remembering That Monarchic Prophets Could Also Be Successful in Their Own Times and Its Significance

אל־תהיו כאבתיכם אשר קראו־אליהם הנביאים הראשנים לאמר כה אמר יהוה צבאות שובו נא מדרכיכם הרעים ומעליליכם הרעים ולא שמעו ולא־הקשיבו אלי נאם־יהוה:

Do not be like your ancestors, to whom the former prophets proclaimed, "Thus says the Lord of hosts, 'Return from your evil ways and from your evil deeds.'" But they did not hear or heed me, says the Lord (Zech 1:4, NRSV).

The prophets of the monarchic past were remembered in Yehud, for the most part, as unsuccessful in their own monarchic historical contexts. This motif, which is explicitly stated in the text cited above (cf. Zech 7:7, 12),[10] played a central role in the construction of "the (generic) prophets" in

---

strength of cohesive tendencies. Needless to say, there were not enough literati or social resources in late Persian Jerusalem to allow for the development of sects and their more rigid and antagonistic viewpoints.

10. J. O'Brien ("Nahum-Habakkuk-Zephaniah: Reading the 'Former Prophets' in the Persian Period," *Int* 61 [2007] 168–83) has maintained that "Hosea–Zephaniah so closely conform to Zechariah's description of the 'former prophets' that these books may have been written or edited as a prelude to Zechariah" (p. 168) and

> [t]he scenario that I have described supports a redactional scheme in which Hosea through Zephaniah were consciously edited as a preface to Zechariah, providing a portrayal of the "former prophets" useful to the writer of Zechariah. . .[w]hile the contrary argument could be made (that Zechariah simply quoted from earlier prophetic books rather than helped create them), this latter scenario would account for neither 1) why the books have been put in this particular order, nor 2) why Zechariah has so many connections with the "happy endings" of the earlier books, which are widely recognized to reflect postexilic sensibilities. (p. 180)

Immaterial of whether one agrees with her redactional proposals or not, the point that Zechariah's description of the "former prophets" is fully consistent with the image that the books associated with prophetic characters ascribed to the monarchic period is certainly well taken and illustrates the point about a shared social memory about these prophets that shaped these books and is reflected in them.

Kings.¹¹ Most of the memories activated/evoked by the prophetic books whose background is set in the monarchic period contributed to this construction of the past, either explicitly (e.g., Jer 7:25, 25:4, 26:9, 35:15, 44:4) or implicitly because the destruction proclaimed in these books did happen from the perspective of the Persian-period readership.¹²

This social memory of the failed prophets was an integral and ideologically necessary part of a central node of social memories that (1) brought together social memories of exile, justified divine punishment, the correlated sinful character of monarchic Israel and (2) due to its *Sitz im Diskurs*, was strongly informed by widely accepted notions of a deity that warns before punishment and uses prophets as its messengers.¹³ This node of related and mutually reinforcing memories and related ideological concepts provided significance to the remembered, central catastrophe and also served clear didactic purposes in Yehud.

---

11. As I discuss in "'The Prophets.'"

12. There is only one salient exception to this construction of the prophets of old, namely, Isaiah. He was the only major late monarchic period prophetic character who was construed as successful. The positive heightening of the character of Isaiah (and Hezekiah) is related to the significance of the memory of the "salvation" of Jerusalem at the time of Hezekiah, which served as the contrasting site of memory for that of the destruction of Jerusalem at the time of Zedekiah. This contrast of sites of memory plays a very important role in the general metanarrative of the fall of Jerusalem and exile and their ideological/theological significance in Yehud. This issue, however, is beyond the scope of this essay; see my "Malleability and Its Limits: Sennacherib's Campaign against Judah as a Case Study," in *'Bird in a Cage': The Invasion of Sennacherib in 701 BCE* (ed. L. L. Grabbe; JSOTSup 363; European Seminar in Historical Methodology 4; Sheffield: Sheffield Academic Press and Continuum, 2003) 73–105. It goes without saying that this unique characterization of Isaiah raises very interesting questions about the array of memories associated with him in the Persian and Early Hellenistic periods and their relative mindshare (cf. Sir 48:24–25). A good dissertation waits to be written on the matter. A second, and far less salient, exception to the characterization of the monarchic prophets as ineffectual at their time within the corpus of prophetic book is the brief reference to the memory of Micah within the world portrayed in Jer 26:18–19. Significantly, this text is about comparing the Assyrian crisis with the Babylonian and their contrasting outcomes.

13. Clearly, this is not an innovation of the Chronicler but part and parcel of the discourse of the late Persian period. It is implicitly and explicitly attested in the prophetic books (e.g., Jer 7:25, 25:4, 26:9, 35:15, 44:4; Ezek 3:16–27) and in Kings (e.g., 2 Kgs 17:13). The "principle" is, as most principles in Chronicles, not absolute, as demonstrated, for instance, by the absence of any narrative about warning in the paradigmatic case of Ahaz or in the very first reference to YHWH in Chronicles (1 Chr 2:3). On the principle of warning before punishment in Chronicles, see Japhet, *Ideology*, 176–91. The argument that most "principles" in Chronicles are not absolute is developed in my *History, Literature and Theology in the Book of Chronicles* (Bible World; London: Equinox, 2006); for a discussion of the account of Ahaz, see pp. 160–73.

Chronicles is no stranger to any of this. In fact, it reminded its target readers of these notions about YHWH as it asked them to remember multiple past cases that embodied and communicated this set of notions, that is, by creating multiple, appropriate "sites of memory." Moreover, in addition to asking its readers to experience vicariously instances in which prophets were unsuccessful in the past (e.g. 2 Chr 24:19), the Chronicler also and most significantly chose to conclude his key interpretive preface to the narrative that leads up to and includes Jerusalem's destruction and exile, with a heightened note (2 Chr 36:15–16) that reflected and shaped a memory consistent with that in Zech 1:4, namely,

וישלח יהוה אלהי אבותיהם עליהם ביד מלאכיו השכם ושלוח כי־חמל על־עמו
ועל־מעונו: ויהיו מלעבים במלאכי האלהים ובוזים דבריו ומתעתעים בנבאיו עד
עלות חמת־יהוה בעמו עד־לאין מרפא:

The LORD, the God of their ancestors, sent persistently to them by his messengers, because he had compassion on his people and on his dwelling place;[16] but they kept mocking the messengers of God, despising his words, and scoffing at his prophets, until the wrath of the LORD against his people became so great that there was no remedy (2 Chr 36:15–16, NRSV).

It is only expected that widespread memories about prophets being rejected, mocked, and the like would lead to memories of their persecution and even murder at the hands of their enemies. Chronicles, Kings, and the prophetic books, all of which evoke memories about rejected prophets in the monarchic period, shape and communicate a topos of (monarchic period) prophetic martyrology.[14] This topos is reflected also in Neh 9:26, which reminds its readers that their ancestors killed the prophets who had warned them in order to turn them back. In turn, memories of martyrdom make even more memorable (that is, increase the mindshare of) the motif

---

14. For Chronicles, see 2 Chr 16:7–10, 24:19–25, and esp. 24:20–22. I discuss the matter in relation to Kings in "'The Prophets.'" See the portrayal of the prophet Jeremiah there. On prophetic martyrology, see also A. Rofé, *The Prophetical Stories: The Narratives about the Prophets in the Hebrew Bible, Their Literary Types and History* (Publications of the Perry Foundation for Biblical Research in the Hebrew University of Jerusalem; Jerusalem: Magnes, 1988) 197–213. The generative power of the topos becomes evident (and the topos even more dominant) in the late Second Temple period, in which even Isaiah (the most "successful" monarchic prophet within the social memory of Yehud) was imagined as suffering martyrdom. It is worth noting that traditions about Isaiah's martyrdom captured the imagination for centuries and had a very long history of reception (for example, note the midrashic characterization of his killer Manasseh as Isaiah's grandson; or the persistent images in medieval Vulgate manuscripts; see R. Bernheimer, "The Martyrdom of Isaiah," *The Art Bulletin* 34 (1952) 19–34.

of rejection of the monarchic prophets. In sum, themes both of prophetic lack of success and of persecution are well ingrained in social memories about monarchic Judah and Israel in Yehud and play important roles.[15]

All this said, it is worth stressing that Chronicles *balances* this construction of the memory of the prophets with a very substantial number of stories about prophets (or prophetic characters) who were successful in the monarchic period, for example, Shemaiah (twice during the days of Rehoboam, see 2 Chr 11:1–4, 12:5–6), Azariah in the days of Asa (2 Chr 15:1–7), Jehoiada in the days of Joash (note that his role is explicitly assigned to prophets in 2 Chr 24:19), the "man of God" in the days of Amaziah (2 Chr 25:7–9), Zechariah in the days of Uzziah (2 Chr 26:5), and Oded in (narratively and ideologically "kingless") northern Israel during the reign of Ahaz (2 Chr 28:8-15). Each of these stories created a particular site or memory for the readers of Chronicles, that is, a kind of memorial that reminded them that monarchic prophets were often successful.

These memorials do not populate the world evoked by Kings or by the prophetic books in the repertoire of Yehud. Had social mindshare on these matters been shaped *only* on the basis of the Deuteronomistic historical collection (hereafter, DH) and the prophetic corpus, the memory of the prophets of the monarchic period would have been very strongly shaped around the topos of the rejected, unsuccessful prophet and its logical counterpart, the usually sinful Israel. Chronicles, however, rebalanced, to the best of its capabilities, the mindshare of such a common topos. It did so not by denying or asking its readers to forget about it—in fact, it actively participated in its promotion—but by setting the topos in proportion. This attitude is typical of Chronicles and is probably necessary for a "national" history that must conform with some set of "facts" about the past that were already agreed on in the community and that can inform and be informed by other constructions of the past in the community, but not replace them.[16]

The ideological and social implications of the mentioned shift in social memory toward which Chronicles led are significant. The shift helped to construe and remember an image of Israel as not necessarily, or not in

---

15. A study of the ideological and didactical role of the martyrdom of the pious one/few stands well beyond the scope of this essay. It suffices here to say that, although this motif became central later on, and particularly since the persecutions of Antiochus IV, it did exist before and is well attested in the discourse and repertoire of the community in late Persian Yehud. To a large extent, in all these cases, the "one/few" pious stood for what Israel should have been and should be.

16. One point I advanced in *History, Literature and Theology in the Book of Chronicles.*

some essential way, sinful. Remembering monarchic Israel as not necessarily sinful was a consistent, underlying theme in Chronicles.[17]

There was also a practical implicature to Chronicles' tendency to shift the relative balance of mindshare on these issues in the community. As the Chronicler reminded the community of numerous cases of prophets and instances of prophetic preaching and teaching that were successful in their own time, it contributed to expectations about the success of preachers in their own time. As it did so, it conveyed an implied sense of continuity between (the Chronicles' construed) monarchic Israel and the (also construed) late Persian-period community as it should be in the view of the Chronicler.

There is another aspect of this particular tendency to balance social memory in this regard that converged to some extent with the preceding observation. As Chronicles drew, to the best of its capabilities, attention to stories of prophetic success, it drew some attention away from the topoi of prophetic rejection and persecution. The latter, however, was deeply linked in the discourse of the period to the ideological construction of the catastrophe of 586 B.C.E. As a result, Chronicles ended up drawing, indirectly, *some* attention away from the overwhelming focus on the catastrophe itself that would have characterized the social memory of Israel,[18] had social mindshare in late Yehud been shaped *only* by the DH and the prophetic books. This was consistent with the tendency in Chronicles not

---

17. In fact, as I suggested in my previous work ("A House of Treasures: The Account of Amaziah in 2 Chronicles 25—Observations and Implications," *SJOT* 22 [2008] 63–85), the Chronicler raised among its target readership an understanding that Israel, including of course their kings, tend by default to behave properly, that is, to follow Yhwh, if the rule of a bad king is removed from upon them. Significantly, kings are more likely to begin their reign piously than impiously till the death of Josiah, at which time Yhwh decided that a drastic purge is needed and will be fulfilled. Of course, initially pious kings and the people they lead show such a strong tendency to go astray at some point or another, but the putative default behavior of Israel may explain, or contribute to an explanation for a resetting of the entropic clock after the death, that is, the removal from power of a sinful king whose presence interfered with the "natural" tendency of the Israelites. Thus, as soon as Ahaz dies, the people, who previously followed his paths, recognize that this sinful king does not deserve to be buried with the kings of Israel/Judah (cf. 2 Chr 28:27; cf. 2 Chronicles 29–31 and note the date in 2 Chr 29:3). See also the beginning of the reign of Amaziah in 2 Chronicles 25. When a sinful king rules over Judah, the Judahites (/Israel) tend, however, to sin (see, for instance, 2 Chr 33:1–9).

18. Instances of implicit or explicit ideological engagement with the significance of the catastrophe, the use of its memory for didactic purposes and as a framing historical event in historiography attest to the mentioned focus, in addition to any direct or indirect report or image relating to the events themselves, to those that led to them and to their immediate aftermath.

to deny but to place in proportion the significance of the catastrophe of 586 and "exile." This tendency cannot be discussed here, but it suffices to state that Chronicles conveyed to its target readership that nothing essential changed because of this catastrophe and that, in fact, the latter did not matter much in the long run. After all, nothing changed in terms of Yhwh's teachings/torah, Israel's obligation to follow them, the need for godly preachers, the essential character of Israel, the centrality of Jerusalem, or Yhwh's ways of governing the world.[19]

None of these positions are really innovations of the Chronicler. They did exist in one way or another within the general discourse of the period. The Chronicler's effect on the relative mindshare of memories of the monarchic past, however, exemplified a tendency to advance memories consistent with and promoting these positions and with *balancing* other memories that lent themselves to other (seemingly contradictory, but discursively complementary) ideological narratives.

Remembering Also That the Prophets Were Not Necessarily Focused on the Far Future of Their Community and Its Significance

There is no doubt that had the mindshare of the community been shaped by the prophetic books alone, images of monarchic period prophets announcing utopian futures would have played a highly prominent role. To be sure, remembering these announcements played a very substantial role in the creation and social impact of a basic and hopeful meta-narrative that moved from a just punishment in the past to a utopian future. Moreover, because in this meta-narrative Yhwh's announcements about Israel's utopian future are set in the period of its extreme sinfulness, it reminded the community that Yhwh's great promises for Israel's future are not conditional on their behavior. This memory contributed to a sense of hope and certitude about the future. Utopia will come and cannot but come; the community can be sure of that, because of the dystopian character of the monarchic past.

But Chronicles kept bringing its target readership to other sites of memory. Those embodied in monarchic period prophets whose messages to their addressees were not about some idyllic situation in the far future

---

19. On the concept of exile in Chronicles, see my "Towards a Sense of Balance: Remembering the Catastrophe of Monarchic Judah/(Ideological) Israel and Exile through Reading Chronicles in late Yehud," in the *Book of Chronicles and Early Second Temple Historiography* [ed. T. F. Williams and P. S. Evans; Winona Lake, IN: Eisenbrauns, forthcoming]).

of their community or Israel in general, but about what they, that is, the addressees should do in their present and the possible implications of their actions for their immediate future. It is not the far future that figures prominently in all these instances but the very near future.

By doing so, Chronicles led, to the best of its influence, to a shift in the relative mindshare of memories about the main contents of past prophetic utterances in monarchic Judah, which was shaped in the main by the prophetic books.[20] This shift is consistent with the tendency in Chronicles to raise the prominence of issues such as following Yhwh's teachings.[21] Although there is a tendency in Chronicles to portray vignettes of the monarchic past as utopian to some extent, and as veiled models for the future of its community,[22] these are a far cry from images such as those of a world in which "the wolf will live with the lamb" (Isaiah 11), of new heavens and a new earth (Isa 65:17), or of a changed Israel that is reshaped by the deity as unable to sin because it is 'programmed' to follow Yhwh (e.g., Deut 30:16; Jer 31:31–34, 32:38–41; Ezek 11:19–20, 36:25–28; cf. Hos 2:21; Jer 24:7), or of a peaceful world in which all the nations will flow to Jerusalem (e.g., Isa 2:2–4, Mic 4:1–4/5) or in which Jerusalem will become the imperial capital (e.g., Isa 60:11–12).

All the utopian futures evoked by prophetic books mentioned in the preceding paragraph involved a drastic transformation of the world in which the primary readers of Chronicles lived.[23] But Chronicles did not ask them to imagine these changes. On the contrary, it tended to reduce the emphasis that the general discourse of the period placed on these memories of a

---

20. Of course, the books of Samuel and Kings contain examples of utterances that are not utopian and have immediate significance. Again, Chronicles is clearly not "inventing" the prophet who spoke about matters of immediate significance. Yet, when it comes to mindshare about post-secession prophets in Judah, the prophetic books clearly carried the day, until Chronicles contributed to a partial rebalancing. On Kings, see pp. 179–180 below.

21. Including, of course, those relevant to proper worship.

22. See S. J. Schweitzer, *Reading Utopia in Chronicles* (OTS 442; New York: T. & T. Clark, 2007); J. Blenkinsopp, "Ideology and Utopia in 1–2 Chronicles," in *What Was Authoritative for Chronicles?* (ed. E. Ben Zvi and D. V. Edelman; Winona Lake, IN: Eisenbrauns, 2011) 89–104. Remembering utopian elements as facts in the monarchic past is consistent with the tendencies mentioned in the previous sections concerning remembering monarchic Israel as not necessarily sinful and about the essential continuity of Israel that bridges and reduces the salience of the fall of Jerusalem and its temple and its exile.

23. One has to keep in mind that the target readership of Chronicles was aware of and most likely read the repertoire of authoritative books of late Persian or early Hellenistic Yehud/Judah.

future, utopian transformation. Instead, Chronicles drew attention toward imagining a world better than the present, but not categorically discontinuous with it. The good future world that Chronicles tended to bring to prominence was still a mundane world in which godly speakers are needed and so are authoritative texts. This approach of Chronicles is again consistent with its inclination to reduce attention and soften—though certainly not eliminate—the discursive heights usually associated with the dystopic catastrophe of 586 B.C.E. and its counterpart, the heightened images of "earth shattering" changes in the world as known to the community.

Kings, like Chronicles, did not draw particular attention to the utopian images of the prophetic books, but unlike Kings, Chronicles did provide many salient memorials (or sites of memory) leading its readers to imagine many particular (post-David/Solomon) Judahite prophetic characters and their speeches.[24] This remark leads us to the next main observation.

Constructing a Temporally and Geographically Additional Distribution of Prophetic Sites of Memory and Its Significance

The book of Kings did not develop a strong mindshare among its target readership for memories of individual prophets in the (separate) Kingdom of Judah from the period it became well established (as a result of the successful secession of the north) to its fall along with that of its capital, Jerusalem.[25] To be sure, generic references to prophets conveyed a general sense that there were always prophets, but the text did not lead to the formation of prominent sites of memory that drew very substantial mindshare. The corpus of prophetic books provided a significant number of central monarchic period characters to remember, but concentrated them

---

24. The exception in Kings concerns Isaiah.

25. As mentioned above, the most salient exception for Judah is Isaiah; see also the case of Hulda. It goes without saying that Kings asked its target readership to remember and imagine multiple prophets in the North and construes some of them as very memorable (for example, Elijah and Elisha) but there are no counterparts to them in Judah. This situation may be explained, but *only in part* by the roles assigned to prophets in reports concerning the ascension or rejection (and disposal) of northern dynasties, which for obvious reasons had no counterpart in Judah's historical narrative once the Davidic dynasty is established.

There is a need for a kind of sibling essay to this one, but dealing with prophetic memories in the Deuteronomistic Historical and the prophetic collections and their *Sitz im Diskurs*. It is worth stressing that Chronicles emerged later than these two collections, and for a substantial period of time social memory about prophets was shaped, in the main, by these two collections. I plan to write an essay on this in the near future.

around either the late northern Israelite period and its counterpart in Hezekianic Judah (e.g., Hosea, Amos, Micah, Isaiah) or the late Judahite monarchic period or its immediate aftermath (e.g., Zephaniah, Jeremiah, Ezekiel). As mentioned above, both periods were closely associated with each other, because they provided the framework to understand the catastrophe of exile and draw significance from it.[26]

Chronicles asked its target readership to remember a significant number of prophets, who are not mentioned elsewhere but who cover precisely the gaps in the geographical or temporal distribution of prophetic images evoked by the other authoritative corpora.[27] In other words, its effect, to the best of its influence, was to rebalance the mindshare of different images of the past in the community and through this rebalancing act to shape a general social memory of the monarchic period in Judah. In this social memory prophets appear as consistent sites of memory throughout the entire temporal and spatial landscape of Judah, as at least the literati in the late Persian period imagined it.[28] This is consistent with two ideo-

---

26. It is worth noting that, unlike the emphasis on Manasseh as responsible for the Exile in some voices in Kings (see 2 Kgs 24:3), there is no prophetic book allocated to that period. Kings drew attention to Manasseh in its metanarrative of exile; the prophetic corpus—just as Chronicles—drew attention away from his reign in their own general metanarratives of exile. A full discussion of this matter and its implications is beyond the scope of this essay.

27. See, for instance, 2 Chr 13:22 (reign of Abijah), 15:8 (reign of Asa), 16:7 (reign of Asa), 19:2 (reign of Jehoshaphat), 20:14 (reign of Jehoshaphat), 20:37 (reign of Jehoshaphat), 24:20 (reign of Joash), 25:7–10 (reign of Amaziah), 28:9 (kingless northern Israel). Jehoiada, the priest, serves the roles often associated with prophets during the reign of Joash, as he directs him to follow in Yhwh's ways. After Jehoiada's death, when the king abandons his counsel, prophets are called to bring him and his elite back, though they fail to do so (2 Chr 24:19). (As required by the narrative world, Jehoida is also a kind of kingly figure who restores to Judah the laws and regulations of both Moses and David, reestablishing the temple and the Davidic dynasty). The role of the prophetic voice during the reign of Uzziah is taken up by Azariah, the priest, and the other priests. L. Jonker associates most of these prophets with reports about war or cult. See Jonker, "Refocusing the Battle Accounts of the Kings: Identity Formation in the Books of Chronicles," in *Behutsames Lesen: Alttestamentliche Exegese im Gespräch mit Literaturwissenschaft und Kulturwissenschaften: Festschrift für Christof Hardmeier zum 65. Geburtstag* (ed. S. Lubs et al.; Arbeiten zur Bibel und Ihrer Geschichte 28; Leipzig: Evangelische Verlagsanstalt, 2007) 245–74. While this might be true, much of the narrative space of the nonformulaic section of the regnal accounts in Chronicles is devoted to these matters.

28. Of course, Chronicles also places prophets in periods that in the memory of the community are already populated by prophets, such as the David-Rehoboam period (cf. DH), the Ahabite period (cf. DH), the Hezekian period (cf. DH and the prophetic books), the Josianic period, and the relatively brief account of the three kings leading to the fall of Jerusalem. It is worth noting, however, that at times Chronicles draws

logical messages that Chronicles frequently communicated to its target readership: (1) Israel could exist without Jerusalem or temple or king, but not without divine instruction or guidance, and (2) the principle of warning mentioned above. Both, within the world construed by Chronicles, required the presence of prophetic voices.

Moreover, by filling the temporal and (theo)polity-bound gaps, Chronicles contributed to balancing mindshare in such a way that resulted in softening of the "heights and valleys" distribution of memorable prophetic figures in the social memory of the community in late Yehud. This in turn was fully consistent with the tendency in Chronicles to soften—though certainly not eliminate—the heights and valleys associated in other literature with the post-Davidic/Solomonic past. After all, for Chronicles, neither exile nor for that matter the reported deeds of Josiah or Hezekiah[29] mattered so much in the long run.[30]

Remembering Also the Wide Range of Potential Intermediaries of Divine Knowledge and of Divine Knowledge and Its Significance

Chronicles also rebalanced the existing memories of the community in terms of who can be intermediaries of the divine for Israel and what they may do. It reminded its target readers that YHWH's intermediaries did not have to be "professional" or "permanent prophets" to fulfill the roles of prophets.[31] It reminded them that these intermediaries may be kings, even

---

attention to prophets known from existing sources that fit the period but advances a reconfiguration of the social memory of the community about them. The most obvious example is the case of Elijah and his letter to Jehoram in 2 Chr 21:11–15. In fact, there is hardly any period within the monarchic past to which the readers of Chronicles were not explicitly asked to associate prophetic voices. (Unlike Kings, in which he is never explicitly mentioned, Chronicles draws attention to Jeremiah in the context of the reign of Zedekiah; see 2 Chr 36:12). The most salient exception is the period of Ahaz.

29. I wrote elsewhere on the account of Josiah in Chronicles. See my "Observations on Josiah's Account in Chronicles and Implications for Reconstructing the World View of the Chronicler," in *Essays on Ancient Israel in Its Near Eastern Context: A Tribute to Nadav Na'aman* (ed. Y. Amit et al.; Winona Lake, IN: Eisenbrauns, 2006) 89–106.

30. The same holds true, of course, for the deeds of kings viewed in an extremely negative way, for example, those of Ahaz, who shut the doors of the temple, among his many other acts of impiety.

31. Y. Amit, among others, maintains that, in Chronicles, "a king, a Levite or any other person, functions as prophet when he utters prophetic statements in the Chronistic sermonizing style" ("The Role of Prophecy and Prophets," 89). The "Chronistic sermonizing style" to which she refers is the style of the "Levitical sermon" as discussed in G. von Rad, "The Levitical Sermon in I and II Chronicles." Contrast Amit's position

a foreign king, priests, or Levites (e.g., 1 Chr 28:19; 2 Chr 20:14–17, 24:20–22, 29:25, 35:20–24, 36:22).[32] It reminded them that monarchic-period prophets may compose and perform cultic music (1 Chr 25:1–8) or laments (2 Chr 35:25). It asked them to keep in mind that these prophets recorded (and interpreted) monarchic history (e.g., 1 Chr 29:30; 2 Chr 9:29, 12:15, 13:22, 23:32, 33:19) and conversely that books consisting of historical (royal) record included prophetic texts (2 Chr 20:34, 32:32, 33:18).[33]

Thus, Chronicles contributed to a reconfiguration of the range of what came to the minds of its target readership when they thought of monarchic-period prophetic personages, that is, it affected the relative mindshare of various prophetic images that existed in the community. Most importantly, it created a conceptual realm that brought together (1) prophecy, in the "narrow" sense, (2) laws and regulations (associated with the intermediary figures Moses or David, who in Chronicles were also considered to be prophetic characters and, accordingly, their inspired words to be some form of prophecy—and *vice versa*),[34] (3) historical writ-

---

with Schniedewind's, for whom prophets are *only* those whom Chronicles explicitly designate as such (e.g., W. M. Schniedewind, "Prophets and Prophecy," 214). Suffice to say that at the very least, Chronicles reflected and shaped a conceptual field populated by both "prophets" and prophetic characters who deliver prophecies, even if they are not *explicitly* called prophets. This shared conceptual field strongly associated one image to the other.

32. *Foreign king*: The text in 2 Chr 35:22 states מפי אלהים, but within the discourse of the target readership of Chronicles, אלהים could only be understood as a reference to YHWH. Most likely, in response to this understanding, in the text in 1 Esd 1:28, Jeremiah replaces Neco as the intermediary for YHWH's words.

Note that mediation in the case of 1 Chr 28:19 is through a written text. This is one of the cases in which David is construed as a kind of necessary complement to Moses, given the importance of the temple and temple cult and above all of the divine instructions necessary for establishing and maintaining it. See S. J. de Vries, "Moses and David as Cult Founders in Chronicles," *JBL* 107 (1988) 619–39; and my own discussion of these matters in "One Size Does Not Fit All: Notes on the Different Ways in Which Chronicles Dealt with the Authoritative Literature of Its Time," in *What Was Authoritative for Chronicles?* (ed. E. Ben Zvi and D. V. Edelman; Winona Lake, IN: Eisenbrauns, 2011) 13–36.

See also 2 Kgs 23:2 and 2 Chr 34:30 and note the exchange between prophets and Levites.

33. See Blenkinsopp, "Ideology and Utopia"; and S. Schweitzer, "Judging a Book by Its Citations: Authority and the Sources in Chronicles," in *What Was Authoritative for Chronicles?* (ed. E. Ben Zvi and D. V. Edelman; Winona Lake, IN: Eisenbrauns, 2011) 37–66.

34. See, for instance, 2 Chr 8:14, noting the concluding expression מצות דויד איש־האלהים, and see 2 Chr 30:16. The term איש־האלהים is used in Chronicles for Moses

ings, and (4) cultic poetry or music.³⁵ In other words, this realm brings together the authoritative repertoire of the community and associated it with prophecy.³⁶

Moreover, Chronicles brought together and brought to the attention of the community's present memories about both *written texts* and *oral exhortations*, encouraging the community to follow these texts and what they stood for. Oral exhortations served to provide memorable examples of what following Yhwh could mean in practical, historically contingent terms (e.g., 2 Chr 28:9–15). In any event, readers were reminded that both (inspired/authoritative) written and oral texts were necessary in monarchic Israel and, by extension, in post-monarchic Israel.

In other words, Chronicles did far more than simply legitimize its work by suggesting that pious or "ideologically" appropriate historiographical works such as Chronicles have some kind of prophetic authority and that, by extension, so did the readings and interpretations of existing authoritative literature that Chronicles advanced. Of course, Chronicles did so. But, in addition, it shifted the web of images about the past that existed in the community so as to include memories that evoked a conceptual realm of prophecy consistent with a large and varied authoritative corpus of written works (including those containing interpretations/readings of other

---

also in 1 Chr 23:14 and for other prophets in 2 Chr 11:2 and 25:9. Significantly, the target readership of Chronicles is asked to evoke a memory of David as a person who, like Moses, knew the distant future (see 1 Chr 16:35). I discussed the matter and its implications elsewhere; see "Who Knew What? The Construction of the Monarchic Past in Chronicles and Implications for the Intellectual Setting of Chronicles," in *Judah and the Judeans in the Fourth Century* B.C.E. (ed. O. Lipschits, G. N. Knoppers, and R. Albertz:Winona Lake, IN: Eisenbrauns, 2007) 349–60.

35. See Gerstenberger, "Prophetie in den Chronikbüchern"; and Z. Talshir, "Several Canon-Related Concepts Originating in Chronicles," *ZAW* 111 (2001) 386–403.

36. This is, of course, the beginning of the process that led eventually to the development of an agreed corpus of inspired (i.e., prophetic) writings and eventually to canon(s). See "the law, the prophets, and the rest of the books" in the foreword in Sirach. It is worth stressing that the realm of prophecy in Chronicles included also, as M. Leuchter correctly noted, prophecy as divine דבר, which may "empower history to unfold and direct empires to rise and fall"; M. Leuchter, "Rethinking the 'Jeremiah' Doublet in Ezra–Nehemiah and Chronicles," in *What Was Authoritative for Chronicles?* (ed. E. Ben Zvi and D. V. Edelman; Winona Lake, IN: Eisenbrauns, 2011) 183–200. This concept of prophecy is not necessarily associated with unitemporality, as a divine word may unfold more than one time and in more than one way. See, for instance, understandings of prophetic portrayals of the "return" (i.e., the removal of "Exile") as something that has already happened, even if partially in Persian times, but at the same time as something to be fulfilled in the future. On these matters, see pp. 184–187 below.

written works, for example, Chronicles) and oral speeches. Each of these references to written or oral texts shaped sites of memory that embodied and communicated what was transmitted through divine intermediation.

The implied conceptualization of this realm of prophecy/authoritative corpus and its retrojection to monarchic Israel is consistent with the sense of continuity between the past brought to the present of the community through the reading of Chronicles and its own present, or what should be, according to Chronicles, its present. But, of course, this must be balanced too. There was no room in the present of the target readers of Chronicles, for instance, for a new Moses or David, for new Mosaic commandments or divine laws identifying the place of the temple or establishing its cult. One may note that despite all its differences (e.g., kings, size of population, and so on), the same holds true for the post-David (or David/Solomon) period portrayed in Chronicles. In any event, the Chronistic prophetic landscape of the post-Davidic/Solomonic, monarchic period, and the memories it evoked were consistent with, and a legitimizing force for a present advocated by Chronicles, that is, for its "down-to-earth" utopia.

Remembering Also That although the Prophets Were Historical Figures Their Words May Be Transhistorical or Multitemporal and Its Significance

Chronicles is a historiographical work. As expected given its literary genre, all its prophetic characters are explicitly anchored to particular historical circumstances. These anchors are crucial to the memory-shaping function of the book. Remembering these characters would not have contributed to the communal memory of any particular set of circumstances, if it were not for these explicit anchors. Moreover, Chronicles often asked its target readership to imagine these prophetic personages as speakers who addressed concrete, particular historical situations in the present of their addressees.[37] In addition, this Chronistic trend is clearly associated with and even required by the general tendency toward drawing attention to the concept of warning before punishment, which is involved in the shaping of multiple sites of memory in the community about people in the monarchic period who were exhorted to turn back from their sinful path.[38]

---

37. Contrast with Amit's assertion that "the prophets of the Deuteronomistic historiography do not react to concrete historical events, ("The Role of Prophecy and Prophets," 88). Amit's statement is a bit too extreme, and she later qualifies it in her essay, but it points at the different balance of attestation of tendencies between Kings and Chronicles.

38. See Japhet, *Ideology*, 176–91.

These tendencies generated a need for the conceptualization of prophecy as anchored in and contingent to the putative historical circumstances of the conveying prophetic voice. After all, prophetic messages and characters had to be imagined as carrying at least the potential to influence the actions of the remembered historical agents in their own (putative) times.

However, Chronicles reminded the community that, whereas the remembered prophets are each to be associated with a particular temporal and spatial place in the array of shared (construed) pasts of the community, prophetic words may and at times did apply to multiple circumstances, including but certainly not limited to those of the prophetic speaker. Thus, prophets in Chronicles may allude to or use words associated with much later prophets in the corpus of prophetic literature,[39] and conversely, prophetic words that refer to the far future in that corpus may be taken as relevant or even partially fulfilled in the monarchic past, without removing their significance as prophecies for the distant future within the discourse of the community.[40]

Thus, Chronicles contributes to a drive toward both close connection and separation between prophet and prophetic words in social memory. For particular purposes and ideological narratives, the two must be remembered together; but at the same time, the prophetic words could be taken as "floating" textual sites of memory by themselves and, as such, be evoked in multiple contexts, to the point that they may significantly contribute to the shaping of memories of multiple events at different times.[41]

The basic atemporality of the prophetic word, as it becomes a site of memory in and by itself, was necessary for assuming its multitemporality. Again, this is no innovation of Chronicles but a very important feature

---

39. E.g. 2 Chr 15:3 (and cf. Hos 3:4), 5 (and cf. Zech 8:10 and Amos 3:9), 6 (and cf. Zech 11:6), 7 (and cf. Jer 31:16 and Zeph 3:16); 2 Chr 16:9 (and cf. Zech 4:10); 20:20 (and cf. Isa 7:9). See P. C. Beentjes, *Tradition and Transformation*, 137–39; Japhet, *Ideology*, 183; Willi, *Auslegung*, 177, 223–29; von Rad, "Levitical Sermon"; Ben Zvi, "Who Knew What."

40. For instance, and as A. Warhurst has shown, some of the attributes of the ideal king in Isaiah 11 contribute to the characterization of Hezekiah in Chronicles. Thus, "the Chronicler retrojects restoration prospects onto descriptions of past history." See Warhurst, "Chronicler's Use of the Prophets," 181. Needless to say, the portrayal of this (partial) fulfillment was not an implied call to reject the future value of the utopian prophecy in Isaiah 11 or diminish its relative mindshare in the memory of the community. In fact, the opposite is likely to be correct. The allusions to Isaiah 11 likely served to draw the attention to the text and its (now double) message.

41. This is consistent with the idea of prophecy as a historical force or agent that actually makes things happen in history. See p. 183 n. 37 above; see also Isa 55:10–11.

of the discourse of the period.[42] It is reflected, for instance, in the strong tendency toward dehistoricizing the present in the prophetic writings, particularly in the majority of the 12 prophetic books.[43] Chronicles and these books contributed, even if implicitly, to the development of a community in which evoking prophetic messages did not necessarily evoke temporal constraints and "historical" contingency. This position allowed for the continuous significance of words set in the past, be they reported in the prophetic books, pentateuchal or historical texts or, for that matter, in any book in the authoritative repertoire of the community. This position allowed for the creation of a sea of images and texts that, though set originally in a particular event in the remembered past, were seen as (at least, potentially) relevant and instrumental for multiple or even all times. In other words, it allowed for the social reproduction of a text-centered community.

In addition, it allowed the community in the late Persian period to strengthen its sense of continuity between itself and the past communities of Israel that it remembered, as it imagined a shared set of crucial and defining texts. Within a discourse in which Israel was conceived as a transtemporal entity and at the same time as a text-centered community, one can only expect the development of a tendency to associate at least some level of trans-temporality to Israel's texts. Moreover, within this *Sitz im Diskurs*, a tendency of this sort toward transtemporality is likely to end up evoking some sense of temporal omnipresence concerning the basic sea of texts that define the community or at least to end up creating the conditions in which this sense may have emerged.[44]

To be sure, the concept of atemporal prophetic words uttered by temporally bound prophets carries within itself some degree of tension. This is particularly so because the temporally bound prophets were to be char-

---

42. For instance, and as mentioned above, the image of the "return" as both fulfilled in Persian times and yet not fulfilled. See the case of the utopian world of Isaiah 11, discussed above.

43. I discussed these matters elsewhere; see my "De-historicizing and Historicizing Tendencies in the Twelve Prophetic Books: A Case Study of the Heuristic Value of a Historically Anchored Systemic Approach to the Corpus of Prophetic Literature," in *Israel's Prophets and Israel's Past: Essays on the Relationship of Prophetic Texts and Israelite History in Honor of John H. Hayes* (ed. B. E. Kelle and M. Moore; (OTS 446; London: T. & T. Clark, 2006) 37–56.

44. Whether this sense of omnipresence is already active in Chronicles, even if in only a partially and strongly balanced way, or whether this book (among others) prepared the way toward its development cannot be answered in any clear way. See my "Who Knew What?"

acterized by their prophetic words and remembered as those who uttered them. Tensions like this often carry some degree of generative power within the discourse of the community. In this case, the tension had the potential to generate some instances of partial "leakages" of atemporality from the *prophetic word* to the prophetic figure.[45] These partial leakages allowed for authors, redactors, and interpreters to imagine themselves as taking on, even if partially, the persona of the prophet and shaping prophetic words. This process was central to the development (including redaction) of the prophetic books, but one wonders whether it was not, even if perhaps in a marginal way, at work when the authorship of Chronicles advanced authoritative readings of the divine teachings associated with Moses.[46] One may wonder if the same does not hold true for cases in which prophetic phrases and expressions, or allusions to them, were embedded in the text of Chronicles—even if, and most likely because, these phrases or expressions were known in the community and remembered as associated with acknowledged prophetic voices.

To Conclude

This essay explored ways in which Chronicles influenced social memory about prophets and prophecy in the community within which it emerged. Carrying out this exploration required a *Sitz im Diskurs* approach to Chronicles' relevant data, which included numerous, and at times seemingly contradictory, images of prophets and prophecy. This essay has shown that Chronicles contributed, to the extent of its capabilities, to a process of balancing the relative mindshare of different memories and sets of memories about prophets and prophecy in the late Persian (or early Hellenistic) Yehudite community in which its primary readership is located. The cumulative weight of the five central cases studied strongly suggests that Chronicles' tendencies to rebalance mindshare about prophets and prophecy were deeply interwoven with substantial ideological trends that already existed in the discourse of the community but that were well represented and even particularly salient in Chronicles.

The question of how effective was Chronicles vis à vis other authoritative works (e.g., Kings, prophetic books, pentateuchal books) in shaping

---

45. There is no point in talking about leakage in the other direction. Clearly, there was much room in the discourse of the community for contingent prophetic words, and there was no need of a "leakage" from the image of a contingent prophet to produce this space.

46. I discussed particular examples and the general issues involved in "One Size Does Not Fit All."

mindshare in flesh-and-blood, historical communities in the late Persian or early Hellenistic period remains open. In fact, it cannot be answered with any degree of certainty. Moreover, its degree of influence might have changed from time to time and be dependent on particular settings. One should keep in mind that although Chronicles most likely presented itself as "less authoritative" than the texts in the primary history (Genesis–2 Kings),[47] it could have strongly influenced mindshare, if it successfully convinced the community that it was bringing forward the true meaning of these texts or authoritative, complementary viewpoints and memories. In any event, Chronicles was accepted by the community, or at least the Jerusalem-centred literati of Yehud, and was read and reread by them. Such a read and reread book could not but inform, at least to some extent, social memory among its historical readers.[48]

---

47. Chronicles was written in Late Biblical Hebrew. I explore elsewhere the communicative message of Late Biblical Hebrew *vis à vis* Standard Biblical Hebrew; see my "Communicative Message of Some Linguistic Choices," in *A Palimpsest: Rhetoric, Ideology, Stylistics and Language Relating to Persian Israel* (ed. E. Ben Zvi, D. V. Edelman, and F. Polak; Piscataway, NJ: Gorgias, 2009) 269–90.

48. An excellent source for the study of the influence of Chronicles in the shaping of memories of the monarchic period in later periods and communities is I. Kalimi, *The Retelling of Chronicles in Jewish Tradition and Literature: A Historical Journey* (Winona Lake, IN: Eisenbrauns, 2009), and see also bibliography there.

Deus ex Machina *and*
Plot Construction in Ezra 1–6

LISBETH S. FRIED

Chapters 1–6 of Ezra tell the story of how the Second Temple came to be built. It begins with Cyrus the Great's decision in 538 B.C.E., the first year of his reign over Babylon, to allow the Judeans in Babylon to return and rebuild their Temple of YHWH in Jerusalem.[1] It ends with the Temple's completion and dedication 18 years later in the 6th year of Darius I (the Great).[2] As described, it is a temple-building story, a genre of literature typical of the ancient Near East. As has been shown, ancient Near Eastern

---

1. That is, if the date is authentic. For a thorough discussion of Cyrus II, the Great, see P. Briant, *From Cyrus to Alexander: A History of the Persian Empire* (trans. P. T. Daniels; Winona Lake, IN: Eisenbrauns, 2002).

2. Although Darius I is generally assumed, some scholars have opted for Darius II, e.g., B. Becking, "Ezra's Re-enactment of the Exile," in *Leading Captivity Captive: 'The Exile' as History and Ideology* (ed. L. L. Grabbe; JSOTSup 278; Sheffield: Sheffield Academic Press, 1998) 40–61. There were three kings named Darius—Darius I (522–486), Darius II (424–405), and Darius III (336–331). Nehemiah was sent to Jerusalem by an Artaxerxes in that king's 20th year (Neh 2:1). Artaxerxes grants him timber to build the wall around Jerusalem and to build a house for himself (Neh 2:8). An Aramaic letter dated to the 17th year of a King Darius (*Textbook of Aramaic Documents from Ancient Egypt*, vol. 4: *Ostraca and Assorted Inscriptions* [ed. B. Porten and A. Yardeni; Jerusalem: Hebrew University Press, 1999] 7–9) was found in an archive on the Nile Island of Elephantine. It is a copy of a letter sent to Bagavahya, the then Persian governor of Yehud. The letter states that the writers had sent a similar letter three years before to Yoḥanan the high priest in Judah and to Delaiah and Shelemiah, sons of Sanballat, governor of Samaria. The answer was received from Bagavahya and from Delaiah. This Sanballat is very likely the one referred to in Nehemiah's memoir. It seems that at the time of the letter he was elderly and his son was acting on his behalf. Since Sanballat and Nehemiah were governors during the reign of an Artaxerxes, the Darius who was king at the time of the letter must have ruled after Nehemiah's Artaxerxes—thus, Darius II or III. Because Darius III did not rule 17 years, this letter must have been written in the 17th year of Darius II (407 B.C.E.), so that Nehemiah—like Sanballat—would have been governor during the reign of Artaxerxes I, the only Artaxerxes who ruled before Darius II. If Nehemiah was governor under Artaxerxes I, and because at that time the temple was already built (Neh 6:10–11), the temple must have been completed during the reign of Darius I, the only King Darius who preceded Artaxerxes I.

temple-building stories exhibit a common pattern, they are based on a common template.³ Being part of this ancient Near Eastern world, the biblical writers based their story of the Second Temple's construction on this same template. This template, or typology, expresses not only the way in which temple restoration is described in ancient Near Eastern historiography, but also the ideology by which temple-rebuilding projects were understood.⁴ The story of the Jews' return to Judah and of the temple's rebuilding as told in Ezra 1–6 is predicated on this same typology of ancient Near Eastern temple rebuilding.⁵

This typology of temple building is composed of 11 fixed components.⁶ Table 1 lists these components in order and compares them to the elements in Ezra 1–6. Although most of the components are present, not all of them are. There is no history of how the temple came to be destroyed, for example, unless we include the letter from Tattenai to Darius in Ezra 5, in which the history of the temple is recorded. Nor does Ezra 1–6 contain a statement confirming that Yhwh did in fact enter his temple, a notable

---

3. For a discussion of the building-story genre, see V. A. Hurowitz, *I Have Built You an Exalted House: Temple Building in the Bible in Light of Mesopotamian and North-West Semitic Writings* (JSOTSup 115; Sheffield: Sheffield Academic Press, 1992); L. S. Fried, "The Land Lay Desolate: Conquest and Restoration in the Ancient Near East," in *Judah and the Judeans in the Neo-Babylonian Period* (ed. O. Lipschits and J. Blenkinsopp; Winona Lake, IN: Eisenbrauns, 2003) 21–54; idem, "Temple Building in Ezra–Nehemiah," in *From the Foundations to the Crenellations: Essays on Temple Building in the Ancient Near East and Hebrew Bible* (ed. M. J. Boda and J. Novotny; AOAT 366; Münster: Ugarit-Verlag, 2010) 319–38; as well as the many fine articles in Boda and Novotny, eds., *From the Foundations to the Crenellations*.

4. For a study of the application of ancient Near East story templates to biblical narratives and ideology, see K. Lawson Younger, *Ancient Conquest Accounts: A Study in Ancient Near Eastern and Biblical History Writing* (JSOTSup 98; Sheffield: Sheffield Academic Press, 1990).

5. It is possible that the author of Ezra 1–6 had the Second Temple's actual building inscription at his disposal even though he does not cite it. K. M. Stott (*Why Did They Write This Way? Reflections on References to Written Documents in the Hebrew Bible and Ancient Literature* [LHBOTS 492; London: T. & T. Clark, 2008] 19–51) points out that it was common for classical historians, like Herodotus and Thucydides, for example, to base their history on inscriptional and literary sources that they do not cite. See also my "Conquest and Restoration"; and my "Ezra's Use of Documents in the Context of Hellenistic Rules of Rhetoric," in *New Perspectives on Ezra–Nehemiah: History and Historiography, Text, Literature, and Interpretation* (ed. I. Kalimi; Winona Lake, IN: Eisenbrauns, 2012) 11–26.

6. R. S. Ellis, *Foundation Deposits in Ancient Mesopotamia* (New Haven, CT: Yale University Press, 1968); Hurowitz, *I Have Built You an Exalted House*; Boda and Novotny, eds., *From the Foundations to the Crenellations*; Fried, "Conquest and Restoration."

Table 1. Elements of Temple-Building in Ancient Near Eastern Building Inscriptions and in Ezra

ANE	Ezra
A. Brief history of the temple—why was it in ruins?	A. Missing
B. The decision to build—The king receives a divine command, usually in the first year.	B. In the first year of King Cyrus, Yhwh stirs up the spirit of Cyrus (1:1–2).
C. Building materials are brought from the ends of the earth.	C. Wood is brought from Lebanon and floated down to Yaffa (3:7).
D. Foundations are laid and the site is prepared.	D. In the second year of their arrival in the second month . . . the builders laid the foundations of the temple of Yhwh (3:10).
E. A ceremony for later building stages is held (e.g., the dedication of the altar).	E. In the seventh month, Jeshua and Zerubbabel set up the altar . . . and they offered burnt offerings upon it (3:1–3).
F. The description of the completed temple and its furnishings plus a statement that the temple has been built.	F. And this house was finished on the third day of the month of Adar in the 6th year of Darius (6:15).
G. The dedication ceremony of the finished building.	G. The people celebrated the dedication with joy (6:16).
H. The god is installed in the temple and takes up residence.	H. Missing
I. Celebration.	I. On the 14th day of the first month the returned exiles kept the Passover (6:19).
J. Presentation of gifts and appointment of temple personnel.	J. They appointed the Levites, from 20 years old and upward, to have oversight of the work on the house of Yhwh (3:8).
K. Prayer or curses.	K. A beam shall be pulled out of the house of anyone who harms this temple, and he shall be impaled on it. His house shall be made a dunghill. May the God overthrow any king or people that shall put forth a hand to alter this, or to destroy this house of God in Jerusalem (6:11–12).

lack that has led the rabbis to conclude that the Shechinah did not dwell in it (*BT Yoma* 21b). It can also be seen by examining the verse numbers that some of the components are out of order. This is because component E, "building and dedicating the altar," has been moved up from its normal position at the end of the building process to the beginning (to Ezra 3:3), displacing everything before it. According to the author of Ezra 1–6, the returnees built the altar and sacrificed on it as soon as they arrived, a very late stage in typical Mesopotamian temple-building projects.

Rhetorical Additions to the Building Story Template

As is obvious, Ezra 1–6 does not consist only of a building story. These chapters include lists of temple vessels and of returnees (Ezra 1:9–11, 2:2–70), of letters to and from a series of Persian kings (4:6–22, 5:6–17, 6:2–12), and a narrative segment about conflict between various groups of people (4:1–5). This conflict results in a threat to the temple-building process, a threat overcome only by the prophesying of Haggai and Zechariah (5:1). None of these elements belongs to the typical ancient Near East temple-building account. So, why have they been added? Why has the dedication of the altar been moved up to the beginning of the building story? Why has the typical ancient Near East temple-building story been deemed inadequate?

To answer these questions, it would help to know who wrote these chapters, why, and when. I have argued previously that one purpose of the narrative in Ezra 1–6 was to describe a community that fulfills Ezekiel's vision of the restoration of Judah.[7] A difficulty with this view is the presence of the prophets Haggai and Zechariah in such a powerful role since Ezekiel condemns the prophets and vows that they shall not return to the land of Israel (Ezek 13:9). Commentators as a rule do not discuss the inclusion of these prophets except to say that the author of Ezra bases these verses on the prophetic books that he evidently had before him[8] or to suggest that the prophetic voice was used to indicate that the necessary divine intervention was available to restart the building process.[9] Both of

---

7. L. S. Fried, "Who Wrote Ezra–Nehemiah and Why Did They?" in *Unity and Disunity in Ezra–Nehemiah: Redaction, Rhetoric, and Reader* (ed. M. J. Boda and P. L. Redditt; Hebrew Bible Monographs 17; Sheffield: Sheffield Phoenix, 2008) 75–97.

8. For example, H. G. M. Williamson, *Ezra, Nehemiah* (Word Biblical Commentary 16; Waco, TX: Word Books, 1985) xxiv, 75.

9. For example, J. Blenkinsopp, *Ezra–Nehemiah: A Commentary* (OTL; Philadelphia: Westminster, 1988) 116; A. H. J. Gunneweg, *Esra* (Kommentar zum Alten Testament 19; Gütersloh: Gütersloher Verlagshaus Mohn, 1985) 95–96.

these interpretations are certainly valid. Nevertheless, they do not explain the full rhetorical force of bringing in the prophets at the end of the narrative in spite of the declaration of Ezekiel, cited above, that they should not enter the land and in spite of the fact that they are missing from the list of returnees.

One way to address this issue is to consider more fully the diverse influences on the writer, but doing this requires knowing when he wrote. It has been shown that Neh 12:10–11 records all the high priests of the Persian period, down to the reign of Darius III,[10] and Williamson has argued convincingly that Ezra 1–6 was composed last, after Ezra 7–Nehemiah 13 was completed.[11] If all this is accepted, then Ezra–Nehemiah and especially these six chapters must have been written after the conquest of Alexander the Great, that is, in the Hellenistic period, in the last third of the fourth century at the very earliest. Thus, we may expect Hellenistic influences on the text including even Aristotelian (384–322 B.C.E.) ideals of rhetorical composition.[12] Greek rhetorical influences on biblical historiography have been studied for a long time now, but not, to my knowledge, with regard to the structure of Ezra 1–6.[13] Gary Knoppers complains that Greek

---

10. L. S. Fried, "A Silver Coin of Yohanan Hakkôhen," *Transeuphratène* 26 (2003) 65–85, pls. 2–5; J. C. VanderKam, *From Joshua to Caiaphas: High Priests After the Exile* (Minneapolis: Fortress, 2004).

11. H. G. M. Williamson, "The Composition of Ezra i–vi," *JTS* n.s. 34 (1983) 1–30. See also my "Who Wrote Ezra–Nehemiah."

12. Even before the advent of Alexander, however, there had been many Greek influences on the Levant. See, e.g., Einat Ambar-Armon and Amos Kloner, "Archaeological Evidence of Links between the Aegean World and the Land of Israel in the Persian Period," in *A Time of Change: Judah and Its Neighbours in the Persian and Early Hellenistic Periods* (ed. Y. Levin; Library of Second Temple Studies 65; London: T. & T. Clark, 2007) 1–22.

13. See, for example, J.-W. Wesselius, *The Origin of the History of Israel: Herodotus' Histories as Blueprint for the First Books of the Bible* (JSOTSup 345; Sheffield: Sheffield Academic Press, 2002); idem, "Towards a New History of Israel," *Journal of Hebrew Scriptures* 3 (2000–2001) 1–21; J. Van Seters, *In Search of History: Historiography in the Ancient World and the Origins of Biblical History* (New Haven, CT: Yale University Press, 1983); T. B. Dozeman, "Geography and History in Herodotus and in Ezra–Nehemiah," *JBL* 122 (2003) 449–66; F. A. J. Nielsen, *The Tragedy in History: Herodotus and the Deuteronomic History* (JSOTSup 251; Sheffield: Sheffield Academic Press, 1997); K. M. Stott, *Why Did They Write This Way? Reflections on References to Written Documents in the Hebrew Bible and Ancient Literature* (LHBOTS 492; London: T. & T. Clark, 2008); S. Mandell and D. N. Freedman, *The Relationship between Herodotus' History and Primary History* (South Florida Studies in the History of Judaism 60; Atlanta: Scholars Press, 1993); G. N. Knoppers, "Greek Historiography and the Chronicler's History: A Reexamination," *JBL* 122 (2003) 627–50. G. F. Davies (*Ezra and Nehemiah* [Berit Olam; Collegeville, MN: Liturgical Press, 1999]) applies an avowedly rhetorical approach to the study of Ezra–Nehemiah, but does not compare

historiography has been fruitfully compared to the writings of the Deuteronomistic Historian and of Genesis, but as yet scholars have ignored Chronicles (and I would add Ezra 1–6) in this rubric.[14] I have suggested recently, however, that the use of the documents in Ezra 1–6 is a technique borrowed from Hellenistic rules of rhetoric.[15] Here, I propose that these Hellenistic rules of rhetoric may explain the very structure of these chapters.

Rhetoric is the art of persuasion, and spans the genres: speeches, histories, tragedies, comedies, all need to persuade the audience.[16] Ezra 1–6 is

---

the book to Hellenistic rhetorical strategies, nor does he look at the rhetorical role of the prophets Haggai and Zechariah in the book.

14. Knoppers, "Greek Historiography and the Chronicler." In contrast, there have been several studies comparing the laws regarding foreign marriages in 5th century Athens and Yehud, e.g., B. Halpern, "Ezra's Reform and Bilateral Citizenship in Athens and the Mediterranean World," in *Egypt, Israel, and the Ancient Mediterranean World: Studies in Honor of Donald B. Redford* (ed. G. N. Knoppers and A. Hirsch; Leiden: Brill, 2004) 439–53; T. C. Eskenazi, ("The Missions of Ezra and Nehemiah," in *Judah and the Judeans in the Persian Period* [ed. O. Lipschits and M. Oeming; Winona Lake, IN: Eisenbrauns, 2006] 509–29; L. S. Fried, "The Concept of 'Impure Birth' in Fifth Century Athens and Judea," in *In the Wake of Tikva Frymer-Kensky: Tikva Frymer-Kensky Memorial Volume* [ed. S. Holloway, J. Scurlock, and R. H. Beal; Gorgias Précis Portfolios 4; Piscataway, NJ: Gorgias, 2009] 121–42). M. Cohen ("Leave Nehemiah Alone: Nehemiah's 'Tales' and Fifth-Century B.C.E. Historiography," in *Unity and Disunity in Ezra–Nehemiah: Redaction, Rhetoric, and Reader* [ed. M. J. Boda and P. L. Redditt; Hebrew Bible Monographs 17; Sheffield: Sheffield Phoenix, 2008] 55–74) compares Greek historiography to Nehemiah suggesting not a direct connection but rather "a commonality in the development of historical writing in the fifth century B.C.E." across the Greek and Judean world. She cites A. Momigliano ("Persian Historiography, Greek Historiography, and Jewish Historiography," in *The Classical Foundations of Modern Historiography* [Sather Classical Lectures 54; Berkeley: University of California Press, 1990] 2) that "both Greek and postexilic Hebrew historiography came into existence against the background of the Persian Empire and clearly show their common origin." Most recently, M. Boda ("Prayer as Rhetoric in the Book of Nehemiah," in *New Perspectives on Ezra–Nehemiah: History and Historiography, Text, Literature, and Interpretation* [ed. I. Kalimi; Winona Lake, IN: Eisenbrauns, 2012] 267–84) compared the narrative devices used in Nehemiah to Hellenistic rules of rhetoric.

15. L. S. Fried, "Ezra's Use of Documents." Momigliano ("Persian Historiography," 12–13) attributes the extensive use of documents to Achaemenid influences. He cites Esther (9:36) as evidence of the importance that the Achaemenids attached to documents. I would rather place Esther in the Hellenistic period and cite Greek influences on the text. See the discussions surrounding the date of Esther in C. A. Moore, *Esther* (AB 7B; New York: Doubleday, 1971) lvii–lx; and in J. D. Levinson, *Esther: A Commentary* (OTL; Louisville: Westminster John Knox, 1997) 26–27.

16. G. F. Davies, *Ezra and Nehemiah*, xiv. See also C. Pelling, *Literary Texts and the Greek Historian: Approaching the Ancient World* (London: Routledge, 2000) 1–2.

narrative, and Aristotle distinguishes two basic kinds: history and poetry. This difference in genre is not a function of the text being written in prose or verse. Aristotle states that "it would be quite possible for Herodotus's work to be translated into verse, and it would not be any the less a history with verse than it is without it" (*Poetics* 3851b1). Presumably, the reverse is also true—tragedies and comedies would be poetry, whether or not they were actually written in verse. I use "poetry" here as Aristotle does, to signify either tragedy or comedy while ignoring the element of versification. All poetry is not history, of course, but history writing can be a type of poetry. To Aristotle, the job of the historian is to report what has happened, while that of the poet is to report what could have happened or what is capable of happening according to the rules of probability or necessity (*Poetics* 3851b1–5). For this reason, Aristotle can maintain that "poetry is a more philosophical and serious business than history, for poetry speaks of universals, whereas history speaks only of particulars" (*Poetics* 3851b5–10). History is a subset of poetry, however, because "what is possible is persuasive . . . and what has happened is, we feel, obviously possible" (*Poetics* 3851b15–20).[17] In that sense, the tasks of the poet and of the historian are the same: to persuade the audience that the events recorded could have (or have) actually happened. Further, the techniques the writers have at their disposal to do this are the same.[18]

I suggest that the lists, the documents, the narrative, and the words of the prophets were all added to the Jerusalem temple's basic ancient Near-Eastern temple-building story in probably the late fourth century B.C.E., the Hellenistic period. Interpreting Ezra 1–6 according to Aristotelian rules of rhetoric may therefore help us to understand why these elements

---

17. Nielsen (*The Tragedy in History*, 27–36) stresses Herodotus's roots in the epic tradition of Homer and notes (p. 29) that the historian's task is not intrinsically different from that of the poet: "both hymn the doings of mankind." In contrast, T. C. Eskenazi (*In an Age of Prose: A Literary Approach to Ezra–Nehemiah* [SBLMS 36; Atlanta: Scholars Press, 1988] 1–2) bases the difference between poetry and prose on the presence or absence of gods and heroes in the stories and claims that we are now in an "Age of Prose." It is certainly true that we no longer have in either Greece or Yehud epic tales with the gods as central characters, but their total absence cannot be derived from this. They are still there, acting, but hidden. Eskenazi states (p. 1) that the words of the prophet have come to a "kind of closure," citing Ezra 1:1 לכלות דבר יהוה. Her book never discusses Ezra 5:1, however, and its numerous references to Ezra 6:14 are always to the last half of the verse, never to the first half where the importance of the prophets is mentioned. I would suggest that even accepting Eskenazi's distinction, that we are still in an Age of Poetry.

18. Nielsen, *The Tragedy in History*, 31. See also Hermann Strasburger, *Homer und die Geschichtsschreibung* (Heidelberg: Carl Winter, 1972).

were added. I have previously discussed the role of the documents;[19] here, I focus on the lists and the inclusion of the prophetic voice.

The Lists

The goal of any text is to persuade the reader, and according to Aristotle, texts have many ways to do this (*Rhetoric* 1356a1). One way is to increase readers' confidence in the reliability of the text and in the author's ability to access relevant sources.[20] Lists were used to accomplish both these goals, and the inclusion of lists was a fixed part of Greco-Roman narrative. Spurious lists were created when actual lists were unavailable.[21] Ctesias, for example, presents his readers with a spurious list of Assyrian kings, which he claims to have derived from Persian royal archives.[22] The fictive list of translators in the *Letter of Aristeas* (47–50) is another example of the addition of lists to increase the credibility of the text and to display the writer's knowledge of his subject.[23] Herodotus's provision of the minutest details of the peoples, places, and events that he describes are likewise intended to persuade the reader of his access to reliable sources rather than to provide historical facts, because his statements and the facts often conflict.[24] Greek historians also included genealogies in their reports to show their command of the subject matter, avoiding gaps by filling in the genealogies with spurious names. Herodotus's genealogies of the Spartan kings (7:204, 8:131), for example, are partly historical and partly fictive, reaching back to Heracles.[25] The genealogies of Jesus (Matt 1:2–16, Luke

---

19. Fried, "Ezra's Use of Documents."
20. Although originally intended for the orator, with the progress of writing, the rules of rhetoric were quickly applied to written texts (T. Morgan, *Literate Education in the Hellenistic and Roman Worlds* [Cambridge Classical Studies; Cambridge: Cambridge University Press, 1998] 190–226).
21. D. Lateiner, *The Historical Method of Herodotus* (Phoenix Journal of the Classical Association of Canada Supplementary Volume 23; Toronto: University of Toronto Press, 1989) 9; S. Honigman, *The Septuagint and Homeric Scholarship in Alexandria: A Study in the Narrative of the Letter of Aristeas* (London: Routledge, 2003) 73.
22. Ctesias' list of kings is quoted in Eusebius' *Chronici canones* and preserved in J.-P. Migne, *Collection Intégrale et Universelle Des Orateurs Sacrés Du Premier et Du Second Ordre* (Paris: Gaume, 1892) 19: 325–28.
23. Honigman, *The Septuagint and Homeric Scholarship*, 72; N. G. Cohen, "Jewish Names as Cultural Indicators in Antiquity: The Vogue of Certain Jewish Names is a Projection of the Surrounding Non-Jewish Cultural Milieu," *JSJ* 7 (1976) 97–128; idem, "The Names of the Translators in the Letter of Aristeas: A Study in the Dynamics of Cultural Transition," *JSJ* 15 (1984) 32–64.
24. S. West, "Herodotus' Epigraphical Interests," *CQ* 35 (1985) 278–305.
25. See G. N. Knoppers, "The Relationship of the Priestly Genealogies to the History of the High Priesthood in Jerusalem," in *Judah and the Judeans in the Neo-Bab-*

3:23–38) link Jesus to David for obvious reasons but do not agree even on the name of his paternal grandfather.

The inclusion of the list of vessels in Ezra 1 and the list of returnees in Ezra 2 serve a similar function. They not only glorify the temple by describing the great wealth and the immense number of people who streamed to Jerusalem to participate in its rebuilding, but the specificity in the names, numbers, family backgrounds, and towns of origin of the returnees, which is recorded in them, increases the reader's confidence in the author, in his access to sources, and in the reliability of his report.

The Narrative Structure

Besides the lists and other proofs or apparent proofs of the things to be persuaded (*logos*), Aristotle distinguishes two other modes of persuasion (*Rhetoric* 1356a1–5): through audience identification with the protagonists (*ethos*) and by the emotions aroused (*pathos*). A major way to persuade depends on eliciting emotional responses from the audience—positive feelings toward the protagonists and negative feelings toward their opponents. When the protagonists are worse than average, comedy results; when they are better than average, when they are people to be taken seriously whose acts have serious implications, then we have tragedy (*Poetics* 3849b10–25). If the writer of Ezra 1–6 is to be taken seriously, then he must relate events about ordinary men and women, people whom the audience can identify with, yet also people who are to be taken seriously and whose acts have serious consequences. In addition, he must produce a catharsis in the reader by arousing pity and fear in him.[26] Indeed, one purpose of adding the narrative in Ezra 1–6 to the text of the underlying building inscription may simply have been to provide the reader pleasure in the building story by building catharsis.

Because in both history and epic poetry, the subject matter is a man or a woman in action, the most important aspect of the writing is the series of narrated events, that is, the plot (*Poetics* 3850a15). The rhetorical handbooks set forth a rigid structure for both historical and poetic narrative, and this is outlined in table 2. It must consist of prologue, narration, proof that the narrative is true or possible, and epilogue. In turn,

---

ylonian Period (ed. O. Lipschits and J. Blenkinsopp; Winona Lake, IN: Eisenbrauns, 2003) 109–33, and the articles cited there for studies of the influence of Hellenistic rules of rhetoric on the biblical genealogies.

26. Aristotle, *Poetics* (trans. G. F. Else; Ann Arbor: University of Michigan Press, 1967) 6–7.

each of these have fixed components that define them (Aristotle, *Rhetoric* 1356a1).[27] The prologue must introduce the protagonist and create in the reader a favorable attitude toward him. It must also convince the reader that the writer's version of events is possible and reliable and that the writer has knowledge and sources that can be trusted. The epilogue should leave the reader in a positive frame of mind. Between the prologue and epilogue falls the narration. The narration provides the author's version of the events narrated, but it must also follow a fixed course (*Poetics* 3853a10–17).

An initial favorable attitude toward the protagonist must be strengthened by describing the good fortune that he enjoys, thus proving that he is favored by the gods. The protagonist must then suffer an unexpected reversal in fortune. This reversal must be from good fortune to bad, for it is only such reversals that arouse pity and fear in the reader. Moreover, the reversal must occur not from the protagonist's wickedness (for then it would be comedy), but from a natural decision, a decision that makes the protagonist the creator of his own undoing. Further, the decision must be the type that any ordinary person would make, so that the audience can easily identify with it. It must be a decision, though, that has great and negative consequences, a decision that results in a dramatic and negative reversal of fortune. In addition, the reversal must be "contrary to the reader's expectations," yet a logical and necessary consequence of the decision nevertheless (*Poetics* 3852a4).

Ezra 1–6 Follows Aristotelian Rules of Rhetoric

The Prologue

As can be seen in table 2, the narrative of Ezra 1–6 follows Aristotelian rules of tragic poetry. Ezra 1 and 2 form the prologue. They set the stage—they indicate the time and place of the action, and they introduce the protagonists—Zerubbabel, Jeshua, and the rest of the community of returnees. The lists of returnees and of temple vessels are added to convince the reader of the writer's knowledge and familiarity with the sources, so that the reader can readily accept the possibility of what follows.[28]

---

27. J. Wisse, *Ethos and Pathos from Aristotle to Cicero* (Amsterdam: Hakkert, 1989) 13.

28. Herodotus begins his history (1.2) with a reference to Persian scholars (οἱ λόγιοι Περσέων) in a similar attempt to gain the trust of the reader that he has special sources that the ordinary person does not have.

Table 2. Elements of Greek Historiography according to Aristotle and in Ezra

Aristotle	Ezra
Prologue	
Sets the stage, the time, and place, and reason for the action. Introduces the characters.	*Ezra 1:1–8.* In the first year of Cyrus, the *Gola* community returns to Jerusalem to build the temple.
Lists are included so that the reader gains an appreciation of the expertise of the author and trusts his story.	*Ezra 1:9–11; Ezra 2.*
Narrative Proper	
Act 1. Positive attitude toward protagonists created.	*Ezra 3:1–7.* Zerubbabel and Jeshua build an altar and begin the sacrifices. *Ezra 3:7–9.* They pay workers according to Cyrus's grant, and appoint temple personnel.
The good fortunes of the protagonists displayed.	*Ezra 3: 10–13.* Zerubbabel and Jeshua have the good fortune to have lived to see the temple's rebuilding in Jerusalem.
Act 2. The protagonists make a fateful decision that has serious and negative consequences.	*Ezra 4:1–3.* Zerubbabel and Jeshua reject the offer of their "enemies," the "people of the land" to help build the temple.
A terrible reversal of fortune happens to the protagonists as a result of the decision.	*Ezra 4:4–5.* The "people of the land" stop the temple building project.
Proofs of the veracity of the narrative inserted. (A tragedy would stop here, but a history must continue to its actual ending.)	*Ezra 4:5–23.* The correspondence with Artaxerxes proves the mendacity and duplicity of the "people of the land."
Act 3. A *deus ex machina* occurs to bring events to their rightful conclusion.	*Ezra 5:1.* Haggai and Zechariah prophesy.
A second *reversal of fortune* from negative to positive occurs to bring events to their actual and necessary conclusion.	*Ezra 5:2.* Zerubbabel and Jeshua begin again to rebuild the temple.
Proofs of the narrative inserted.	*Ezra 5:3–6:12.* The correspondence with Darius.
Epilogue. The audience is put in a positive frame of mind.	*Ezra 6:13–22.* The temple is completed and dedicated with joy. The Passover is celebrated with joy.

Narrative—Act 1, The Good Fortune of the Protagonists Revealed

The narrative proper begins in Ezra 3, and is intended to arouse a favorable attitude toward the protagonists. We read that as soon as the returnees are settled in their towns, they gather as one man in Jerusalem to build an altar to the God of Israel and to offer burnt offerings on it according to the law of Moses (Ezra 3:1–6a). The reader becomes favorably disposed toward them, for not only do they carefully follow the law of Moses, but they dutifully obey the edict of Cyrus too by preparing to lay the foundations of the temple according to his mandate, by paying the carpenters and masons their correct fees, and by bringing cedar trees from Lebanon by sea to Jaffa as Cyrus had authorized (3:6b–7). The enthusiasm and concern shown by Zerubbabel, Jeshua, and the rest of the returnees for the laws of both God and Cyrus testify to their high moral character and their good will toward God, toward the Persian king, and toward the Judean community—the community to which the implied reader presumably belongs.

By moving the altar-building scene from the end of the building story to its beginning, the author immediately conveys the enthusiasm of the protagonists—Zerubbabel, Jeshua, and the whole community—for the laws of God and Moses. In the process, however, the story is transformed from a Mesopotamian temple-building story to a Greek story. Building an altar and sacrificing on it before a temple is built is anomalous according to ancient Near Eastern theological understandings.[29] Sacrificing on an isolated altar with no temple present at all is typical of Hellenistic and Greek ritual practices, however. Indeed, building the altar is the necessary first step when establishing a Greek cult site.[30]

The narrative continues in Ezra 3:10–13, where the ceremony celebrating the dedication of the Second Temple's foundations is described. This is the climax of the chapter and portrays the great good fortune of the protagonists, for they and they alone have lived to see YHWH's Temple rebuilt.

---

29. See the articles in Boda and Novotny, eds., *From the Foundations to the Crenellations*.

30. A. Burford, *The Greek Temple Builders at Epidaurus: A Social and Economic Study of Building in the Asklepian Sanctuary During the Fourth and Early Third Centuries B.C.* (Liverpool Monographs in Archaeology and Oriental Studies; Liverpool: Liverpool University Press, 1969) 47. I thank Prof. B. A. Levine for calling Burford's book to my attention. Greek cult sites are created by building an altar and sacrificing on it. Only then is a temple built. As is clear from the Homeric myths, in contrast to the Mesopotamian gods, Greek gods did not dwell in a temple but lived on Mt. Olympus. Sacrificial altars could be anywhere; the god would come, participate in the sacrificial meal, and leave (W. Burkert, *Greek Religion* [trans. J. Raffan; Cambridge, MA: Harvard University Press, 1985] 55–59).

They and they alone have lived to witness in that rebuilding God's eternal loyalty to the people Israel.

Narrative—Act 2, The Protagonists Make a Fateful Decision

Aristotelian rules of rhetoric require that a reversal of fortune now occur. If good fortune is symbolized by rebuilding the temple, then the reversal of fortune must be a halt to the building process. Aristotle requires, moreover, that this reversal come about as a result of an ordinary decision by the protagonists, a decision that anyone might make. Accordingly, we read next of the natural, but ill-advised, decision of Zerubbabel and Jeshua, the primary protagonists:

> When the enemies of Judah and Benjamin heard that the returned exiles were building a temple to Yhwh, the God of Israel, they approached Zerubbabel and the heads of families and said to them, "Let us build with you, for we worship your God as you do, and we have been sacrificing to him ever since the days of King Esar-haddon of Assyria who brought us here."
>
> But Zerubbabel, Jeshua, and the rest of the heads of families in Israel said to them, "You shall have no part with us in building a house to our God; but we alone will build to Yhwh, the God of Israel, as King Cyrus of Persia has commanded us" (Ezra 4:1–3).

When Zerubbabel and Jeshua make the rash decision to resist their "enemies'" participation in the temple-building project, these "enemies" react angrily: they "bribe officials to frustrate the plan [to build the temple] throughout the reign of King Cyrus of Persia and until the reign of King Darius of Persia" (Ezra 4:5), and the building process is stopped until the reign of Darius. Stopping the construction of the temple is a sharp reversal in the fortunes of our protagonists, a reversal intended to arouse pity in the reader. The involvement of high Persian officials in the stoppage is intended to arouse fear as well.

Is the incident historical? Did Persian officials really stop the temple-building process? No. We have not history-writing here but drama. The incident is created to comply with Hellenistic, particularly Aristotelian, rules of poetic tragedy. The letter offered as proof of the perfidy of "the people of the land" who supposedly bribe officials to stop work on the temple-building project (Ezra 4:11–22) has nothing to do with temple-building at all.[31] It concerns Jerusalem's city wall and indicates that only

---

31. For a discussion of why a letter aimed at stopping the building of a city wall around Jerusalem is included at this point of the narrative about the Jerusalem temple, see my "Ezra's Use of Documents."

the construction of Jerusalem's city wall was stopped, not work on the temple.[32] Moreover, the correspondence is addressed to neither Cyrus nor Darius but to an Artaxerxes, probably the first of that name, Darius's grandson (465–24 B.C.E.). Tattenai's letter to Darius confirms, moreover, that there was no interruption in temple-building. By the time of Tattenai's arrival, probably in Darius's second year, work on the temple was progressing nicely, and it "prospered in their hands" (5:8).[33] The writings of Haggai and Zechariah, moreover, firmly dated to the beginning years of Darius I,[34] know of no halt in the construction of the temple caused by Persian authorities, nor do they know of any disputes with them. These prophetic writings reveal no problems with the Samaritans or any foreign-

---

32. A. Schenker and D. Böhler argue that the version of the letter to Artaxerxes in Ezra 4 was originally in the form it takes in 1 Esdras, that is, that it included a reference to the temple as well as the city walls (2:18, 20). See A. Schenker, "La Relation d'Esdras A' au Texte Massorétique d'Esdras-Néhémie," in *Tradition of the Text: Studies Offered to Dominique Barthélemy in Celebration of His 70th Birthday* (ed. G. J. Norton and S. Pisano; OBO 109; Göttingen: Vandenhoeck & Ruprecht, 1991) 218–48; idem, "The Relationship between Ezra–Nehemiah and 1 Esdras," in *Was 1 Esdras First? An Investigation into the Priority and Nature of 1 Esdras* (ed. L. S. Fried; Ancient Israel and Its Literature 7; Atlanta: Society of Biblical Literature) 2011; D. Böhler, *Die Heilige Stadt in Esdras a und Esra–Nehemia: Zwei Konzeptionen der Wiederherstellung Israels* (OBO 158; Göttingen: Vandenhoeck & Ruprecht, 1997); idem, "On the Relationship between Textual and Literary Criticism: The Two Recensions of the Book of Ezra: Ezra–Neh (MT) and 1 Esdras (LXX)," in *The Earliest Text of the Hebrew Bible: The Relationship between the Masoretic Text and the Hebrew Base of the Septuagint Reconsidered* (ed. A. Schenker; Septuagint and Cognate Studies 52; Atlanta: Society of Biblical Literature, 2003) 35–50. For a full discussion of all the issues surrounding 1 Esdras, see now the articles in L. S. Fried, ed., *Was 1st Esdras First? An Investigation into the Nature and Priority of 1 Esdras* (SBLSymS; Atlanta: Scholars Press, forthcoming).

33. A cuneiform tablet found in Babylon and dated to 502 B.C.E. refers to the servant of "Ta-at-tan-nu, satrap (*piḫatu*) of Ebir-nari," that is, to Tattenai, satrap of Beyond the River (Arthur Ungnad, "Keilinschriftliche Beiträge Zum Buch Esra und Ester," *ZAW* 57 [1941] 240–44). Scholars conclude that Tattenai's letter is the oldest and most authentic section in Ezra 1–6. See, for example, J. Pakkala, *Ezra the Scribe: The Development of Ezra 7–10 and Nehemiah 8* (BZAW 347; Berlin: de Gruyter, 2004) 3; R. G. Kratz, *The Composition of the Narrative Books of the Old Testament* (trans. J. Bowden; London: T. & T. Clark, 2005) 53–55; L. L. Grabbe, "The 'Persian Documents' in the Book of Ezra: Are They Authentic?" in *Judah and the Judeans in the Persian Period* (ed. O. Lipschits and M. Oeming; Winona Lake, IN: Eisenbrauns, 2006) 546–48; H. G. M. Williamson, "The Aramaic Documents in Ezra Revisited," *JTS* 59 (2008) 41–62.

34. Pace D. Edelman, *The Origins of the 'Second' Temple: Persian Imperial Policy and the Rebuilding of Jerusalem* (BibleWorld Series; London: Equinox, 2005); cf. R. W. Klein, "Were Joshua, Zerubbabel, and Nehemiah Contemporaries? A Response to Diana Edelman's Proposed Late Date for the Second Temple," *JBL* 127 (2008) 697–701.

ers, nor do they indicate that there were any divisions at all between the returnees and any other group.[35]

The biblical writer evidently created the event in order to add drama and tension to his text[36] and also perhaps because he believed that something like this "must have happened" to cause Tattenai, the governor of the sub-satrapy Beyond the River, to investigate the temple-building project in Jerusalem (5:3). The writer likely assumed that Tattenai would not have investigated the temple unless there had been some complaints about it, and so he created the incident described in 4:1–5. In fact, Tattenai needed no complaints to prompt his inspection. He was simply taking an appropriate tour of his jurisdiction in the first year of his appointment as satrap of Beyond the River in the second year of Darius I and then sending his findings on to the king who appointed him.[37]

Though not historical, the incident in Ezra 4:1–5 is consistent with Hellenic rules of rhetoric. As required, the resulting reversal in the fortune of our protagonists is caused by an ordinary decision, a decision that anyone could imagine himself making. Second, the "enemies" naturally become very angry when their offer is repulsed. According to Aristotle (*Rhetoric* 1378b), anger is defined as a "conspicuous impulse for revenge . . . [commonly] for a slight directed without justification towards oneself or one's friends." "Slighting" consists of (1) exhibiting contempt for someone, (2) thwarting someone's wishes for no reason, or (3) shaming the victim for no reason. Because whoever paid the officials to write accusing letters to the Persian kings obviously acted out of anger and out of a desire for revenge, they must have felt slighted. The biblical writer created an event in which our protagonists inadvertently slight those who come to offer help, causing them to react in anger, to seek revenge, and to try to stop the building process. Thus, a natural decision on the part of our protagonists brings about their sharp reversal of fortune, a reversal intended to arouse pity and fear on the part of the reader. This conforms to Aristotelian rules of plot construction.[38]

---

35. P. R. Bedford, *Temple Restoration in Early Achaemenid Judah* (SJSJ 65; Leiden: Brill, 2001).

36. So also C. C. Torrey, *Ezra Studies* (Library of Biblical Studies; New York: Ktav, 1970).

37. Reports such as these from the satrap to the king were a vital part of Achaemenid rule; see my *The Priest and the Great King: Temple-Palace Relations in the Persian Empire* (Biblical and Judaic Studies 10; Winona Lake, IN: Eisenbrauns, 2004).

38. Of course, it would have been more to the master's liking if the so-called "enemies" of the Jews turned out to be their long-lost cousins, descendants perhaps of those not deported, and would have been even better if our protagonists gradually recognized

Narrative—Act 3, A Second Reversal of Fortune, from Bad to Good: The God on the Machine

A tragic poet should end his tale here, with the temple-building's cessation. To Aristotle, the better stories end unhappily, tragically. There should be only one reversal of fortune—from good to bad, with no reversal from bad to good fortune again. However when the audience knows how the story ends, the poet has no choice but to report the known ending. Thus, the author of Ezra 1–6 has no choice but to report the temple's completion. Many Greek plays, for example, are dramatic retellings of familiar myths, myths whose positive ending was already known to the audience. Even when the Greek poets retold familiar stories, however, they embellished them by putting the protagonists in precarious and dangerous positions in order to arouse pity and fear in the audience. In those cases, when a positive ending was already known to the audience, the poet would often find himself unable to extricate the hero from his tragic circumstances to bring about the known positive ending. The plot would become so tangled that it would frequently be necessary for a god to appear to untangle the plot and bring the matter to its rightful and appropriate conclusion.[39] At other times, the appearance of the god was necessary just to let the audience know what the rightful ending ought to be, that is, the ending desired by the gods. In these types of cases, the god would be lowered onto a roof or balcony by means of a crane and either magically bring about the desired ending or at least tell the protagonists—and the audience—what the desired outcome was. In fact, the *deus ex machina*, "the god on the crane," eventually became a standard ending in Greek tragedy.[40] In Sophocles' *Philoctetes*, for example, Heracles appears to tell both the protagonists and the audience that the gods wanted Philoctetes to go with Odysseus to conquer Troy. Often, as in Euripides' *Electra*, the play would include the erection of a temple and the establishment of a cult for just those gods who had been lowered onto the stage—a temple and a cult whose shrine and rites were well known to the audience. This

---

this after work on the temple had been stopped (*Poetics* 3852a30–35). Unfortunately, there is nothing of this in the text. For a discussion of the identity of these "enemies," see L. S. Fried, "The ʿAm Haʾaretz in Ezra 4:4 and Persian Imperial Administration," in *Judah and the Judeans in the Persian Period* (ed. O. Lipschits and M. Oeming; Winona Lake, IN: Eisenbrauns, 2006) 123–45, and the literature referred to there.

39. A. Spira, *Untersuchungen zum Deus ex Machina bei Sophokles und Euripides* (Kallmünz, Opf: Lassleben, 1960); Rush Rhem, *Greek Tragic Theatre* (Theatre Production Series; London: Routledge, 1992).

40. Spira, *Untersuchungen Zum Deus Ex Machina*.

technique would bring the mythical actions presented in the play into the present real time of the audience.[41] In spite of the popularity of the *deus ex machina,* however, Aristotle fulminates against it. According to Aristotle (*Poetics* 1454a33–1454b9):

> In character portrayal also, as in plot construction, one should always strive for either the necessary or the probable, so that it is either necessary or probable for that kind of person to do or say that kind of thing, just as it is for one event to follow the other. It is evident, then, that the dénouements of plots also should come out of the character itself, and not from the "machine" as in the Medea or with the sailing of the fleet in the Aulis. . . . let there be no illogicality in the web of events.

The "god on the machine" is, by definition, illogical, an event that comes neither out of the character of the *dramatic personae* nor out of the sequence of events that formed the plot. It is extraneous to both. To Aristotle, tragedies should end unhappily but logically, and the only purpose for the god to be lowered on to the stage was simply to avoid the natural and logical ending.

As was often the case in Greek theater, the implied reader of the biblical text also knew the story's ending; he knew that the temple stood, and so knew that it had been completed and dedicated. The problem for the author then was to get from the low-point of the drama, the pathetic and frightening reversal of fortune when temple building seems to have been stopped irrevocably, to the known happy outcome—the temple's successful completion and dedication under Darius I. The author solves the problem in the usual way: he brings in a god.

The presence of the *deus ex machina* is not unknown in biblical literature. Isaac is dramatically rescued from Abraham's knife when an angel (or God himself) stays Abraham's hand (Genesis 22). Indeed, if the story were acted out, the angel would have to have been lowered down by a crane. Because the audience knows that Isaac survives to sire children, the author cannot have him sacrificed.[42] The only way out of the dilemma then, was apparently to have a god appear, save Isaac, and grant Abraham numerous blessings to boot.

A much less flamboyant type of *deus ex machina* is depicted here in Ezra 5. The reader knows that the temple was eventually built, and so in

---

41. Rehm, *Greek Tragic Theatre,* 70–71

42. Although there is a Jewish legend that Isaac was actually sacrificed, goes to heaven for three years, and is then resurrected to sire children (L. Ginzberg, *The Legends of the Jews* [vol. 1 of Bible Times and Characters From the Creation to Moses in the Wilderness; trans. H. Szold; Philadelphia: Jewish Publication Society, 1947] 279–86).

spite of the fact that construction has been stopped by order of the king himself, the author must somehow get around to the temple's completion and dedication. Because late 4th-century B.C.E. Judean theology would not have permitted the aniconic god to appear on a rooftop,[43] lowered down by a crane, the author brings in the prophets Haggai and Zechariah to prophesy.

According to the text, as soon as they prophesy (5:1), Zerubbabel and Jeshua rise to begin work on the temple (5:2). Tattenai comes just at that moment to investigate (5:3) and reports back to his king, Darius, that the temple is progressing "quickly," and the work "prospers in their hands" (5:8). There is no evidence in Tattenai's letter that the work had ever been stopped, nor could there be, because the letter was written in the reign of Darius I, and the putative stoppage occurred in the reign of his grandson, Artaxerxes I. Saying this, however, denies the role of the prophets and denies God's ultimate sovereignty over his temple. It also denies the intention of the writer. By having the prophets prophesy, the writer creates a type of *deus ex machina*. The prophesying results in God's forcing the action to the ending God desires—the completion and dedication of his temple. Like the role of the *deus* in Greek tragedy, the role of the prophets here is to inform the reader what God's true desire is (that the temple be rebuilt) and God's effectiveness in bringing his desires about. In spite of Aristotle's caveat against the "machine" and in spite of Ezekiel's hostility toward the prophets, our author succumbs and uses the prophetic voice to represent God himself, the "*deus ex machina*," to bring the story to its rightful and obvious conclusion (Ezra 5:1–2, 5; 6:14).

Epilogue

As discussed above, the epilogue follows the drama and is intended to create a positive frame of mind in the audience. As is seen in the epilogue of Ezra 1–6 (Ezra 6:14–22), great good fortune reigns for all the protagonists as the temple is completed and dedicated through the prophesying of Haggai and Zechariah and by the commands of the God of Israel and the decrees of Cyrus, Darius, and Artaxerxes king of Persia. The epilogue stresses the great joy that is experienced by the community of returnees.

> The people of Israel, the priests and the Levites, and the rest of the returned exiles, celebrated the dedication of this house of God with joy (Ezra 6:16).

---

43. An angel would have been appropriate here as well to announce that the temple will go forward; cf. 1 Chronicles 21.

The dedication of the temple occurs on the (twenty-)third of Adar (Ezra 6:15)[44] and is quickly followed by the celebration of the Passover holiday on the 14th of the following month:

> With joy they celebrated the festival of unleavened bread seven days; for Y{\sc hwh} had made them joyful, and had turned the heart of the king of Assyria to them, so that he aided them in the work on the house of God, the God of Israel.

Conclusion

It can be concluded from the above analysis that the structure of the plot in Ezra 1–6 has been revised from the traditional ancient Near East temple-building story to conform to Aristotelian rules of tragic drama. This is true in both the creation of the character of the protagonists (*ethos*) and in the development of a plot (*pathos*). Neither character nor plot would have been present in the original temple-building story around which these chapters were built. In good Aristotelian fashion, Ezra 1–6 begins by describing the great good fortune of the returning community in that the decree of Cyrus (in conformity with the predictions of Jeremiah) enables them to finally return to Judah and to rebuild their temple. As required by Aristotelian rules of tragic poetry, however, a reversal of this good fortune occurs. Moreover, it occurs as a result of the natural decision of the protagonists, the type of decision that anyone would make. According to the story, a hasty decision to reject the "enemies" of the Judeans participation in the temple-building project leads to their feeling slighted, their resulting anger, their desire for revenge, and the eventual cessation of all work on the temple. This pitiable and fearful situation is rectified only by Haggai and Zechariah's prophesying—by the appearance of the god whose temple it is, a 4th-century Judean version of the god on the machine.

---

44. Reading with 1 Esdr 7:5.

Is the Governor Also among the Prophets? Parsing the Purposes of Jeremiah in the Memory of Nehemiah

DAVID SHEPHERD

In light of the fact that the book of Nehemiah is not located among the canonical Nevi'im, nor is the character of Nehemiah obviously included in the company of the prophets, it seems unlikely that the question 'Is Nehemiah also among the prophets?' should be answered in the affirmative. Recently, however, C. Karrer-Grube has suggested that the restoration programme described in the composition of Ezra–Nehemiah as a whole should be understood as a fulfilment of the divine promises found in Jeremiah.[1] While Karrer-Grube discusses a variety of resonances between Jeremiah and Ezra–Nehemiah, some of which will be discussed below, a fundamental contention of her argument is that Nehemiah's first-person report as well as chaps. 8–10 should be read as a fulfilment of "the word of the LORD spoken by Jeremiah" (Ezra 1:1), particularly those words of Jeremiah found in chaps. 30–33 and 17:19–27.

There is much that is stimulating and illuminating in Karrer-Grube's analysis, but her proposal depends, and unfortunately also founders, first on her suggestion that the clear centrality of the temple in the composition of Ezra–Nehemiah as a whole is a "far-reaching correction" of Jeremiah's apparent disinterest in the reconstruction of the temple. The difficulty is that a correction this far reaching can only be considered "fulfilment" in the loosest possible sense of the word.[2] Moreover, as T. C. Eskenazi notes, Nehemiah 9 is at pains to emphasize that the covenant entered into by the community at the Water Gate is as old as the Abraham, with whom the community identifies—the Abraham who was found to

---

1. C. Karrer-Grube, "Scrutinizing the Conceptual Unity of Ezra and Nehemiah," in *Unity and Disunity in Ezra–Nehemiah: Redaction, Rhetoric, and Reader* (ed. M. J. Boda and P. L. Redditt; Hebrew Bible Monographs 17; Sheffield: Sheffield Phoenix, 2008) 156.

2. J. Blenkinsopp, "Ezra–Nehemiah: Unity or Disunity?" in *Unity and Disunity in Ezra–Nehemiah: Redaction, Rhetoric, and Reader* (ed. M. J. Boda and P. L. Redditt; Hebrew Bible Monographs 17; Sheffield: Sheffield Phoenix, 2008) 308.

be faithful (9:8) and to whom God was in turn faithful (9:32). Whatever then the covenant in Nehemiah 9 is, the one thing it is not is "new," as in Jer 31:31–34.[3] Finally, Karrer-Grube is hard-pressed to prove that the word Ezra–Nehemiah fulfils must belong to Jeremiah (rather than another prophet), given that others of the period are often found to voice common concerns.[4] Undoubtedly, Jeremianic influence has been felt in some way in the redaction of Ezra–Nehemiah as a whole (see Ezra 1:1), but the apparent resonances of the final composition to Ezekiel's restoration programme—with its interest in the cult and its apparatuses—suggests that scholarship has yet to account fully for the complexity of Ezra–Nehemiah's indebtedness to various prophetic traditions.[5]

While the exploration of this influence of prophetic traditions on the redactional shaping of Ezra–Nehemiah as a whole is thus to be encouraged, this study is much more modest in its aims. I will argue only that the self-presentation of Nehemiah in his so-called Memoir reflects an awareness of his own sense of identification with and participation in the fulfilment of the prophetic purposes associated with Jeremiah.

Though there is not, admittedly, universal agreement as to the authenticity or extent of Nehemiah's own record of his exploits, the position that Neh 1:1–2:20, 4:1–7:5, 12:31–43, and 13:6–31 (more or less) reflect his personal account is perhaps widely enough held to allow us to consider how various elements within it might support the above suggestion.[6]

---

3. T. C. Eskenazi, "Unity and Disunity in Ezra–Nehemiah: Responses and Reflections," in *Unity and Disunity in Ezra–Nehemiah: Redaction, Rhetoric, and Reader* (ed. M. J. Boda and P. L. Redditt; Hebrew Bible Monographs 17; Sheffield: Sheffield Phoenix, 2008) 325; See also A. Steinmann's review of Karrer-Grube's essay (*Review of Biblical Literature* 2 [2009]. On-line: http://www.bookreviews.org/bookdetail.asp?TitleId=6677&CodePage=6677.pdf). Rather more impressive are the resonances of theme and vocabulary between Jeremiah 31 and Ezra 8–9 detected by J. G. McConville, "Ezra–Nehemiah and the Fulfilment of Prophecy," *VT* 36 (1986) 205–24. Though again, the situation is complicated by apparent allusions to the Isaianic tradition.

4. Eskenazi, "Unity and Disunity," 326.

5. For the suggestion of the influence of Ezekiel on the composition of Ezra–Nehemiah as a whole, see L. S. Fried, "Who Wrote Ezra–Nehemiah and Why Did They?" in *Unity and Disunity in Ezra–Nehemiah: Redaction, Rhetoric, and Reader* (ed. M. J. Boda and P. L. Redditt; Hebrew Bible Monographs 17; Sheffield: Sheffield Phoenix, 2008). While Fried highlights the "Ezekielian" editor's exclusion of prophetic figures from the list of returnees, she also suggests that this same editor presents Ezra's reading of the law and Nehemiah's erection of the wall as symbolic enactments of the prophet whom God told Ezekiel would build a *gader*. While the suggestion is attractive (and capitalizes on the verbal parallels between Neh 3:3–5 and Ezek 13:4–5), one might wish for more concrete evidence in support of it.

6. For a recent survey of opinions on the existence and extent of the NM, see M. J. Boda, "Redaction in the Book of Nehemiah," in *Unity and Disunity in Ezra–*

Perhaps the most obvious point of departure for an assessment of the extent of Nehemiah's identification with the purposes of the Jeremianic tradition is the beginning of Nehemiah's own account, particularly given that some have sensed a resonance between the initiation of Nehemiah's ministry and the stereotypical form(s) of initiation associated with the prophetic tradition.[7] While H. G. M. Williamson declines P. R. Ackroyd's suggestion that the opening words of the book ("the words of Nehemiah the son of Hacaliah"[8]) reflect the influence of the prophetic books, his detection of a call and a commission in Nehemiah's Memoir resonates with initiation patterns most frequently associated with prophets.[9] Indeed, the presence of a first-person narrative, the clear sense of a divine catalyst/support (2:8) for a new role or course of action (2:5), the self-identification of Nehemiah with the community to which he is "called" (1:5–11), and even the appearance of initial resistance to the divinely imposed burden (1:4) might all be seen to contribute to the "prophetic" impression of the beginning of Nehemiah's self-portrait.[10] Whether such a constellation of features suffices to establish Nehemiah's prophetic "calling" may, however, be doubted given the absence of other elements commonly found in narratives such as these.[11] Moreover, the impression of a prophetic vocation for Nehemiah diminishes when one considers both that many of these same form-critical features may be detected in those who are leaders (e.g., Gideon) but not obviously prophets[12] and that one of the hallmarks of

---

Nehemiah: Redaction, Rhetoric, and Reader (ed. M. J. Boda and P. L. Redditt; Hebrew Bible Monographs 17; Sheffield: Sheffield Phoenix, 2008) 25 nn. 1 and 2.

7. P. R. Ackroyd, *I and II Chronicles, Ezra, Nehemiah* (TBC; London: SCM, 1973) 274; R. J. Coggins, *The Books of Ezra and Nehemiah* (New York: Cambridge University Press, 1976) 69–70.

8. Unless otherwise noted, English translations are taken from the RSV.

9. H. G. M. Williamson characterizes Neh.1:1–11 as "Nehemiah's Vocation" and 2:1–10 as "Nehemiah's Commission" (*Ezra, Nehemiah* [WBC 16; Waco: Word, 1985] 175–76). In a similar vein, see also Ackroyd, *I and II Chronicles, Ezra, Nehemiah*, 269; and Coggins, *The Books of Ezra and Nehemiah*, 68–71. Because this study does not detect in Nehemiah any formal equivalent to a *prophetic* call, the further elaboration by W. Zimmerli of two types of call is, for our purposes, a moot point (*Ezechiel* [BKAT 13, Neukirchen-Vluyn: Neukirchener Verlag, 1969] 15–21).

10. For the drawing of such parallels, see especially Coggins, whose comparison of Nehemiah's reluctance (1:4) with Jer 1:6, however, seems especially strained (*The Books of Ezra and Nehemiah*, 70).

11. For all the petitionary piety conveyed in the opening of Nehemiah's account, the sense of an immediate divine audience/exchange (or indeed an explicit commission of any sort) so characteristic of the classic prophetic call is notably lacking.

12. So N. Habel, "The Form and Significance of the Call Narratives," ZAW 77 (1965) 297–323.

the prophets is their function as divine messenger.[13] Indeed, the accounts found in Amos, Isaiah, Ezekiel, and Jeremiah suggest that the role of mediating the divine word (Amos 7:15–16, Isa 6:9, Ezek 2:3–4, Jer 1:6) is virtually the *sine qua non* of a specifically prophetic call, and however the "Word of God" may or may not be present in the introductory chapters of Nehemiah, Williamson is surely right to note that it is the *absence* of the prophetic mediating of the word of the Lord, which is most conspicuous at the beginning of Nehemiah, particularly when contrasted with the highlighting of Jeremiah, Haggai, and Zechariah in the book of Ezra.[14]

While the call narratives of Isaiah, Ezekiel, and Amos accordingly describe the prophetic purpose entirely in terms of the mediation of the divine word,[15] the same cannot be said for the prophet Jeremiah, whose divinely expressed purposes in Jeremiah 1 extend beyond the mere delivery of the divine message (vv. 6, 9, 17): "See, I have set you this day over nations and over kingdoms, to pluck up and to break down, to destroy and to overthrow, to build and to plant" (Jer 1:10).[16]

The fact that all six of these verbs recur in subsequent texts within the book of Jeremiah (12:14–17; 18:7, 9; 24:6; 31:28, 38, 40; 42:10; 45:4) supports R. P. Carroll's suggestion that v. 10 serves as a summary, cataloguing Jeremiah's prophetic purposes within his call or commissioning narrative.[17] R. Bach's analysis of the final pair of verbs in this sequence ("to build and to plant") strongly suggests that, within the book of Jeremiah and beyond, this word pair is used to represent the notion of a settled and sustainable life. While the history and development of its use within the

---

13. J. F. Ross, "The Prophet as Yahweh's Messenger," in *Israel's Prophetic Heritage: Essays in Honor of James Muilenburg* (ed. B. W. Anderson and W. Harrelson; London: SCM, 1962) 98–107.

14. H. G. M. Williamson ("More Unity Than Diversity," in *Unity and Disunity in Ezra–Nehemiah: Redaction, Rhetoric, and Reader* [ed. M. J. Boda and P. L. Redditt; Hebrew Bible Monographs 17; Sheffield: Sheffield Phoenix, 2008] 336) in response to the suggestion of Nykolaishen ("The Restoration of Israel by God's Word," 176–99) that the divine word is manifest in the opening chapters through inscripturated prayer.

15. Isa 6:10b establishes that the call of Isaiah to dull the perceptions of the people is inextricably linked with (and arguably simply a recapitulation of) the particular divine word Isaiah is called on to deliver: "Go, and say to this people: 'Hear and hear, but do not understand; see and see, but do not perceive'" (6:9).

16. R. Bach, "Bauen und Pflanzen," in *Studien zur Theologie der alttestamentlichen Überlieferung* (ed. R. Rendtorff and K. Koch; Neukirchen-Vluyn: Neukirchener Verlag, 1961); and, recently, J. Smoak, "Building Houses and Planting Vineyards: The Early Inner-Biblical Discourse on an Ancient Israelite Wartime Curse," *JBL* 127 (2008) 19–35.

17. R. P. Carroll, *Jeremiah: A Commentary* (London: SCM, 1986) 95.

book of Jeremiah may be debated, Bach argues persuasively that the pairing originates with Jeremiah himself.[18] So while the exiles are encouraged in Jer 29:5 to remain in Babylon to "build houses and live in them; plant gardens and eat their produce" until the completion of Babylon's "seventy years" (29:10), it is clear from 24:6 that the ultimate reconstruction will be undertaken by God himself on their eventual return to the land: "I will build them up and not tear them down; I will plant them and not uproot them." This abstract expression of the "building up" of the people finds its concrete counterpart in Jer 30:18–21:

> Thus says the LORD: "Behold, I will restore the fortunes of the tents of Jacob, and have compassion on his dwellings; the city shall be rebuilt upon its mound, and *the citadel*[19] shall stand where it used to be. Out of them shall come songs of thanksgiving, and the voices of those who make merry. I will multiply them, and they shall not be few; I will make them honored, and they shall not be small. Their children shall be as they were of old, and their congregation shall be established before me; and I will punish all who oppress them. Their prince shall be one of themselves, their ruler shall come forth from their midst; I will make him draw near, and he shall approach me, for who would dare of himself to approach me? says the LORD.

While the notion of the concrete "rebuilding" of Jerusalem is not of course limited to Jeremiah (see also Ezek 36:10, 33–36; 48:15–35; Isa 44:26–28; 49:16–26; 61:4), and other prophetic passages do evoke the image of repopulation (see Ezek 36:33–36, Isa 49:17–22) and even the motif of ultimate subjugation of oppressors (49:26), what is unique to Jeremiah is this painting of a programmatic picture of restoration. This unique programmatic picture begins with physical reconstruction (v. 18) but also includes the sounds of celebration (v. 18) the restoration of honor (v. 19b) and population (v. 19b), the establishment of the congregation (v. 20a), punishment of oppressors (v. 20) and the leadership of one belonging to the community who is divinely summoned but not specifically of the line of David (v. 21).[20] Given that prophecies of the reconstruction of the physical (and societal) infrastructure of Jerusalem feature more prominently in the latter portions of Jeremiah, it is perhaps not surprising that in the call/commission narrative's summary (1:10), "to build" is left

---

18. Bach, "Bauen und Pflanzen," 19–35.
19. NRSV; MT: ארמון
20. That the royal status of this leader is not specified (and thus potentially or intentionally excluded) seems clear. See Carroll, *Jeremiah*, 584; and J. R. Lundbom, *Jeremiah 21–36* (AB 21b; New York: Doubleday, 2004) 408.

to the end, for while the purposes of plucking up, breaking down, destroying, and overthrowing had been amply accomplished by the end of Jeremiah's ministry, the purpose of (re)building (amplified in Jer 30:18–21) evidently remained unfulfilled.[21]

That this prophetic purpose of building, uniquely associated with Jeremiah among the prophets and yet to be completely fulfilled in Nehemiah's time, found a resonance in the latter's own sense of motivation seems very likely. Indeed, according to Nehemiah's own account, it is the very news of the ruin of Jerusalem's physical integrity (1:3) that is the initial impetus for all the activity that follows, including his relaying of the troubling news (2:3) along with his request to the king in which his own purpose is made clear: "send me to Judah, to the city of my fathers' graves, that I may rebuild it" (2:5). So too, Nehemiah's articulation of his purpose (v. 17 and exhortation, v. 18) to the Judahites on his arrival in the city is framed entirely in terms of "building" in order to remedy the ruin of Jerusalem: "Then I said to them, 'You see the trouble we are in, how Jerusalem lies in ruins with its gates burned. Come, let us build the wall of Jerusalem, that we may no longer suffer derision.'"[22] Nehemiah goes on to use the verb (בנה) repeatedly in chaps. 4 (vv. 4, 11, 12 [twice]) and 6 (vv. 1, 6) to describe the construction of the wall; however, he reminds the reader in 7:4 that his purpose is not merely "to build" the wall but ultimately to build the city itself through repopulation and the construction of accommodation.[23]

While it is thus clear that Nehemiah's own account of his work does not contain a prophetic call/commission in any recognizable sense, the above suggests that it does disclose that the primary and initial intent and purpose of Nehemiah was "to build"—a purpose that is, among the prophets, uniquely associated with the call/commission of Jeremiah.[24]

What makes Nehemiah's identification with the purposes of the Jeremianic tradition more than merely plausible is the fact that Jeremianic influence is clearly reflected in a variety of other texts within Nehemiah's account, including the record of his encounter with false prophets.

---

21. Jer 24:6, 31:4–5, 31:28, 42:10. Hence, W. Brueggemann, *To Build and To Plant: A Commentary on Jeremiah 26–52* (ITC; Grand Rapids: Eerdmans, 1991); though see also Jer 18:9.

22. See also Neh 2:20.

23. The city was wide and large, but the people within it were few, and no houses had been rebuilt (Neh 7:4).

24. For this consonance of purpose between Jeremiah and Nehemiah, see Eskenazi, "Unity and Disunity," 326.

While various passages within the Hebrew Bible attest an interest in the "problem" of false prophecy,[25] an encounter with Jer 23:9–40 and chaps. 27–29 establishes not only the importance of this topic for Jeremiah but also the importance of Jeremiah's contribution to discussions of false prophecy across the canon.[26]

It is clear even from a cursory reading of Jeremiah that prophets may attract Jeremianic criticism for a variety of behaviors including prophesying by Baʿal (2:8), worshiping the host of heaven (8:2), committing adultery (23:14, 29:23), and even fomenting rebellion against the LORD (28:16, 29:32). It is also true, however, that a large proportion of Jeremiah's accusations against prophets and prophecies revolve around issues of falsehood and deceit, particularly in relation to erroneous predictions of peace and well-being.[27] These erroneous predictions come clearly to the fore in the prelude to and narrative of Jeremiah's encounter with Hananiah in Jeremiah 28.

In Jeremiah 27, the prophetic word delivered by Jeremiah to the rulers of the neighboring nations not only insists on service to Babylon or the payment of a heavy price but also warns against the fatal, divinely inflicted consequences of listening to local prophets whose lies might suggest otherwise (27:9–10). In vv. 14–15, where Jeremiah directs a comparable warning toward Zedekiah, accusations of prophetic deceit (vv. 14, 16) envelope an extension of the fatal consequences to include the death of the guilty/false prophets themselves (v. 15)—an extension that in turn serves to foreshadow this same motif in the Hananiah narrative, which opens chap. 28.

In chap. 28, Jeremiah begins by relating Hananiah ben Azzur's oracular claims that the yoke of the king of Babylon would be broken and the treasures plundered in 597 B.C.E. returned to their rightful place in the temple (vv. 1–4). Jeremiah then reports his response (vv. 5–9) in which he expresses his hope, whether heartfelt or facetious, that these words of Yahweh might be fulfilled, but also the warning that it is only the prophet whom Yahweh has sent whose prophecies are fulfilled (v. 9). As in other

---

25. See e.g., 1 Kings 22; Ezekiel 13, 22:25–28; Micah 3.
26. For a brief but useful survey of the history of scholarly interest in false prophecy in Jeremiah in particular, see C. Sharp, *Prophecy and Ideology in Jeremiah: Struggles for Authority in the Deutero-Jeremianic Prose* (OTS; London: T. & T. Clark, 2003) 103–5.
27. Sharp, *Prophecy and Ideology*, 112–13. For predictions of peace and well-being in Jeremiah, see 5:12, 6:13–15//8:10–12, 14:13, 23:15–17, chaps. 26–29, 37:19). For an exploration of the abstract concept of "falseness," see T. W. Overholt, *The Threat of Falsehood: A Study in the Theology of the Book of Jeremiah* (Naperville: Allenson, 1970).

passages in Jeremiah (e.g., 23:21, 32; 27:15), the issue of prophetic provenance is central—has the prophet been sent by Yahweh or not? The fact that Jeremiah's test of the prophecy's provenance and authenticity hinges on its (lack of) fulfilment has rightly been seen by many to resonate with Deut 18:20–22's warning:[28]

> But the prophet who presumes to speak a word in my name which I have not commanded him to speak, or who speaks in the name of other gods, that same prophet shall die. And if you say in your heart, "How may we know the word which the LORD has not spoken?"—when a prophet speaks in the name of the LORD, if the word does not come to pass or come true, that is a word which the LORD has not spoken; the prophet has spoken it presumptuously, do not stand in dread of him.[29]

Hananiah's dramatic rebuttal of Jeremiah and reiteration of the imminent end of Babylon and the exile leads to Jeremiah's silent withdrawal, perhaps to allow for "time to tell" who was the true prophet (vv. 10–11). Verses 12–14 then narrate Jeremiah's delivery of his surrejoinder in which he confirms Yahweh's granting of authority to Babylon before communicating the divine judgment on Hananiah himself (vv. 15–17).

> And Jeremiah the prophet said to the prophet Hananiah, "Listen, Hananiah, the LORD has not sent you, and you have made this people trust in a lie. Therefore thus says the LORD: 'Behold, I will remove you from the face of the earth. This very year you shall die, because you have uttered rebellion against the LORD.'" In that same year, in the seventh month, the prophet Hananiah died.

It is again made clear that the falseness of the prophet lies in the falseness of his message, but it is the sentence of death and Hananiah's subsequent demise that confirms beyond any credible doubt the connection with Deut 18:20–22 and its provision for capital punishment of the false prophet (v. 20).[30]

It has been suggested that the final insistence of Deut 18:22 (לא תגור ממנו 'Do not stand in dread of him [the false prophet]') implies that the

---

28. See for example, W. McKane, *A Critical and Exegetical Commentary on Jeremiah* (2 vols.; ICC; Edinburgh: T. & T. Clark, 1986–96) 2:719; Carroll, *Jeremiah*, 544; J. A. Thompson, *Jeremiah* (NICOT; Grand Rapids: Eerdmans, 1980) 539; Lundbom, *Jeremiah 21–36*, 335–36.

29. NJPSV; MT: לא תגור ממנו

30. Lundbom, *Jeremiah 21–36*, 339; Thompson, *Jeremiah*, 541; For a thorough analysis of the association of false prophecy with the sentence of death in Jeremiah 28 and Deut 18:20, see F. L. Hossfeld and I. Meyer, *Prophet gegen Prophet* (Fribourg: Verlag Schweizerisches Bibelwerk, 1973) 98–99.

original fulfilment criterion was applied particularly to "prophets" of woe who resorted to prophetic scare-mongering and that Jeremiah is thus here extending or reapplying the fulfilment criterion to a "false" prophet of peace.[31] While Deut 18:22 does speak to the alleged and actual provenance of the prophecy as well as the fatal consequences for the one uttering the unfulfilled prophecy, the passage does not obviously imply anything in particular regarding the character or content of the prophecy except that it is false. As in Deut 1:17, where this same formulation, לא תגורו מפני־איש 'Do not be afraid of any man' is used to warn against yielding to intimidation that might otherwise impugn the judicial process; in Deut 18:22 we find a warning against being intimidated not by the message, but by the prophet him/herself.[32] That a prophet of peace might seek to intimidate is of course amply demonstrated by Hananiah's confrontational actions in these chapters.[33] Indeed, whatever the cause of Jeremiah's initial retreat (v. 11),[34] the fact that Jeremiah returns to rebut and refute Hananiah, despite the latter's dramatic and violent attack on him demonstrates that Jeremiah not only stands by and applies the test of a false prophet in Deut 18:20–22 but also that he heeds Deuteronomy's command not to be intimidated by him.[35]

---

31. As suggested by, for instance, J. Crenshaw, *Prophetic Conflict: Its Effect on Israelite Religion*, (BZAW 124; Berlin: Walter de Gruyter, 1971) 53.

32. In v. 22, the nearest and most obvious antecedent of the prepositional phrase ממנו is clearly הנביא. So TNK, KVJ, RSV, ESV, NASB, NIV.

33. As McKane indicates, Kimḥi's suggestion that Hananiah broke only the "straps" (מוסרות), which he then equates with the "bars" (מטות) of the yoke is unconvincing (see 27:2) and avoids the plain implication of the text: Hananiah's physical removal of the yoke from Jeremiah's neck and breaking of the bars (rather than merely the straps) was intended as an intimidating demonstration of power (*Jeremiah I*, 720).

34. While McKane is sympathetic to the suggestion that Jeremiah's withdrawal was added by a redactor who (mis)understood "Go and speak to Hananiah" (v. 13) as implying some passage of time between Hananiah's actions and Jeremiah's eventual reply, the absence of any explicit explanation for Jeremiah's departure in the present form of the text and the confrontational nature of Hananiah's interaction with him invites the suggestion that initially Jeremiah may well have been intimidated (*Jeremiah I*, 720–22).

35. Opinions regarding the direction of influence between Deuteronomy and Jeremiah ebb and flow on the rising and falling tides of presumed compositional and redactional dates for both. By way of illustration, while the influence of the Deuteronomy passage on Jeremiah was originally defended by E. W. Nicholson (*Preaching to Exiles: A Study of the Prose Tradition in the Book of Jeremiah* [Oxford: Blackwell, 1970] 113–15), later Nicholson ("Deuteronomy 18.9–22, the Prophets and Scripture," in *Prophecy and the Prophets in Ancient Israel*, [ed. J. Day; London: T. & T. Clark, 2010] 154–56) sees Jeremianic influence on Deuteronomy. What is crucial for the purposes of this study is that the narrative in Jeremiah 27–28 provides a striking illustration of not merely the

When we consider Nehemiah's Memoir, it is quite clear that his interest in prophets/prophecy is likewise focused squarely on the threat posed by their falseness. That this interest reflects a specifically Jeremianic (as opposed to Ezekielian) influence is suggested by a closer examination of Nehemiah's own account in chap. 6.[36] While there is neither space nor need here for a detailed rehearsal of a case that I have made elsewhere, it will perhaps be helpful to summarize what seems to me to be the most straightforward and satisfactory reading of the two episodes in Nehemiah 6.[37]

Faced with allegations that prophets are proclaiming him as king (Neh 6:5–8), Nehemiah reports his own response, characterizing the prophecies as fabrications (perhaps of Sanballat himself; v. 9) and disclosing his awareness that his enemies were deploying false prophets in order to cause him to fear. When a second prophecy (that Nehemiah's assassination is imminent should he not retreat to the temple) follows hard on the heels of the preceding episode, Nehemiah's recognition of the previous pattern of intimidation through false prophecy allows him to unmask Shemaiah and his prophecy as yet another tool of Sanballat (and this time Tobiah). In this case the prophecy is intended to hasten Nehemiah's public retreat to the temple in response to a prophecy that his enemies might easily ensure to be false.[38] From Nehemiah's own perspective, the sinfulness (v. 13) of a retreat such as this and resulting discrediting of his leadership lies not in some supposed illegitimate encroachment on the temple precincts but rather in his very visible violation of the insistence that the false prophet must not be feared in Deut 18:21–22.

That it is specifically Jeremiah's engagement with false prophets that Nehemiah's Memoir reflects is suggested by what is present in both their accounts (but absent from, for instance, Ezekiel), namely, a narrative in

---

discernment of false prophecy by means of the fulfilment criteria, but also an awareness and heeding of Deuteronomy's insistence that the false prophet must not be feared.

36. In the penitential prayer of Nehemiah 9, the prophets are mentioned collectively on three occasions: twice eulogized in the historical recital for calling the people to repentance despite being persecuted (v. 26) and ignored (v. 30) and then finally included alongside the great and good of Israelite society (v. 32) in a plea for divine clemency.

37. D. Shepherd, "Prophetaphobia: Fear and False Prophecy in Nehemiah vi," *VT* 55 (2005) 232–50.

38. That the deuteronomic characterization of "false prophecy" as a capital crime should not have deterred Sanballat, Shemaiah, and the rest is likely to be explained by the absence in Deuteronomy of any specific directions as to the false prophet's elimination, which would instead presumably be left to the deity to undertake (see v. 19). See Nicholson, "Deuteronomy 18.9–22," 156; and Hossfeld and Meyer, *Prophet gegen Prophet*, 97–99.

which: (a) false prophecy is confronted, (b) the deuteronomic fulfilment criteria are clearly and explicitly in view, (c) the prophecy is preemptively unmasked as false by other means, and (d) the deuteronomic exhortation to resist the intimidation of the "false prophet/prophecy" is clearly demonstrated.[39] Given these parallels, it seems more than plausible to suggest that Nehemiah's self-understanding as reflected in his Memoir reflects an awareness of Jeremiah's own engagement with false prophecy and Nehemiah's identification with the purposes of the latter.[40]

Another point in the Nehemiah Memoir where this identification is apparent is Neh 13:15–22, when Nehemiah comments on his defense of the Sabbath in Jerusalem. While the Sabbath is by no means an unknown topic among the prophets,[41] the striking resonance of Neh 13:15–22 with Jer 17:19–27 has been observed widely by commentators.[42] Both passages are peculiarly focused on preventing the bearing of burdens (משא: Neh 13:15, 19; Jer 17:21, 22, 24, 27) through the gates of Jerusalem (שער: Neh 13:19 [twice], 22; Jer 17:19 [twice], 20, 21, 24, 27) due to the undesirable interference of this activity with Sabbath observance. Moreover, in both passages this particular form of Sabbath desecration is linked explicitly to the apostasy of "your fathers" אבתיכם (Jer 17:22, Neh

---

39. Jeremiah is, of course, not the only prophet of his or a later time to rail against others whom he sees to be "false." The book of Ezekiel, too, especially in chap. 13, offers a denunciation in striking language of those who would prophesy "lies," and unsurprisingly it shares with Jeremiah and Nehemiah a resonance both with Deuteronomy's denial of the false prophecy's divine provenance (vv. 6–7) and the lack of fulfillment as the criteria by which it is to be judged (v. 6).

40. Hossfeld and Meyer also highlight the awareness of and resistance to prophetic intimidation found in Deut 18:21–22 and Nehemiah 6 and recognize the resonance of the latter with the Hananiah episode in Jeremiah 27–28. While their suggestion that the fear to be resisted was being induced by postexilic prophets parroting the doomsday prophecies of the past is not impossible, it goes beyond the evidence of Deut 18:21–22 and could only be in the background in Nehemiah 6 where the content of the false prophecies (including the allegations of Nehemiah's royal ambitions) is focused first and foremost on inducing fear in Nehemiah (*Prophet gegen Prophet*, 155–56).

41. N. E. Andreasen, *The Old Testament Sabbath: A Traditio-Historical Investigation* (SBLDS 7; Missoula, MT: Society of Biblical Literature, 1972).

42. See, for example, Blenkinsopp, *Ezra–Nehemiah*, 359; Williamson, *Ezra, Nehemiah*, 395; D. Kidner, *Ezra and Nehemiah* (Downers Grove, IL: InterVarsity, 1979) 130; Ackroyd, *I and II Chronicles, Ezra, Nehemiah*, 317; F. C. Fensham, *The Books of Ezra and Nehemiah* (NICOT; Grand Rapids: Eerdmans, 1982) 264. In Ezekiel, we find general references to Sabbath violation (e.g., 22:8, 26, 23:38; on one occasion within a recital of the Exodus tradition [20:11–24]); encouragement for the "prince" to provide suitable resources for the observance of the Sabbath (45:17) and legislation for the proper observance of the Sabbath within the temple gates and precincts (46:1, 3, 4, 12).

13:18) as well as the potential (Jer 17:27) and past (Neh 13:18) punitive destruction of the city. While the suggestion that the Jeremiah passage primarily depends on Neh 13:15–22 has gained some adherents in recent years,[43] the case for Jeremianic priority (and thus influence on Nehemiah) has received renewed support from the work of J. Wright.[44] Wright notes that the resonance of Jer 17:19–27 with other passages in Jeremiah (esp. chap. 22) removes the need to explain it on the basis of the Nehemiah passage.[45] Moreover, Nehemiah's lack of justification or even explanation for the otherwise unprecedented interdiction of bearing burdens (specifically to Jerusalem) on the Sabbath is really only intelligible against the backdrop of the divine sanction supplied by Jer 17:21: "Thus says the LORD: 'Take heed for the sake of your lives, and do not bear a burden on the sabbath day or bring it in by the gates of Jerusalem.'"

So too, whereas one struggles to understand how Nehemiah's specific intervention, namely, the closing of the gates, could fail to be included in the Jeremianic prophecy to Judah's kings if Nehemiah's account was the source, the closing of the gates by Nehemiah makes perfect sense as an example of a practical intervention/application arising from his rigorous interpretation of Jeremiah's more generic injunction.[46] Finally, the careful omission of reference to the Davidic monarchy (Jer 17:25) is perfectly intelligible given Nehemiah's obvious concern to avoid any hint of his (or anyone else's) royal aspiration in Judah (Neh 6:1–9).[47]

While this clear Jeremianic influence on Neh 13:15–22 is attributed by Wright to subsequent redaction of Nehemiah's originally independent account, it is not clear that the obstacles to the traditional attribution of the passage as a whole to Nehemiah's original memoir require a redactional scheme of the complexity that Wright advances.[48] If, as seems reasonable, Nehemiah's initial, temporary stationing of his own servants to guard the

---

43. See, for instance, T. Veijola, "Die Propheten und das Alter des Sabbatgebots," in *Prophet und Prophetenbuch: Festschrift für Otto Kaiser zum 65. Geburtstag* (ed. V. Fritz, K.-F. Pohlmann, and H.-C. Schmitt; BZAW 185; Berlin: de Gruyter, 1989) 246–64; and more recently, T. Reinmuth, *Der Bericht Nehemias* (OBO 183; Fribourg: Universitätsverlag Freiburg, 2002) 295–96.

44. J. Wright, *Rebuilding Identity: the Nehemiah-Memoir and Its Earliest Readers* (BZAW 348; Berlin: de Gruyter, 2004) 221–42 (esp. p. 242 n. 34).

45. See Lundbom for the ways in which 17:19–27 resonates with its immediate context and beyond, including the striking parallel between 17:24–27 and the "*bona fide* Jeremianic poetry of 13:15–17" (*Jeremiah 1–20*, 803).

46. Wright, *Rebuilding Identity*, 231.

47. See Karrer-Grube, "Scrutinizing the Conceptual Unity," 155.

48. Wright, *Rebuilding Identity*, 232 n. 34.

gates (v. 19) was followed by his subsequent more permanent appointment of the Levites in the same role (in v. 22a) and if this explanation also accounts, as it plausibly might, for Nehemiah's servants' not requiring the purification required by the Levites (v. 22a),[49] then there are no obvious grounds for relegating v. 22a to a hand other than Nehemiah's. If this line does indeed come from Nehemiah's hand, then the latter's reference to לקדש את־יום השבת 'to keep the Sabbath day holy' (v. 22a) in the concluding line of his report surely serves as an ample and appropriate summary of a purpose that the Jeremiah passage rhetorically underlines (vv. 22, 24, 27) and with which Nehemiah evidently and uniquely identifies.[50]

Yet another instance of Nehemiah's identification with Jeremiah's prophetic programme and purposes is to be found in Nehemiah's description of his confrontation of debt slavery in Neh 5:1–13. Commentators have noted frequently an array of pentateuchal texts (Exodus 21 and 22, Leviticus 25, Deuteronomy 15 and 24), and less often a parallel with Jeremiah 34, that speak to this issue and with which Nehemiah's situation and approach may thus be compared.[51] In a recent monograph, T. Reinmuth explores the most obvious of the legal texts, Leviticus 25 and Deuteronomy 15 along with Jeremiah 34 for potential resonances with Neh 5:1–13. While neither Leviticus 25 nor Deuteronomy 15 is found to have substantial or significant connections to the Nehemiah passage, Reinmuth highlights unmistakeable resonances between Neh 5:1–13 and Jer 34:8–22. Significantly, in both texts, political leaders address issues of debt servitude that pit the upper classes (Jer 23:10, Neh 5:7) against the people (Jer 34:10; Neh 5:1, 13). While a certain amount of shared terminology might be expected (מכר, עבד) in texts that take up a common topic, Reinmuth highlights two parallels that point to textual influence.[52] While Jer 34:14 reuses the terminology of Deut 15:12 (אחיך העברי 'your Hebrew brother') where it cites this passage in relation to debt servitude, when taking up the same subject, Neh 5:1 prefers אחיהם היהודים 'their Jewish brothers'. Significantly, the only other text in the Hebrew Bible in which this particular collocation is used is this Jeremiah text on this same topic: ביהודי אחיהו 'a Jew, his brother' (Jer 34:9). Moreover, the terminol-

---

49. So Williamson, *Ezra, Nehemiah*, 396.
50. Contra Wright, *Rebuilding Identity*, 232 n.34.
51. Some or all of the legal texts have been noted by, for example, Williamson, *Ezra, Nehemiah*, 238; Kidner, *Ezra and Nehemiah*, 96; Ackroyd, *I and II Chronicles, Ezra, Nehemiah*, 282; Coggins, *The Books of Ezra and Nehemiah*, 91; Blenkinsopp, *Ezra–Nehemiah*, 257–260, who also notes the parallel in Jeremiah 34 (see esp. p. 259).
52. Reinmuth, *Der Bericht Nehemias*, 176–79.

ogy used by Nehemiah in describing the process of enslavement: כבשים לעבדים . . . 'to indenture . . . as servants' (5:5) is again virtually unique to this text and the Jeremiah passage (34:11, 16) ויכבישום . . . לעבדים.[53] Most strikingly of all, the parallels between the Jeremiah and Nehemiah passages extend beyond shared topic and terminology to include the plot. In neither text is it merely a matter of confronting and condemning inappropriate indenturing of fellow community members. Rather, just as the Jeremiah text describes the prophet's confrontation of reenslavement (34:11) following an initial manumission of slaves (34:9–10), so too Nehemiah's own account describes his confrontation of the intramural indenturing of servants (5:5) after his own prior attempts to liberate these same people from debt servitude (in this case to non-Jews; 5:8a). When this parallel of plot is coupled with those of topic and terminology and when the dependence of Nehemiah on Jeremiah has already been suggested, it is difficult to escape the conclusion that here again Nehemiah's Memoir reflects his own awareness of and identification with yet another of the prophetic purposes and actions of Jeremiah as recorded in the book that bears his name.

While it is clear that Nehemiah's own memoir documents a gubernatorial programme that extends beyond and is thus not limited to his sympathy and identification with Jeremiah's prophetic purposes, the fact that Nehemiah does see fit to include episodes that illustrate this identification suggests that it is not an insignificant aspect of the persona he wishes to project and memorialize. That this is so is finally and firmly suggested by the illustration of Jeremiah's influence on the prayers with which Nehemiah's account is seasoned.

Whether or not some (5:14–19; 13:4–14, 15–22, 23–31) or indeed all (1:4–11, 4:4–5, 6:14) of the prayers that the text associates with Nehemiah were included by him as part of his own revision and supplementation of an earlier report, as Williamson suggests, the case for attributing them to Nehemiah at some point in his recollection of his work is easily defensible and indeed quite reasonable.[54]

---

53. The only other appearance of this terminology in the Hebrew Bible is found in 2 Chr 28:10, where it is used to describe the enslavement of Judahites by Israel in the time of Ahaz.

54. Williamson, *Ezra, Nehemiah*, xxvi–xxviii. While the unexpected introduction of the "remember" formula in Neh 6:14 in (for Williamson) earlier material may well be explained by its redactional insertion, it seems more plausible that both Neh 3:36–37 and 6:14 are imprecations offered up *in media res*, which may then have triggered the more intentional and extensive use of the "remember" formula in the prayers that were (subsequently?) added.

Prominent among the prayers included by Nehemiah in his memoir is his appeal to "remember." This so-called *Gedächtnismotiv* has often been compared (particularly when considered along with the rest of Nehemiah's first person account) to similar formulas in other ancient Near Eastern texts.[55] However, even those who advocate these comparisons also recognize that the self-portrait Nehemiah paints does make use of the same palette as other (auto)biographical traditions within the Hebrew Bible.[56]

While the prayer in Neh 1:5–11 has been attributed by some to a later hand, the case for its primary association with Nehemiah continues to prove persuasive to many.[57] What is widely agreed is that the prayer resonates clearly with the penitential prayer tradition (Nehemiah 9, Ezra 9, Daniel 9) and draws extensively on the repertoire of Deuteronomy, including especially the near-verbatim use in Neh 1:5 of Deut 7:21 ("a great and terrible God") and 7:9 ("who keeps covenant and steadfast love with those who love him and keep his commandments").[58] Unlike Deuteronomy 7, however, Nehemiah explicitly articulates the divine keeping of the covenant (1:5) in terms of the need for God to "remember" (1:8–9) his promise through Moses, to return to the land those people who will return to Him. While this notion of God's "remembering" the covenant is clearly paralleled (or indeed undergirded) by Leviticus 26 (vv. 42, 45) and other priestly texts,[59] one searches the rest of the Hebrew Bible in vain for texts that turn this particular language of promise into an explicit petition to remember the covenant. Indeed, it is only Jer 14:20–21 that provides

---

55. For recent research along these lines, see for instance, J. Blenkinsopp, "The Nehemiah Autobiographical Memoir," in *Language, Theology and the Bible: Essays in Honour of James Barr* (ed. S. E. Balentine and J. Barton; Oxford: Clarendon, 1994) 199–212; idem, "The Mission of Udjahorresnet and Those of Ezra and Nehemiah," *JBL* 106 (1987) 409–21.

56. See J. Blenkinsopp, *Judaism: The First Phase: The Place of Ezra and Nehemiah in the Origins of Judaism* (Grand Rapids: Eerdmans, 2009) 97.

57. For a useful summary of the evidence for the former position, see U. Kellermann, *Nehemia: Quellen, Überlieferung und Geschichte* (BZAW 102; Berlin: Alfred Topelmann, 1967) 9; and for more recent but not entirely persuasive advocacy of it, see Wright, *Rebuilding Identity*, 9–24; Reinmuth, *Der Bericht Nehemias*, 44–54. See M. J. Boda for a list of authorities supporting the latter position (*Praying the Tradition*, 70, n. 14); and Williamson for a robust defence of it (*Ezra, Nehemiah*, 167–68).

58. K. Balzer "also draws parallels to 1 Kings 8" ("Moses Servant of God and the Servants: Text and Tradition in the Prayer of Nehemiah [Neh 1:5–11]," in *The Future of Early Christianity: Essays in Honor of Helmut Koester* [ed. B. A. Pearson; Minneapolis: Fortress, 1991] 121–30). See also Wright, *Rebuilding Identity*, 14–17.

59. See for instance Ezek 16:61–63.

the precedent for Nehemiah's prayerful but imperious insistence that God "remember":

> We acknowledge our wickedness, O LORD, and the iniquity of our fathers, for we have sinned against thee. Do not spurn us, for thy name's sake; do not dishonor thy glorious throne; remember and do not break thy covenant with us.

Like Nehemiah, Jeremiah confesses not merely his own sins but his fathers' as well (v. 20; see Neh 1:6) and most crucially, Nehemiah's prayer follows the example of Jeremiah's unique use of the imperative of זכר (14:21) in boldly exhorting God to זכר־נא 'remember' (1:8) the covenant he has made with His people in the time of Moses.[60]

Of course, Jeremiah's prayers that God would "remember" extend beyond the covenant to include both himself and those who opposed his purposes, as may be seen in 18:19–23:

> Give heed to me, O LORD, and hearken to my plea. Is evil a recompense for good (טובה)? Yet they have dug a pit for my life. Remember how I stood before thee to speak good (טובה) for them, to turn away thy wrath from them. Therefore deliver up their children to famine; give them over to the power of the sword, let their wives become childless and widowed. May their men meet death by pestilence, their youths be slain by the sword in battle. May a cry be heard from their houses, when thou bringest the marauder suddenly upon them! For they have dug a pit to take me, and laid snares for my feet. Yet, thou, O LORD, knowest all their plotting to slay me. Forgive not their iniquity, nor blot out their sin from thy sight. Let them be overthrown before thee; deal with them in the time of thine anger.

The influence of Jeremiah's prayer on Nehemiah's Memoir becomes clear when it is compared with Nehemiah's report regarding the local (and very vocal) opposition of Sanballat, Tobiah, and their associates to the rebuilding of the wall (Neh 3:33–5[4:1–3]). In 3:36–37[4:4–5], Nehemiah records a prayer of imprecation against them that includes the words אל־תכס על־עונם וחטאתם מלפניך אל־תמחה 'Do not cover their guilt, and let not their sin be blotted out from thy sight'. While Nehemiah's prayer of imprecation is not dissimilar in spirit or intent to those found elsewhere in the

---

60. Boda provides a helpful discussion of the numerous parallels between Jer 14:17–21 (1 Kings 8) and esp. Leviticus 26 (*Praying the Tradition*, 54 n. 43). See also D. R. Jones, *Jeremiah* (NCB; Grand Rapids: Eerdmans, 1992) 212–13. While the Chronicler's version of Solomon's prayer (2 Chr 6:42) also includes an exhortation to "remember," it is clearly the Davidic covenant that is in view.

Hebrew Bible, especially the Psalms,[61] its resonance with the prayer in Jer 18:23 could not be more clear: אל־תכפר על־עונם וחטאתם מלפניך אל־תמחי. While others have noted this parallel, Williamson is quite correct to suggest that Nehemiah literally makes Jeremiah's prayer his own.[62] Indeed, apart from minor lexical and grammatical adjustments,[63] Nehemiah's use of Jeremiah's words of imprecation extends even to the order in which they appear. While the context in which Jeremiah's words are used by Nehemiah is of course different, his precise reproduction of Jeremiah's words appears to confirm that Nehemiah's identification with the Jeremianic tradition within his first-person account includes his willingness to invoke, as Jeremiah does, God's vengeance against those whom he perceives to be obstructing his purposes.[64]

Indeed, the influence of the Jeremianic prayer tradition (including this passage) on Nehemiah extends still further.[65] Jeremiah's imprecation of others (18:21–23) in the same breath as he explicitly appeals to God to "remember" him and his work (v. 20; see also 15:15)[66] provides a unique precedent within the Hebrew Bible for Nehemiah's own repeated request that God "remember" both him and his enemies, as may be seen specifically in Neh 13:28–31:

> And one of the sons of Jehoiada, the son of Eliashib the high priest, was the son-in-law of Sanballat the Horonite; therefore I chased him from me. Remember them, O my God, because they have defiled the priesthood and the covenant of the priesthood and the Levites. Thus I cleansed them from everything foreign, and I established the duties of the priests and Levites, each in his work; and I provided for the wood offering, at appointed times, and for the first fruits. Remember me, O my God, for good.

---

61. See, for instance, Ps 137 and especially Ps 109:6–19.

62. Williamson, *Ezra, Nehemiah,* 217. The parallel is noted also by Kidner, *Ezra and Nehemiah,* 91; and Ackroyd, *I and II Chronicles, Ezra, Nehemiah,* 277.

63. The more generic כסה employed by Nehemiah is used occasionally elsewhere with the meaning 'forgive' (see Ps 32:1 // כפר); whereas Neh 3:37 uses a passive construction אל־תמחה (Niphal 3fs) 'Let their sin not be blotted out', Jer 18:23 makes use of the Hiphil 2ms: אל־תמחי 'Do not blot out (their sin)'.

64. See also Neh 6:14 for Nehemiah's prayer that God would remember his prophetic opponents.

65. As has been observed by F. C. Holmgren, "Remember Me, Remember Them," in *Scripture and Prayer: A Celebration for Carroll Stuhlmueller* (ed. C. Osiek and D. Senior; Wilmington: Michael Glazier, 1988) 33–45.

66. Jer 15:15: "You understand, O Lord; remember me and care for me. Avenge me on my persecutors. You are long-suffering—do not take me away; think of how I suffer reproach for your sake."

While Nehemiah's insistence on requesting God's remembrance of both his enemies for evil and himself for good strongly suggests his indebtedness to this otherwise unique prayer practice of Jeremiah, there is still further indication of the latter's influence. At the heart of Jeremiah's prayer is his deep concern for 'good' (טובה), evil, and his experience of injustice. Jeremiah prays that because the good he has done to his enemies (by speaking 'good' [טובה] for them; v. 20) has been repaid with evil, so God in his justice should repay their evil with evil in return (vv. 21–23). At the same time, because the good that Jeremiah has done has been not only for "them," but also before "you" (v. 20, God), God's willingness to repay his enemies' evil is an act of "goodness" to Jeremiah and proof that God does indeed remember (and care for, see Jer 15:15) him.

That Nehemiah himself viewed his activities in quite literally the same terms (that is, as good) is confirmed by his report of the people's response to his proposal to rebuild the wall: "So they strengthened their hands for (the) טובה good (work)" (2:18). It is thus not surprising that when the recounting of his activities is supplemented with prayers for his own remembrance, they are offered in terms of the divine repayment of טובה. So, following his return to Jerusalem, his eviction of Tobiah from the temple chamber and its cleansing, and his restoration of the cultic infrastructure and resourcing, Nehemiah's prayer is that "my good deeds" (rather than his enemies' sins; see 4:4–5) would not be blotted out (that is, "remembered"; 13:14).[67] Again, after describing his intervention in the debt-slavery crisis and his seeming resolution of it, Nehemiah prays, "Remember for (my) טובה 'good', O my God, all that I have done for this people" (5:19). Finally, at the conclusion of his account, and with the prayer that God would remember those who have desecrated the sacred offices still ringing in the reader's ears, Nehemiah concludes a note of his good work in relation to the provision for the cultus with the by-now familiar prayer for a divine righting of the scales of justice: "Remember me, O my God, for טובה 'good'"(13:31).

Later Jewish tradition (e.g., *b. Sanh.* 93b) has often remembered Nehemiah for worse rather than for better (especially in comparison with Ezra), but it is clear that the eventual incorporation of Nehemiah's first-person account into the wider framework of Ezra–Nehemiah both reflected the tradition's memory of Nehemiah and also ultimately served to perpetuate

---

67. Here the terminology used is (חסדי) 'my good deeds'. In 13:22, Nehemiah prays: "Remember this also in my favor, O my God, and spare me according to the greatness of thy steadfast love."

it.⁶⁸ While it remains to be seen in what ways (if at all) these redactors remembered Nehemiah's identification with the prophetic purposes of Jeremiah, the above has suggested that the latter is evident in Nehemiah's account of not only his basic purpose ("to build") but also his engagement with false prophecy, his interventions in relation to Sabbath-keeping and the debt slavery crisis and finally his prayers that God remember both him and his enemies. Thus, whether or not Nehemiah's identification with Jeremiah lingered in the memory of his redactors, it seems that the purposes of Jeremiah did live long at least in the memory of Nehemiah.

---

68. It is unclear whether the unique resonance of Neh 1:1 ("The words of Nehemiah son of Hekaliah") with Jer 1:1 ("The words of Jeremiah son of Hilkiah") reflects a particular redactional awareness of the common purpose 'to build' (articulated at the beginning of both Nehemiah and Jeremiah) or the broader constellation of connections between the two books (so M. Leuchter, "The Politics of Ritual Rhetoric: A Proposed Sociopolitical Context for the Redaction of Leviticus 1–16," *VT* 60 [2010] 361).

The Use and Non-Use of Prophetic Literature in Hellenistic Jewish Historiography

ANDREW W. PITTS

In recent research on the use of scriptural sources among the Hellenistic Jewish historians, rewritten Bible for the Torah and historical-political concerns for the prophets have dominated the discussion. Narratological and Greek historiographic models for understanding these historians' relation to their scriptural sources have not been seriously considered. In this essay, I argue that both the use and non-use of prophetic literature in the Jewish historians from the Hellenistic period has significance for their narratives based on models for source integration derived from Greek historiography. I suggest that prophetic literature does not receive as much coverage as many have expected because the historians reserved the citation of these texts for the more marked/emphatic dimension of their source framework, which required selective usage. At the unmarked/nonemphatic level of their source framework, pentateuchal and narrative-historical materials were more appropriate.

Quite unlike the situation with Greco-Roman historiography from the Hellenistic period, the corpus of study for Hellenistic *Jewish* historiography remains rather limited. Some of the earliest historical narratives from this period document the Maccabean history, 1–2 Maccabees—*3* and *4 Maccabees* can hardly be called history. *Jubilees* and 1 Esdras attempt to provide a continuation of biblical historiography. Certainly, Josephus deserves serious consideration as the most extended set of historical works during this time. While the Philonic corpus contains a few works that can be considered properly historical, Philo's writings consist mostly of philosophy, theology, and biblical commentary. He is an epic poet primarily and a historian only secondarily. Beyond this, we possess a number of fragmentary histories that have come down to us through Josephus, Clement, and Eusebius, such as the important but now lost work of Alexander Polyhistor (e.g., Clement, *Strom.* 1.23.154.2–3). But due to my focus on the narrative function of scriptural source implementation within Jewish historiography, I have chosen not to consider the fragmentary histories and to mention Philo only in passing within the analysis of mimesis. Even in the histories that are considered, sometimes the results yielded are not as interesting as we would hope, but I have considered these sources in the interest of providing solid chronological movement while also being as comprehensive as possible because we have so few complete histories of the Jews from this period. As we consider texts in their chronological location, I hope to illustrate a gradual development toward Greek citation strategies—in its most primitive form in *Jubilees* and most developed in Josephus—within Jewish historiography.

Narrative and Intertextuality in Hellenistic Jewish Historiography

The traditional paradigm has typically preferred using histories of the Jews from the Hellenistic period *as* sources rather than assessing their use of sources as part of a monolithic literary paradigm at work within the historian.[1] Although Mason's observation of a recent movement in Josephan studies toward "reading Josephus *through*, and not merely reading *through* Josephus to external realities"[2] has some merit, questions concerning the relationship of sources to the literary strategies of the historians, including Josephus, still—sadly—have received little to no attention. This tendency has, I believe, been an impediment to serious consideration of the intertextual relations of the historians' sources to one another and, more importantly, to the narrative agenda that shapes a given historical work. I grant that intertextual phenomena in these works has, at least

---

1. Many recent treatments, however, show that the use of Josephus as a source remains very much a concern in contemporary Josephan scholarship. See, for example, T. E. Goud, "The Sources of Josephus 'Antiquities' 19," *Historia* 45 (1996) 472–82; R. C. Steiner, "Incomplete Circumcision in Egypt and Edom: Jeremiah (9:24–25) in the Light of Josephus and Jonckheere," *JBL* 118 (1999) 497–505; C. Begg, *Josephus' Story of the Later Monarchy (AJ 9,1–10,185)* (BETL 145; Leuven: Peeters, 2000); L. L. Grabbe, "Jewish Historiography and Scripture in the Hellenistic Period," in *Did Moses Speak Attic? Jewish Historiography and Scripture in the Hellenistic Period* (ed. L.L. Grabbe; JSOTSup 317; Sheffield: Sheffield Academic Press, 2001) 130–55; T. Rajak, *Josephus: The Historian and His Society* (London: Duckworth, 2002). Even some of Mason's own work exemplifies these efforts, e.g. S. Mason, *Flavius Josephus on the Pharisees: A Composition-Critical Study* (Boston: Brill Academic, 2001), though Mason does desire to separate carefully his compositional method from older source-critical frameworks.

2. S. Mason, "Contradiction or Counterpoint? Josephus and Historical Method," *RRJ* 6 (2003) 145–48, quoting p. 46.

at some level, been the object of serious study. Those familiar with the rapidly growing corpus of secondary literature will immediately think of the use of the so-called rewritten Bible by the historians (and other second temple writers), which has been subjected to extensive investigation in recent years, a question we will revisit below.[3] When interpreters take up the direct use of scriptural sources in these contexts, however, they typically focus on how the historian has altered or adapted their biblical resources for local narrative purposes (for example, an alteration in the biblical sequence), but do not give sustained attention to the structural significance of this material within the global narrative agenda.[4] These assessments rarely consider, for instance, how the rewritten Bible and other forms of historiographic imitation might fit into a larger source framework and specifically how these forms of source implementation relate to more explicit citation strategies (that is, those integrated into the narrative through citation formulas of varying kinds). Studies such as these naturally exclude reference to the literature of the classical prophets because this literature was seldom subjected to "rewriting" in the way that

---

3. See especially R. Bauckham, "The Liber Antiquitatum Biblicarum of Pseudo-Philo and the Gospels as 'Midrash,'" in *Gospel Perspectives*, vol. 3: *Studies in Midrash and Historiography* (ed. R. T. France and D. Wenham; Sheffield: JSOT Press, 1983), 33–67; G. E. W. Nickelsburg, "The Bible Rewritten and Expanded," in *Jewish Writings of the Second Temple Period: Apocrypha, Pseudepigrapha, Qumran Sectarian Writings, Philo, Josephus* (ed. M. E. Stone; CRINT; Philadelphia: Fortress, 1984) 33–156; P. S. Alexander, "Retelling the Old Testament," in *It Is Written: Scripture Citing Scripture: Essays in Honour of Barnabas Lindars* (ed. D. A. Carson and H. G. M. Williamson; Cambridge: Cambridge University Press, 1988) 99–121; D. A. Harrington, "Palestinian Adaptations of Biblical Narrative and Prophecies: Part I, Rewritten Bible (Narrative)," in *Early Judaism and Its Modern Interpreters* (ed. R. A. Kraft and G. E. W. Nickelsburg; Atlanta: Scholars Press, 1986) 239–46; C. A. Evans, "Luke and the Rewritten Bible: Aspects of Lukan Hagiography," in *The Pseudepigrapha and Early Biblical Interpretation* (ed. J. H. Charlesworth and C. A. Evans; JSPSup 14; Sheffield: Sheffield Academic Press, 1993) 170–201; P. Borgen, *Philo of Alexandria: An Exegete for His Time* (NovTSup 86; Leiden: Brill, 1997) 46–79; L. H. Feldman, *Josephus's Interpretation of the Bible* (HCS 27; Berkeley: University of California, 1998) 14–73; L. H. Feldman, *Studies in Josephus' Rewritten Bible* (JSJSup 58; Leiden: Brill, 1998); S. W. Crawford, *Rewriting Scripture in Second Temple Times* (Grand Rapids: Eerdmans, 2008).

4. In addition to the material cited above, see specifically, e.g., N. Cohen, "Josephus and Scripture: Is Josephus' Treatment of the Scriptural Narrative Similar throughout the 'Antiquities' I–XI?," *JQR* 54 (1964) 311–32; L. H. Feldman, "Hellenizations in Josephus' Version of Esther," *TAPA* 101 (1970) 143–70; F. J. Murphy, "Retelling the Bible: Idolatry in Pseudo-Philo," *JBL* 107 (1988) 275–87; G. J. Swart, "Rahab and Esther in Josephus: An Intertextual Approach," *Acta Patristica et Byzantina* 17 (2006) 50–65.

term is typically used.⁵ Of course, as long as the discussion has existed, there has been talk of the sources themselves, but these (sometimes quite extended) treatments often remain circumscribed to the identity, nature, and authenticity (especially whether rhetorical invention was involved) of the relevant sources.⁶ Even the more recent investigations of sources in Hellenistic Jewish historians have been dominated almost exclusively by these concerns,⁷ not to mention the older German source-critical studies (*Quellenkritik*) and their predecessors.⁸ The role of source citation as a

---

5. The chapter titles for Crawford, *Rewriting Scripture*, are telling: 1. Introduction; 2. The Text of the Pentateuch at Qumran; 3. Reworked Pentateuch; 4. The Book of Jubilees; 5. The Temple Scroll; 6. The Genesis Apocryphon; 7. 4Q Commentary on Genesis A; 8. Conclusions. Rewritten Bible tends to focus mainly on the Pentateuch with some attention given to Deuteronomistic History.

6. It is interesting that G. E. Sterling, (*Historiography and Self-Definition: Josephos, Luke–Acts, and Apologetic Historiography* [NovTSup 64; Leiden: Brill, 1992] 291–97) configures his narrative analysis strictly in terms of Josephus's omissions, alterations and additions of source material. The closest we come to arriving at a sustained treatment of how the citation of source material may relate to a historian's narrative program are the various treatments of an author's alleged apologetic concerns in the citation of some sources over others—a concern also present throughout Sterling's analysis. But these interpretations typically amount to a *historical* explanation of a *literary* phenomenon rather than providing genuine insight into how sources contribute to narrative fabric of a text. See, for example, L. H. Feldman, "Restoration in Josephus," in *Restoration: Old Testament, Jewish and Christian Perspectives* (ed. J. M. Scott; JSJSup 72; Leiden: Brill, 2001) 223–61, esp. pp. 251–52. I shall interact more with this essay below in light of these considerations. As another example, A. Kasher ("Polemic and Apologetic Methods of Writing in Contra Apion," in *Josephus' Contra Apionem: Studies in Its Character and Context with a Latin Concordance to the Portion Missing in Greek* [ed. L. H. Feldman and J. R. Levison; AGJU 34; Leiden: Brill, 1996] 143–86, esp. pp. 158–59) argues in a typical fashion that Josephus cites his sources and other literature in order to bolster his reliability by appearing, for example, well educated. Other authors often discuss how sources are adapted to suit the historian's literary aims: Borgen, *Philo*, 46–79; see also M. Alexandre, "Rhetorical Hermeneutics in Philo's Commentary of Scripture," *Revista de Retórica y Teoría de la Comunicación Año* 1 (2001) 29–41.

7. E.g., H. W. Attridge, "Historiography," in *Jewish Writings of the Second Temple Period Apocrypha, Pseudepigrapha, Qumran Sectarian Writings, Philo, Josephus* (ed. M. E. Stone; LJPSTT 2; Assen: Van Gorcum, 1984) 157–83; D. R. Schwartz, *Agrippa I: The Last King of Judaea* (TSAJ 23; Tübingen: Mohr Siebeck, 1990) esp. pp. 31–38, 176–82, but also passim; Rajak, *Josephus*, passim; S. J. D. Cohen, *Josephus in Galilee and Rome: His Vita and Development as a Historian* (Boston: Brill, 2002) 24–66; B. E. Scolnic, *Alcimus, Enemy of the Maccabees* (Studies in Judaism; Lanham, MD: University Press of America, 2005) 12–49.

8. E.g., H. Bloch, *Die Quellen des Flavius Josephus in seiner Archäologie* (Leipzig: B.G. Teubner, 1879); J. Destinon, *Die Quellen des Flavius Josephus 1, Die Quellen des Flavius Josephus in der Jüd. Arch. Buch XII–XVII = Jüd. Krieg Buch I* (Kiel: Lipsius & Tischer, 1882); E. Schürer, *A History of the Jewish People in the Time of Jesus Christ, Second Division* (trans. S. Taylor and P. Christie; 3 vols. Edinburgh: T. & T. Clark, 1890)

narrative strategy rarely receives consideration. Even when it does, with very few exceptions, only local-level phenomena are discussed with little consideration for broader narrative structure[9] or, in other cases, narrative analysis merely serves as a tool for detecting underlying sources.[10] Evaluations of this sort are not intended to minimize the importance of any of these foundational works. It is a good sign that the literary function of sources, mostly under the umbrella of *kompositionskritische*, is getting the attention that it is. Nevertheless, the need remains for further investigation of the relationship between the historians' paradigm for systematic source integration and global narrative considerations. It is in this direction that I hope to make some initiatory remarks on how this sort of investigation might proceed, at least with respect to how prophetic literature might be configured within a framework such as this.

In the Greek historians, the predecessors of the Hellenistic Jewish historiographers, two forms of intertextuality can be identified: mimesis/imitation and direct citation.[11] These refer to two distinct ways of citing sources. The former method introduces material into the historical narrative without indicating that the material is incorporated from sources.[12]

3:6–15; Gustav Hölscher, "Josephus," in *PWRE* 18 (1916) cols. 1966, 1981–83, 1992–93; W. Weber, *Josephus und Vespasian: Untersuchungen zu dem juedischen Krieg des Flavius Josephus* (Berlin: Kohlhammer, 1921) passim; R. Laqueur, *The Jewish Historian Flavius Josephus: A Biographical Investigation based on New Critical Sources* (trans. C. Disler; ed. S. Mason; Gießen: Münchow'sche Verlagsbuchhandlung, 1920) passim; H. S. Thackeray, *Josephus, the Man and the Historian* (Hilda Stich Stroock Lectures; New York: Jewish Institute of Religion, 1929) vxiii, 3, 36–39, 48, 59–70, 109, 120.

9. E.g., Cohen (*Josephus in Galilee and Rome*, 44–45, esp. n. 78), following Niese, discusses the local level usage of the Josephan formula πρότερον ἐν ἄλλοις δεδηλώκαμεν when citing the Maccabean history as an instance of meaningless narrative punctuation. His later discussions of "literary technique" in Josephus (pp. 90–91, 110–114) are mostly concerned with how source material is brought into the narrative (i.e., whether it is integrated smoothly), whether it is consistent with other material, whether the data in Josephus provide a complete account, various characterizations and narrative interest. See also Sterling, *Historiography and Self-Definition*, 236.

10. E.g., Mason, "Contradiction," 158–88.

11. What I have summarized here in two paragraphs, I have developed in great detail in A. W. Pitts, "Source Citation in Greek Historiography and in Luke(–Acts)," in *Christian Origins and Greco-Roman Culture* (ed. S. E. Porter and A. W. Pitts; Texts and Editions for New Testament Study 9; Leiden: Brill, 2012), 349–88.

12. On the origins of mimesis in the classical tradition of Aristotle and Plato, see O. B. Hardison, "Epigone: An Aristotelian Imitation," in *Aristotle's Poetics* (ed. L. Golden and O. B. Hardison; Englewood Cliffs: Prentice Hall, 1968) 281–96; P. Simpson, "Aristotle on Poetry and Imitation," *Hermes* 116 (1988) 279–91 (p. 279); L. Golden, *Aristotle on Tragic and Comic Mimesis* (Oxford: Oxford University Press, 1992); B. Earle, "Plato, Aristotle, and the Imitation of Reason," *Philosophy and Literature* 27 (2003) 382–401. On the use of mimesis in the historians, see F. Jacoby,

The historian simply imitates and adapts it from a literary predecessor. This can, therefore, include a whole spectrum of parallel material, ranging from a simple verbal cue that may or may not invoke other literary associations in the minds of the audience to the exact repetition of wording from a previous literary text without formally indicating that the tradition is being taken over from a source. Direct citations are identified through the use of citation formulas to introduce source material.[13]

In terms of the function of these two respective levels of source integration within Hellenistic historical narratives, I employ a linguistic-narrative

---

"Über dei Entwicklung der grieschischen Historiographie und der Plan einer neuen Sammlung der drieschischen Historiographie und der Plan einer neuen Sammlung der drieschischen Historikerfragmente," *Kilo* 9 (1909) 1–44; D. A. Russell, "De Imitatione," in *Creative Imitation and Latin Literature* (ed. D. West and T. Woodman; Cambridge: Cambridge University Press, 1979) 1–16; V. Gray, "Mimesis in Greek Historical Theory," *AJP* 8 (1987) 467–86; V. Gray, *The Character of Xenophon's Hellenica* (Baltimore: Johns Hopkins University Press, 1989) 1–2; T. F. Scalon, "Echoes of Herodotus in Thucydides: Self-Sufficiency, Admiration and Law," *Historia* 43 (1994) 143–76; J. Marincola, *Authority and Tradition in Ancient Historiography* (Cambridge: Cambridge University Press, 1997) 3–33; E. J. Bakker, "Verbal Aspect and Mimetic Description in Thucydides," in *Grammar as Interpretation: Greek Literature in Its Linguistic Contexts* (ed. E. J. Bakker; Mnemosyne Bibliotheca Classica Batava 171; Leiden: Brill, 1997) 7–54; D. S. Potter, *Literary Texts and the Roman Historian* (London: Routledge, 1999) 62–66; G. Schepens, and J. Bollansée, *The Shadow of Polybius: Intertextuality as a Research Tool in Greek Historiography: Proceedings of the International Colloquium, Leuven, 21–22 September 2001* (Studia Hellenistica 42; Leuven: Peeters, 2005).

13. On direct citation of source material in Greek historiography, see M. I. Finely, *Ancient History: Evidence and Models* (New York: Viking, 1986) 27–46; S. West, "Herodotus' Epigraphical Interests," *CQ* 35 (1985) 278–305; D. Fehling, *Herodotus and His "Sources": Citation, Invention, and Narrative Art* (trans. J. G. Howie; ARCA Classical and Medieval Texts, Papers, and Monographs 21; Wiltshire: Cairns, 1989); S. Hornblower, "Introduction," in *Greek Historiography* (ed. S. Hornblower; Oxford: Clarendon, 1993) 54–72; R. Osborne, "Archaic Greek History," in *Brill's Companion to Herodotus* (ed. I. de Jong and H. van Wees; Leiden: Brill, 2002) 497–520; D. R. MacDonald, "Introduction," in *Mimesis and Intertextuality in Antiquity and Christianity* (ed. D. R. MacDonald; SAC; Harrisburg: Trinity Press International, 2003) 1–9; V. Gray, "Interventions and Citations in Xenophon's Hellenica and Anabasis," *CQ* 53 (2003) 111–23; J. T. Dillery, "Greek Sacred History," *AJP* 126 (2005) 505–26. B. Smarczyk, "Thucydides and Epigraphy," in *Brill's Companion to Thucydides* (ed. A. Rengakos and A. Tsakmakis; Brill's Companions in Classical Studies; Leiden: Brill, 2006) 495–522; P. J. Rhodes, "Documents and the Greek Historians," in *A Companion to Greek and Roman Historiography* (ed. J. Marincola; Blackwell Companions to the Ancient World; Malden, MA: Blackwell, 2007) 56–66. On the use of Greek historiography in Jewish history, see G. E. Sterling, "The Jewish Appropriation of Hellenistic Historiography," in *A Companion to Greek and Roman Historiography* (ed. J. Marincola; Blackwell Companions to the Ancient World; Malden, MA: Blackwell, 2007) 231–43, esp. pp. 238–39.

tool known as markedness in which, on a scale of markedness or narrative prominence, more specific narrative elements are marked and less specific elements are unmarked.[14] This places mimetic elements of the historian's source framework on the background of the narrative and directly cited material on the foreground. Material can also be frontgrounded in cases where the source is cited by name or quoted directly rather than paraphrasing material. Foreground/frontground material such as this tends to appear at points in the narrative where additional validation is needed in Greek historiography, such as reference to the supernatural, hard-to-believe accounts, major narrative movements (birth or death of a major character).[15] They are reserved and used selectively "for emphasizing special sources and as a validation for exceptional events."[16] For less-important material, but where sources are still needed, historians draw from the mimetic dimension of their source framework. This is the story in Greek historiography, anyway.[17] I want to argue that the Hellenistic Jewish historians adopted the same methodology in their use of sources and that prophetic texts were particularly well suited for direct citation within their wider narrative strategies. So at the background mimetic level, prophetic resources are neglected, while at the marked, direct citation level, they are strategically employed.

The Non-Use of Prophetic Literature: Mimesis and Rewritten Bible

In Greek historiography, complete or partial originality was never the expectation, at least not in the way that we typically think of it. Instead,

---

14. On this method and its application, see Pitts, "Source Citation." See also, on markedness, E. L. Andrews, *Markedness Theory: The Union of Asymmetry and Semiosis in Language* (Sound and Meaning; Durham, NC: Duke University Press, 1990); E. L. Battistella, *Markedness: The Evaluative Superstructure of Language* (SUNY Series in Linguistics; Albany, NY: State University of New York Press, 1990); S. Fleischman, *Tense and Narrativity: From Medieval Performance to Modern Fiction* (London: Routledge, 1992) 52–56; E. L. Battistella, *The Logic of Markedness* (New York: Oxford University Press, 1996).

15. See Fehling, *Herodotus*, 143; G. S. Shrimpton and K. M. Gill, "Herodotus' Source Citations," in *History and Memory in Ancient Greece* (McGill-Queen's Studies in the History of Ideas 23; Montreal: McGill-Queen's University, 1997) 231–65, esp. p. 240); Marincola, *Authority*, 86; Gray, "Interventions," 118; Diller, "Greek Sacred History," 521.

16. Marincola, *Authority*, 86.

17. On the use of Greek historiography by Jewish historians, see Attridge, "Historiography," 157; Feldman, *Josephus' Interpretation of the Bible*, 3–13; Sterling, "Jewish Appropriation," 231–43.

historians took over the essential material of their predecessors and moderately adapted it for their purposes through mimesis.[18] As Marincola's analysis shows, historical compositions were quite unoriginal, based primarily on imitation of previous works, seeking to only make gradual advances within and alterations on the prevailing tradition.[19] We see this, for example, in the relationship between Herodotus and Homer/Hesiod in which Herodotus had little historical material to draw from (other than scholars, such as Hecataeus, Charon, Dionysius, and Xanthus), using the epic tradition as his model. Thucydides then appears to have imitated Herodotus and perhaps Hecataeus at places. Xenophon then imitated Thucydides and/or Herodotus. Dionysius of Halicarnassus, in fact, wrote a historiographic treatise on mimesis (*De Imitatione*), now only preserved in fragments, where he attempted to identify the mimetic sources behind a number of the historians. In what we do know from the fragments that remain, the aim of mimesis, according to Dionysius, was often to bring divergent works on a topic together to form a single running narrative with only subtle alterations to suit the narrative framework.[20] The art of this kind of history was expressed in the skill of uniting various streams of tradition into a single contemporary version of the history. This mimesis was, in fact, so essential to Greek historiography that Duris criticized two fourth-century B.C.E. historians, Ephorus and Theopompus, for lacking mimesis in their accounts (*FGrH* 76 F1). The paucity of extant historical sources that served as models, however, remains a significant obstacle for understanding fully the extent, nature, and form of mimetic appropriation that took place.

When we approach Hellenistic Jewish historiography, we encounter the same problem at one level, but not at another—at least not in the same degree. A classification of the kinds of sources used by these historians in terms of nonscriptural and scriptural sources helps illustrate this point. As with the Greek historians, many of their Jewish successors utilized now non-extant sources, causing substantial problems for modern interpreters when citation formulas are lacking. Most of the histories Josephus refers to and apparently imitates (e.g., Alexander Polyhistor, Demetrius) are now

---

18. See C. J. Kraemer, "Imitation and Originality," *The Classical Weekly* 20 (1927) 135–36.

19. Marincola, *Authority*, 14.

20. For reconstructions and analysis of this treatise, see M. Heath, "Dionysius of Halicarnassus 'On Imitation,'" *Hermes* 117 (1989) 370–73; R. L. Hunter, *Critical Moments in Classical Literature: Studies in the Ancient View of Literature and Its Uses* (Cambridge: Cambridge University Press, 2009) 107–27.

lost.²¹ When Josephus does not cite his source directly but appears to borrow material, much debate ensues over the identity of his literary model/source text(s). The discussion of whether or not Josephus used an unknown Latin senatorial source or some other source(s) in *Ant.* 19 provides one example.²² Many believe the historian Eupolemus may have provided one of the sources that 1 and 2 Maccabees imitated,²³ but due to the Maccabean history's use of mimesis rather than direct citation for this source (if it was indeed used) and the fragmentary nature of the source as we now have it, whether Eupolemus was a model text for the Maccabean history will remain an anomaly. Philo's writings present similar problems. Scholars tend to think Philo used sources, but these nonscriptural sources apparently typically occupy the mimetic dimension of his source framework, leaving the identity of Philo's nonscriptural sources, for the most part, unknown.²⁴ Due to these complexities, it will not serve the purposes of this essay to probe these mysteries except to say that these sources, whatever their identity, fit into the mimetic level of the historians' source framework and help shape the background of the narrative.

The situation changes, however, when we turn to the scriptural sources used by the historians. These sources typically reveal themselves in the form of the so-called rewritten Bible genre, which, in addition to some unknown nonscriptural sources, seems to help form the mimetic component of the source configuration utilized by Jews in the Hellenistic period to write the histories of their people. But at this level of source integration, the use of prophetic literature remains conspicuously absent. The historians reserve mimetic techniques for narrative literature, especially the Pentateuch. This may be observed in several of the histories from this period. In *Jubilees*, we find an attempt to rework Jewish history from Genesis 1 through Exodus 24 while integrating traditions from *1 Enoch* (*Jub.* 5 //

---

21. See Sterling, *Historiography and Self-Definition*, 137–225, for assessment of the role of several of these now-lost Jewish historians used by Josephus.

22. See Goud, "Sources," 472–82, esp. pp. 472–73, for discussions in the secondary literature.

23. E.g. B. Wacholder, *Eupolemus: A Study of Judaeo-Greek Literature* (HUCM 3; New York: Hebrew Union College–Jewish Institute of Religion, 1974) 27–40; J. A. Goldstein, *II Maccabees* (AB 41A; Garden City, NY: Doubleday, 1983) 37–41.

24. For attempts to identify these sources, however, see R. G. Hamerton-Kelly, "Sources and Traditions in Philo Judaeus: Prolegomena to an Analysis of His Writings," *SPhilo* 1 (1972) 3–21; and the source-critical analysis of Philo's interpretation of the Pentateuch in R. Goulet, *La philosophie de Moïse: Essai de reconstitution d'un commentaire philosophique préphilonien du Pentateuque* (Histoire des doctrines de l'Antiquité classique 11; Paris: Vrin, 1987).

1 En. 10–11; but imitates many other features of the Enoch circle, e.g., the *Letter of Enoch*, throughout), the *Testaments of Judah* (e.g., *Jub.* 34:1–9 // *T. Jud.* 3–7), *Reuben* (e.g., *Jub.* 33:1–9 // *T. Reu.* 3), and *Levi* (e.g., *Jub.* 34:20 // *T. Lev.* 9) as well as nonextant works such as the *Book* or *Apocalypse of Noah* (*Jub.* 10:1–15; 7:20–39).[25] In each of these and many other instances, the author does not cite his sources directly but takes them over from his predecessors and weaves them seamlessly into his retelling of early Israelite history. The writings of Moses, nevertheless, remain the principle source for the work, only being cited directly in the introductory material.[26] Besides perhaps an allusion to the first part of Daniel (1 Esd 3:1–5:6), 1 Esdras imitates the Chronicler, Ezra, and Nehemiah (see pp. 241–244 below on the priority of the canonical books to 1 Esdras).[27] While large sections of biblical text are not taken over and reworked directly in 1 and 2 Maccabees (see 2 Macc 2:29–31), we do discover, at least in 1 Maccabees, a tendency to blend the telling of the story of the Hasmonean dynasty with the retelling of the biblical story, presenting the Hasmoneans as a continuation of it (e.g., 1 Macc 2:49–70 // Num 24:5–9; 1 Macc 14:5–14 // 1 Kgs 4:25), but again, without reference to the prophetic corpus. We know that Josephus uses Moses as his principal source for the first 10 chapters of his *Antiquities* because he tells us this much. And when one assesses how this source finds its way into Josephus's narrative, it very much resembles the mimetic tendencies of his Greek predecessors rather than constituting a new specifically Jewish genre, now known to scholars in the last 50 years as the rewritten Bible. Moses gets some coverage in the preface and the first chapter of *Antiquities*, but *as a source* drops quickly into the background after this, resurfacing only on rare occasions. Yet when Josephus turns to his prophetic sources, he tends to prefer direct citation to mimesis techniques.

The writings of the prophets are noticeably absent at this level of source utilization. We seldom see imitation of prophetic literature. Only in rare

---

25. On the use of traditions in *Jubilees*, see R. H. Charles, *The Book of Jubilees or The Little Genesis* (London: Black, 1902) xliv–xlv.

26. As with mimetic practices in Greco-Roman historiography, there is a discussion of the sources in the introductory material (preface/prologue), but in the remaining narrative the author integrates much source material (those mentioned and those not mentioned) without citation (e.g. Diodorus, 1.4.1–4; Dionysius of Halicarnassus, *Ant. rom.* 1.7.1–3).

27. See 2 Chr 35:1–9 // 1 Esd 1:1–22; 2 Chr 35:20–36:21 // 1 Esd 1:25–58; 2 Chr 36:22–23/Ezra 1:1–3a // 2 Esd 2:1–5a; Ezra 1:3b–11 // 1 Esd 2:5b–15; Ezra 4:7–24 // 1 Esd 4:16–27; Ezra 2:1–4:5 // 1 Esd 5:7–73; Ezra 5:1–10:44 // 1 Esd 6:1–9:36; Neh 7:73–8:13a // 1 Esd 9:37–55.

or fringe cases does this occur. For example, in *The Story of Zosimus* or *The History of the Rechabites* we find a compilation of the Exodus story, Daniel 10 and 12, and especially Jeremiah 34 in chaps. 8–10, which may be the most primitive portion of the document.[28] But this text, although highly Hellenistic and likely originally composed in Greek, hardly represents mainstream Jewish historiography and may turn out to be quite late.[29] Another text on the margins, as far as history is concerned, *Lives of the Prophets*, weaves data from biblical prophetic texts into its narrative as it documents the *vita* of 23 prophets, but as Satran shows, we have no antecedent to its genre of "compressed, anecdotal biography" within the literature of the Second Temple period, and we should probably date the text to the early Byzantine era rather than the first century C.E. in any case.[30]

Within mainstream historiography the mimetic models remain the historical books of the Hebrew Bible, especially the writings of Moses. In their article entitled "Palestinian Adaptations of Biblical Narratives and Prophecies," Harrington and Horgan illustrate this point when they focus only on the historians' use of rewritten biblical narrative and consign the appropriation of prophetic literature exclusively to Qumran practices, especially within the pesher literature.[31] Similarly, Brooke can write an entire article entitled "Rewritten Law, Prophets and Psalms" that includes no analysis of the latter two categories—likely because it rarely happened. The article contains only a single passing reference to a prophetic text, Isaiah 36–39 with parallels in 2 Kings 18–20.[32] Why the disparity of prophetic literature as literary models for the Hellenistic Jewish historians? A number of factors are no doubt at work here. Certainly narrative histories will provide more content for creating new histories and can likely be more naturally reworked into the new compositions. But it seems, more fundamentally, that the authors did not desire to background these important

---

28. On *The History of the Rechabites*, see C. H. Knights, "Towards a Critical Introduction to 'The History of the Rechabites,'" *JSJ* 26 (1995) 234–42.

29. Knights argues for a possible date as late as the seventh century C.E. ("Towards a Critical Introduction," 331).

30. D. Satran, *Biblical Prophets in Byzantine Palestine: Reassessing the Lives of the Prophets* (SVTP 11; Leiden: E.J. Brill, 1995) 79–96, 98.

31. D. J. Harrington and M. P. Horgan, "Palestinian Adaptations of Biblical Narratives and Prophecies," in *Early Judaism and Its Modern Interpreters* (ed. R. A. Kraft and G. W. E. Nickelsburg; The Bible and Its Modern Interpreters 2; Atlanta: Scholars Press, 1986) 239–58.

32. G. J. Brooke, "The Rewritten Law, Prophets and Psalms: Issues for Understanding the Text of the Bible," in *The Bible as Book: The Hebrew Bible and the Judaean Desert Discoveries* (ed. E. D. Herbert and E. Tov; London: British Library, 2002) 31–40, esp. p. 32.

prophetic texts but sought to project them onto the foreground of the narrative through direct citation to help substantiate important narrative movements or instances their audience(s) might find difficult to believe.

The Use of Prophetic Literature: Direct Citation

Whereas mimesis and autopsy remained the most common ways of maintaining historical authority, Marincola shows that explicit reference to sources in the Greek historians more generally was reserved "for emphasizing special sources and as a validation for exceptional events."[33] Exceptional events here can range from the miraculous to key literary developments to special circumstances that need further endorsement (for example, where the historical reliability of the event is disputed). Direct citation of sources, then, remained a rare phenomenon so that it had its desired narrative impact when it was used, a feature which, according to Potter, distinguished Greek history from biography:

> In terms of form, perhaps the most important point is that [biography] allowed for direct quotation of documents in a way that the generic rules for narrative history did not. It is not altogether clear why this should be so, but it may be that the tradition of the eyewitness memorialist influenced the later practitioners in such a way that they too wished to include first-hand statements about their subject.[34]

I will argue in this section that Hellenistic Jewish historians, especially Josephus, took over this literary strategy from their Greek predecessors and that, among others, the prophetic writings from the Hebrew Bible served their interests well in this respect. This position contrasts with that of Begg, for example, who sees the historian as mainly interested in adopting narrative portions of prophetic writings.[35]

Most assert that the pseudepigraphal book of *Jubilees* provides the first example of reworked Jewish history during the Hellenistic period (150 B.C.),[36] a text originally composed in Hebrew (as evidence from Qumran reveals), then translated into Greek (and possibly Syriac), and then Latin.

---

33. Marincola, *Authority*, 86.
34. Potter, *Literary Texts and the Roman Historian*, 67.
35. C. Begg, "The 'Classical Prophets' in Josephus' *Antiquities*," *LS* 13 (1988) 341–57; repr., *"The Place Is Too Small for Us": The Israelite Prophets in Recent Scholarship* (ed. R. P. Gordon; Sources for Biblical and Theological Study 5; Winona Lake, IN: Eisenbrauns, 1995) 547–62.
36. E.g., Alexander, "Retelling the Old Testament," 100; Fröhlich, *Time and Times and a Half*, 92.

Though we possess an Ethiopian version of *Jubilees*, only fragments remain from these more primitive versions. The Hebrew text appears to have been composed in order to help Jews under foreign control resist assimilation into Hellenistic culture.[37] Due to these linguistic, social, and literary (it appears that the text attempts to be a further development in, rather than a hellenization of, biblical historiography) considerations, this text might not be as relevant as some of the others for our purposes. Nevertheless, we may begin to detect here some early movements toward the mimetic practices that would dominate historical works written shortly after its composition. While this earliest history-like Jewish text from the Hellenistic period does not directly cite prophetic literature, it does cite Moses, who was clearly considered a prophet. As with the Greek historians, when the author cites his Mosaic source, he does so at significant points within the narrative. Recall that he only cites Moses explicitly within the programmatic introductory material, highlighting his source as special and prominent at this juncture before turning to imitate it throughout the remainder of his work.[38] We may see, then, in this work the first reflections of Greek models of source integration working themselves into the literature of the Jewish historians. Even if adapting the Greek model is not intentional at this stage, it appears to have provided precedent for later practice.

In following the historical trajectory, 1 Esdras[39] is worth mentioning in that it seems to be an attempt to follow a type of biblical historiography (mid-second century to early-first century B.C.E.); as with *Jubilees*, the major Hellenistic development being original composition in Greek.[40] As a sort of prologue, the book begins with what essentially amounts to a

---

37. J. C. VanderKam, "The Origins and Purposes of the Book of *Jubilees*," in *Studies in the Book of Jubilees* (ed. M. Albani, J. Frey, and A. Lange; TSAJ 65; Tübingen: Mohr Siebeck, 1997) 3–24, esp. p. 22.

38. In 50 chapters, the author only mentions him by name 13 times, 7 of which appear in the first chapter, one in the second chapter, and the remaining 5 scattered throughout the rest of the narrative, starting in chap. 23. But these figures are more revealing still. The author only cites Moses as source in the opening verses of chaps. 1 and 2 and here only indirectly, as it is really God/an angel who is communicating to Moses, who then in turn communicates through his writings. In the remaining instances, Moses gets mention only as a narrative figure.

39. M. Bird graciously allowed me to use the manuscript for his forthcoming commentary on 1 Esdras in my preparations of this essay. My analysis in these paragraphs has greatly benefited from his work: M. F. Bird, *First Esdras* (Septuagint Commentary Series; Leiden: Brill, 2012).

40. On 1 Esdras as a translation of a Vorlage similar but not identical to the MT, see Z. Talshir, *I Esdras: From Origin to Translation* (SBLSCS 47; Atlanta: Society of

reworking of the narrative of 2 Chr 35:1–36:23, in which Jeremiah plays a central role. The author recruits Josiah's religious reform according to the law as a kind of historical-narrative introduction to Ezra's ministry in an attempt to unite the two traditions.

In addition to subtle revisions/additions/omissions to the Chronicles narrative at the mimetic level, the author employs a direct citation of Jeremiah that amounts to a conflation of a prophecy from Jeremiah's writings (Jer 25:12, 29:10) with material from the Chronicles narrative (2 Chr 36:21) and/or Lev 26:34: "and they were servants to him and to his sons until the Persians began to reign, in fulfillment of the word of the Lord by the mouth of Jeremiah, saying, 'Until the land has enjoyed its sabbaths, it shall keep sabbath all the time of its desolation until the completion of seventy years'" (1 Esd 1:57–58). When the time comes to cite a source directly, he does not cite his narrative material about Jeremiah from Chronicles, but the prophetic text itself. The location of this passage is highly programmatic, functioning as a transition between the Chronicles and the Ezra tradition and as the trajectory-setting conclusion to the extended historical prologue.[41]

The author then carries this momentum directly into his narrative by recapitulating the emphasis on his story as a fulfillment of the words of Jeremiah at the beginning of the second chapter (1 Esd 2:1 // Ezra 1:1) and then Jeremiah as both a source and a narrative figure disappears from the story, never to return. The author seems to avoid citation of sources beyond this intentionally. His main sources, the Chronicler, Ezra, and Nehemiah, certainly are not mentioned. Even when prophets issue prophecies within the narrative, the author does not transmit a record of what they said, through direct citation or any other means (e.g., Aggaeus and Zacharias the son of Addo, 1 Esd 6:1; cf. 1 Esd 7:3). In 1 Esd 8:83, the author attributes a citation concerning intermarriage to "the prophets," but this seems to be some kind of adaptation of Ezra's pronouncement

---

Biblical Literature, 1999) passim. See also L. W. Batten, *A Critical and Exegetical Commentary on the Books of Ezra and Nehemiah* (ICC; New York: Scribners, 1913) 6–13.

41. Although a number of interpreters comment on this text, to my knowledge, no one has yet observed this narrative strategy: e.g., C. C. Torrey, *Ezra Studies* (Chicago: University of Chicago Press, 1910) 286; R. H. Charles, *The Apocrypha and Pseudepigrapha of the Old Testament in English: With Introductions and Critical and Explanatory Notes to the Several Books* (2 vols.; Oxford: Clarendon, 1976) 1:25; J. M. Myers, *I and II Esdras: A Translation with Introduction and Notes* (AB 43; New York: Doubleday, 1974) 34; R. W. Klein, "I Esdras," in *The HarperCollins Bible Commentary* (J. L. Mays and J. Blenkinsopp; San Francisco: HarperSanFrancisco, 2000) 698–704, esp. p. 699; Bird, *First Esdras*, ad loc.

(Ezra 10:10–11). No extant prophetic text contains exactly these words (but see Leviticus 18).

Although not as Hellenized as some of the later texts from our period, notably Josephus, 1 Esdras fits the pattern employed by the Greek historians, who only employed direct citation at highly strategic points in the narrative. And the author appears particularly concerned to reserve prophetic literature (in this case, Jeremiah), a special source, for these purposes. Indeed, the Jeremiah text seems to provide forward-looking prophetic validation for the entire narrative with its scarcity making it highly marked within the literary structure of the work. Although this text appears more slavish and less literary, it still seems to align with Greek mimetic practice.

First Esdras, then, appears to function as a kind of transitional text, with some initial signs of Hellenization surfacing in its citation strategies. Of course, one may naturally object to positioning 1 Esdras at this point in the chronological development, or its dependence on prior canonical literature due to the complex web of issues that form around the date, composition, and relationship of this work to its sources. Beginning especially with the seminal work of Pohlmann,[42] some have argued for the so-called *Fragmenthypothese*: that 1 Esdras constitutes a Greek translation of a fragment of a larger work that included 1–2 Chronicles.[43] This view and other (canonical) literary independence theories propose that 1 Esdras goes back to a primitive tradition independent of Ezra–Nehemiah, the

---

42. But before Pohlmann, note the similar views and foundational work of H. Howorth, "Some Unconventional Views on the Text of the Bible. I: The Apocryphal Book of Esdras A and the Septuagint," *Proceedings of the Society of Biblical Archaeology* 23 (1901) 147–59; idem, "Some Unconventional Views on the Text of the Bible. II: The Chronology and Order of Events in Esdras A, Compared with and Preferred to those in the Canonical Ezra," *Proceedings of the Society of Biblical Archaeology* 24 (1902) 147–72; C. C. Torrey, "The Nature and Origin of 'First Esdras,'" *AJSL* 23 (1907) 116–41; R. H. Pfeiffer, *History of New Testament Times with an Introduction to Apocrypha* (New York: Harper, 1949) 243; see also A. E. Gardner, "The Purpose and Date of 1 Esdras," *JJS* 37 (1986) 18–27, esp. p. 18. Although these authors differ in various respects (Pfeiffer criticizes Howorth, for example, for understanding 1 Esdras as the original form of the canonical books), they view 1 Esdras independently of the present form of the canonical tradition, whether drawing on the same body of tradition that the canonical writings did or from a prior form of the canonical literature.

43. K.-F. Pohlmann, *Studien zum dritten Esra: Ein Beitrag zur Frage nach dem ursprünglichen Schluß des chronistischen Geschichtswerkes* (FRLANT 104; Göttingen: Vandenhoeck & Ruprecht, 1970); W. O. E. Oesterley, *An Introduction to the Books of the Apocrypha* (London: SPCK, 1935) 136–37; F. M. Cross, "A Reconstruction of the Judean Restoration," *JBL* 94 (1975) 4–18, esp. pp. 6–15; *The First and Second Books of Esdras* (ed. R. J. Coggins and M. A. Knibb; CBCNEB; Cambridge: Cambridge University Press, 1979) 5.

latter providing a reworking of the same or very similar material. Nevertheless, in defense of the traditional literary dependence thesis, several scholars have undermined these conclusions. Talshir, for example, shows that the typical evidence marshalled by Pohlmann and his followers remains entirely circumstantial.[44] Bird mentions a number of further problems with the theory.[45] Several others still have substantiated points of correlation that strongly suggest literary dependence on the parallel canonical accounts.[46] We continue to have, then, solid precedent for recognizing the priority of Ezra–Nehemiah plus the Chronicler as significant sources for 1 Esdras so that a date in the mid-second to early-first century B.C.E. and dependent relation to biblical sources as a transitional piece of Hellenistic Jewish historiography seems likely.

The first two books of the Maccabean history provide a different kind of history from those reviewed so far, because both volumes focus specifically on contemporary history. A scarcity of scriptural materials results from this reality in terms of the source framework, but, at least in the case of 2 Maccabees, we find in the second letter appended to the beginning of the work a discussion of scriptural sources, including "the records of the prophet Jeremiah" (2:1), a citation of Moses (2:11–12), "the archives or memoirs of Nehemiah" as well as a library including books about the kings and prophets and the writings of David (2:13). However, the relationship of this sort of introductory epistolary material to the history itself, apparently beginning in 2:19, remains unclear so that the value of this material for understanding the nature of the entire document is inconclusive. In 1 Maccabees there appears to be an intentional strategy to avoid, in many cases even echoing prophetic language. While the author freely imitates OT narrative material in his hero characterizations, as Goldstein notices, on most occasions, he "seems deliberately to have departed from or to have avoided the wording of biblical prophecies." Although in telling the conquests of the Hasmonaean brothers, reference to prophetic material would have greatly supported the narrative development, "not once does

---

44. Talshir, *I Esdras*, 21–34. See also H. G. M. Williamson, *Israel in the Books of Chronicles* (Cambridge: Cambridge University Press, 1977) 14–23.

45. Bird, *First Esdras*, "Introduction."

46. O. Eissfeldt, *The Old Testament, An Introduction* (trans. P. R. Ackroyd; Oxford: Blackwell, 1965) 574; T. C. Eskenazi, *In an Age of Prose: A Literary Approach to Ezra–Nehemiah* (SBLMS 36; Atlanta: Scholars Press, 1988) 155–74; T. C. Eskenazi, "The Chronicler and the Composition of 1 Esdras," *CBQ* 48 (1986) 39–61; Williamson, *Israel in the Books of Chronicles*, 21–36; H. G. M. Williamson, *Ezra–Nehemiah* (WBC 16; Dallas: Word, 2002) xxii–xxiii.

he echo the prophecies of conquests there."[47] It seems that 1 Maccabees, which prefers imitation as a general model over citation, adopts scriptural sources almost entirely restricted to narrative material.[48] I interpret this phenomenon as the continuation of a tendency within Second Temple historiography to avoid sourcing biblical prophetic materials for mimesis.

It is not until Josephus that we witness the full dawn of Hellenism within Jewish historiography. As noted above, Josephus adopts his historiographic framework explicitly from the Greek historians, including his method for source utilization and citation, as I hope to show in the remainder of this section. Josephus knew and used 1 Esdras and 1 Maccabees and both provided literary models for him at some level. Whereas Josephus does cite Moses directly—in the preface and in his creation account, especially (both highly programmatic locations)—when he chooses to cite his scriptural source directly, he apparently prefers prophetic writings. We observe this phenomenon when we look at how Josephus handles his prophetic sources.

Of the Hebrew prophets, it is Jonah, a somewhat unlikely candidate, perhaps, who makes the first appearance in Josephus's *Antiquities* and not until book 9. In citing and reworking his Jonah material, Josephus conflates material from 2 Kings 14 and the book of Jonah. Josephus presents Jonah as a "prophet" who "foretold" Jeroboam's victory over Syria and whose writings are contained in Josephus's "Hebrew books" (*Ant.* 9.205–208). This seems significant because the biblical book does not describe itself as prophetic.[49] As Begg notices, Josephus shows a concern to portray Jonah as an accurate predictor of the future.[50] Due to the function of the quotations to provide credibility to the history, this focus would need to play an important part in his portrayal, especially if some had questioned Jonah at this level. The direct citations come in the midst of the reworking

---

47. J. A. Goldstein, "How the Authors of 1 and 2 Maccabees Treated the 'Messianic Prophecies,'" in *Judaisms and Their Messiahs at the Turn of the Christian Era* (ed. J. Neusner, W. S. Green, and E. S. Frerichs; Cambridge: Cambridge University Press, 1987) 69–96, quoting p. 77.

48. Goldstein ("How the Authors of 1 and 2 Maccabees Treated the 'Messianic Prophecies,'" 76–77) acknowledges "echoes" of a few prophetic texts within 1 Maccabees, but these for the most part amount to slight parallels in language (restricted to his "Ode to Judas") and certainly no direct citations. He reinforces that "Indeed, relatively infrequent are the Hasmonaean propagandist's allusions, in telling of his heroes, to the books of the Writing Prophets" (p. 76).

49. L. H. Feldman, "Josephus' Interpretation of Jonah," *AJSR* 17 (1992) 1–29 (6–7).

50. Begg, "Classical Prophets," 346.

of 2 Kgs 15:23–27. While Jonah only receives passing mention in 2 Kings, Josephus makes him into a significant focus, recruiting his prophetic utterances as a validation for the military success of Jeroboam. Josephus shows his reluctance to employ material affirming the miraculous in Jonah, however, through his use of qualifying language (e.g., "the story has it"; see *Ant.* 9.208, 213).[51] Miracles were often viewed with suspicion in ancient history. In addition to reasons mentioned below, this may have provided incentive for Josephus to deploy a quotation from Nahum in support of the same event in the subsequent context.

Josephus cites Nahum at a highly strategic point in chap. 11 of book 9, but here the citation takes over a decently sized section of text from Nah 2:8–13 verbatim rather than citing the prophet's name and summarizing his material. However, Josephus refrains from citing more of Nahum's oracles because he does not want to "appear troublesome to [his] readers" (*Ant.* 9.242). Feldman and Begg both interpret this statement to mean that prophecy in general would be overbearing to Josephus's ancient readers,[52] but when interpreted in the context of ancient (Greek) historiography where the citation of sources was reserved for special narrative movements and events, we see that Josephus was concerned here to handle his sources according to the appropriate standards, including his prophetic ones. In the text he does cite, Nahum predicts the fall of Nineveh. The citation functions in the narrative as a conclusion to the 11th chapter of book 9, giving literary closure to Josephus's recounting of Assyria's conquest over Israel in the preceding paragraphs (*Ant.* 9.228–35). He uses the citation to resolve the narrative tension of Israel, on the one hand, being God's chosen people, while on the other hand, God providentially allowing his people to be taken as Tiglath-Pileser's prisoners (*Ant.* 9.235). The quote also functions in a supporting role, as Begg notes, "to confirm and reinforce the announcement about Nineveh's overthrow made by Jonah earlier."[53] The Jonah material may have needed further endorsement

---

51. See Thackeray, *Josephus*, 90; Begg, "Classical Prophets," 346; Feldman, "Josephus' Interpretation of Jonah," 3, 14–15; T. M. Bolin, *Freedom beyond Forgiveness: The Book of Jonah Re-examined* (JSOTSup 236; Sheffield: Sheffield Academic Press, 1997), 15.

52. L. H. Feldman, "Prophets and Prophecy in Josephus," in *Prophets, Prophecy, and Prophetic Texts in Second Temple Judaism* (ed. M. H. Floyd and R. D. Haak; LHBOTS 427; New York: T. & T. Clark, 2006) 210–39, esp. p. 216; Begg, "Classical Prophets," 347–48.

53. Begg, "Classical Prophets," 348. In a later study, Begg (*Josephus' Story*, 302) states, "by positioning his quotation of Nahum's word of doom for Assyria where he does, i.e. not long after his citation of Jonah's similar message, Josephus underscores the

due to perceptions in some circles that he may have been a false prophet (Tob 14:4).[54] Josephus's own remarks further substantiate this function of the citation by emphasizing that everything Nahum predicted regarding Nineveh "happened about . . . a hundred and fifteen years afterward" (*Ant.* 9.242). And with this, the chapter concludes.

Isaiah surfaces for the first time toward the end of book 9 of the *Antiquities*, where Josephus refers to him as the prophet who knew all future events and on whom King Hezekiah depended (*Ant.* 9.276). Again, Josephus combines material from 2 Kings 18–20 and Isaiah 36–39 in the composition of his account. Isaiah figures as a significant character within book 10, acting as a prophetic consultant to the king, especially with respect to the fate of Israel in relation to Assyria. Josephus relates that Isaiah "wrote down all his prophecies, and left them behind him in books" (*Ant.* 10.35), apparently acknowledging his access to these prophetic texts. Although he seems to employ a different Vorlage than the one behind the MT, Josephus cites Isa 44:28 directly from "the book which Isaiah left behind of his prophecies" (*Ant.* 11.5–6) as the text that gave Cyrus the incentive to send the Jews back to their native land (see Xenophon, *Cyr.* 1.1).[55] And as with the quotation given from Nahum, the biblical text here functions in two ways. First, it substantiates a significant narrative turn in Josephus's portrayal of Israel's history related specifically to the theme of exile and return. Second, it provides further validation for the prophecies of Jeremiah in the preceding descriptions (*Ant.* 11.1–2). Haggai and Zachariah help further substantiate these realities. They assure the Jews that the

---

certainty of Assyria's demise as something announced by two different prophets. Such a 'confirmation' of Jonah's announcement would be all the more in order." This kind of function for the quotation indicates a direct parallel with practices of source citation found among the Greek historians.

54. So B. Ego, "The Repentance of Nineveh in the Story of Jonah and Nahum's Prophecy of the City's Destruction: A Coherent Reading of the Book of the Twelve as Reflected in the Aggada," in *Thematic Threads in the Book of the Twelve* (ed. P. L. Redditt and A. Schart; BZAW 325; Berlin: de Gruyter, 2003) 155–64, esp. pp. 157–58.

55. Feldman (*Studies*, 379) remains puzzled as to why Josephus used Isaiah so infrequently and suggests that this may have been due to a priestly preference to Jeremiah over Isaiah. While such considerations certainly could have factored into the selections Josephus made in the end, we must remember that according to the canons of historiography, citation is kept to a minimum so that taking over large portions of Isaiah 7 in support of Ahaz's alliance with Assyria, for example (as Feldman thinks we might expect), may not have been as much of an option as one would think. Such an event likely did not need the heavy endorsement of prophetic citation in Josephus's mind. Some of the other events, notably those prophesied in Jonah, Nahum, and Jeremiah, clearly did. These seem more integral to his narrative strategy and, therefore, require substantiation.

Persians will not interfere with their efforts to rebuild the temple (*Ant.* 11.96), and it was in fact their prophecies that helped bring the structure of the temple to conclusion (*Ant.* 11.106; see also *J.W.* 6.270). The pattern resurfaces: the citation confirms other prophecy/history and relates to themes of exile/restoration. Josephus also cites Isa 19:18–23 toward the end of his account of the Jewish War, again on this theme of the history of the rebuilding of the temple (*J.W.* 7.432). This citation illustrates Feldman's point that these restoration themes in Josephus take on a clear orientation toward the temple.[56]

If the rabbis favor Isaiah, the Hellenistic Jewish historians favor Jeremiah, who makes an appearance not only in 1 Esdras and 2 Maccabees but receives extensive treatment in Josephus as well. Scholarship in this domain of Josephan studies has tended to focus on Josephus's typology of Jeremiah in relation to his own life and ministry.[57] That Josephus draws significantly on Jeremiah to show that the Jews' war against Rome was the result of divine judgment also remains a consistent emphasis.[58] Besides the analysis of Begg,[59] little attention has been given to the function of the citations themselves. Josephus first refers to the prophet's "lament, which is extant to this time also" (*Ant.* 10.78). He goes on to insist that Jeremiah predicted the destruction of Jerusalem by Rome (10.79). Much of the account focuses on Jeremiah's story in the context of the reigns of Jehoiakim and Zedekiah rather than his writings (*Ant.* 10.84–154). Josephus summarizes his ministry, apparently including the prophecies recorded in the book that bears his name, when he says that Jeremiah "foretold every day" (*Ant.* 10.89) how the king of Babylon would overthrow Jehoiakim. Josephus continues to reiterate these predications and

---

56. Feldman, "Restoration," 254.

57. See esp. J. Blenkinsopp, "Prophecy and Priesthood in Josephus," *JJS* 25 (1974) 239–6, esp. pp. 244–46; D. Duabe, "Typology in Josephus," *JJS* 31 (1980) 18–36, esp. pp. 26–27; S. J. D. Cohen, "Josephus, Jeremiah and Polybius," *History and Theory* 21 (1982) 366–81, esp. pp. 367–69; Begg, "Classical Prophets," 354; R. Gray, *Prophetic Figures in Late Second Temple Jewish Palestine: The Evidence from Josephus* (New York: Oxford University Press, 1993) 72–74; L. H. Feldman, "Josephus's Portrait of Isaiah," in *Writing and Reading the Scroll of Isaiah: Studies of an Interpretive Tradition* (ed. C. C. Broyles and C. A. Evans; VTSup 70; Leiden: Brill, 1997) 583–608, esp. p. 586. In each of these sources and others we often find an attempt to compare various historical details between Josephus's account and Jeremiah's. Beyond these, see, e.g., R. C. Steiner, "Incomplete Circumcision in Egypt and Edom: Jeremiah (9:24–25) in the Light of Josephus and Jonckheere," *JBL* 118 (1999) 497–505.

58. N. Kelly, "The Cosmopolitan Expression of Josephus's Prophetic Perspective in the 'Jewish War,'" *HTR* 97 (2004) 257–74, esp. p. 260.

59. Begg, "Classical Prophets," 352–55.

their accuracy throughout his narrative (*Ant.* 10.104, 106, 112, 114–20, 124, 141; see *Ant.* 10.176–80; so also *J.W.* 5.391–92). He recruits Ezekiel within the Jeremiah narratives as well, but—as Begg observes—these typically amount to "a confirmatory echo" to the prophecies of Jeremiah.[60] He introduces Ezekiel for the first time as a contemporary of Jeremiah, who wrote two books (*Ant.* 10.79). Each citation of Ezekiel seems to strengthen Jeremiah's prediction regarding the fate of Israel in relation to Babylon (*Ant.* 10.98, 104–6; see *Ant.* 10.141). This set of summarizing citations from Jeremiah–Ezekiel shows again the dual function of Josephus's use of prophetic literature, serving to confirm the development of the important narrative themes revolving around the issue of Israel's exile and return.[61] As with Isaiah, Jeremiah's restoration focus remains oriented toward the temple. As Gray notices, he even sometimes adds temple references to Jeremiah where none exist in the source text (e.g., *Ant.* 10.128 // Jer 38:20–23).[62]

Although not considered among the "classical prophets" in the Jewish tradition, Daniel stands among Josephus's most beloved prophets, receiving more attention than any of the others. Most of his account of Daniel consists of reworked narrative material.[63] Duabe, Gray, and especially Gnuse connect his portrayal of Daniel in the *Antiquities* with Josephus's own life, particularly as it is represented in the autobiographical material in his *Life* (77–79, 80–82, 84–85).[64] Besides the narration of Daniel's interpretation of the king's dream, Josephus first emphasizes the genuinely prophetic character of Daniel's writings when he says if one "cannot curb his inclination for understanding the uncertainties of the future, and whether they will happen or not, let him be diligent in reading the Book of Daniel, which he will find among the sacred writings" (*Ant.* 10.210). Again, with Daniel, we see Josephus highlight prophecies concerning the destruction

---

60. Begg, "Classical Prophets," 355.
61. See Kelly, "Cosmopolitan Expression," 260.
62. Gray, *Prophetic Figures*, 74.
63. On Josephus's numerous allusions to Daniel, see F. F. Bruce, "Josephus and Daniel," *ASTI* 4 (1965) 148–62; repr., in F. F. Bruce, *A Mind for What Matters: Collected Essays of F.F. Bruce* (Grand Rapids: Eerdmans, 1990) 19–31.
64. Duabe, "Typology," 28; Gray, *Prophetic Figures*, 74–75; R. K. Gnuse, *Dreams and Dream Reports in the Writings of Josephus: A Traditio-Historical Analysis* (AGAJU 36; Leiden: Brill, 1996) 29–30. See also O. Betz, *Offenbarung und Schriftforschung in der Qumransekte* (WUNT 6; Tübingen: Mohr, 1960) 341–43; T. W. Franxman, *Genesis and the "Jewish Antiquities" of Flavius Josephus* (Biblica et orientalia 35; Rome: Biblical Institute, 1979) 215; G. L. Johnson, "Josephus: Heir Apparent to the Prophetic Tradition," in *SBL 1983 Seminar Papers* (ed. K. H. Richards; SBLSP 22; Chico, CA: Scholars Press, 1984) 337–46.

of Jerusalem and the temple (*Ant.* 10.264–68; see *Ant.* 10.272–80, 11.337, 12.332), themes connected with exile and restoration.

It is within Josephus' use of Daniel that we begin to get a sense of the purposes for which Josephus employed prophetic texts within his narrative. He says in *Ant.* 10.277: "All these things did this man leave in writing, as God had showed them to him, insomuch, that such as read his prophecies, and see how they have been fulfilled, would wonder at the honour wherewith God honoured Daniel; and may there discover how the Epicureans are in an error," referring to the Epicurean denial of divine providence (*Ant.* 10.278–79). Following right on the heels of this programmatic statement about the narrative function of at least Daniel's prophecy, we have the direct citation of the prophet Isaiah about Cyrus at the beginning of book 11 roughly four verses later (one of a small handful of direct citations from prophetic literature). Josephus then appears to deploy prophetic literature in direct support of the providential activity of Israel's God.[65]

It seems that, for Josephus, the theme of judgment/exile and return/restoration was most well suited for demonstrating divine providential intervention, specifically the Assyrian/Babylonian judgments and the restoration of Jerusalem/the temple.[66] Although the use of Jonah may not appear at first to fit this pattern as neatly as the others, perhaps Josephus cites him first in support of a conquest theme before pronouncing God's providential judgment and restoration of the nation. Then Josephus cites Nahum's extended prophecy of judgment along with Isaiah's in book 11 on restoration, both high marked (front grounded) due to their exact reproduction of the text. Therefore, Josephus weaves prophetic writings and direct citations from the prophets into these narratives to support his illustration of divine providence through them.

This fits well with the function of direct citation within the Greek historians. As Gray observes in Xenophon's writings: "The major function of citation is to validate content that the reader might find too hard to

---

65. Attridge (*The Interpretation of Biblical History*, 103–4) suggests that Josephus's primary motivation in using prophecy was to substantiate Yahweh's providential relationship with his people. See Bruce, "Josephus," 22; Gray, *Prophetic Figures*, 39.

66. This emphasis may have helped Josephus sort through his material from Daniel, neglecting much of the apocalyptic contained in chaps. 7–12. On Josephus's nonapocalyptic reading of Daniel, see A. Momigliano, "What Josephus Did Not See," in *Essays on Ancient and Modern Judaism* (Chicago: University of Chicago Press, 1994) 67–78; S. Mason, "Josephus, Daniel, and the Flavian House," in *Josephus and the History of the Greco-Roman Period: Essays in Memory of Morton Smith* (ed. F. Parente and J. Sievers; StPB 41; Leiden: Brill, 1994) 161–91.

believe. The writer engages with his reader to authorize: excessively large or small numbers, sensational deaths, significant reputations, great impiety or the activities of gods, significant sayings, and that which is generally excessive."[67] In the case of Josephus, he cites his prophetic sources in support of the "the activities of gods" so as to refute the Epicurean doctrine to the contrary.

This basic literary strategy can be generalized and applied to Josephus's source framework more broadly. Josephus only cites Moses, for example, as a source (rather than a narrative figure) in the preface and then extensively the first chapter on the creation of the world. Moses, as a source, then begins to drop quickly into the background mimetic level of Josephus's source framework, only resurfacing to validate hard-to-believe points in his narrative. For example, after the creation story, he cites Moses again in *Ant.* 1.93, combining his pentateuchal source with several other secular sources, in order to support the flood. As Franxmen notes, "Jos. has not much interest in employing source citation in his Genesis narrative after Abraham." He notes that "his purpose in invoking outside authority seems to be the historical substantiation of the slightly fabulous."[68] Josephus has clearly imitated his Greek predecessors in this and his use of prophetic literature constitutes a more specific function of this broader literary-historiographic strategy.

My conclusion here runs contrary to that of Begg, who argues that Josephus chooses the prophetic literature that he does (and neglects other prophetic texts) due to their distinct narrative material, accurate predictions, and contribution in terms of historical content.[69] Understanding Josephus's use of prophetic literature against the background of Greek historiography in this way helps provide answers to the anomalies created by Begg's proposal. It explains why Josephus cited some of the prophets he did and also why he excluded some (but not all) of the minor prophets; his concern was with divine providence through exile/restoration. It also makes his use of Nahum (which Begg admits remains odd on his proposal) and neglect of so much of Ezekiel's narrative-historical material intelligible. It explains another of Begg's and Feldman's proposed difficulties as well (why so few prophets are cited because Josephus clearly knew other texts[70]) and cuts against the conclusions of scholars such as Schwartz

---

67. Gray, "Interventions," 116–17.
68. Franxman, *Genesis*, 23.
69. Begg, "Classical Prophets," 341–57.
70. Feldman ("Restoration," 252) thinks Josephus failed to cite the prophets more frequently for nationalistic and political reasons. However, the prophets Josephus does

who postulate that Josephus likely used the prophets so infrequently due to partial ignorance.[71] Within Greek historiography, source citation was highly selective, being carefully reserved for those places in the narrative where special validation was needed. Therefore, as a historian, Josephus could only cite a small range of material and he did so only at the most crucial junctures within his narrative so that a neglect of large amounts of prophetic material can hardly count as proof of ignorance.

Conclusions

Recent research has neglected the narrative function of source implementation in the Hellenistic Jewish historians. I have argued that configuring their source framework in the context of Greek historiography seems to provide more adequate descriptive resources for understanding their use of the rewritten Bible and direct citation of sources. Rewritten Bible seems to be better assessed as a distinct Hellenization of Jewish history using Greek mimetic practice. Historical material from the Pentateuch and narratives within the Jewish Scriptures were ideal for this purpose, and historians tended to project these sources onto the background of their own narratives. In terms of the development of the citation of sources and specifically biblical prophetic materials in the Jewish historians, we see a chronological trajectory toward Hellenism and with it implementation of methods for source citation from Greek historiography, culminating in Josephus. *Jubilees* merely adopts mimetic practices, probably inspired by Chronicles. First Esdras, slightly further along the continuum of Hellenism, evidences a model of source integration much closer to Greek historiography, but still primitive in its applications. 1–2 Maccabees represent contemporary history and so, with respect to the use of scriptural materials, their composition remains difficult to assess at this level. Finally, with Josephus, biblical law and narrative are reworked through mimesis on the background of the narrative and prophetic literature is highlighted through direct citation at particularly strategic or marked points in the composition. For Josephus, this marks divine providence in God's interactions with his people through conquest, exile, and restoration.

---

cite remain as politically charged as any.

71. S. Schwartz, *Josephus and Judean Politics* (Columbia Studies in the Classical Tradition 18; Leiden: Brill, 1990) 45–46. That Josephus himself acknowledges that he was aware of other prophecies but intentionally did not include them (*Ant.* 9.242) reinforces my assessment here. See Feldman, "Josephus' Portrait of Isaiah," 584.

Part 2

Historiography in Israelite Prophetic Books

The Poetics of History and the Prophecy of Deutero-Isaiah

Danielle Duperreault

Prior to the events of 597–586 B.C.E., Judah's sense of corporate identity was defined in terms of a geographical place: "I have set my King on Zion, my holy mountain."[1] The retributive acts of Nebuchadnezzar II (605–562 B.C.E.) obliterated Judah's given symbolic order and gave rise to a profound exegetical reconsideration of Judahite historical self-understanding.[2] Deutero-Isaiah's conceptual framework, which he shares with ancient Near Eastern theologians generally, leads him to draw a correlation between divine intentions—the דבר or 'word'—and historical events.[3] Deutero-Isaiah (DI) interprets the military advance of Cyrus of Persia (ca. 576–530 B.C.E.) as an oracular "sign." He moreover suggests that this favorable sign was already augured in the writings of Israel's prophets. In order for him to be able to establish formal continuity between the Judahite prophetic past and his policy of Achaemenid collaboration, DI must situate his exegetical work within the context of a revised historical self-understanding. Indeed, the prophecy of DI presupposes a reformulation of historical consciousness as both the condition and the ground of its coming into being.

History is retrospectively and poetically endowed by writers with whatever meaning it comes to possess. Any sort of writing that involves historical reflection necessitates a process of interpretation: past events must first be constituted as such before they can be organized into a coherent whole.[4] DI's prophetic message relies very much on the careful and deliberate se-

---

1. Ps 2:6.
2. For an account of the eradication of Judahite memory sites, see Lam 2:6. Also see 2 Kgs 24–25.
3. B. Albrektson, *History and the Gods: An Essay on the Idea of Divine Manifestations in the Ancient Near East and in Israel* (ConBOT 1; Lund: Berlingska Boktryckeriet, 1967) 11–122.
4. H. White, "Literary Theory and Historical Writing," in *Figural Realism: Studies in the Mimesis Effect* (Baltimore: Johns Hopkins University Press, 1999) 1–26.

lection and organization of historical events.⁵ The complex prophetic form—a hallmark of traditional Judahite self-understanding—recodes and reorients the pool of textual iconography to which DI gives very particular shape. This essay will explore the complex interdependence of history and prophecy as it is expressed in both the form and the content of DI's poetics, and will proceed as follows: the first section will consider DI's teleological understanding of the oracular and text-derived word (דבר) which runs like an authoritative thread all the way through his commentary. The authority of this traditional word is always already inscribed in the prophetic *genre* which DI seeks to reproduce even as he reconfigures Israel's past. Section two will explore DI's poetics of history, paying particular attention to the mobilization and deployment of beginnings. DI, who seeks to reconcile Israel to the reality of Persian imperialism, can legitimate his collaborationist claims only by drawing typological analogies between repatriation on the one hand and creation and the patriarchal promise theme on the other. DI's chronology differs from that of other prophetic books in that he explicitly and consistently situates the beginning point of Israel's history at the moment of creation.⁶ DI's expanded timeline of events moreover constitutes key elements of Yahwist historiography *as* the history of Israel. DI's historiography therefore deviates significantly in terms of content from the past prophetic writings with which he seeks to establish continuance.⁷ The essay will conclude with a summary and synthesis of both sections.

Prophecy

Isa 40:8   יבש חציר נבל ציץ   The grass withers, the flower fades
           ודבר אלהינו יקום לעולם   but the word of our god will stand forever

---

5. First, I recognize that the term *prophecy* is problematic in light of divinatory practices common to Israel/Judah and the rest of the ANE. Second, I largely adopt the view that DI is a unit, albeit layered.

6. With an emphasis on creation comes a monotheistic conception of the divine. See G. von Rad, *Old Testament Theology* (trans. D. M. G. Stalker; 2 vols.; Louisville: Westminster John Knox, 2001) 1:240–43. Also see R. E. Clements, "Monotheism and the God of Many Names," in *The God of Israel* (ed. R. P. Gordon; University of Cambridge Oriental Publications 64; Cambridge: Cambridge University Press, 2007) 56–59.

7. J. Van Seters, "Confessional Reformulation in the Exilic Period," *VT* 22 (1972) 448–59.

The above-quoted verse at first reads very much like something one might find stitched on a pillow. Upon closer inspection however, the passage gestures towards a reflection on the nature of language, and on the relationship of the created order to the divine. The דבר, or word, is a binary term. The דבר first and foremost signifies the oracular word of Yahweh.[8] Indeed, DI constitutes the דבר as a fixed and irrefutable point in the face of change: יקום לעולם. DI constructs his entire exegetical argument on precisely this epistemological foundation: the דבר, synonymous with oracular authority, is made manifest by events that unfold on the practical field of worldly events. In short, Yahweh acts in history and keeps his (messenger-mediated) word—albeit fluidly, as will become apparent later in this essay.

The דבר, however, is also a "technical term" that refers to actual material texts (signs) that can be read and that lend themselves to interpretation by DI.[9] The passage cited below is from First Isaiah:

Isa 30:8	עתה בוא	Go now—
	כתבה על לוח אתם	Write it before them on a tablet
	ועל ספר חקה	and inscribe it on a scroll
	ותהי ליום אחרון	that it may be for a time to come
	לעד עד עולם	as a witness forever

Regardless of its "authenticity," this verse speaks to the way preexilic texts were read by subsequent scribal agents. Jan Assmann aptly describes writing as a "place of refuge."[10] The writings attributed to preexilic prophetic writers became the fixed word around which Judahite collective identities—both diasporic and autochthonous—began to reformulate themselves.[11] Indeed, for DI, the "time to come" was now.[12]

---

8. C. Levin, "The 'Word of Yahweh': A Theological Concept in the Book of Jeremiah," in *Prophets, Prophecy, and Prophetic Texts in Second Temple Judaism* (ed. M. H. Floyd and R. D. Haak; LHBOTS 427; New York: T. & T. Clark, 2006) 42–62, esp. pp. 42–43, 60.

9. M. Fishbane, *Biblical Interpretation in Ancient Israel* (Oxford: Oxford University Press, 1985) 469. Also, H. G. M. Williamson, *The Book Called Isaiah: Deutero-Isaiah's Role in Composition and Redaction* (Oxford: Clarendon, 1994) 29.

10. J. Assmann, *Religion and Cultural Memory: Ten Studies* (trans. R. Livingstone Cultural Memory in the Present; Stanford: Stanford University Press, 2006) 99.

11. M. Nissinen, "The Historical Dilemma of Biblical Prophetic Studies," in *Prophecy in the Book of Jeremiah* (ed. H. M. Barstad and R. G. Kratz; BZAW 388; Berlin: de Gruyter, 2009) 117–20. Also, see R. P. Carroll, *From Chaos to Covenant: Prophecy in the Book of Jeremiah* (New York: Crossroad, 1981) 71; Fishbane, *Biblical Interpretation in Ancient Israel*, 15.

12. Williamson, *The Book Called Isaiah*, 100–107.

Despite the author's adherence to the formal conventions of prophetic writing—which suggest that speech is being enacted—DI's erudite דבר displays a profound preoccupation with its relation to other texts, be they prophetic, psalmic, or historiographic.[13] Texts are never spoken of explicitly as text in DI.[14] Nonetheless, the word does not simply float around in the air. DI is deeply concerned with the interpretation of past writings, and in fact presupposes them in terms of being able to resituate the community in relation to its history. The דבר encapsulates the (decontextualized) past in textual form and transports it to the present. The written word, the actual physical materiality of the texts themselves, is precisely what allows DI to establish what is most important to his project: the conservation and rearticulation of tradition.

DI breaks with popular exilic opinion when he writes that oracles of salvation are actually on the cusp of fulfillment.[15] The דבר is dynamic and teleological: DI has scrutinized the horizon of worldly events, both past and present, and on this basis has ascertained that Yahweh's as-yet unfulfilled salvific acts are imminent. DI correlates signs on the practical field of human events with the promises encoded in the written oracular דבר. It is by this divinatory process that DI can gauge the status of Israel's covenantal relationship with Yahweh.

Prophecy, first and foremost a literary genre, is made up of various subgenres that constitute its distinctly formal aspects. The text under consideration is largely a product of scribal techniques that function either to affirm the oracle under scrutiny or to demonstrate that the oracle has been, or is on the verge of being, fulfilled. When DI interprets former oracles, he also lays bare the process of his own methodology:

Isa 48:3	הראשנות מאז הגדתי	the former things I declared of old
	ומפי יצאו	they went out from my mouth
	ואשמיעם	and I made them known
	פתאם עשיתי	suddenly I did them
	ותבאנה	and they came to pass

---

13. C. Westermann, *Isaiah 40–66: A Commentary* (OTL; Philadelphia: Westminster, 1969) 21–27. Also see Williamson, *The Book Called Isaiah*, 241.

14. The idea of actual writing occurs only twice in DI. Both instances deal with inscribed flesh (44:5, 49:16).

15. See 40:1–2, 9–11, 27–31; 41:8–10, 14–20; 43:1–7, 14–15, 16–17, 18–21; 44:1–5, 21–22, 24–28; 45:1–7, 22–25; 46:3–4, 8–11, 12–13. See R. Albertz, *Israel in Exile: The History and Literature of the Sixth Century* B.C.E. (trans. David Green; Studies in Biblical Literature 3; Atlanta: Society of Biblical Literature, 2003) 379–80.

The passage quoted above suggests that the forensic proofs appealed to by DI are to be found in the written word, specifically past prophecies. The "former things" are predictions—in this case the destruction of Jerusalem—formulated in writing: Yahweh "made them known" through his mediators, the prophets.[16] As text, past oracles can be evaluated in the present in light of the evidentiary support of actual historical events. DI correlates preexisting prophetic accounts with events, or signs, in the "practical field."[17] DI determines that oracular fulfillment has indeed taken place through the (always retrospective and divinatory) process of interpretation.

DI's rhetorical strategy deals largely in the juridical language of proofs.[18] Interestingly enough, none of DI's proofs of fulfilled oracles are actually put forward in oracular form. They instead take the form of disputations.[19] Unlike preexilic prophetic disputations—where Israel stood accused—DI emplots Yahweh as the defendant:[20]

| Isa 43:26 | הזכירני נשפטה | Put me in remembrance, let us argue together |
| | יחד ספר אתה למען תצדק | set forth your case that you may be proved right |

DI's argumentation depends on the establishment of the "fact" that past oracles have been fulfilled. With a few bold strokes, DI sketches out a story—complete with Aristotelian beginning, middle, and end[21]—that encompasses the entire Deuteronomistic History: "your first father sinned / your mediators transgressed against me / therefore I profaned the princes of the sanctuary" (43:27b–28). DI offers a historical summary of the experience of exile from Yahweh's point of view. The accused—Yahweh—defends

---

16. See H. Tadmor, "Autobiographical Apology in the Royal Assyrian Literature," in *History, Historiography, and Interpretation: Studies in Biblical and Cuneiform Literatures* (ed. H. Tadmor and M. Weinfeld; Jerusalem: Magnes, 1983) 51–52.

17. P. Ricoeur, *Time and Narrative* (vol. 1; Chicago: University of Chicago Press, 1983) 53–55.

18. Yahweh in fact seems to exist in a permanent state of litigation, either with "Israel," other nations, or foreign gods.

19. Isa 42:18–25, 43:25–28, 48:1–16; the only exception is the oracle at 48:16–22, which includes a sort of historical synopsis as motivation for the final exodus from Babylon.

20. J. Harvey, *Le Plaidoyer Prophétique Contre Israel Après la Rupture de l'Alliance: Étude d'une Formule Littéraire de l'Ancien Testament* (Studia 22; Paris: Desclée de Brouwer, 1967) 9.

21. Aristotle, *Aristotle's Poetics: Translated and with a Commentary by George Whalley* (trans. G. Whalley; ed. J. Baxter and P. Atherton; Montreal: McGill-Queens University Press, 1997) §27.

his past actions and takes full responsibility for them. Yahweh was provoked. DI lays the blame squarely on an eponymically troped Jacob / Israel, who behaved badly (43:27a).

DI, however, ironically interprets the destruction of Jerusalem as proof, in a positive way, that Yahweh's oracular דבר taught via his messengers the prophets, still stands (יקום לעולם). Indeed, DI is later able to reframe 43:27 in positive terms: "I have swept away your transgressions like a cloud, and your sins like mist / return to me for I have redeemed you" (44:22). DI carefully and strategically situates the whole of the experience of exile—as effect of the cause of sin—as at an end. The events leading up to and including the destruction of Jerusalem, likened to cloud and mist, are rendered insubstantial, and situated squarely in the past. By formulating the dispute in a way that presupposes exile is something that exists in the past, new future possibilities immediately open themselves up in terms of the narrative arc. The exile becomes yet another contiguous event in a series of contiguous events that DI can emplot as he wishes in the service of his teleology.

The writer establishes formal and cognitive continuity with past prophecy in order to claim authority for his current interpretive claims. Continuity—albeit a selective one—exists in the present with the prophetic past. The fact that DI exists in the (generically mixed) form of prophecy already sends out a reified signal that the דבר continues to be active in the world. By applying a process of interpretation—presented as legal proof—to establish that past prophecies have indeed been fulfilled, DI paves the way for an application of deductive logic to the contemporary situation.[22] When DI writes that he tells "a new thing / now it springs forth" (43:19), his predictions are anchored already to the 'fact' that Israel's impending fate was correctly diagnosed in previous prophetic texts. The דבר is authoritative not only in terms of "former things"—namely, the augured destruction of Judah and its symbolic universe—but also in terms of the future, as interpreted by DI. Yahweh is still active in history because some prophecies are as yet unfulfilled. If the "former things"—oracles of Judah's doom—indeed have come to pass, then the restoration—oracles of salvation—will also come to pass:[23]

---

22. There is nothing inductive about DI's very conclusive "word," although see Isa 51:9–11.

23. P. Ackroyd, *Exile and Restoration: A Study of Hebrew Thought of the Sixth Century B.C.* (OTL; Philadelphia: Westminster, 1968) 243–44.

Isa 46:8	זכרו זאת והתאששו	Remember this and consider,
	השיבו פושעים על לב	recall it to mind, transgressors.
Isa 46:9	זכרו ראשנות מעולם	Remember the former things of old
	כי אנכי אל ואין עוד	because I am El and there is no other,
	אלהים ואפס כמוני	Elohim, and there is none like me,
Isa 46:10	מגיד מראשית אחרית	declaring the end from the beginning
	ומקדם אשר לא נעשו	and from ancient times things not yet done
	אמר עצתי תקום	saying: "I will establish my plan
	וכל חפצי אעשה	and I will accomplish all my purpose."

In the above proclamation of salvation, the inscribed audience is exhorted to remember the "former things of old" as proof of Yahweh's action in history. DI's reasoning in this transitional passage is absolutely clear: a "thing not yet done," an event promised by Yahweh in "ancient times," is on the threshold of being made manifest. The plan and purpose of 46:10 refer specifically to a political event. Unlike the prophetic דבר, עצה is a technical term relating to statesmanship.[24] DI suggests that the locus of political power exists outside the created realm and is exclusively the purview of Yahweh.

DI's interest in past prophetic oracles is not merely academic. In 45:1, Cyrus of Persia is controversially identified as Yahweh's משיח. Indeed, Cyrus of Persia will implement Yahweh's plan (46:11).[25] The Cyrus oracle (44:24–45:7) is arguably the most striking in DI and certainly describes the quintessential "new thing" about to come to pass. The passage as a whole is framed by eschatological hymns (44:23, 45:8) and begins and concludes with cosmogonic accounts (44:24 and 45:7). The fanfare associated with the advent of Cyrus is a crucial component of DI's *telos*. Nowhere in the text is DI's rhetoric as effectively deployed as it is here. Indeed, the writer legitimates his political claims via the appropriation of divinatory norms:

| Isa 44:26a | מקים דבר עבדו | the one who establishes the word of his servant |
| | ועצת מלאכיו ישלים | and fulfills the plan of his messengers |

Authority structures are encoded in the logic of the text's articulation. The teleological aspect of the technical term דבר, in parallel with עצה ('plan'),

---

24. W. McKane, *Prophets and Wise Men* (SBT 44; London: SCM, 1965) 113.
25. I am reading the Qere.

is given concrete political specificity.²⁶ DI proposes to rewrite Israel's past in such a way as to incorporate the advent of Cyrus into the plot line of Israel's history:

Isa 44:28a   האמר לכורש רעי   the one who says of Cyrus "He is my shepherd,
                וכל חפצי ישלים   and he fulfills all my purpose"

Cyrus's divinely ordained "purpose," expressed in the typologized linguistic medium of ancient Near Eastern royal cosmogonies, is to restore Jerusalem, rebuild the temple (44:28b), and free the exiles (45:13).²⁷ In each instance and without exception, divine intentions—Yahweh's word/plan/purpose—are configured to be in alignment with contemporary affairs of state. Yahweh's current purpose is identical to the plan of DI. The political aspirations of the writer are thereby explicitly troped to signify divine intentionality.

Yahweh is in the process of fulfilling his preexisting word through the unfolding of history. Indeed, contemporary political events are troped to signify oracular fulfillment:

Isa 55:11   כן יהוה דברי אשר יצא מפי   so shall be my word that goes out from my mouth
           לא ישוב אלי רקים   it shall not return to me empty
           כי אם עשה את אשר חפצתי   but shall accomplish that which I purpose
           והצליח אשר שלחתי   and cause to prosper that for which I send it

The oft-cited Deutero-Isaian דבר, grounded in past writings and always on the cusp of actualization, is the repatriation of the exiles to Jerusalem: "For you shall go out in joy / and be led forth in peace" (55:12).²⁸ Repatriation under the auspices of the Achaemenid Empire is the political moment of "salvation" DI has in mind, and it governs the composition of this prophetic text.²⁹ The formal medium of prophecy functions to authorize DI's agenda. Indeed, prophetic literature shapes and legitimates DI's understanding of history, because the דבר manifests itself as a dynamic present and ongoing reality—insofar as DI interprets it that way.

---

26. Albrektson, *History and the Gods*, 70, 96–97. See Isa 46:10.
27. Particularly relevant to this discussion is L. Fried, "Cyrus the Messiah? The Historical Background to Isaiah 45:1," *HTR* 95 (2002) 373–93. Also see Albrektson, *History and the Gods*, 96. Also see J. Van Seters, *Prologue to History: The Yahwist as Historian in Genesis* (Louisville: Westminster John Knox, 1992) 184.
28. Von Rad, *Old Testament Theology*, 246.
29. Isa 46:8–11 heralds the advent of Cyrus.

History

Up until this point, I have stressed the formal continuity maintained by DI between past literary prophetic traditions and the contemporary situation. The (real or imagined) Babylonian present, however, was anything but continuous with the monarchic Judahite past. The events of 597–586 B.C.E. meant different things to subsequent groups of theological tradents. Everyone had an opinion, and DI was no exception. Territorial conquest—tiny Judah being only one example—probably signified proof of Marduk's magnificence to Nebuchadnezzar II's priestly entourage.[30] Judahite theologians, who responded quite differently, had a tendency to gaze fixedly and with nostalgia toward a symbolic order that in any "real" technical sense was defunct: the Deuteronomistic History is a self-castigating eulogy of epic proportions,[31] "Jeremiah" interprets exile as a lost opportunity for salvation,[32] and the book of Lamentations poignantly depicts the destruction of Jerusalem as evidence of the stilled voice of Yahweh:[33]

Lam 2:17a	עשה יהוה אשר זמם	Yahweh has done what he purposed
	בצע אמרתו	he has cut off his word
	אשר צוה מימי קדם	which he commanded long ago

In fact, Lam 2:17a can be set in direct contrast to Isa 40:8:

| Isa 40:8 | יבש חציר נבל ציץ | the grass withers, the flower fades |
| | ודבר אלהינו יקום לעולם | but the word of our god will stand forever |

There are as many interpretations of the "fact" of exile as there are those who write about it. It is precisely within this purview that we can theoretically assess the poetic "work" of the text of Deutero-Isaiah. A great cognitive divide separates any "event" from the written word that is used to describe it. Events in and of themselves are "contingent and discontinuous."[34] H. White points out that "there is no such thing as raw facts but only

---

30. Albertz (*Israel in Exile*, 58) makes a safe assumption in reading the mind of Nebuchadnezzar II.
31. DtrH traffics in the subtext of prophecy and fulfillment.
32. Albertz, *Israel in Exile*, 6–7.
33. The polyvalent term בצע can mean either "to cut off" or "to fulfill."
34. L. Mink, "History and Fiction as Modes of Comprehension," in *Historical Understanding* (ed. B. Fay, E. Golub, and R. Vann; Ithaca: Cornell University Press, 1987) 49. Also see H. White, "The Value of Narrativity in the Representation of Reality," in *The Content of the Form: Narrative Discourse and Historical Representation* (Baltimore: Johns Hopkins University Press, 1984) 10; White, *Theory*, 9; Ricoeur, *Time and Narrative*, 65.

events under different descriptions."[35] Historical self-understanding is necessarily a narrative understanding: the individual or collective selectively "grasps together" disparate past elements and constitutes them as a coherent "whole."[36] We impose meaning on carefully selected past events by the application of chronological and linguistic codes, each of which is culturally predetermined.[37] Texts are therefore always discursive things, as we are only ever able to approximate the real but never to know it.[38] While this assessment may seem somewhat negative, it is precisely the moment of disjunction inaugurated by the encounter between language and the events it seeks to represent that provides the critical space for interpretation to do its work.

Unlike his contemporaries, DI does not fixate on the event of exile. The careful scrutiny applied to "ancient" prophetic literature by DI has also been applied to creation psalms and the Yahwist. History can only constitute identity if that history has been internalized by the contemporary community.[39] But in the process of writing his exegetical commentary, DI, who relies on alternate historiographies, generates an entirely new narrative self-understanding. Past events—both real and invented—are selected, rearranged, and deployed in such a way as to reconstitute, or resituate, the community's narrative identity. DI looks to origins—as many of them as he can—and with a shift in orientation away from the singularity of exodus-to-exile historiography comes the possibility for a reenvisionment of the future—a reorientation of the Israelite narrative arc—as eschatological, replete with possibilities.

Creation

While emplotment is always selective and retrospective, the anchor of any plot is its beginning. Beginnings are not natural occurrences. Beginnings are strategically determined, and always situated in relation to the teleology of the plot.[40] The beginning is determinative of the narrative

---

35. White, *Theory*, 18. Also see Aristotle, *Poetics*, §27.27–28.
36. Mink, "History and Fiction as Modes of Comprehension," 47.
37. White, *Narrativity*, 10.
38. Idem, *Theory*, 6.
39. Idem, "What Is a Historical System?" in *Biology, History and Natural Philosophy* (ed. A. D. Breck and W. Yourgrau; New York: Plenum, 1972) 236. Also E. Hobsbawm,"Introduction: Inventing Tradition," in *The Invention of Tradition* (ed. E. J. Hobsbawm and T. Ranger; Past and Present Publications; Cambridge: Cambridge University Press, 1983)1–15, esp. p. 9.
40. N. Partner, "Narrative Persistence: The Post-Postmodern Life of Narrative Theory," in *Re-Figuring Hayden White* (ed. F. Ankerschmidt, H. Kellner, and

arc of DI's philosophy of history, which extends through to the present and gestures toward an eschatological future.[41] DI seeks to correlate the beginning point of Israel's history with the event of creation. While not absent from other prophetic books, creation constitutes a key moment in the plot of DI's historiography. Creation is explicitly historicized.[42] This is not the case in Hosea, Ezekiel, or Jeremiah, certainly not in the same chronologically intentional way as it is in DI. What changes in DI is that the iconography of beginnings is not only recast in prophetic form (which already makes for a significant difference), but also that creation is prioritized specifically as the beginning point of a chronology, one that is particularly relevant to the present political situation:

Isa 40:21	הלוא תדעו הלוא תשמעו	Do you not know? Have you not heard?
	הלוא הגד מראש לכם	Has it not been declared from the beginning?
	הלוא הבינתם מוסדות הארץ	Have you not understood the foundations of the earth?

The above-quoted verse is situated in the midst of a complex and lengthy legal disputation (40:12–31) the objective of which is the "descriptive praise" of the deity.[43] While the verbs ידע and שמע seem to imply that events speak themselves, Westermann asserts that in this instance—as in most others—verbs of speaking and hearing in DI refer specifically to pre-existing written texts.[44] The prepositional phrase 'from the beginning', or מראש, exists in a relation of semantic parallelism with מוסדות הארץ. In parallel poetic structures, the *b* strophe restates the contents of the *a* strophe "while adding precision or emphasis."[45] The prepositional phrase "from the foundations of the earth"—in combination with the ambiguous yet loaded term מראש—alludes to the act or event of creation.

E. Domansak, *Cultural Memory in the Present*; Stanford: Stanford University Press, 2009) 81–104, esp. p. 17.

41. Eschatological hymns are not in short supply: Isa 42:10–13, 44:23, 45:8, 51:3, 51:9–11, 52:9–10, 55:12–13.

42. See von Rad, *Old Testament Theology,* 240. Also, Clements ("Monotheism and the God of Many Names," 57–59), who neglects to consider the effect of a monotheistic conception of the divine on questions of temporality and history. Also see K. J. Dell ("God, Creation, and the Contribution of Wisdom," in *The God of Israel* [ed. R. P. Gordon; University of Cambridge Oriental Publications 64; Cambridge: Cambridge University Press, 2007] 63) who maps out the context of the debate.

43. Westermann, *Isaiah 40–66*, 48–49.

44. Ibid., 55–56. See Pss 33; 104:7; 147.

45. P. -E. Dion, *Hebrew Poetics: A Student's Guide* (Mississauga: Benben Publications, 1988) 10.

Isa 40:28a	הלוא ידעת אם לא שמעת	Have you not known, or have you not heard?
	אלהי עולם יהוה	Yahweh is an everlasting god
	בורא קצות הארץ	creator of the ends of the earth.

In his analysis of this verse, Westermann writes that "one of the creator's properties is his limitless extension in time (everlasting) and in space (the ends of the earth)."[46] Like the דבר—discussed in section one—Yahweh is also עולם. Indeed, the national deity of Judah, is specifically identified as the orchestrator of creation. Verse 28, which reiterates the questions posed in 40:21 above, counters the preceding verse (v. 27), which is a community lament: "My way is hid from Yahweh / and my right is disregarded by my god."[47] Because creation is one of Yahweh's functions, DI can refute, with "evidence" that is both textual and cosmic, lament theologies that are in some way grounded in, or constrained by, nationalist ideologies.

DI wields creation in a way that combines "history" with rhetoric. Creation not only works to put the past in its place but it also demands an orientation toward the future. The future in DI means Persian imperialism (as discussed above) with the result that theology and propaganda unsurprisingly overlap.[48] Creation plays a crucial role in the articulation of contemporary Judahite identity and functions as the authoritative ground from which the fortuitous advent of Cyrus is announced:

Isa 44:24b	אנכי יהוה עשה כל	I am Yahweh who makes all things,
	נטה שמים לבדי	stretching the heavens alone,
	רקע הארץ מי אתי	beating out the earth—who was with me?

The Cyrus salvation oracle (44:24–44:28)—governed by the messenger formula כה אמר יהוה—is addressed to Jacob / Israel, whom Yahweh formed "in the womb," a point I shall return to shortly (see 44:2, 21). The announcement of Cyrus's status in the Israelite community is proclaimed, by DI, in relation to the act of creation. The authoritative דבר of 44:26 is propped up by v. 24b, where Yahweh identifies himself as the sole founder of the created order.[49]

---

46. Westermann, *Isaiah 40–66*, 55–56.
47. Ibid., 60.
48. My thanks to a colleague for drawing my attention to the following quotation from Orwell's *1984*: "who controls the present controls the past, who controls the past controls the future." Cited in C. Sulzbach, *From Here to Eternity and Back: Locating Sacred Spaces and Temple Imagery in the Book of Daniel* (Ph.D. diss., McGill University, 2009) 100.
49. See 44:6, 8, 24; 45:5 (twice); 45:6 (twice), 18, 21 (twice), 22; 46:9.

The following verse concludes the Cyrus oracle and functions to re-affirm DI's דבר to Jacob / Israel. The rhetoric of creation is a preemptive move anticipating dispute in the context of collaboration with foreign rule:

Isa 45:7   יוצר אור ובורא חשך   the one who forms light and creates darkness,[50]
          עשה שלום ובורא רע   who makes peace and creates evil—
          אני יהוה עשה כל אלה   I am Yahweh who makes all these things.[51]

Albrektson writes that historical events—in this case the calling of Cyrus by Yahweh—in and of themselves "cannot possibly disclose (Yahweh's) reasons and causes, purposes or intentions."[52] Indeed, the correlation between the Cyrus event and the oracles to which it are said to refer is not always clear to the encoded and inscribed audience. Disputations in fact ensue that DI takes pains to quell: "Woe to him who strives with his maker / an earthen vessel with the potter / Does the clay say to him who fashions it 'what are you making?' or 'Your work has no handles?'" (45:9; see 40:27). The ריב generic justifies DI's primary claim, namely, that Yahweh is the Lord of history.[53] Westermann astutely (and optimistically) points out that Yahweh's designs "infinitely outstrip those possibilities for the future which Israel herself can see."[54] As creator of the cosmological order, Yahweh's intentions are at once unimpeachable and ultimately unfathomable: "for as the heavens are higher than the earth / so are my ways higher than your ways / and my thoughts than your thoughts" (55:9). The act of creation, insofar as Jacob / Israel is concerned, is an uncaused cause. The same preemptive rhetoric vested in the unknowability of creation is transferred to the Cyrus event.

DI transforms the self-evident fact of the created order, there for all to see, into an identifiable, chronological event. The formal constraints of prophecy lend a sense of legal authority and political imperative to DI's figuration of creation. While creation recodes the past, it is *genre*—the

---

50. DI maintains an uneasy relationship with proto-Genesis 1 (see the disputation in Isa 45:18–19). Indeed, (Fishbane, *Biblical Interpretation*, 414) assumes that Genesis 1 exists already *as* Genesis 1 prior to the composition of DI. We cannot assume however that "Genesis 1" antedates DI. Scribal debates relating to the minutiae of the enactment/figuration of creation would have been particularly heated. There is no reason to suppose that P wrote off the top of his head. No doubt, P also worked within an exegetical tradition that had its roots in exilic scholarship.

51. See *Enuma Elish*, tablet 4.20: "Your destiny, O Lord, shall be foremost of the Gods/Command destruction or creation, they shall take place."

52. Albrektson, *History and the Gods*, 117.

53. Harvey, *Plaidoyer*, 61. The only "technically correct" exemplar of the ריב formula in DI occurs in 42:18–25.

54. Westermann, *Isaiah 40–66*, 60.

configuration of prophecy as a whole—that inscribes the event of creation with a predisposition toward the future. Indeed, within the context of prophecy, creationist historiography provides a rationale for both the continued existence of Judah and the maintenance of Israelite identity within the confines of Persian imperialism.

Jacob/Israel[55]

It is a truism of narrative theory that the beginning launches the trajectory of events that constitutes the narrative arc.[56] The beginning point of creation in DI in fact reorients the Israelite narrative arc. J. Van Seters significantly points out that "writers in the Deuteronomic tradition made Yahweh's self-disclosure, election, covenant and promises begin with the exodus just as in Jeremiah and Ezekiel."[57] Prior to Yahwist historiography, the patriarchal past was not a strategic chronological point in the articulation of Judahite collective identity. If the community Jacob/Israel understood its historical relationship with Yahweh to begin with the deliverance from Egypt, then exile from the promised land would truly have signified the end of the story. By emplotting creation as the beginning point of Israel's history, DI can effectively rewrite that history as a series of events subsequent to creation (as indeed all events are subsequent to creation). Proofs of fulfilled oracles, while crucial in terms of persuasive rhetoric, are not enough. DI also situates his proofs within the context of a historical consciousness that has been reconfigured: DI looks to contemporary historiographical texts for typological proofs. DI's finely tuned literary ear enables him to generate complex and multilayered typologies. DI's plot has more than one beginning, with the result that narrative arcs proliferate, and a multiplicity of future possibilities typologically come into play:

Isa 43:1	ועתה כה אמר יהוה	But now thus says Yahweh,
	בראך יעקב	the one who created you, Jacob,
	ויצרך ישראל	and who formed you, Israel
	אל תירא כי גאלתיך	do not be afraid for I have redeemed you
	קראתי בשמך לי אתה	I have called you by name, you are mine.

---

55. I wish to thank Professor J. Van Seters for bringing to my attention the following article: "In the Babylonian Exile with J: Between Judgement in Ezekiel and Salvation in Second Isaiah," in *The Crisis of Israelite Religion: Transformation of Religious Tradition in Exilic and Post-Exilic Times* (ed. B. Becking and M. C. A. Korpel; OtSt 42; Leiden: Brill, 1999) 71–89.

56. Ricoeur, *Time*, 31–51; White, *Theory*, 9; Van Seters, *Prologue*, 332: "origin discloses character and destiny."

57. Van Seters, "Confessional," 54.

The ועתה—which marks the disjunctive transition from retrospective legal curse (42:25) to future oracular hope—points to the inauguration of Yahweh's salvific acts in the present. The verb ברא is conspicuously present throughout DI. Yahweh is not only the creator of the cosmos (40:12–31; 42:5; 44:24; 45:9–13, 18; 47:13; 51:13, 16), he is also the creator of Jacob/Israel. By metonymically linking the creation of Jacob/Israel with the creation of the cosmos and by specifying that the eponymous Jacob/Israel being thus described is the ancestor of the contemporary community Israel, this collective identity is redefined in cosmogonic terms. The oracle in fact concludes by giving a very clear account of those who make up the (dispersed) community:

Isa 43:7	כל הנקרא בשמי	everyone who is called by my name,
	ולכבודי בראתיו	whom I created for my glory,
	יצרתיו אף עשיתיו	whom I formed and made.

Jacob/Israel is no longer circumscribed by identity categories limited to a geographical space, a monarchy, or the exodus from Egypt. The contemporary community Jacob/Israel is constituted by an election that predates the former identity categories of Judah (see 44:1; also Gen 28:13–15). Eponymy is further specified as follows:

Isa 44:2	כה אמר יהוה עשך	Thus says Yahweh who made you,
	ויצרך מבטן יעזרך	who formed you from the womb[58] and will help you:
	אל תירא עבדי יעקב	"Do not fear, Jacob my servant,
	וישרון בחרתי בו	Jeshurun, whom I have chosen."

The above-quoted oracle of salvation also deals in the utopian future of repatriation (see 43:1–7). DI intensifies and personalizes the eponymic moment of the creation of Jacob/Israel. The verbs עשה and יצר—cognates of ברא—are now metaphorically applied to the act of human conception. Jacob/Israel, formed and made מבטן—'from the womb' (see Isa 44:24a, Gen 25:23–24)—has a relationship with Yahweh that is preontological. The genesis of Jacob/Israel, itself a literary trope, is naturalized in its Deutero-Isaian literary context as an epochal event of world-historical proportions. The creation of Jacob/Israel in this passage rivals that of creation in DI's cosmogonic world view. The community is living now also in the midst of an epochal event, a beginning.

---

58. See 44:2, 24; 46:3; 49:1, 5. Also see Tadmor, "Autobiographical Apology in the Royal Assyrian Literature," 39.

M. Fishbane writes that, while typologies tend toward homology, the fact that the data being correlated (that is, the Cyrus event) exist in real time means that "no new event is ever merely a 'type' of another, but always retains its historically unique character."[59] Typologies are points of alignment between events that are chronologically distinct. They moreover presuppose "older datum."[60] Like beginnings, typologies are not natural occurrences but rather must always be "exegetically established."[61] DI makes a direct correlation between the cosmogonic beginning and the present and restates in explicit terms what in J was only implicit:

Isa 41:4	מי פעל ועשה	Who has performed and done this,
	קרא הדורות מראש	calling the generations from the beginning
	אני יהוה ראשון	I, Yahweh, the first
	ואת אחרנים אני הוא	and with the last, I am he.

The above-quoted participial phrase קרא הדורות מראש is also situated in the legal context of a ריב. The passage in question (41:1–4) is the first intimation, in DI, of the advent of Cyrus. It is unclear in this passage whether DI refers to the generations of the primordial history, to later patriarchal generations, or to the exodus generation, and the ambiguity is probably deliberate.[62] DI transforms what was previously a series of contiguous events linked by genealogies in J into one comprehensive and overarching trope. In DI, J's work of contiguity gives way to synecdoche: the "generations" have always already been called by Yahweh, who is eternally present.

Isa 51:1	שמעו אלי רדפי צדק	Harken to me those who pursue righteousness
	מבקשי יהוה	those who seek Yahweh;
	הביטו אל צור חצבתם	look to the rock from which you were hewn,
	ואל מקבת בור נקרתם	and to the quarry from which you were dug;
Isa 51:2	הביטו אל אברהם אביכם	look to Abraham your father,
	ואל שרה תחללכם	and to Sarah who bore you,
	כי אחד קראתיו	for he was but one when I called him,
	ואברכהו וארבהו	and I blessed him and made him many.

The beginning of the exilic community Jacob/Israel is the call of Abraham. In this passage, the promise theme is retrojected onto the epony-

---

59. Fishbane, *Biblical Interpretation*, 351.
60. Ibid., although see Hobsbawm, "Introduction: Inventing Tradition," 1–15.
61. Fishbane, *Biblical Interpretation*, 72.
62. P. Ricoeur, *Interpretation Theory: Discourse and the Surplus of Meaning* (Fort Worth: Texas Christian University Press, 1976) 47.

mous ancestor. The promise of numerous progeny (Gen 15:5, 22:15–17; see Isa 54:1) is extended to the contemporary community, who are urged to follow Abraham's typological example in terms of repatriation. The ambiguous "generations" of 41:4 are here identified as the patriarchal generations. The beginning of the created order and the beginning of the generations are deliberately not given a cause other than being an act of the deity: Yahweh tautologically chooses and calls Abraham because Abraham is the father of Jacob/Israel.[63]

DI draws a typological analogy between Abraham and the exiled remnant.[64] Typologies ultimately function as proofs in DI. The Cyrus event is typologically illuminated by the Abraham story, and vice versa, which in the verses following gestures toward the timely (new) exodus theme:[65]

Isa 41:8	ואתה ישראל עבדי	But you, Israel my servant
	יעקב אשר בחרתיך	Jacob, whom I have chosen
	זרע אברהם אהבי	offspring of Abraham, who loves me,
Isa 41:9	אשר החזקתיך מקצות הארץ	you whom I took from the ends of the earth
	ומאציליה קראתיך	and called from its farthest corners
	ואמר לך עבדי אתה	saying to you: 'You are my servant,
	בחרתיך ולא מאסתיך	I have chosen you and not cast you off'
Isa 41:10	אל תירא כי עמך אני	fear not, for I am with you,
	אל תשתע כי אני אלהיך	be not dismayed, for I am your god;
	אמצתיך אף עזרתיך	I will strengthen you, I will help you
	אף תמכתיך בימין צדקי	I will uphold you with my righteous right hand.[66]

Though it lacks the messenger formula, both the language and the disjunctive ואתה marks this passage as a (royal) oracle of salvation.[67] One of

---

63. See M. Noth, *A History of Pentateuchal Traditions* (trans. B. W. Anderson; Englewood Cliffs, NJ: Prentice-Hall, 1972) 57–58.

64. See Isa 54:1.

65. J. Van Seters, "Babylonian Exile," 81. See Isa 41:25.

66. A. Laato, *The Servant of Yahweh* (ConBOT 35; Stockholm: Almqvist & Wiksell, 1992) 48–58. Every line of the oracle corresponds to an element of ANE royal ideology. Also see Van Seters, *Prologue*, 256.

67. Westermann, *Isaiah 40–66*, 69. Also see Van Seters who writes, citing Schmid, that "because the language is clearly original to royalty, it could only be separated from this *Sitz im Leben* and applied to the people as a whole after the demise of the monarchy." (*Prologue*, 255).The exception is, of course, Cyrus of Persia.

the most interesting literary effects of typologies is that of the effacement of temporal boundaries. In this passage, Jacob/Israel is being called now, in the present. DI again provides no explanation as to *why* Yahweh chose the servant Israel (or for that matter, Abraham). He just *did*: "his understanding is unsearchable" (40:28). It is hubris to question the motives of the deity (45:9–11).

DI draws typological comparisons between the Cyrus event on one hand, and the Abrahamic call, the (new) exodus, and Yahweh's marriage to Israel/Zion on the other. The prophetic wedlock trope—Hosea (1–3), Jeremiah (2–3), and Ezekiel (16; 23)—inspires DI to draw complex typological comparisons between a motif that is historiographic, and a prophetic motif that is analogical. Both rest on the notion of election. Yahweh's ongoing relationship with Jacob/Israel calls to mind, for DI, the loyalty of a husband to his wife. The symbolic language in the passage quoted below, also part of a "fear not" promise of salvation, is reminiscent of similar passages in Hosea and Jeremiah:

Isa 54:5	כי בעליך עשיך	for your maker is your husband
	יהוה צבאות שמו	Yahweh of hosts is his name
	וגאלך קדוש ישראל	your redeemer is the holy one of Israel
	אלהי כל הארץ יקרא	god of the whole earth he is called
Isa 54:6	כי כאשה עזובה	For like a wife forsaken
	ועצובת רוח	and grieved in spirit
	קראך יהוה	Yahweh has called you,
	ואשת נעורים כי תמאס	like a wife of youth when she is cast off,
	אמר אלהיך	says your god.

The patriarchal election theme and the idea of marriage as a covenantal alliance are typologically analogous.[68] Zion, the "wife of youth" (see Hos 2:17, Jer 2:2), like the dispersed patriarchs (Isa 41:10), is "called" by Yahweh (see Isa 41:9). She is reassured by Yahweh-the-husband, her "maker" (see Hos 8:14), that she, like Jacob/Israel, is not "cast off" (see Isa 41:9). Indeed, in DI's symbolic imaginary, the forsaken wife metaphor invites additional typological comparisons: (1) to a Rahab-esque figure who is

---

68. Covenant is eternal in DI, as it is in the Nathan oracle: "When he commits iniquity, I will chasten him with the rod of men, with the stripes of the sons of men; but I will not take my steadfast love from him, as I took it from Saul" (2 Sam 7:15). This sounds about right, except that what applies to David now applies to Jacob. The Davidic line was merely another covenantal point (ברית עולם) in the time-line of eschatological history (Isa 55:3).

no longer barren[69] and (2) to Noah, the cosmogonic flood waters, and the promise of restoration.[70] Jacob/Israel in exile is now being called, like Israel in Egypt, like the forsaken wife, like Noah. Each tells the story of devastation followed by redemption. Typological proofs serve very much the same rhetorical function as did the oracular proofs described earlier in this essay.[71]

Because he locates divine intentionality at the moment of creation, DI sets the groundwork for a typological momentum that is self-sustaining: the beginning is retrojected from the present situation of impending repatriation to the exodus out of Egypt, to the call of Jacob in the womb (46:3–4), to the cosmogonic calling of Abraham from the ends of the earth (41:8–10), to the forsaken wife, to Noah and the flood (54:9–10), to the slaying of the chaos dragon (51:9–11), and ultimately to creation itself. Complex narrative structures do their poetic work, so that temporality is reconfigured, and all the epochal events of Israel's invented past come to be not only strategically articulated but also conceptually and symbolically bound one to the other.[72] The consistency of the imagery is such that the merest mention of resonant typological symbols sets the whole construct ringing like a set of finely balanced bells. The eschatological future (under Achaemenid rule) now gapes wide open. Only Eden-like possibilities remain.

Conclusion

The prophetic word in DI is troped to signify a permanent, continuous link between the dispersed generations and their deity. Indeed, the דבר is the principle of order and coherence in the cosmos that "stands forever" (Isa 40:8). The prophecy of DI, however, exists as an *effect* of exilic historiography. It is precisely the poetic work of J that enables DI to draw, within the formal constraints of the prophetic genre, a continuous, chronological, and typological link between cosmogonic accounts, the patriarchal

---

69. Isa 54:1–3: הרחיבי מקום אהלך; see Gen 26:22; Josh 2:1, 3; 6:17, 23, 25.

70. Isa 54:10, וברית שלומי; see Gen 9:9–15.

71. The exodus is a seminal "event" in the history of Israel that DI never once explicitly mentions. Indeed, he only alludes to the exodus, and I would suggest even seeks to resituate it within the broader context of eschatological history. The only passages in DI where the exodus is clearly alluded to are 43:16–17 and 48:21; also see 51:10, where the story of the chaos dragon becomes typologically linked to the crossing of the sea (see 44:27).

72. See B. Anderson, *Imagined Communities: Reflections on the Origin and Spread of Nationalism* (rev. ed.; New York: Verso, 1991) 4.

past and the (post)exilic present. The political event of repatriation under Aechemenid rule—typologized as a new exodus, a new creation, an election, a covenantal promise, a marriage—is troped, in its prophetic context, to signify oracular fulfillment. The text of DI provides us with a glimpse of the process of identity formation as it unfolds: the narrative identity categories of Israel—both ontological and epistemological—are completely reformulated. Indeed, despite DI's claims to the contrary, the immutable written דבר paradoxically functions as the ground and enablement of change.[73]

---

73. Van Seters, "Confessional," 10.

Personal Missives and National History: The Relationship between Jeremiah 29 and 36

Mark Leuchter

Few chapters in the study of Israelite historiography have occasioned more interest than Jeremiah 36. Standing somewhere between genuine history and symbolic drama, it purports to relay a moment in the development of the book of Jeremiah where the prophet's word and the scribe's pen intersect, together forging a powerful vehicle that transcends the limits of the royal court and its alleged loci of power.[1] The narrative sees the constant introduction of various characters, the looming threat but ultimate folly of the king, and the delineation of categories of fidelity and apostasy.[2] In the end, though, the chapter is a testament to the importance of the Jeremiah tradition as a textual legacy, one that survives the slings and arrows of politics and that embodies, expresses, and preserves revelation in the face of political obstacles. Though the chapter functions as a metaphor for the elevation of the scribal office to the same degree of authority as that of the prophet—several commentators note that Jeremiah fades into the background while the scribes of Jerusalem become the principal actors in the drama[3]—the final sentiment expressed in the

---

1. The opinions on the degree of historicity versus design are varied. See J. Muilenberg, "Baruch the Scribe," in *Proclamation and Presence: Old Testament Essays in Honour of Gwynne Henton Davies* (ed. J. I. Durham and J. R. Porter; Macon, GA: Mercer University Press, 1983) 215–38, esp. p. 245; C. Rietzschel, *Das Problem der Urrolle: Ein Beitrag Zur Redaktionsgeschichte des Jeremiasbuches* (Gutersloh: Gutersloher Mohn, 1966) 105–8; E. Nicholson, *Preaching to the Exiles: A Study of the Prose Tradition in the Book of Jeremiah* (Oxford: Blackwell, 1970) 43; G. Wanke, *Untersuchungen der sogennanten Baruchschrift* (BZAW 122; Berlin: de Gruyter, 1971) 74; W. Thiel, *Die deuteronomistische Redaktion von Jeremia 26–45* (WMANT 41; Neukirchen-Vluyn: Neukirchener Verlag, 1981) 49–51; W. M. McKane, *A Critical and Exegetical Commentary on Jeremiah* (2 vols.; ICC; Edinburgh: T. & T. Clark, 1986–96) 2:911; J. R. Lundbom, *Jeremiah 21–36* (AB; New York: Doubleday, 2004) 298.

2. For a more detailed discussion of these features and their connection to the preceding chapters, see M. Leuchter, *The Polemics of Exile in Jeremiah 26–45* (Cambridge: Cambridge University Press, 2008) 99–112.

3. The best treatment of this theme in Jeremiah 36 is still J. A. Dearman, "My Servants the Scribes: Composition and Context in Jeremiah 36," *JBL* 109 (1990) 403–21.

chapter focuses attention not on human agents but on the literary/redactional enterprise as the vehicle for revelation:

> Then Jeremiah took another roll, and gave it to Baruch the scribe, the son of Neriah; who wrote in it from the mouth of Jeremiah all the words of the book that Jehoiakim the king of Judah had burned in the fire; *and to these were added many similar words.* (דברים רבים כהמה; Jer 36:32)

This enigmatic verse certainly "covers" the multiple layers of redaction that scholars have long noted within the Jeremianic corpus, attempting to qualify those redactional layers as ideological/theological accretions consistent with the initial prophetic enterprise itself.[4] The concept of an internally motivated and thematically consistent redaction had indeed already obtained in the preexilic book of Deuteronomy, a text that ensured its own ongoing vitality by legislating the circumstances under which it could be redacted.[5] The same impulse underlies the events within Jeremiah 36, which uses the historiographic form to spell out, in no uncertain terms, that the process of textual expansion and emendation is a fundamental qualification of a text's status as sacred Scripture. Within Jeremiah 36, and in fact throughout the entire unit of Jeremiah 26–45, outstanding characters of Jerusalem's scribal class are highlighted by name; given the role of scribes by the late seventh century B.C.E. as redactors and exegetes of earlier written tradition, the naming of these characters would appear to reinforce the chapter's interest in legitimizing the redactional process.[6] But Jer 36:32 goes beyond even this in its implications, for it makes no mention of *who* is responsible for adding the "many similar words," how they were added, and most significantly, whence they were derived.[7] Despite the fact that the verse ends a particularly eloquent and detailed example of biblical historiography, sources and redaction are completely abstracted from discernible historical contexts, rendered as conceptual principles rather than part of a tangible social setting.

---

4. Dearman, "My Servants the Scribes," 419.

5. See Deut 17:8–13. This passage is widely regarded as a mechanism for creating new and binding law (v. 13, especially, clarifies this point), but given the expressly literary form of law in the deuteronomic world view (Deut 6:9, 10:1–5, 11:20, 31:11), this new law must be conceived as literary in ultimate form as well.

6. On the historical character of the names in Jeremiah 36, see Dearman, "My Servants the Scribes," 409–17. On scribes in the late seventh century as exegetes and mediators of tradition and law, see the classic study by B. M. Levinson, *Deuteronomy and the Hermeneutics of Legal Innovation* (New York: Oxford University Press, 1997) esp. pp. 144–51.

7. So also Y. Hoffman, "Aetiology, Redaction and Historicity in Jeremiah xxxvi," *VT* 46 (1996) 186.

Jer 36:32 thus closes a chapter so concerned with the persistence of written prophecy in a variety of contexts on a decidedly ambiguous note, and this can hardly be an incidental flourish. Though the events it depicts are set in the year spanning 605–604 B.C.E. (Jer 36:1, 9), most scholars would place the composition of the narrative at a much later point in time, namely, the Exilic or Postexilic Period.[8] Regardless of whether one opts for the former or latter background, both periods were witness to a dispersed Israel, with communities in Egypt, the homeland of Judah (or, if under Persia, Yehud), and the Eastern Diaspora in Babylon and Persia, and all such communities seem to have possessed or had access to the Jeremiah tradition.[9] However, this tradition was not a unified, systematized entity fitting neatly into a single scroll one could simply label ספר ירמיהו. Different communities who claimed to possess Jeremianic materials were apparently in possession of different ספרי ירמיהו, with remarkable variation in terms of content and scope. In this sense, Jeremiah 36 may contain a hermeneutical statement on the inconsistent diversity of Jeremianic materials scattered throughout Israel's social landscape. C. J. Sharp has suggested that Jeremiah 36 provides hermeneutical insight into the growth of different protocollections (e.g., the LXX or the MT) that possessed legitimacy within the communities that preserved them:

> The text-critical development of the book of Jeremiah is of course far more complex than Jer. xxxvi shows. But the fact that Jer. xxxvi preserves the literary memory of a shorter (but neither deficient nor secondarily abbreviated) earlier scroll and a longer (but neither corrupted

---

8. For the exilic composition of the chapter, see Leuchter, *Polemics of Exile*, 99–112. On the chapter as part of a postexilic stratum, see E. Otto, "Scribal Scholarship in the Formation of Torah and Prophets: A Postexilic Scribal Debate between Priestly Scholarship and Literary Prophecy. The Example of the Book of Jeremiah and the Its Relation to the Pentateuch," in *The Pentateuch as Torah: New Models for Understanding Its Promulgation and Acceptance* (ed. G. N. Knoppers and B. M. Levinson; Winona Lake, IN: Eisenbrauns, 2007) 177–80; Hoffman, "Aetiology," 187. Hoffman suggests a relatively late, Persian-period date contemporaneous with Ezra–Nehemiah for its composition (p. 183 n. 9), citing the linguistic work of F. H. Polak to support this dating. However, Polak has since published several essays indicating that the linguistic profile of the Jeremianic prose evidences an earlier period than that of Ezra–Nehemiah, and Polak himself places the text in a late seventh to mid-sixth century context. See his essays "The Oral and the Written: Syntax, Stylistics, and the Development of Biblical Prose Narrative," *JANES* 26 (1999) 59–105, esp. pp. 69–71, 93–95; "The Style of the Dialogue in Biblical Prose Narrative," *JANES* 28 (2001) 53–95, esp. pp. 58–59, 69.

9. The production of the LXX Vorlage among the Jewish scribes of Egypt is generally recognized; see J. R. Lundbom, *Jeremiah 1–20* (AB; New York: Doubleday, 1999) 100–101.

nor secondarily expanded) later scroll suggests that our text-critical categories for evaluating the provenance of texts may not provide appropriate parameters for understanding the genesis of the written text(s) of Jeremiah held in the most ancient circles that guarded and transmitted the prophet's words. . . . At the least, it should no longer be assumed that secondary editorial activity, whether reflected in expansion in individual readings or in the larger literary ordering of the OAN, precludes the possibility of original variants existing as well.[10]

Sharp's observation closes her study of the divergences between the OAN (Oracles against the Nations) in the MT and LXX collections and carries implications for the text-critical study of these works.[11] However, it applies also to the smaller subcollections of Jeremianic writings that existed in antiquity. At a time well before the standardization of an authoritative Jeremianic corpus (of which Jeremiah 36 was a central part),[12] a fragmented and fluid stream of Jeremianic literature was possessed by the communities the prophet addressed.

A prime example of this is the collection of personal missives preserved in Jeremiah 29. Most scholars recognize that genuine dispatches between Jeremiah, the community of captives exiled to Babylon in 597, and various intermediaries lay beneath the current form of this chapter.[13] As we will see, this community had a particular and exclusivist understanding of history, politics, social identity, and the cosmic dimensions of each, and these perceptions were shaped in no small part by their ownership of this textual collection. The contents of Jeremiah's missive(s) lay out a plan for exilic life as divinely ordained for this group, on which future blessing and restoration to the homeland is entirely contingent. They provide this community with an immutable sacred charter legitimizing subsequent measures and doctrines conceived to reinforce and actualize it in contradistinction

---

10. C. J. Sharp, "'Take Another Scroll and Write': A Study of the LXX and MT of Jeremiah's Oracles against Egypt and Babylon," *VT* 47 (1997) 487–516, esp. pp. 508–9.

11. See also Hoffman's discussion of the distinctions between the two OAN collections in relation to the compositional strategy of Jeremiah 36 ("Aetiology," 188–89).

12. See similarly Hoffman regarding the role of the author of Jeremiah 36 in creating a comprehensive Jeremiah scroll incorporating different streams of discourse, though he dates this process later than what I propose herein ("Aetiology," 187).

13. See, among others, Dearman, "My Servants the Scribes," 420; M. Dijkstra, "Prophecy by Letter (Jer xxix 24–32)," *VT* 33 (1983) 419–22; B. D. Sommer, "New Light on the Composition of Jeremiah" *CBQ* 61 (1999) 646–66, esp. p. 661–63 with references cited there. K. Schmid (*Buchgestalten des Jeremiabuches: Untersuchungen zur Redaktions und Rezeptionsgeschichte von Jer 30—33 in Kontext des Buches* [WMANT 72; Neukirchen-Vluyn: Neukirchener Verlag, 1996] 211), however, ascribes a different origin to the text.

to other groups whom the prophet had addressed in different terms and tones. With the prophetic legitimation of life in exile came a new understanding of the cosmos: life within a Mesopotamian milieu over against a still-standing Jerusalem not yet demolished by Babylonian fury. To live in the latter was, for this group, to live at a distance from Yhwh's chosen *axis mundi* as attested by Jeremiah's own written word.

At the same time, the chapter is not simply an archive of independent letters but a carefully arranged composition that carries the rhetorical and lexical hallmarks of the rest of the Jeremianic corpus.[14] The collection of missives worked into this single chapter delineates a specific group of people who are still deemed worthy of the prophet's interest, instruction, and support. It is they—not the other scattered communities—who receive his unmitigated written word, a factor of great importance at a time when prophetic texts had obtained an importance paralleling (if not surpassing) the potency of oral oracles delivered by prophets themselves.[15] Moreover, these texts are presented as conveyed through the agency of trusted scribal associates, ensuring their authenticity.[16] And yet, these unique missives bear the linguistic flourishes common to virtually all strata within the book of Jeremiah, including oracles directed to other groups and with diametrically opposed messages.[17] It is the balance between this chapter's uniqueness and general traits that suggests its fitness for evaluation under the hermeneutical implications of Jer 36:32, as the text makes clear that these words that are now part of an expanded ספר ירמיהו once had a life of their own.[18]

In this study, our attention will focus on a tripartite literary relationship involving three textual sources: (1) the historiographic episode in

---

14. The שקר motif surfaces here (29:9, 23), along with the sword/pestilence/famine triad found throughout other prose sections of Jeremiah.

15. On the increased status of written prophecy as a primary medium (as opposed to the emphasis on oral delivery only secondarily transcribed), see K. van der Toorn, "Mesopotamian Prophecy between Immanence and Transcendence: A Comparison of Old Babylonian and Neo-Assyrian Prophecy," in *Prophecy in Its Ancient Near Eastern Context: Mesopotamian, Biblical and Arabian Perspectives* (ed. M. Nissinen; SBLSymS 13; Atlanta: Society of Biblical Literature, 2000) 71–87.

16. Jer 29:1 provides the legitimizing factor here by clarifying that these Jeremianic utterances were delivered through trusted, official personnel; for the significance of tracing these texts to legitimate scribal officials, see Hoffman, "Aetiology," 185.

17. The specific language shared by Jeremiah 29 and these other units will be explored in more detail below.

18. For the view (with other commentators) that Jeremiah 27–29 was once an independent collection predating the redaction of Jeremiah 26–45 more generally, see Leuchter, *Polemics of Exile*, 40–49.

Jeremiah 36 regarding the prophet's rewritten oracles, (2) the "original" material in Jeremiah 29 (that is, the message directed to the exiles of 597), and (3) the "redactional" stratum in the chapter. This stratum is responsible not only for orchestrating the collection of missives preserved therein into a particular sequence but also for the stereotyped language woven into this matrix of text that is identical to tropes found elsewhere in the book of Jeremiah and directed to different communities. This derives from writers who were not part of the 597 community, which saw itself as distinct from all other exiled groups. But concomitant with the notice in Jer 36:32 that "many similar words" were added to authentic Jeremianic writings, the later redactional stratum in Jeremiah 29 represents an attempt to render the prophet's message in that chapter applicable to all those enduring exile. In doing so, the redactors tied a once-independent collection and once-independent community to a much grander literary project with demographic and social parameters far greater than those represented by earlier versions of Jeremiah's written words.

Redactional Stereotyping in Jeremiah 29

Though Jeremiah 29 contains several addresses from (and to) the prophet, it is the first dispatch that governs the manner in which the others are perceived, and it is only with regard to the first that the others make any sense as witnesses to the turbulence of the period. This first missive begins with a carefully focused directive:

> Thus says Yhwh of hosts, the God of Israel, to all the captivity whom I have caused to be carried away captive from Jerusalem to Babylon: build houses, and dwell in them, and plant gardens, and eat their fruit; take wives, and bear sons and daughters; and take wives for your sons, and give your daughters to husbands, that they may bear sons and daughters; and multiply there, do not be diminished. And seek the peace of the city to which I have caused you to be carried away captive, and pray to Yhwh for it; for in its peace shall you have peace. (Jer 29:4–7)

The emphasis on the founding of familial institutions in a new geopolitical context is a fitting point of order for a group that had been subject to the trauma of captivity and transplantation into an alien social world. E. Assis, for example, points to a number of exilic psalms that seem to liturgize Jeremiah's prophetic word to families torn away from the religious modalities that had characterized their lives for generations, demonstrating the degree to which family structures could provide some surrogate for the other bastions of Judahite life no longer available to exilic populations.[19] Much of this is preconditioned by the failure of Josiah's reform and the related attempt in Deuteronomy to unify the entire Israelite population under the banner of an undifferentiated type of kinship (Deut 5:2–3), overturning kinship allegiances (Deut 13:2–6), and leveling the autocratic basis for religious authority (Deut 17:15, 18:15).[20] Though Jeremiah's words in Jer 29:5–7 take up deuteronomic concepts,[21] the emphasis on family units and the acceptance of their new geographic conditions must account for the failure of some aspects of Deuteronomy to prove practical at an earlier time. They attest to the difficulty in sustaining the macrostructure of its ideology at the outset of the sixth century.

As the missive continues, however, it quickly turns into a platform for sermonizing typical of other prose sermons in the book of Jeremiah that were conceived for audiences still living in Judah. The closing verses constitute the missive's rhetorical apex:

> For thus says YHWH concerning the king that sits upon the throne of David, and concerning all the people that dwell in this city, your brethren that are not gone forth with you into captivity; thus says YHWH of hosts: Behold, I will send upon them the sword, the famine, and the pestilence, and will make them like vile figs, that cannot be eaten, they are so bad. And I will pursue after them with the sword, with the famine, and with the pestilence, and will make them a horror unto all the kingdoms of the earth, a curse, and an astonishment, and a hissing, and a reproach, among all the nations where I have driven them; because they have not listened to My words, says YHWH, by which I sent to them my servants the prophets, sending them early and often; but you would not hear, says YHWH. So you, hear the word of YHWH, all of the captives I have sent from Jerusalem to Babylon! (vv. 16–20)

The secondary nature of these verses is recognized due to their absence from the LXX tradition. But it is nigh well impossible *not* to hear other

---

19. E. Assis, "Psalm 127 and the Polemic of the Rebuilding of the Temple in the Post-Exilic Period," *ZAW* 121 (2009) 256–72, esp. pp. 262, 266–67; idem, "Temple Substitutes in Exile" (paper presented at the annual meeting of the SBL, New Orleans, November 22, 2009).

20. This is further reflected throughout the book of Jeremiah with regard to gentilics associated with individual prophets (and with Jeremiah himself), highlighting the clan/kinship/lineage affiliations that intensified in the wake of the failure of the alleged deuteronomic social program. See M. Leuchter, "The 'Prophets' and the 'Levites' in Josiah's Covenant Ceremony," *ZAW* 121 (2009) 36–40.

21. On the deuteronomic influence within the letter, see A. Berlin, "Jer 29:5–7: A Deuteronomic Allusion?" *HAR* 8 (1984) 3–11.

Jeremianic oracles in these closing verses of the letter, recalling the vision of the figs in Jeremiah 24,[22] the repeated sword/famine/pestilence triad (e.g., Jer 14:12, 21:9) and, especially, the common "prophets" refrain found throughout the book (Jer 7:25, 25:4, 26:5). One may view these images and formulas as simply a witness to the forms of expression common at the time, as this expression is prominent in the very significant late seventh century meditation in 2 Kgs 17:13, 23.[23] If (as is often thought) Jeremiah and those scribes close to him who developed his book were closely associated with the Deuteronomistic movement,[24] then the manner of scribal training and thinking espoused by this movement would certainly shape the parameters of discourse even in the formation of a letter directed to a limited community experiencing unique circumstances.[25] However, the recurrence of motifs or lexemes in Jeremiah is typically a sign of redactional stereotyping or deliberate citation/allusion, not inadvertent

---

22. D. Rom Shiloni has argued recently that Jeremiah 24 was a post-Jeremianic accretion deriving from the exilic period; see her essay "Group Identities in Jeremiah: Is It the Persian Period Conflict?," in *A Palimpsest: Rhetoric, Stylistics, and Language Relating to Persian Periods* (ed. E. Ben-Zvi, D. Edelman, and F. Polak; Perspectives on Hebrew Scriptures and its Contexts 5; Piscataway: Gorgias Press, 2009) 17–24, 35. Rom-Shiloni's thorough discussion warrants close attention, especially regarding the lexical evidence she highlights. In an earlier work, however, I noted that Gedaliah's decree in Jer 40:9–10 draws from oracles authentic to Jeremiah, including terms and images from Jeremiah 24, and that the specificity of the reference relates closely to the agricultural/seasonal experience of people still residing in the land (*Polemics of Exile*, 121–22). In light of Rom-Shiloni's discussion, I would adjust my position and suggest that Jeremiah 24 is based on an authentic sentiment, teaching, or even *mashal* that was known to have been spoken by Jeremiah (echoed in Jer 29:17) but which was later developed as the book grew to account for disparate social collectives in exile.

23. On 2 Kings 17 as primarily a late seventh century passage, see J. C. Geoghegan, *The Time, Place and Purpose of the Deuteronomistic History: The Evidence of "Until This Day"* (BJS 347; Providence, RI: Brown University Press, 2006) 92 and passim. This does not preclude the possibility of later accretions in the chapter dating from the Exilic or even Postexilic Periods, but Geoghegan's discussion establishes that a substantial form of the chapter is preexilic. The connection between the book of Jeremiah and this particular passage in Kings has been discussed by C. J. Sharp, *Prophecy and Ideology in Jeremiah: Struggles for Authority in the Deutero-Jeremianic Prose* (OTS; London: T. & T. Clark, 2003) 144–45; H. Weippert, *Die Prosareden des Jeremiabuches* (BZAW 132; Berlin: de Gruyter, 1973) 218.

24. Thiel, *Jeremia 26–45*, passim; Dearman, "My Servants the Scribes," 418–19; Lundbom, *Jeremiah 1–20*, 92 (Jeremiah and the scribes as deriving from a common "rhetorical school"); Leuchter, *Polemics of Exile*, 9–11.

25. See D. M. Carr, *Writing on the Tablet of the Heart: Origins of Scripture and Literature* (Oxford: Oxford University Press, 2005) 148–49.

or incidental expression.²⁶ One example of each will suffice, namely, the characterization of national transgression in Jer 2:7:²⁷

> And I brought you into a land of fruitful fields, to eat the fruit thereof and the good thereof; but when you entered, you defiled (ותטמאו) My land (ארצי), and made My heritage (נחלתי) an abomination (תועבה). (Jer 2:7)

This brief passage alludes to the earliest days of Israel's life in the land and then offers a criticism of the manner of Israel's subsequent conduct, but this criticism draws word for word from an earlier source in Deut 24:4:

> Her former husband, who sent her away, may not take her again to be his wife, after that she is defiled (הֻטַּמָּאָה); for that is abomination (תועבה) before YHWH; and you shall not cause the land (ארץ) to sin, which YHWH your God gives you for an inheritance (נחלה). (Deut 24:4)

Here, it is clear that Jeremiah's critique is not generic; it is carefully and deliberately founded on deuteronomic concepts, and attempts to extend to the entire nation a binding piece of legislation once intended for a more protracted social circumstance. The lexemes from Jer 2:7 are repeated very closely in Jer 16:18:

> And first I will recompense their iniquity and their sin double; because they have profaned (חללם)²⁸ My land (ארצי); they have filled my inheritance (נחלתי) with the carcasses of their detestable things and their abominations (תועבותיהם). (Jer 16:18)

Most scholars date Jer 2:7 to the early period of the prophet's career; the primary contents of Jeremiah 16 appear to derive in large part from a subsequent (but still originally preexilic) context.²⁹ What is significant

---

26. Stereotyped tropes are a key to the redactional growth of the book; for a full study, see G. H. Parke-Taylor, *The Formation of the Book of Jeremiah: Doublets and Recurring Phrases* (SBLMS 51; Atlanta: Society of Biblical Literature, 2000).

27. Though these lexemes do appear in other contexts unaffiliated with the Deuteronomistic modality, their presence in Jeremiah in relation to discourses on marital fidelity and family integrity suggest Deut 24:1–4 as the source.

28. This discussion follows my earlier analysis of the allusion to these same verses in the book of Ezra; see M. Leuchter, "Ezra's Mission and the Levites of Casiphia," *Community Identity in Judean Historiography: Biblical and Comparative Perspectives* (ed. G. N. Knoppers and K. A. Ristau; Winona Lake, IN: Eisenbrauns, 2009) 187–88. As I note in that study, the variant חללם in this instance is so minor it may be attributed to an inadvertent alteration in the textual transmission of the original material.

29. On Jer 2:7 as part of the prophet's Josianic era career, see M. A. Sweeney, *King Josiah of Judah: The Lost Messiah of Israel* (Oxford: Oxford University Press, 2001)

is that during the course of redaction (perhaps the redactional enterprise resulting in Jeremiah 1–20, as suggested by Lundbom) this later oracle has been recast according to the terms of the earlier one, establishing consistency in texts deriving from disparate historical and social contexts.[30] These examples fit neither into the category of historiography nor of personal missive, but they are representative of a compositional protocol that permeates most of the book of Jeremiah and are suggestive of the origins, function, and purpose of the stereotyped tropes currently extending the first missive in Jeremiah 29. Though the language is distinctively Jeremianic, its appearance in the missive should be seen as emerging from a redactor who obtained the sources underlying Jeremiah 29 and sought to build on them.[31] The characteristic phraseology now found in vv. 16–20 attempts to subordinate the older material composed for a limited audience to a much larger enterprise and purpose represented by the developing Jeremianic corpus *en masse*. The social implications of this redactional addition are made clear in the final verse: "all of the captives" to Babylon, those of the 597 community and those beyond it, are subject to its terms (v. 20).

This redactional move does not reduce the value or authenticity of the source material but, instead, suggests that it cannot be seen as an independent work or collection. Jer 36:32 identifies the existence of "many similar words" beyond the original literary collection emanating from the prophet and his immediate circle of supporters, but it also specifies that these words were "added" to the authoritative corpus that they produced. Thus, the authors of Jeremiah 36 waver between recognizing the pro-

---

215–25. Jeremiah 16 presupposes a different social context with the prospect of exile more imminent and contains a tenor of threat speaking to the dismantling of family structures (symbolized by the prohibition placed on the prophet himself to have children of his own [Jer 16:1–2]). This emphasis best fits a post-Josianic context, reflecting the inward turn to atomistic lineage identity over against the monolithic national kinship of Deuteronomy, but still a preexilic time when lineage structures and expectations regarding progeny were presupposed. Some verses, of course, may reflect exilic glosses (e.g., v. 13). Verse 18 may well be a secondary redactional addition to the chapter (suggested by its formulaic commonality with Jer 2:7 and the original source in Deut 24:4), but this could also be a preexilic redactional development associated with the early literary coordination of the prophet's oracles (see immediately below). The chapter may have eventually become a palimpsest for redactional development, however; see Rom-Shiloni, "Group Identity," 33–34.

30. See Lundbom, *Jeremiah 1–20*, 93–94 regarding these chapters as part of an early collection or edition of Jeremiah's oracles.

31. Leuchter, *Polemics of Exile*, 40–60.

phetic origins of other collections and demanding that they be part of a metacollection in order to retain their worth. The original missive is subjected to a shaping that allows it to contribute to the multivalence of the book of Jeremiah, attesting to the geographical and demographic jurisdiction that the redactors wished to ascribe to the book.[32] It retains its place as a specific mandate for the captives of 597 by virtue of its superscription (Jer 29:1), but the infusion into the missive of lexemes from throughout the book makes clear that it can only be understood in light of the book's larger discourse. The community to which it pertains is subject to the same standards and channels of authority delineated in Jeremiah 36. In order to qualify as a "similar word," it must fall under the authority of the scribe(s) entrusted with the prestige and legacy of the prophet.

The Cosmic Categories of History

The direction of influence, however, runs both ways. Just as Jeremiah 29 was redacted to resonate with the larger corpus developed by Jeremiah's support group, the author of Jeremiah 36 shaped his narrative in awareness of concepts that surfaced for the first time in Jeremiah 29. Immediately preceding the finale of the narrative where a second scroll is produced, the prophet is reported to have an oracle cursing Jehoiakim, presumably for destroying the *Urrolle*:

> Therefore thus says Yhwh concerning Jehoiakim king of Judah: He shall have none to sit on the throne of David; and his dead body shall be cast out in the day to the heat, and in the night to the frost. And I will visit upon him and his seed and his servants their iniquity; and I will bring upon them, and upon the inhabitants of Jerusalem, and upon the men of Judah, all the evil that I have pronounced against them, but they did not listen. (Jer 36:30–31)

Widely recognized is the fact that this oracle clashes with the account of Jehoiakim's death as reported in 2 Kgs 24:6 and the fact that this king did indeed have a son who ruled after him (however briefly). This inconsistency has led some scholars to discount the report in 2 Kgs 24:6 as stereotyped and concealing a more gruesome end to Jehoiakim's life, while

---

32. Here Sharp's astute observation regarding textual diversity in antiquity requires a caveat ("Take Another Scroll," 508–9). While the hermeneutical implications of Jeremiah 36 do indeed legitimize the viability of multiple textual collections, the circumstance concluding the chapter clearly subordinates these collections to one overarching metatext.

others (myself included) have viewed the inaccuracy of the prediction as evidence of its authenticity and origin with the prophet; its position in the chapter reflects the polemical design of the later authors of Jeremiah 36.[33]

Konrad Schmid has recently offered an additional insight that makes the latter possibility more likely, but moves beyond matters of rhetoric or polemic and considers the oracle's exegetical implications.[34] Schmid notes that the curse on Jehoiakim relates to Nebuchadnezzar's victory at Carchemish that secured Babylon's place as the dominant power in the ancient Near East. As such, the year 605 sees the Davidic dynasty lose any and all claims to standing at the center of Israel's cosmic order. This sensibility pervades throughout much of the book of Jeremiah and motivated the inclusion of the Jehoiakim oracle into Jeremiah 36 according to Schmid. Regardless of when the oracle was first generated, its current place within Jeremiah 36 orchestrates the stage of history according to the leading role of Babylon. That the expansion of the book via the inclusion of "many similar words" takes place immediately after this oracle suggests that the other Jeremianic collections alluded to within Jer 36:32 relate closely with the same concept of a shift in the cosmic balance and the role of Babylon in Israel's national destiny. This must have been all too clear to the captives of 597 addressed by Jeremiah's missives; the desperate prophetic oracles anticipating a swift return to Jerusalem that Jeremiah counters later in Jeremiah 29 only attest to the astonishment and trauma that the captives must have experienced. Against this background, a feature elsewhere in the chapter refers explicitly to this political/cosmic shift:

> For thus says Yhwh: After seventy years are accomplished for Babylon, I will remember you, and perform my good word toward you, in causing you to return to this place. (Jer 29:10)

---

33. See my discussion in Leuchter, *Polemics of Exile*, 11–112, 239 n. 122.

34. See K. Schmid, "Nebuchadnezzar, the End of Davidic Rule, and the Exile in the Book of Jeremiah" (paper presented at the annual meeting of the SBL, New Orleans, November 22, 2009). Schmid views the entire oracle as deriving from a fifth century context that looks back on the rise and eventual fall of Babylon in light of Jeremiah's 70 year oracle, connecting the 70 years in that oracle with the rise of Cyrus in 539 B.C.E. and thus reading the start of Jehoiakim's own reign (in 609) as the initiating moment of that 70-year period. As I have argued elsewhere (M. Leuchter, "Jeremiah's 70-Year Prophecy and the לב קמי/ששך *Atbash* Codes" *Bib* 85 [2004] 503–22), however, the 70-year oracle is not a postexilic retrospective categorization of events but a reference to the shift in international politics and the deity behind it. The matter remains open to debate. Nevertheless, Schmid is absolutely correct that both the Jehoiakim oracle in Jer 36:30–31 and the 70-year prophecy in Jer 29:10 (see also Jer 25:14) signify the shift in Babylon's role in history and the cosmos in the Jeremianic world view, as the ensuing discussion makes clear.

The 70-year oracle refers to a famous inscription from the reign of Esarhaddon celebrating that king's restoration of Babylon 11 years after its devastation by his father and predecessor, Sennacherib.[35] In the Esarhaddon inscription, the cuneiform symbol for 11, when inverted, is the symbol for 70; the inscription informs the audience that Marduk's initial intention to leave Babylon in a state of ruin for 70 years was overturned (literally), leading to Esarhaddon's restoration. Jer 29:10 revisits this motif and reminds the audience that Babylon had emerged as an undeniable power under YHWH's auspices, and its fortunes would not be overturned for a long time.

Jeremiah's 70-year oracle carried tremendous force in the mind of its various audiences. It reappears in Jer 25:14 (a later redactional accretion) and became the basis for inner-biblical meditation well into the Postexilic Period (Zech 1:12; 2 Chr 36:20–21; Dan 9:2).[36] As the author of Daniel 9 reveals, the oracle was eventually seen in temporal terms rather than as an allusion to the political culture of late seventh–mid-sixth century Mesopotamia, but the earlier literary responses to this oracle emphasize its cosmic/political dimensions.[37] This already begins in Jer 36:30–31, though the author of this passage does not openly invoke the 70-year prophecy, his categorization of the political cosmos is guided by the same sensibility. For this author, the rise of Babylon was to replace Jerusalem-centric ideology in defining Israel's social purpose and covenantal responsibilities, and that this occurred under Jehoiakim's "watch" as king. This is evident in passages such as Jer 25:1 and Jer 27:1,[38] and the author of Jer 36:30–31 relates this concept to the growth of the book of Jeremiah itself (v. 32).

Cosmic Shift and In-Group Elitism

The accounting for this larger cosmic/historical trend in the historiography of Jeremiah 36 addressed a serious problem that had obtained

---

35. Leuchter, "*Atbash* Codes," 509–16.

36. Jeremiah 25 is best viewed as reflecting a post-597 context and establishes connections between the preceding materials in Jeremiah 1–24 and the Babylon Oracle of Jeremiah 50–51. The chapter thus postdates the composition of that oracle (according to the superscription of Seraiah's colophon, ca. 594/593 B.C.E.) but caps a collection that was already known to the Judahites who fled to Egypt between 587 and 582 B.C.E. For a brief overview, see W. M. Schniedewind, *How the Bible Became a Book: The Textualization of Ancient Israel* (Cambridge: Cambridge University Press, 2004) 154–57.

37. Zechariah, for example, incorporates the oracle into his own message (Zech 1:12), and in the context of the rebuilding of the Jerusalem Temple (the locus of the cosmic interface in the priestly world view espoused by Zechariah).

38. So also Schmid, "Nebuchadnezzar."

by the time the redactors of the Jeremianic corpus began their activity. Jeremiah's missive had identified the captives of 597 as the community of covenantal promise over against those remaining in the land, and subsequent dispatches make clear that any prophets surfacing in that captive group prophesying a return to Zion were illegitimate (Jer 29:20–32). This dovetails with the categorization of history according to Nebuchadnezzar's rise to power: Jerusalem is not, nor could it ever be, the center of Israel's universe so long as YHWH had deemed Babylon the *Axis Mundi*. Doubtless, the acceptance of these words by this community led to the formation of Jeremiah's view regarding the good/bad figs preserved in Jeremiah 24, leading to the redaction of earlier oracles of hope and restoration directed to the exilic population (Jeremiah 30–31).[39] However, in their current form and literary context, these oracles of hope are directed not only to the captives of 597 but to those who suffered exile after 587 as well; despite similar conditions of forced migration and captivity, distinctions must be drawn between these two groups.[40] By the time of the second exilic wave, Ezekiel had already begun his prophetic work within the captive community of 597 and had identified them and them alone, as a viable covenantal group.[41] Ezekiel's attitude toward the later wave of exiles is exclusive and condemnatory, directing his audience to view their plight as the rightful punishment of a deserving horde. One example, regarding the Judahites of the post-597 homeland, is particularly representative:

> And, behold, though there will be left a remnant therein that shall be brought forth, both sons and daughters; behold, when they come forth unto you, and you see their way and their doings (את דרכם ואת עלילותם), then you shall be comforted concerning the evil that I have brought upon Jerusalem, even concerning all that I have brought upon it. (Ezek 14:22)

What is particularly notable here is Ezekiel's echo of Jeremiah's rhetoric, not only in terms of condemning the community that had lived in Judah between 597 and 587 but, specifically, his use of the phrase את דרכם ואת עלילותם, which recalls the words from Jeremiah's famous Temple Sermon (דרכיכם ומעלליכם in Jer 7:3). This lexical commonality is part of a broader pattern that uses Jeremiah's time-tested oracles as the basis for legitimacy

---

39. On the pre-587 redaction of these oracles and the post-587 addition concluding them but expanding their applicability, see Leuchter, *Polemics of Exile*, 50–60.

40. Leuchter, *Polemics of Exile*, 60–64.

41. For a detailed examination of this feature in Ezekiel and its impact on subsequent communities, see D. Rom-Shiloni, "Ezekiel as the Voice of the Exiles and Constructor of Exilic Ideology," *HUCA* 76 (2005) 1–45.

and rhetorical force within those of Ezekiel,[42] but it is hardly a coincidence that in Ezek 14:22, the condemnation of the exiles of 587 is qualified by terms lifted from Jeremiah's temple sermon. Ezek 14:22 suggests that it is *their* apostasy of which Jeremiah spoke, and that this apostasy must relate to their own neglect of the cosmic shift to Babylon at an earlier time. Bolstered by the earlier missive of Jeremiah and the subsequent dispatches and exchanges delineating misguided theological perspectives, Ezekiel's prophetic ministry stressed the uniqueness of the 597 community as one that had reconciled itself to the genuine balance of the cosmos; this contributed to the dissonance between the needs and self-conceptions of the different Judahite communities now all residing in Mesopotamia.

The composition of the literary unit spanning Jeremiah 26–45 and the redaction of the larger corpus surrounding these chaps. (Jer 1–25+OAN) attempt to address this circumstance, arguing that people who remained in the land down to 587 were still worthy of Jeremiah's favor. Repeatedly, these chapters highlight the very close relationship between the prophet and the Shaphanide scribal group, several of which were decidedly *not* taken captive to Babylon in 597 B.C.E.[43] Baruch ben Neriah, for example, is given charge of a land redemption document during a transaction dated to 587 and symbolizing the eventual return to ancestral territory for all exiles (Jer 32:6–15). Furthermore, the "colophon" of Baruch in Jeremiah 45 specifies that Yhwh will bless him no matter where or when he is to find himself (Jer 45:5)—including Jerusalem, Mizpah, or even Egypt (Jeremiah 40–44). Likewise, his brother Seraiah is entrusted with facilitating an apotropaic ritual involving a harsh anti-Babylonian oracle (Seraiah's "colophon," Jer 51:59–64). This act is dated to a few years after the 597 exile (51:59), and the closing דברי ירמיהו formula following this episode creates an *inclusio* with the same formula appearing in Jer 1:1, extending the significance of Seraiah's deed back over the entirety of the work.[44] But

---

42. Leuchter, *Polemics of Exile*, 158–59.
43. Ibid., passim.
44. Debate ensues, of course, over the priority of the MT sequence over that of the LXX, the latter of which places Baruch's colophon at the finale of the work. I will reiterate what I have suggested in several other publications, namely, that the LXX should indeed be viewed as a repository of earlier versions of chapters and parallel units found in the MT, but that the MT sequence—which saw the expansion of those parallel units—was orchestrated prior to the LXX. The "capping" of Seraiah's colophon with terminology from the beginning of the book accompanied the introduction of the supplement material (Jeremiah 26–45 MT) into an extant earlier and shorter corpus, facilitating its message as consistent with the authoritative status of Jeremiah's existing oracles. Additional hermeneutical considerations favor the temporal priority of the MT

the Shaphanide figures mentioned in Jeremiah 36 and their role as the licensed trustees of Jeremiah's written oracles makes the strongest statement about the fitness of groups exiled only in 587 to share in the covenantal qualifications Jeremiah had earlier bestowed on the captives of 597. Of special importance is the question/answer exchange between the Shaphanides in the Temple and Baruch, who has just read to them the written words of Jeremiah:

> And they asked Baruch, saying: "Tell us now: How did you write all these words from his mouth? (את כל הדברים האלה מפיו)" Then Baruch answered them: "He declared to me all these words from his mouth (מפיו יקרא אלי את כל הדברים האלה), and I wrote them with ink in the book." (Jer 36:17–18)

As I have discussed elsewhere, this exchange highlights the typological equivalency between the word of Yhwh as placed in the prophet's mouth (Deut 18:18, Jer 1:9) and that same word transmuted into the written work of a scribe.[45] Thus, even the early collection of the prophet's words is subjected to the scribal process, and the scribes responsible for this include those who remained with the prophet in the land past the year 597 b.c.e. It is for this reason that a Shaphanide such as Gedaliah is able to assume a position of political leadership entirely consistent with Jeremiah's own oracles even after the destruction of Jerusalem, and it is notable that the decree ascribed to him in Jer 40:9–10 draws heavily from Jeremiah's missive to the captives of 597 and the collection in which it was preserved (cf. Jer 27:12–17; 29:7, 10).

The rhetorical strategy of this account is meant to fill temporal and literary chasms between exilic groups following the captivity in 587. The author of the account suggests that even those remaining in the land under Gedaliah could, theoretically, share in the conditions of an ongoing covenant as defined by the words of Jeremiah initially applied to Jehoiachin and those accompanying him to Babylon. All of these figures and words and deeds attributed to them fall under the rubric of the "many similar words" in Jer 36:32 that draws these diverse sources together just as it opened the door for the redacted version of the missives in Jeremiah 29 to enter the growing corpus.[46] Oracles addressed to specific communi-

---

(in an early form) over the LXX; see C. R. Seitz, "The Prophet Moses and the Canonical Shape of Jeremiah," *ZAW* 101 (1989) 18–27.

45. Leuchter, *Polemics of Exile*, 34–35.

46. The passive voice noted by Hoffman regarding the addition of these similar words (נוסף) certainly facilitated this process ("Aetiology," 186).

ties were redacted to apply broadly, and the central figures in the prophet's ministry during Judah's final decade are highlighted as the inheritors of his authority.[47] Others who subsequently found their way into Babylon are therefore presented as benefitting from the same good graces that Jeremiah's words had applied to the captives of 597. This very idea has now been introduced into Jeremiah 29 though the formulaic language in vv. 16–19, leading to the apex of the passage in v. 20: *all* the exiles from Jerusalem to Babylon—the 597 group and those who arrived after 587—are part of a single community commonly addressed by the current form of the chapter.

Summary and Conclusion

The relationship between the dispatches in Jeremiah 29 and the narrative of Jeremiah 36, then, provides one very important reason behind the creation of an authoritative, single Jeremianic corpus in exile. A fractious culture characterized the period, where homeland groups, émigrés to Egypt and exiles to Babylon eyed each other with suspicion and bitterness.[48] But it is clear that within the populations taken to Babylon, intra-group conflict persisted throughout the course of the Neo-Babylonian period (and beyond this time as well).[49] Within part of this population —the captives of 597—a view developed that the cosmic shift from Jerusalem to Babylon had been recognized by the prophet Jeremiah himself, and for this reason their forced migration away from Jerusalem provided them with a theologically exalted status and positioned them for ongoing blessing. As Jeremiah's 70-year prophecy implied, YHWH had allowed for Babylon to flourish, and those who recognized this were those who lived in Babylonian lands and who built distinct kinship structures according to YHWH's will.[50]

---

47. Dearman, "My Servants the Scribes," 420. One should note that the redactional addition in Jer 29:16–19 specifies that the individuals exiled after 597 are the "brethren" of the Jehoiachin group (v. 16) and that the lack of attention paid to the prophets is addressed to that latter group via the second-person address (v. 19). Thus, the redaction blurs the lines between these two communities and contributes to the view that the redacted corpus applies equally to exiles of various waves.

48. Both the Jeremiah and Ezekiel traditions witness this, as both contain a strong antipathy for Judahites who fled to Egypt (e.g., Jeremiah 43–44, Ezekiel 29–30).

49. Rom-Shiloni, "Group Identity," 39–46.

50. Assis, "Psalm 127," 266–67. The family/kinship emphasis noted by Assis may have led to the exclusivity espoused by Ezekiel and adopted by the 597 community, viewing themselves as a pseudo-clan of sorts in contradistinction from the later captives. This may have some bearing on the development of the kinship organization known

This view was not extended to the newly exiled population following the events of 587, witnessed especially within the oracles of Ezekiel and their contribution to an alternate sacral hierarchy and strict social boundaries in exile. The exilic redaction of the Jeremianic corpus fires back by infusing stereotyped materials into the prophet's original missive(s), situating the community to which it was directed on a level playing field with other groups addressed by the prophet in similar terms. The missives, in essence, became but another collection accounted for within the growing Jeremianic corpus, and the diversity of these corpora are alluded to within the "many similar words" notice in the closing verse of Jeremiah 36. But the construction of this chapter, as part of a larger historiographic project, also specified that the figures most closely trusted by the prophet were scribes who had *not* been sent to Babylon alongside Jehoiachin in 597. Rather, many of these characters appear elsewhere in the narrative matrix of the book as agents of prophecy, effectors of history, and facilitators of blessing. Against the claims of the Ezekiel tradition that the exiles of 597 were the only true Israel, the book of Jeremiah binds representatives of different post-597 communities to Jeremiah's prophecies (Gedaliah, who governed from Mizpah; Baruch, who eventually went to Egypt; Seraiah and the other Shaphanides eventually exiled to Babylon) and identifies them as the executors of divine will.

That this argument hinges on material conveyed through the historiographic form says something important about the role of historiography during the course of the exile. D. M. Carr has insightfully noted that national historiography is primarily a product of the state, and that the development of the epic/ancestral narratives regarding the ancestors takes place beyond the reaches of the royal court, among people separated from it and, in his view, reacting to its loss.[51] Many scholars, of course, see the epic/ancestral narratives as having roots in times earlier than the exile, but Carr is correct that the production of historiography with a na-

---

in Ezra–Nehemiah as the בית אבות as opposed to the earlier בית אב. On the distinction between the two, see H. G. M. Williamson, "The Family in Persian Period Judah: Some Textual Reflections," in *Symbiosis, Symbolism, and the Power of the Past: Canaan, Ancient Israel, and Their Neighbors from the Late Bronze Age through Roman Palaestina* (ed. W. G. Dever and S. Gitin; Winona Lake, IN: Eisenbrauns, 2003) 469–85, esp. pp. 472–78. Williamson considers a number of factors leading to the terminological change, including the possibility of larger mixed groups constituting kinship units emerging from the exile (p. 479).

51. D. M. Carr, "The Rise of Torah," in *The Pentateuch as Torah: New Models for Understanding Its Promulgation and Acceptance* (ed. G. N. Knoppers and B. M. Levinson; Winona Lake, IN: Eisenbrauns, 2007) 39–56, esp. pp. 48–49.

tional scope is the precinct of institutions that were greatly compromised by the destruction of 587 B.C.E. This is actually implied within Jeremiah's missive, instructing its recipients to turn inward to family/kinship structures and not to remain concerned with the passé fixtures of the Judahite monarchy.[52] But the authors of Jeremiah 36 (and the related Jeremianic historiography) proclaim this to be an invalid view: any and all "similar words" recalled as spoken by Jeremiah are not the province of disconnected groups but address a nation enduring a common experience. The scribes who redacted Jeremiah's missives and other independent text collections wove the trustees of those collections into a single nation even as they wove the collections into a single book. By doing so, they affirmed that even without a functioning royal court and despite the debates between communities taken from their homeland, Israel was still a single nation with a national history worth telling.

52. As per the implications of Assis' examination ("Psalm 127") and the trends characterizing the post-Josianic situation in Judah (Leuchter, "The 'Prophets' and the 'Levites,'" 36–40).

Ezekiel's Perspective of Israel's History: Selective Revisionism?

Brian Peterson

Steven Tuell perhaps sums up Ezekiel's recitation of history best when he compares Gerhard von Rad's assessment of Israel's history to Ezekiel's. Whereas von Rad saw the Hebrew Bible as a recitation of Israel's *Heilsgeschichte*, Ezekiel presents Israel's history as *Unheilsgeschichte*.[1] But what is the reason for Ezekiel's negative retrospection—a perspective so radically different from that of other Hebrew prophets and historians? In this essay I hope to answer this question by focusing on Ezekiel's overall presentation, his purposes, and the texts that deal almost exclusively with Israel's history as viewed by the prophet, namely, chaps. 16, 20, and 23.[2] My emphasis will not be so much on "how" Ezekiel is different, for few would disagree that Ezekiel's history is indeed that, but rather I will focus more on "why" he is so radical in his presentation.

If every book of the Hebrew canon were lost and only the book of Ezekiel remained, trying to gain a clear picture of Israel and its history

---

[1]. S. Tuell, *Ezekiel* (NIBCOT 15; Peabody, MA: Hendrickson, 2009) 126. Tuell here is speaking specifically of chap. 20 in Ezekiel but does note the tenor of Ezekiel in this vein.

[2]. I will not focus on these chapters in their totality but rather I will deal only with portions of the text that relate specifically to historical recitations. Also, while I understand the interpretive and sociological concerns these chapters create for some readers (specifically chaps. 16 and 23), I will not address those issues here. Others have attempted to offer approaches to these texts that may ameliorate their harshness. See, for example, K. Pfisterer Darr, "Ezekiel's Justifications of God: Teaching Troubling Texts," *JSOT* 55 (1992) 97–117, esp. pp. 113–16. See further, C. L. Patton, "Should Our Sister Be Treated Like a Whore? A Response to Feminist Critiques of Ezekiel 23," in *The Book of Ezekiel: Theological and Anthropological Perspectives* (ed. M. S. Odell and J. T. Strong; SBLSymS 9; Atlanta: Society of Biblical Literature, 2000) 221–38; R. J. Weems, *Battered Love: Marriage, Sex, and Violence in the Hebrew Prophets* (OBT; Minneapolis: Fortress, 1995); M. Shields, "Multiple Exposures: Body Rhetoric and Gender Characterization in Ezekiel 16," *JFSR* 14 (1998) 5–18; and F. van Dijk-Hemmes, "The Metaphorization of Women in Prophetic Speech: An Analysis of Ezekiel xxiii," *VT* 43 (1993) 162–70.

would indeed be difficult. In fact, one could conclude it is lopsided. As one reads through Ezekiel a picture of Israel's history appears glum and depressing with nothing meritorious to cling to. It does not take long when reading the book of Ezekiel before you realize that the prophet's selectivity in the recitation of Israel's history is not just bordering on selective revisionism but is indeed just that![3] Ezekiel, though, is not the only biblical writer to construe history a certain way in order to gain a desired response. One need only look to the Chronicler to realize that without the alternate perspective of the Deuteronomistic Historian,[4] David's life, for example, would appear almost saintly.[5] Thus, before we indict the prophet for historiographic malfeasance, we must step back from the text and assess the prophet's motives for writing from this perspective. I believe that, once this facet is investigated along with the prophet's literary and geographical context, new light will be shed on why Ezekiel's overview of Israel's past is so morose.

Ezekiel's Context: The Crux of the Prophet's Revisionism

Three aspects of Ezekiel's context play a vital role in understanding the man and his message. Foremost of these three is his setting. One of the key things to remember about Ezekiel when comparing his prophecy to the works of other prophets is the fact that Ezekiel is the first of the 'writing' prophets to live and minister from outside the land of Israel.[6] The traumatic displacement of the leadership of Jerusalem's cult (not to mention the people) from service and worship in the temple would have caused a serious reevaluation of who YHWH was. In this regard, many questions needed to be answered. What was the nature of Israel's relationship *vis à vis* YHWH in light of an absent temple and its ritual? Was YHWH weaker than Marduk and the Babylonians' gods? Could YHWH even help or speak

---

3. So too D. I. Block, *The Book of Ezekiel Chapters 1–24* (NICOT; Grand Rapids: Eerdmans, 1997) 614.

4. I do not mean to suggest any preference for the Deuteronomistic Historian's version of history over that of Ezekiel's, but rather I seek to point out that the "truth" of Israel's history must lay somewhere between that presented in the Deuteronomistic History and the negative assessment of Ezekiel.

5. See also comments by E. F. Davis, *Swallowing the Scroll: Textuality and Dynamics of Discourse in Ezekiel's Prophecy* (JSOTSup 78; Sheffield: Almond, 1989) 110, esp. n. 13.

6. Notwithstanding arguments for the possibility that Moses, Elijah, or Jonah may have written portions of their prophecies and/or ministered from outside of the land of Israel proper (especially Moses).

to his people in a foreign land? Early on, these, and I am sure many other questions, must have confronted the prophet on a daily basis. Yhwh did indeed use Ezekiel to answer these questions whether the people wanted to listen or not (see Ezekiel 3).

To begin with, the very calling of Ezekiel within the land of exile (chaps. 1–3) served as an answer to the latter question—a break from the normative understanding of geographically centralized deities (see 1 Kgs 20:23, 28). As for the former two, Ezekiel's central message would answer these nagging questions. Chapters 1–3, 8–11, and, more specifically, 21:18–23, show in vivid detail who is in control of not only the future of Israel, but also the very king of Babylon himself, and by extension, his gods.[7] Jerusalem would not be the spoil of the nations because Yhwh was in some way too weak to defend it; on the contrary, Jerusalem would fall because Yhwh had abandoned it and had sent Babylon to punish his wayward people for their sin. They were the ones responsible for their own plight. Destruction of the city, temple, and land, followed by an extended exile was the just reward for a nation plagued by wanton sin and rebellion since their inception. As Block points out, "before Yahweh could effect the new community of faith, the evils of the past must be purged."[8] Only after this extended period of punishment and exile would Yhwh once again remember his covenant with his people (Ezek 16:60–62) and act on their behalf, not on account of their faithfulness, but rather for the sake of his name (20:9, 14, 22; 36:22).

Second, as a priest, Ezekiel's purpose in life, namely, to serve Yhwh within the confines of the temple and its cult, was unattainable. This reality alone would have caused Ezekiel to write from a jaded perspective as he sought to assign blame for the predicament in which he found himself. Beyond the psychological facets of the prophet himself, though, the exiles would have had to deal with the dilemma of whether to integrate into their new culture or hold out hope for a quick return. It is perhaps this latter issue that may have fueled Ezekiel's need to downplay any positive vestiges of Israel's past. Both Jeremiah and Ezekiel engaged in this ongoing dispute with the false prophets both in Jerusalem and among the exilic community (see Ezek 13; 22:25–28; Jer 5:31; 14:13–15; 23; 26:5–16;

---

7. I have argued the merits of these aspects in detail elsewhere. See my *Ezekiel in Context: Ezekiel's Message Understood in Its Historical Setting of Covenant Curses and Ancient Near Eastern Mythological Motifs* (Princeton Theological Monograph 182; Eugene, OR: Pickwick, 2012).

8. Block, *Ezekiel 1–24*, 470.

27:9–18; 29; 37:19).⁹ For Ezekiel, it appears his desire to paint the history of Israel's past inimically lay in his need to extinguish any hope of a quick return because of the present community's refusal to acknowledge their complicity in their present plight (chaps. 18 and 20). Even in the midst of the horrors of exile, the people still refused to acknowledge and adhere to the message of the prophet (33:29–33). Ezekiel's need to shock a stubborn and unrepentant people out of their lethargy required a literary style unlike any before. In light of this stubbornness and the prophet's exilic context, Ezekiel was forced to adopt an approach that was unorthodox. No favorable or encouraging depiction of Israel's history would serve the prophet's purposes to shake such an obstinate audience (3:7–8), on the contrary, only a negative assessment of all they were now, and had been in the past, could possibly rouse them.

Finally, at no point in Israel's history had the nation deserved the grace and favor of Yhwh.¹⁰ The perpetual kindness of Yhwh, whether in the past or future, could only be linked to *his* covenant loyalty (חסד) and desire not to profane his holy name.¹¹ Although Israel may have thought that they had been deserving of Yhwh's favor because of *their* association with the covenant and because of the presence of the temple (Jer 4:7), both Ezekiel and Jeremiah dismantle this assumption. Because Israel had constantly broken that covenant, it became obvious that only Yhwh had kept his side of the agreement. Again, the reason for this was in order that his holy name might not be profaned among the nations (Num 14:12–20; Ezek 20:9, 14, 22; 36:20–23), which no doubt stemmed from Yhwh's desire to remain loyal to the covenant despite his people's actions (see Num 14:13–

---

9. Specific false prophets living among the exilic community are named by Jeremiah, that is, Ahab son of Kolaiah and Zedekiah son of Maaseiah (Jer 29:21).

10. One could argue that the wilderness generation was the first to experience this undeserved love especially after the golden calf incident in Exodus 32. However, in Ezek 20:1–9 and 23:1–3, the prophet begins their rebellion even earlier during their sojourn in Egypt. We will pick these texts up in more detail below.

11. While the technical term for covenant loyalty (חסד) does not appear in Ezekiel, the term רחם ("to be compassionate" in the Piel) is present in 39:25 and contextually reflects this covenant love. It is important to point out, however, that although the term חסד is absent in the book of Ezekiel, this does not negate Yhwh's demonstration of his undying covenant love. Yhwh demonstrated his love for his people by restoring all that the people held dear, viz., the temple, land, and king, along with abundance, provision, and prosperity (see chaps. 40–48). These, in whole or in part, are hallmarks of Yhwh's love present at the inception of the covenants with Abraham, the nation at Sinai, and David. Note also that the reason for Yhwh's actions throughout Israel's history in Psalm 106 rests both in his covenant love (106:1, 44–46) and for the sake of his name (106:8).

20 esp. vv. 16 and 19). For this reason, Ezekiel recounted Israel's history not just once from a negative perspective, but rather three different times, each time arguably harsher, in order to reaffirm the content of his message.

The Texts

Ezekiel 20

Having established the context of the prophet's message and the probable psychological[12] nuances behind Ezekiel's prophecy, we are now ready to examine the texts themselves. Because chap. 20 is the classic chapter in Ezekiel dealing with the selective history of Israel, we will focus most of our attention here, with discussions on chaps. 16 and 23 to follow.[13] The concepts and historical retrospection used by the prophet are very

---

12. Numerous studies have been done dealing with the possible mental state of Ezekiel, which may account for his strange visions and his graphic detail. For example, K. Jaspers ("Der Prophet Ezechiel: Eine pathologische Studie," in *Arbeiten zur Psychiatric, Neurologie und ihren Grenzgebieten: Festschrift für Kurt Schneider* [ed. H. Kranz; Willsbach: Scherer, 1947] 1–9) argues that Ezekiel was a schizophrenic. E. C. Bloome, "Ezekiel's Abnormal Personality," *JBL* 65 (1946) 277–92; D. J. Halperin, *Seeking Ezekiel: Text and Psychology* (University Park: Pennsylvania State University Press, 1993); J. Stiebert, *The Exile and the Prophet's Wife: Historical Events and Marginal Perspectives* (Interfaces; Collegeville, MN: Liturgical Press, 2005) 84–108; and B. Bron, "Zur Psychopathologie und Verkündigung des Propheten Ezechiel: Zum Phänomen der prophetischen Ekstase," *Schweizer Archiv für Neurologie, Neurochirurgie und Psychiatrie* 128 (1981) 21–31.For an overview of a few of these key studies see K. F. Pohlmann, *Ezechiel: Der Stand Der Theologischen Diskussion* (Darmstadt: Wissenschaftliche Buchgesellschaft, 2008) 184–87.

13. Entire monographs (or chapters) have been written on this chapter specifically dealing with theological and compositional concerns. E.g., F. Sedlmeier, *Studien zu Komposition und Theologie von Ezechiel 20* (SBB 21; Stuttgart: Katholisches Bibelwerk, 1990); and S. Ohnesorge, *Jahwe gestaltet sein Volk neu. Zur Sicht der Zukunft Israels nach Ez 11,14–21; 20,1–44; 36,16–38; 37,1–14.15–28* (FB 64; Würzburg: Echter, 1991) esp. pp. 78–202. For an analysis of these two works, see Pohlmann, *Ezechiel: Der Stand*, 148–52. For a discussion on the structure and literary nuances of this chapter, see L.Eslinger, "Ezekiel 20 and the Metaphor of Historical Teleology: Concepts of Biblical History," *JSOT* 81 (1998) 93–125; J. Lust, "Ez., XX, 4–26 une parodie de l'histoire religieuse d'Israel," *ETL* 43 (1967) 489–502; and L. C. Allen, "The Structuring of Ezekiel's Revisionist History Lesson (Ezekiel 20:3–31)," *CBQ* 54 (1992) 448–62. See also proposed structural divisions by S. Herrmann, *Die prophetischen Heilserwartungen im Alten Testament: Ursprung und Gestaltwandel* (BWANT 85; Stuttgart: Kohlhammer, 1965) 262–63; and G. Bettenzoli, *Geist der Heiligkeit: Traditionsgeschichtliche Untersuchung des QDŠ-Begriffes im Buche Ezechiel* (Quaderni di Semitistica 8; Florence: Istituto di Linguistica e di Lingue Orientali, Università di Firenze, 1979) 195–98, as noted by Allen, "Structuring," 452 nn. 16 and 17, respectively.

similar to those used by the psalmist in Psalm 78,[14] and later by Stephen in Acts 7.[15] In chap. 20, as in chap. 23, the prophet begins by noting the rebellion of the people in the land of Egypt. Unlike his predecessor, Hosea (Hos 2:14–15, 11:1) and his contemporary Jeremiah (Jer 2:1–3), Ezekiel looked back on Israel's earliest history as a period of rebellion and idolatry.[16] Indeed, this approach was something radically new in the prophetic corpus and would have been shocking for his audience. In this vein, Blenkinsopp insightfully notes that Ezekiel's opening indictment "would be comparable to a leading churchman arguing that Christianity had taken a wrong direction from apostolic times."[17]

Ezekiel wastes no time in getting to his point by eliminating any favorable "back story" in the Egyptian sojourn and the exodus events.[18] No mention of Moses as lawgiver (Exod 24:12) or intercessor (Exod 32:11–14; Num 14:13–16, 21:7) is presented. There is no recollection of the former promises to the patriarchs (Exod 2:24; see Gen 12:1–3) or of the very motive for Yhwh calling forth his people out of bondage (Exod 3:7–9). The mutually agreed-on Sinai covenant is only implied (20:11), whereas the curses of the same covenant are stressed (compare 20:23 to Lev 26:33; Deut 4:27, 28:64).[19] The complete silence of any level of hope or innocence and merit on the part of the people is deafening.[20]

When we compare Ezekiel's recollection of the Egyptian sojourn (20:5–10) to the pentateuchal account (Exodus 1–13), the differences are immediately apparent. In Exodus, the children of Israel living in bondage in Egypt accept Moses' message of deliverance (Exod 4:31). Aside from

---

14. J. Blenkinsopp, *Ezekiel* (IBC; Louisville, KY: Westminster John Knox, 1990) 87. See also Block, for a comparison of chap. 20 with Psalm 106 and Ezekiel 36 (*Ezekiel 1–24*, 615–16).

15. R. W. Jenson, *Ezekiel* (Brazos Theological Commentary on the Bible; Grand Rapids: Brazos, 2009) 154.

16. Tuell, *Ezekiel*, 128. See also Psalm 106 for a negative review of Israel's history albeit with a positive conclusion in vv. 44–48.

17. Blenkinsopp, *Ezekiel*, 88.

18. M. S. Odell, *Ezekiel* (Smyth & Helwys Bible Commentary; Macon, GA: Smyth & Helwys, 2005) 246. See also Eslinger, "Ezekiel 20," 102. Eslinger points out the absence of the "idealized exodus experience" and the "honeymoon in the Sinai desert."

19. Ezekiel's ongoing focus on the curses of the law makes rhetorical sense here. The mentioning of causing the nation to pass "under the rod" תחת השבט and bringing them "into the bond of the covenant" במסרת הברית in v. 37, no doubt refers to the curses of the law (see Deuteronomy 28 and Leviticus 26). While Blenkinsopp does point out that "passing under the rod" had shepherding implications focusing on counting sheep for tithing/slaughtering purposes, the context clearly suggests curses of the law (*Ezekiel*, 91).

20. So too Darr, "Justifications," 98.

a couple of brief notations of unbelief stemming from the taskmasters' harsh treatment of the people (see Exod 5:21; 6:9, 12), the nation obeyed. Therefore, we are left wondering from the outset why the prophet begins his indictment of the people with their sojourn in Egypt. Whether or not the prophet is privy to sources and information apart from the Hebrew text is not known and is purely speculative. But it does appear that he has some knowledge of a time in the inchoate period of the nation when the people refused to give up their idols in Egypt (20:7–8).[21]

Several possibilities lay behind Ezekiel's motivation for beginning with the Egyptian sojourn and for eliminating Israel's "back story." First, it was in Egypt that Israel grew from one family into a nation. These national roots in Egypt must have served as the incipient moment when their rebellion (as a nation) began.[22] Some scholars even postulate that the reason for the immense suffering in Egypt may have been due to the people's desire for Egypt's gods.[23] Second, it is also conceivable that the prophet is focusing on the possible correlation between the gods of Egypt and the golden calf incident[24] or Jeroboam's connection to Egypt as a fugitive (1 Kgs 11:26–40) and his later establishment of calf worship at Dan and Bethel (1 Kgs 12:28–29).[25] In the former case, scholars have noted the close connection between Aaron's golden calf and the Egyptian god, Apis.[26] Third, it is possible that Ezekiel is recalling an earlier oral or textual

---

21. Jenson posits that Ezekiel does not want to leave any period in Israel's history "untainted"; therefore, he begins his address by indicting the nation even before they came into covenant with Yhwh (*Ezekiel*, 156).

22. It seems evident that the extended oracles against Egypt in chaps. 29–32 may have arisen from Ezekiel's loathing of Egypt due to their negative influence on Israel. So too, Blenkinsopp, *Ezekiel*, 88.

23. R. H. Alexander, *Ezekiel* (Expositor's Bible Commentary 6; Grand Rapids: Zondervan, 1986) 833. W. Eichrodt (*Ezekiel: A Commentary* [trans. Cosslett Quin; OTL. Philadelphia: Westminster, 1970] 323) suggests that Israel may have involved themselves in "Egyptian heathenism."

24. Note the judgment associated with this incident where 3000 people are killed by the Levites (see Exod 32:28).

25. Note the similar language used by Jeroboam in 1 Kgs 12:28 and Aaron in Exod 32:4, viz., "These are your gods, which brought you up out of Egypt" (אלה אלהיך ישראל אשר העלוך מארץ מצרים). See also R. H. Pfeiffer, "Images of Yahweh," *JBL* 45 (1926) 217. Pfeiffer suggests that Ezekiel is making a connection to Jeroboam's possible alliance with Sheshonk I (Shishak).

26. See C. F. Keil, *Ezekiel* (COT 9; Peabody, MA: Hendrickson, 2001) 466. Also, contra D. Slivniak ("The Golden Calf Story: Constructively and Deconstructively," *JSOT* 33 [2008] 22), who asserts that the golden calf was "authentically Israelite." The use of bull and calf iconography spanned a wide area of Canaan during this period; see, for example, "'Golden Calf' Found," *ChrCent* 107 (1990) 728. For a literary analysis

tradition much like that presented in the Deuteronomistic History. In this vein, we can point to textual evidence recalling the conquest period that suggests that Israel's idolatry began in Egypt and even earlier with Abraham's ancestry in Ur (see Josh 24:2, 14–15).[27] Finally, it is possible that the answer may lay closer to Ezekiel's own day and the events taking place around him. The opening date in chap. 20 (August 14, 591 B.C.E.) seems to correspond very closely to the timing of the political intrigues of the period. Pharaoh Psammetichus II (595–589 B.C.E) had been successful in his military campaign against Cush, and now the rulers in Syria-Palestine (including Zedekiah) hoped for his incursion into the Levant to loosen the grip of the Babylonians.[28] The nation of Israel once again was looking to their old "lover," Egypt, to save them from their predicament (see Ezekiel 29–32).[29] If in fact the elders were seeking Ezekiel's approval of this possible liaison between Zedekiah and Psammetichus II in order to bring about a quick end to the exile, they were sadly mistaken (20:1–4). Whatever the case may be, Ezekiel had a solid basis both textually and politically to connect Israel's rebellion to their nascent period.

The next section of Ezekiel's account (20:10–17) does resonate with the pentateuchal sources concerning the actions of the first Exodus generation while in the wilderness (20:10–17).[30] Here, Ezekiel appears to be focusing on the people's constant rebellion and murmuring (e.g., Exod 15:24; 16:7–9, 12; Num 14:27; 17:5, 10) and their "violation of the Sabbath ordinance" (compare Exodus 16 to Ezek 20:12–24).[31] For the first generation of the Exodus period idolatry, exemplified in the golden calf incident (Exodus 32–34) and rebellion against YHWH and his appointed leaders (Numbers 12, 16), epitomized in the evil report of the spies

---

of Exodus 32–34, see H. Chanan Brichto, "The Worship of the Golden Calf: A Literary Analysis of a Fable on Idolatry," *HUCA* 54 (1983) 1–44.

27. So too Blenkinsopp, *Ezekiel*, 88; and Lust, "Ez., XX, 4–26," 516. Lloyd R. Bailey ("The Golden Calf," *HUCA* 42 [1971] 97–115, esp. pp. 102–3) argues against any Egyptian connection. He avers that the Israelites would not have looked to the gods of the land that had just been defeated by YHWH. He instead suggests that the bull-god is to be linked to the "god of the fathers" which finds its root in Abraham's ancestry in Ur (pp. 112–14).

28. Odell, *Ezekiel*, 248.

29. Alexander, *Ezekiel*, 833.

30. Contra R. H. Pfeiffer (*Introduction to the Old Testament* [London: Black, 1953] 546), who avers that Ezekiel was unable to "see the historical reality because he lived in an imaginary world."

31. Blenkinsopp, *Ezekiel*, 89. Blenkinsopp goes on to note the close association of the priestly tradition and Sabbath keeping as a sign of true devotion to YHWH.

(Numbers 13–14), served as the capstones of their rebellion.³² In similar fashion, Ezekiel's indictment of his current generation highlighted these two recurring sins. The nation practiced unrelenting idolatry (Ezekiel 6, 8–11, 16) and rebellion against Yhwh and his prophets (Ezek 3:7, 20:8). Thus, Ezekiel's presentation of the sins of the Exodus generation is indeed parallel with other sources and, if one were to focus on only the negative reports in the Pentateuch, may even be less intense. For example, the rebellion of the first generation reaches its apex in Num 14:26–45 when the people refuse to listen to the judgment of Yhwh but instead try to possess the land of Canaan without Moses or the Lord's presence. Yhwh decreed that this first generation would die in the wilderness and their offspring would possess the land. Ezekiel's statement in 20:17 that Yhwh did not completely "annihilate" (כלה) this first generation in the wilderness is again reflective of the Pentateuchal account in that their offspring and Joshua and Caleb (a small "remnant") entered Canaan. The parallel with Ezekiel's day is glaring. Yhwh would punish the exilic generation in the "wilderness" of Babylon, but their offspring (a "remnant") would be allowed to reenter the land of promise. I will develop this in more detail below.

The next part of Ezekiel's historical revision appears in 20:18–26. Here, the prophet rehearses the actions of the second generation in the wilderness. Again, the people rejected Yhwh's statutes (חקות) and followed the statutes (חקים) of their fathers.³³ We also find in v. 25 the shocking notation concerning the "not good" (לא טוב) laws of Yhwh.³⁴ There can be little doubt that the wilderness generation's willingness to follow the statutes of their forefathers was an analogy of rebellion just waiting to be exploited by Ezekiel. The "not good laws," contextually associated with child sacrifice (20:26), does create a degree of tension in the account.³⁵ Suffice it

---

32. Note also the Dathan and Abiram account in Numbers 16.

33. There may be an intentional play on the masculine and feminine forms of "statutes" here in chap. 20, denoting those of Yhwh and those of the forefathers. W. Zimmerli (*Ezekiel 1–24* [Philadelphia: Fortress, 1979] 411) and Block (*Ezekiel 1–24*, 636) also point out this gender fluctuation.

34. The Targum tries to mitigate the theological implications of this text by translating it, "They followed their stupid inclination and they obeyed religious decrees which were not proper and laws by which they could not survive." See Blenkinsopp, *Ezekiel*, 90.

35. The theological issues stemming from this debate are beyond the scope of this essay. Note, for example, that this translation has pitted Ezekiel against the law of Moses, Deuteronomy in particular. E.g., see J. L. Crenshaw, "Theodicy and Prophetic Literature," in *Theodicy in the World of the Bible* (ed. A. Laato and J. C. de Moor; Boston: Brill, 2003) 247. See further, S. W. Hahn and J. Sietze Bergsma, "What Laws Were 'Not

to say that if indeed Ezekiel is using the very law of Yhwh as a means of judgment, then his perspective on the law would definitely be a revision of pentateuchal and Prophetic history.³⁶ These concerns aside, Ezekiel makes a startling statement in v. 23 concerning the second wilderness generation. Somewhere along the line, whether in the sin of Baal of Peor (Numbers 25) or in their general rebellion, this generation had accumulated enough wrath from Yhwh to elicit the judgment of exile *before* they entered the land.³⁷ Therefore, they were living on borrowed time once they did enter Canaan. The people's continued violation of the covenant laws (that is, their rebellion) and their propensity to follow the statutes (חקים) of their forefathers only sealed the already-determined future of the nation.³⁸

Finally, the last period presented in chap. 20 highlights the actions of the people once they entered the land of Canaan (20:27–29). Ezekiel completely bypasses the relatively positive history of Joshua and the conquest³⁹ and instead focuses on the negative facets of Israel's early history in the land. It is possible that Ezekiel is here underlining the Judges period and the repeated cycle of sin recorded there,⁴⁰ but even then, no mention is made of the arguably positive judgeships of Othniel, Deborah, or Barak.

Good'? A Canonical Approach to the Theological Problem of Ezekiel 20:25–26," *JBL* 123 (2004) 201–18. In this article, the authors suggest that Yhwh gave the bad laws of Deuteronomy in order to bring about the covenant curses, namely, the exile. G. C. Heider ("A Further Turn on Ezekiel's Baroque Twist in Ezek 20:25–26," *JBL* 107 [1988] 721–24) argues that Ezekiel is in a way reinstituting the tenth plague formerly used against Egypt as a means of punishing his own people. See further Lust, "Ez., XX, 4–26," 510–13.

36. Darr notes that whereas the people had rejected the life-giving laws earlier, now the people practiced the "bad laws" "religiously" ("Justifications," 99).

37. See Hos 9:10. See also Darr, "Justifications," 99. Blenkinsopp avers that Ezekiel is trying to explain the "why" of the exile by suggesting it was "preordained" by God from Israel's earliest history (*Ezekiel*, 86).

38. On the tensions within Ezekiel's argumentation of a promised exile (especially in light of Ezekiel 3 and 18), see M. J. Boda, *A Severe Mercy: Sin and Its Remedy in the Old Testament* (Siphrut 1; Winona Lake, IN: Eisenbrauns, 2009) 279–83, 292.

39. The sin of Achan (Joshua 7) is the main blot found in the book of Joshua. Nevertheless, it appears that even Joshua recognized the people's penchant to sin and rebel against Yhwh when he told the people at the covenant renewal ceremony at Shechem that they were not able to keep the covenant (Josh 24:19–20).

40. There are those who argue that the books of Joshua and Judges are parallel accounts of the settlement of the land. One by rapid military conquest (i.e., Joshua) and one by slow integration (i.e., Judges). See H. J. Flanders Jr., R. W. Crapps, and D. A. Smith, *People of the Covenant: An Introduction to the Hebrew Bible* (4th ed.; New York: Oxford University Press, 1996) 228, 231, 236, 239; V. H. Matthews and J. C. Moyer, *The Old Testament: Text and Context* (Peabody, MA: Hendrickson, 1997) 81; J. Bright, *A History of Israel* (4th ed.; Louisville, KY: Westminster John Knox, 2000) 129; G. E.

As for the monarchy, the prophet completely overlooks the pious phases of the reigns of Saul,[41] David, Solomon, Hezekiah, and Josiah. Instead, he jumps over the period of the united kingdom and focuses on the later period of the divided kingdom when worship on the high places (במות) dominated the cultic scene. Again, only the negative aspects of Israel's kings are emphasized in his account.[42]

Ezekiel closes out his historical retrospection by turning to his listeners and drawing stark parallels between their early history and their present realities (20:30–39). Yhwh reaffirms his commitment to effect judgment on the nation. He parallels the exilic period as the "wilderness," where he will judge those who rebel (מרד) against his statutes and commands. Even though they may think they can be like the other nations (20:32) and in so doing avoid the plans of Yhwh, Yhwh will have the final say. Darr aptly concludes,

> Relentlessly, Ezekiel 20 insists that the exiles cannot base their hopes for release and restitution on past righteousness or divine mercy. They cannot claim that they differ from their wicked ancestors, and they cannot conceal in their unspoken thoughts any idea of avoiding Yahweh's plans for their future. Moving from retrospect to prospect, this chapter proclaims with absolute certainty that no action on the exiles' part can ever interfere with God's determination to see that plan fulfilled, the rebellious purged, cultic purity enforced, and human willfulness quelled in a morass of shame and contrition.[43]

We may conclude this section by reaffirming that the prophet's purposes and setting dictated his selectivity of Israel's history and how he presented it—Ezekiel is indeed "sovereign" over his rendition of the past.[44] Ezekiel sees in the exile a perfect chance to highlight effective parallels with the first "exile" in Egypt. Israel had not deserved Yhwh's help in the first exile because of their constant rebellion. And similarly, the present exilic generation does not deserve his help now. With rhetoric *par excellence*, the

---

Mendenhall, *Ancient Israel's Faith and History: An Introduction to the Bible in Context* (Louisville, KY: Westminster John Knox, 2001) 101.

41. There is textual evidence that Saul's early reign was marked by pious acts of reform (see 1 Sam 28:9).

42. One could argue that the sins of Ahaz (2 Kgs 16:2–3) and Manasseh (2 Kgs 21:1–18; 2 Chronicles 33) may have colored Ezekiel's thinking here due to his focus on child sacrifice. Moreover, there is a close thematic and theological connection between Ezekiel 20 and 2 Kgs 17:7–23. Ezekiel may in fact be reiterating aspects of that part of Israel and Judah's history.

43. Darr, "Justifications," 101–2.

44. Davis, *Swallowing the Scroll*, 113.

prophet resorts to an earlier refrain reminiscent of the exodus generation. Yhwh would bring the exilic nation into the "land" he had "sworn" to give their fathers (20:42) with or without their consent (Exod 6:8; 13:5, 11; 33:1; Num 14:23, 30; 32:11; Deut 1:8, 35; 6:10, 18, etc.).[45] Ezekiel ends his selective history in chap. 20 by making sure one thing was clear for his listeners (20:1): that, while they may be determined to renege on their end of the covenant and repeat the rebellion of their forefathers, Yhwh will remain faithful to his word and the covenant. This, along with Yhwh's need to vindicate himself before the nations becomes the basis for the unifying refrain "for the sake of my name" (למען שמי; see 20:9, 14, 22, 44).

Ezekiel 16

In Ezekiel 16, the prophet moves away from the exodus tradition analogy of chap. 20 and opts for an extended allegory depicting Jerusalem as the bride of Yhwh with a focus on cultic nuances.[46] Ezekiel's use of the marriage metaphor no doubt finds its beginning in Hosea's marital analogy (see Hosea 1–3).[47] The metaphor allowed for the full range of the feelings of love, betrayal, retribution, and restoration to play out in the minds and emotions of the recipients of the oracle.[48]

The prophet begins this chapter with the abandoned-child motif (16:3–13)—which would normally elicit pathos in an audience.[49] However, even

---

45. It is perhaps from this perspective that one could see the merits of B. J. Schwartz's argument, as stated in "Ezekiel's Dim View of Israel's Restoration," in *The Book of Ezekiel: Theological and Anthropological Perspectives* (ed. M. S. Odell and J. T. Strong; SBLSymS 9; Atlanta: Society of Biblical Literature, 2000) 43–67.

46. For a discussion on the role of cities being classified as female (goddesses) married to the patron deity of the nation (especially in West Semitic literature), see A. Fitzgerald, "The Mythological Background for the Presentation of Jerusalem as a Queen and False Worship as Adultery in the OT," *CBQ* 34 (1972) 403–16, esp. pp. 405, 414–16. See further, J. Lewy, "The Old West Semitic Sun-God Hammu," *HUCA* 18 (1944) 429–81.

47. See also Isa 49:14–23, 54:1–8, 62:3–5, 66:7–13.

48. B. Brown Taylor ("Betrothed by God," in *Gospel Medicine* [Cambridge, MA: Cowley, 1995] 50–56) points out the value of the marriage metaphor based on Hosea's use of it. See also R. D. Patterson, "Metaphors of Marriage as Expressions of Divine-Human Relations," *JETS* 51 (2008) 689–702, esp. pp. 689–98; and S. L. McKenzie, *Covenant* (Understanding Biblical Themes; St. Louis: Chalice, 2000) 57–58.

49. The exposure of children, especially unwanted female children, was an effective means of "abortion" in the ANE. Moreover, this motif is often linked to the beginnings of great leaders who are miraculously saved and destined for great things (e.g., Sargon, Moses, Romulus, and Remus). In this case, Ezekiel seems to be implying that Israel was intended to be great and be a great leader but failed miserably because of its rebellion. See further the work of J. E. Coleson, "Israel's Life Cycle from Birth to

before the prophet allows his listeners to feel a hint of pity for themselves, he has insulted them by associating them with pagan ancestry (16:3; see also vv. 43b–45) and the defiling aspects of birth and blood (Lev 12:1–8, 17:10–14).[50] In Ezekiel's retrospection of Jerusalem's early history, only Canaanite beginnings from an Amorite father and a Hittite mother, matter.[51] It is true that originally the capital was neither a Judahite nor an Israelite city, having its roots in Jebusite culture,[52] but Ezekiel strategically overlooks David's capture of it and Solomon's establishment of the temple on Mount Moriah. Here, the prophet practices selective revisionism by purposely abandoning any positive historical beginnings as envisioned within the Deuteronomistic History (see 2 Samuel 5). Rather, he stresses the city's pagan and defiling beginnings well before David's capture of it.

As the metaphor unfolds, the prophet recalls happier times in Israel when YHWH loved and cared for his "bride." Unlike chap. 20, in v. 8 the prophet clearly implies that the period associated with the Sinai covenant was a time of positive beginnings. Furthermore, the prophet's description of Israel's clothing in vv. 9–10 along with her food in v. 19 has tabernacle and sacrificial nuances.[53] Finally, the notation about placing a crown on the bride's head evokes memories of the establishment of the monarchy with possible references to Solomon's fame (v. 14—perhaps referencing the queen of Sheba's visit?).

Ezekiel's pleasant "walk down memory lane," though, quickly turns ugly in v. 15 and continues this way until v. 59. The prophet rehearses

---

Resurrection," in *Israel's Apostasy and Restoration: Essays in Honor of Ronald K. Harrison* (ed. A. Gileadi; Grand Rapids: Baker, 1988) 237–50; B. R. Foster, trans., "The Birth Legend of Sargon of Akkad," (*COS* 1.133:461); and B. Lewis, *The Sargon Legend: A Study of the Akkadian and A Tale of the Hero Who Was Exposed at Birth* (American Schools of Oriental Research Dissertation Series 4; Cambridge, MA: ASOR, 1980). See also the Babylonian Talmud version of the birth of Moses (*Sotah* 12a–13b), Joshua the son of Nun (*Rab Pe'alim* 12a), and Abraham (*Shevet Musar* 52), as noted by Lewis, *The Sargon Legend*, 153–55.

50. What is more, Jerusalem is described as a female child, for which the defilement period is twice as long as for a male (Lev 12:5).

51. For a technical discussion on the possibilities of Ezekiel's reference here, see J. T. Luke, "'Your Father was an Amorite' (Ezek 16:3, 45): An Essay on the Amorite Problem in OT Traditions," in *The Quest for the Kingdom of God: Studies in Honor of George E. Mendenhall* (ed. H. B. Huffmon, F. A. Spina, and A. R. W. Green; Winona Lake, IN: Eisenbrauns, 1983) 221–37, esp. pp. 222–24.

52. Block points out that the Hittite and Amorite comment is not necessarily connected to Jerusalem but is to be associated with the general inhabitants of Canaan at the time of the conquest. They "represent human depravity at its worst" (*Ezekiel 1–24*, 475).

53. See Darr, "Justifications," 102, esp. nn. 14 and 15.

the "wife's" numerous dalliances and the resulting punishments.[54] On the theological level, most of these liaisons reflect Judah's penchant for foreign gods. Because of this debauched behavior, Ezekiel insists that Jerusalem is worse off than Sodom and Samaria. While the majority of the Hebrew Bible may not explicitly support Ezekiel's denigration of Jerusalem to such a level, his approach does resonate with similar indictments found in the prophetic corpus (see Isa 3:9, Jer 23:14, Lam 4:6, Amos 4:11). The chapter ends on a quasi-positive note (vv. 60–63), calling to remembrance the covenant of Yhwh and his willingness to forgive. However, even this act of benevolence is merely to shame the nation—an act that will cause them to keep their "mouth" (פה) shut in the future (v. 63).

While Darr is perhaps correct when she cautions against the need to scour Israel's history to explain every aspect of this allegory, there still is enough detail within the account to merit an analysis of valid parallels.[55] To begin with, in this chapter Ezekiel is somewhat more irenic when compared to chap. 20. His presentation of the nation's history, although in allegorical form, nonetheless resonates with the picture presented in the Deuteronomistic History and the Pentateuch. The theological lesson that Israel owed its complete existence to the covenant love of Yhwh seems to be fair in light of what is known from the canonical text. Ezekiel is cautious to get the chronological aspects of the nation's beginning and growth correct. But his indictment of the nation for idolatry and covenant violation once again overlooks the Deuteronomistic Historian's positive aspects of Israel's history, especially during the conquest and the early monarchy, namely, the Judahite kings. Also, no mention is made of either Hezekiah's reforms or Josiah's more-recent program of cultic centralization in Jerusalem (see 2 Kings 18, 23; 2 Chronicles 34–35). The only possible

---

54. I believe that many of these punishments (e.g., cutting with swords, stripping, etc.) are not to be found in the curses of the Law but rather in Neo-Assyrian and Neo-Babylonian marriage contracts. See M. T. Roth, "'She Will Die by the Iron Dagger': Adultery and Neo-Babylonian Marriage," *JESHO* 31 (1988) 186–206; idem, *Babylonian Marriage Agreements 7th–3rd Centuries* B.C. (AOAT 222; Kevelaer: Butzon & Bercker, 1989); idem, "Marriage and Matrimonial Prestations in First Millennium B.C. Babylonia," in *Women's Earliest Records: From Ancient Egypt and Western Asia* (ed. B. S. Lesko; BJS 166; Atlanta: Scholars Press, 1989) 245–55; S. Lafont, *Femmes, Droit et Justice dans l'Antiquité orientale: Contribution à l'étude du droit penal au Proche-Orient ancient* (OBO 165; Göttingen: Vandenhoeck & Ruprecht, 1999); E. Meier Tetlow, *Women, Crime, and Punishment in Ancient Law and Society* (2 vols.; New York: Continuum, 2005) 1:110; and R. Westbrook, "Adultery in Ancient Near Eastern Law," *RB* 97 (1990) 542–80. I have also handled this in detail elsewhere, see my *Ezekiel in Context*, 173–225.

55. Darr, "Justifications," 104.

conclusion for such a revision must rest in the wickedness of Mannaseh's reign (2 Kgs 23:26, 24:23) and the rapid backsliding of Josiah's successors (2 Kgs 23:37; 24:9, 19). It appears tenable that Ezekiel is here following theological assertions of the Deuteronomistic Historian and his/their negative assessments of the last of the Judahite kings.

Another interesting factor to consider that we touched on above is the affinity Ezekiel's message has with those of other prophets when it comes to likening Israel and Judah to unfaithful brides. Of course, Hosea and Gomer immediately come to mind, but other prophets have developed a similar notion of Israel and YHWH's relationship. Jeremiah, for example, notes the cultic harlotries practiced by both Israel and Judah (see Jer 2:20, 3:13), while Isaiah compares Jerusalem to a harlot (זונה; 1:21) due to covenant violations. Also, Jeremiah notes the accoutrements and attire of a bride in relation to Judah (Jer 2:32), which Ezekiel elaborates on (16:10–18). Finally, the association of Judah with harlotries coupled with the stripping and nakedness motif finds an earlier connection to Nahum and his prophecy against Assyria (see esp. Nah 3:4–6). It is clear that a precedent had been set before the period of Ezekiel to present Israel and Judah in negative caricatures of a harlot and all the repugnant associations that accompanied such a metaphor. However, Ezekiel develops this metaphor well beyond that of his contemporary Jeremiah and his predecessors. Ezekiel's message and approach while repulsive to many interpreters, meshed historically with similar prophetic perspectives.

Ezekiel 23

In chap. 23, our final text, Ezekiel again presents Israel's history in allegorical form. The content of this chapter follows closely to that of chap. 16, the difference being that here in chap. 23 the prophet focuses on Israel's history from an angle of political intrigues. This chapter is much like chap. 20 in that it denies any positive retelling of Israel's history and begins with a historical retrospection in the land of Egypt. In Ezekiel 23, the prophet separates Jerusalem and Samaria into two separate entities (which he labels "sisters") with the names Oholibah and Oholah, respectively (see also Jer 3:6–11). Ezekiel begins with the "elder" of the two sisters and rehearses Samaria's alliances with Assyria, which ended in its destruction and exile in 722 B.C.E. (see vv. 5–10). Because his focus is on Judah, this truncated history of the Northern Kingdom serves comparative needs only (see v. 11).[56] For example, in both the Deuteronomistic

---

56. Although laconic, this brief history highlights the main political interactions which brought down the Northern Kingdom.

History and several prophetic texts, the Northern Kingdom had gone after foreign gods (e.g., 1 Kgs 16:30–32 and 1 Kings 18) and had made alliances with foreign nations (e.g., Hos 7:11, 9:1–9; 1 Kgs 20:34; Isaiah 7; Jeremiah 2). These political intrigues and idolatrous actions had been denounced by the prophets of those generations, and now Ezekiel uses these former acts of Oholah as an object lesson for her younger sister Oholibah.

Ezekiel's use of the political analogy appears to reflect the warnings of Hosea to the Northern Kingdom at an earlier period in the divided monarchy (see Hosea 9). The female imagery of Hosea 9 along with the singling out of Assyria and Egypt as "lovers" reinforces this conclusion. Ezekiel here plays on these earlier prophetic warnings of ill-founded alliances with Assyria and Egypt as a means of indicting Judah for their refusal to learn from her sister. Furthermore, Ezekiel's contemporary Jeremiah had also used the political waywardness of Israel as an object lesson for instructing Judah (see Jer 2:14–18; 3:6–12). Thus, in vv. 11–21 the prophet relates the long history of Oholibah's similar political intrigues with Assyria, Egypt, and Babylon followed by a list of soon-to-be enacted punishments (vv. 21–49).

In vv. 11–21, the prophet's rendition of the past seems closely equated to the actual political dealings between the kings of Judah and the surrounding superpowers during the eighth to the sixth centuries B.C.E. For this section we will begin our analysis by examining Judah's political posturing with Assyria and Egypt and end with Babylon, the most difficult of the three.

We first encounter Judah's direct rebellion in forging a political alliance with Assyria during the reign of Ahaz (741–722 B.C.E.) and the prophetic ministry of Isaiah. Ahaz's fear of the Syro-Ephraimite coalition caused him to seek an alliance with Assyria's Tiglath-pileser III (2 Kgs 16:7; 2 Chronicles 28) despite warnings from Isaiah against such a pact (Isaiah 7).[57] Judah's vassalage to Assyria would continue in some form until Assyria's final defeat at Carchemish in 605 B.C.E. Interestingly, Ezekiel does not mention Hezekiah's rebellion against Assyria at the behest of Isaiah in 701 B.C.E., nor does he note the salvation of Jerusalem by YHWH when Sennacherib attempted to take the city at that time (2 Kgs 18:13; 19; 2 Chronicles 32; Isaiah 36; 37). This may have been due to the historical ambiguity of the failed siege.[58]

---

57. According to 2 Kgs 16:10–18, Ahaz built a pagan altar in the temple and remodeled aspects of the temple furniture due to Assyrian influence.

58. Isa 1:5–8 seems to reflect the desolation of the land by Sennacherib, whereby Jerusalem is left as a "flag" on a hill. See G. W. Grogan, *Isaiah* (Expositor's Bible Com-

In the case of Egypt, Ezekiel's message again appears "historically" accurate. Egypt had always been the go-to nation for Israel when it sought protection against northern aggressors in the Levant. Throughout the later period of Judah's existence as a nation, Egypt had been an inviting prospect to rely on for security from Babylon and Assyria. However, every prophet who prophesied during the period of these political dealings warned Judah's rulers against such an action. Isaiah (see Isaiah 30; 31), Jeremiah (Jeremiah 37; 43; 44), and Ezekiel all warned against these ill-fated endeavors (Ezek 17:15).[59] In this recitation of Israel's past, it appears that the prophet is highlighting the strong political pull Egypt had over the nation from its inception.[60] Indeed one need only look at the wilderness generation to note the constant desire of the people to return to a life of captivity (Exod 17:3; Num 11:5, 18–20; 14:3–4; 20:5; 21:5; Deut 1:27; Neh 9:17), captivity which would later be reflected in vassal alliances. Ezekiel's constant reiteration of this specific alliance and Judah's dalliances with Egypt can only be attributed to the immediate context of Zedekiah's desire to rid himself of Yhwh's "servant," Nebuchadnezzar.[61] Because Judah refused to listen to Yhwh's voice through the prophets, but instead tried to ward off the hardships and certainty of imposed exile, Ezekiel once again reaffirms the veracity of Yhwh's wrath and of the coming destruction of Jerusalem.

Finally, Ezekiel's reference to the political alliances with Babylon creates the most problems in this text (23:14–17). Aside from the possible allusion to Hezekiah's interaction with Merodach-baladan (2 Kgs 20:12–15; Isaiah 39), no clear reference is made in the OT to Judah sending envoys to Babylon to seek help (v. 16).[62] Furthermore, one of the key problems with Ezekiel's presentation concerning political alliances with Babylon is that Zedekiah, as do his predecessors, constantly tries to break away from

---

mentary 6; Grand Rapids: Zondervan, 1986) 30. Historically, we know that Judah remained a vassal state of Assyria throughout this period into the reign of Manasseh, Hezekiah's son. In the annals of Esarhaddon, Manasseh is mentioned by name among 12 vassal kings. See R. Borger, *Die Inschriften Asarhaddons Königs Assyrien* (AfOB 9; Graz, Austria: E. Weidner, 1956) 60, §27: Nin. Episode 21 line 55b lists "*Me-na-si-i šàr* ᵘʳᵘ*Ia-ú-di*" among vassal kings paying tribute to Assyria.

59. For a discussion, see P. S. Evans, *The Invasion of Sennacherib in the Book of Kings: A Source-Critical and Rhetorical Study of 2 Kings 18–19* (VTSup 125; Leiden: Brill, 2009).

60. Even before the nation left Egypt, Yhwh knew that Israel would not desire to remain free if they immediately encountered war; see Exod 13:17.

61. So too Darr, "Justifications," 108.

62. There may be implicit reference to a treaty between Josiah and Nabopolassar in 2 Kgs 23:29 and 2 Chr 35:20. See Zimmerli, *Ezekiel 1–24*, 486.

Nebuchadnezzar.⁶³ But both Jeremiah and Ezekiel warn against actions of this sort (Jer 20:4; 21; 25; 27; Ezekiel 17; etc.). Some of the tension may be resolved in Ezekiel's case if in fact Zedekiah had sworn an oath of allegiance to Nebuchadnezzar in the name of Yhwh. This appears to have indeed been the case.⁶⁴ Thus, Yhwh required an honoring of the treaty despite Zedekiah's attempts to break it. Furthermore, because Judah's time for judgment had arrived, Nebuchadnezzar became the "servant" of Yhwh in this process (Jer 25:9; 27:6; 43:10; Ezek 21:19–22).

In the second half of chap. 23 (vv. 22–49), Ezekiel moves away from a historical recitation in order to present a declaration of future punishment and the accompanying harshness associated with conquest and overthrow. Throughout this section, the prophet alludes to past cultic corruptions such as spiritual adultery and child sacrifice (23:37, 39) while interspersing them with the common prophetic motifs of stripping and nakedness (23:26, 29—see discussion on chaps. 16 and 20 above). It is in this section of prophetic utterance that Ezekiel steps outside the canonical "world" and invokes ancient Near Eastern realities of war and conquest coupled with the punishments reserved for spousal unfaithfulness (see 23:24–26, 45, 47).⁶⁵ While Ezekiel may adopt punishments not mentioned in the earlier accounts of the Law, he is nonetheless accurate to the historical context of his day.

Conclusion

The three texts that we have examined all have a common focus on Israel's negative history, and yet each presents that history from a slightly nuanced perspective. Canonically, chaps. 16, 20, and 23 of Ezekiel offer an incessant negative perspective of Israel's history where the Deuteronomistic Historian, the psalmists, and other prophets tended to balance the negative features with some form of hope and reassurance. In this vein, Ezekiel's negative recitation of history in the three chapters we examined is tempered with messages of hope in diminishing fashion until chap. 23

---

63. E.g., Jehoiakim's rebellion, which brought about the 597 b.c.e. exile (2 Kgs 24:1).

64. See G. E. Mendenhall, "Puppy and Lettuce in Northwest–Semitic Covenant Making," *BASOR* 133 (1954) 26–30. At p. 30 n. 16, Mendenhall points out Zedekiah's implied taking of an oath in the name of Yhwh before Nebuchadnezzar. Also, H. Tadmor, "Treaty and Oath in the Near East," in *Humanizing America's Iconic Book: Society of Biblical Literature Centennial Addresses 1980* (ed. G. M. Tucker and D. A. Knight; SBLBSNA 6; Chico, CA: Scholars Press, 1982) 149–52.

65. See p. 308 n. 54 above.

where no reassurance is offered (see 16:53–54, 60–63 and 20:40–42). Fittingly, chap. 23 precedes the parable of the boiling pot (24:3–14) and the prophecy of Jerusalem's fall (see 24:25). Ezekiel's historical recitations capped by chap. 23 serve as a crescendo to the indictments of the nation in chaps. 13–24.

I began this essay by asking simply *why* Ezekiel revised the history of his people. Throughout, I have tried to answer this query while examining whether or not this revision was accurate to the other accounts of Israel's past found in the biblical text. It appears that what is recorded, for the most part, can be traced to some recognizable negative facet of Israel's past recorded by others throughout the Hebrew Bible. There can be no doubt that Ezekiel knew of a more "balanced" history of his nation but opted for a retrospection focused on the negative as opposed to the positive. We have discovered that Ezekiel's penchant for stressing the negative appears rooted in his greater purposes and the prophet's very call (see 3:3–9). He was called to deliver a message to a people who were thickheaded (חזקי מצח), hard-hearted (קשי לב), and had foreheads (מצחות) harder than flint (חזק מצר; see 3:7–9).[66] Ezekiel's purposes merited an innovative approach to the task, one that would bring into stark relief a predominant pattern of rebellion and sin throughout Israel's history.[67] According to the prophet, it was only the grace and sovereignty of Yhwh that had brought the nation into the land in the first place. Furthermore, it would be a similar act of grace that would effect an end to the exile and bring about a second return to the "promised land."[68] Ezekiel therefore needed to select specific aspects of Israel's past in order to highlight these unmerited acts of grace. The exilic community had failed to recognize these previous deeds, or for that matter, to acknowledge their own complicity in bringing about the predicament they found themselves in. As Davis comments,

> however just the punishment of exile may be, that in itself cannot bring Israel to self-recognition and thus to repentance. Only God's *prior* act of deliverance from the effects of sin makes it possible for Israel to stand at some critical distance from its own conduct. Encouraged by the demonstration of God's undeserved favor, the nation can begin to make proper

---

66. Note also Ezekiel's use of "heart of stone" (לב האבן) in 36:26.
67. See Ezek 2:3, 5–8; 3:9, 26, 27; 12:2, 3, 9, 25; 17:12; 24:3, for references to the "rebellious" house motif.
68. Lust asserts that Ezekiel's rendition of history is radically different from the earlier sources because the prophet felt the true exodus, entry into the promised land, and kingship, had not yet been established—it was still a futuristic event ("Ez., XX, 4–26," 527).

use of its memory by entering into honest assessment of the past and assuming full responsibility for what it has done.⁶⁹

Ezekiel has therefore utilized a selective revision of Israel's history for a greater purpose. Yes, to show that Israel was indeed culpable for their current state of affairs but more importantly, to demonstrate that the God who had sworn to their forefathers to give them the land and the God with whom they had entered into covenant in the wilderness, was indeed sovereign and in full control of their destiny, whether past or present. For Ezekiel, history is only the game board on which this reality was played out, a history inundated with sin, rebellion, and defiance of the greater purposes of Yhwh. Even now as the nation pondered their predicament and the words of Ezekiel, they once again resorted to old familiar methods of dealing with their God, namely, rebellion (Ezek 20:32). In Ezekiel's world this could not stand; Israel's history may have been pockmarked with rebellion, but Yhwh would have the final say, "with a strong hand and a mighty arm and with wrath poured out, I will be king over you!" (20:33).

---

69. Davis, *Swallowing the Scroll*, 115, emphasis original.

The Ordering of the Twelve as Israel's Historiography

GRACE KO

In the past two decades, the study of the Twelve has focused on the debate about whether the twelve Minor Prophets should be read as a book of the Twelve or as twelve individual books. Proponents of the former do not suggest abandoning reading the Twelve as individual books, but rather advocate that reading the Twelve as a whole provides a canonical perspective and supplements insights that might be missed by reading the books individually.[1] They also tend to pay attention to the redactional processes and seek to reconstruct the redactional history of the Book of the Twelve.[2] Paul House is one of the few scholars who take a literary approach rather than a historical redactional approach.[3]

Building on the work of those who read the Twelve as a literary whole, particularly House's work, this essay seeks to discern if the ordering of the Twelve in the Masoretic Text can shed new light on Israel's historiography. As a case in point, it examines the placement of Habakkuk in the Book of the Twelve to see how it fits in the bigger picture of the history of Israel.

In this essay, I intend to use a synchronic approach and begin looking for possible literary clues that link the Twelve together and warrant reading them as a literary whole. Then I discuss the sequence of the Twelve

---

Author's note: I wish to thank Professors Marion Taylor, John Kessler, and Mark Boda for reading and commenting on a draft of this essay. Their insightful comments are invaluable to me, and I am solely responsible for any mistakes that remain.

1. For a concise summary of the recent literature on reading the Twelve as a whole, see P. L. Redditt ("Recent Research on the Book as One Book," *CurBS* 9 [2002] 47–80). For an opposing view, see E. Ben Zvi ("Is the Twelve Hypothesis Likely from an Ancient Readers' Perspective?" in *Two Sides of a Coin: Juxtaposing Views on Interpreting the Book of the Twelve/the Twelve Prophetic Books* [E. Ben Zvi and J. D. Nogalski; Analecta Gorgiana 201; Piscataway, NJ: Gorgias, 2009] 47–96).

2. Ben Zvi questions the reliability and certainty of the redactional reconstructions proposed by scholars. He also argues that ancient readers would not have been concerned with the redactional history of the books. See ibid., 58–63.

3. P. R. House, *The Unity of the Twelve* (JSOTSup 97; Sheffield: Sheffield Academic Press, 1990).

to find out whether the ordering demonstrates the final editor's intentionality.[4] I then examine the placement of Habakkuk in the Twelve to show how it fits in the overall plot of the Twelve and how it contributes to the historiographical record of Israel's exile and restoration found in the Twelve. Last, I draw a conclusion from the above investigation to show how the Book of the Twelve as a whole presents Israel's historiographical record of the period from the eighth century B.C.E. to the Persian Period.

The Unity of the Twelve

While no one denies that the Book of the Twelve is a collection of twelve prophetic books bearing the names of the prophets who purport to have written them,[5] scholars have long noticed signs of editorial activity,[6] which suggest that the Twelve be read as a literary whole.[7] Literary techniques such as *inclusio*, repetition of phrases, catchwords, motifs, and themes are employed to link them into a composite unity.[8]

---

4. Here the final editor is taken as a collective singular. Recently, Nogalski ("One Book and Twelve Books: The Nature of the Redactional Work and the Implications of Cultic Source Material in the Book of the Twelve," in *Two Sides of a Coin: Juxtaposing Views on Interpreting the Book of the Twelve / the Twelve Prophetic Books* [E. Ben Zvi and J. D. Nogalski; Analecta Gorgiana 201; Piscataway, NJ: Gorgias, 2009] 11–46) identifies a group of Levites, who were associated with the Jerusalem temple during the later part of the Persian Period, as the final editors.

5. Ben Zvi avers that the Twelve were preserved as one scroll since antiquity but questions its unity and sees little evidence that it is intended to be read as a whole. He contends that the most significant internal evidence is the titles of the twelve prophetic books which set them apart as individual books, just like Isaiah or Jeremiah or Ezekiel. See his essay "Twelve Prophetic Books or 'The Twelve': A Few Preliminary Considerations," in *Forming Prophetic Literature: Essays on Isaiah and the Twelve in Honor of John D. W. Watts* (ed. J. W. Watts and P. R. House; JSOTSup 235; Sheffield: Sheffield Academic Press, 1996) 125–56.

6. Even Ben Zvi does not deny that redactional activity took place in prophetic literature, but he doubts whether one can reconstruct the redactional layers. Also he focuses on the reader, not the redactor. See "Is the Twelve Hypothesis," 63.

7. Most contemporary scholars read the Book of the Twelve as a literary unit. For some of the scholarly works in this area, see J. W. Watts and P. R. House, eds., *Forming Prophetic Literature: Essays on Isaiah and the Twelve in Honor of John D. W. Watts* (JSOTSup 235; Sheffield: Sheffield Academic Press, 1996); J. D. Nogalski and M. A. Sweeney, eds., *Reading and Hearing the Book of the Twelve* (SBLSymS 15; Atlanta: Society of Biblical Literature, 2000); P. L. Redditt and A. Schart, eds., *Thematic Threads in the Book of the Twelve* (BZAW 325; Berlin: de Gruyter, 2003). For a canonical view of the Twelve, see C. R. Seitz, *Prophecy and Hermeneutics: Toward a New Introduction to the Prophets* (Studies in Theological Interpretation; Grand Rapids: Baker, 2007) 195–219.

8. Nogalski observes that there are at least five types of intertextuality in the Book of the Twelve: quotations, allusions, catchwords, motifs, and framing devices. See the

It is at the seams between individual books that one sees clearly traces of unifying literary techniques. For instance, Joel 4:16[3:16] (cf. Hos 11:10), "The Lord will roar from Zion, and from Jerusalem he will give his voice," is repeated at Amos 1:2, the book that follows Joel. Another deliberate link between Joel and Amos is the portrayal of the fertility of the land in the day when God's people are restored in Joel 4:18[3:18] and Amos 9:13.[9] Similarly, at the end of Amos (9:12), "Edom" is mentioned (cf. Joel 4:19[3:19]) and then picked up by Obadiah (Obad 1). Both Jonah (4:2) and Micah (7:18) end with partial quotations from Exod 34:6–7, while Nahum, which follows Micah, begins with God's character as portrayed in the Exodus 34 passage (Nah 1:2–3; cf. Exod 34:6–7, 14). The command given in Hab 2:20 that the earth is to keep silent (הס) before the Lord is repeated in Zeph 1:7 and Zech 2:17[2:13].[10]

Other literary links in the Book of the Twelve include agricultural motifs of the fertility and famine of the land and locust imagery.[11] Nogalski points out that the famine and fertility of the land serve as God's judgment and restoration, and that locust imagery suggests both natural calamity and foreign invasion.[12] Themes such as judgment and restoration of God's people, the Day of the Lord, and theodicy also serve as threads that bind the books together.[13] These and other literary devices argue for reading the Twelve as a complex, yet unified whole.

---

detailed discussion in his essay, "Intertextuality in the Twelve," in *Forming Prophetic Literature: Essays on Isaiah and the Twelve in Honor of John D. W. Watts* (ed. J. W. Watts and P. R. House; JSOTSup 235; Sheffield: Sheffield Academic Press, 1996) 102–24.

9. Nogalski mentions that by reading these two links between Joel and Amos synchronically, Joel then "effectively encompasses the beginning and end of Amos." See his essay, "One Book and Twelve Books," 12.

10. For a summary of Nogalski's study on catchwords between the Twelve, see P. L. Redditt, "The Formation of the Book of the Twelve: A Review of Research," in *Thematic Threads in the Book of the Twelve* (ed. P. L. Redditt and A. Schart; BZAW 325; Berlin: de Gruyter, 2003) 1–26.

11. Agricultural motifs such as grain, wine, oil, wool, linen, vine, figs, olive, food, and so on abound in the Twelve, e.g., Hosea 2, 14; Joel 1:2–2:17; 4:19; Amos 4:6–11, 9:13–14; Hab 3:17; Hag 1:6, 10–11; 2:15–19; Zech 8:12; Mal 3:8–11. For the significance of the land theme in the Twelve, see also L. J. Braaten, "God Sows: Hosea's Land Theme in the Book of the Twelve," in *Thematic Threads in the Book of the Twelve* (ed. P. L. Redditt and A. Schart; BZAW 325; Berlin: de Gruyter, 2003)104–32.

12. J. D. Nogalski, "Recurring Themes in the Book of the Twelve: Creating Points of Contact for a Theological Reading," *Int* 61 (2007) 125–36.

13. *Day of the Lord*: D. L. Petersen, who refuses to call the Twelve a book, nevertheless suggests the Day of the Lord as the thematic thread of the Twelve. He also notes that this theme is present explicitly in all of the Twelve except Jonah and Nahum (Hos 9:5, Joel 3:4, Amos 5:18–20, Obad 15, Mic 2:4, Hab 3:16, Zeph 1:7–16, Hag 2:23, Zech 14:1, and Mal 3:19; and implicitly in Nah 1:7). See his essay, "A Book of the

The Ordering of the Twelve Minor Prophets

Ben Zvi notes that there are five different sequences of the twelve books, and that the diverse orderings of the twelve books undermines the hypothesis that the Twelve is supposed to be read as a single book.[14] However, the diverse sequences may reflect the redactors' and translators' theological concerns[15] and their understanding of the Twelve as a whole.[16]

Chronology as an Ordering Principle

Chronology plays an important part in the positioning of the writings of the Twelve. Several dated superscriptions and incipits located strategically in the Twelve give a rough chronological framework from the eighth century B.C.E. to the Persian period.[17] These dated superscriptions and

---

Twelve?" in *Reading and Hearing the Book of the Twelve* (ed. J. D. Nogalski and M. A. Sweeney; SBLSymS 15; Atlanta: Society of Biblical Literature, 2000) 3–10.

Theodicy: Van Leeuwen notices that the scribal redactors use Exod 34:6–7 as a base text to elaborate a theodicy in the first six books of the Twelve. He also shows its use in the naming of Hosea's children in Hosea 1–2; Joel 2:13; Jonah 4:2; Mic 7:18–20; and Nah 1:2–3. See his essay, "Scribal Wisdom and Theodicy in the Book of the Twelve," in *In Search of Wisdom: Essays in Memory of John G. Gammie* (ed. L. G. Perdue, B. B. Scott, and W. J. Wiseman; Louisville: Westminster John Knox, 1993) 31–49. For the theme of theodicy in the Twelve, see also J. L. Crenshaw, "Theodicy in the Book of the Twelve," in *Thematic Threads in the Book of the Twelve* (ed. P. L. Redditt and A. Schart; BZAW 325; Berlin: de Gruyter, 2003) 175–91.

Nogalski identifies four themes that provide a lens for reading the book of the Twelve as a composite unity: the Day of the Lord, the fertility of the land, the fate of God's people, and theodicy. For a detailed discussion, see, "Recurring Themes," 125–36.

14. Ben Zvi, "Twelve Prophetic Books," 134.

15. M. A. Sweeney, "Sequence and Interpretation in the Book of the Twelve," in *Reading and Hearing the Book of the Twelve* (ed. J. D. Nogalski and M. A. Sweeney; SBLSymS 15; Atlanta: Society of Biblical Literature, 2000) 49–64.

16. A. Schart, "Reconstructing the Redaction History of the Twelve Prophets: Problems and Models," in *Reading and Hearing the Book of the Twelve* (ed. J. D. Nogalski and M. A. Sweeney; SBLSymS 15; Atlanta: Society of Biblical Literature, 2000) 34–48.

17. J. D. W. Watts defines an incipit as "a sentence which begins a narrative or a narrative book," and a superscription as "a title, sometimes expanded, over a book, a portion of a book, or a poem." See his essay "Superscriptions and Incipits in the Book of the Twelve," in *Reading and Hearing the Book of the Twelve* (ed. J. D. Nogalski and M. A. Sweeney; SBLSymS 15; Atlanta: Society of Biblical Literature, 2000) 110–24. According to the superscriptions, the three eighth-century prophets are Hosea, Amos, and Micah, and the seventh-century prophet is Zephaniah; whereas the incipits in Haggai and Zechariah put them in the Persian Period. In addition, Nogalski argues that Jonah, Nahum, Habakkuk, and Malachi also owe their location to the chronological framework. See Nogalski, "One Book and Twelve Books," 12–13.

incipits indicate that the editor of the Twelve intended to put them in a historical framework so as to provide the reader with contours of Israel's history to understand better the messages of the prophets.[18]

While chronology is one of the principles that determine the positioning of the Twelve, the chronological order of the Twelve is only a rough approximation. For example, chronologically, most scholars favor the primacy of Amos. The superscription of Amos situates him in the reign of the Judean king Uzziah (783–742 B.C.E.) and the Israelite king Jeroboam ben Joash (786–746 B.C.E.), while the historical setting of Hosea ranges from 786 B.C.E. (Jeroboam's reign) through 687/6 B.C.E. (Hezekiah's reign). Hence, chronologically Amos is prior to Hosea. More troublesome is the placement of Joel after Hosea, for Joel, which lacks a historical superscription, is routinely dated to the Persian period.[19] Other factors such as the length of the text, catchwords and comparable material at the seams of the books also play a role in the ordering of the books.[20]

Narrative Unity Following a U-Shaped Comedy Framework

Sweeney explains that, while each prophetic book is distinct in terms of its content and literary communication, its placement within the Twelve subsumes its communicative autonomy and changes its communicative functions and outlook to that of the book as a whole.[21] Thus, the overall arrangement of the Twelve affects not only how the individual prophets are heard but also the theological emphasis of the final editor.

House proposes that the positioning of the twelve books highlights the main points of the prophetic message, which are: the sin of Israel and the nations (Hosea–Micah), the punishment of the sin (Nahum–Zephaniah), and the restoration of both from that sin (Haggai–Malachi).[22] He further observes that the plot of the Twelve forms a U-shaped comic framework:[23]

---

18. They also provide important clues for the redactional reconstruction. For example, the similarities among the four dated superscriptions in Hosea, Amos, Micah, and Zephaniah prompt some scholars to group them together as a Deuteronomistic Corpus. Meanwhile, Haggai–Zechariah 1–8 also exhibits editorial connections. See ibid., 14–16.

19. Petersen, "A Book of the Twelve," 6.

20. Ibid., 6.

21. Sweeney, "Sequence and Interpretation," 56.

22. House, *Unity of the Twelve*, 68. See the charts for the structure of the Twelve on p. 72.

23. Comedy usually portrays a hero overcoming obstacles to come to a positive resolution and is best represented by a U. The main character in a comedy may slide to the bottom but will ultimately triumph and rise to the top. The history of Israel as portrayed in the Twelve is a comedy because of its hopeful future. The opposite of comedy

the fortune of Israel and other nations begins with Hosea and spirals downward until it hits the lowest point at Habakkuk, then starts to inch upward to Malachi.[24]

House's scheme is not without criticism: Schart calls it "too imprecise," for all three elements—sin, punishment, and restoration—are present in each book.[25] Ben Zvi accuses House of minimizing the hope marker in the individual books such as Hosea, Joel, Amos, and Micah in order to promote the overall plot of the Book of the Twelve.[26] Mark Boda accuses him of discounting the sin/punishment markers in the Haggai–Malachi sections.[27] Redditt suggests that the Twelve consists of a double plot developing the dual theme of progress (comedy) and regress (tragedy).[28]

Despite these criticisms, House's proposal of a U-shaped comic plot for the Book of the Twelve seems to fit the historical context: the fate of Israel and Judah spiraled down from the mid-eighth century (Hosea–Micah) to the darkest period of universal mayhem during the late-seventh to early-sixth century B.C.E., especially after the death of Josiah in 609 B.C.E. (Nahum–Zephaniah);[29] then the restoration came during the Persian period with the return of the Exile and the rebuilding of the temple (Haggai–Malachi).[30] Donald E. Gowan observes that there is a clustering of the prophetic books around the three key moments in Israel's history,

---

is tragedy, which involves taking a hero, who possesses better quality than others, from glory to defeat. Tragedy is usually represented by an inverted *U*. See ibid., 113–14.

24. Ibid., 123–24.

25. Schart, "Reconstructing the Redaction History," 39.

26. Ben Zvi, "Twelve Prophetic Books," 128.

27. M. J. Boda, "Messengers of Hope in Haggai-Malachi," *JSOT* 32 (2007) 113–31.

28. Redditt, "The Formation of the Book of the Twelve," 6.

29. A. J. Everson suggests that both the location of Habakkuk in the Book of the Twelve and the theme of the Day of the Lord indicate that Habakkuk was remembered in conjunction with the tragic death of Josiah in 609 B.C.E. See his essay, "The Canonical Location of Habakkuk," in *Thematic Threads in the Book of the Twelve* (ed. P. L. Redditt and A. Schart; BZAW 325; Berlin: de Gruyter, 2003) 165–74.

30. Here restoration is not to say that the postexilic community did not have their share of problems and difficulties. Rather, it shows that Yahweh's promise of restoration was partially fulfilled as it pertains to the return of the remnants and that the community is a people of Yahweh, notwithstanding their internal disputes and disappointments and their struggle to keep the relationship with Yahweh and the hope of salvation alive. Some of the problems facing the postexilic community are recorded in Zechariah and Malachi, for example, the wicked leadership in Zech 10:1–3a; 11:1–3, 4–17; 13:7–9; Mal 2:1–4, 8; the issue of sin and idolatry in Zech 5:3–4, 6–8; 7:8–10; 8:16–17; 13:1–2; Mal 2:11; the threat of foreign power in Zech 13:7–8; 14:1–2. I will discuss later how these three books could be on the upswing of the comic plot.

namely, the fall of Samaria in 722 B.C.E., the fall of Jerusalem in 587 B.C.E., and Cyrus' Decree in 538 B.C.E.[31] His observation confirms the *U*-shaped comic plot of Israel's history, which the Twelve helps to portray.

A brief description of the positioning of the Twelve is in order. The choice of Hosea as the introduction of the Twelve is to depict the covenant between Yahweh and his people within a familial setting: the marriage bond between a husband and wife, the relationship between parents and their children.[32] This is the closest circle for a person. Yahweh portrays himself as a husband betrayed by his unfaithful wife (Israel) to illustrate the hurt he endures (Hos 3:1) and to make the indictment against Israel of breaking the covenant by worshiping idols that much more poignant (Hos 2:2, 5). Idol worshiping is the primary sin for it breaks the first three commandments of the Decalogue (Exod 20:2–5a). Furthermore, the lack of "knowledge of God," which is the direct result of idol worshiping, is regarded as the root cause for all social sins and crimes committed by the Israelites against each other (Hos 4:1).[33] God then calls the people to repent and offer divine forgiveness and restoration (Hos 3:4–5, 14:2–10[14:1–9]). Thus, this sets the tone for the rest of the Twelve.[34]

The placement of Joel after Hosea focuses intentionally on the centrality of Jerusalem, as well as the outworking of the program set by Hosea, that is, repentance brings restoration.[35] Joel calls for repentance after a

---

31. See table 2 in his book, *Theology of the Prophetic Books: The Death and Resurrection of Israel* (Louisville: Westminster John Knox, 1998) 8.

32. Watts sees that Hosea 1–3 and Malachi function as a frame for the Book of the Twelve because they both use domestic relations to tell "the theme of the love of God for Israel." See his essay "A Frame for the Book of the Twelve: Hosea 1–3 and Malachi," in *Reading and Hearing the Book of the Twelve* (ed. J. D. Nogalski and M. A. Sweeney; SBLSymS 15; Atlanta: Society of Biblical Literature, 2000) 209–17. G. Baumann also recognizes marriage in Hosea 1–3 and Malachi as the framing theme in the Book of the Twelve to portray "the love of God and the response from the Israelites." See her essay, "Connected by Marriage, Adultery and Violence: The Prophetic Marriage Metaphor in the Book of the Twelve and in the Major Prophets," in *Society of Biblical Literature 1999 Seminar Papers* (SBLSP 38; Atlanta: Society of Biblical Literature, 1999) 552–69.

33. For more specific charges against Israel, see Hos 4:1–14. Amos takes it even further, specifying many universal crimes committed by humanity in his book.

34. Sweeney calls Hosea a "programmatic introduction" to the Twelve ("Sequence and Interpretation," 56).

35. Sweeney thinks that the MT places the two programmatic books (Hosea and Joel) at the beginning of the Twelve: Hosea deals with the disrupted relationship between Israel and the Lord and calls for Israel's repentance while Joel outlines the threat posed against Israel by a foreign nation and envisions the defeat of the enemy and the restoration of Jerusalem in the Day of the Lord. See ibid., 59.

serious plague in Judah, which he attributes to divine judgment.[36] His ministry seems to be successful, for a salvation oracle is pronounced (Joel 2:19–27).[37] He ends the book with the judgment of the nations and the roaring of the Lord from Zion to protect his people (cf. Hos 11:10).

Amos is regarded as the earliest prophetic book written within the Twelve, but it is placed canonically after Joel. The reason for this may be that, in Joel, there is still a chance for repentance (Joel 2:12–27), while in Amos, Israel seems to have forfeited the opportunity and, hence, judgment is inevitable (Amos 7:7–9, 8:3–9:4).[38] The rejection of the prophetic message by Amaziah seals the fate of the Northern Kingdom (Amos 7:10–17).[39] Thus, the editor of Amos resumes the catchword of the "roaring of the Lord" from the previous book and picks up the theme of the sins of the nations and Israel to portray the spiraling down of Israel's fate. However, judgment would never have the last word, because Yahweh's judgment always has the purpose of bringing Israel back, so Amos ends with the restoration of Israel and Edom (9:11–15).

The mention of Edom at the beginning and end of Amos (1:11–12, 9:12; cf. Joel 4:19[3:19]) anticipates Obadiah. Obadiah continues the plot with an accusation against Edom for its aloofness and lack of compassion toward Judah (vv. 11–14). The placement of Obadiah after Amos also serves as an elaboration of the sins of the nations described in Amos 1:3–2:3. Edom is singled out because of its relationship with Israel: Edom, the descendants of Esau, is Israel's brother (Amos 1:11, Obad 10). The familial motif serves to emphasize Edom's sin against Judah.

While Obadiah indicts Edom for its cruelty toward Judah, Jonah shows the aloofness of Israel (in the person of Jonah) and Jonah's lack of compassion toward a foreign nation (Assyria). Jonah's story demonstrates that God desires sinners to repent—even a wicked nation such as Assyria is given a chance to repent; how much more he would wish Israel to heed his voice and repent. Also, while Nineveh is given only 40 days to repent and

---

36. R. Simkins opines that Joel's call for the people to "return to Yahweh" is not a call to repentance because no specific sin is mentioned in Joel. Rather, it is a call to honor Yahweh by participating in proper acts of mourning appropriate to their suffering of natural catastrophe. See his article "'Return to Yahweh': Honor and Shame in Joel," *Semeia* 68 (1994) 41–54.

37. Nogalski indicates that while the opportunity to repent "is not explicitly actuated, the promise remains in effect" ("Recurring Themes," 128).

38. Nogalski also notices that "Israel is given a chance to repent at the end of Hosea, but Amos, from the outset, assumes Israel's chance has passed" (ibid., 128).

39. So H. Lalleman-de Winkel, *Jeremiah in Prophetic Tradition: An Examination of the Book of Jeremiah in the Light of Israel's Prophetic Traditions* (CBET 26; Leuven: Peeters, 2000) 237–38.

the Ninevites grasp that opportunity to avert their doom,[40] Israel, from the time of Amos to its exile, is given 40 years to repent before calamity comes, but the people ignore the prophetic warning that resulted in their exile in 722 B.C.E.[41] Moreover, as Julia O'Brien suggests, reading Jonah retrospectively would show that the fall of Nineveh is not due to Yahweh's lack of compassion for other nations.[42] Nineveh's ultimate downfall is due to her own wickedness. Jonah's recital of Yahweh's attributes in 4:2 anticipates both Micah and Nahum.[43]

The historical datum in the superscription of Micah situates it in the second half of the eighth century B.C.E. Micah focuses on the sins of Israel and Judah and their judgment. To Micah, divine judgment seems inescapable, though he tries in vain to stop Judah from following Israel's fate (Mic 1:8–16, 6:16). Though devastation seems imminent, the prophet still gives them hope for the future restoration, based on Yahweh's attributes as proclaimed in Exod 34:6–7 (Mic 7:18–20).

While both Jonah and Micah end with Yahweh's compassion and mercy, Nahum begins with Exod 34:6–7 and prophesies Yahweh's punishment on Nineveh, the destroyer of Israel. This distinctive use of Exod 34:6–7 emphasizes another aspect of Yahweh's attributes—his justice. In Jonah and Micah, Yahweh's mercy is the basis for Nineveh's deliverance and Israel's hope for future restoration; but in Nahum, Yahweh's justice is the reason for Nineveh's downfall. Hence, Yahweh's dual attributes of grace and righteousness as proclaimed in Exod 34:6–7 are manifested in his dealings with Israel and Nineveh. The destruction of Assyria in Nah 3:18–19 then forms a thematic transition to the book of Habakkuk with the coming of Babylon, the destroyer of Assyria.[44]

Habakkuk speaks of the inevitability of the Babylonian invasion but at the same time assures the people of Yahweh's destruction of Babylon.

---

40. The penitent language of the Ninevites in Jonah 3:9, "Who knows? He may relent and have compassion" recalls Joel 2:14. Also both repentant communities receive divine forgiveness (Jonah 3:10, Joel 2:18).

41. Van Leeuwen, "Scribal Wisdom and Theodicy," 45.

42. J. M. O'Brien,"Nahum-Habakkuk-Zephaniah: Reading the 'Former Prophets' in the Persian Period," *Int* 61 (2007) 168–83.

43. Some scholars attribute passages that allude to Exod 34:6–7 (Joel 2:12–14; Jonah 3:9; 4:2; Mic 7:18–20; Nah 1:2b, 3a; Mal 1:9a) to a "grace" redaction layer. See J. Wöhrle, "A Prophetic Reflection on Divine Forgiveness: The Integration of the Book of Jonah into the Book of the Twelve," *JHS* 9 (2009) 1–17; Van Leeuwen, "Scribal Wisdom and Theodicy," 31–49; Seitz, *Prophecy and Hermeneutic*, 216. For a critique of this view, see K. Spronk, "Jonah, Nahum, and the Book of the Twelve: A Response to Jakob Wöhrle," *JHS* 9 (2009) 1–9.

44. Redditt makes a citation error of Mic 7:18–19 instead of Nah 3:18–19 ("The Production and Reading," 15).

Both Nahum and Habakkuk deal with Israel's and Judah's archenemies, Assyria and Babylon, respectively, so it is only logical that both contain a theophanic hymn celebrating Yahweh as divine warrior fighting on behalf of Israel—Nahum begins with a hymn (Nah 1:3b–6) and Habakkuk ends with a hymn (Hab 3:3–15).[45] Duane L. Christensen proposes a chiasmus in the structure of Nahum and Habakkuk:[46]

A. Hymn of Theophany	Nahum 1
B. Taunt Song against Nineveh	Nahum 2–3
X. The Problem of Theodicy	Habakkuk 1
B′. Taunt Song against the Wicked Ones	Habakkuk 2
A′. Hymn of Theophany	Habakkuk 3

These two books also serve to vindicate God's righteousness by punishing the wicked nations, Assyria and Babylon, who are God's instruments to judge Israel and Judah but have overstepped their mandate (cf. Zech 1:15).

The superscription of Zephaniah dates it to the seventh century before the fall of the Judean kingdom. While Nahum and Habakkuk focus on Assyria and Babylon, Zephaniah describes the awesome Day of the Lord when the universal judgment[47] purges the sin of all nations, and ends with a future restoration of Jerusalem with worshipers from all nations. Hence, Zephaniah begins the upward trend of the *U*-shaped narrative arc.

The three postexilic prophets are at the restoration phase of the "comic" framework, because from the perspective of the preexilic prophets, the return of the remnants signals Israel's restoration. The incipits in Haggai (1:1, 15; 2:1, 10, 18, 20) give dates ranging from the 1st day of the 6th month in the second year of King Darius to the 24th day of the 9th month in the same year (August 29–December 18, 520 B.C.E.); and in Zechariah (1:1, 7; 7:1) from the 8th month of the 2nd year of Darius to the 4th day of the 9th month in the 4th year of Darius (October 520–December 7, 518 B.C.E.).[48] Haggai mainly concerns the rebuilding of the temple, which

---

45. For a discussion on the different rhetorical functions of the divine warrior hymn in Nahum and Habakkuk, see O'Brien, "Nahum-Habakkuk-Zephaniah," 177.

46. D. L. Christensen, "The Book of Nahum: A History of Interpretation," in *Forming Prophetic Literature: Essays on Isaiah and the Twelve in Honor of John D. W. Watts* (ed. J. W. Watts and P. R. House; JSOTSup 235; Sheffield: Sheffield Academic Press, 1996) 187–94.

47. The scope of the universal judgment in Zeph 1:2–3 is not just on humanity but also includes all creatures on earth (animals, birds, and fishes), and its description is a reversal of the creation account in Gen 1:20–27.

48. J. W. Rogerson, "Haggai," in *Eerdmans Commentary on the Bible* (ed. J. D. G. Dunn and J. W. Rogerson; Grand Rapids: Eerdmans, 2003) 718–20.

signifies the presence of God and the restoration of the relationship between Yahweh and his people.[49]

Zechariah continues Haggai's plot of the restoration of Jerusalem. He focuses on Yahweh's intervention for Jerusalem: by turning his wrath against the nations (Zech 1:15, 21; cf. 9:1–8), by bringing back the exiles (2:6–9), by eliminating the sins and wickedness of the land (5:1–11), by providing them with a righteous king to save them (9:9–10), and by restoring Jerusalem as God's holy city where Yahweh reigns (14:16–21).[50]

Some scholars contend that the pessimistic elements and darker tone present in Zechariah, especially the shepherd units in 10:1–3a; 11:1–3, 4–17; 13:7–9, and the devastation of the Day of the Lord described in Zech 13:7–14:2, argue against the positive trend of the comic narrative arc.[51] However, the Day of the Lord is depicted as a distant future[52]—the *eschaton*—when the Lord will come to win the final battle and to settle all accounts.[53] This futuristic outlook serves as a warning to those who are bent on sinning, and as a comfort to the suffering righteous. Thus, Zechariah ends on a high note of the restoration and consecration of Jerusalem (14:8–11, 16–21).

Malachi gives a reality check and records six disputations between the prophet and the people (1:2–5, 1:6–2:9, 2:10–16, 2:17–3:5, 3:6–12, 3:13–21[4:3]). As such, Malachi seems to stall the upward trend, but still

---

49. For a discussion on the significance of the editorial framework of the book of Haggai, see R. A. Mason, "The Purpose of the 'Editorial Framework' of the Book of Haggai," *VT* 27 (1977) 413–21.

50. Many scholars see Zechariah as a composite production of chaps. 1–8 and 9–14 and conclude that it has undergone a complex redactional process to come to its present form. For a summary of the history of research, see D. L. Petersen, "Zechariah 9–14," in *ABD* 6:1065–66.

51. The negative tone in Zechariah may be the prophetic reactions to his contemporary situation, that is, the issues of wicked leadership, sin, and idolatry, which need purging.

52. The phrase "in that day" (ביום ההוא), which indicates a futuristic outlook, abounds in Zechariah. This phrase appears 16 times in merely three chapters (Zechariah 12–14).

53. The Day of the Lord, a key theme that runs through the Twelve, could be seen as the Day of Israel's and Judah's calamity (Joel 1:15–2:11, Amos 5:18–20, Obad 10–14, Hab 3:16, Zeph 1:4–18), as well as a future day of *eschaton* (Joel 3:1–5[2:28–32]; 4:1–21[3:1–21]; Amos 9:11–15, Obad 15–21, Mic 4:1–7, Zech 14:1–21, Mal 3:2, 23[4:5]). The preexilic prophets tend to see this day as a national day of calamity and the eschaton as God's bringing back of the exiles and restoring the fortunes of Jerusalem, e.g., in Amos 9:14 (ושבתי את־שבות); cf. Joel 4:1[3:1]. However, due to the disappointing realities in the Persian Period, the postexilic prophets then reiterate the future Day of the Lord to admonish the people.

it provides the Twelve with an open end and a high expectation of the coming of the Lord (3:1). Thus, Haggai, Zechariah, and Malachi witness the faithfulness of the Lord in bringing the people back from the Exile, which is the first step of restoration. Then, the rebuilding of the temple signifies a reestablishment of their relationship with Yahweh. Though their current realities are worse than previously prophesied, these prophets urge their compatriots to keep their covenant with God, and insist that God would one day come to fulfill all of his promises. House points out that Malachi, as the book end of the Twelve, summarizes major themes found in the Book of the Twelve:[54] the emphasis on love and marriage faithfulness reminds the reader of Hosea (Mal 2:11–16);[55] the admonition of priests echoes Joel and Zechariah (Mal 2:1–9); the stressing of the Day of the Lord as a day of punishment links the book with previous books, particularly Amos and Zephaniah (Mal 3:19–21[4:1–3]); finally, Malachi's conclusion ties together the Haggai–Zechariah–Malachi corpus by claiming that all facets of restoration will indeed take place, and that the Messiah will help the restoration.[56]

In sum, this section has argued that the historical data contained in the superscriptions and the incipits help to give the Twelve a rough chronology and to set them in their historical context. Additionally, this section has argued that the narrative schema of the Twelve fits a *U*-shaped comedy framework. Hence, it is obvious that the ordering of the Twelve is a deliberate and careful endeavor to highlight the theological messages that its editor tries to convey, that is, Israel's sin, judgment, repentance, and restoration. Israel's sin brings divine judgment. However, divine judgment is not an end in itself; rather, it calls for repentance. Repentance then leads to restoration. This principle not only applies to Israel but also to the other nations as well so as to affirm Yahweh's sovereignty over all nations.

The Placement of Habakkuk in the Twelve

When the book of the Twelve is read as a composite whole with a *U*-shaped comedy framework, Habakkuk is placed at the lowest point of the *U*; the nadir of the narrative schema, for Judean society is in a state that

---

54. House, *Unity of the Twelve*, 108.
55. Other than the marriage theme, the word *land* in Hos 1:2 and Mal 3:24[4:6] also form an inclusio for the Book of the Twelve. See Braaten, "God Sows," 105.
56. Boda argues that the "messenger of the Lord" (מלאך יהוה) is the *leitmotif* that ties together the Haggai–Zechariah–Malachi corpus. See his "Messengers of Hope in Haggai–Malachi," 113–31.

is beyond repair and the divine judgment through Babylonian invasion seems inevitable.

The dating of Habakkuk's setting is closely related to the identification of the "wicked" and the "righteous" in the book.[57] I concur with the majority of the scholars who see the reign of King Jehoiakim (609–598 B.C.E.) as the most likely period for Habakkuk's ministry.[58] It was a time when Israel's hope of restoration was crushed following the humiliating defeat at Megiddo when Josiah's attempt to stop the Egyptian Pharaoh Neco from assisting the doomed Assyrians resulted in Josiah's death (2 Kgs 23:29–30). Though Neco failed to save Assyria from the Babylonians, on his way back, he deposed Jehoahaz and placed Josiah's other son Jehoiakim on the throne as an Egyptian vassal. Jehoiakim proved to be an unworthy successor of his father. He showed no concern for the misery of his people by taxing them heavily in order to pay for the heavy tribute imposed on Judah (2 Kgs 23:33–35) and by building for himself a new and magnificent palace with forced labor, an act sternly condemned by Jeremiah (Jer 22:13–14, 17).[59] He abolished the religious reform started by Josiah, and let the pagan practices creep back in. He threatened and persecuted the prophets who spoke out against him: Jeremiah had to go into hiding, while another prophet, Uriah, son of Shemaiah was captured and put to death (Jer 26:20–23). Furthermore, Jehoiakim showed no respect for the Lord by cutting up and burning the scrolls that contained Jeremiah's warnings (Jer 36:1–26).

This brief description of Jehoiakim's reign fits the depiction of Judean society in Habakkuk's initial complaint in 1:2–4 perfectly:[60] the prophet

---

57. For a summary of various positions in the 1990s, see O. Dangl, "Habakkuk in Recent Research," *CurBS* 9 (2001) 131–68.

58. Among those who date the book to Jehoiakim's reign are D. W. Baker, *Nahum, Habakkuk, and Zephaniah: An Introduction and Commentary* (TOTC; Leicester: Inter-Varsity, 1988) 44–45; K. L. Barker and W. Bailey, *Micah, Nahum, Habakkuk, Zephaniah* (NAC 20; Nashville: Broadmen & Holman, 1998) 259; O. P. Robertson, *The Books of Nahum, Habakkuk, and Zephaniah* (NICOT; Grand Rapids: Eerdmans, 1990) 36–7; J. J. M. Roberts, *Nahum, Habakkuk, and Zephaniah: A Commentary* (OTL; Louisville: Westminster John Knox, 1991) 63.

59. Jeremiah's woe oracle against Jehoiakim was similar to the second woe oracle pronounced by Habakkuk on the Babylonians in Hab 2:9. This shows that Jehoiakim's crime was known to Habakkuk.

60. Although "the wicked" remain anonymous in 1:2–4, that the "law grows numb," indicates that they are likely members of the Judean community. The reason for the anonymity of the wicked may have been to avoid possible reprisal against the lamenter by the wicked, especially if the wicked are the powerful ones in the community. Some scholars, such as Floyd, Cleaver-Bartholomew, and Prinsloo, view the

uses words such as *violence, iniquity,* and *trouble* and phrases such as, *destruction and violence* and *strife and contention* to describe the mayhem in the society. He also complains that "law grows numb," "justice never goes forth," for "the wicked surrounded the righteous,"[61] and "judgment goes forth perverted." Under such a tyrannical rule, when prophetic warnings were not only rejected but silenced, God's words were blatantly repulsed, social justice was not carried out, murder and persecution of the prophets were ordered and supported by the state, and lamenting to God was the only recourse that was left for the righteous. It is little wonder that the whole book of Habakkuk is set in the form of a lament.[62]

When facing calamity, questions about theodicy usually surface. Thus, it is only appropriate that theodicy is the theme of Habakkuk; and it may also explain the prophet's use of lament to express himself. For in situations when one is in great distress and desperation, lament is the most appropriate language one can use to cry out to the Lord, complain to him, and expect him to give a response. Westermann helpfully pointed out that the cry of distress (and hence the lament) plays an important part in the event of exodus, which leads to the deliverance of the Israelites.[63] This foundational event in Israel's history gives the assurance for God's people that Yahweh hears their lament.[64] Hence, the framework of lament seems to indicate that Habakkuk's setting is during a time of great calamity.

Chaldeans as the "wicked" throughout the book. But this requires rearrangement of the text to fit their conjecture. For their proposals, see M. H. Floyd, "Prophetic Complaints about the Fulfillment of Oracles in Habakkuk 1:2–17 and Jeremiah 15:10–18," *JBL* 110 (1991) 397–418; D. Cleaver-Bartholomew, "An Alternative Approach to Hab 1,2–2,20," *SJOT* 17 (2003) 206–25; G. T. M. Prinsloo, "Habakkuk 1—A Dialogue? Ancient Unit Delimiters in Dialogue with Modern Critical Interpretation," *OTE* 17 (2004) 621–45.

61. The fact that "the wicked surrounded the righteous" is flanked by the failure of justice implies that Habakkuk is concerned about the existential question of the survival of the righteous.

62. Habakkuk is the only prophetic book that uses lament as its overall framework. E. R. Wendland identifies all six elements of a communal lament in the book of Habakkuk; see his "'The Righteous Live by Their Faith' in a Holy God: Complementary Compositional Forces and Habakkuk Dialogue with the Lord," *JETS* 42 (1999) 591–628. Habakkuk also lacks the messenger formula that frequently appears in prophetic books.

63. For the significance of lament in the Old Testament, see C. Westermann, "The Role of the Lament in the Theology of the Old Testament," *Int* 28 (1974) 20–38.

64. Brueggemann thinks that lament concerns a redistribution of power: the lesser petitionary party is given a voice, and his speech is taken seriously and heard by the greater party (God). For a detailed discussion, see his article, "The Costly Loss of Lament," *JSOT* 36 (1986) 57–71.

God's surprise answer—that he is about to bring in the Chaldeans as judgment (1:5–11)[65]—provokes further complaint from Habakkuk, for to him, the coming of the Chaldeans could only bring more grievances to the people who have already suffered greatly. Thus, Habakkuk uses divine attributes to call into question divine actions to show the incongruities between the two (1:12–14). He further complains against the Chaldeans (1:15–17), hoping that it would arouse the compassion of God.

In the midst of great national crisis, Habakkuk stands on the side of the oppressed people and employs the traditional lament cries of "How long?" and "Why?" The book conveys that his cries obviously reach God, for God responds to him (2:2–5). Moreover, by standing on the side of the people, Habakkuk would no doubt gain a wide audience, for he acts as their spokesman before God. While other prophets usually justify divine acts by accusing the people of sinning and by condemning them, Habakkuk is the only prophet who challenges God's rightness of choosing the Chaldeans as an agent to judge Judah. As such, Habakkuk is placed at this juncture of the Twelve to take up an important lacuna in the other prophetic books by presenting, from a humanistic perspective, the existential question and the "theodic protest"[66] of the righteous during the lowest point in Israel's history.

Yahweh's answer in 2:2–5 marks the turning point of the book. This section and the ensuing five woe oracles (2:6–19) against the wicked let the prophet know that though the invasion by the Babylonians is inevitable, Yahweh does have a plan and a final destruction awaits the wicked.[67] Meanwhile, the righteous ones should persevere in their faithfulness (2:4b).[68] The theophany, which portrays Yahweh as a warrior coming to

---

65. The purpose of Yahweh's raising up the Chaldeans is not explicitly mentioned here, but Habakkuk understood this to be God's judgment according to 1:12b, "O Lord, you have set him (שמתו) as a judgment (למשפט), O Rock, you have established him (יסדתו) to requite (להוכיח)." However, Sweeney ("Structure, Genre, and Intent in Habakkuk," *VT* 41 [1991] 63–83) insists that the Chaldeans are raised not as a judgment but as a cause of injustice.

66. A term coined by W. Brueggemann, by which he means the protest against Yahweh for not carrying out the divine justice according to the covenantal promise. See his article "Some Aspects of Theodicy in Old Testament Faith," *PRSt* 26 (1999) 253–68.

67. The recipient of the oracles is not explicitly mentioned; however the content of the oracles reveals that it is likely to be the Babylonians, especially 2:8–9, where plundering of the nations and pillaging of the peoples are mentioned, which fit the descriptions of the Chaldeans in 1:5–11, 15–17. Also, this section addresses the prophet's previous concern that the Chaldeans pillage the nations without ending.

68. There is an ambiguity as to whose faithfulness the writer has in mind in the divine response "But the righteous (וצדיק) in his faithfulness (באמונתו) shall live" (2:4b).

fight for his people (3:3–15), not only provides assurance that God has the power and the passion to see his grand plan accomplished but it also gives Habakkuk the much needed boost to his faith, for when one is privileged to be privy to the glory of God as manifested in the theophany, the impact on one's faith is tremendous. Habakkuk's resolution in 3:16–19 gives a concrete example of a righteous person living out his faith in the face of great calamity: to trust and to wait patiently for the Lord, to rejoice in the Lord and to draw strength from him, even when all of life's necessities are deprived. This requires great determination and resolution to persevere through extreme atrocity. Thus, Habakkuk embodies the divine message that "the righteous in his faithfulness will live" (2:4) and becomes a paradigm for all the suffering righteous to follow. While this message may be suitable in many situations, it is particularly important during the great national crisis when Yahweh seems to have repudiated his covenant with David (cf. Ps 89:40[39]) and to have forsaken his people. This message assures the righteous that God has not abandoned them and that they are admonished to persevere and trust God for their survival. Hence the combination of all three elements: Habakkuk's lament framework, its theme of theodicy, and its message of admonishing the righteous to persevere in faithfulness during calamity, confirms Habakkuk's position at the nadir of the *U*-shaped narrative arc, the lowest point in Israel's history.

In sum, Habakkuk differs from other prophetic literature in both form and content. It plays a unique role in the Twelve by providing a humanistic perspective to give a voice to the suffering righteous during Judah's national crisis. Instead of being Yahweh's mouthpiece to condemn the people and to call them to return, the prophet represents the people and employs the form of lament to question God's theodicy. Through his lament and dialogues with God, he finally resolves the issue of theodicy and comes to a conclusion. Habakkuk's resolution to trust God demonstrates to the people in the Judean community how to live a faithful life during times of atrocity so as to prepare them for the "day of distress" (יום צרה) that is yet to come.

There have been three proposals: (1) God's faithfulness, supported by LXX, and (2) the trustworthiness of the vision. See J. G. Jansen, "Habakkuk 2:2–4 in the Light of Recent Philological Advances," *HTR* 73 (1980) 59–62, and (3) the faithfulness of the righteous person since he is the closest antecedent. I opt for the third meaning for this addresses: Habakkuk's existential concern of the survival of the righteous during adversity.

Conclusion

While it is important to read individual prophetic messages as separate units,[69] the editorial activities in the Book of the Twelve encourage the reader to read these individual books as a composite whole. This new paradigm of treating the Twelve as a literary whole is not to supplant the older paradigm of reading them individually but to introduce another dimension that is pertinent to the interpretation of the Twelve.[70] Moreover, the positioning of the Twelve shows that the sequence is a thoughtful and deliberate editorial arrangement that involves chronological and thematic considerations.

The Book of the Twelve as a whole emphasizes the relationship between Yahweh and his people, Israel. The prophets explain Israel's historical experience of the fall of both the Northern and Judean kingdoms in terms of their covenantal relationship with Yahweh. They view Israel's history as a dynamic interaction between Israel and Yahweh. Through his judgment and deliverance, Yahweh reveals himself as the Lord of history.[71] Von Rad aptly observed that Israel "could only understand her history as a road along which she traveled under Jahweh's protection. For Israel, history consisted only of Jahweh's self-revelation by word and action."[72] He further commented that the ancient writers of Israel's history were men of faith and that no matter how diverse their theologies, "their conceptions of history centered completely on God."[73]

By recounting Israel's unfaithfulness of breaking the covenant with Yahweh, Hosea sets the stage for the history of Israel to unfold. He warns the Israelites of the imminent divine judgment and calls for repentance, as well as promises restoration. This principle of "sin brings judgment, judgment calls for repentance, and repentance leads to restoration" reflects Yahweh's dual attributes of mercy and justice as proclaimed in Exod 34:6–7. That

---

69. Ben Zvi argues that one would reach different conclusions for each individual book if the twelve prophetic books are read individually. For his critiques on House and Nogalski, see "Twelve Prophetic Books," 128–29.

70. Sweeney, "Sequence and Interpretation," 50.

71. V. P. Long calls this notion "the very center of Old Testament historiography." See his "Historiography of the Old Testament," in *The Face of Old Testament Studies: A Survey of Contemporary Approaches* (ed. D. W. Baker and B. T. Arnold; Grand Rapids: Baker, 1999) 145–75.

72. G. von Rad, *Old Testament Theology* (trans. D. M. G. Stalker; 2 vols.; New York: Harper & Row, 1962–65) 2:418.

73. Ibid.

explains the prominence of the Exodus passage in the Twelve. The sovereignty of Yahweh over all nations is also demonstrated by the application of this universal principle, particularly in Yahweh's dealings with foreign nations in Obadiah, Jonah, Nahum, and Habakkuk. Thus, the final editor uses Israel's historical experience to remind Israel that its life depends on Yahweh, and that natural catastrophe and foreign nations are merely divine agents to bring judgment to Israel for its unfaithfulness. The purpose of the prophetic messages in the Twelve is to admonish Israel to guard its relationship with Yahweh by keeping his covenant.

If we allow House's proposal of the *U*-shaped comedy framework for the Book of the Twelve to stand, then Habakkuk is found at its lowest point. The placement of Habakkuk at this point is due to the national catastrophe that befalls Judah, which then raises the issue of theodicy. Crenshaw concludes that theodicy arises when life anomalies clash with theological belief and that the prophets who are caught between the tension of divine justice and compassion refuse to relinquish either one.[74] Habakkuk's unique role is that it allows the righteous to pose the issue of theodicy to God. Its placement also explains why this prophetic book is set in a lament framework—for it is the most appropriate genre to express pain and doubt caused by the extreme atrocity during the darkest hour in Israel's history. Habakkuk's final resolution to wait for the Lord serves as a paradigm for all suffering righteous to persevere during the time of adversity, and looks beyond the Day of calamity as described in Zephaniah to the restoration phase.

The glorious, elevated state of restoration portrayed by the preexilic prophets makes the restoration phase described in the three postexilic prophetic writings disappointing by comparison. Nonetheless, Haggai, Zechariah, and Malachi illustrate the partial fulfillment of Yahweh's promise of restoration as it pertains to the return of the Exile and the rebuilding of the temple. This signifies a reconciliation of Israel's relationship with Yahweh, and most importantly, conveys the message that Yahweh is with Israel and is not done with it yet. Thus, the Book of the Twelve ends with a high hope of the coming of the Holy One in the future (Mal 3:1).

In sum, the Book of the Twelve provides not just the individual prophetic messages but, as a whole, reflects Israel's historiography by giving an account of Yahweh's historical dealings with Israel from mid-eighth century B.C.E. to the Persian period.

---

74. "Theodicy in the Book of the Twelve," 191.

The "Exilic" Prophecy of Daniel 7: Does It Reflect Late Pre-Maccabean or Early Hellenistic Historiography?

RALPH J. KORNER

The historiographical elements in the symbolic dream vision of Daniel 7 locate the Jews, God's people, within the broad sweep of human (not just Jewish) history, a history that is periodized (Babylon, Media, Persia, Greece) and divinely determined.[1] Daniel 7 pictures the four Gentile empires as four beasts that are judged by the "Ancient of Days," a prophetic vision that is purported to have taken place within the context of an exilic timeframe ("In the first year of King Belshazzar of Babylon," 7:1). But what is its historiographical context? If one assumes that "predictive" elements in Daniel are *ex eventu*, then the *crux interpretum* for discovering the historical backdrop for the apocalyptic vision of Daniel 7 is one's identification of the historical referent for the main antagonist in chaps. 7 and 8—the "little horn" (7:8, 11, 20–21, 24–26; 8:9–12, 23–25).[2] The candidate forwarded by the majority of scholars is Antiochus IV Epiphanes (175–64 B.C.E.), which then places the composition of Aramaic Daniel 7 into the late pre-Maccabean period, just prior to the desecration of the

---

1. A. Momigliano ("The Origins of Universal History," in *The Poet and the Historian: Essays in Literary and Historical Biblical Criticism* [ed. R. E. Friedman; HSS 26; Chico, CA: Scholars Press, 1983] 133–154, esp. p. 141) argues that Daniel's four kingdom schema finds its precursor in the three kingdom paradigm (Assyria, Media, and Persia) that was codified by Herodotus (fifth century B.C.E.) and described by Ctesias (fourth century B.C.E.). J.-D. Kaestli ("Les rapports entre apocalyptique et historiographie: réflexions à partir du livre de Daniel," in *Ancient and Modern Scriptural Historiography L'historiographie biblique, ancienne et moderne* [ed. G. Brooke and T. Römer; BETL 207; Leuven: Leuven University Press, 2007] 191–202, esp. 193–98) emphasizes that, unlike pseudepigraphic apocalypses, but not unlike ancient historiographers, the author of Daniel is at the very least concerned with reliably situating his material within the historical epoch in which his narrative unfolds.

2. J. J. Collins (*Daniel* [Hermeneia; Minneapolis: Fortress, 1993] 278) notes that "the crucial arguments for a pre-Maccabean vision focus on v. 8, where we find the first clear reference to Antiochus Epiphanes as the 'little horn.'"

333

temple in Jerusalem (167 B.C.E.).³ This date ties its compositional history to that of the Hebrew chapters (1–2:4a; chaps. 8–12; ca. 164 B.C.E.), rather than to that of the rest of the Aramaic corpus (2:4b–6:29; hereafter, chaps. 2–6).⁴

The purpose of this essay is to assess the historiographical implications of identifying the "little horn" in chap. 7 (but not in chap. 8) with Ptolemy I Soter (323–282 B.C.E.), as opposed to Antiochus IV Epiphanes.⁵ Two primary questions guide this investigation. First, can Daniel 7 function as a symbolic history of Judean events in the early Hellenistic, rather than only in the late pre-Maccabean, period? Second, because the early Hellenistic era is the period in which the rest of the Aramaic corpus (chaps. 2–6) purportedly was written, can the compositional history of Aramaic Daniel 7, in its entirety, be tied to that of chaps. 2–6?⁶ By way of concluding comments, I will offer suggestions for further study with respect to the social setting of Daniel 7 in relation to early Hellenistic Jewish Second Temple writings.

The Symbolic History of Daniel 7:
Late Pre-Maccabean or Early Hellenistic?

There is general agreement among scholars that the "little horn" of Daniel 7 and 8, represents, at the very least, a Hellenistic king who arises out of 10 horns (the Diadochoi, "Successors," of Alexander the Great)

---

3. Commentators who date chap. 7's composition to approx. 167 B.C.E. include: Collins, *Daniel*, 35; J. Montgomery, *A Critical and Exegetical Commentary on The Book of Daniel* (ICC; New York: Scribners, 1927) 96; N. Porteous, *Daniel: A Commentary* (OTL; Philadelphia: Westminster, 1965) 20; A. Lacocque, *The Book of Daniel* (trans. D. Pellauer; Atlanta: John Knox, 1979) 9–10; W. Sibley Towner, *Daniel* (IBC; Atlanta: John Knox, 1984) 5; P. L. Redditt, *Daniel* (NCB; Sheffield: Sheffield Academic Press, 1999) 25.

4. The Hebrew framework of Daniel (1–2:4a; chaps. 8–12; hereafter chaps. 1, 8–12) was written sometime after the desecration of the temple (167 B.C.E.) but prior to its purification and rededication (164 B.C.E.). Collins aptly sums up the tensions associated with the compositional dating of chap. 7: "while Daniel 7 is bound to chaps. 2–6 by language and concentric arrangement, it is bound to 8–12 by chronological sequence [that is, Maccabean history] and content" (*Daniel*, 34). See also 29 n. 285, 34 n. 321.

5. Historical dates in this essay follow chart 1 in J. H. Hayes and S. R. Mandell (*The Jewish People in Classical Antiquity: From Alexander to Bar Kochba* [Louisville: Westminster John Knox, 1998] 22–24).

6. See J. G. Gammie ("The Classification, Stages of Growth and Changing Intentions in the Book of Daniel," *JBL* 95 [1976] 191–204, esp. p. 191) for arguments for an early Hellenistic dating of chaps. 1 and 2–6.

which sit on the head of the fourth, and final, beast (Alexander the Great). This "little horn," who gains ascendancy over the inhabited world (or, at the very least, the inhabited "world" of Judea) through the removal of 3 of the 10 horns, is said, among other things, to speak arrogantly against God (7:8, 11, 20, 25) and to make war against the "holy ones of the Most High" (7:21, 25). But what are the interpretive possibilities for an identification of the original referent for Daniel 7's "little horn"?

Two "Little Horns," One Referent?

Commentators who situate Daniel 7 within the late pre-Maccabean era (167 B.C.E.), do so primarily in light of one specific historical criterion: the clear identification of the "little horn" in chaps. 8–12 with Antiochus IV Epiphanes. The "little horn" of Daniel 7 is then presumed to represent the same person.

The "little horn" of Daniel 8 is said to grow out of one of "four prominent horns" (8:8; the Diadochoi, cf. 8:22) that arise out of "the great horn" of the male goat (8:8), which represents Alexander the Great (8:21).[7] This "little horn" is readily identifiable as the Seleucid king, Antiochus IV Epiphanes who, in 167 B.C.E., along with his supporters, replaced the temple's offerings with sacrifices to Zeus (1 Macc 1:45–49; 2 Macc 5:15, 6:2–6; cf. Dan 8:11), and set up "a desolating sacrilege on the altar of the burnt offering" (1 Macc 1:54; cf. Dan 8:13).

Antiochus IV Epiphanes is introduced again in chap. 11 (vv. 21–28). He is described as the "contemptible person" (11:21) whose anti-Judean sentiments (11:28) are translated into overt actions (11:29–39) that profane even the temple itself (11:31; "they shall set up the abomination that makes desolate").[8]

But how does Antiochus IV Epiphanes accord with Daniel 7? Any monarchial referent for the "little horn" must conform to at least 3 essential historical criteria: (1) he is of the lineage of the "10 horns" and must have reigned over Judea, the land of the "holy ones"; (2) he can somehow be associated with a sufficient level of antagonism toward God and his "holy ones" to merit apocalyptic judgment; and (3) his rise to power over Judea is in tandem with the "demise" of 3 other kings ("3 horns") who had influence in the Land.

These three criteria in Daniel 7 are met in the reign of Antiochus IV Epiphanes. If one assumes, as the majority of commentators do, that the

---

7. All scripture quotations are from the NRSV, unless otherwise noted.
8. See also P. L. Redditt, "Daniel 11 and the Socio-historical Setting of the Book of Daniel," *CBQ* 60 (1998) 463–74.

"10 horns" are chronologically sequential, then Antiochus IV Epiphanes is the most appropriate referent for the 11th, or "little," horn."[9] If one assumes that the "10 horns" are contemporaneous, irrespective of whether the number *10* is meant literally or symbolically, Antiochus IV Epiphanes still is a suitable candidate.[10] Antiochus IV Epiphanes not only qualifies as a possible original referent for the "little horn" in both Aramaic Daniel 7 and Hebrew Daniel 8, he is the only Hellenistic king who can do so in both chapters.

Two "Little Horns," Two Referents?

Historical referents notwithstanding, the textual descriptions do not, though, *necessitate* an identification of the "little horn" of Daniel 7 with the "little horn" of Daniel 8. The "little horn" is portrayed in differing, though not necessarily contradictory, ways in the two chapters. In Daniel 7, the "little horn" arises out from the midst of the "10 horns" of the 4th beast, either as a contemporaneous, or a chronologically sequential, king. At the very least, 4 of the 11 "horns" appear to be contemporaneous—the "little horn" and the "three horns" which it supplants (7:8, 20).[11] In Daniel 8, by contrast, five "horns" are in view, only four of which appear to be contemporaneous, with the fifth (the "little horn") being a "second" generational one only, in that it arises out from one of the "four prominent horns" (8:8, 9).[12]

While Antiochus IV Epiphanes is the only satisfactory referent for the "little horn" of Daniel 8, regarding the "little horn" of Daniel 7, he is but

---

9. Because only 7 of the 10 horns correlate clearly with Seleucid kings, some commentators resort to a mixture of Ptolemies and Seleucids (Collins, *Daniel*, 320).

10. A. A. di Lella and L. F. Hartman (*The Book of Daniel: A New Translation with Introduction and Commentary* [AB23; Garden City, NY: Doubleday, 1978] 208, 216–17) follow Porphyry's lead in suggesting that the 10 horns are contemporaneous kings within the Greek empire. Collins notes that "the number ten may well be a round, schematic number" (*Daniel*, 321). The three contemporaneous "horns" removed by Antiochus IV Epiphanes were Ptolemy VI Philomator, Ptolemy VIII Euergetes, and Artaraxias, king of Armenia.

11. The Aramaic of Dan 7:8 reads, in part, ואלו קרן אחרי זעירה סלקת ביניהון ותלת מן־קרניא קדמיתא אתעקרו מן־קדמיה ('and behold, another horn, a little [one], came up between them, and three from [among] the earlier horns were dehorned from before it'); 7:20 reads תלת ועל־קרניא עשר די בראשה ואחרי די סלקת ונפלו מן־קדמיה ('and concerning the ten that [were] on its head, and the other [horn] that came up and three [horns] fell from before it').

12. The Hebrew reads of 8:9 reads ומן־האחת מהם יצא קרן־אחת מצעירה ותגדל־יתר אל־הנגב ואל־המזרח ואל־הצבי ('and [out] from one of them came one horn from [being] little and it grew exceedingly toward the south [Egypt?], toward the east [Mesopotamia?] and toward the beautiful land [Judea?]').

one of three possible candidates. Lebram argues that the Seleucid king, Antiochus III the Great (223–187 B.C.E.), is one possible candidate.[13] Viewing Antiochus III as the "little horn" of Daniel 7 helps to explain why his life is so extensively retold in Daniel 11. But Lebram's view does not fulfill all three essential criteria for an identification of the "little horn" in Daniel 7. Specifically, as Albertz notes, the reign of Antiochus III "cannot explain . . . the three horns which are torn out" (7:8, 24).[14]

There is an even earlier candidate, however, whose reign also fits all three of the essential criteria for an identification of the "little horn" of Daniel 7—Ptolemy I Soter, "Savior," (satrap, 323–305; king, 305–282 B.C.E.). Like the later Seleucids (198–164 B.C.E.), he too governed Judea. He established Ptolemaic control over Judea which continued unabated for over 100 years (301–198 B.C.E.). But unlike the Seleucid king, Antiochus IV Epiphanes, Ptolemy I Soter only fits a "contemporaneous" scenario in which the "10 horns" are a "round, schematic number."[15] He neither corresponds with the "little horn" descriptions in Daniel 8, nor can he be a chronologically sequential "little horn" in Daniel 7.

Although he is not the "little horn" of Daniel 8, Ptolemy I Soter may very well be presupposed as one of the "four prominent horns." If so, then the "four prominent horns" allude to the fourfold division of the Alexandrian empire among the Diadochoi who defeated another Alexandrian general, Antigonus Monophthalmus, "one-eyed," at the battle of Ipsus (301 B.C.E.) in northern Syria.

This victorious alliance of four Diadochoi was comprised of Cassander (Macedonia), Lysimachus (Thrace), Seleucus I Nicanor (Babylon), and Ptolemy I Soter (Egypt). Antiochus IV Epiphanes, the undoubted "little

---

13. J. C. Lebram, *Das Buch Daniel* (Zürcher Bibelkommentare Alte Testament 23; Zürich: Theologischer, 1984) esp. pp. 21, 84 (as cited in R. Albertz "The Social Setting of the Aramaic and the Hebrew Book of Daniel," in *The Book of Daniel: Composition and Reception* [ed. J. J. Collins and P. W. Flint; 2 vols.; Leiden: Brill, 2000] 1:171–204, esp. p. 187).

14. Albertz, "Social Setting," 1:187. There is no evidence to tie Antiochus III with the murder of his brother (223 B.C.E.), whom he succeeded to the throne, or that there ever were two other rivals whom he supplanted.

15. See Collins in n. 9 above. If the "10 horns" represent the 13 contemporaneous satraps who were confirmed by the Council of State immediately following Alexander the Great's death, then "10" is a round number: Perdiccas, Ptolemy I, Lysimachus, Craterus, Antipater, Antigonus Monophthalmus, Leonnatus, Menander, Philotas, Laomedon, Eumenes, Peithon, and Archon. For their territorial assignments, see N. Davis and C. M. Kraay, *The Hellenistic Kingdoms: Portrait Coins and History* (London: Thames & Hudson, 1973) 137–40. Cassander is a son of Antipater. Seleucus I was a lieutenant of Perdiccas in Babylon.

horn" of Daniel 8, was a descendant of Seleucus (358–281 B.C.E.), thereby making Seleucus I Nicanor, and by extension his three allies, fitting referents for the "four prominent horns."

If one assigns differentiated historical identities for the "little horns" in Daniel 7 and 8, then not only can a diachronic development of the text of Daniel 1–12 be presupposed, but at least one historiographical implication can be suggested. By recontextualizing the "little horn" of Aramaic Daniel 7 for a Maccabean readership, the author of Hebrew Daniel 8–12 also implicitly subsumes chap. 7's historiographical elements—divine determinacy, as evidenced in the periodization of history, guarantees divine judgment on the Hellenistic king and deliverance for God's people, the Jews.

Ptolemy I Soter and the Balance of Daniel 7

Aside from being in concord with the three essential criteria of a historical referent for the "little horn" of Daniel 7, Ptolemy I Soter, not unlike Antiochus IV Epiphanes, also accords with at least six historiographical details in the balance of chap. 7.

The "Three Horns" (7:8, 20, 24)

Daniel 7 talks about "three horns" that "were plucked up by the roots" (7:8), "fell out" (7:20), and represent "three kings" whom the "little horn" "shall put down" (7:24).[16] There are two "threesomes" that accord with the reign of Ptolemy I Soter. The first "threesome" is the three foes that Ptolemy I Soter encountered in his ongoing bid for control of Coele-Syria (323–301 B.C.E.)—Perdiccas (321 B.C.E.), Antigonus Monophthalmus (306 B.C.E.), and Demetrius, his son (312 B.C.E.).[17] The armies of all three foes would realistically have been encountered by Judeans, making the references in Daniel 7 to the "three horns," which were uprooted, fell down, and were put down, by Ptolemy I Soter, very relevant for a Judean, and even a Jerusalemite, readership in the late fourth–early third century B.C.E.

---

16. See p. 336 n. 10. Dan 7:24 reads, ותלתה מלכין יהשפל.

17. In its original sense "Coele-Syria" ("hollow Syria") encompassed southern Syria from Lebanon southward to and including the depression of the Jordan Valley, that is, Judea. Cf. E. Bevan, *The House of Ptolemy: A History of Egypt under the Ptolemaic Dynasty* (Chicago: Ares, 1968) 24. In 321 B.C.E., Perdiccas was repulsed by Ptolemy I near Memphis. In 306 B.C.E., Antigonus led a large force over land against Egypt while Demetrius brought the fleet down the coast. Ptolemy I was confirmed as satrap in Egypt after his defeat of Demetrius at Gaza in 312 B.C.E. (L. Grabbe, *A History of the Jews and Judaism in the Second Temple Period* [2 vols.; Library of Second Temple Studies 68; T. & T. Clark, 2008] 2:278–80). For a concise, yet detailed, history of the reign of Ptolemy I Soter, see Davis and Kraay, *Hellenistic Kingdoms*, 140–49.

The second set of possible referents for the "three horns" are the three Diadochoi with whom Ptolemy I Soter made formal alliances—Cassander and Lysimachus (311 and 302 B.C.E.), and Seleucus (316 and 302 B.C.E.)—and through whom Antigonus Monophthalmus was defeated at the Battle of Ipsus (301 B.C.E.).[18] Ptolemy I Soter, however, did not participate in the actual battle itself.[19] Instead, he consolidated his holdings in Judea and broader Coele-Syria during 302 B.C.E. and returned to Egypt in 301 B.C.E.[20] Following Ipsus, Seleucus gained control over, and remained in, Syria-Mesopotamia, while Cassander and Lysimachus returned to Macedonia and Thrace, respectively. Ptolemy remained the sole sovereign over his recently reoccupied territory of Coele-Syria (302 B.C.E.), in which he had established military garrisons and centralized administration of agricultural production, finances, and record-keeping.[21] For the first time since the death of Alexander the Great, Judeans again were under the hegemony of an uncontested Hellenistic ruler.

The limitations of interpreting the "three horns" as the three allies of Ptolemy I Soter are twofold. First, aside from Seleucus's four-year stay in Ptolemaic Egypt (316–312 B.C.E.), there does not appear to be any historical record of a military or political presence in Judea by Cassander or Lysimachus.

Second, it is difficult to imagine, at least insofar as a modern readership with the benefit of historical hindsight is concerned, why his three victorious allies would be described in such defeatist terms (uprooted, fallen, and put down). Through the eyes of a Judean readership, however, the rationale may have been more apparent. The three allies' absence in Coele-Syria, particularly after the conclusive battle of Ipsus, could have been misperceived as an involuntary removal at the hands of Ptolemy I Soter, because he was the sole remaining Hellenistic king in the Land. If so, then, the clause 'and three kings he shall put down' (or 'subdue'; ותלתה מלכין יהשפל), may even allude to the refusal of Ptolemy I Soter to recognize Seleucus's legitimate "right" to sovereignty over Coele-Syria after the battle

---

18. Grabbe, *History*, 2:280.
19. The diminutive descriptor "little" for the regnal title "horn" in Daniel 7 becomes more understandable given the lack of military involvement by Ptolemy I Soter at the decisive battle of Ipsus—although a "horn" (ruler over Judea), his absence allows him to be ascribed, at best, only "little" honor in comparison with his allies (the "three [normal-sized] horns").
20. Grabbe, *History*, 2:287.
21. R. S. Bagnall, *The Administration of the Ptolemaic Possessions outside Egypt* (Columbia Studies in the Classic Tradition 4; Leiden: Brill, 1976) 11–24.

of Ipsus, and Seleucus' subsequent choice not to press his claim through military action.[22]

The Arrogant Little Horn (7:8, 11, 20)

The "little horn" of Daniel 7 is portrayed quite negatively as a vehement enemy of God and his "holy ones" (either angels or pious/priestly people).[23] He is said to have a mouth that speaks 'arrogantly' (7:8, 11, 20; רברבן) against "the Most High" (7:25) and to be one who makes "war with the holy ones and was prevailing against them" (7:21). Would Ptolemy I have been viewed so negatively by a Judean readership of Daniel 7? Tcherikover states that there are "two threads of historiographical tradition, one describing Ptolemy as their enemy and the other as their friend."[24]

The felicitous tradition is represented by Hecataeus of Abdera, a Greek writer and contemporary of Ptolemy I Soter. Writing about the victory of Ptolemy I (not yet "Soter") over the Antigonid Demetrius at Gaza in 312 B.C.E., Hecataeus is said to describe a chief priest (but probably not the high priest) Hiskias, or Ezechias, who may also be the same person as Hezekiah, the governor of Judea.[25] Hiskias willingly chose, along with

---

22. In 311 B.C.E., Ptolemy I Soter was promised Coele-Syria by Cassander, and Lysimachus, once Antigonus was defeated. Given the absence of Ptolemy I Soter at Ipsus, in 301 B.C.E. Seleucus, instead, was given the right to rule Coele-Syria. Ptolemy I Soter, however, refused to give up the holdings he had consolidated in Coele-Syria in 302 B.C.E.

23. According to Collins, the substantival use of קדישין ('holy ones') in Daniel 7, and elsewhere in the HB and DSS (Hebrew קדשים), has primary reference to celestial beings (*Daniel*, 313 n. 322). See also, idem, *The Apocalyptic Imagination: An Introduction to Jewish Apocalyptic Literature* (2nd ed.; Bible Resource Series; Grand Rapids: Eerdmans, 1998) 123–55. C. Fletcher-Louis ("The High Priest as Divine Mediator in the Hebrew Bible: Dan 7:13 as Test Case," in *Society of Biblical Literature 1997 Seminar Papers* [Atlanta: Scholars Press, 1997] 161–193, esp. pp. 186–92) interprets "holy ones" as a reference to pious Jews such as priests; idem, *All the Glory of Adam: Liturgical Anthropology in the Dead Sea Scrolls* (STDJ 42; Leiden: Brill, 2002) 142 n. 16, 83 n. 82.

24. V. Tcherikover, *Hellenistic Civilization and the Jews* (trans. S. Applebaum; New York: Atheneum, 1975) 55.

25. Numismatic evidence for the historicity of Josephus's chief priest, Hiskia, includes coins bearing the inscription "Hiskia the governor" in ancient Hebrew script. Under Ptolemaic administrative policies for temple states, the union of religious and political power was not unusual. Schäfer (*The History of the Jews in the Greco-Roman World* [rev. ed.; London: Routledge, 2003] 9) suggests that "Hiskia was possibly Judaism's last governor at the end of Persian rule, who then decided in 312 B.C.E. that he would rather go into Egyptian exile with Ptolemy."

1500 priests, to follow Ptolemy I back to Egypt because of "his kindness and love of mankind" (*C. Ap.* I, 186ff., cf. *Ant.* XII, 9).[26]

Agatharchides (second century B.C.E.) portrays Ptolemy I in a much more negative light. Josephus cites Agatharchides as claiming that Ptolemy I was "a hard master" (*Ant.* XII, 6) over Jerusalem after he "captured Jerusalem by deceit and treachery . . . on the Sabbath" (*Ant.* XII, 4).[27] Schäfer cites scholarly consensus in affirming that "this report of a conquest of Jerusalem by Ptolemy on the Sabbath is not contested as such."[28] Thus, although in 312 B.C.E. Judeans might have rightly viewed Ptolemy I (not yet Soter) as a "savior," in 302 B.C.E., after his deceitful conquest of Jerusalem, Ptolemy I (now Soter; 305 B.C.E.) would no doubt have been viewed in the exact opposite light. If the author of Daniel 2–7 moved among the Jerusalem elite, he may well have been pro-Antigonid.[29] This mixture of political discontent with religious fervor would have been an inflammatory scenario indeed, out of which a scathing literary attack against the Ptolemaic foe in the form of Daniel 7 would not have been surprising.

In summary, then, if Josephus accurately reproduces Agatharchides' words, and if Agatharchides is referring to the conquest of Jerusalem in 302 B.C.E., and if his more negative assessment of Ptolemy I Soter reflects the actual historical experiences, and perspectives, of Jerusalemites in 302 B.C.E., then this suggests the plausibility of locating the composition of Daniel 7's symbolic vision sometime soon thereafter.

"Greater Than (and Different from) the Others" (7:20, 24)

The Judean author of Daniel 7 writes that the "little horn" "seemed greater than the others [the 10 horns]" (7:20; וחזוה רב מן־חברתה) and "different from the others" (7:24; והוא ישנא מן־קדמיא). How would these two descriptions fit Ptolemy I Soter, especially after the battle of Ipsus? The phrase "greater than the others" describes him well as the sole uncontested sovereign over Judea. But how is Ptolemy I Soter "different from the others," that is, the 10 horns?

---

26. Josephus's citation, though, is likely of a Jewish writer about 100 B.C.E. (Pseudo-Hecataeus), which reduces its credibility (Grabbe, *History*, 2:283).

27. See also Appian (*Syr.* 50), but he gives no indication of a date for Jerusalem's conquest.

28. Schäfer, *History of the Jews*, 10. The historically suspect *Letter of Aristeas* describes Ptolemy I as forcibly resettling up to 100,000 Jews in Egypt (v. 12), but, because no mention is made of a conquest of Jerusalem, it is dated either to 320 B.C.E. or 312 B.C.E.(Grabbe, *History*, 2:282).

29. Ruling classes of Jerusalem before its conquest can be said to have sided with Antigonus (Schäfer, *History of the Jews*, 10).

Aside from his obvious discontinuity with Antigonus, he differs from his three allies in at least two ways. First, he did not participate with them in the battle of Ipsus (301 B.C.E.). Second, prior to that decisive battle, his three new allies were only minimally evident during the other battles across Coele-Syria (320–301 B.C.E.). At most, Seleucus I joined Ptolemy I in Egypt (316 B.C.E.) but only until the battle of Gaza (312 B.C.E.), after which point he returned to Babylon.[30] In other words, a Judean audience would have, at best, rarely noticed that any army outside of Ptolemy's was ever on Judean soil.

"Eyes" (7:8)

If Daniel 7 was written to an early third-century B.C.E. Judean readership (post–battle of Ipsus), then two possible referents, each of whom had occupied the land repeatedly during the years 320–301 B.C.E., would no doubt have come to mind to a Judean readership—Antigonus Monophthalmus and Ptolemy I Soter. Both would have been perceived as deserving divine judgment for their arrogant rule over the "holy ones of the Most High" (7:21, 25). While the "mouth" of the "little horn" serves a narratological function (arrogant speech), the "eyes" do not.[31] Perhaps the inclusion of "eyes" (plural) is meant to hint at the fact that Antigonus Monophthalmus, the "one-eyed" tyrant, was not the "little horn" with two eyes. Hope is thus instilled in a Judean readership that Ptolemy I Soter was not the agent of God's judgment, but rather is still the target of divine retribution, a comforting message in light of his apparently harsh rule after taking Jerusalem the year prior.

"Change Sacred Seasons and Laws" (7:25b).

If one supports a late pre-Maccabean date for Daniel 7, then a correlation of v. 25 ("changing sacred seasons and laws") with the reign of Antiochus IV Epiphanes seems straightforward. He is the quintessential example, in Jewish history, of a Gentile king who introduced a foreign calendar thereby making it impossible to celebrate Sabbaths and feasts properly (cf. 1 Macc 1:45; 2 Macc 6:6). The relevance of v. 25 within the reign of Ptolemy I Soter is less obvious.

Albertz suggests that the author of the Aramaic section of Daniel (2:4b–7:28; hereafter, chaps. 2–7), excluding the "little horn" references, is a learned psalmic poet who worked not only for the temple, but also

---

30. Grabbe, *History*, 2:286.
31. Dan 7:8b reads, "And behold, eyes like the eyes of a human in this horn and a mouth speaking abundantly/arrogantly" (ואלו עינין כעיני אנשא בקרנא־דא ופם ממלל רברבן).

for pious communities.³² If his social reconstruction is to be believed, it is easier to see why the actions of Ptolemy I Soter in 302 B.C.E. would have evinced religious rhetoric from the author of Daniel 7: (1) "shall attempt to change sacred seasons" may refer to the profanation of the Sabbath by Ptolemy I Soter in his devious conquest of Jerusalem; and (2) "shall attempt to change . . . the laws" may refer to purity laws that were abrogated through the undoubted subsequent placement of a Gentile military garrison in the holy temple city, Jerusalem.³³

A further aggravating factor that may have prejudiced a pious Jew to more readily indict Ptolemy I Soter on religious charges is the conferral of divine honors, though not deification proper, on him by Greeks, Egyptians, and other nationalities alike.³⁴ In 304 B.C.E., the league of the Islanders (particularly Rhodes) was the first to grant Ptolemy I "honors equal to the gods."³⁵ The Rhodians conferred on Ptolemy I the ascription "Soter" (Savior) after his help in repelling the Antigonid attack against their island (305/304 B.C.E.) that was led by Antigonus's son Demetrius, who thereafter was named *Poliorcētēs* 'Besieger of Cities'. The Rhodians consulted the oracle temple at the Oasis of Siwah, as the Egyptian priesthood had done years earlier, prior to conferring the Pharaonic title of "Son of Ammon" on Alexander the Great.³⁶ With the oracle's agreement, the Rhodians dedicated to Ptolemy I, now Soter, a sacred enclosure (*temenos*) with adjoining stoas, naming it the Ptolemaion.³⁷

The Egyptians too offered Ptolemy I Soter deifying honors. Although he took on himself the title "king" in 305 B.C.E., it was not until 304 B.C.E. that the Egyptian priesthood formally crowned Ptolemy I Soter in native fashion as a pharaoh. At this point he took on himself the same throne name as Alexander ("beloved of Amun, Chosen by Ra"). Prior to this, in a bid to unite his country still further, while he was only satrap of

---

32. "Social Setting," 186–87.

33. Bagnall notes that it was common Ptolemaic practice to place garrisons in the main cities of Phoenicia and Syria (*Administration*, 14).

34. Ptolemy II Philadelphus (283–246 B.C.E.) formally deified Ptolemy I Soter and his third wife, Berenice, as "Savior Gods" and inaugurated the festival of the Ptolemaieia in their honor (280 B.C.E.; G. Shipley, *The Greek World after Alexander: 323–30 BC* [London: Routledge, 2000] 159).

35. At least so the Rhodians claimed in 280 B.C.E. (ibid., 159; see also p. 138).

36. Alexander went to the oracle at Siwah, some 500 miles from Memphis. The oracle of Siwah was associated with Ammon (or Amun). Ammon became associated with Zeus and was depicted as a Greek god with ram horns (W. Ellis, *Ptolemy of Egypt* [London: Routledge, 1994] 6–7).

37. Shipley, *Greek World*, 162. See also Ellis, *Ptolemy of Egypt*, 49.

Egypt (323–305 B.C.E.), Ptolemy I formally established the cult of Serapis (or Sarapis), a syncretistic religious amalgam to which both Greeks and Egyptians/non-Greeks could adhere.[38] The cult of Serapis (also known to Greeks as the healing god, Asklepios), was centred in Memphis and grew in popularity throughout the Ptolemaic empire.[39] An incursion of the Serapis cult into the "holy" land would not have been looked on favorably by anyone associated with the Yahwistic cult centered in the Temple in Jerusalem.[40] Given this context, it is not inconceivable that Ptolemy I Soter's sacrilegious conquest of Jerusalem was the "last straw" (so to speak) which set on fire the righteous ire of a pious Jew, maybe even a learned psalmic poet, who then "penned" Daniel 2–7.[41]

The anomalous portrayal of the four "beasts" (Gentile kings) as being in some way contemporaneous with each other (7:11, 12) may also support a compositional date for Daniel 7 soon after the takeover of Jerusalem. Ginsberg notes that right through the Greek age there existed residual Median and Persian kingdoms (Atropatene and Persis, respectively), and, for two brief periods, there existed a Babylonian kingdom (307–301 B.C.E. and 292–261 B.C.E.).[42] If one presupposes that texts inform the reader, not of the period(s) about which they are written, but primarily of the period(s) in which they were written, then either of the two dates for the Babylonian kingdom, both of which overlap with the reign of Ptolemy I Soter, suggest a terminus ad quem for the composition of Daniel 7.

"A Time, Two Times, and Half a Time" (7:25c)

In Dan 7:25, the readership is told that the "holy ones of the Most High . . . shall be given into his power for a time, two times, and half a time." How might this reference relate to Judea, the land associated with

---

38. The Serapis cult appears to be an amalgamation of the Egyptian god, Osir-Hapi, and the Serapis at Alexandria, which was a Greek bearded god, resembling Zeus or Hades or Asklepios (Bevan, *Ptolemy*, 44). See also Grabbe, *History*, 137.

39. Bevan, *Ptolemy*, 45.

40. Jewish polemic against Memphis is unambiguously evident by at least the last quarter of the second century B.C.E. in Pseudo-Ezekiel (4Q385, 4Q385b, 4Q386, 4Q388, 4Q391). D. Dimant ("Pseudo-Ezekiel," in *Qumran Cave 4.21 Parabiblical Texts*, part 4: *Pseudo-Prophetic Texts* [DJD 30; Oxford: Clarendon, 2001] 57) notes the centrality of Memphis during the time of Ptolemaic Egypt (4Q386 1 ii 2–6).

41. The inclusion of Jewish "hero" stories in Daniel 3 and 6, in which pious Jews refuse to bow in worship to a Gentile king, or to his statue, takes on greater relevance for an early third century B.C.E. readership within the context of the progressive bestowal of divine honors on Ptolemy I Soter and his institution of the Serapis cult.

42. H. L. Ginsberg, *Studies in Daniel* (Texts and Studies of the Jewish Theological Seminary of America 14; New York: Jewish Theological Seminary, 1948) 7.

the "holy ones of the Most High," particularly after Ptolemy I Soter's conquest of Jerusalem, and the rest of Coele-Syria, which territory he retained after the battle of Ipsus?[43] The question in Dan 7:25 might then be restated as, "How long shall Judeans be given into the power of Ptolemy I Soter?" The answer ("a time, two times, and half a time") may refer to three possible timeframes—one distant and two imminent—relative to the conclusion of the fourth century B.C.E.

First, the most distant deliverance envisioned would be sometime during the reign of Ptolemy V Epiphanes (204–180 B.C.E.), whose reign was preceded by three Ptolemaic kings after Ptolemy I.[44] In this regard, the phrase "half a time" could then be a veiled reference to his loss of Coele-Syria, and Jerusalem, "halfway" through his reign (198 B.C.E.) to Antiochus III the Great (223–187 B.C.E.) in the Fifth Syrian War. While possible, this option is problematic. It would require either a lucky guess on the part of the author of Daniel 7 or an *ex eventu* insertion of the three and a half "times" during the early second century B.C.E.[45]

Second, an imminent deliverance may instead be implied if one equates "two times" and "a half a time" with "defeats" suffered by Ptolemy I after his initial conquest of Coele-Syria in 320 B.C.E. ("a time"). He abandoned Coele-Syria in 315 and 311 B.C.E. ("two times").[46] The year 306 B.C.E. appears to be a time both of victory and defeat for Ptolemy I Soter ("a half a time"?). In 306 B.C.E., Demetrius fought Ptolemy I's fleet at Cyprus in the battle of the Cyprian Salamis and "the whole fabric of Ptolemaic sea-power collapsed."[47] But out of the jaws of defeat, Ptolemy I (not yet Soter) somehow found a way to snatch victory. Within a year he began to regain

---

43. Whether the "holy ones" are celestial or pious/priestly human beings (see p. 340 n. 23 above), Judea, or at the very least, Jerusalem, remains the geographical ground over which the "little horn" wields power for "a time, two times, and half a time."

44. The three Ptolemaic kings between Ptolemy I Soter and Ptolemy V Epiphanes are Ptolemy II Philadelphus (283–246 B.C.E.), Ptolemy III Euergetes I (246–222 B.C.E.), and Ptolemy IV Philopator (222–204 B.C.E.; Hayes and Mandell, *Jewish People*, 22–23).

45. If Daniel 7 was emended during the reign of Ptolemy V, its apocalyptic message would have countered any Jewish group who championed human agency for the earthly establishment of "God's kingdom" (e.g., the Hebrew section of Ben Sira).

46. Ptolemy abandoned Coele-Syria in 315 B.C.E. after Antigonus had defeated Perdiccas in eastern Mesopotamia (316 B.C.E.) and then again in 311 B.C.E. when a Ptolemaic force was defeated in northern Syria by Demetrius (Bevan, *Ptolemy*, 24–25). See also, Grabbe, *History*, 2:287.

47. Bevan, *Ptolemy*, 27. Grabbe, however, anomalously dates the battle of Salamis to 307 B.C.E., without explanation (*History*, 2:280).

the upper hand against his Antigonid foes by stymieing, first, Antigonus's land attack on Egypt (306 B.C.E.) and, second, Demetrius's 15-month naval siege on the great maritime and commercial state of Rhodes (305–304 B.C.E.).[48] Around 305 B.C.E. he assumed the title "king," not too long after Antigonus had done the same thing (306 B.C.E.).[49]

One limitation of this second option is that the Judean readership of Daniel 7 would then have expected the imminent establishment of God's kingdom (7:14, 27) soon after ca. 305 B.C.E. (the "half a time"?). But this predates the "sacrilegious" Ptolemaic conquest of Jerusalem in 302 B.C.E., which makes it more difficult, then, to justify why Ptolemy I Soter would be the object of Daniel 7's portrayal of the "little horn" in such vitriolic fashion. It is really only subsequent to the battle of Ipsus that Ptolemy I Soter would have established himself as a fitting arrogant "little horn," given his more overt anti-Judean sentiments and his uncontested sovereignty over Judea.

The third, and best, interpretive option with respect to an apocalyptic expectation of the imminent arrival of God's kingdom is to equate the "times" with Ptolemy's "three and a half" victories. This then suggests a dating of Daniel 7 subsequent to the battle of Ipsus. There are three victories that are ascribable to direct Ptolemaic military action (320 B.C.E.; 312 B.C.E., Gaza; and 305–304 B.C.E., Rhodes). One could conceivably portray Ipsus, the fourth Ptolemaic victory (301 B.C.E.) as a "half" victory, in that it was more won *for* Ptolemy I Soter, than *by* him.

The Compositional History of Daniel 7: Late Pre-Maccabean or Early Hellenistic?

As noted at the outset of this essay, the *opinio communis* ties the compositional history of Daniel 7 to that of the Hebrew chapters (chaps. 1, 8–12; 164 B.C.E.), rather than to that of the Aramaic corpus (chaps. 2–7). This necessitates a theory for the diachronic development for Daniel 1–12 that can become quite complex.[50]

---

48. Bevan, *Ptolemy*, 34. See also, Grabbe, *History*, 2:287.

49. Ibid., 2:280. Prior to his self-proclamation as "king," Antigonus was still technically a satrap of the kings Philip Arrhidaeus and Alexander, even though both were murdered previously (317 B.C.E. and 311 B.C.E., respectively; Bevan, *Ptolemy*, 27).

50. Collins suggests the following diachronic development of Dan 1–12: (1) each of the tales of chaps. 2–6 were originally distinct; (2) the initial collection probably represented 3:31–6:29; (3) in the Hellenistic period all of the Aramaic tales were collected, along with the introductory chap. 1; (4) Daniel 7 was composed in Aramaic before the desecration of the temple (167 B.C.E.), with all seven chapters circulating for a short time as an Aramaic book; and (5) some time before the death of Antiochus IV

Rainer Albertz, among others, cuts across the grain of scholarly consensus with a simpler solution. He asserts that (1) the compositional history of Aramaic Daniel 7 is tied to that of Daniel's other Aramaic chapters (2:4b–6:29), and (2) the Aramaic corpus (chaps. 2–7) can be formally classified as an "apocalypse."[51] Albertz affirms Lebram's thesis that the original Aramaic corpus should be dated to Antiochus III, but, contra Lebram, he still argues that late pre-Maccabean era textual emendation is responsible for the "little horn" references.[52]

Given the number of secondary emendations required, however, Albertz admits that "the assumption of a literary reworking of Daniel 7 is the only weak point of the thesis that Daniel 2–7 constitutes an older apocalypse."[53] This essay suggests, rather, that the weak point of Albertz's (and others') thesis is a different assumption; it is the assumption that the only plausible historical referent for the "little horn" of Daniel 7 is Antiochus IV Epiphanes. If one grants the possibility of Ptolemy I Soter as the original referent for the "little horn" of Daniel 7, the need for an "assumption of a literary reworking of Daniel 7" becomes a moot point.

Regardless of one's stance with respect to Albertz's controversial claim that the Aramaic chapters of Daniel (chaps. 2–7) can be formally classified as an "apocalypse," his argument that they form a cohesive literary unit with a contemporaneous compositional history in the early Hellenistic period stands on its own merits. His argument for the literary unity of Daniel 2–7 provides additional evidence for a consideration of chap. 7 as an early Hellenistic composition, and to an identification of the "little horn" with an early Hellenistic referent, the most plausible candidate of whom appears to be Ptolemy I Soter.

Albertz identifies three primary criteria—linguistic, thematic, and structural—whose combined witness, he claims, favors viewing Daniel 2–7 as a

---

Epiphanes in 164 B.C.E., the Hebrew chaps. 8–12 were added, and chap. 1 was translated into Hebrew to provide a Hebrew frame for the Aramaic chapters (*Daniel*, 38). For a suggested compositional history of chaps. 8–12, see di Lella and Hartman, *The Book of Daniel*, 13–14.

51. Albertz, "Social Setting," 176–79. Other modern commentators who hold to an early Hellenistic dating of Daniel 7 are noted by Collins (*Daniel*, 28). Early 20th century commentators are listed by H. H. Rowley (*Darius the Mede and the Four World Empires in the Book of Daniel: A Historical Study of Contemporary Theories* [Cardiff: University of Wales Press, 1935] 4).

52. J. C. Lebram, *Das Buch Daniel*, esp. pp. 21, 84 (as cited in Albertz, "Social Setting," 187). Albertz identifies the secondary verses as 7bβ, 8, 11, 12, 20–21, 22b, 24–25, and 26bβ ("Social Setting," 188 n. 59). See also di Lella, *The Book of Daniel*, 209.

53. Albertz, "Social Setting," 188, n. 59.

unified literary corpus with respect both to their organization and to their compositional history.[54]

Linguistic Unity of Daniel 2–7

Dan 2:4b–7:28 is written not only in the same language (Aramaic) but in the same dialect (Achaemenid Imperial Aramaic).[55] Achaemenid Imperial Aramaic is the official, literary, and commercial language of the Persian Empire and is consistently found in texts of the fifth–third centuries B.C.E.[56] There is commonality of language between Daniel 2–7 and Imperial Aramaic, although not uniformity.[57] While acknowledging that a "precise dating on linguistic grounds is not possible," Collins concludes that the Aramaic of Daniel is later than that of the Samaria papyri (Wadi Daliyeh, fourth century B.C.E.) but earlier than that of the *Genesis Apocryphon* (1Q20).[58]

Thematic Unity of Daniel 2–7

In addition to the general linguistic continuity of chap. 7 with chaps. 2–6, Albertz underscores their thematic unity as well. He argues that the theme of God's global supremacy over earthly kingdoms "links each chapter like a chain," but "is completely absent in the Hebrew chaps. 8–12."[59]

---

54. Ibid., 176–79.
55. K. Beyer, *The Aramaic Language: Its Distribution and Subdivisions* (trans. J. F. Healey; Göttingen: VandenHoeck & Ruprecht, 1986) 19. See also, F. Rosenthal, *A Grammar of Biblical Aramaic* (5th ed.; Wiesbaden: Harrassowitz, 1983) 6.
56. Beyer, *Aramaic Language*, 19.
57. J. Lund ("Aramaic Language," in *Dictionary of the Old Testament: Prophets* [ed. M. J. Boda and J. G. McConville; Downers Grove, IL: Intervarsity, 2012] 43–52) provides an extensive analysis of language features in Daniel 2–7 that are in common with, and different from, Achaemenid Imperial Aramaic. For source divisions based on differences in language features see, for example, di Lella and Hartman (*The Book of Daniel*, 210) and F. Polak ("The Daniel Tales in their Aramaic Literary Milieu," in *The Book of Daniel in Light of New Findings* [ed. A. S. van der Woude; BETL 106; Leuven: Leuven University Press, 1993] 249–265, esp. pp. 259–60). Collins maintains a late pre-Maccabean dating for Daniel 7 by claiming it was carefully written in imitation of the Aramaic of the earlier, Hellenistic chaps. 2–6 (*Daniel*, 38).
58. Collins, *Daniel*, 16, 17. D. Machiela's seminal study of 1Q20 (*The Dead Sea Genesis Apocryphon: A New Text and Translation with Introduction and Special Treatment of Columns 13–17* [STDJ 79; Leiden: Brill, 2009] 140) assigns "the brunt of Daniel's Aramaic to the early 3rd cent. B.C.E." rather than following "the assumption of some [that is, most scholars working on Qumran Aramaic] that the 'Aramaic of Daniel' must date to around 165 B.C.E."
59. Albertz claims that Hebrew Daniel (1–2:4a, 8–12) focuses only on how the stories and visions of Daniel 2–7 relate specifically to Israel and not to the rest of the world as do Aramaic chaps. 2–7 ("Social Setting," 175–79, esp. p. 176).

Although acknowledging that fact, Collins problematizes its value by noting the discontinuity between chap. 7 and chaps. 2–6 in the imagery used to fill out that kingdom theme.[60]

Structural Unity of Daniel 2–7

The chiastic organization of chaps. 2–7 is also used to support the view that, contra Collins's diachronic theory, they once comprised an independent and unified Aramaic book.[61] Albertz, among others, affirms Lenglet's claims that the contents of chaps. 2, 3, and 4 are redescribed in chaps. 7, 6, and 5, respectively: (1) chaps. 2 and 7 each have a four-kingdom schema; (2) chaps. 3 and 6 affirm the covenantal faithfulness of Jewish statesmen amidst Gentile royal courts by recounting tales of their miraculous deliverance from certain death; and (3) chaps. 4 and 5 describe the humbling of two Babylonian kings (Nebuchadnezzar and Belshazzar) and their resultant ascription of glory to God.[62] The message of divine supremacy over human government in chaps. 4 and 5 forms a fitting narratological centerpoint for the entire content of chaps. 2–7.

Dorothy Peters notes that the "bookending" of Aramaic Daniel (2:4b–7:28) by the Hebrew chapters of Daniel (1:1–2:4a and 8:1–12:13) is not unique among Jewish Second Temple scribal practices.[63] She claims that "bookending was a scribal strategy . . . whereby a reinterpreted version of a previously known text was adapted within a fresh retelling of the narrative and anchored to another text or figure" (for example, Moses).[64] Peters identifies two ideological motives for this diachronic literary strategy.

---

60. Collins, *Daniel*, 294.
61. See p. 346 n. 49 for Collins' diachronic theory. Albertz appears to mislabel Daniel 2–7 as a "concentric symmetry" because a chiastically structured narrative forms parallel centerpoints (A B C C′ B′ A′), while a concentrically symmetrical narrative forms a single centerpoint (A B C B′ A′) ("Social Setting," 176–79).
62. A. Lenglet, "La structure littéraire de Daniel 2–7," *Biblica* 53 (1972) 169–90. See Albertz, "Social Setting," 176–79. Another literary support for the unity of chaps. 2–7 is the inclusio formed by the ideologically contrastive expressions מלכות עלם, "everlasting kingdom" (7:27) and עלם in 2:4 (in the expression "O King live forever"; A. E. Portier-Young, "Languages of Identity and Obligation: Daniel as Bilingual Book," *VT* 60 [2010] 98–115, esp. p. 113).
63. D. M. Peters, "The Scrolls and Scriptures on the Margins: Remembered in Canon and Forgotten in Caves," in *The World of Jesus and the Early Church: Identity and Interpretation in Early Communities of Faith* (ed. Craig A. Evans; Peabody, MA: Hendrickson, 2011) 37–52, esp. pp. 41–42, 44, 50.
64. Ibid., 41. Bookending also occurs in the Book of Watchers (*1 Enoch* 1–36), wherein the oldest stratum, chaps. 6–11, was "bookended by Enoch's speeches in *1 En.* 1–5 and *1 En.* 12–36, [such that] the primary authoritative figure in *Watchers* is no longer Noah, but Enoch" (ibid., 42).

First, bookending allows time-bound Aramaic writings to be recontextualized for new cultural and political settings.[65] The differentiated descriptions of the "little horn" in Aramaic Daniel 7 and Hebrew Daniel 8 may very well be a witness of this phenomenon. If so, it suggests the validity of postulating Ptolemy I Soter as the original, time-bound referent for the "little horn" (Aramaic Daniel 7), which would then have required its historiographical recontextualization for a later Maccabean-era readership into a Seleucid "little horn" (Hebrew Daniel 8).

Second, Peters states that bookending helped to maintain the authority of time-bound Aramaic writings.[66] By the Maccabean era, the use of Aramaic for writing authoritative texts was on the decline.[67] The "Back to Torah movement" increasingly came to use Hebrew as "the language in which authoritative texts were written, particularly given its connection to Moses traditions."[68] Thus, with respect to the authoritative status of Aramaic Daniel 2–7, bookending them with the Hebrew chaps. 1 and 8–12 maintains their authority for a new Maccabean audience because the Hebrew chapters, particularly Daniel 9, shift "the focus from Daniel as the primary revealer and interpreter of dreams and vision to Moses and the written Torah."[69]

Although literary factors favor a unified compositional history for the Aramaic chapters of Daniel, Collins rightly observes that structural cohesion in and of itself "does not necessarily warrant the conclusion that these

---

65. Ibid., 42, 51.

66. Ibid. See also A. Sérandour, "Hébreu et Araméen dans la Bible," *REJ* 159 (2000) 345–55. He argues that Hebrew, as a local and sacred idiom, served to support religio-cultural identity formation, a factor of crucial importance during the Maccabean crisis.

67. Peters notes "a trend towards the centralization of authority in Moses [such that some] . . . texts were bookended by and subordinated to newly authoritative texts anchored to Moses while the authority of Aramaic texts not reworked into Hebrew compositions seems to have diminished" (ibid., 51; cf. also pp. 46, 48).

68. Ibid., 48.

69. Ibid., 44. Daniel 9 "introduces deuteronomic language of confession and repentance, of curse and oath, and the trangression of Torah" (ibid., 44); see also Peters, *Noah Traditions in the Dead Sea Scrolls: Conversations and Conversations in Antiquity* (SBLEJL 26; Atlanta: Society of Biblical Literature, 2009) 61, 184–89. Rather than Peters's diachronic approach, though, Portier-Young's sociolinguistic perspective uses a synchronic approach to argue that the very bilingual nature of Daniel 1–12 itself "project[s] a particular construction of the world, invite[s] the reader to adopt a particular identity and position within that world, and establish[es] a set of rights and obligations counter to those of the Seleucid empire." But her approach requires that "the entire book of Daniel was composed in the 2nd cent. B.C.E." ("Languages of Identity," 114).

chapters originated as a coherent composition."⁷⁰ It would seem, however, that when one combines the three factors of linguistic, thematic, and structural evidence, that their combined weight tips the scales in favor of a shared compositional history for chaps. 2–7, and, thus also, for a shared historical setting—the early Hellenistic period.

Some Implications for Second Temple Judaism(s) Studies

If one accords with this essay's contention that not just Daniel 7 but the entire Aramaic corpus of Daniel (chaps. 2–7) may very well reflect the socioreligious turmoil associated with the reign of Ptolemy I Soter, the study of early Hellenistic Jewish literature gains a new and important witness. Of particular value, then, would be an investigation both into the social history of the author/community behind the composition of Daniel 2–7 (dare one use the term *Danielic Judaism?*) and into its comparison with the social history of those groups of Jews who composed and read the Enochic corpus of literature, three of whose oldest writings are purported to date from early Hellenistic times (*1 Enoch* 6–11, 12–16, 72–82).⁷¹ Nickelsburg suggests that the Watchers in *1 Enoch* 6–11 allude to the Diadochoi ("the Giants") in their repetitive warfare between 323 B.C.E. and 302 B.C.E.⁷² Tigchelaar claims that *1 Enoch* 12–16 reflect an allegorical allusion to the Samaritan schism (ca. mid-fourth century B.C.E.), which Josephus reports in his *Antiquities* (11.306–12).⁷³ Albertz sees in

---

70. Collins, *Daniel*, 34.

71. G. Boccaccini argues for so-called Enochic Judaism, that is, a coherent social movement behind the writing of the five books of *1 Enoch* (late fourth century B.C.E. to the first century C.E.). See esp. his 1991 book (*Middle Judaism: Jewish Thought, 300 B.C.E. to 200 C.E.* [Minneapolis: Fortress, 1991]) and the four volumes edited by Boccaccini from the Enoch Seminar (2002, 2005, 2007, 2009). The Aramaic Enochic texts found at Qumran include: 4Q201, 202, 204–7, 212 (the Book of Watchers, the Book of Dreams, and the Epistle of Enoch); 4Q208–11 (the Astronomical Book); the Book of Giants (1Q23, 24, 26; 4Q203, 530–33).

72. *1 Enoch 1: A Commentary on the Book of 1 Enoch, Chapters 1–36; 81–108* (ed. K. Baltzer; Hermeneia; Minneapolis: Augsburg Fortress, 2001) 170.

73. Although the historicity of Josephus's complete account (*Ant.* 11.97–347) of the Samaritan schism has long been questioned, E. Tigchelaar (*Prophets of Old and the Day of the End: Zechariah, the Book of Watchers and Apocalyptic* [OtSt 35; Leiden: Brill, 1996] 199) suggests that, since the discovery of the Wadi Daliyeh papyri, the reliability of chaps. 306–12 is now more credible to scholars. At least one of Josephus's claims remains suspect though. Y. Magen ("The Dating of the First Phase of the Samaritan Temple on Mount Gerizim in Light of Archaeological Evidence," in *Judah and the Judeans in the Fourth Century B.C.E.* [ed. O. Lipschits, G. N. Knoppers, and R. Albertz; Winona Lake, IN: Eisenbrauns, 2007] 157–212) cites incontrovertible archaeological

the Chronicles' emphasis on the centrality of the temple cult and Davidic lineage another implicit polemic against the schismatic priests in Jerusalem who joined the Samaritan temple cult.[74]

If one allows for the possibility of Fletcher–Louis' argument that the high-priestly office is being alluded to in the vision of "the one like a son of man" (7:13, 14), then both a religious and a political polemic may be implicit.[75] Religiously, chap. 7 may be said to give implicit affirmation of the Jerusalem priesthood in its struggle against the Samaritan schismatics. Politically, an ironic polemic may be implicit therein such that the exaltation of the "the one like a son of man" could be interpreted as undermining Ptolemy I Soter's claim to sovereignty over Judea by exalting his Judean *prostasias* (the high priest in Jerusalem) as the "real" sovereign over the Judean temple state.[76]

Conclusion

It was the expressed intent of this essay to explore the historiographical implications of identifying the "little horn" in chap. 7 (but not in chap. 8) with Ptolemy I Soter (323–282 B.C.E.). Two primary implications were identified. First, it was seen that the differentiated descriptions of the "little horn" make it possible to suggest that the "little horn" of chap. 7 represents Ptolemy I Soter (323–282 B.C.E.) while the "little horn" of chap. 8 has as its original referent Antiochus IV Epiphanes (175–164 B.C.E.). This literary reapplication of the "little horn" implicitly serves to appropriate Aramaic Daniel's assumptions of divine determinacy, as evidenced in the periodization of history, within the historiography of Hebrew Daniel (chaps. 1, 8–12), thereby creating hope of divine deliverance

---

evidence that the first phase of the Samaritan temple's construction on Mt. Gerizim was in the fifth century B.C.E., rather than after Alexander's campaign in the Levant in 332 B.C.E. (*Ant.* 11.324).

74. R. Albertz, *A History of Israelite Religion in the Old Testament Period* (trans. J. Bowden; 2 vols.; OTL; Louisville: Westminster John Knox, 1994) 523–33.

75. See p. 340 n. 23.

76. Hecataeus calls the Jewish high priest a *prostasias*, "the people's representative" (Diod. XL, 3, 5). The extent of power accorded a *prostasias* in third century B.C.E. Judea is uncertain. Tcherikover (*Hellenistic Civilization*, 59) claims that, under Ptolemaic rule, "the *prostasias* was a permanent position . . . in the hands of the high priest . . . [and was not unlike] a petty monarch." Schäfer (*History of the Jews*, 16), however, doubts that "the Ptolemies treated the temple state of Judea differently than other temple cities in Egypt whereby, in addition to the high priest, an official was appointed with a function similar to that of the *epistates* (financial official) . . . who was directly responsible to the King."

for a new generation of Jews facing a Gentile antagonist. Second, the literary strategy of bookending may very well have functioned to impute the authoritative status of Daniel's Aramaic chapters to the subsequently written Hebrew chapters, which were specifically created for a Maccabean readership. Both historiographical implications allow for an early Hellenistic, rather than only for a late pre-Maccabean origin, for the "exilic" prophecy of Daniel 7.

Two primary questions were asked with respect to the validity of identifying the "little horn" of Daniel 7 with Ptolemy I Soter. First, can the rest of Daniel 7, not just the "little horn" imagery, function as a symbolic history of Judean events in the early Hellenistic, rather than only in the late pre-Maccabean, period? The combined witness of six historiographical elements in the rest of Daniel 7 seems to correlate as well with the reign of Ptolemy I Soter as it does with the reign of Antiochus IV Epiphanes. Based on *ex eventu* assumptions, it does not appear unrealistic, then, to suggest a compositional date for Daniel 7 sometime soon after the battle of Ipsus (301 B.C.E.).

The second question asked was whether the entire Aramaic corpus of Daniel demonstrates sufficient internal unity to support a contemporaneous compositional history for chaps. 2–7, rather than only for chaps. 2–6. If so, chap. 7 could then be linked literarily and not just historiographically, with an early Hellenistic compositional date. Linguistic, thematic, and structural evidence supports such a thesis, thereby placing into question the necessity of explaining the "little horn" in Daniel 7 as a secondary redaction.

But many more questions still remain to be asked, let alone answered. This study is but a small beginning in a potentially fruitful direction, particularly as it relates to an analysis of the intersections between the social histories of so-called Enochic Judaism and what one might perhaps call "Danielic Judaism." That study, however, remains for another day, and perhaps even, another author.

(Re)Visionary History: Historiography and Religious Identity *in the* Animal Apocalypse

COLIN M. TOFFELMIRE

The *Animal Apocalypse* of *1 Enoch* 85–90 offers an example of ancient historiography in the form of a prophetic vision of the history of the people of Israel in which the players are represented by animals.[1] By assuming the mantle of Enoch, the pseudonymous author is able to offer his comments regarding Israelite history and identity as an authoritative prophet/sage/ revealer and perfect priest living in the ancient past.[2] As prophet, sage, and revealer, Enoch sees the close resemblance between the primordial deluge, the exodus, and the Seleucid-era sufferings of YHWH's people, implying that readers or listeners should respond as did their ancient forebears with faithfulness to YHWH and revolt against apostasy and foreign rule. As priest, Enoch draws divisions between the elect and nonelect based on

---

1. By "historiography," I mean history writing as an interpretive act, or as a way of organizing and accounting for both past events and present circumstances. For various definitions of and distinctions between "history" and "historiography," see S. D. Beeson, "Historiography Ancient and Modern Fact and Fiction," in *Ancient and Modern Scriptural Historiography* (ed. G. Brooke and T. Römer; Leuven: Leuven University Press, 2007) 3–4; J. Van Seters, *In Search of History: Historiography in the Ancient World and the Origins of Biblical History* (New Haven, CT: Yale University Press, 1983) 1, 2, 5; E. Breisach, *Historiography: Ancient, Medieval, and Modern* (2nd ed.; Chicago: University of Chicago Press, 1994) 3, 7, 13.

2. Though I recognize that questions of authorship and redaction are relatively complicated with regards to the *Animal Apocalypse*, I am concerned in this essay with a synchronic examination of the final form of the apocalypse as it has been reconstructed by modern scholarship. I will, for the sake of ease, refer to the author(s) and redactor(s) of the *Animal Apocalypse* as either "the author" or "pseudo-Enoch" throughout this essay. For an examination of authorship and redaction in relation to the *Animal Apocalypse* and the Book of Dreams generally, see: P. Tiller, *A Commentary on the Animal Apocalypse of 1 Enoch* (SBLEJL 4; Atlanta: Scholars Press, 1993) 61–79; G. Nickelsburg, *A Commentary on the Book of 1 Enoch Chapters 1–36; 81–108* (Minneapolis: Fortress, 2001) 347, 360–63. References to "Enoch," consequently, indicate the prophetic figure who serves as visionary within the discourse world of the dream visions of *1 Enoch*.

cultic categories of clean versus unclean, thus establishing the "sides" in the revolutionary conflict. Through Enoch's dream-vision, pseudo-Enoch retells Israelite history in order to establish a religious history and identity for Jews living in Seleucid-era Yehud. History thus becomes a frame in which the author sets his message of religious and militant resistance.

One might ask whether pursuing the historiography of an apocalypse is warranted. U. Rappaport suggests that apocalyptic literature has no real interest in history apart from as a springboard for a vision of the future.[3] Rappaport pits the historiography found in apocalyptic literature (Daniel 11 in particular) against his definition of "scientific" history, which he never strictly defines but suggests is better represented by an ancient Greek view of historiography and which has a different outlook in terms of "criterion for truth; what really happened; beginnings; causes; human behaviour."[4] In the first place, it should be noted that Rappaport's "scientific" standard involves the external imposition of a different cultural standard. Second, even if Rappaport's point is given, it does not follow that apocalyptic literature has no interest in the past or that it is interested only in the future. Neither Daniel 11 nor the *Animal Apocalypse* could ever meet the requirements of this sort of definition, principally because the authors of these works did not understand the world in terms of human conditions, terms, or deeds. It does not follow, however, that apocalyptic literature has no interest in the past or that it is interested only in the future. As J.-D. Kaestli notes in response to Rappaport, apocalyptic literature is concerned with all realities, "spatiales et temporelles."[5] Indeed, as I will demonstrate below, if the *Animal Apocalypse* is more concerned about any particular point in time it is the present and not the future.[6] Therefore, though we can expect no adherence to modern historiographical methods,[7] the *Animal Apocalypse* does operate within the confines of a

---

3. U. Rappaport, "Apocalyptic Vision and Preservation of Historical Memory," *JSJ* 23 (1992) 226.

4. Rappaport, "Vision," 219 n. 5.

5. J.-D. Kaestli, "Les Rapports Entre Apocalyptique et Historiographie," in *Ancient and Modern Scriptural Historiography* (ed. G. Brooke and T. Römer; Leuven: Leuven University Press, 2007) 199.

6. See also A. Portier-Young, *Theologies of Resistance in Daniel, the Apocalypse of Weeks, the Book of Dreams, and the Testament of Moses* (Ph.D. diss., Duke University, 2004) 134; Tiller, *Commentary*, 15.

7. As both Beeson and Breisach note, modern historiographies are historiographies nonetheless, and are founded on ideological and methodological assumptions of their own. See Beeson, "Historiography," 10; and Breisach, *Historiography*, 407–8.

kind of historiography, and that historiography is concerned with the past, the present, and the future.[8]

This essay will examine the *Animal Apocalypse* in an attempt to uncover the function of the historical account as it is presented in the dream vision.[9] Though this will be primarily an examination of literature, the historical milieu in which the work was likely created, Seleucid-controlled Yehud between 165 and 160 B.C.E., will play a role in the discussion below.[10] The exploration of historiographical function will involve two particular elements of the allegory. First, Enoch functions as prophet, sage, and revealer, creating a type/antitype relationship between past and present. Second, Enoch functions as priest, leading to the clean-versus-unclean metaphor that controls the allegory and creating a division between the elect and the nonelect.[11] I will begin with an examination of the use of Enoch as visionary, examining his sapiential, revelatory, and prophetic roles. In the following section I will turn my attention to Enoch's role as priest and the presentation of the clean/unclean division that is found in the *Animal Apocalypse*, examining the hierarchy of election that is created by means of this controlling metaphor. Though some analysis of the historiographical function of various elements will be provided throughout, I will reserve the majority of this discussion for the fourth section.

---

8. As A. Portier-Young (*Apocalypse against Empire: Apocalyptic Theologies of Resistance in Early Judaism* [Grand Rapids: Eerdmans, 2010] 13) notes, apocalyptic literature like the *Animal Apocalypse* "[turns] to history as a means of revealing the contingency of present realities." With sincere thanks to Dr. Portier-Young for a prepublication draft of a portion of her recently released work.

9. Nickelsburg demonstrates the close resemblance of the events in the animal history to the accounts found in the Pentateuch, the Deuteronomistic History, *1 Enoch* 6–11, and possibly Ezra–Nehemiah, but correctly states that "[the] author of the Vision has constructed his allegory through the *creative and tendentious* use of traditional materials" (*Commentary*, 358, emphasis added).

10. For the date, see Portier-Young, *Theologies of Resistance*, 131; J. C. VanderKam, *Enoch and the Growth of an Apocalyptic Tradition* (CBQMS 16; Washington, DC: Catholic Biblical Association of America, 1984) 161; Tiller, *Commentary*, 63–78. See Tiller especially for a more extensive discussion of the date and provenance of the *Animal Apocalypse*. He suggests the *Animal Apocalypse* was probably written closer to 165 B.C.E. See also Russell, *Divine Disclosure: An Introduction to Jewish Apocalyptic Literature* (Minneapolis: Fortress, 1992) 40. For a contrasting view, see C. Rowland, *The Open Heaven: A Study of Apocalyptic in Judaism and Early Christianity* (New York: Crossroad, 1982) 252.

11. It should be noted that there is a degree of overlap between these two elements and their historiographical function in the *Animal Apocalypse*. As will become clear below the theme of election is tied to the roles of Enoch as well as to the clean versus unclean division.

Enoch the (Re)Visionary

The pseudepigraphical use of a visionary figure such as Enoch is not uncommon for prophetic literature of the Second Temple period. A. Jassen notes, "[unlike] the classical presentation of prophets in the Hebrew Bible, the Qumran documents and related Second Temple period texts rarely introduce any particular contemporary individual with a prophetic title or identify prophetic activity as such."[12] Jassen goes on to suggest that Enoch was not considered a prophet by Second Temple authors and readers,[13] but it may be more accurate to say he was not a prophetic figure in the traditional sense. Enoch's role as prophet functions as an extension of his more common role as sage and revealer of divine mysteries. By taking on the mantle of Enoch, the great sage, revealer, and prophet, pseudo-Enoch creates a bridge between the primordial past and the conflicted present and helps to show the faithful their place in Israel's history.

As J. VanderKam notes, the oldest extant Enochic compositions are the Astronomical Book, the Book of the Watchers, and the Book of Dreams (which includes the *Animal Apocalypse*).[14] The first two compositions have "an emphatic scientific interest" and paint a picture of Enoch as a wise sage who has an intimate knowledge of the truths of the universe.[15] Enoch is the ultimate sapiential sage, equal to or possibly greater than Moses himself.[16]

In his discussion of the relationship between the *Genesis Apocryphon* and *1 Enoch* 13, D. Machiela makes note of the highly influential role played by Enoch.[17] In both accounts, the fallen angelic beings ask Enoch to make petition on their behalf to God. Enoch's status is so great that even heavenly beings recognize his importance and authority, as well as his unique relationship to God. In both the Book of Watchers and the *Genesis Apocryphon*, Enoch "is the veritable embodiment of divine revelation—an enfleshed apocalypse."[18] Enoch is the perfect revealer of divine mystery.

---

12. A. Jassen, *Mediating the Divine: Prophecy and Revelation in the Dead Sea Scrolls and Second Temple Judaism* (STDJ 68; Leiden: Brill, 2007) 6.
13. Jassen, *Mediating*, 260.
14. VanderKam, *Growth*, 140–41; Russell, *Divine*, 38–40.
15. VanderKam, *Growth*, 141. Note also *Jub.* 4:16–25, where Enoch appears as the progenitor of all knowledge and wisdom (ibid., 9–10).
16. Jassen, *Mediating*, 265–66.
17. D. A. Machiela, "Genesis Revealed: The Apocalyptic Apocryphon from Qumran Cave 1," in *Qumran Cave 1 Revisited: Texts from Cave 1 Sixty Years after Their Discovery* (ed. D. K. Falk et al.; STDJ 91; Leiden: Brill, 2010) 4. With sincere thanks to Dr. Machiela for providing me with a prepublication draft of this article.
18. Machiela, "Genesis," 8–9.

In the Book of Dreams, this revelatory role is developed into a prophetic role, as the content of divine revelation shifts from present to future. As VanderKam notes, this makes Enoch's "understanding of the course of history as comprehensive and insightful as his grasp of the universe."[19] Enoch knows not only the mysteries of the universe and the divine will, but the mystery of the complete future history of the people of Israel as well.

This portrait of Enoch as the ultimate sage, revealer, and prophet is vital to the *Animal Apocalypse*. As L. Stuckenbruck suggests, framing the animal history as an Enochic vision allows pseudo-Enoch to tie the events of his own time to events in the distant, primordial past.

> With respect to the *Animal Apocalypse*, the author(s) found in "Enoch" a way to coordinate the inner frames of *Urzeit* and *Endzeit*: During a remote era of increasing destruction and evil, Enoch is made to recount visions that anticipate a decisive divine intervention in the Great Deluge. By analogy, a real writer, as "Enoch," was interpreting contemporary events to support his conviction that a final eradication of evil powers and the reestablishment of a new world order were imminent.[20]

Of particular importance is the message that the trajectory of history is about to change dramatically, just as it did at the time of the Flood.

Enoch's perfect knowledge as sage, revealer, and prophet allows him to assess correctly his present and near future (pseudo-Enoch's past), and tie this to God's distant future plans (pseudo-Enoch's present). This creates a type/antitype motif that connects the antediluvian generation with pseudo-Enoch's apostate contemporaries, as well as the exodus from Egypt and desert wanderings with the final eschatological judgment. As in much apocalyptic literature, here in the *Animal Apocalypse*, "[eschatology] and protology are in fact two sides of the same coin."[21]

---

19. VanderKam, *Growth*, 141.
20. L. T. Stuckenbruck, "'Reading the Present' in the Animal Apocalypse (*1 Enoch* 85–90)," in *Reading the Present in the Qumran Library: The Perception of the Contemporary by Means of Scriptural Interpretations* (ed. K. De Troyer and A. Lange; SBLSymS 30; Atlanta: Society of Biblical Literature, 2005) 92. See also Koch, "The Astral Laws as the Basis of Time, Universal History, and the Eschatological Turn in the Astronomical Book and the Animal Apocalypse of *1 Enoch*," in *The Early Enoch Literature* (ed. G. Boccaccini and J. J. Collins; SJSJ 121; Leiden: Brill, 2007) 134.
21. P. Sacchi, "The Theology of Early Enochism and Apocalyptic: The Problem of the Relation between Form and Content of the Apocalypses. The Worldview of Apocalypses," in *The Origins of Enochic Judaism* (ed. G. Boccaccini; Torino: Silvio Zamorani Editore, 2002) 77–85.

As Stuckenbruck suggests, the final age described in the *Animal Apocalypse* (that is, pseudo-Enoch's present) was seen as equal in evil and wickedness to the antediluvian age. Just as that age led to the great Flood, so this age leads inexorably to God's final intervention on behalf of his elect. "The dimensions of antediluvian evil show themselves once again, though with a different face. On this point, the fictive and 'real' horizons of the present converge."[22] The other point of commonality between the two eras is the promise of God's salvation for the elect. Here we find a connection between the first and second dream visions. Enoch's prayer in 84:1–6 that a remnant be saved is fulfilled in 89:1–9. "The author's own community were to self-identify as antitypes of the righteous Noah, the remnant saved from the Flood, and Enoch, whose intercession helped effect that salvation."[23]

Combined with this flood/final age motif is the exodus-desert/eschaton motif. The exodus and desert wanderings represent, in the *Animal Apocalypse*, "an ideal period."[24] A. Portier-Young makes note of several points of similarity between the exodus and God's final intervention in the *Animal Apocalypse*. These include "themes of darkness (90:15), splitting (now the earth 90:18), sinking of the enemies (now into the earth 90:18) and covering (90:18)."[25] The parallel leads to the conclusion that this final eschatological event and the following new age are the culmination of God's work. Here what was begun in the Flood and the exodus from Egypt will be made complete. And at the close of this strongly deterministic history,[26] the faithful elect, represented by the lambs, must play their part.[27]

This type/antitype motif thus creates a portrait of both an entirely unacceptable state of affairs and an ideal period. The unacceptable state of the past (*1 Enoch* 87–88) is mirrored in the unacceptable state of the present

---

22. Stuckenbruck, "Reading," 101.
23. Portier-Young, *Theologies of Resistance*, 140; see also VanderKam, *Growth*, 170.
24. Idem, *Enoch: A Man for All Generations* (Columbia: University of South Carolina, 1995) 78.
25. Portier-Young, *Theologies of Resistance*, 182. See also Tiller, *Commentary*, 286–87; and Nickelsburg, *Commentary*, 379, 401.
26. Koch, "Astral Laws," 133. See H. Kvanvig ("Cosmic Laws and Cosmic Imbalance," in *The Early Enoch Literature* [ed. G. P Boccaccini and J. J. Collins; SJSJ 121; Leiden: Brill, 2007] 139–58), who suggests that we find the opposite situation in the book of the Watchers, where "the cosmos is out of divine control."
27. M. Henze, "Enoch's Dream Visions and the Visions of Daniel Reexamined," in *Enoch and Qumran Origins: New Light on a Forgotten Connection* (ed. B. Boccaccini; Grand Rapids: Eerdmans, 2005) 17–22.

(90:1–5). Likewise, the ideal period of the past (89:16–40) is mirrored in the ideal period of the future (90:6–38). Thus, the present state of foreign rule must end, and the ideal period of God's rule and the supremacy of the elect must be reinstated. This can only be brought about if the actions of the faithful (that is, those who hear and accept the teaching of pseudo-Enoch) echo the actions of Noah, Moses, and Enoch himself.

Clean and Unclean

The division between Israel and the nations of the world envisaged by the author of the *Animal Apocalypse* is drawn precisely along the line between clean and unclean animals.[28] In all cases, Israel is depicted by ritually pure animals and in all cases Israel's earthly enemies are depicted by ritually impure animals. What is more, all of the enemies of God are depicted as unclean, even when these enemies belong by nature to Israel. Enoch, the perfect priest, demonstrates that he is able to divide clean from unclean, elect from nonelect. This clean/unclean division represents the controlling metaphor for the animal imagery in the allegory.[29] The connections between this controlling metaphor and the historiography of the *Animal Apocalypse* will, for the most part, be drawn in the fourth section of this essay.

In addition to his role as perfect sage/revealer/prophet, Enoch also plays the role of the perfect priest in both the Book of the Watchers (*1 Enoch* 14:8–23) and in the *Animal Apocalypse* (*1 Enoch* 87:3). There, he is shown the heavenly temple itself, the only human to receive this honor. This priest, who is fit for service in the heavenly temple, is thus able

---

28. Note that significant portions of this section have been adapted from my M.A. thesis. For the original version, see my "White Bulls and Wild Goats: Animal Imagery in Daniel 7 and 8 and the Animal Apocalypse of *1 Enoch*" (M.A. thesis, Ambrose Seminary, 2008) esp. pp. 59–66.

29. Though I use the term *allegory* to describe the *Animal Apocalypse*, it is important to note that the *Animal Apocalypse* is not an allegory in the traditional, Western sense. That is to say, it is not a tale in which abstract virtues or ideas are personified (see J. Whitman, "Allegory," in *The Princeton Encyclopedia of Poetry and Poetics* (ed. A. Preminger and T. V. F. Brogan; Princeton: Princeton University Press, 1993) 31–35; S. Taylor Coleridge, "From The Statesman's Manual," in *Critical Theory since Plato* (ed. H. Adams; New York: Harcourt Brace Jovanovich, 1971) 468. Instead, it is a historical survey in which the various actors are represented (generally) as animals. When I speak in terms of a "controlling metaphor," I am attempting to describe the way in which the selection of the various images that represent humans and angels in the allegory has been made. The most important criterion for selection is not related to the level of the individual image (bull, hyrax, raven, and so on) but is related instead to the level of the entire system of images.

to see the truth of God's system of election by means of the division of animals in his dream vision.

As an extension of this status as priest (and of sage, revealer, and prophet), Enoch is also the very definition of God's elect. He is the ultimate example of faith and obedience, and of God's favor. Note that in the *Animal Apocalypse* he is the only human figure who does not appear to die and who is translated into the heavenly realm, and more specifically to the heavenly temple, before the destruction of the earth in the flood (87:1–4). Even Noah and Moses do not receive this honor. The use of Enoch suggests that the author of the *Animal Apocalypse* is not only making a bid for legitimacy by aligning his work with that great and holy prophet, but he is laying claim to his own status as one of God's elect. "The future generations who will gain access to Enoch's writings and thus to divine knowledge are singled out as appropriate recipients because they are deemed to be righteous."[30] All who read and align themselves with the *Animal Apocalypse* gain knowledge of Enoch's hierarchy of election, and demonstrate their own place with the elect in that hierarchy.

Just as the priestly dietary laws of Leviticus and Deuteronomy set up a hierarchy of holiness within the animal kingdom and the human community, so also the use of clean and unclean animals in the *Animal Apocalypse* sets up a hierarchy of holiness and rightness.[31] This hierarchy exists with God at its head, followed closely by all of those who have taken on (and maintained) human form, followed again by the ritually clean animals that represent the majority of the people of Israel, followed finally by the ritually unclean animals that represent the nations that conspire against the people of God and continually attempt to destroy them.

One of the significant clues to the hierarchical nature of the structure of the allegory is the inclusion and the behavior of the angelic beings. The first mention of nonanimal beings in the *Animal Apocalypse* is the description of the fallen star that becomes a bull. It falls to earth and becomes a participant in what occurs there. It is difficult to determine from the text whether this first fallen star is responsible for the violence of the oxen in 86:2, but it is certainly possible and probably implied by the closeness of the two events.[32] Regardless of the measure of culpability that can be as-

---

30. Jassen, *Mediating*, 271.

31. For an alternate view in which the clean/unclean division is only a component of the selection criteria in the *Animal Apocalypses*, see Tiller, *Commentary*, 28–29.

32. This first star is almost certainly Asael, who in the Book of Watchers taught humanity metallurgy and warfare (*1 En.* 8:1) and was primarily responsible for introducing sin into the world (*1 En.* 10:8). See Tiller, *Commentary*, 236; Nickelsburg, *Commentary*, 372.

signed to the first star in those early acts of destruction, there is no doubt that the subsequent fallen stars of 86:3–4 are completely responsible for the production of the first unclean animals in the vision. As in the story of the Watchers found in *1 Enoch* 6–16, it is these fallen stars that provide the first true division among the races.

The introduction of the heavenly beings that become oxen and the consequent advent of the unclean animals comprise a single metaphorical system. This particular passage is important because it is the first instance of interaction between different species or types of being, represented by different kinds of creatures. The heavenly beings are represented first by stars (86:1) and then by "white men" (87:2). These represent the highest order of creature in Enoch's hierarchy of created beings. That these are of the highest order is demonstrated in the descent of the watchers (chap. 86) and in the promotion of Noah (89:1) and Moses (89:36) from clean animals to human forms.[33] After the heavenly beings come the clean animals, which are represented by two subtiers: the bulls and oxen first, and the rams and sheep second. Finally, we have the unclean animals, which include both the animals that are specifically referred to by Leviticus and Deuteronomy and the animals that do not meet the criteria of clean animals. The culmination of Enoch's vision demonstrates that the unclean animals occupy the lowest place in the vision's hierarchy and that the clean bulls are considered a higher form than the clean sheep. Though all of these animals are redeemed in Enoch's new world (90:29–33), their redemption is made complete only when they are all transformed into white bulls (90:38).

Concerning P. Tiller's suggestion that the use of clean animals to represent Israel denotes their "acceptance by God,"[34] it is important to note that the type of animal used to represent a character in the vision does not, in and of itself, reliably predict whether that character will be accepted or judged harshly by God. The watchers who become bulls (the highest level of the clean animal) are, at the end of the vision, "judged and found guilty, and [taken] to the place of condemnation, and they were cast into an abyss, full of flaming fire, and full of pillars of fire" (90:24). Likewise,

---

33. Lange's suggestion that Moses and Noah move into the heavenly realm is only accurate to a degree. Note that both Noah (89:9) and Moses (89:38) die human deaths. They are not, therefore, translated into the heavenly realm but instead move up one level in the cosmic hierarchy. Compare this with Enoch's translation into heaven (87:3–4). Armin Lange, "Dream Visions and Apocalyptic Milieus," in *Enoch and Qumran Origins: New Light on a Forgotten Connection* (ed. G. Boccaccini; Grand Rapids: Eerdmans, 2005) 28–29.

34. Tiller, *Commentary*, 29.

the sheep who were blinded (and remained so; 89:74; 90:7) are later cast into "a like abyss . . . and they burned" (90:26). It is clear, therefore, that judgment is not reserved for the unclean animals. Indeed, the unclean animals do not suffer the judgment of the abyss but are instead transformed into clean animals and become a part of the perfect eschatological community (90:38).

More important than the initial nature of a given group is its trajectory. Note that the stars are demoted to the tier of the bulls (86:3). Though they may have begun their existence at the highest level of God's hierarchy of election, they willfully removed themselves from that standing. After that point they are no longer stars but fallen stars (88:1). Additionally, these fallen stars have genitalia "like horses" (86:4). It is possible that this suggests an element of defect or uncleanness, thus including the fallen stars within the realm of the unclean animals.[35]

A similar change of nature is found in the blind sheep that are cast into the abyss. Blindness is taken almost universally by scholars as a metaphor for some kind of spiritual or ethical defect in these particular sheep. L. Stuckenbruck sees this as a sign of a lack of discernment.[36] Portier-Young sees a double layer of signification in which sight indicates both right understanding and right action.[37] G. Nickelsburg provides a brief excursus on sight and blindness where he presents a similar interpretation, suggesting that blindness is related to following or not following God's law.[38] Tiller suggests that sight and blindness are related to the Enochic wisdom tradition.[39] All of these interpretations are sound, but they neglect an important component of the image of the blind sheep, namely, the consequent cultic defilement of the sheep.

Blindness in a sacrificial animal makes that animal unfit for sacrifice (Lev 22:22), and the use of this sort of animal defiles the altar (Mal 1:6–8). The affliction of blindness on some of the sheep pushes them into the category "unclean" and consequently pushes them out of the category "elect."[40] So Portier-Young is incorrect when she suggests that the lambs of *1 En.* 90:6

---

35. Admittedly, this second element is rather tenuous. Tiller suggests, quite legitimately, that this may be a proverbial reference related to lust or size of genitalia, and found in earlier biblical literature like Ezek 23:20. Tiller, *Commentary*, 240. So also Nickelsburg, *Commentary*, 372.

36. Stuckenbruck, "Reading," 99.

37. Portier-Young, *Theologies of Resistance*, 159.

38. Nickelsburg, *Commentary*, 380–81.

39. Tiller, *Commentary*, 26.

40. This is contra Koch, who suggests that "Enoch narrates that the sheep went astray again and again and became blind but nevertheless retained their special rela-

are "continuous with the white sheep who in *Animal Apocalypse* symbolize the elect of Israel."[41] The opening of the eyes of the lambs indicates that, unlike their blind forebears, these new lambs are not defiled and maintain their status as part of the elect. They are not continuous with the blind sheep that immediately precede them but with preexilic sheep.[42]

This is a question of particular importance because of the connection between the blind sheep of 89:73 and the lambs of 90:6–9. If, as VanderKam suggests, 90:16–17 represent the tipping point between past and future from the point of view of the author of the *Animal Apocalypse*, then the behavior of the lambs in 90:8–18 represents the behavior (or desired behavior) of the author's compatriots and thus the heart of the message of the *Animal Apocalypse*. These lambs who have begun "to open their eyes" (90:6) are the first generation to do so since the Preexilic Period. They are the first of God's people to fall legitimately into the category of clean/elect for many generations. As we will see below, the relationship between the lambs and the "extremely and excessively" (90:7) blind sheep that precede them will be central in our understanding of pseudo-Enoch's view of history and election.

Also notable is the relationship between the clean and unclean animals in the allegory, which offers an insight into the nature of election in the Enochic system. The nations represented by the unclean animals are never thought of as unrelated to Israel, nor are they necessarily its enemies (though many of them will become enemies over the course of time).[43] They are simply considered inferior by nature. The inferiority of the unclean animals is a product of being born outside the line of election. No rationale for election is ever offered. The author simply assumes that all who are clearly of Israel are elect, and all others are not. Therefore, only the descendants of Adam who make up the line of descent that will become the nation of Israel are depicted as clean animals.

---

tion to the God of *ʿalam* (84:54) throughout the whole history." Koch, "Astral Laws," 130–31.

41. Portier-Young, *Theologies of Resistance*, 157.

42. Both Nickelsburg (*Commentary*, 395 n. 18) and Tiller (*Commentary*, 340) make note of the relationship between the defiled table of *1 En.* 89:73 and the condemnation of priests in Mal 1:8, but neither draw a connection between the blindness of the sheep in the allegory, the impure table in both passages, and the blindness of the sacrifice in Malachi.

43. As Tiller notes regarding the swine and hyrax, "[their] presence in this list reminds the reader that as all of the animals listed are unclean, whether or not they are harmful to sheep, so no Gentile nation is acceptable to God, whether or not it is harmful to Israel" (Tiller, *Commentary*, 31).

This tie to the past and the unbroken line of election that leads even to the author's own time demonstrates that the people of Judea are God's elect, and that they are therefore intrinsically superior. All other nations and peoples are merely the inferior offspring of the elect and as such, should not rule over the elect. They are, in fact, so inferior that no Gentile leader is ever singled out or represented by a specific animal.[44] This is a tale only of the elect. Regarding the relationship between the elect and the nonelect, note particularly *1 En.* 90:37–38. Here, we are told that "all the wild beasts and all the birds of heaven were afraid of [the white bull] and made petition to it continually" (v. 37). This precedes the translation of the unclean animals into "white cattle" (v. 38). Only after giving obeisance to the great messianic/patriarchal figure,[45] the ultimate among the human elect, are the unclean peoples transformed and admitted into the eschatological community.

This emphasis on election and on the intrinsic superiority of the Jewish people is a keystone of the *Animal Apocalypse*'s historiography. The function of Enoch as heavenly priest and the consequent clean-versus-unclean structure of the allegory emphasizes this central concept. This vision is, at its core, a tale of the necessity of the superiority and triumph of God's elect over their oppressors.

Tying the Present to the Past

In this final section, I will examine the historiography of the *Animal Apocalypse*, particularly in light of the preceding two sections, against the background of mid-second-century B.C.E. Yehud. The two components of the *Animal Apocalypse* that I have identified, both of which are connected to the concept of election, reflect two elements of the social reality undergirding the historiography of the *Animal Apocalypse*. The function of Enoch and the type/antitype motif reflect pseudo-Enoch's deep concern with foreign rule. The clean/unclean division is tied to his concern with dividing the elect from the nonelect and is consequently connected to current conflicts and tensions among his fellow Jews. Those conflicts are in turn connected to pseudo-Enoch's concerns with the current state of the temple and cult. Consequently, in this section I will examine the interrelated issues of the relationship between the *Animal Apocalypse* and various

---

44. Nickelsburg, *Commentary*, 396.
45. It is unclear which term most accurately describes the great white bull. VanderKam uses both (*Man*, 84) and Nickelsburg suggests that it is a messianic figure (*Commentary*, 406).

proposed "groups" operating at the time, the treatment of temple and cult in the *Animal Apocalypse,* and the current, unacceptable state of foreign rule. I will demonstrate that the historiography of the *Animal Apocalypse* is born out of a theology of election and superiority and is designed to encourage vehement religious and militant resistance.

Though reconstructing the history of Persian-period Yehud is intrinsically problematic due to the paucity of sources,[46] P. Sacchi suggests that according to some evidence there may have existed a two-part power structure in Jerusalem throughout the Persian and Greek periods, legitimized by foreign imperial power.[47] Regardless of whether this was the case throughout the Persian period, during the Greek period foreign powers certainly dictated much of the politics of Jerusalem.[48] In describing the attempt by Simon of Bilgah (see 2 Macc 3:4–6) to gain power of the temple by essentially bribing the Seleucids, Sacchi notes that this suggests the power of the priesthood in Jerusalem derived from external sources. "It was only because of their fidelity to the succession of kings who dominated Palestine that the priests had been able to maintain their power."[49] This seems to be precisely the thing that the author of the *Animal Apocalypse* despises.

As noted above, the concern of the *Animal Apocalypse* is with the behavior of God's people in the present. It is, of course, necessary to ask: what is pseudo-Enoch's present? The tipping point between past and present in the vision can be fixed quite clearly at 90:16–17.[50] Here, history as pseudo-Enoch knew it ends, and we see the beginnings of God's active and irrevocable intervention in the story. If the message of the *Animal Apocalypse* is concerned with the present behavior of pseudo-Enoch's generation, then it seems advisable to reflect briefly on the sociocultural milieu suggested by various apocalypses, as well as the relationship between the *Animal Apocalypse* and what, for the sake of convenience, we might refer to as Jewish society at large.

There is currently a great deal of debate concerning the notion of apocalyptic groups or sects that may have been responsible for the various pieces of extant literature from the Second Temple period.[51] First of all,

---

46. L. Grabbe, *Judaism from Cyrus to Hadrian* (Minneapolis: Fortress, 1992) 142.
47. P. Sacchi, *The History of the Second Temple Period* (JSOTSup 285; Sheffield: Sheffield Academic Press, 2000) 166. See also pp. 14 and 116 n. 5.
48. VanderKam, *Growth*, 142.
49. Sacchi, *History*, 222; see also p. 224.
50. VanderKam, *Growth*, 163.
51. See Henze's description and summary of the debate between Collins and Hengel over the so-called "Hasidim" ("Dream Visions," 18).

what do we mean by "group" or "sect"? A. Yarbro Collins suggests that "it has something to do with people who hold themselves as exclusive in some way, as those exclusively saved, righteous, or elect."[52] As we have seen, the author of the *Animal Apocalypse* saw himself, and likely some subset of the Jewish people, in terms like this. But is it therefore possible to identify a particular "Enoch" group or "Book of Dreams" group that might be set against, for instance, a "Sirach" group or a "Daniel" group?[53] Even among specialists, there is little agreement on what can or cannot be said about groups such as these.[54] A. Lange suggests that it is more helpful to speak in terms of "a wider apocalyptic milieu" in order to explain the various points of similarity and difference between the Daniel and Enoch texts,[55] but as J. Davila's response demonstrates, the similarities are so generic and the differences so pronounced that any such category loses all meaningful value.[56]

Perhaps the most helpful suggestion at this stage is Tiller's view:

> Nothing in Daniel, Enoch, or Sirach can be taken as evidence for the existence of a community, group, or movement. There is evidence only for the existence of a class of professional sages and teachers, trained in the traditions of their aristocratic or apocalyptic wisdom, whose politically charged teachings had an impact on their own and subsequent generations.[57]

Certainly, the existence of diverse religious literature, sometimes with competing aims, reinforces the conflicted nature of Jewish society under Greek rule. But what we find in the *Animal Apocalypse* is not the manifesto of a clearly defined sociological group, but a piece of religious literature composed for the purpose of influencing Jewish society at large.

With regard to the relationship between the message of the *Animal Apocalypse* and larger Jewish society, there are some things that can be said

---

52. A. Yarbro Collins, "The Theology of Early Enoch Literature," in *The Origins of Enochic Judaism* (ed. G. Boccaccini; Torino: Silvio Zamorani Editore, 2002) 112.

53. See P. Tiller, "The Sociological Settings of the Components of *1 Enoch*," in *The Early Enoch Literature* (ed. Boccaccini and J. J. Collins; SJSJ 121; Leiden: Brill, 2007) 237–55, esp. p. 254.

54. See Yarbro Collins's description of the panel discussion at the 2001 *Enoch* Seminar, "Theology," 112.

55. Lange, "Dream Visions and Apocalyptic Milieus," 34.

56. J. R. Davila, "The Animal Apocalypse and Daniel," in *Enoch and Qumran Origins: New Light on a Forgotten Connection* (ed. B. Boccaccini; Grand Rapids: Eerdmans, 2005) 35–38.

57. P. Tiller, "The Sociological Context of the Dream Visions of Daniel and *1 Enoch*," in *Enoch and Qumran Origins: New Light on a Forgotten Connection* (ed. G. Boccaccini; Grand Rapids: Eerdmans, 2005) 23–26.

with relative surety, and other things that are matters of debate. Stuckenbruck summarizes three characteristics of the *Animal Apocalypse*:[58] it presents a divinely revealed message, it supports Judas both militarily and religiously (though perhaps with reservations), and it believes that the lines between the powers of good and evil had been clearly drawn. The first and third conclusions are essentially certain. Regarding the second, it is clearly the case that pseudo-Enoch supported the military campaign of Judas, but as for support for Judas's temple cleansing (see 1 Macc 4:36–61; 2 Macc 10:1–8), this does not appear at all in the *Animal Apocalypse*. It seems far more likely that the author of the *Animal Apocalypse* wrote his message before Judas's cultic activity and saw the revolt as the final sign of the very end of the age. It can clearly be seen that in *1 En.* 90:14–19 the revolt is brought to a conclusion when YHWH himself (that is, the Lord of the sheep) intercedes and ushers in the new age. Having said this, Stuckenbruck is correct in that the question of pseudo-Enoch's concern for the temple is of significant importance.

The question of the pseudo-Enoch's attitude toward the temple and the cult is also a matter of significant disagreement. Some, with VanderKam, would suggest that "[it] remains a fact . . . that no emphasis is placed on the Mosaic law. . . . It simply plays no role for this writer."[59] Others, with Portier-Young, assert that "[the] author emphasized Torah fidelity, particularly with regard to cult."[60] Though *1 En.* 89:73 is unequivocal in its rejection of the Second Temple and its cult, Collins is correct to caution against the assumption that this entails a wholesale rejection of temple and cult.[61] It is much more likely that pseudo-Enoch was deeply concerned with the temple and the cult, as the reverence for both the heavenly temple (87:3) and the Solomonic temple (89:50) indicate, but that

---

58. Stuckenbruck, "Reading," 96. It should be noted that Stuckenbruck accepts the idea of a defined group behind the *Animal Apocalypse* and the Enoch literature, but even though I disagree that this sort of group can be designated with any confidence, his three points certainly do correspond to the message of the *Animal Apocalypse*.

59. VanderKam, *Man*, 80. See also M. Himmelfarb, "Temple and Priests in the Book of the Watchers, the Animal Apocalypse, and the Apocalypse of Weeks," in *The Early Enoch Literature* (ed. G. Boccaccini and J. J. Collins; SJSJ 121; Leiden: Brill, 2007) 219–36; Henze's summary of Boccaccini's view, and the consequent critique of H. Najman, "Dream Visions," 19.

60. Portier-Young, *Theologies of Resistance*, 130. See also Nickelsburg, *Commentary*, 355.

61. J. J. Collins, *The Apocalyptic Imagination* (2nd ed.; Grand Rapids: Eerdmans, 1998) 69. Ellens and García Martínez suggest the same is true of the altered Enochic calendar in the Astronomical Book. J. H. Ellens and F. García Martínez, "Enochians and Zadokites," in *The Origins of Enochic Judaism* (ed. G. Boccaccini; Torino: Silvio Zamorani Editore, 2002) 147–53.

there was some conflict between pseudo-Enoch and the current temple establishment.[62]

Additionally, the centrality of clean and unclean categories suggests that pseudo-Enoch is not disinterested in the Mosaic law, nor in matters concerned with cult and religious ritual. In his fascination (one might even say obsession) with categorizing and subcategorizing angelic beings, people, and nations, pseudo-Enoch shows a concern for boundaries and divisions that is distinctly priestly.[63] Though the *Animal Apocalypse* is clearly an entirely different genre of literature from the law codes of the Pentateuch, there remains a significant overlap between the law codes and the apocalypse. Pseudo-Enoch is interested in defining who is in and who is out and uses ritual cleanliness as a framework to draw his boundaries. Given this, it is difficult to justify the suggestion that the *Animal Apocalypse* is not concerned with the Mosaic law.

M. Knibb suggests that the assault on the Second Temple and its cult is part of a wider set of motifs that work together to indicate that, for pseudo-Enoch, "Judah continued in a state of exile after the return [from Babylon], a state that would only be finally brought to an end with the inauguration of the new age."[64] Knibb's insight is important, as it suggests that if the author of *Animal Apocalypse* saw the exile as ongoing, this may have been because even after the return from exile the Jews were still *de facto* servants of one empire or another. What changes drastically with the advent of the eschatological age is that all other nations are subordinated to the Jews and they are finally a truly triumphant people. Tiller's suggestion that the final eschatological reality is "universalist" is true only insofar as all nations submit universally to God's elect people, and thus are themselves included among the elect.[65]

As discussed above, one of the most important components of the imagery of the *Animal Apocalypse* is the blindness (and consequent uncleanness) of the sheep in the Postexilic Period. This blindness reaches its height in the sheep that beget the lambs who will become the key contem-

---

62. M. A. Knibb ("Temple and Cult in Apocryphal and Pseudepigraphical Writings from before the Common Era," in *Essays on the Book of Enoch and Other Early Jewish Texts and Traditions* [SVTP 22; Leiden: Brill, 2009] 377) suggests that this may have been another, disenfranchised, priestly group, but Tiller counters this argument by noting that a priestly faction would likely have made room for a new Temple in the eschatological vision (Tiller, *Commentary*, 109). Of course there is no need to posit an explicit priestly group behind the *Animal Apocalypse* for this disillusionment with the Temple to be significant.

63. With thanks to R. Werline for pointing this out to me.

64. Knibb, "Temple," 375–76.

65. Tiller, *Commentary*, 20.

porary protagonists for pseudo-Enoch. These sheep ignore the pleas of the lambs and are described as "extremely and excessively blinded" (90:7). Immediately following this in 90:6–9, the young lambs revolt against the old regime by revolting against the foreign powers that stand behind it. This scene is the only explicit indication of what the blindness of the sheep means.[66]

We can see what blindness means to pseudo-Enoch by examining what it means for the lambs to become sighted. The key factor that distinguishes the two groups is that the sighted lambs are unwilling to submit to the rule of a foreign power. What else but a position of rebellion such as this would have provoked the wrath of the ravens (the Seleucids) in 90:7? Note also the earlier situation in 89:41 (the summary of the time of the Judges), in which the sheep vacillate between sight and blindness. In both situations, blindness most likely indicates religious betrayal or apostasy, and in all cases of blindness in the *Animal Apocalypse* the apostate live under foreign rule. The two situations are so closely bound that it is difficult to see if apostasy leads to foreign rule or if allowing foreign rule is a brand of apostasy. Likely, it is a rather muddled combination of the two that is at work in the *Animal Apocalypse*. In any case, this is, perhaps, the most important and fundamental division of the *Animal Apocalypse*. Animals that are clean, that are elect, are the ones that do not countenance foreign, pagan rule.

The historical individuals represented by the image of sighted lambs are (possibly) Onias III and Judas Maccabeus. If the commonly used translation of 90:8 is accepted ("and seized one of those lambs"),[67] Onias is almost certainly the lamb who is murdered by the ravens for resisting their rule. Judas Maccabeus is the lamb who grows horns in 90:9 and leads the other sheep in a military campaign against the unclean birds that represent the pagan Greeks.[68] Like Noah, Moses, and Enoch himself, these are paragons of election pseudo-Enoch means his readers to emulate.

But militant resistance is not the only point. In addition to this role of violent resistance, Portier-Young suggests that readers of the *Animal*

---

66. Though see above for alternate explanations presented by other scholars.
67. I follow the translation of Nickelsburg and VanderKam, *1 Enoch*, throughout this essay. M. Black (*The Book of Enoch or 1 Enoch* [SVTP; Leiden: Brill, 1985]) renders the phrase: "and seized *the leader* of the rams" (emphasis original). Tiller points out the significant textual difficulties with this verse and suggests a translation of "and seized those lambs" (*Commentary*, 352–54). Even if Tiller's translation is accurate, the point remains fundamentally the same and the ravens attack those Jews who resist the program of forced Hellenization.
68. Tiller, *Commentary*, 62–63, 355.

Apocalypse are also encouraged to take up the prophetic mantle of Enoch in "lament and petition."[69] As Enoch petitioned for a remnant from the flood, so also pseudo-Enoch and his readers are to petition God for a remnant among the elect. As Tiller notes, "the Enochic band . . . was fighting the enemies of God as a prelude to the final judgment of its Jewish enemies and the establishment of justice and peace in a New Jerusalem."[70] The *Animal Apocalypse* is not only about militant resistance, though this is key. It is more deeply about proclaiming that God's elect should and will be raised above their enemies.

Here, we have an instance of what Portier-Young refers to as "critical inversion," wherein the cosmology and imagery of the apocalypse provides an entirely different way of seeing the world. Thus, in the *Animal Apocalypse* it is the use of "counter-mythologies that make it possible to re-imagine a world governed not by the empires, but by God."[71] The goal for pseudo-Enoch is not only to overthrow or destroy the oppressors and to set up an autonomous, separate kingdom. The goal, as the final heavenly vision makes abundantly clear, is that the entire world, including the empires, should be brought under the rule of the clean animals.[72]

An interesting twist to this inversion is that in the final scene of judgment, while the unclean animals bow down and obey the sheep, they are not themselves thrown into the fires of judgment. Instead, it is the fallen stars, the unjust shepherds, and the blinded sheep who are thrown into the fire and destroyed (90:20–27). We might compare this to Portier-Young's analysis of the Book of Watchers, where she notes that "the book's composers symbolically locate the practices of local religious authorities within the broader hegemonic system and hold them accountable alongside the Hellenistic rulers with whom they now appear to be complicit."[73] But in the *Animal Apocalypse*, the Hellenistic rulers get off rather lightly compared with the judgment reserved for those who, while apparently among the elect, function as though they were among the unclean or nonelect.

The *Animal Apocalypse*, then, seems to occupy an interesting position of tension. Whereas it is strongly concerned with priestly matters and

---

69. Portier-Young, *Theologies of Resistance*, 157.
70. Tiller, *Commentary*, 126.
71. Portier-Young, *Apocalypse*, 15.
72. Portier-Young's concept of critical inversion also suggests that after the inversion the new ruler (in this case, the clean animals) "retains the polarities and value structures of inside/outside, civilized/uncivilized, ordered/violent, moderate/excessive" (*Apocalypse*, 20). Note, for instance, the laying down of the sword given to the sheep in 90:34. Here, the violent sheep have taken on the role of peaceful rulers.
73. Portier-Young, *Apocalypse*, 34.

draws clear in/out divisions based on imagery tied to ritual cleanness, it simultaneously functions as a very harsh and unyielding critique of the Jerusalem cult, its temple, and the priests who are complicit in the crimes of the oppressive imperial regime. This suggests that, while underwriting local religions and their legal codes may indeed have functioned as a form of imperial "domination and exploitation,"[74] both under the Persians and the Greeks, here in the *Animal Apocalypse* we have a subversive writer who maintains a strong interest in religious legal codes and yet opposes the officially sanctioned cult precisely because it is a form of imperial domination.

Conclusion: The Last Are First

We have seen thus far that pseudo-Enoch feels a strong tie between himself, along with all faithful Jews, and the elect of the past, particularly as represented by Enoch as priest and his descendents. Just as all of the truly faithful Israelites are represented as clean animals in the *Animal Apocalypse*, so also pseudo-Enoch's compatriots are depicted as the sighted lambs of chap. 90. What is more, these sighted lambs are particularly great and notable because they have thrown off the defiling blindness of their immediate forebears.

In addition to this connection to the faithful Israelites of the past, the use of Enoch as sage, revealer, and prophet has also created a connection to central events in Israel's past. By means of the type/antitype motif, pseudo-Enoch shows that just as God has worked in great and wonderful ways in Israel's past, so also will he work in great and wonderful ways in pseudo-Enoch's present. This present will not, however, involve a simple recurrence of past events but will be the very culmination of what was begun in those past events. For pseudo-Enoch, "now" is the most important time in all of history.

By tracing the heritage of the group of elect lambs back through history and connecting them to all of the other elect that have come before and by tying the events of Israel's past to the events of his present, pseudo-Enoch has carved out a place of eminent importance for himself and his compatriots in this final age. They are the culmination of the elect and they live at the greatest moment in history. It is their militant resistance and their clarion call that will demonstrate their loyalty and election and help to bring about the final reorientation of the universe.

---

74. R. Horsley, "Empire, Temple, and Community—But No Bourgeoisie! A Response to Blenkinsopp and Petersen," in *Second Temple Studies*, vol. 1: *Persian Period* (ed. P. R. Davies; JSOTSup 117; Sheffield, JSOT Press, 1991) 163–74.

Index of Authors

Ackroyd, P. R.   146, 164, 211, 219, 221, 225, 244, 260
Aharoni, Y.   159
Albertz, R.   33, 258, 263, 337, 342, 347, 348, 349, 351, 352
Albrektson, B.   255, 262, 267
Alexander, P. S.   231
Alexander, R. H.   301, 302
Alexandre, M.   232
Allen, L. C.   299
Ambar-Armon, E.   193
Amit, Y.   44, 45, 49, 50, 51, 66, 67, 167, 181, 184
Anderson, B.   271, 273
Andreasen, N. E.   219
Andrews, E. L.   235
Aristotle   195, 196, 197, 198, 199, 201, 203, 204, 205, 206, 233, 259, 264
Arnold, B. T.   76
Assis, E.   51, 280, 281, 291, 293
Attridge, H. W.   232, 235, 250
Auld, A. G.   46, 143

Bach, A.   64, 212, 213
Bagnall, R. S.   339, 343
Bailey, L. R.   302, 327
Baker, D. W.   327
Bakhtin, M. M.   4, 5, 145, 146
Bakker, E. J.   234
Balzer, K.   223
Barker, K. L.   327
Bar-On, S.   8, 15
Barstad, H. M.   25, 26
Barth, K.   107, 108
Barton, J.   164
Batten, L. W.   242
Battistella, E. L.   235
Bauckham, R.   231
Beaulieu, P.-A.   157
Becking, B.   189

Bedford, P. R.   203
Beentjes, P. C.   155, 167, 185
Beeson, S. D.   355, 356
Begg, C. T.   167, 230, 240, 245, 246, 248, 249, 251
Begrich, J.   153
Ben Zvi, E.   185, 188, 315, 316, 318, 320, 331
Berlin, A.   281
Bernheimer, R.   174
Bettenzoli, G.   299
Betz, O.   249
Bevan, E.   338, 344, 345, 346
Beyer, K.   348
Birch, B. C.   80
Bird, M. F.   241
Blenkinsopp, J.   178, 182, 192, 209, 219, 221, 223, 242, 248, 300, 301, 302, 303, 304
Bloch, H.   232
Block, D. I.   43, 45, 46, 49, 51, 52, 55, 58, 60, 62, 64, 66, 67, 111, 296, 297, 300, 303, 307
Bloome, E. C.   299
Bluedorn, W.   51, 67
Boda, M. J.   194, 210, 304, 320, 326
Bodner, K.   71, 85, 163
Böhler, D.   202
Boling, R. G.   53, 62
Bollansée, J.   234
Borgen, P.   231, 232
Borger, R.   311
Bowman, R. G.   55
Braaten, L. J.   317, 326
Bray, J. S.   58
Breckelmans, C.   38
Breisach, E.   355, 356
Brekelmans, C.   37, 38
Brenner, A.   51
Brensinger, T. L.   60
Brettler, M. Z.   3, 4, 19, 45

Briant, P. 169, 189
Brichto, H. Chanan 302
Bright, J. 304
Bron, B. 299
Brooke, G. J. 3, 4, 239, 333
Brooks, S. S. 59, 65
Brown Taylor, B. 306
Brueggemann, W. 77, 83, 138, 151, 214, 328, 329
Burford, A. 200
Burkert, W. 200
Burney, C. F. 60
Butler, T. C. 43, 45, 46, 47, 51, 53, 54, 58, 60, 62

Campbell, A. F. 70
Carr, D. M. 282, 292
Carroll, R. P. 25, 133, 212, 213, 216, 225, 257
Cassuto, U. 10, 13
Chapman, S. B. 23, 27, 29, 32, 35, 36
Charles, R. H. 238, 242
Childs, B. S. 5, 8, 10, 14, 146, 160
Chisholm, R. B. 46
Christensen, D. L. 324
Cleaver-Bartholomew, D. 327, 328
Clements, R. E. 145, 153, 154, 256, 265
Coats, G. W. 14, 15
Cogan, M. 116, 147, 149, 150, 152, 157, 158
Coggins, R. J. 211, 221, 243
Cohen, M. 194
Cohen, N. 196, 231
Cohen, S. J. D. 232, 248
Cohn, R. 107, 115
Coleson, J. E. 306
Collins, J. J. 333, 334, 336, 337, 340, 346, 347, 348, 349, 350, 351, 369
Crapps, R. W. 304
Crawford, S. W. 231, 232
Creach, J. F. D. 29, 32, 34, 35, 36, 38
Crenshaw, J. 217, 303, 318, 332
Cross, F. M. 99, 100, 108, 129, 157, 243

Cryer, F. H. 93, 94
Czövek, T. 71, 77, 79

Dangl, O. 327
Darr, K. 295, 300, 304, 305, 307, 308, 311
Davies, P. R. 133, 164, 193, 194, 275
Davila, J. R. 368
Davis, E. F. 296, 314
Davis, N. 337
Dearman, J. A. 275, 276, 278, 282, 291
Dell, K. J. 265
Dennerlein, N. 155
Destinon, J. 232
Dietrich, W. 127
Dijk-Hemmes, F. van 295
Dijkstra, M. 278
Dillard, R. B. 143, 144, 147, 148, 158, 161
Di Lella, A. 336, 347, 348
Dillery, J. T. 234
Dimant, D. 344
Dion, P.-E. 265
Dozeman, T. B. 193
Driver, S. R. 5, 25
Duabe, D. 248, 249
Duke, R. K. 146
Durham, J. I. 5, 14, 29
Dutcher-Walls, P. 39

Edelman, D. 202
Eerdmans, B. D. 5
Ego, B. 247
Eissfeldt, O. 244
Ellens, J. H. 369
Ellis, R. S. 190, 343
Eskenazi, T. C. 194, 195, 209, 210, 214, 244
Eslinger, L. 80, 120, 299, 300
Evans, C. A. 231, 311
Everson, A. J. 320
Exum, J. C. 46, 58, 61, 64
Eynikel, E. 64

Fehling, D. 234, 235

Feldman, L. H.   231, 232, 235, 245, 246, 247, 248, 251, 252
Fensham, F. C.   219
Fernández Marcos, N.   46
Finely, M. I.   234
Fishbane, M.   257, 267, 270
Fitzgerald, A.   306
Flanders, H. J., Jr.   304
Fleischman, S.   235
Fletcher-Louis, C.   340
Floyd, M. H.   327, 328
Foster, B. R.   307
Franxman, T. W.   249, 251
Freedman, D. N.   193
Fretheim, T. E.   5, 49, 83
Friebel, K.   34, 35, 111
Fried, L. S.   189, 190, 192, 193, 194, 196, 204, 210, 262
Friedman, R. E.   10, 18
Fritz, V.   28, 150

Gammie, J. G.   334
García Martinez, F.   369
Garcia-Treto, F. O.   163
Gardner, A. E.   243
Geohegan, J. C.   282
Gerstenberger, E. S.   33, 167, 183
Gill, K. M.   235
Ginsberg, H. L.   344
Ginzberg, L.   205
Gnuse, R. K.   249
Golden, L.   233, 302
Goldstein, J. A.   237, 244, 245
Goud, T. E.   230, 237
Goulet, R.   237
Grabbe, L.   39, 202, 230, 338, 339, 341, 342, 344, 345, 346, 367
Gray, J.   53, 106, 150, 152, 156, 234, 235, 248, 249, 250, 251
Green, B.   5, 35, 163, 258
Greenspahn, F. E.   44
Grogan, G. W.   310
Gunn, D. M.   44
Gunneweg, A. H. J.   192

Haak, R. D.   49, 167
Habel, N.   211
Hahn, S. W.   303

Halperin, D. J.   299
Halpern, B.   194
Hamerton-Kelly, R. G.   237
Handy, L. K.   53
Hanspach, A.   168
Hardison, O. B.   233
Harrington, D. A.   231, 239
Hartman, L. F.   336, 347, 348
Harvey, J.   259, 267
Hawk, L. D.   29, 33, 35
Hayes, J. H.   334
Hays, J.   120
Heath, M.   236
Heider, G. C.   304
Heinisch, P.   6, 19
Heller, R. L.   46, 55
Hentschel, G.   60
Henze, M.   360, 367, 369
Herodotus   190, 193, 195, 196, 198, 236, 333
Herrmann, S.   299
Hess, R.   35
Hobsbawm, E.   264, 270
Ho, C. Y. S.   143
Höffken, P.   168
Hoffman, Y.   276, 277, 278, 279, 290
Hoglund, K. G.   164
Holmgren, F. C.   225
Holquist, M.   5
Hölscher, G.   233
Honeyman, A. M.   17
Honigman, S.   196
Horgan, M. P.   239
Hornblower, S.   234
Horsley, R.   373
Hossfeld, F. L.   216, 218, 219
House, P. R.   315, 331
Houtman, C.   6, 9, 16, 17
Howorth, H.   243
Hubbard, R. L.   35, 37
Hudson, D. M.   61
Hunter, R. L.   236
Hurowitz, V. A.   190

Jansen, J. G.   330
Janzen, W.   5, 49
Japhet, S.   143, 144, 146, 148, 149, 158, 161, 167, 173, 184, 185

Jaspers, K. 299
Jassen, A. 358, 362
Jenson, R. W. 300, 301
Jeppesen, K. 26
Jobling, D. 79
Johnson, G. L. 249
Johnstone, W. 144, 164
Jones, G. H. 106, 224
Jonker, L. C. 167, 171, 180

Kaestli, J.-D. 333, 356
Kalimi, I. 155, 158, 164, 188, 190, 194
Kalmin, R. 125
Karrer-Grube, C. 209, 210, 220
Kasher, A. 232
Kegler, J. 168
Keil, C. F. 301
Kelly, N. 248, 249
Keulen, P. S. F. Van 131
Kidner, D. 219, 221, 225
Kissling, P. J. 30, 136
Klein, J. 157
Klein, L. R. 66
Klein, R. W. 80, 84, 202, 242
Kloner, A. 193
Knibb, M. A. 370
Knights, C. H. 239
Knohl, I. 12, 14
Knoppers, G. N. 100, 143, 155, 168, 193, 194, 196, 351
Koch, K. 359, 360, 364, 365
Köckert, M. 26
Koopmans, W. T. 35, 37, 38
Kraay, C. M. 337, 338
Kraemer, C. J. 236

Laato, A. 271
Lacocque, A. 334
Lafont, S. 308
Lalleman-de Winkel, H. 322
Lange, A. 359, 363, 368
Laqueur, R. 233
Lateiner, D. 196
Lattimore, R. 93
Latvus, K. 48
Lebram, J. C. 337, 347

Lemaire, A. 156
Lemke, W. K. 99, 108, 109
Lenglet, A. 349
Lenzi, A. 54
Leuchter, M. 183, 227, 275, 277, 279, 281, 282, 283, 284, 286, 287, 288, 289, 290, 293
Levin, C. 257
Levinson, B. M. 16, 17, 133, 194, 276
Lewis, B. 307
Lewy, J. 306
Lohfink, N. 27, 29
Long, B. 111, 137, 151, 331
Long, V. P. 77
Lubetski, M. 154
Lundbom, J. R. 213, 216, 220, 275, 277, 282, 284
Lund, J. 348
Lust, J. 299, 302, 304, 313

MacDonald, D. R. 234
Machiela, D. 358
Mandell, S. 193, 334, 345
Marincola, J. 234, 235, 236, 240
Martin, L. R. 46
Mason, R. A. 168, 230, 233, 250, 325
Matheney, M. 111
Matthews, V. H. 50, 54, 56, 60, 64, 66, 304
Mayes, A. D. H. 25, 44, 56
May, H. G. 10, 15, 69, 125, 184, 224
McCann, J. C. 49
McCarter, P. K., Jr. 80, 82, 84
McCarthy, D. J. 29
McConville, J. G. 24, 26, 210
McKane, W. M. 133, 216, 217, 261, 275
McKenzie, S. L. 100, 129, 136, 143, 146, 147, 164, 165, 306
McNeile, A. H. 5, 8, 17
Mead, J. K. 110, 113, 114
Meier Tetlow, E. 308
Mendenhall, G. E. 305, 307, 312
Meyer, I. 216

Micheel, R.   167
Migne, J.-P.   196
Millar, J. G.   57
Miller, P.   25
Mink, L.   263, 264
Mitchell, C.   145, 163
Moberly, R. W. L.   83, 85, 91, 137
Momigliano, A.   194, 250, 333
Montgomery, J.   334
Morgan, T.   196
Morgenstern, J.   13
Moscovitz, L.   125
Moyer, J. C.   304
Mroczek, E.   3
Mueller, E. A.   56, 58, 59
Mullen, E. T.   150
Murphy, F. J.   231
Myers, J. M.   242

Najman, H.   3, 4, 369
Na'aman, N.   56, 150, 151
Nelson, R. D.   24, 25, 26, 28, 29, 32, 33, 35, 45, 56, 57, 106, 129, 134, 137
Newsome, J. D.   167
Nicholson, E. W.   217, 218, 275
Nickelsburg, G. E. W.   231, 239, 351, 355, 357, 360, 362, 364, 365, 366, 369, 371
Niditch, S.   51, 64
Nielsen, F. A. J.   193, 195
Niessen, C.   60
Nissinen, M.   93, 126, 133, 257
Nogalski, J. D.   315, 316, 317, 318, 322, 331
Noll, K. N.   70, 126, 127, 133, 142
Noth, M.   5, 8, 38, 56, 95, 126, 127, 157, 271

O'Brien, J.   172, 323, 324
O'Brien, M.   38, 39
O'Connell, R. H.   44, 46, 48, 49, 55, 56, 59, 64, 66, 67
Odell, M. S.   295, 300, 302
Oesterley, W. O. E.   243
Ohnesorge, S.   299
Osborne, R.   234

Otto, E.   277
Overholt, T. W.   215

Pakkala, J.   131, 202
Parker, S. B.   126
Parke-Taylor, G. H.   283
Parpola, S.   94
Partner, N.   264
Patterson, R. D.   306
Patton, C. L.   295
Pedersen, J.   13
Pelling, C.   194
Peters, D. M.   349, 350
Petersen, D. L.   25, 167, 317, 319, 325
Pfeiffer, R. H.   243, 301, 302
Pitts, A. W.   229, 233, 235
Plato   233, 361
Pohlmann, K.-F.   243, 244, 299
Polak, F. H.   277, 348
Polzin, R.   58, 81, 163
Porteous, N.   334
Porter, J. R.   29
Portier-Young, A.   349, 350, 356, 357, 360, 364, 365, 369, 371, 372
Potter, D. S.   234
Prinsloo, G. T. M.   327, 328
Propp, W. H. C.   6, 8, 9, 10, 16, 17
Provan, I. W.   120, 155

Rajak, T.   230, 232
Rappaport, U.   356
Redditt, P. L.   315, 317, 320, 323, 334, 335
Rehm, R.   205
Rengakos, A.   234
Revell, E. J.   60
Rhem, R.   204
Rhodes, P. J.   234, 343, 346
Ricoeur, P.   259, 263, 268, 270
Rietzschel, C.   275
Roberts, J. J. M.   327
Rofé, A.   174
Rogerson, J. W.   324
Rom-Shiloni, D.   282, 284, 288, 291
Rooy, H. F. van   168

Ross, J. F. 212
Roth, M. T. 308
Rowland, C. 357
Rowlett, L. 29
Rubenstein, J. L. 125
Russell, D. A. 234, 357, 358

Sacchi, P. 359, 367
Satran, D. 239
Satterthwaite, P. E. 55, 60, 61, 62
Scalon, T. F. 234
Schäfer-Lichtenberger, C. 27, 28, 29, 31
Schäfer, P. 340, 341, 352
Schaper, J. 156
Schart, A. 316, 317, 318, 320
Schenker, A. 131, 202
Schepens, G. 234
Schmid, K. 278, 286
Schneider, T. J. 51, 58, 66, 299
Schniedewind, W. M. 144, 168, 182, 287
Schwartz, D. R. 232, 251, 252, 306
Schweitzer, S. J. 178, 182
Scolnic, B. E. 232
Sedlmeier, F. 299
Seeligmann, I. L. 167
Segal, J. B. 9, 17, 19
Seitz, C. R. 290, 316, 323
Selmen, M. 155
Sérandour, A. 350
Sharp, C. J. 215, 277, 278, 282, 285
Shepherd, D. 218
Shields, M. 295
Shipley, G. 343
Shrimpton, G. S. 235
Sibley Towner, W. 334
Sietze Bergsma, J. 303
Simkins, R. 322
Simpson, P. 233
Sjöberg, M. 48, 63
Smarczyk, B. 234
Smith, D. A. 304
Smoak, J. 212
Soggin, J. A. 60
Sommer, B. D. 278
Sparks, K. L. 93
Spira, A. 204

Spronk, K. 51, 323
Stacey, W. 111
Steiner, R. C. 230, 248
Steinmann, A. 210
Sterling, G. E. 232, 233, 234, 235, 237
Steussy, M. J. 71, 80
Stiebert, J. 299
Stott, K. M. 190, 193
Strasburger, H. 195
Stuckenbruck, L. T. 3, 4, 359, 360, 364, 369
Sulzbach, C. 266
Swart, G. J. 231
Sweeney, M. A. 55, 107, 121, 131, 283, 316, 318, 319, 321, 329, 331

Tadmor, H. 116, 147, 149, 150, 152, 158, 259, 269, 312
Talshir, Z. 183, 241, 244
Tcherikover, V. 340, 352
Thackeray, H. S. 233, 246
Thiel, W. 275, 282
Thompson, J. A. 216
Tiemeyer, L.-S. 133
Tigay, J. H. 56
Tiller, P. 355, 356, 357, 360, 362, 363, 364, 365, 368, 370, 371, 372
Toorn, K. van der 279
Torrey, C. C. 203, 242, 243
Trebolle Barrera, J. C. 46
Trompf, G. W. 44
Tsakmakis, A. 234
Tuell, S. 295, 300

Ulrich, E. C. 46

VanderKam, J. C. 193, 241, 357, 358, 359, 360, 365, 366, 367, 369, 371
Van Leeuwen, R. C. 318, 323
Van Seters, J. 6, 10, 93, 100, 130, 131, 193, 256, 262, 268, 271, 274, 355
Vaux, R. de 9, 13
Veijola, T. 220

Index of Authors

Von Rad, G. 94, 95, 96, 97, 99, 102, 126, 168, 181, 185, 256, 262, 265, 295, 331
Vries, S. J. de 106, 147, 167, 182

Wacholder, B. 237
Walsh, J. T. 107, 109, 110, 120
Wambacq, B. N. 15
Wanke, G. 275
Warhurst, A. 167, 185
Waterfield, R. 93
Watts, J. W. 3, 4, 316, 317, 318, 321
Webb, B. G. 45, 49, 50, 62, 64, 67
Weems, R. J. 295
Weidner, E. 311
Weinberg, J. P. 167
Weinfeld, M. 24, 29, 129
Weippert, H. 282
Wendland, E. R. 328
Wenham, G. J. 24, 28, 29, 30
Werline, R. 370
Wesselius, J.-W. 193
Westbrook, R. 308
Westermann, C. 32, 33, 35, 36, 258, 265, 266, 267, 271, 328
West, S. 196, 234
White, H. 255, 263, 264, 268

Whitman, J. 361
Widmer, M. 89
Wildberger, H. 145, 153, 154, 161
Williamson, H. G. M. 144, 146, 147, 148, 149, 158, 160, 161, 192, 193, 202, 211, 212, 219, 221, 222, 223, 225, 244, 257, 258, 292
Willi, T. 146, 164, 167, 185
Winkle, D. W. van 119
Winnett, F. V. 6
Wiseman, D. J. 158
Wisse, J. 198
Wöhrle, J. 323
Wolff, H. W. 41
Wong, G. T. K. 55, 56, 63, 67
Wray Beal, L. M. 105, 121
Wright, C. J. H. 37, 100, 220, 221, 223
Würthwein, E. 127, 140

Yarbro Collins, A. 368
Yee, G. E. 55, 58
Younger, K. Lawson 190

Zimmerli, W. 211, 303, 311

Index of Scripture

Old Testament / Hebrew Bible

Genesis
1   237
1:20–27   324
2:2–3   12, 13
6:5   89
8:21   89
9:9–15   273
9:16   10
12:1–3   300
12:16   57
15:5   271
15:18   158
18   89, 162
18:22   28
20:7   89
22   205
22:15–17   271
25:22   56, 57
25:23–24   269
26:22   273
28:7   151
32:11–13   32
32:30   49
48:16   46

Exodus
1–13   300
1:20   57
1:42–43   30
2:24   300
3   86
3:7–9   300
3:13–15   49
4:13–14   30
4:13–15   49
4:24–26   16, 30
4:31   300
5:4–5   30

Exodus (cont.)
5:21   301
6:1   30
6:2–9   30
6:3   49
6:8   306
6:9   151, 301
6:9–10   27
6:12   301
7:19–20   30
9:12   30
9:35   33
10:28–29   6
11:1–3   5, 6, 7, 19
11:1–10   4, 5, 6, 7, 8, 19
11:1–12:13   11
11:1–12:28   3–21, 4, 19, 20
11:2   7
11:2a   5
11:3   7
11:4   10
11:4–6   7
11:4–7   16
11:4–8   5, 9, 10, 14, 19, 20
11:4–10   7, 8
11:4–12:13   8
11:4a   6
11:4b   5, 6
11:4b–7   6
11:4b–8   6
11:5   9
11:6   10
11:7   6, 7, 10
11:7–8   7, 8, 11
11:7b   6

Exodus (cont.)
11:8   6, 10
11:8–9   6
11:8a   6
11:8b   6
11:9–10   5, 6, 7
12   30
12:1–11   7, 8, 11
12:1–13   4, 7, 8, 9, 10, 12, 13, 15, 16, 20
12:1–20   8, 13, 14
12:1a   14
12:3b   8, 15
12:3b–6   14
12:4a   8, 15
12:4b   8, 13, 15
12:5b   15
12:6   9
12:6b   15, 18
12:7   8, 9, 14
12:7a   15, 16
12:7b   8, 9, 13, 15
12:8–11   15
12:8a   8, 9, 13, 14
12:8b   8, 13
12:9a   8, 13
12:10   9, 15, 16
12:11a   8, 13
12:11b   8, 13
12:12   9
12:12a   14, 15
12:12b   10
12:12–13   7, 9, 10, 14, 17, 20
12:13   10, 17, 18, 20
12:13a   8, 10, 15
12:13b   8, 10, 15

Exodus (cont.)
12:14 11
12:14–20 4, 9, 11, 12, 13, 20
12:14a 13, 14
12:15 11, 12
12:15a 13, 15, 17
12:15b 13
12:16 11, 12
12:17 11, 14
12:17a 13, 14
12:17b 14
12:18 11, 12, 14
12:18–20 12
12:18a 13
12:19–20 11, 12
12:19a 12, 13, 15
12:19b 12, 13
12:20a 12, 13
12:20b 12, 13
12:21–23 8, 15
12:21–24 17
12:21–28 4, 15, 19
12:21b 14, 15, 18
12:22 14, 15, 16, 17
12:22–23 20
12:22–24 18
12:22–27a 8
12:22a 15
12:22b 15, 17, 19
12:23 14, 17, 18, 19
12:23a 15
12:23b 10, 15
12:24–28 15
12:26 30
12:27a 15
12:27b 15
13:5 30, 306
13:11 306
13:14 10
13:14–15 18
13:15 10
13:17 311
14:21–22 30
15:8 30
15:24 302
15:26 56

Exodus (cont.)
16:7–9 302
16:12 302
17:3 311
17:8–16 80
17:10–13 30
18:15 57
20 89
20:2–5a 321
20:4–6 89
20:5–6 90
20:8–11 12, 13
21 221
22 221
22:16–17 64
23:20 46
24 237
24:12 300
27 30
29:34 9
31 30
31:19–22 30
32 298
32–34 89, 302
32:1–6 89
32:4 301
32:9–10 89
32:11–14 300
32:21–24 89
32:28 301
33:1 306
33:2 46
33:12–34:7 49
34 317
34:6–7 90, 317, 323, 331
34:25 9

Leviticus
7:15 9
8:32 9
10:11 33
12:1–8 307
12:5 307
14:2–9 19
17 9
17:10–14 307

Leviticus (cont.)
18 243
22:22 364
22:29–30 9
23:5–8 14
25 221
26 223, 300
26:33 300
26:34 242
26:42 223
26:45 223

Numbers
4:13–16 300
11:5 311
11:18–20 311
12 302
13–14 30, 303
14:3–4 311
14:10 302
14:12–20 298
14:13–20 298
14:16 299
14:19 299
14:23 306
14:26–45 303
14:27 302
14:30 306
16 302, 303
16:40 33
17:5 33, 302
19:2–10 19
20:5 311
21:5 311
21:7 300
23:19 82, 83
23:20 83
24:1 83
24:5–9 238
24:7 83
24:20 83
25 304
27:21 66
27:23 33
28:16–18 14
31:7–12 80
31:17–18 80

Index of Scripture

Numbers (cont.)
32:11   306
34:5   158

Deuteronomy
1–34   40
1:5   30
1:6–8   27
1:8   306
1:9–19   39
1:17   30, 217
1:27   311
1:35   306
1:37–38   28
2–3   39
2:7   30
2:34–35   80
3:2   27
3:12–20   30
3:18–20   31
3:21–22, 28   28
4:2   134
4:10–14   134
4:13–14   134
4:25–31   133
4:27   300
5   39
5:1–5   134
5:2–3   281
5:5   134
5:5–6   27
5:22   4, 134
6:5   16
6:9   276
6:10   306
6:18   56, 306
6:20   10
6:20–25   134
7   223
7:1–5   30
7:9   223
7:21   223
8:21–22   218
8:22   138
9:5b   128
9:13   27
9:25–29   30

Deuteronomy (cont.)
10:1–5   276
10:17   137
11:20   16, 276
11:24   30
12   56
12:2   56
12:5   56
12:8   56, 63, 65
12:25   56
12:32–13:5   24
13   24, 26
13:1   29, 33, 134
13:1–5   26, 38
13:1–6   24, 26
13:2   26
13:2–6   134, 281
13:3   24
13:5   24
13:7   29
13:19   56
15   221
16:4   9
16:18–18:22   24, 133
17   30
17:8–13   39, 276
17:13   276
17:14   130
17:14–20   39
17:15   281
18   26
18:1–8   39
18:9–13   24
18:9–22   24, 26
18:11   56, 57
18:14   25
18:15   23, 25, 26, 30, 31, 37, 41, 89, 281
18:15–18   31, 36
18:15–19   25, 28
18:15–20   134
18:15–22   37, 39, 134
18:16   25
18:17   89

Deuteronomy (cont.)
18:18   23, 25, 26, 27, 30, 31, 37, 38, 41, 290
18:19   25
18:20   26, 38, 216
18:20–22   26, 216, 217
18:21–22   26, 38, 219
18:22   132, 134, 135, 136, 139, 216, 217
19:1–3   30
20:1–10   30
20:13–14   80
21:9   56
21:10–14   80
22:8   138
22:16   138
22:17   139
22:18   138
22:19–23   139
22:24   139
22:28–29   64
22:34   139
23–33   134
24   221
24:1–4   283
24:4   283, 284
25:17–19   80
27:2–8   30
28   300
28:64   300
28:64–68   133
29:14   28
29:27   133
30:1–10   133
30:11–14   134
30:12   141
31   30, 36
31:2–6   28
31:6–7   29
31:7–8   23, 28, 29, 37, 39
31:10–13   134
31:11   276

Deuteronomy (cont.)
  31:14–15 28
  31:14–15, 23 28
  31:23 28, 29
  32:44 28
  33 30
  33:1 49, 108
  34:5 36
  34:6 36
  34:7 36
  34:9 28, 29
  34:9–10 28
  34:10 26, 27, 28, 36, 39, 108
  34:10–12 26, 27, 134
  34:11 24, 26

Joshua
  1 31
  1–11 35
  1–24 40
  1:1 31, 36, 39
  1:1–2 31
  1:1–9 37
  1:2 30, 31, 37
  1:2–9 28, 41
  1:2–18 30
  1:6–9 29, 31
  1:7–9 27, 28
  1:10–11 31
  1:11 30
  1:12–15 31
  1:17 31
  1:17, 151
  1:38 28
  2 30
  2:1 273
  2:3 273
  2:24 32
  3–4 33
  3:5 33, 127
  3:5 38
  3:8 33, 34
  3:9 32, 33
  3:10 34
  3:10–13 34

Joshua (cont.)
  3:13 30, 33
  3:13–16 38
  3:15–16 33
  3:17 30
  4:4–7 34
  4:10 40
  4:14 41
  4:14 33
  4:18 33
  4:22–24 30
  4:24 33
  5 38
  5:2–7 30
  5:10 30
  6:2 32
  6:2–5 127
  6:5 128
  6:16 32
  6:17 30, 273
  6:20 128
  6:23 273
  6:25 273
  6:26 33, 38, 128, 129
  7 32, 304
  7:1–9 32
  7:6–8 32
  7:7–9 30
  7:13 32
  7:13–15 32
  7:14 32
  7:15 32
  7:16–18 73
  8:1 32, 127
  8:18 32, 35
  8:18–23 30
  8:28 80
  8:29 81
  8:30–35 30
  9:14 66
  10 34
  10:8 32, 127
  10:19 32
  10:22–25 35
  10:30 32
  10:32 32

Joshua (cont.)
  11 32
  11:6 127
  11:7, 9, 14 80
  11:8 32
  11:12 38
  11:15 31, 38, 40
  11:20 30
  11:22 40
  11:23 38
  12:1–6 30
  12:7–24 30
  13:8 30
  14 37
  14–19 30
  14:2 38
  14:6 23, 50
  15 37
  15:13 38
  15:47 158
  16 37
  17 37
  17:4 38, 41
  18 32, 37
  18:1 59
  19 32, 37
  19:49–50 37
  19:51 59
  20 37
  20:1–20 30
  20:2 33
  20:28 62
  20:41–43 140
  21 37
  21:2 38, 59
  21:8 38
  21:19 140
  21:28–29 140
  21:44 32
  22 37
  22:5 38
  22:7 30, 41
  22:9 38, 59
  22:15–28a 140
  22:23 139
  22:26–27 140
  22:26–28 34

Joshua (cont.)
22:29   59, 140
22:37–38   140
23   35, 37
23:7–8   38
23   30
24   30, 31, 35, 36, 37, 38, 41
24:1–28   35
24:2   32, 37, 302
24:2–13   35, 38
24:2–24   37
24:2–28   38
24:8   32
24:10   37
24:14   35, 37
24:14–15   36, 37, 302
24:14–28   35
24:15   37
24:16   37
24:17   37
24:19–20   34, 36, 38, 40, 304
24:26–27   34
24:28–32   36
24:29   37
24:30   37
24:31   37, 40
24:32   37

Judges
1   40, 58, 67
1:1   39, 58, 60, 61, 66
1:1–2   66
1:1–2:5   43, 56, 66, 67
1:2   61
1:3   66
2:1–5   34, 38, 53, 58, 66, 67
2:6–3:6   54
2:6–16:31   43, 44, 49, 52, 54, 55, 65, 67
2:10–11   34

Judges (cont.)
2:11–19   48
2:12   44
2:12–13   36
2:14   40, 44
2:15   44, 54
2:16, 18   44
2:18   44, 45
2:19   45
2:20   44
2:20–22   54
3:6–8   34, 38
3:7   44, 53, 56
3:7–11   45, 48
3:8   44, 53
3:9   53, 44
3:9a   53
3:9b   45, 53
3:10   45
3:11   45
3:11a   53
3:11b   53
3:12   44, 53, 56
3:12–30   53
3:12b–14   53
3:15   44, 53
3:15b–30a   53
3:19   53
3:20   53
3:30   45
3:30b   53
4   130
4:1   44, 45, 50, 53, 56
4:1–5:31   50
4:2   44, 50
4:3   44, 50
4:4   50, 51
4:4–5   39
4:4–10   52
4–5   50
4:5   50, 51
4:6–9   51, 129
4:9   130
4:15–23   129
4:23   45
4:24   45

Judges (cont.)
4:31   45
6:1   44, 56
6:1–8:32   45
6:1a   45
6:1b   45
6:6   44
6:6, 7   44
6:6–10   46, 47
6:6a   45
6:6b   45
6:7–10   46, 53
6:8   27, 51
6:8–9   47
6:8–10   39, 48, 50, 67
6:11   51
6:11–24   67
6:11–25   46, 47
6:12   45
6:13   47
6:14   127
6:16   127
6:20   50
6:21   50
6:22   50
6:22–23   50
6:23   50
6:25–27   48
6:34   45
7:2–11   48
7:9–11   48
7:13–15   48
8:28   45
8:32   45
8:32–33   45
8:33–10:2   52
8:33–35   52
9   52
9:1–6   52
9:1–22   52
9:7–22   52
9:20   127
9:22   44
9:23   45
9:23–10:1   52
9:57   33

Judges (cont.)
 10:1 44
 10:2, 3 45
 10:2, 5 45
 10:2a 52
 10:2b 52
 10:6 44, 56
 10:6–12:7 48
 10:6–16 36, 48
 10:7 44
 10:8 44
 10:9 44
 10:10 44
 10:11–14 48, 67
 10:13–14 34, 38
 10:16 49
 11:29 45
 11:29, 30 52
 11:30–31 63
 11:32 45
 11:33 45
 12:3 45
 12:7 45
 13 49, 50, 123
 13–16 65
 13:1 44, 49, 56
 13:1–16:31 49
 13:2–5 49
 13:3 127, 128
 13:3–23 67
 13:6 49
 13:6, 8 50
 13:9 49
 13:10 50
 13:11 50
 13:12 51
 13:19 50
 13:20 50
 13:21 50
 13:22–23 50
 13:23 50
 13:24 128
 13:25 45
 14 44
 14:6 45
 14:19 45
 15:14 45

Judges (cont.)
 15:20 45
 16 55
 16:25 45
 16:30 45
 16:31 45
 17 55, 57
 17–18 55, 57, 58, 59
 17–21 43, 55, 56, 57, 58, 59, 64, 65, 66, 67
 17:1–21:25 65
 17:2 33
 17:6 55, 65
 17:16 58
 18:1 55, 65
 18:3–6 57
 18:5 60, 66
 18:5–6 62
 18:10 58
 18:30 66
 18:30–31 62
 19 59
 19–21 55, 58
 19:1 55, 65
 19:9 59
 19:10–12 59
 19:18 59
 19:27 17, 59
 20 59, 60, 61
 20:1 60, 62
 20:1–17 62, 64
 20:3 60
 20:7 60
 20:9–11 60
 20:18 60, 61, 62, 66
 20:18–21 60
 20:18 58
 20:18–48 60, 62
 20:19–20 60
 20:21 60
 20:22 60, 61, 62
 20:22–25 60
 20:23 58, 60, 61, 62, 66
 20:24–25 60

Judges (cont.)
 20:26 62, 63, 65
 20:26–28 60, 62
 20:26–48 60
 20:27 58, 66
 20:27–28 52, 66
 20:28 62
 20:29–30 60
 20:31–48 60
 20:36b–48 60
 21 63
 21:1 63
 21:1–5 63, 67
 21:2–3 63
 21:2–5a 63
 21:3 64
 21:4–5a 63
 21:5 60
 21:5b 63
 21:6 64
 21:6–14 63, 64
 21:6b–7 63
 21:8–12 64
 21:13–15 63
 21:14 64
 21:15 64
 21:15–23 64
 21:16–18 64
 21:19–23 64
 21:24–25 64
 21:25 55, 65

1 Samuel
 1 71
 1–2 39
 1:3 59
 1:20 71
 1:28 72
 2 69, 88
 2:18–26 69
 2:22 59
 2:25–26 130
 2:27 32, 50
 2:27–36 95, 129
 2:30 130
 2:34 33
 2:35 88

1 Samuel (cont.)
  3   51, 69, 88
  3:1–18   95
  3:3   59
  3:11–14   129
  3:15   59
  3:19   87
  3:19–20   87
  3:20   39
  3:21   59
  4:4, 12   59
  7   51, 86
  7–12   38
  7–13   69
  7:3   86
  7:4   86
  7:6   39
  7:7–11   39
  7:15–16   39
  7:15–17   39
  8   72, 85, 132
  8–12   80
  8–15   71
  8:1–3   130
  8:1–10   130
  8:4–18   72
  8:6–7, 21–22   39
  8:7   72, 86
  8:7–9   72
  8:8   86
  8:9   72
  8:10–18   72
  8:11–18   129, 130
  8:19–22   72
  8:21   72
  8:22a   72
  8:22b   73
  9   73, 77, 79
  9–11   73
  9:6–7   50
  9:9   56
  9:15–16   127
  9:15–17   78, 128
  9:21   86
  9:26–10:1   73
  10   73, 76, 77
  10:2   73
  10:2–8   129, 130

1 Samuel (cont.)
  10:3–4   74
  10:5–7   74
  10:7   74
  10:8   74, 75, 76
  10:9   86
  10:9–11   129
  10:17–27   73
  10:18   27, 32
  10:22   58, 60, 66
  10:25   39
  11   76, 77
  11–16   129, 130
  11:1–7   35
  11:14–15   73
  12   36, 38, 40, 74, 75, 86, 108
  12:3   75
  12:3–4   39
  12:4–5   75
  12:6–13   39
  12:8–11   48
  12:10   86
  12:11   75
  12:14–15   39, 75
  12:17   75
  12:17–18   75
  12:18   75
  12:19   75, 79
  12:19–25   32
  12:20–25   39
  12:21   86
  12:23   75, 91
  12:24–25   75
  12:25   109
  13   75, 76, 77, 87
  13:1   77
  13:8   76
  13:8–15   95, 96
  13:13   39, 75, 76
  13:14   77
  14   77
  14:37   58, 60, 66
  15   70, 71, 73, 77, 78, 79, 80, 81, 83, 85, 87, 89, 90, 91, 96
  15–16   69

1 Samuel (cont.)
  15:1   39, 78, 82
  15:1–16:13   96
  15:2   32
  15:2–3   79
  15:3   80
  15:4–9   81
  15:10   39
  15:10–11   86
  15:11   81, 82, 85, 87
  15:12   86
  15:14   79
  15:15   79, 90
  15:16   86
  15:16–19   86
  15:17   86
  15:20–21   86
  15:21   79
  15:22–23   86
  15:23   82, 86, 87, 90
  15:23–26   84
  15:24   79
  15:24–31   96
  15:26   82, 87
  15:27   84
  15:28   83, 84
  15:29   81, 82, 83, 84, 87
  15:30   79
  15:34   87
  15:35   81, 82
  16   83
  16:13   34
  19   69
  20:20–22   35
  20:35–39   35
  22:3   69
  22:4   60
  22:10   58, 60, 66
  22:13   58, 60, 66
  22:15   58, 60, 66
  23:1–13   132, 135
  23:2   58, 60, 66
  23:4   58, 66
  25:1   69
  27   70, 80
  28   69, 79
  28:1   69

Index of Scripture

1 Samuel (cont.)
28:3–25   96
28:6   58, 60, 66
28:9   305
30   70, 80
30:8   58, 60, 66
32:14   90
32:31–32   90
33:12–13   90
33:16–17   90
34:6–7a   90
34:9   90

2 Samuel
2:1   58, 60, 66
5   307
5:19   58, 60, 62, 66
5:23   58, 60, 66
6   76
6:17–18   152
7   69, 70, 83, 89, 94, 95, 96, 130
7:3   91
7:4–17   91
7:5   32
7:11b–16   129
7:12b–13b   130
7:13a   130
7:14   25
7:14b   131
7:15   89, 272
7:16   130, 153
7:18   86
8:17   130
11:1–12:25   96
11:27   97
11:27b   97
12   69, 70, 91, 130
12:1–14   40
12:1–15   53
12:7   32
12:7–12   129
12:9   97
12:10   131
12:14   127
12:15–23   129
12:24–25   130
13–16   130

2 Samuel (cont.)
13–19   129
16:9   33
17:14   130, 131, 132
17:28   17
24   69
24:12–13   127
24:16   10
26:19   156

1 Kings/3 Kingdoms
1–10   130
1:7–8   130
2:2–4   119
2:27   129, 130
2:30   32
2:35   130
3–10   129
3–11   121
3:1   119
3:1–3   119
3:5–15   121
3:7–8   86
3:14   119
4:18–37   127
4:25   238
5–9   129, 130
5:1   158
6–7   119
6:11–13   121
6:12   119
8   223, 224
8:53   33
8:56   33
8:65   158
8:63   152
9:1–9   121
9:4–6   119, 120
9:6–9   120
11   107, 110, 113, 119, 131
11–12   131
11–14   105, 106, 107, 110, 111, 117, 121, 129
11:1   119
11:1–11   120
11:4–6   119

1 Kings/3 Kgdms (cont.)
11:10–11   119
11:11–13   120, 121
11:12–13   120
11:26–40   301
11:29   113
11:29–33   34
11:29–39   106, 110, 111, 113, 129, 131
11:29–40   96
11:30   118
11:30-31   113
11:30–31   111
11:31   32
11:32   131
11:35–36   131
11:36   120
11:37   113
11:37–38a   131
11:38   113
11:38–39   116
11:38b–39   131
12   32, 110
12:15   33, 151
12:21   131
12:22   50
12:22–24   110, 121
12:24   32
12:24a–z   131
12:24b   131
12:24g–n   131
12:24o   131
12:24o–z   131
12:24x   131
12:25–13:10   115
12:26–33   108, 114, 131
12:28   301
12:28–29   301
12:32   100, 130
12:32–33   114
13   96, 99, 100, 101, 102, 106, 107, 108, 109, 110, 113, 132, 136
13:1–2   50
13:1–3   40

1 Kings/3 Kgdms (cont.)
13:1–5 34
13:1–10 106, 110,
   111, 113, 115,
   117
13:1–19 113
13:2 32, 117, 136
13:3 24, 33, 112
13:5 33
13:11–24 136
13:15–16 102
13:18b 136
13:19–20 102
13:20–25a 106,
   110, 111, 112,
   113, 116
13:20–32 113
13:22 116
13:29 116
13:29–31 116
13:33–34 108
13:34 109
13:34–14:20 131
14 98, 100, 107,
   110, 113, 131
14:1 114
14:1–8 112
14:1–10 114
14:1–18 96, 106,
   110, 111, 113,
   116, 117, 129
14:2 113, 114
14:3 114
14:4 113
14:7 113
14:7–11 115, 117
14:8 113, 115
14:9 113
14:9–10 114
14:10–11 113
14:11 114, 116
14:11–19 114
14:13 114, 116
14:14 113, 114
14:15–16 113, 115
14:15–18 114
14:18 33, 116

1 Kings/3 Kgdms (cont.)
14:18b 114
14:20 114
14:20–25a 114
14:21 114, 115
14:22 114
14:24–25a 114
14:25b 114
14:25b–32 114
14:26 114
14:27 114
14:28 114
14:29 114
14:30 114
14:31–32 114
15 32
15:4 129, 162
15:5 56
15:11 56
15:14 120
15:16–22 150
15:26 117
15:27–30 96
15:29 33, 129, 132
15:30 117
15:34 117
16:1–4 96, 111,
   128, 129, 132
16:1–7 117
16:7 111
16:12 33, 128
16:13 117
16:19 117
16:26 117
16:29–22:40 136
16:30–32 310
16:30–33 136
16:31 117
16:31–32 137
16:34 33, 38, 129
17 123
17–22 136
17:1–22:40 132
17:4 127
17:13–16 127
17:14 127
17:16 33

1 Kings/3 Kgdms (cont.)
17:17–24 127
17:18 108
17:21–23 132
18 310
18:19–40 137
18:20–40 136
18:21 40
18:22 108
19:1–3 137
19:15–18 111
19:18 137
20:1–12 136
20:13 27, 32
20:13–14 127, 137
20:22 126, 127, 137
20:23 297
20:28 32, 127, 137,
   297
20:34 310
20:35–36 136
20:35–43 34
20:39–43 137
21 32
21–24 136
21:3 123
21:10–15 123
21:13 118
21:16 136
21:17–24 117
21:17–29 111
21:26 137
21:27 137
21:27–29 96
22 215
22:1–38 122
22:5 137
22:5–6 58
22:6 32
22:6–7 137
22:8 137
22:11 32, 138
22:13–14 138
22:17 139
22:20 137
22:22 137
22:22–23 137

1 Kings/3 Kgdms (cont.)
  22:25 138, 139
  22:31 139
  22:36 139
  22:43 56

2 Kings
  1:2 159
  1:2–16 128
  1:2–17 129
  1:3 159
  1:6 159
  1:16 159
  1:17 128
  2:21 32
  3 126
  3:4–27 132, 135
  3:11 108
  3:11–19 122
  3:18 32
  4:16 127
  4:16–17 127
  5:8 108
  5:10 127
  7:1 32
  7:1–2 127
  8:7–15 132, 135
  8:19 120
  9:1–10 111
  9:6–10 40
  9:7–10 117
  9:22–37 132
  9:36 33
  10:10 33
  10:28–29 117
  10:30 56
  12:3 56
  12:14 17
  13:11 117
  13:14–19 132, 135
  13:25b 132
  14 245
  14:3 56
  14:23–27 135
  14:24 117
  14:25 33, 132
  15:3 56

2 Kings (cont.)
  15:9 117
  15:18 117
  15:23–27 246
  15:24 117
  15:28 117
  16 143, 144, 145, 148, 149, 153, 155, 156, 158, 159, 161, 162, 163
  16:2 56, 151
  16:2–3 305
  16:2–4 151
  16:3 149, 154
  16:3–4 152
  16:4 149, 155
  16:5 149, 150, 159, 160
  16:5–6 152
  16:6 150, 158
  16:7 310
  16:7–8 152
  16:8 150
  16:9 151, 152, 161
  16:10 156
  16:10–11 151
  16:10–18 310
  16:11 156
  16:34 128
  17 107, 108, 119, 122, 147, 282
  17:2 117
  17:4 148
  17:7–23 37, 305
  17:12 137
  17:13 41, 173, 282
  17:13–14 122
  17:17 25
  17:21–23 129
  17:23 33, 282
  17:29–34 102
  18 308
  18–20 144, 239, 247
  18:3 56, 122
  18:3–6 122

2 Kings (cont.)
  18:4 152
  18:5 150
  18:9–10 147
  18:9–12 147
  18:13 147, 310
  18:15–16 150
  18:19 32
  19 132, 136, 310
  19:6 32
  19:6–7 122
  19:20–34 122
  19:34 122
  20:1 32, 122
  20:1–19 132, 135
  20:4–6 122
  20:5–6 128
  20:6 122
  20:12–15 311
  20:12–19 151
  20:16–18 122
  21:1–18 305
  21:6 25
  21:10–15 128, 129
  21:11 137
  21:21 137
  22–23 40, 107, 118, 123
  22:2 56
  22:11 118
  22:14–20 132, 135
  22:15 32
  22:15–17 123
  22:15–20 135
  22:20 118
  23 106, 109, 110, 123, 308
  23:2 182
  23:15 101
  23:15–16 109
  23:15–20 99, 100, 102, 106, 118, 132
  23:19 109
  23:24 137
  23:25 118
  23:26 309

2 Kings (cont.)
23:26–27 121, 123
23:29 135, 311
23:29–30 327
23:30 118
23:33–35 327
23:37 309
24–25 255
24:1 312
24:2 33, 128
24:3 180
24:6 285
24:9 309
24:19 309
24:23 309
25 40

Isaiah
1:1 145
1:5–8 310
1:10 32
2:2–4 178
3:9 308
6 145
6:1 145
6:4 17
6:9 212
6:10b 212
7 145, 155, 160, 161, 162, 164, 247, 310
7:1 153, 162
7:2 162
7:3–9 162
7:4 153, 160
7:4–9 153
7:7 153, 160
7:7–9 160
7:8 161
7:9 153, 160, 161, 162, 185
7:10 153
7:11 66
7:16 153
7:17 153, 161
7:18 154, 158, 159
7:23 154
7:23–25 161

Isaiah (cont.)
7:24 154
7:25 154, 155
8:2 152
8:19 57
19:3 57
19:18–23 248
20:2 33
27:12 158
30:1–2 66
30:1–7 148
30:8 257
31:1 148
31:3 148
31:5 10
32 310
36–39 144, 239, 247
37 310
39 311
40:1–2 258
40:8 256, 263, 273
40:9–11 258
40:12–31 265, 269
40:21 265, 266
40:27 266, 267
40:27–31 258
40:28 266, 272
40:28a 266
41:1–4 270
41:4 270, 271
41:8 271
41:8–10 258, 273
41:9 271, 272
41:10 271, 272
41:14–20 258
41:25 271
42:5 269
42:10–13 265
42:18–25 259, 267
42:19 46
42:25 269
43:1 268
43:1–7 258, 269
43:7 269
43:14–15 258
43:16–17 258, 273
43:18–21 258

Isaiah (cont.)
43:19 260
43:25–28 259
43:26 259
43:27 260
43:27a 260
43:27b–28 259
44:1–5 258
44:2 266, 269
44:5 258
44:6 266
44:8 266
44:21 266
44:21–22 258
44:22 260
44:23 261, 265
44:24 261, 266, 269
44:24–28 258
44:24–28 266
44:24–45:7 261
44:24a 269
44:24b 266
44:26 46, 266
44:26–28 213
44:26a 261
44:27 273
44:28 247
44:28a 262
44:28b 262
45:1–7 258
45:5 266
45:6 266
45:7 261, 267
45:8 261, 265
45:9 267
45:9–11 272
45:9–13 269
45:13 262
45:18 266, 269
45:18–19 267
45:21 266
45:22 266
45:22–25 258
46:3 269
46:3–4 258, 273
46:8 261
46:8–11 258, 262
46:9 261, 266

Isaiah (cont.)
  46:10 261
  46:11 261
  46:12–13 258
  47:13 269
  48:1–16 259
  48:3 258
  48:16–22 259
  48:21 273
  49:1 269
  49:5 269
  49:14–23 306
  49:16 258
  49:16–26 213
  49:17–22 213
  51:1 270
  51:2 270
  51:3 265
  51:9–11 265, 273
  51:10 273
  51:13 269
  51:16 269
  52:9–10 265
  53 162
  54:1 271
  54:1–3 273
  54:1–8 306
  54:5 272
  54:6 272
  54:9–10 273
  54:10 273
  55:3 272
  55:9 267
  55:10–11 185
  55:11 262
  55:12 262
  55:12–13 265
  60:11–12 178
  61:4 213
  62:3–5 306
  66:7–13 306

Jeremiah
  1 86, 212
  1–20 284
  1–24 287
  1:1 227, 289
  1:3 214

Jeremiah (cont.)
  1:6 211, 212
  1:8 224
  1:9 212, 290
  1:10 212, 213
  1:17 212
  2 310
  2–3 272
  2:1–3 300
  2:2 272
  2:3 214
  2:4 32
  2:5 214
  2:7 283, 284
  2:8 215
  2:14–18 310
  2:20 309
  2:32 309
  3:6–11 309
  3:6–12 310
  4:7 298
  5:12 215
  5:31 297
  6:13–15 215
  7:3 288
  7:19–27 219
  7:25 173, 282
  8:2 215
  8:10–12 215
  9:24:6 212
  9:26 159
  12:14–17 212
  14:12 282
  14:13 215
  14:13–15 297
  14:17–21 224
  14:20 224
  14:20–21 223
  14:21 224
  15:15 225, 226
  16 283
  16:18 283
  17:19 219
  17:19–27 209, 220
  17:20 219
  17:21 219, 220
  17:22 219

Jeremiah (cont.)
  17:24 219
  17:24–27 220
  17:25 220
  17:27 219, 220
  18:7, 9 212
  18:9 214
  18:19–23 224
  18:20 225
  18:21–23 225
  18:23 225
  20:4 312
  21 312
  21:9 282
  22 220
  22:13–14 327
  22:17 327
  23 297
  23:9–40 134, 215
  23:10 221
  23:14 215, 308
  23:15–17 215
  23:21 216
  23:32 216
  24 282, 288
  24:6 213, 214
  24:7 178
  25 134, 287, 312
  25:1 287
  25:4 173, 282
  25:9 312
  25:12 242
  25:14 286, 287
  26 224
  26–29 215
  26–45 276, 279, 289
  26:5 282
  26:5–16 297
  26:9 173
  26:18–19 173
  26:20–23 327
  27 215, 312
  27–28 217, 219
  27–29 215, 279
  27:1 287
  27:2 217
  27:6 312

Jeremiah (cont.)
27:9–10   215
27:9–18   298
27:12–17   290
27:14   215
27:14–15   215
27:15   215, 216
27:16   215
28   215, 216
28:1–4   215
28:2   80
28:5–9   215
28:9   215
28:10   80
28:10–11   216
28:11   217
28:12–14   216
28:13   217
28:15–17   139, 216
28:16   215
28:20   216
28:22   217
29   278, 279, 280, 284, 285, 286, 290, 291, 298
29:1   279, 285
29:4–7   280
29:5   213
29:5–7   281
29:7   290
29:9   279
29:10   213, 242, 286, 287, 290
29:16   291
29:16–19   291
29:16–20   281, 284
29:17   282
29:19   291
29:20   284, 291
29:20–32   288
29:21   298
29:23   215, 279
29:32   215
30–31   288
30–33   209
30:18–21   213, 214
31   210

Jeremiah (cont.)
31:4–5   214
31:16   185
31:28   212, 214
31:31–34   178, 210
31:38   212
31:40   212
32:6–15   289
32:38–41   178
34   221, 239
34:8–22   221
34:9   221
34:10   221
34:11   222
34:14   221
34:16   222
35:15   173
36   275, 276, 277, 278, 280, 285, 286, 287, 291, 292
36:1   277
36:1–26   327
36:9   277
36:17–18   290
36:30–31   285, 286, 287
36:32   276, 277, 279, 280, 284, 286, 290
37   311
37:2   33
37:6–8   148
37:19   215, 298
38:20–33   249
40–44   289
40:9–10   282, 290
42:10   212, 214
43   311
43–44   291
43:10   312
44   311
44:4   173
45:4   212
45:5   289
46:25   148
49:18   213

Ezekiel
49:19b   213
49:20   213
49:20a   213
49:21   213
49:26   213
50–51   287
50:1   33
51:59   289
51:59–64   289
52:19   17
1–3   297
1:4   174
1:21   309
2:3   313
2:3–4   212
2:5–8   313
3   297, 304
3:3–9   313
3:7   303
3:7–8   298
3:7–9   313
3:9   313
3:16–27   173
3:26   313
3:27   313
6   303
8–11   297, 303
11:19–20   178
12:2   313
13   134, 215, 297
13–24   313
13:4–5   210
13:9   192
14:3–4, 7   58
14:22   288, 289
16   272, 295, 299, 302, 303, 306, 312
16:3   307
16:3–13   306
16:10–18   309
16:43b–45   307
16:53–54   313
16:60–62   297
16:60–63   313
16:61–63   223

Ezekiel (cont.)
17   312
17:12   313
17:15   311
18   298, 304
20   295, 298, 299, 300, 303, 304, 305, 306, 308, 309, 312
20:1–4   302
20:1–9   298
20:5–10   300
20:7–8   301
20:8   303
20:9   297, 298, 306
20:10–17   302
20:11   300
20:12–24   302
20:14   297, 298, 306
20:17   303
20:18–26   303
20:22   297, 298, 306
20:23   300
20:26   303
20:27–29   304
20:30–39   305
20:32   305, 314
20:33   314
20:34   27
20:40–42   313
20:42   306
20:44   306
21:18–23   297
21:19–22   312
21:26   60, 66
22:8   219
22:25–28   215, 297
23   272, 295, 299, 300, 309, 312, 313
23:1–3   298
23:14–17   311
23:20   364
23:24–26   312
23:26   312
23:29   312
23:37   312

Ezekiel (cont.)
23:38   219
23:39   312
23:45   312
23:47   312
24:3   313
24:3–14   313
24:20–24   24
24:25   313
26   219
29–30   291
29–32   301, 302
29:6–7   148
32–34   302
33–36   213
33:29–33   298
36   300
36:10   213
36:20–23   298
36:22   297
36:25–28   178
36:26   313
36:33–36   213
38:17   33
39:25   298
40–48   298
45:17   219
45:18–20   19
45:21   14
46:1   219
46:3   219
46:4   219
46:12   219
48:15–35   213

Hosea
1–2   318
1–3   272, 306, 321
1:2   326
2   317
2:2   321
2:5   321
2:14–15   300
2:17   272
2:21   178
3:1   321
3:4   185

Hosea (cont.)
3:4–5   321
4:1   32, 321
4:1–14   321
4:12   60, 66
4:15   67
7:11   310
8:14   272
9   310
9:1–9   310
9:5   317
9:10   304
9:15   67
11:1   300
11:10   317, 322
12:2   148
12:5   46
12:11   67
14   317
14:2–10   321

Amos
1:2   317
1:3–2:3   322
1:11   322
1:11–12   322
3:1   32
3:9   185
4:1   32
4:4   67
4:6–11   317
4:11   308
5:5   56, 67
5:18–20   317, 325
7:7–9   322
7:10–17   322
7:15–16   212
8:3–9:4   322
9:1   17
9:4   58
9:11–15   322, 325
9:12   317, 322
9:13   317
9:13–14   317
9:14   325

Obadiah
1 317
10 322
10–14 325
15 317
15–21 325

Jonah
3:9 323
3:10 323
4:2 317, 318, 323

Micah
1:8–16 323
2:4 317
3 215
4:1–5 178
4:1–7 325
6:16 323
7:18 317
7:18–19 323
7:18–20 318, 323

Nahum
1 324
1:2–3 317, 318
1:2b 323
1:3a 323
1:3b–6 324
1:7 317
2–3 324
2:8–13 246
3:4–6 309
3:18–19 323

Habakkuk
1 324
1:1 33
1:2–4 327
1:5–11 329
1:12–14 329
1:12b 329
1:15–17 329
2 324
2:1 33
2:2–4 330
2:2–5 329
2:4 330

Habakkuk (cont.)
2:4b 329
2:6–19 329
2:8–9 329
2:9 327
2:20 317
3 33, 324
3:3–15 324, 330
3:16 317, 325
3:16–19 330
3:17 317

Joel
1:2–2:17 317
1:15–2:11 325
2:12–14 323
2:12–27 322
2:13 318
2:14 323
2:18 323
2:19–27 322
3:1–5 325
3:4 317
3:19 159
4:1 325
4:1–21 325
4:16 317
4:18 317
4:19 317, 322

Zephaniah
1:2–3 324
1:4–18 325
1:7–16 317
3:16 185

Haggai
1:1 324
1:6 317
1:10–11 317
1:15 324
2:1 324
2:10 324
2:13 46
2:15–19 317
2:18 324
2:20 324
2:23 317

Zechariah
1–8 325
1:1 324
1:7 324
1:12 287
1:15 324, 325
1:21 325
2:6–9 325
2:17 317
4:10 185
5:1–11 325
5:3–4 320
5:6–8 320
7:1 324
7:7 33, 172
7:8–10 320
7:12 172
8:10 185
8:12 317
8:16–17 320
9:1–8 325
9–14 325
9:9–10 325
10:1–3a 320, 325
11:1–3 320, 325
11:4–17 320, 325
11:6 185
12 33
12–14 325
13:1–2 320
13:2–6 134
13:7–8 320
13:7–9 320, 325
13:7–14:2 325
14:1 317
14:1–2 320
14:1–21 325
14:8–11 325
14:16–21 325

Malachi
1:1 33, 46
1:2–5 325
1:6–2:9 325
1:6–8 364
1:8 365
1:9a 323
2:1–4 320

Malachi (cont.)
  2:1–9   326
  2:8   320
  2:10–16   325
  2:11   320
  2:11–16   326
  2:17–3:5   325
  3:1   46, 326, 332
  3:2   325
  3:6–12   325
  3:8–11   317
  3:13–21   325
  3:19   317
  3:19–21   326
  3:23   325
  3:24   326

Psalms
  2:6   255
  32:1   225
  33   265
  77:3   57
  78   300
  89:40   330
  90:10   161
  104:7   265
  106   298, 300
  106:1   298
  106:8   298
  106:44–46   298
  109:6–19   225
  110:4   83
  132:11   83
  137   225
  147   265

Job
  33:23   46

Qoheleth
  2:19   58
  5:5   46
  10:1   159

Lamentations
  2:17a   263
  4:6   308

Esther
  9:36   194

Daniel
  1   346, 350, 352
  1–2:4a   348
  1–12   338, 346, 350
  1:1–2:4a   349
  2   349
  2–6   334, 348, 349, 353
  2–7   341, 342, 344, 346, 347, 348, 350, 351, 353
  2:4b–6:28   334, 347
  2:4b–7:28   342, 348, 349
  3   349
  3:31–6:29   346
  4   349
  5   349
  6   349
  7   333, 334, 335, 336, 337, 338, 339, 340, 341, 342, 344, 345, 346, 347, 348, 349, 352, 353, 361
  7:1   333
  7:8   333, 335, 336, 337, 338, 340, 342
  7:8b   342
  7:11   333, 335, 340, 344
  7:12   344
  7:13   352
  7:14   346, 352
  7:20   335, 336, 338, 340, 341
  7:20–21   333
  7:21   335, 340, 342
  7:24   337, 338, 341
  7:24–26   333
  7:25   335, 340, 342, 344, 345
  7:27   346, 349

Daniel (cont.)
  8   334, 335, 336, 337, 338, 350, 352, 361
  8–12   335, 338, 346, 347, 348, 350, 352
  8:1–12:13   349
  8:8   335, 336
  8:9   336
  8:9–12   333
  8:11   335
  8:13   335
  8:21   335
  8:22   335
  8:23–25   333
  9   134, 223, 350
  9:2   287
  10   239
  11   356
  11:21   335
  11:28   335
  11:29–39   335
  11:31   335

Ezra
  1–6   190, 192, 193, 194, 195, 197, 198, 206, 207
  1:1   195, 209, 210, 242
  1:1–2   191
  1:1–3a   238
  1:1–8   199
  1:3b–11   238
  1:4   211
  1:5–11   211
  1:9–11   192, 199
  2   197, 199
  2:1–4:5   238
  2:2–70   192
  2:5   211
  2:8   211
  3   200
  3:1–3   191
  3:1–6a   200
  3:1–7   199
  3:3   192

Ezra (cont.)
3:6b–7   200
3:7   191
3:7–9   199
3:8   191
3:10   191
3:10–13   199, 200
4:1–3   199, 201
4:1–5   192, 203
4:4–5   199
4:5   201
4:5–23   199
4:6–22   192
4:7–24   238
4:11–22   201
5   190, 205
5:1   192, 195, 199, 206
5:1–2, 5   206
5:1–10:44   238
5:2   199, 206
5:3   203, 206
5:3–6:12   199
5:6–17   192
5:8   202, 206
6:2–12   192
6:11–12   191
6:13–22   199
6:14   206
6:14–22   206
6:15   191, 207
6:16   191, 206
6:19   191
7   193
8–9   210
9   223
10:10–11   243

Nehemiah
1:1   227
1:1–2:20   210
1:4   211
1:4–11   222
1:5   223
1:5–11   223
1:6   224
1:8–9   223

Nehemiah (cont.)
2:18   226
2:20   214
3:3–5   210
3:33–5   224
3:36–37   222, 224
3:37   225
4:1–7:5   210
4:4–5   222, 226
5:1   221
5:1–13   221
5:5   222
5:7   221
5:14–19   222
5:19   226
6   218, 219
6:1–9   220
6:5–8   218
6:9   218
6:10–11   189
6:13   218
6:14   222, 225
7:4   214
7:73–8:13a   238
9   209, 218, 223
9:8   210
9:17   311
9:26   174, 218
9:30   218
9:32   210, 218
12:10–11   193
12:31 43   210
13   193, 219, 221
13:4–14   222
13:6   219
13:6–7   219
13:6–31   210
13:14   226
13:15   219
13:15–22   219, 220, 222
13:18   220
13:19   219, 221
13:22   219, 221, 226
13:22a   221
13:23–31   222
13:24   221

Nehemiah (cont.)
13:27   221
13:28–31   225
13:31   226

1 Chronicles
2:3   173
10:13   60, 66
14:10   60, 66
16:35   183
21   206
21:12   10
23:14   183
25:1–8   182
28:19   182
29:11   84
29:30   182

2 Chronicles
1:5   56
5:1–13   221
6:42   224
8:14   182
9:26   158
9:29   182
10:15   33
11:1–4   175
11:2   183
12:5–6   175
12:15   182
13   146, 148, 149
13:8   146
13:8–9   146
13:11   147
13:22   180, 182
14:1   56
15:1–7   175
15:3   185
15:5   185
15:6   185
15:7   185
15:8   180
15:12   221
16:1–12   150
16:2–9   148
16:7   180
16:7–10   174

2 Chronicles (cont.)
  16:9 185
  19:1–2 148
  19:2 180
  20 162
  20:1 162
  20:3 162
  20:14 180
  20:14–17 162, 182
  20:20 162, 165, 185
  20:32 56
  20:34 182
  20:37 180
  21:11–15 181
  22:3–6 148
  23:32 182
  24:2 56
  24:19 174, 175, 180
  24:19–25 174
  24:20 180
  24:20–22 174, 182
  25 176
  25:2 56
  25:6–10 148
  25:7–9 175
  25:7–10 180
  25:9 183
  25:26 145
  26:4 56
  26:5 175

2 Chronicles (cont.)
  26:16–21 76
  26:22 145
  27:2 56
  28 143, 145, 147,
      148, 149, 158,
      160, 161, 163,
      164, 310
  28:1 56
  28:2 146
  28:3 155
  28:5 147, 159
  28:5–7 161
  28:6 160
  28:8 147, 161
  28:8–15 159, 175
  28:9 180
  28:9–15 183
  28:10 148, 222
  28:10–16, 23 146
  28:12 160
  28:13 148
  28:17 147
  28:18 158, 159
  28:19 161
  28:20 159
  28:23 146
  28:24 147, 157
  28:25 155
  28:26 145
  28:27 176

2 Chronicles (cont.)
  29–31 176
  29:2 56
  29:3 176
  29:25 182
  30:6 147
  30:16 178, 182
  32 156, 310
  32:32 144, 145, 182
  33 305
  33:1–9 176
  33:18 182
  33:19 182
  34–35 308
  34:2 56
  34:30 182
  35:1–9 238
  35:1–36:23 242
  35:6 33
  35:20 311
  35:20–24 182
  35:20–36:21 238
  35:22 182
  35:25 182
  36:12 181
  36:15–16 46, 174
  36:20–21 287
  36:21 242
  36:22 182
  36:22–23 238
  36:23 157

Deuterocanonical Literature

1 Maccabees
  2:49–70 238
  4:36–61 369
  14:5–14 238

2 Maccabees
  2:1 244
  2:11–12 244
  2:13 244
  2:19 244
  2:29–31 238
  3:4–6 367
  10:1–8 369

Sirach
  46:1 23

Tobit
  14:4 247

Pseudepigrapha

1 Enoch
1–5   349
1–36   349
6–11   357
6–16   363
8:1   362
10–11   238
10:8   362
12–36   349
13   358
14:8–23   361
84:1–6   360
85–90   355
86   363
86:1   363
86:3   364
86:3–4   363
86:4   364
87–88   360
87:1–4   362
87:2   363
87:3   361, 369
87:3–4   363
88:1   364
89:1   363
89:1–9   360
89:9   363
89:16–40   361
89:36   363
89:38   363
89:41   371
89:50   369

1 Enoch (cont.)
89:73   365, 369
89:74   364
90   373
90:1–5   361
90:6   364, 365
90:6–9   365
90:6–38   361
90:7   364, 365, 371
90:8   371
90:8–18   365
90:9   371
90:14–19   369
90:15   360
90:16–17   365, 367
90:18   360
90:20–27   372
90:24   363
90:26   364
90:37–38   366
90:38   363, 364

Jubilees
1:5–7   3
1:26–2:1   3
4:16–25   358
5   237
7:20–39   238
10:1–15   238
33:1–9   238
34:1–9   238
34:20   238

Testament of Judah
3–7   238

Testament of Levi
9   238

Testament of Reuben
3   238

1 Esdras
1:1–22   238
1:25–58   238
1:28   182
1:57–58   242
2:1   242
2:5b–15   238
2:18   202
2:20   202
3:1–5:6   238
4:16–27   238
5:7–73   238
6:1   242
6:1–9:36   238
7:3   242
7:5   207
8:83   242
9:37–55   238

2 Esdras
2:1–5a   238

New Testament

Matthew
1:2–16   196

Luke
3:23–38   197